THE BOYS FROM THE 'BRIG

THE LIFE AND TIMES OF ALBION ROVERS

by

R.W. MARWICK

Published by Monklands Library Services Department

ISBN 0 946120 19 6

© World Copyright

		Page
ACKNOWLEDGEMENTS		5
LIST OF PHOTOGRAPHS		6
INTRODUCTION		11
CHAPTER ONE — AN HISTORICAL PERSPECTIVE	1882-91	13
CHAPTER TWO — THE FIRST TENTATIVE STEPS	1891-03	27
MR. ALBION ROVERS No. 1 — SIMON SCOTT		52
CHAPTER THREE — A SEARCH FOR STATUS	1903-15	54
CHAPTER FOUR — MARKING TIME	1915-19	81
MR. ALBION ROVERS No. 2 — HUGH THOM		91
CHAPTER FIVE — GREAT EXPECTATIONS	1919-23	93
CHAPTER SIX — THE LONG WAY BACK	1923-34	114
MR. ALBION ROVERS No. 3 — EDDIE McLAREN		147
CHAPTER SEVEN — IT'S TOUGH AT THE TOP	1934-39	148
CHAPTER EIGHT — THE LOST FORTIES	1939-45	169
MR. ALBION ROVERS No. 4 — W. WEBBER LEES		185
CHAPTER NINE — THE FIGHT BACK TO THE TOP	1945-49	187
CHAPTER TEN — IN THE WILDERNESS	1949-61	207
MR. ALBION ROVERS No. 5 — TOM FAGAN		254
CHAPTER ELEVEN — THE NEW DEAL	1961-82	256
CHAPTER TWELVE — THE SECOND CENTURY	1982-	340
APPENDIX 'A' ROVERS' INTERNATIONALISTS		366
APPENDIX 'B' LIST OF MANAGERS		367
APPENDIX 'C' SCOTTISH CUP DETAILS		368
APPENDIX 'D' LEAGUE PLACINGS		374

ACKNOWLEDGEMENTS

In the compilation of this book, I am deeply indebted to many people for their interest, encouragement and helpful advice. Many of those who would have been most useful in advising me about the early years of the Club were long gone before I was able to seek their advice. Nevertheless, it has been a life-long, pleasurable task to uncover all those details with a relevance to Albion Rovers. Even after forty years of hard slog, the story is by no means complete and it is unlikely that it can ever be totally so.

The Club is currently in its one hundred and fourth year and information covering the first three years is extremely brief, even if it exists at all. The initial decade is not well documented and continues to be the subject of research in much of my spare time.

With little printed documentation of the Club in existence, and even some of what is available found to be subsequently misleadingly inaccurate, it has been a labour of love to winnow out the details contained in this book. Regrettably there are no Club Minutes available for consultation, which is particularly unfortunate during the formative years. Nevertheless, it is most satisfying to be able to connect the names of the past with real people, not just from old photographs but also by finding out many details about their achievements, both on and off the field.

This task would have been impossible without the local newspaper material contained on microfilm in the local Libraries and the help and consideration of John Fox and his staff has been much appreciated. Mrs. Holness at the Hamilton Advertiser office and the staff at the Mitchell Library in Glasgow with their material have also been splendid sources of information.

Mrs. Margaret Lees, widow of Webber, has contributed much detail, whilst Eric Murray of the Airdrie & Coatbridge Advertiser has been of real assistance from a photographic point of view.

The various supporters and friends who have contributed anecdotes, memorabilia, observations and even at times admonitions, are all gratefully and humbly acknowledged.

Ian Wheeler of the Dundee Courier was a rich source of old photographs and his enthusiasm for the project was uplifting. Grant Cullen also produced several photographs of great interest and I am further indebted to him for carrying out the onerous task of proof reading, which he did willingly and enthusiastically.

Betty Paterson patiently typed the final manuscript, having been ably assisted in the initial typing by Moira McKenna and my thanks are due to both.

A list of photographs and suppliers of photographs is acknowledged elsewhere and my thanks are due to them all for without the illustrations the book would be less readable.

LIST OF PHOTOGRAPHS	SOURCE
1. FRONT COVER – 1961 – Action in first match with new strip against East Stirlingshire.	Author
2. 1892/93 Team Group.	Miss Margaret Gray
3. Individual Photos: Bruce Chalmers, Matt Rorke, Willie Roberts, Archie Sergeant.	Author
4. 1903/04 Qualifying Cup Finalists Group.	Mrs. May Boyd
5. 1906 Postcard of Leith Athletic match.	Tom Boyd, Caldercruix
6. 1913/14 Qualifying Cup Winners Group.	T. Grant Cullen
7. Individual Players: Guy Watson, Robbie Ewing, Davie Ewing, Bobby Archibald.	Author
8. 1913 President Thom and Sime Scott with the Qualifying Cup.	Author
9. 1914/15 Minor Team Group at the Meadow.	John S. Laird
10. 1919/20 Team Group.	The Courier Dundee
11. 1920/21 Team Group.	The Courier Dundee
12. 1920/21 Players sitting on the fence.	The Courier Dundee
13. Rovers' sole Internationalist – John White.	T. Grant Cullen
14. 1921/22 Team Group.	Author
15. Individual Players: Willie Reid, Bob Penman, Peter Bennie, Bob McSkimming.	Author
16. 1927/28 Team Group.	The Courier Dundee
17. 1928/29 Team Group.	The Courier Dundee
18. 1931/32 Team Group.	The Courier Dundee
19. Individual Players: John Donnelly, Alec Browning, Murdy Walls, Bobby Beath.	Author
20. 1933/34 Championship Winning Group.	Author
21. 1934 Civic Reception Programme.	Andrew Liddell
22. 1934/35 Team Group.	Author
23. Individual Players: John Renwick, Willie Bruce, Andy Waddell, John Barclay.	Author
24. Cartoon from "News of the World".	Mrs. Margaret Lees
25. 1936/37 Team Group.	Author
26. Supporters' Club Committee.	Author
27. 1937 Johnny Bell being welcomed to Coatbridge.	Author
28. 1937/38 Team Group.	Author
29. Promotion Winning Dance.	Mrs. Margaret Lees
30. A happy group of Rovers, plus friends.	Mrs. Margaret Lees
31. The Directors Box.	Mrs. Margaret Lees
32. 1940 D.O.R.A. Cartoon in "Evening Times".	Author
33. 1944/45 Team Group.	Author.
34. 'Cigarette' Cards: Jock Stein, Johnny McIlhatton, Willie Hannah, Tommy Kiernan, Willie Findlay.	Author
35. 1947 Leaving on Cup Business at Dundee.	Author
36. 1947/48 Team Group.	The Courier Dundee

LIST OF PHOTOGRAPHS   **SOURCE**

37. Lindsay Cartoon of Hibs Cup match.   Mrs. Margaret Lees
38. 1948 Johnny Love signing for Rovers.   Mrs Margaret Lees
39. 1948/49 Training Group.   Author
40. 1948/49 Team Group.   Author
41. 1948 Old Crocks match against Airdrieonians. Jimmy Cannon
42. Individual Players: Jock Stein, 'Chic' Muir, Johnny Craig, Bobby Kerr.   Author
43. 1949/50 Team Group.   T. Grant Cullen
44. 1950 Training Group.   Archie Fleming
45. 1951 Cliftonhill after the Stand blaze.   The Courier Dundee
46. 1985 Cliftonhill same view.   Author
47. 1951 Cliftonhill general view to East.   The Courier Dundee
48. 1985 Cliftonhill same view.   Author
49. 1950/51 Players taking the field for Cup Tie against Clyde.   Archie Fleming
50. 1952/53 Team Group.   Archie Fleming
51. 1953/54 Team Group.   Author
52. 1954/55 Programme.   Author
53. Individual Players: Matt Carson, John McGuinness, John McPhail, Jim McCracken.   Author
54. 1957/58 Team Group.   Author
55. 1961/62 Team Group.   Glasgow Herald
56. 1964/65 Team Group.   T. Grant Cullen
57. 1965/66 Team Group.   Author
58. 1968/69 Team Group.   Author
59. 1970/71 Team Group.   Author
60. 1973/74 Team Group.   Author
61. Individual Players: John Brogan, Tommy Sermanni, Sam Malcolmson, Bert Rice.   Airdrie & Coatbridge Advertiser
62. 1974 Inaugural football match at Meadowbank Stadium against Meadowbank Thistle.   Edinburgh Evening News
63. 1974/75 Team Group.   T. Grant Cullen
64. 1975/76 Spring Cup tie at Arbroath.   Author
65. 1976/77 Team Group.   Author
66. 1977/78 League match at Shawfield.   Author
67. 1978 Goal at Stair Park, Stranraer.   Author
68. 1979/80 Team Group.   Author
69. 1981 Ballboys.   Airdrie & Coatbridge Advertiser
70. 1981/82 Team Group.   Airdrie & Coatbridge Advertiser
71. 1982 Centenary Civic Reception.   Airdrie & Coatbridge Advertiser

LIST OF PHOTOGRAPHS   **SOURCE**

72. 1982 Civic Reception Programme.   Monklands District Council
73. 1982 Civic Presentation.   Airdrie & Coatbridge Advertiser
74. 1983 crowds at Cliftonhill for cup tie.   Author
75. 1984/85 Team Group.   Airdrie & Coatbridge Advertiser
76. 1984 Top money transfer Bruce Clelland.   Airdrie & Coatbridge Advertiser
77. Individual Players: Alan Rodgers, Victor Kasule, Tony Gallagher, Jim Deakin.   Airdrie & Coatbridge Advertiser
78. 1984/85 Bernie Slaven Scottish Top Scorer.   Airdrie & Coatbridge Advertiser
79. 1985/86 Team Group.   Airdrie & Coatbridge Advertiser
80. 1984 Grandstand before resurfacing.   Author
81. 1985 Grandstand after resurfacing.   Author
82. 1985/86 Directors.   Airdrie & Coatbridge Advertiser
83. Captain Sam Conn welcoming Manager Tommy Gemmell to Cliftonhill.   Airdrie & Coatbridge Advertiser
84. 1985 Broomfield 'home' match.   Author
85. Back cover 1986/87 Team Group.   Author

MR. ALBION ROVERS
1. Simon Scott   Author
2. Hugh Thom   Author
3. Eddie McLaren   Author
4. W. Webber Lees   Author
5. Tom Fagan   T. Fagan

TO FIONA

Without whose generous forbearance
of the many "lost" hours spent in
Libraries and elsewhere this book
might never have been written.

INTRODUCTION

Every one of us, so I am told, has 'a book in him'. If that is fact then this book has been a long time coming but who knows it may be like good wine and well worth the wait.

My researches started more than thirty five years ago with a simple Scrap Book. This encouraged my delving into the past to uncover the names of the heros of earlier times, a recording of the successes of the team and eventually an attempt to get behind these bare facts and put some meat on the skeleton.

There was nowhere to turn for anything other than very basic information and no source of reference to settle an argument or nudge a failing memory. Little of Rovers' history appears to have been recorded over the years. Even Club Minute Books are unavailable for the vast majority of the one hundred and four year existence of the Club.

Much of my knowledge of the earlier days had been handed down by those of an older generation by word of mouth. Local legend also has a major part to play in the story but much of this has been either omitted or watered down somewhat to spare the blushes of those concerned. By far the most prolific source of information was the local Library and the pages of newspapers both local and national.

Many hours have been expended in research and it is my determination to give as detailed a history of the Club since its earliest days by recording, in chronological order, each and every match and important happening.

This may make the book a bit of a bore for those who are neither avid Rovers Fans nor Football Buffs. I make no apologies for that as the intention is for a full and detailed, warts and all, history of the Life and Times of Albion Rovers, who are the 19th oldest team currently playing in Scottish Senior Football.

Due to the sheer lack of detail covering the early years of the Club, my information over this period is still incomplete and my researches will continue. The results perhaps may well be the subject of a further 'tome' — who knows?

CHAPTER ONE

AN HISTORICAL PERSPECTIVE

This story starts one hundred and four years ago when life was very much different from that experienced today and from all points of view.

1882 was the hey-day of Victorian Britain, when the sun never set on the British Empire, the Industrial Revolution was in full swing and Britain was the foremost producer of goods for the World Market Place. Generally the time was one of prosperity and full employment for those who wanted to work but at the same time life was hard, hours were long and recreation not considered to be essential.

Although it was to be a further three years before Coatbridge became a Burgh, the zenith had already been reached in the prosperity and importance of the Town which had begun a few short decades earlier as a series of outlying villages— Langloan, Summerlee, Coatdyke, Whifflet and Dundyvan developed into the Town we know today.

On the football front the game was totally amateur with Queen's Park being the foremost team in Scotland. All Scottish players were fair game for the "unofficial" professional clubs in the north of England and many opted for a spell in the paid ranks. Professionalism was to be legalised south of the border in 1885 but didn't come to pass in Scotland until 1893, when, after several attempts by various advocates, Glasgow Celtic were successful in sponsoring the change from a solely amateur game to one which included professionals.

At the start of the 1880s the top teams were as likely to be found in the villages as the towns and cities, with Renton, Vale of Leven, Shotts and Cambuslang vying with the likes of Queen's Park, Glasgow Rangers, Dumbarton, Third Lanark, Hearts of Midlothian, Hibernian and the like.

Locally the "big" teams were Drumpellier, Airdrieonians, Plains Blue Bells and Airdriehill, whilst the main outdoor sports were cricket in the Summer and curling and quoits in the Winter. The game was not organised as we know it today and teams relied on their match secretaries being very active to ensure an attractive fixture list.

Early on it was realised that friendlies had only a limited appeal and there was a flurry of knock-out tournaments with a Cup as a trophy for the winner. The Premier Tournament was the National or what became known as the Scottish Football Association Cup first played for in Season 1873/74. The Lanarkshire Cup first saw the light of day in 1879/80 and other County Cups such as the Dunbartonshire, Ayrshire, Renfrewshire, Linlithgowshire, Forfarshire, etc., were all augmented by other more local cups such as the Airdrie Charity Cup, the Larkhall Charity Cup and the 'Coatbridge Express' Consolation Cup. The Scottish League was not to be formed until Season 1890/91, when Dumbarton and Rangers tied to be declared joint champions. Several "non league" groupings were set-up as early attempts to organise an ordered fixture list of some competitive nature to last throughout the season.

It was in this background that a bunch of enthusiastic sporting youths came to the new outdoor sport of football who were playing with the local junior teams who eventually took that momentous decision in October 1882, when a Public Meeting was held and the Albion Rovers Football Club (Coatbridge) was formed. The first

Office Bearers were President, Mr. R.S. Crombie, Sunnyside Road, Coatbridge, Vice-President, Mr. Thomas Simpson, Main Street, Coatbridge, Treasurer, Mr. Alexander Harvey, Baird Street, Coatbridge and the Secretary, Mr. George Smellie of Bank Buildings, Coatbridge. The players were drawn from two local junior teams, the Rovers and the Albion.

Times were difficult for a Club starting as late in a season as this. Most teams already had their fixture list completed and the initial season was spent playing against many of the minor teams and the second strings of the more established clubs. The first game played under the chosen colours of royal blue jerseys and white knickers was on the 11th of November 1882, when at their home ground of Cowheath, which was situated on what is today the Asda Car Park, Glencairn were visitors and resulted in a resounding 6-0 defeat. It was clearly brought home to the fledgling local team that success was not going to be automatic or immediate and that much hard work was ahead of the Committee.

The following week saw a 4-3 defeat, at Airdrie Cricket Ground, at the hands of Airdrieonians second eleven and the remainder of the season was made up with victories against Craigfield Seconds by 3-0 and Alpha from Motherwell by 6-1 and Chryston by 3-2.

All was not, of course, hard work and football matches as there was a good social side to things as well. The first supper of the Club was held in the Crown Restaurant on Friday, 21st April, 1883 and the President duly occupied the chair whilst croupier for the evening was Tom Simpson and it is noted in the local press that "after supper, which was splendidly purveyed in Mr. Cumming's best style, song, toast and sentiment prevailed, until the small hours of the morning when the company broke up singing Auld Lang Syne, all thoroughly satisfied with the evening's entertainment".

The first full season of the Club saw a change from the central Cowheath Park to Whifflet where Meadow Park was leased from the North British and Caledonian Railway Companies. This was a more commodious stadium and, although there was much criticism that the Club was no longer centrally situated, it was generally considered by Members to be a good move.

Nothing much of note occurred during the season but the Club was slowly building up a reputation which was to hold them in good stead in the years to come as far as the making up of a fixture list was concerned.

Season 1884/85

This was memorable because of several firsts. The most notable of these was the first meeting of the two Coatbridge Senior Clubs with Drumpellier visiting Meadow Park and losing by a 4-1 scoresheet. Rovers, just to underline the fact, had to resort to playing seven reserves in the team which made the victory all the more gratifying.

The team were invited to open the new ground of Campsie and it was a Gala Day for the Home Club who inflicted a severe 8-2 victory over the Young Rovers. High scoring was a feature in those days and that season great changes in fortune were noted in succeeding weeks. On the 14th February, at home against Airdrie a 8-0 victory was recorded but the following week against Airdrieonians (note two quite distinctly different teams) at Mavisbank a 9-0 defeat was the result. On the 28th March at home against the Alpha Seconds a 6-2 defeat was received but a week later against Airdrieonians justice was done when the Young Rovers won by 6-5 at home.

Two elevens were being fielded in those days and at the end of the season the First team had played twenty-three, won ten, lost nine, drawn four, scored ninety-three and conceded sixty-two goals, whilst the Second eleven played ten games, won six, lost three, drew one whilst scoring thirty goals and conceding eighteen. Mr. R.B. Crombie was again elected President with his Vice-President being Tom Smith. The Committee consisted of S. Scott, W. Howatt, W. Cairns, T. Craig, A. Millar with the Treasurer being Alex Harvey and Secretary William Haining from Tenants Place.

Now quite well established, the teams looked forward to the 1885/86 season with some relish and in mid-September the Town was buzzing for the long awaited Scottish Cup first round match against Drumpellier which was played at the Meadow. Rovers won this in a 6-2 romp but were eventually knocked out of the National Cup by Wishaw Swifts who, after a 2-2 draw at Coatbridge, won the replay very easily by 5-0. Rovers protested following this match on the basis that there were no corner flags, no proper touch lines and rough play by the Swifts. On considering their appeal, the Cup Committee threw it out and Rovers lost their deposit. Protests were very common in those days and it was rare for a team to lose a cup tie and not submit a protest.

The results continued to be very inconsistent with unknown Vulcan Rovers taking a creditable 2-2 draw and a 4-1 defeat at the hands of Third Lanark R.V. Second team. A victory over Airdrieonians, at Whifflet on the 21st of November, saw Rovers lead 5-2 at half-time to hang on for a 6-5 victory. Lanarkshire Cup second round match saw the local team Broomfield swamped by a massive 17-0 followed the next week with a 13-0 victory over Queens Park Hampden Eleven. A visit up to Arbroath to play Strathmore ended in a high scoring 5-5 draw.

Another protested cup tie took place against Rutherglen in the third round of the Lanarkshire Cup when Rovers lost 5-2. This time the protest was that, although the match was played at Rutherglen, the home team turned up twenty-five minutes late, one of the Rutherglen players was not registered and spectators interfered with play. This time the appeal was upheld and the match was scheduled to be replayed. The tie eventually went to Rutherglen by 3-2 due to a late winner and so perhaps the inevitable took place.

The season continued in haphazard fashion with a 9-2 defeat at the hands of Airdrieonians followed by successive home wins over Rutherglen by 4-1, Thornliebank by 5-3 and Cambuslang by 2-1. On the 29th May, in the Airdrie Charity Cup second round match, Royal Albert had a fine 3-2 win up at Mavisbank Park. Rovers by this time in the year were depleted with several of their regulars playing cricket for the local teams. There was a 4.30 p.m. kick-off for this match and admission was 3d. with the grandstand an additional 3d. Ladies were admitted free as was normal in those days.

SEASON 1886/87
At the outset of the season, and with the five years experience at senior level now behind them, the established stars were looking forward to the campaign ahead. The opening game of the season was on the 4th September against Dumbarton Union and this resulted in a very satisfactory 7-1 home victory. This set them up very well for the first round Scottish Cup tie against Clydesdale, who were routed by the score of 5-1, at Rutherglen, on a day of stormy, torrential rain. The high scoring and winning streak continued in the next round when Dykehead were despatched by 7-0 at Coatbridge.

However, the bubble was to burst with two away defeats, by 4-2 against West Calder and then 4-3 against First R.R.V. at Greenock, both in Friendly matches. On the 23rd October, it was back to the Cup and Thistle were roundly trounced 4-2 at Coatbridge. Changing Cups, this time to the Lanarkshire variety, a first round tie against Royal Albert ended in a resounding 13-1 victory.

A week later, Cambuslang were the visitors to the Meadow as Lanarkshire's Premier team borne out by the fact that they were to be losing finalists to Renton in the next season's National Cup tournament. Cambuslang easily won 6-1 leaving Rovers only the Lanarkshire Cup, to which they returned the next week at home, against Motherwell (formerly Alpha), but could only manage a 3-3 draw, losing the following week at Motherwell by a 3-1 scoreline. A Friendly against East Stirlingshire at Falkirk saw a 3-3 draw in December before the team left for a New Year holiday tour down to the North of England.

Three matches were set up, the first being against Black Watch Shankhouse who were holders of the Northumberland County Cup. Rovers team in this first "Foreign" match was Hodson, Calder, Cowan, Barr, Howatt, Harvey, McEwan, S. Scott, J. Morton, White and J. Scott. On Monday 3rd January, Bishop Auckland were the opposition and a resounding 9-3 victory took place over the Durham County Cup-Holders and Rovers' tails were up. The tour finished on the Tuesday with a game against Newcastle West End but by this time, the Lads' tongues were hanging out and they had to fight back from a one goal deficit at half-time before John Scott equalised late in the game to make a most satisfying scoreline, three games played and none lost.

Back home on the 15th of January at Motherwell a 2-0 defeat was suffered but the next week saw a 1-1 draw against Wishaw Thistle before, against King's Park at Stirling, Rovers really got back on the rails by a 7-0 victory and Simon Scott scoring four of the goals. This game started a surge of six victories on the trot, the next scalp being Airdrieonians who lost 5-4 at Coatbridge. This was followed by Glasgow University who lost by 8-0 and then Armadale at 2-1.

Dunblane was the next port of call and a 2-1 victory was notched up followed by a visit to Blair Lodge Park to play old rivals Drumpellier who were thoroughly despatched by 8-1. Motherwell were next due at Coatbridge but arrived fifty minutes late. Due to the late start, the game was abandoned at 2-2 each as darkness fell and it was not possible to follow play.

The 9th April saw the Airdrie Charity Cup recommenced and at Mavisbank Park a 6-1 victory over Cambuslang Hibs. was the net result, with Simon Scott notching yet another hat-trick. The next week, East Stirlingshire were the visitors and, despite Captain Sandy Harvey playing for the Lanarkshire Select, an 8-1 victory was achieved to be followed by a 5-1 victory the following week against First R.R.V. from Greenock.

On the last day of April, the Airdrie Charity Cup Final was played at Mavisbank against Airdrieonians who ran out narrow winners by 3-2, brothers John and Simon Scott scoring Rovers' goals. There were over three thousand at the game at which the gate amassed the vast sum in those days of £35. Rovers Final team was Hodson, Calder, Cowan, Howatt, Barr, Harvey, McEwan, S. Scott, Baird, White and J. Scott.

Next came the long trip to Angus and a game against Forfar Athletic, who ran out winners by a 9-2 scoreline. It was back to winning ways the following Saturday, which was a Benefit game for the Coatbridge Brass Band, when Linthouse were the guests and they went home with their tails between their legs after a 3-1 defeat. Next visitors to Coatbridge were Clydesdale Harriers who drew 4-4 on Monday, 16th of May, and the following Monday returned to lose by 4-2 with Rovers new signing, Fraser from Rangers, scoring two of the goals. McFarlane from Airdrie and Anderson from Motherwell took up the full-back positions in this game.

Airdrieonians now organised a tournament at their Mavisbank pitch and Rovers defeated Dykehead by a John Scott goal to nil and the following week were required to play two games on the one day beating Carfin Shamrock 2-0 before losing in the Final to Motherwell by the only goal of the game. There was considerable crowd trouble at this game after Simon Scott had been badly injured by a Motherwell defender and indeed was out of football and cricket for many weeks.

Season 1887/88
This started with a bang with nine victories out of the first ten matches played. The opening game on the 27th August was against First R.R.V. at Greenock and despite missing five regular first team players a 5-4 victory was secured. The following Saturday at Meadow Park, Airdriehill were the opposition in a Scottish Cup tie which was easily won by 12-0. Rovers' team that day was Hudson, Cowan, Gaylor, Howatt, Barr, Miller, S. Scott, Anderson, Addie, J Scott and Baird. This is Rovers highest score in the Scottish Cup Competition.

Flushed with this outstanding success, a visit was then made to Dalhousie Park, Perth to play Fair City Athletic and another 5-2 victory was noted in the record books. Returning to the Scottish Cup on the 24th September, Rutherglen were defeated in an away victory of 6-3. The following game at Dumbarton saw the homesters win by 7-2 and thus stop in its tracks the current Rovers' good fortune. Nevertheless, a 3-1 victory was gained over Monkcastle Kilwinning at Coatbridge by 3-1 and the powerful Northern were defeated on their own Hydepark, Glasgow in the Scottish Cup third round by 4-3.

At this stage, the Committee were obviously looking to the future and thought that they had a fair old team gathered together and Meadow Park was fitted with payboxes at the Entrances and a Stand erected for the next home game against King's Park which was won by 4-0. The Lanarkshire Cup was next on the scene and the first round tie at Coatbridge against Dykehead saw another resounding victory this time by 8-0 followed by the fourth round Scottish Cup against Third Lanark R.V. at home where, in front of a two thousand crowd, the 'Hi-Hi' were defeated 4-2 with the Scott brothers sharing the goals two apiece.

Continuing on their winning way Couther Villa were next on the scene at Coatbridge in a Lanarkshire Cup second round tie and were soundly trounced by 14-0, seven goals being scored in each half. Simon Scott was top marksman with five. McEwan had three and Anderson and J. Scott two each, with the remaining goals coming from Baird and Howatt. On this very important day, Rovers were represented by Hudson, Cowan, Walker, Howatt, Chalmers, Watson, Baird, S. Scott, McEwan, J. Scott and Andrew. With such a high scoring team, the support was optimistic that the fifth round Scottish Cup visit to West Cragie Park in Dundee to play Our Boys the next week would be no different.

However, the Rovers were in for a shock and only Bruce Chalmers could get on the scoreline at the end of a 4-1 defeat. In fact, the Rovers' team walked off the park prematurely and despite remonstrations from the referee, the cause was considered lost and the towel was flung in. County rivals, Cambuslang, beat Our Boys 6-0 in the semi-final eventually losing 6-1 to Renton in the Final.

Back home at the Meadow, Linthouse were the next visitors, the winning ways were re-found and a 4-1 scoreline was the end result as the forerunner of a seven games without defeat run. This match was followed by a 5-0 romp against Drumpellier, in the third round of the Lanarkshire Cup, with Tommy McEwan scoring a hat-trick and was followed by 6-2 and 5-2 victories over Campsie and Rutherglen respectively. The year was rung out with a 5-4 victory over Monkcastle Kilwinning and the news that a Coatbridge Charity Cup was to be inaugurated in commemoration of the Jubilee of Queen Victoria.

Neilston were the first foots on the 7th January and a 4-1 score was the outcome. Northern were dealt with likewise the following week but the current run of success dried up in the Lanarkshire Cup semi-final against Airdrieonians at Coatbridge when, in front of four thousand spectators, on a drizzling, strong windy day, Rovers threw away a 4-2 lead just after half-time and eventually lost 6-4. Rovers' team in this final was Hudson, T.G. Calder, H. Calder, Howatt, Watson, Chalmers, McEwan, S. Scott, Baird, J. Scott and Andrew.

A return visit to Linthouse at their Langlands Park, Govan Ground achieved a 5-1 victory and on the visit to Neilston a 4-3 victory was attained. Port Glasgow Athletic put paid to these good results with a 6-1 victory 'Doon the Watter'. On the 5th of February, Glasgow Rangers were visitors to the Meadow and Rovers won 2-0 in a keenly contested game with Anderson and Colquhoun scoring the goals. On the day, Rangers played in their Black and White striped jerseys and the conditions were cold and the pitch snow covered. The good form continued with an 8-3 victory over Jamestown but the following week King's Park were visited for a 3-2 defeat which saw a single goal half-time lead thrown away.

At the end of March, with three players engaged for the Lanarkshire Select in Dumbarton, Port Glasgow Athletic were defeated at Coatbridge by 3-2 and Glasgow University were the first of three home draws in succeeding weeks at 2-2 and the two Saints, Mirren and Bernard's, drawing 3-3 and 1-1 respectively, the latter in front of a home crowd of more than two thousand.

Continuing at the Meadow, Kilbirnie, the Ayrshire Cup holders, lost 3-2 before Glasgow University made a welcome return but lost 3-1 for their trouble. On the 28th April, when Third Lanark R.V. visited the Meadow, a 1-1 draw took place. In a hurricane wind, the 'Hi-Hi' turned up two men short and two Rovers' men, Robertson at left-half and Anderson at inside-left, were 'loaned' for the day. With the season fast coming to a close, Partick Thistle visited and went home easy winners by 5-0 and when Clydesdale Harriers arrived on Monday the 14th May for the last home match of the season, finishing an astonishing run of ten home games on the trot, a 3-1 score was chalked up with Simon Scott scoring his usual two and Anderson the other. Bob Baird played for the Harriers during this match on loan.

A week later the Edinburgh Hibernians visited Coatbridge to play at School Park, Whifflet in a Benefit match for Whifflet Shamrock and Rovers were defeated by 2-1 in an interesting game against the First Leaguers.

Thus ended a season with thirty-six games played, twenty-five won, seven lost, four drawn and an amazing one hundred and forty-nine goals with only seventy-nine conceded. The Committee sat back complimenting themselves on the giant step forward they had made in the senior game in such a short space of time and already were looking forward to the new season.

Season 1888/9
The new season opened with all the old stars available, which was quite a feather in the cap for the Committee as Scottish Clubs were having difficulty holding onto their amateur players with the poaching taking place by English teams. The first game was played in Falkirk against East Stirlingshire and was a 4-3 win but on Wednesday, 13th August, Airdrieonians were played in the opening home game of the season in a 1-1 draw in front of four thousand fans with the kick-off being delayed due to Rovers' players being involved in the Glasgow Cricket Cup at the Glasgow Exhibition. John Scott, Simon Scott, Tom McEwan, Sandy Harvey and Andrew Johnstone made up the team who defeated Govan Athletic. Despite this, Airdrieonians could only start the game with nine men, although they made up their numbers as the game proceeded. Rovers' team was Haddow, Walker, H. Calder, Howatt, Chalmers, Barr, McEwan, Gray, Dally, Baird and J. Scott.

A first defeat was inflicted by Northern away from home by 6-2 and the following Thursday, in the Exhibition tournament, St. Mirren trounced Rovers by 4-0 but this was compensated by a 4-2 win at Perth against Fair City Athletic on the following Saturday.

The following week was Scottish Cup first round day and Bellshill were due to visit the Meadow. The Bellshill Committee asked for a five o'clock kick-off but even then they incredulously failed to turn up by the appointed time. Accordingly, Rovers claimed the tie which situation was confirmed by the Association. Despite or perhaps because of, the inactivity that Saturday, Mossend Swifts ran up a 4-1 victory at Mossend before the team got back on the lines on the 15th September with a 7-1 win over Bo'ness with the Scott brothers scoring five goals and Harvey and Anderson the other two.

Flushed with this success, the second round Scottish Cup match, at home against Rutherglen, saw a mammoth 9-1 scoreline with McEwan scoring five, Simon Scott two and John Scott and Johnstone one apiece. Renton quickly brought the team back to earth with an 8-2 win down in Dunbartonshire. The see-saw form continued the following week with a 5-1 away win at Maryhill followed by a Scottish Cup third round exit at the hands of Glasgow Celtic by 4-1. Rovers complained bitterly about the rough play by the Celtic team to no avail.

Licking their wounds from defeat in that Cup, Royal Albert from Larkhall were hosts the following week in the Lanarkshire Cup Tourney when a 4-4 draw was played out in gale conditions. Rovers were 4-0 up just after half-time and by the end were hanging on grimly to achieve a draw. Before two thousand spectators the following week the replay took place at Coatbridge with the Albert running off easy winners by 4-0 in very soft conditions.

A visit to Alexandria to take on the mighty Vale of Leven was the next hurdle which Rovers failed. The score was 3-1 but Rovers were four men short of their usual team and two halves of thirty-five minutes each were played in this match.

There were many problems for match secretaries in these days with players being unable to obtain leave from their places of employment or inability to arrive in time and there are many indications of players and even full teams finding themselves on the wrong train. There are also many episodes related in the popular press of teams taking one train whilst their hamper with all their playing gear ended up on another going in the opposite direction.

Such a situation befell Dumbarton Athletic the following week on their visit to Coatbridge but they eventually arrived one hour late and the game finally finished in darkness with a 2-0 victory for Rovers. The following week at Beechwood Park,

Glasgow Thistle provided the opposition but Rovers ran out narrow winners by 3-2. The ground was in such a condition that the game was shortened to two halves of thirty minutes each.

Weather conditions at this time were atrocious and the Meadow was considered unplayable and the match against Arthurlie was played at Blair Park Lodge, Drumpellier, home of the team of that name but this made no difference to Rovers who chalked up a 5-1 score. The next match was at Battlefield when a narrow 1-0 victory was achieved.

On the 15th November, Port Glasgow Athletic made the trip from the Tail of the Bank and on a frost covered pitch, the game started half an hour late and ended up 6-2 for Rovers. The visitors' left-back walked off in a huff in the second half when the score was 4-2 but, after pressure from his Committee Members, came back to finish the game. This match was followed by a visit from the Maryhill Giants, Partick Thistle, who came, saw and conquered to the tune of 3-1, thus ending a reasonably successful 1888.

Another Tour to foreign parts took place, again to the North East of England, and two matches were fixed up. The first was against Darlington on New Year's Day, when a 7-0 score was attributed to the Scots, and on the following Saturday, the other Darlington team—St. Augustine's were similarly dealt with, only this time the score was 9-0. The Town Crier was used prior to the game and this helped to ensure the gate was over the thousand.

Back at home, Cowlairs were the First Foots and they suffered a 4-0 defeat whilst Kilbirnie were next to fall to the tune of 4-1 down in Ayrshire in a game in which Rovers turned up late and both halfs were restricted to thirty-five minutes.

A high-scoring game took place as the last match in January, and a return fixture with Partick Thistle which ended up with the odd goal in thirteen giving victory to the Jags. The following two matches saw defeats; first of all at home against Mossend Swifts at 3-1 and away against King's Park at 6-4.

A new tournament took place under the auspices of the Lanarkshire Football Association and Linthouse were the visitors on the 2nd March. A Willie Baird goal was sufficient in front of nearly three thousand fans to see the points go to Rovers, who should have played Uddingston but they refused and Linthouse were called in at the last moment. It was back to high-scoring the next week, when Ayr Athletic visited and went home losing by 8-0 and St. Mirren fared no better the following Saturday, losing by 3-2.

On the 23rd March, Vale of Leven arrived and, in a quagmire of a pitch, produced the biggest score to date against Rovers at the Meadow, winning by 7-3, and this reverse was followed the following week by King's Park going home victors by 3-2. However, all was not lost, and Glasgow Thistle opened April with a visit and a 7-2 victory for Rovers, made all the more meritorious as five players were representing Lanarkshire in the County game against Renfrewshire.

In the Final of the Lanarkshire Trophy against Airdrieonians, with a four o'clock kick-off, and the gate prices increased to six pence, two thousand people saw Rovers lose at the Meadow by 2-1, Rovers team being Haddow, Cowan, Walker, Harvey, Chalmers, Howatt, McMillan, S. Scott, Baird, Anderson and J. Scott.

There then followed two games against Edinburgh Hibernians, starting with a first appearance at Easter Road, when a very creditable 3-3 draw was achieved with Rovers leading 3-1 at half-time, and the equalising goal for Hibs late on being hotly disputed. The following week the Hibernians returned to Coatbridge, when another draw—this time at 2-2 each—was the result, and would you believe—Hibs. equalising in the last minute. As the First Leaguers had failed to best the non-leaguers over these two matches, the players were feeling quite pleased with themselves.

Dumbarton were next to come to the Meadow and lost 4-1, with Airdrie losing 3-1 on the Wednesday at Mavisbank. The following Wednesday, Zingari, a team made up chiefly by Queen's Park players, but who free-lanced, arranged matches and were a good crowd drawer, were roundly defeated by 7-4. This was the first of a five game home end of season run with Carfin Shamrock featuring in a 0-0 draw and then Edinburgh Hibernians losing 4-0 in a Benefit match for the family of James McGinty, who was killed by falling down a pit shaft at Drumpellier. This game had an evening kick-off and twenty Pounds were raised for McGinty's dependents. Big reputation Renton then scored the only goal of the game, whilst Glasgow Celtic managed a 2-1 victory to end the season.

Season 1889/90
As preparations were being concluded for the new season, left-back Harry Calder signed with Preston North End, and his full-back partner Walker moved on to Burnley. But apart from this, most of the players of the previous season were willing and eager for the matches ahead and the team got off to the best possible start, with a visit to new territory to play Arbroath, the Forfarshire champions, and, although losing 1-0 at half-time, the men from the 'Brig scored three goals through John Scott, Thomson and Bryson, to return home victorious. The team for this match was Haddow, A. Scott, Duff, Galloway, Chalmers, Howatt, J. Scott, Thomson, Baird, Rorke and Bryson.

The following Saturday was a bit of a disaster, with Abercorn failing to turn up and at short notice a home fixture was arranged against the unknown quantity Methlaw Park from Dumbarton, and the visitors surprised everyone with the quality of their play to run off winners by 4-1. Defeat continued in the next game played at Byreknowe Park, Carfin, against the local Shamrock, who easily disposed of a poor Rovers' team by four goals without reply.

Disappointingly, another home fixture was cancelled when Battlefield failed to turn up but on the 21st September, the highest defeat to that date was inflicted by Vale of Leven to the tune of 10-4. As often happens in these circumstances, the team bounced back in the next game, which was against Partick Thistle at the Meadow. The game was close until half-time when at 3-2 the result could have gone either way, but in the second-half Rovers popped in another three goals to run out convincing winners by 6-2. Maybe because of this result, the following week yet another team failed to turn up for their fixture. This time it was Maryhill, which left severe problems for the Committee, as all these games were a financial loss.

The next match was against local rivals, Airdrieonians at Mavisbank Park, where in front of over three thousand fans a tight 3-3 draw was played out. Rovers introduced inside-left Rogerson from Carluke and he opened the scoring with Sandy Rowan scoring the others. The topsy-turvy form continued the following week against Broxburn at home, where a 3-1 defeat was inflicted. Rovers started this game with ten men plus a substitute, awaiting the arrival of Rowan, and when he arrived a swap took place on the pitch. Who said substitutes were a modern phenomenon?

On the 26th of October came the first of the Cup ties with a visit to Larkhall against Royal Albert. This finished up a 2-2 draw and the Royalists had difficulty in fielding a team. Firstly, the game started ten minutes late and, under protest the homesters kicked off with only ten men and had to make up the numbers later on in the game. A protest was made to the Lanarkshire F.A. by the Royalists on the conduct of Mr. Rose of Partick Thistle, who refereed the tie. More important for Rovers was the loss of John Scott to Sunderland as a Professional, leaving behind brothers Simon and Adam.

The Association threw out the protest and required the replay to take place the following week at Meadow Park with Mr. Harrison, of the Ayrshire Association, this time in charge. This replay ended once more in a 2-2 draw.

Neilston were next to bow the knee at the Meadow, losing 6-2. Partick Thistle took revenge for their earlier defeat by winning 4-2 in Glasgow before Uddingston arrived to receive a 3-0 drubbing. The visitors came two men short and, as frequently happened in those days, two spectators who "just happened" to have their boots with them were called on. Another favourite was lost prior to this game, with Willie Howatt deciding his future lay with Blackburn Rovers.

With Meadow Park being the venue for the Lanarkshire -v- Northumberland County Match, Rovers visited Hamilton West End and had a straightforward 3-1 victory, but on the first Saturday in December, a visit to Edinburgh to play Leith Athletic was not successful and the team came home 4-2 down.

The Lanarkshire Cup second round match against Motherwell saw a return to the winning standard, with a 5-3 victory moving Rovers into the Semi-Final. But with the traditional seasonal bad weather, Wishaw Thistle visited Coatbridge to find the Meadow waterlogged and a match of two thirty-five minute halves was played for a 3-1 Wishaw victory. The last home match of the year, on the 28th December, saw a visit by the Edinburgh Hibernians which, again due to ground conditions being very hard with frost, allowed only two half hour halves to be played. This saw a 3-1 victory for Rovers with Simon Scott opening the scoring and Archie Sergeant notching a double.

Another tour was undertaken to the North of England and on the last day of the year a game was played against Bishop Auckland with a fine 4-3 victory the result. This was followed on Wednesday the 1st against Darlington when a 6-4 victory was logged. However, with the legs starting to go, on the following Saturday and in the fourth game in eight days against Stockton, the best that could be achieved was a 2-1 defeat. Top scorer over the tour was Duncan Smith with four goals then Matt Rorke with three and Archie Sergeant had two.

The Airdrieonians' team came to first-foot their Coatbridge neighbours, but arrived two men short and Willie Baird was co-opted to the opposition for the day. Despite this, Rovers ran out emphatic winners on a 5-1 scoreline. In exactly the same soft underfoot conditions the following week, Battlefield this time forming the opposition, Rovers had to lend reserve forward McMillan to the visitors, but still managed to chalk up a 5-2 victory.

Two visits in successive weeks to the 'Tail of the Bank' saw first of all Greenock Morton secure a 2-2 draw, but then Port Glasgow Athletic were defeated by 5-2 when Rovers were not extended. On the 8th February, Mossend Swifts also arrived two men short and again Rovers lent Anderson and Donald to the visitors. Led by an Archie Sergeant hat-trick, Rovers, who were winning 5-0 at half time, could not improve things in the second-half on the frost bound ground, but confidently looked forward to their Lanarkshire Cup semi-final the next week against Royal Albert, following their recent run of success.

When the due day arrived the ground was very frosty and the referee, Mr. Bishop from Falkirk, agreed that riddled ashes should be laid on the pitch, but the crowd of upwards of three thousand could only watch the visitors pocket the tie by 2-1 with Rovers seemingly strangely disinterested. The next match was against Motherwell at Dalziel Park and, despite being several first team players short, Rovers managed a 4-2 victory. But the following week Airdrieonians again visited the Meadow, where, in front of fifteen hundred spectators, a fiercely contested game saw Airdrie win by the odd goal in seven.

Two victories then followed, the first by the only goal of the game at Uddingston and then ample revenge against Methlan Park from Dumbarton, with Rovers scoring five goals without reply. The first match in April brought the Ayrshire Cup holders, Annbank, who proved to be a big draw at Coatbridge and, despite Davie Haddow being injured early in the game and Sandy Harvey having to take over in goal, it wasn't until the second-half that Annbank took over and eventually ran out worthy winners by 3-1. Two 5-1 home victories occurred, the first against Port Glasgow Athletic, who again arrived with only nine men and Rovers doing the usual lending. Kilmarnock Athletic the following week were similarly dealt with.

The first Competition for the Larkhall Charity Cup was held and Rovers were drawn to meet Airdrieonians in a match with considerable bad feeling, which Rovers eventually won by 2-0. The two thousand fans were entertained with a stand-up fight between Traquair of Rovers and Davidson of Airdrie, into which big Dave Haddow joined. Eventually after Mr. Young of Clyde restored order, the pugilists were ordered off and Haddow was severely warned. Despite the ill-feeling, a gate of £30.10.0d. was the satisfactory outcome to the Sponsors. In continuing the ill-feeling after the game, Airdrie protested that Rovers had not handed in their team lines before the game, but this was turned down by the Committee.

In mid-week Hamilton Accies. were trounced 8-0 in a Coatbridge Express match but a visit to Barrowfield the following Saturday saw a hard fought 3-3 draw against Clyde. The next week it was back to the Larkhall Charity Cup, this time for the Final match which Royal Albert won, much to the glee of their Support, by 7-1 with a gate of £35 this time.

The sporting Monklanders saw the Airdrie Charity Cup take place at Mavisbank and in the first round Rovers had a 2-2 draw against Carfin Shamrock. The following Tuesday saw English Leaguers Sunderland play another 2-2 draw before a visit was made to Motherwell in the Express Cup. Rovers won this game 5-4 but Motherwell protested on the grounds of rough play, which was upheld by the Committee and the match ordered to be replayed.

However, before this could take place, it was back to the Airdrie Charity Cup and Mavisbank, where the undecided tie against Carfin Shamrock was played out. This finished a 1-1 draw at full-time and, despite playing an extra five minutes each way, there was no further score and the following Wednesday the game was replayed with Rovers going down narrowly by 5-4.

The final game of the season was the replayed Express Cup match at Motherwell, when Rovers went down by 2-1. Whilst Rovers protested that the game should have been played on neutral territory, the Sponsors rejected the protest and confirmed the Motherwell victory.

More importantly for Rovers, however, this saw a decimation of their amateur team to the English professional ranks. Already during the season, J. Scott and Howatt had gone to Sunderland and Blackburn Rovers respectively. Big Dave Haddow moved on to Derby County. He was to return to Rangers and play for

Scotland against the Auld Enemy in due time. Adam Scott left for an illustrious career with Nottingham Forest and Bruce Chalmers followed Haddow to Derby County, whilst Matt Rorke joined Scott at Notts Forest along with Sandy Rowan. Archie Sergeant signed for Middlesborough Ironopolis and Duncan Smith for less fashionable Accrington.

Thus nine first team players had decided to seek their fortunes away from Coatbridge and this was a severe blow to President Crombie and his Committee. But, as Rovers were running three teams at that time, the reserves were looked to to provide the new nucleus. Willie Roberts, who had made his debut at the end of the season, Jack Russell, Hudson, Marshall and Bruce all were added to the pool.

Season 1890/91

With such a loss of first team players the Faithful were not looking for too much at the beginning of the season and this was fortunate because, on the last day of August at home to Royal Albert, a 5-0 defeat was inflicted on the following team — Galbraith, Russell, McKim, Galloway, Traquair, Roberts, J. Bryson, Hislop, Templeton, Thomson and C. Bryson.

However, the heads were up the next week in the Scottish Cup first round against Carrington at Hanover Park, Glasgow when a 2-1 victory was recorded. In the visit to Battlefield, with a five o'clock kick-off, a 4-1 defeat was experienced as the first of seven straight defeats. West End from Newcastle won by three clear goals before St. Mirren had a crushing 5-1 victory in the second round of the Scottish Cup.

This was followed by a 5-2 drubbing at home against Airdrieonians and a 9-2 annihilation at Falkirk before Port Glasgow Athletic came to Coatbridge to win 2-1. With the Supports' spirits down in their boots, Kilbirnie won 6-1 down in Ayrshire. It took a Lanarkshire Cup tie against Motherwell Shamrock to bring this miserable list of defeats to a halt, although this was only a 2-2 draw but it was enough and the following Saturday the replay at Ladywell Park was scheduled but due to bad ground conditions and weather, only a Friendly was played for thirty-five minutes but a 4-1 victory was achieved in that short time.

The following Saturday, the Cup tie proper took place with the result being a very encouraging 8-1 victory. The next match was against Burnbank Swifts, who were Scottish Junior Cup holders, having their first game at the Meadow but due to very heavy rain, the game was restricted to a thirty minute first half with only fifteen minutes being played in the second half. There was sufficient time however for Rovers to score a 3-1 victory before time was called.

Two further victories took place at Whifflet, firstly against East Stirlingshire by 4-1 and then 2-1 against Uddingston. Captain Jimmy Galloway and his boys were stopped in their tracks on the 13th of December by Battlefield in a 1-1 draw with Galbraith of Rovers guesting with the visitors in what turned out to be the last game played by Rovers in the year.

Another tour was undertaken to the North of England but with Rovers' much weakened team, the results were very discouraging. On New Year's Day, Stockton were the opposition, but a 2-0 defeat was the result and the following day Bishop Auckland ran out easy winners by 6-2. So finished a most disappointing tour from a result point of view although the social side was as successful as ever.

On the 10th January, the Lanarkshire Cup second round tie took place at Caldercruix, against Glengowan, which resulted in a victory for Rovers by means of the only goal of the game. Conditions were very bad with the pitch being frost bound and both Clubs submitted protests and the L.F.A. sustained them and ordered a replay. Meanwhile, Motherwell visited the Meadow and ran off 2-0 victors before the replayed Glengowan match saw Rovers finally win 3-1

Back to the bad old days of the previous season when Clydesdale failed to appear for their fixture but the month of February started off with a visit to Barrowfield against Clyde but the team was well defeated by 4-3. Uddingston were next to visit Coatbridge in the Lanarkshire Cup semi-final when Billy Baird scored a goal late on to equalise a half-time deficit to take the tie into a replay. Despite being away from home, the following Saturday saw a 5-1 victory at Uddingston with Charlie Bryson scoring three of the goals. He also got on the score sheet the following week at home against Kilbirnie but couldn't save a 3-1 defeat to be followed by a visit from Falkirk who won by 4-3 as a prelude to the Lanarkshire Cup Final against Airdrieonians played at Motherwell.

This was the sixth final tie in various cups that Rovers had contested but they were still to collar their first trophy. A four thousand crowd saw Rovers leading by one goal to nil with ten minutes to go and the Coatbridge support licking their lips in anticipation for Cup glory. It was not to be and Airdrie lifted the Cup at full-time by a 2-1 margin. The defeated team was Henderson, Traquair, Martin, Galloway, S. Scott, Harvey, Marshall, Anderson, Baird, Thompson and C. Bryson.

A hilarious situation took place two weeks later against Clydesdale in the Coatbridge Express Cup. The match was played at Southcroft Park, Rutherglen and Rovers ran out winners by 4-3. They had to play one man short for the first twenty minutes by which time they were 2-0 up. Then with ten minutes to go and Rovers winning 4-3, goalkeeper Hudson had to leave his goal and go and catch a train leaving Rovers to hang on for the remainder of the tie.

The following Tuesday, a celebration supper was held for the vanquished Lanarkshire Cup Finalists in the Masonic Hall when a good time was had by both Players and Supporters. East Stirlingshire were visited in Falkirk for a 4-3 defeat and a depleted team visited Hamilton to play Burnbank Swifts the following week to lose by a numbing 10-1 whilst Hudson, Martin and Harvey were all playing for the Lanarkshire Select against Cumberland in the 6-1 victory at Meadow Park. The following Wednesday at Motherwell saw a 3-1 defeat to be followed by a 4-1 defeat by Glasgow Wanderers at Coatbridge when Mr. Smellie the referee caused a great commotion by ordering the wrong man to the pavilion following a fracas on the field. Consequently the game was stopped until both sets of Committee-men remonstrated with the Referee, justice was finally done and the game re-started.

Up to this time, the task of the Match Secretary had been very onerous and it was a great struggle each season to compile a satisfactory fixture list with many of the Saturdays being meaningless friendlies interspersed between the various Cup ties. It had long been the intention to form other groupings similar to the Scottish League, which was now in operation and in His Lordship's Larder, an hostelry in Glasgow, during April 1891 the Scottish Federation was formed. This combined the following teams — Albion Rovers, Arthurlie, Burnbank Swifts, Falkirk, Glasgow Wanderers, Hurlford, Kilmarnock Athletic, King's Park, Motherwell, Pollokshaws, Royal Albert and Wishaw Thistle and was scheduled to start for season 1891/92. There was much congratulation in the non-league that success had been achieved in gaining access to this grouping.

Returning to Cup football and the Larkhall Charity Cup in particular, Airdrieonians were the opposition at Larkhall on the 3rd May in a match which cost Rovers dear as Simon Scott fractured his collar bone during the game and thus would be out of Football and Cricket for some considerable time. The score was also unpalatable with a 2-0 defeat.

Rovers hardworking Committee announced they had negotiated a 5 year lease of Meadow Park with the Railway Company in time for the Wednesday match against Airdrieonians in the Airdrie Charity Cup which ended up a 2-2 draw but the final of this Cup was to be contested between Motherwell and Royal Albert, the latter team winning by 3-0 at Mavisbank. Guesting for the Albert on the day were ex-Rovers Haddow and Chalmers, now of Derby County who picked up a winners badge. The season finished with a match at Beechwood Park, Glasgow against the Thistle when Rovers won by 2-1, thus ending a disappointing season when again no cups had been won for the sideboard but also some satisfaction in a period of transition and re-building an entire eleven, some successes had been achieved. The Committee re-doubled their efforts and set to work over the summer to sign up experienced players in an attempt to become a force in the County.

CHAPTER TWO

THE FIRST TENTATIVE STEPS

Season 1891/92
The Committee were very successful in signing players and were pleased to welcome back several disillusioned players following their season in the English League. Chalmers, Rowan, Sergeant, Smith and Rorke all returned to the fold to be joined by Paterson Sergeant, a young talented full-back from Glenboig, and goalkeepers Allan and Young.

Thus the new season optimistically started with a friendly match arranged for the 7th August against Bathgate Rovers at Coatbridge when a 2-2 draw was the result. Rovers team was Young, P. Sergeant, Martin, Galloway, Chalmers, Roberts, Rowan, A. Sergeant, Buchanan, Gray and Smith.

Much was looked forward to in the league grouping called the Federation, and also the new rule which gave a penalty kick for a foul given within the box which was hereafter the full width of the pitch.

The season proper started on the 15th August against Glasgow Wanderers in the Federation and, with Mr. T. Watson the Federation Secretary refereeing, an easy 7-2 victory was recorded. This good form continued in the next match against Wishaw Thistle, away from home, this time by 5-2. The third victory on-the-trot was logged at home by 2-0 against Pollokshaws with this game starting fifty minutes late due to two of the visiting team missing their train connection.

All this good work came to an end when another visit was paid to Old Public Park, Wishaw against the local Thistle in the Scottish Cup, when the homesters won by 7-3. Salt was rubbed in the wound by Chalmers missing a penalty. The next week it was back to Federation business against Kilmarnock Athletic at Coatbridge and this time a Chalmers penalty score was enough to divide the points.

A trip to Barrhead was next on the cards to play Arthurlie, who were second top of the Federation, and despite Smith scoring two goals in the second half, the homesters ran out deserved winners by 3-2. Two home victories in a row then saw Rovers go top of the League. First of all against Kilbirnie when a 4-0 result was the satisfactory outcome but this was bettered on the third week in October against Clydebank when a 7-5 score was notched with Sandy Rowan scoring a club record — six goals. The winning ways continued the following week at Holm Quarry, Kilmarnock, against the local Athletic with a 4-2 victory.

Flushed with this success, and with a vacant Saturday available, a friendly was quickly set up against old friends King's Park at Stirling, who were to run out deserved winners by 4-2. Despite this set-back, optimism was running high in the support, and when Royal Albert were next to visit Meadow Park on Federation business, a crowd of two thousand saw a deserved Rovers win by 3-1.

In time for the Lanarkshire Cup Tie, against Airdrieonians at Coatbridge, came the announcement that an additional dressing room was to be provided under the Grandstand and spray and plunge baths were to be fitted for the players. However, this good news did not spread itself to the playing pitch and Airdrie went back up the road with a 5-3 win under their belt.

It was back to the Federation the following week when Motherwell visited the Meadow and whilst Rovers were top, the 'Well were bottom of the table and it was no surprise when Rovers won this one by 3-1. Two friendly defeats then took

27

place, the first down at Port Glasgow by 6-2 and the second at home against Dykebar by 3-1.

Meanwhile in the Federation, Rovers had been supplanted at the top of the League and were now sitting in second place when Falkirk came to visit. There was nothing Rovers could do to stop the Bairns going off with a 4-2 victory. The following week, in another friendly against Royal Albert on a wet, stormy day, a 5-2 defeat was inflicted by the visitors. This score was reversed the following week against Burnbank, in the last game of the year at Hamilton, to go second top of the Federation. The 9th of January, in a friendly at Clydebank, Rovers won by 5-0 and a visit to an ice-covered pitch 'Doon the Watter' against Saltcoats Victoria which the Ayrshire club won by 2-0.

Mixed fortunes then occurred in the Federation with the return match against Motherwell, with Rovers leaders and the Steelmen third bottom. The homesters more than made up for their earlier defeat with a resounding 7-3 victory. Rovers bounced back immediately trouncing Burnbank Swifts by 5-1 although the Swifts played with only eight signed men and two substitutes gained from the terracing. Pollokshaws also righted the scales with a 4-2 victory in Glasgow before two friendly matches saw Cambuslang lose 2-1 at the Meadow, whilst at Falkirk a 1-1 draw was played. This game was rescheduled as a friendly because the Federation fixture, which had been due to be played, was cancelled due to a hard pitch.

Back on Federation business the following week saw a visit from Hurlford which Rovers won by 7-0 and, as the official referee did not appear, Mr. Hutton of Rovers became the man in the middle with the approval of the opposition. A 6-0 victory at Clydebank was next in line and the fans were then convinced of the great potential of their team. This faith was badly shaken when after fifteen minutes in the next match, at home against Wishaw Thistle, the local favourites were losing by two clear goals. However, the half time score was 4-2 in favour of Rovers and a further three goals were put on for no reply in the second half making a tremendous twenty goals for two against over the previous three Federation games.

The away match at Eglinton Park, Glasgow to play Glasgow Wanderers, who had earlier lost by 7-2, looked an easy fixture as Wanderers were firmly fixed at the bottom of the League but they surprised Rovers in a 2-1 victory. The Lanarkshire Cup got a turn with a fixture at Douglas Park against Hamilton Academical and a 4-2 victory ensued. Missing from this one was Willie Roberts who was being married.

On the 2nd April a friendly was played against Airdrieonians at Coatbridge with a 3-2 victory being the satisfactory result. However, the following week against Leith Athletic at Bank Park, Edinburgh, three clear goals were lost although the team was depleted with Archie Sergeant and Bruce Chalmers playing for Lanarkshire against Cumberland, at Workington, in a 4-1 victory. The latter captained his County team.

Arthurlie were the next visitors at Coatbridge to be trounced 6-1 even although they were current League leaders and the following week, in the Coatbridge Express Cup, Wishaw Thistle were beaten by the only goal of the match. The last day of the month found Airdrie fighting out a 3-3 draw at the Meadow in a friendly, whilst Royal Albert were the next victims, in the Coatbridge Express Cup, by 5-3 at Larkhall. The following Wednesday saw the return match go Royal Albert's way by four clear goals giving them the tie by 7-5.

There was still a chance of lifting the Federation title and hopes were high when the postponed match at Falkirk took place on the 21st of May and a 4-2 victory was achieved but all was thrown away in the last fixture at Hurlford when Rovers lost by 6-1 to finish in second place. So near and yet so far! The fans and players alike were sure that the good days were just around the corner however, and that this was only the start of better times.

It was again time for the Charity Cups and the first of these was the early stages of the Larkhall Variety with Hamilton Accies being promptly seen off by a 6-2 drubbing putting Rovers into the final yet again. The following Saturday saw the Airdrie Charity Cup preliminary rounds take place and Rovers met the strong-going Airdriehill team. The royal blue shirted Rovers defeated their red shirted opponents at Mavisbank Park by 3-2 to move into another final. Airdrieonians had just moved headquarters to Broomfield but were allowing the pitch time to knit for the new season and the Charity matches were being played on their old stamping ground. Thus the scene was set for a grand finale to the season with two Charity Cup Finals due in succeeding weeks.

The first took place at Raploch Park, Larkhall, against Royal Albert in the third final of the Local Charity Cup. Following heavy rain, the ground was slippery and Rovers were represented by Allan, P. Sergeant, Martin, Galloway, Chalmers, Roberts, A. Sergeant, Marshall, Rowan, Rorke and Smith and there was great excitement when Galloway opened the scoring in ten minutes. This was equalised a few minutes later and that's how the teams stood at half time. Marshall regained Rovers lead but the homesters drew level before, after some fine play by Sergeant and Marshall, Smith scored Rovers' third goal with only ten minutes to go and Rorke scoring a fourth goal virtually from the kick-off. With the referee looking at his watch, Archie Sergeant settled the tie beyond all possible doubt at a resounding substantial 5-2 and Rovers thus took possession of their first cup after having so many runners-up medals.

A telegram was sent home 'A CUP AT LAST' and the whole town set about receiving the team with due honours. When the train arrived at Whifflet Station, a brake awaited the Heroes of the Hour. The horses were done away with in favour of willing hands of the supporters and, to the strains of the Coatbridge Brass Band, a triumphant entry was made onto the Main Street to the Temperance Hall where the team and support spent a jubilant sociable half hour together.

Naturally, the following Saturday couldn't come quickly enough and on the 18th June, the old rivals Airdrieonians and Albion Rovers met at Mavisbank Park before a disappointing crowd of only two thousand five hundred amidst more heavy rain. Rovers were represented by the same team as had won the Cup at Larkhall the previous week. After twenty minutes Airdrie drew first blood and shortly after scored for a second time with Rovers' fans despondent at the inability of their team to break down a sound Airdrie defence. Sergeant gave the 'Blues' some hope in the fifty-second minute with a fine goal but Rovers' defence then had a series of miraculous escapes when the goal which Airdrie deservedly merited seemed ready to appear at any moment. A goal at that stage would have finished the game as a spectacle but it was not to be and Rovers gained the ascendancy. As often happens in these situations, the underdogs scored and again, immediately after the kick-off, Sergeant rose like a salmon to head a fine goal from a cross by Smith. Archie then had a goal rightly chalked off for offside but Matt Rorke scored two goals to make the score an amazing 5-2. Not to be outdone, on the final whistle, Airdrie scored again to make the final score 5-3. Players and fans alike couldn't believe it. Ten years without a trophy for the sideboard and all of a sudden two Cups within eight days!

ALBION ROVERS SEASON 1892/93
Back: P. Sergeant, B. Chalmers, J. Allan, J. Martin.
Centre: J. Galloway, T. Marshall, W. Roberts, D. Smith.
Seated: A. Sergeant, J. McGeechan, J. Gray, M. Rorke, D. Millar, Trainer.
Airdrie Charity Cup, Larkhall Charity Cup.

After the teams had dined together and the Cup had been presented to Rovers, the official party were driven home on a couple of waggonettes. At the Gushet House, where the Airdrie War Memorial is now sited, they were met by an enormous crowd and again, headed by the Coatbridge Brass Band, the procession wound its way down into Coatbridge. At the Clyde Tube Works, the horses were unyoked and, until the end of the journey deliriously joyful fans conveyed the Rovers triumphant along the Main Street down to the Fountain.

All the disappointments of the past ten years had been put behind them and no-one could wait until the new season was underway.

Season 1892/93
At last the great day dawned on the 13th August, when on Federation business the short journey was made to Falkirk. Although the homesters scored the first two goals, Rovers added five in an amazing ten minute spell to lead 7-3 by half-time. By the time the referee called an end to hostilities, a glorious 12-5 score in favour of Rovers had been recorded. Rovers were represented by Allan, P. Sergeant, Martin, Johnston, Chalmers, Roberts, A. Sergeant, Gray, Rowan, Rorke and Smith. What a start, and more was to follow with two straight home wins in the Federation, firstly against Royal Albert by 3-0 and then Clydebank by 5-0 in which game Matt Rorke scored a hat trick.

The following week in the Scottish Cup first round, Shettleston Swifts played in their light blue jerseys with Rovers wearing their black and white stripes. A quick exit resulted for the Glasgow team at 9-1 with Matt Rorke again top scorer, this time with four. However, to ensure they didn't grow too big for their boots, a competent Neilston team were visited and, although Rovers led 3-1 at one stage in the second half, they were soundly beaten by 5-3. The following week Wishaw Thistle were defeated 2-1 at the Meadow, both matches being in the Federation.

Continued success in the Scottish Cup came in the second round, when Carfin Hibs were defeated at Coatbridge by the mammoth score of 10-0 and again Matt Rorke had a hat-trick. This was followed by a remarkable double the following week when Falkirk came in search of Federation points but lost by a prodigious 12-3 scoreline, a result which put Rovers on top of the Federation League Table. Top dog was John Gray with five goals and Simon Scott had four. Great stuff for the fans!

Airdriehill were next to feel the strength of the new, confident Rovers' team and in the Lanarkshire Cup first round were soundly defeated by 6-3. The third round of the Scottish Cup saw Port Glasgow Athletic routed by 4-2. Arthurlie were visited in the Federation and they had been undefeated at home for eighteen months, and this trend continued with an emphatic 3-1 victory. Due to some crowd trouble the referee stopped the game in the seventy-fifth minute when the score was 2-1 for the homesters but eventually law and order was returned and the match finished.

A friendly took place the following week at Logie Green, Edinburgh, against St. Bernards, who won convincingly by three goals to no reply. However, with Cup Tie fever gripping the town, the fourth round tie at Pollokshaws saw a special train take a fair support to watch a 2-1 victory. The following week a friendly was arranged with Airdrieonians, to keep the team in match practice, but the Diamonds won this one by 3-2 at Coatbridge. Due to the generally foggy atmosphere, only two thirty-five minute periods were played in this match.

The fifth round of the cup was a home draw against Kilmarnock, who had been recently formed out of the old Kilmarnock Athletic. Whilst a Rorke goal was disallowed when there had been no score and the same man scored again with a penalty before half time, it was Kilmarnock who were the eventual winners by 2-1, thus ending the Premier Cup run for this season. This also saw Bruce Chalmers' last game meanwhile as a Rover, as he left to play for Sheffield Wednesday.

A friendly arranged with Vale of Leven the following week was thirty minutes late in starting due to the late arrival of the opposition, but the 4-1 scoreline was the first-ever win over Vale of Leven and Simon Scott proved to be an able deputy over the departed Chalmers at centre half. On Christmas Eve, Wishaw Thistle were engaged in a friendly match at Old Public Park in what should have been a Lanarkshire Cup match, but two thirty-five minute halfs were played due to ground conditions and it was just as well as Rovers lost 2-0.

Bruce Chalmers
1886-90, 1891-93, 1895-97

Willie Roberts
1890-94

Matt Rorke
1889-90, 1891-93

Archie Sergeant
1891-94, 1898-99

Monday, 2nd January, saw Rovers' first visit to Broomfield but for their trouble received a severe 4-0 thrashing. Due to weather conditions it was three weeks before the next match which was a Lanarkshire Cup tie with Wishaw Thistle at Old Public Park, when the 'Jags' won easily by a 6-2 scoreline. Motherwell were First Foots at the Meadow on the 28th January on Federation business and finding Rovers still in a Spirit of Goodwill, received a satisfactory 4-1 victory. However, the following week saw Rovers go to the top of the League by means of a comprehensive 6-0 drubbing of Clydebank, who at that time had no home ground.

Glasgow Northern were hosts at Hyde Park, Springburn, in the first of three friendly matches which ended up with the amazing score of 6-6, to be followed by a home draw against Bathgate Rovers which this time ended up 2-2 in a game of two thirty-five minute halves. The third draw at 3-3 was achieved over Arthurlie in the Federation, with McGeechan scoring a hat-trick and with Harry Gray of Mossend Brigade and Jimmy McEwan of Albion making their debut.

The return to the winning standard came the following week at the Meadow with Cambuslang as visitors, when the light blue shirted County rivals were defeated by 6-2 with Rovers playing the first ten minutes without Burns. The referee insisted that Rovers change their royal blue shirts to black and white stripe shirts in the second half. A 4-0 victory at home against Neilston, in the Federation, came before a Coatbridge Express Cup Tie was scheduled against Airdrieonians. In front of one thousand fans Rovers started the match with ten men and had to wait for twenty-five minutes before Sneddon showed up with the score at 1-1. He would have been better staying away as the final result was 7-1 for the Diamonds.

Around this time there was considerable talk of a split with the Lanarkshire Association but the next Federation game was switched to Coatbridge, due to an Inter-Association match being played at Falkirk. East Stirlingshire lost out all round with the final score being 7-1 for Rovers. On the same day Rovers won the Second Eleven Final at Broomfield against Royal Albert with a high-scoring 8-3 scoreline and were represented by Young, Donald, Carson, Johnston, Pollock, Harvey, Marshall, Foy, Addie, J. Bryson and C. Bryson.

Another high-scoring draw Federation match took place at Motherwell on the opening day of April when ten goals were shared at Dalziel Park. Wishaw Thistle the following week managed to win 3-2 in a very tight game before the Edinburgh Hibs visited Coatbridge to be defeated by 4-2 in a friendly. East Stirlingshire were then the rearranged hosts in the Federation and a 3-3 draw was the result. This match was followed by a Coatbridge Express Cup match against Hamilton Accies which ended up 2-1 in favour of Rovers. Further interest in the Federation title was ended with two consecutive defeats; the first away against Royal Albert by 6-2, and the second at home by 4-2 against Pollokshaws. Baird and Galbraith made up the Pollokshaws' team in the fortieth minute with the visitors winning at that stage by 1-0.

Slamannan Wanderers were then defeated in the Coatbridge Express Cup by 2-1 but in the final at Broomfield, Motherwell won by 4-1 in front of fifteen hundred fans and a subsequent Rovers' protest that a Motherwell player had played in a Cup tie with Rangers against St. Bernards was thrown out. Rovers were represented by Allan, P. Sergeant, Donald, Beveridge, Burns, Roberts, A. Sergeant, Addie, Gray, Rorke and Bryson.

The final game in the Federation took place at Pollokshaws with a 4-2 defeat being the disappointing result and this, despite the fact that Matt and Bob Scott of Airdrie were co-opted for the day. Continuing with the agreed allowance of two imported players, the Airdrie Charity Cup first round match against Airdrieonians saw Rovers field ex-players Haddow and McPherson, both from Rangers but neither could stop the Diamonds from winning 3-1.

Thus ended a most disappointing season, with none of the promise being fulfilled from the previous season and, as so often happens, it was back to the drawing board. The transfer of Johnny Gray to Rangers during the close season did nothing to endear the Committee to the fans.

Season 1893/94
A change was made from the Federation League to the Scottish Alliance League for the new season. The opening game on the 12th August was a Friendly against old rivals Pollokshaws. This was an 8-2 home victory with Davie Beveridge scoring a fine hat-trick. Rovers were represented by Traynor, P. Sergeant, Harvey, Thomson, Burns, Roberts, Stewart, D. McGeechan, Beveridge, J. McGeechan and McDonald. The following week saw the first game in the Alliance, at home against Cambuslang, with a 3-2 defeat being the net result. This was followed up with an away win in the same League against Royal Albert, who could feel aggrieved at the 4-3 scoreline considering they played all the second half with only ten men and had three goals disallowed.

The red striped Broxburn team were next to visit Meadow Park in a Friendly and a 2-1 score for the homesters was chalked up which was followed by a fine Alliance home victory over Arthurlie by the only goal of the game. Trialist Cross from Vale of Leven, who made a promising debut, refused to sign unless on a Professional form. He did not appear in the next match, which again took place at the Meadow, in the second round of the Scottish Cup against Dykehead and saw a 5-1 victory for Rovers. There was a very poor attendance for this match, possibly greatly attributable to the Brass Band Competition in Coatbridge Town Centre.

In the Alliance at Wishaw the next game against the local Thistle saw a 4-3 defeat but this was followed with a home friendly victory by 8-0 over Hurlford. This again set the team up for the Scottish Cup third round match against Neilston at home. An historic occasion this as the match was the first time nets were used at an Albion Rovers' home game. The score ended up 7-0 for Rovers and both McGeechan and Thomson had hat-tricks, giving the new nets a good first test.

Next was a Lanarkshire Cup tie at Hamilton which saw the Accies win by 2-1. It was the habit in these days of both the opposing teams providing a linesman, with a neutral referee. Rovers changed linesmen at half time from Cairns to President Baird but, after objection from the Hamilton team, Cairns completed the second half. There was crowd trouble at the end of this game and much ill-feeling.

Falkirk was the next venue for the fourth round Scottish Cup Tie and a 3-3 draw was realised with Rovers throwing away a 3-0 half time lead. In the replay a week later, a 5-2 victory saw Rovers safely into the fifth round. On the evening before the next match, which was a friendly against Annbank, a great storm blew down the grandstand at an estimated £120 cost but the game took place on the Saturday with a 2-1 victory for Rovers in very cold, windy conditions. The next Scottish Cup match in the fifth round was again a home draw against the Black Watch team and two thousand fans saw Rovers completely dominate this game and run out easy winners by 6-0. In the Alliance at home Airdrieonians won 4-2. Airdrie in their red and white stripes were easy winners in this game which started ten minutes late. Captain Willie Roberts missed this match due to a family bereavement.

With a Cup Tie looming against Celtic, a match was arranged with Clyde at Barrowfield Park but the move misfired and Rovers were beaten 5-2. On the 16th December, Parkhead was visited but in five minutes outside left Willie McFarlane broke his leg and Rovers went to pieces eventually losing by 7-0. In the last game of 1893, Linthouse were the visitors in a friendly which ended 4-1 for Rovers and this game is memorable mainly for right back Cross scoring a hat-trick. The night before a Concert was held to help defray the costs for the new grandstand.

Monday the 1st January saw the visit from Airdrieonians on Alliance business but they proved to be ungracious first-foots, pocketing the points in a 4-0 victory. Bad crowd trouble occurred at the next home match in the Alliance when Royal Albert were the visitors. The game was ten minutes late in starting and there were two separate punch-ups involving players and spectators before Rovers eventually won by 5-4 after trailing 2-3 at half-time. The Royalists left the field in protest at 5-4 but the referee, Mr. Drysdale of Arthurlie, was successful in getting them to return and complete the match.

The return match against Linthouse took place at Langlands Park, Govan but the same score of 4-1 for Rovers was the end result. This was followed by victories of 8-0 over Carrington and a 5-2 over Battlefield in Friendly matches before a 4-1 defeat was inflicted by Stenhousemuir at Larbert.

The following week Rovers cancelled an Alliance game with Airdrieonians at the last minute and were fined one Pound by the Alliance Committee. Cambuslang were next to be visited for a 2-2 draw before Arthurlie had an easy 5-1 home victory in a match in which President Baird had to strip to field a full team but he was injured and was off all the second half. The Second Battalion of the Black Watch visited Coatbridge for the second time this season and this time got off with only a 5-1 defeat.

George Bruce now took over as Match Secretary as from this date and the first match he was officially involved in was the Coatbrige Express Cup, when Dykehead came and were soundly defeated 8-2. The new pavilion behind the West goal was erected in time for this game, which saw Cross sign as a Professional for Notts Forest and get his wish of long-standing.

Four Friendly matches then took place with Cambuslang winning 2-1 and Morton being defeated 3-2, both away from home, before two home matches saw Stenhousemuir lose 4-2 but Annbank winning 3-1.

The next week it was back to Coatbridge Express business when the Glengowan team was defeated 12-0 but on more serious business the Wishaw Thistle team lost 2-1 in the Alliance before losing again at Meadow Park in the Semi Final of the Coatbridge Express Cup by 2-0. This match saw the return of right back Cross from Nottingham as a disillusioned young man. This caused Rovers Committee to consider turning fully professional from now on. The following Wednesday the newly-erected grandstand was blown down in a gale but the fixture against Airdrieonians in the Alliance Championship still took place with Rovers winning 2-1.

On the 26th May the fifth Coatbridge Express Final took place at Meadow Park against Airdriehill and Rovers ran out easy winners by 4-0. The home team also won the toss for the ball played and the gate money to be shared was £11.11.6d. plus £3.0.0d. for the hire of the ground. Rovers team was Campbell, Cross, Martin, Beveridge, Burns, Roberts, Sergeant, Stewart, Thomson, McGeechan and Addie.

This match turned out to be the last match by Rovers popular Captain — Willie

Roberts — who died in tragic circumstances on Saturday, 6th June, at the Falls of Clyde. He had been visiting the local beauty spot in a Rachabite outing and witnessed a young girl, Agnes Gray from Buchanan Street, fall some twenty metres to the bottom of a cliff. Although separated by the fast flowing water, he attempted to jump to her assistance but fell into the water and was engulfed by the current. His death was almost instantaneous and the following Wednesday saw a large turn-out for this popular twenty-four year old moulder from Paul's Land in Whifflet.

The same day as this tragic occurrence was taking place, Airdrie were defeating Rovers in the Airdrie Charity Cup at 4-2, with Reid and Aitken of Stenhousemuir guesting for Rovers. The season ended on the last day of June with Glasgow Rangers visiting the Meadow in a Benefit for Willie Roberts' widow and family.

Rovers agreed to encompass professionalism at their A.G.M. and President Baird was returned for yet another year in office. More success was looked for than had been achieved during the previous twelve months. The old Committee received a real rough passage on the matter of the grandstand which had been blown down twice during the past season, but agreement was eventually reached when the new Committee agreed to ensure that the edifice was properly tied down.

Season 1894/95

The season ahead was looked forward to with great anticipation by Committee and fans alike and it was considered that the playing staff were a bunch of young go-ahead players who could develop very well during the next twelve months. On the 18th August, Wishaw Thistle came to visit on Alliance business and immediately set the cat among the pigeons by winning 5-2. Rovers team was Young, Cross, Martin, Sergeant, Burns, Cowan, Stewart, Brown, Thomson, Stevenson and Murdoch.

Captain Cross was livid at the ineptness of his defence and some changes were made for the visit to Johnstone the following week, the most notable of which being the return to goal of Dave Campbell. The big stick seemed to work for a 5-0 victory was recorded. This was made much easier with the Johnstone goalkeeper being off injured all of the second half.

Thus early in the season with an unsettled team, the Scottish Cup first round tie against Carfin at Coatbridge caught Rovers cold and five more goals were lost with only three in reply. Right winger Stewart played his last match before going off to Blackburn.

The next Alliance match was at Larkhall against Royal Albert which, with ten minutes to go, was 5-4 to the home team when Jack Martin and McMaster of the Royalists got involved in a punch-up which quickly spilled over to the spectators. In no time a full-scale riot was on hand, leaving the referee no option but to abandon the game. The League Programme was eventually completed with this game not being replayed. Back home the following week the Gordon Highlanders visited in a friendly to be hammered 8-2.

The next match at the Meadow in the Alliance was against Cambuslang, which was to be Archie Sergeant's last game before leaving for Liverpool. The game ended all square at 4-4. The next week the newly-formed Coatdyke Gaelic team visited the Meadow in a game which Rovers won easily by 3-0. Again the following week, at Dunterlie Park, Barrhead, the Arthurlie team were defeated by 3-1 in the Alliance. Hamilton Accies were next on the chopping block and at the receiving end of a 5-0 drubbing at Coatbridge.

A special train taking two hundred and fifty supporters up to Shotts on Lanarkshire Cup business saw a hard fought 2-2 draw forcing a replay the following week at the Meadow and to the delight of the home support, a two clear goal scoreline helped to offset the ordering off of outside right Brown and the loss of a third player to English football, Willie Burns the popular centre-half, who left for Bolton Wanderers.

A Friendly was fixed for the 10th November against Northern at Coatbridge and the homesters were short of Cross and Murdoch, who were representing the Lanarkshire F.A. against Ayrshire down in Burns' country. Cross in fact Captained the Lanarkshire team. Again Rovers rang the changes with Brady, signed from Whifflet Rangers, at right back and old stalwart Simon Scott at centre half, together with new signing Matt Cullen from Airdrieonians at outside right. In a well contested match a 2-2 draw was a fair result. The same scoreline covered the next match against the Clyde 'A' team and two other home Friendlies saw Vale of Leven lose by 3-0 but Stenhousemuir won by 2-0 in front of a small attendance.

The Lanarkshire Cup was next in line and Hamilton Accies were defeated narrowly by 3-2. They immediately appealed on the scoreline but this was thrown out by the F.A. Rovers played a new centre half in this match, ex-Western Athletic, Forrest who had been playing his football in America. Dalziel Park, Motherwell was the venue for the next match which Rovers won by 2-1 in a game of two thirty-five minute halves. Prior to the game a severe gale blew down the surrounding fencing and also the stand roof. The year ended with a visit to Shotts against Dykehead when a 3-2 victory was recorded.

There was very bad weather at the beginning of the New Year and, in an attempt to play the Semi-Final of the Lanarkshire Cup, two visits were made in succeeding weeks to Hamilton to play Burnbank Swifts but both games had to be called off. On the second visit a Friendly was arranged and on the badly frozen ground a 1-1 draw was the result.

The Club was deeply saddened with news of the death of ex-President W. Haining after a long illness. Due to continuing bad weather, no football was possible in the month of February and when on the 2nd March the Semi-Final tie against Burnbank Swifts was played, this was only the second game in ten weeks. Even so, a result could not be achieved and a 1-1 draw was the outcome with centre forward Murdoch being the hero and villain of the piece by scoring Rovers' goal but then being ordered off allowing the Swifts to come back and fix up a rematch. For the third time in three weeks the opponents were the Swifts, this time at Meadow Park, and Rovers turned up trumps by 5-2.

Despite this encouraging result it was clear that the present playing staff had to be augmented as the Club was feeling the loss of Stewart, Sergeant and Burns. Former Airdrieonians Goldie and Thomson were signed up and they appeared in the Alliance fixture against Wishaw Thistle when a 3-3 draw was the controversial result. There were no nets at the ground and it was maintained by Rovers that the third Wishaw goal had travelled outside the posts, but the referee would have none of it.

There followed a series of victories in the Alliance starting off against Arthurlie at Coatbridge by 4-1 and against the Accies at Hamilton by 6-1, whilst Johnstone visited Coatbridge for a 5-2 defeat.

The 27th of April saw the Lanarkshire Cup Final at Broomfield against Motherwell and, due to both teams having the same blue colours, Rovers played in their alternative strip of black and white stripes. Things did not go well and five thousand enthusiastic fans saw Rovers 3-1 down at half time but by the end of the match despite scoring a further three goals the defence conceded seven and yet another trophy had gone at the last hurdle. Rovers were represented by Stewart, Brady, Martin, Beveridge, Cross, Cowan, Bruce, Thomson, Murdoch, Smith and Scott.

The following match was against Royal Albert in the Coatbridge Express Cup but further disaster followed in this match with an 8-4 defeat at Larkhall. Meanwhile back in the Alliance, Dykehead were trounced 4-0 at Shotts and the following Wednesday Airdrieonians gave best in a friendly at Broomfield by 3-0.

Ample revenge for the Express Cup defeat was gained over Royal Albert by 4-0 at the Meadow, in the Alliance, whose final game saw Rovers make a tremendous effort to catch the leaders with an astonishing 12-2 victory against Cambuslang. Nevertheless, the Alliance was won on the same day by Wishaw Thistle which left only the Charity Cup as a possible trophy for the sideboard.

Airdrieonians were matched in a 2-2 Friendly at the Meadow before the Airdrie Charity Cup saw Rovers dumped unceremoniously out in the first round by Dykehead by 2-1. A season which started in defeat ended in similar fashion with the fans and players alike contemplating on what might have been.

Season 1895/96
Under President Robert Baird's direction, the Committee were very active with prominent newcomers Boyle and Connolly signed from Coatdyke Gaelic and Brown from Airdrie West End. These, together with a mixture of the established players who, although young, were now a season more established. Much was looked for in the coming season which had another innovation in the new throw-in Law which required players to stand and not jump when balls were being put into play.

The season opened with a couple of friendlies; the first against Airdrieonians on the 3rd August resulted in a 6-4 victory with Rovers team being Clark, Cross, Boyle, Beveridge, Ross, Cowan, Bruce, Thomson, Murdoch, Brown and Connolly. An away draw at Greenock Morton set the team up for the season proper in the Alliance where, to the strains of the Coatbridge Brass Band, Hamilton Accies were the visitors and recipients of a 5-0 drubbing. Bob Roberts from Airdrieonians made his debut in this match. All the good work went for nought with a visit to Burnbank Swifts, when a 2-1 defeat was inflicted.

However the team bounced back for the Scottish Cup match against Dykehead at Coatbridge which Rovers won by the only goal of the match. Despite this encouragement, Arthurlie won rather easily by 3-2 at Barrhead in the Alliance. A lack of rhythm was evident at Falkirk in a friendly in a 4-2 defeat before first season seniors, Blantyre, were visited for a 4-4 draw in the Alliance. Bob Smellie moved on to Airdrieonians, with Bob Walkinshaw making the reverse journey, in time for the second round Scottish Cup match at Wishaw against the local Thistle. Rovers had the promise of an extra 5/-d. per man to win, but 1-1 was the best that could be gained on the day. This game was stopped for a ten minute period due to a break-in by the crowd.

The following week the replay took place at Meadow Park with Rovers running off easy winners by 5-1. Wishaw protested against the incompetency of Messrs. Cowan, Walkinshaw and McRoberts, but this was subsequently withdrawn by Thistle and Rovers went on to meet East Stirlingshire the next week in Round three knowing that the winners must play Blantyre in the fifth round having received a bye at the fourth stage. This was an important match and in front of two thousand disappointed supporters the Falkirk team were successful by 2-0.

With Rovers' tails right down, Royal Albert extracted a 7-1 defeat at Larkhall before Battlefield were defeated, at Coatbridge in a friendly, by 2-0. Further disappointment was to follow at Fir Park when Motherwell had an easy 4-2 victory in the Lanarkshire Cup. The next week, despite welcoming Bruce Chalmers back to the fold at centre half, the visit to Wishaw Thistle saw the Alliance Champions rout the Coatbridge lads by 6-3 before Rovers eventually got it right against Cambuslang by 5-2 with trialist Reid scoring a hat-trick. Mercurial as ever the following week saw a 3-2 defeat at Broomfield at the hands of local rivals Airdrieonians.

Next, on Alliance business, came Northern and after a whirlwind start Rovers were 6-1 up at half-time and slackened off somewhat in the second half to run out easy winners by 10-2 with Hardie and Murdoch both scoring hat-tricks. All this good work went to waste the following week in a friendly at Larbert when Stenhousemuir won by 11-3.

This topsy-turvy form was very frustrating for the fans and everyone was thankful for a couple of weeks respite due to bad weather before another New Year tour of the North East of England was embarked upon. The first match was played against Stockton when a 2-2 draw was secured but on Thursday, 2nd January, Darlington extracted a 5-1 victory and on the following Saturday Bishop Auckland rubbed salt in the wound to the tune of 6-2.

Back home bad weather saw enforced rests for the next two Saturdays but instead of being rusty from disuse the team swiftly clicked into gear when the Alliance games started with firstly Neilston being hammered 8-0 and then County rivals Cambuslang defeated by 2-0. This result was all the more satisfying as 'Fister' Cowan was ordered off leaving the team shorthanded. A couple of friendlies were then embarked upon, both away from home, with first of all Port Glasgow Athletic defeated by 3-2 before East Stirlingshire won by 5-4 at Merchiston Park.

When Rovers moved to Meadow Park from their original ground at Cowheath in 1883, there was a considerable band of their supporters who felt that this was a retrograde step and that the team would only command a wide support if it had a more centrally positioned ground. It was at this time that one of a series of attempts was made to move the Club either back to Cowheath or to the grounds of Cliftonhill House, but there was sufficient opposition for the argument to be set aside for another day.

Back on the Alliance trail, the Accies were defeated 2-1 at Hamilton and then a 2-2 draw against Blantyre and a 1-0 victory over Arthurlie gave great heart to the team before, in the Coatbridge Express Cup, Blantyre were defeated 3-2. Neilston caused a halt to the current good Alliance form with a 5-2 victory in Glasgow before the white shirted Royal Albert were defeated 3-1 at Coatbridge. In a match which was advertised as a Coatbridge Express Cup Tie, Hamilton Harp were defeated 6-2 in a rescheduled friendly match and four Rovers' reserves were co-opted to the Harp and Davie Beveridge missed a penalty.

Wishaw Thistle came to Coatbridge as top of the league by four clear points and in the last game of the Alliance Championship lost by 4-1 with Bob Walkinshaw scoring a hat-trick. Rovers made a quick exit from the Express Cup at the hands of Airdrieonians by 2-0 and reversed this score on the final game of the season against Burnbank Swifts.

Thus finished a poor season for the first eleven although a young second eleven won the Lanarkshire Second Eleven Cup at Broomfield against Royal Albert by 7-2, the young Rovers' team on that occasion being Stewart, Donald, Carson, Sneddon, Bryson, Pollock, Lumsden, Scott, Eadie, McEwan and Paterson.

The A.G.M. was also a stormy affair and, although Bob Baird was confirmed as President, great dissatisfaction was commented upon regarding the Alliance arrangements and the Committee were exorted to seek other arrangements for the coming season.

By the time the Alliance A.G.M. was held on the 3rd of July, Royal Albert, Wishaw Thistle and Albion Rovers all intimated their intention not to join for the coming season. The former two were now fully fledged members of the new Scottish Combination which Rovers were hoping to join but Arthurlie, Hamilton Academical and Albion Rovers were all applying for places and it was by no means certain that this would be attained.

However, there was a great shock in store for the Whifflet team who were rejected in favour of Hamilton Academical. Rovers were proposed for membership by Stenhousemuir but Mr. Nutt of Wishaw Thistle made a statement to the effect that the Rovers were on the point of going defunct. There was no-one present from Rovers to confirm or deny this statement and the slur on the Club proved to be very serious and it was no consolation to the Whifflet team for Mr. Nutt to withdraw his statement a couple of weeks later. The matter is supposed to have originated from Rovers' representative promising to support Mr. Nutt for the Lanarkshire F.A. Presidentship but when it came to the vote the Rovers' man voted elsewhere. Sour grapes or not, it was to have a very adverse affect on Albion Rovers' playing fortunes in the following year. It was not possible to return to the Alliance as it had now made up its members and the fixtures for the coming season. Rovers were in a no-mans-land — a limbo caused entirely by their own ineptitude and lack of foresight.

Season 1896/97
After the disappointments of the close season it was like putting the clock back for the Committee and Sime Scott the Match Secretary. Apart from the usual Cup Competitions it would only be possible to fix up friendly matches with the teams who had vacancies in their fixtures lists which would include many of the lesser lights and reserve teams of the more established clubs. Most of the previous season's player pool was again available and when the fateful day dawned Duntocher Harp were visitors to the Meadow where Rovers won most convincingly by 5-0. Rovers were represented by Cross, Aitken, Boyle, Robertson, Chalmers, Sneddon, W. Scott, Hamilton, Murdoch, MacKenzie and Downie.

Next visitors to Coatbridge were Annbank, who were Scottish Qualifying Cup holders, and it was quickly underlined to Rovers that the season whilst meaningless in one sense was not going to be a series of easy victories in another sense. The visitors trooped home winners of a closely contested match by 2-1.

Distaster was to follow the next week in the major tournament, the Scottish Cup, with Rovers in deep trouble fielding a team. Sandy Slaven ex-Airdrie and Motherwell was fielded at right half but when Walkinshaw did not appear until after kick-off, Thompson took his place. Rovers went into an early lead when Hamilton scored but Rovers were reduced to nine men after thirty minutes when both

Hamilton and Willie Scott had to leave the field and eventually Royal Albert ran out easy winners by 4-1.

Only two matches were played in the month of September, both away from home and both were appalling disasters. The Heart of Midlothian 'A' team won by 7-1, whilst the Vale of Leven crushed a poor Rovers team by 8-2. October was an improvement starting with a 4-4 draw at Blantyre in the fourth consecutive away match but the Hearts 'A' team came to the Meadow and won 3-0. The Cameronians were then defeated at Whifflet by 3-2 before Queen's Park Strollers scored a fine 7-2 victory in Glasgow.

A further loss was the transfer of Irishman Peter Boyle to Aston Villa for £50 on the eve of the Hamilton Accies game which was lost by the only goal of the game. In the Lanarkshire Cup, Motherwell won by 3-2 but on appeal Rovers were successful in having the match replayed. Thornliebank then came to visit and in front of a paltry one hundred gate, a game of two half-hour halves was played which was sufficient time for the Bankies to win 4-0. The unknown Camelon were visited and in a match of two thirty-five minute halves the home team started the game with ten men but they were sufficiently strong to win 3-2 over the seventy minutes.

The replayed Lanarkshire Cup match at Motherwell was next on the agenda where in front of one thousand fans the homesters romped home to the tune of 5-2, thus ending quite clearly the worst six months in the history of the Club. There were no further games arranged over the next four weeks but on the 16th of January, Vale of Leven visited Whifflet in a 2-2 draw after which goalkeeper Clark packed his bags and moved to Motherwell who had been impressed by his display in the Lanarkshire Cup tie. Troubles were queuing up for the luckless Rovers and when Camelon made their return visit to Coatbridge and gained a 1-1 draw the total gate receipts were £1.10/- which was a financial disaster as Rovers had to feed the Camelon contingent and pay a £3 guarantee.

A further break for a month then took place before Ayr Parkhouse were visited with 1-1 being the score. Thornliebank being next visited and another defeat, this time by 4-2, was the outcome. The last game of March saw Third Lanark 'A' team at Coatbridge in a 1-1 draw.

Needless to say Members were very unhappy with the current state of affairs, the quality of football and standard of opposition, blaming the Committee with gross incompetence. In an attempt to mollify the fans an attractive fixture was arranged for Broomfield with the local rivals and this ended up in a creditable 2-2 draw. The following Wednesday gave the team an opportunity to redeem themselves with a Coatbridge Express match at the Meadow against Motherwell and despite the snow-covered pitch, a clear cut 3-1 victory was the result. However, just to prove that Rovers' good fortune this season had completely deserted them, Motherwell were successful in protesting that the match be replayed, much to the disgust of the local fans.

Two home friendlies then took place with Ayr Parkhouse drawing 2-2 and the Argyll and Sutherland Highlanders being trounced by 4-1 and then, 'glory be!' Motherwell scratched from the Express Cup and to take the place of this fixture at very short notice a game was set up with Blantyre and in the only bright spot in an overall grey landscape of a season they were defeated by an incredible 14-0, with Rovers having the temerity to complain about the poor quality of the opposition.

The following Monday Airdrie visited Meadow Park in a Benefit Match for Sime Scott, which, of course, made Sime a professional after fourteen years of amateur status. He was to promptly seek reinstatement prior to the forthcoming season. The Airdrie team walked off winners by 2-1.

The much awaited semi-final of the Express Cup was next on the agenda as a last hope for glory but the Royal Albert were successful on their home patch by 3-2 leaving the season to fritter out with defeats against Hamilton Academical and Wishaw Thistle.

Season 1897/98
Much behind the scenes activity took place during the close season by the Committee and a successful application was made to join the Scottish Combination. At least there was a guarantee of more competitive football in the year ahead.

The opening fixture was a friendly against King's Park at Stirling which ended in a 5-4 defeat but new ground was covered in the first round of the Scottish Qualifying Cup against Carfin Rovers when a special train took the faithful to see a memorable 4-3 victory with Willie Scott notching a hat-trick.

A first game in the Scottish Combination was at home against Royal Albert and two goals by Alec Mitchell the new left winger from Baillieston was sufficient to see a satisfactory start made. Rovers were represented by Stewart, Walker, Boag, Galloway, Ross, Devine, W. Scott, Brodigan, Smellie, Murdoch and Mitchell.

It was back to the Premier Cup the following week and Longriggend were suitably despatched by 3-0 before a visit to Wishaw in the Combination saw Thistle lose by 2-1. The Scottish Cup run was to come to an end against Port Glasgow Athletic by 4-2 in a match which Rovers were fated never to win, losing their goalkeeper before half-time and Jack Martin taking over between the posts.

Ayrshire Cup holders Kilmarnock Athletic were next to visit the Meadow and after an interesting and close game were the winners by 4-3 and in the third home game in a row Third Lanark 'A' team won by 3-1 in the Combination on the week that the Renton team resigned from the Second Division of the Scottish League. There was then an almighty scramble by other clubs to take over their fixtures and eventually Hamilton Academical were elected over both Rovers and Royal Albert. This cost the Accies a £20 fine for leaving the Combination but that was a very small price to pay for League status.

A series of four defeats then took place with first of all a visit to Johnstone in a friendly ending up 2-1 but three home games saw Queen's Park Strollers win 4-1 in the Combination. Motherwell won the second round Lanarkshire Cup match by three clear goals and in the Combination Rangers 'A' team won convincingly by 4-1. Thornliebank were elected to take Hamilton Accies' place in the Combination thus ensuring there would be no blank Saturdays from now on. In two friendly matches Longriggend secured a 2-2 draw before, on a foggy day with two thirty-five minute halves, Dykehead were defeated at the Meadow by 3-1.

New Year started off with new boys Thornliebank being defeated by 3-2 and then, in a friendly at Ayr, the local Parkhouse were trounced 5-2. On a muddy pitch the following week, Rovers came back from a 2-1 half time deficit against Wishaw Thistle in the Combination with a Mitchell hat-trick to pick up the points but the next two matches were a couple of Friendlies which saw Airdrieonians defeated 3-1 at Broomfield and Charlie Dobbins ordered off for fighting with Willie Main, and Glasgow University smashed 5-0 at the Meadow with Thomson scoring a hat-trick.

This good series of results came to an abrupt halt at Ibrox against Rangers 'A' team, who were sitting top of the Combination, when a very heavy 9-1 defeat was received. In the next match, Queen's Park Strollers were dumped 4-3 at Hampden in what was the Strollers first defeat of the season.

King's Park came to the 'Brig in a Friendly in a high-scoring 6-4 victory before Arthurlie won easily 6-0 at Barrhead in the first of two Combination matches; the second was against the Third Lanark 'A' team when a 2-2 draw was secured in Glasgow.

The Coatbridge Express Cup then hoved over the horizon at the end of the season but after a no-scoring draw at the Meadow, Carfin Rovers were finally defeated in the replay by 4-1. The last game in the Combination then took place at the Meadow, when, against Arthurlie ample revenge was achieved for the earlier defeat, with a 4-1 victory.

This left the last game of the season the Express Cup final against Longriggend, which was played at Broomfield. This was a game which Rovers were confidently expected to win against the Miners and it was no surprise when they scored first. When Longriggend equalised before half-time, it was the thin end of the wedge and the village team ran out easy winners by 3-1 and the Trophy was eventually handed over in the Miners Arms over a "tea of pies and ginger".

Rovers' team that day was—Stewart, Boag, Martin, Galloway, Dobbins, Welsh, Marshall, Hamilton, Thomson, Mitchell and McLean.

Season 1898/99
Considerable behind-the-scenes activity took place in the close season, which resulted in several new faces being signed on the dotted line, and the fans appetite for the new season was whetted by a couple of friendlies. First of all against Airdrieonians, when a match of two thirty-five minute halves took place at home for a 1-1 draw, when Rovers were represented by Hunter, Fleming, Ostler, Galloway, Dobbins, Welsh, Marshall, Maxwell, McNellish, Ferguson and Hamilton. The other friendly was a visit to Stirling against King's Park when a 4-2 victory was run up.

The season proper started on the 27th August with a Scottish Combination match against Third Lanark 'A' which was won by 4-0. Thirds were pushed to provide a team and three substitutes were weaned from the spectators to make up the Thirds numbers. This was followed by a remarkable 7-1 victory over Hearts 'A' with Ferguson scoring three and Maxwell and Docherty two each before Dykehead were the visitors in the Scottish Qualifying Cup, but Rovers carried the day winning 4-2.

Back in the Combination the following week Wishaw Thistle were the visitors, playing in their new strip of blue jerseys, they easily crushed the Rovers' best efforts by 3-0. Vale of Leven were next at Coatbridge, in the second round of the Qualifying Cup, to be defeated 4-2 but this fine result was tempered by the news that Wishaw Thistle were drawn away in the Third Round. Before this match there was a friendly against Carfin which resulted in a 2-1 victory but in the 'Big Match', Thistle easily crushed the Rovers' best efforts by 5-1 at the Old Public Park much to the disappointment of the six hundred travelling support who journeyed by special train. Both teams ended up playing with ten men after injuries after sixty minutes. Following this disappointment, a friendly was set up at Broomfield which resulted in a 4-0 victory before three home Combination games took place. Johnstone firstly lost 2-0 then Royal Albert won 3-2 before Queen's Park Strollers defeated Rovers by 2-0.

The next match was the Lanarkshire Cup second round against Dykehead which was abandoned due to darkness with Rovers winning 2-1. The following week was a 1-1 rematch before the Shotts team were finally beaten 2-0 at Coatbridge. Dykehead played with ten men for most of the game in what turned out to be a very tough encounter. Dykehead protested on the grounds that Shaw was ineligible and this was upheld by the L.F.A. and the match ordered to be replayed. However, before this could happen, Hearts 'A' exacted ample revenge by 7-0 through in Edinburgh. The fourth match in five weeks against Dykehead took place with the rematched second round Lanarkshire Cup replay, which Rovers won convincingly by 3-0.

The following week saw the third round of the County Cup at Benhar against East Lanarkshire in a match where there was considerable ill-feeling and talk of boycotting the final. The players agreed to play without wages, otherwise the team would have been withdrawn from the competition. In the event an easy 4-1 victory was secured.

There were then four away successive defeats in the Combination, the first against Johnstone by 7-1 which was made all the more difficult with right back Boag being off injured after five minutes. At Hampden Queen's Park Strollers won 1-0 in a match where, due to incredibly bad weather conditions, the teams had to leave the field several times for shelter. Old rivals Wishaw Thistle took best by 3-2 which could have been worse but for Thistle missing a penalty late on in the match. Ibrox was the venue of a 4-2 defeat at the hands of Rangers 'A' with both Rovers' goals coming from penalties scored by Archie Sergeant. This slump fixed Rovers firmly at the bottom of the Combination.

Davie Rombach, a full-back was signed from Clyde who had set a £20 fee on his head for a league club and Rovers, who were non-league, paid no fee for him. Rovers bad luck continued in the home Combination fixture against Thornliebank, when although winning 3-2, the game was abandoned due to bad fog. The twentieth Lanarkshire Cup final eventually took place at Broomfield with a gate of £50, against Motherwell who ran out easy winners by 3-0. Rovers being represented by Hunter, Boag, Rombach, Dobbins, Sergeant, Walsh, Nangle, Hamilton, Ferguson, Main and McLean.

Next to visit the Meadow were Rangers 'A' for a 1-1 draw, thanks to a Hamilton goal. The following week in the newly-formed Lanarkshire League, the first match at Douglas Park against Hamilton Accies who ran out winners by 2-0, Rovers' Captain Boag was ordered off. A couple of weeks later the referee failed to turn up at Broomfield for the game against Airdrieonians which Rovers lost 5-1. Jack Russell refereed this match, who was acceptable by being a former player of both clubs. In the same league, Hamilton Accies came for the return match at Coatbridge and ran out easy winners by 5-2 before Motherwell scored in the last minute to win by the odd goal in three.

Two Combination matches then took place, both against Arthurlie and resulting in wins for the Renfrew team by 3-1 at Coatbridge and 4-2 at Barrhead. Rovers' first victory in the Lanarkshire League by 3-0 over Royal Albert at Larkhall was followed in quick succession by another over Motherwell by 2-1 but 'Well protested due to darkness setting in. Airdrieonians the following Saturday won by 2-0. On the Monday came a visit to Royal Albert and a very rough game, saw a convincing 5-2 defeat. Dobbins was ordered off and Rovers' bus was attacked by stones with Boag and President Baird being cut by flying glass before receiving a police escort out of the town.

Royal Albert came to visit in a Lanarkshire League match which Rovers won easily by 4-0 before the last Combination match saw a 1-1 draw in Glasgow against Third Lanark 'A'. The season finished in a visit to Longriggend when the Villagers were beaten convincingly by 4-1. Thus ended a very poor season for Rovers, who finished well down the Combination Table after an early defeat in the Scottish Qualifying Cup, a disappointing result in the final of the Lanarkshire Cup saw the sideboard bare of any trophies.

Season 1899/1900
A preliminary match to the season opening took place on Tuesday, 14th August, against new club Wishaw at Meadow Park when Rovers, represented by Hunter, Boag, Rombach, Devlin, Lyons, Welsh, Hughes, Hamilton, O'Rorke, O'Brien and Shaw, fought out a 1-1 draw. The following Saturday the season proper started against Wishaw Thistle in the Combination with a no-scoring draw before Renton were soundly defeated 7-0 in the third home game on the trot.

A visit to Bainsford saw East Stirling win 4-1 in a friendly before the new club, Carfin Emmett, were visited in the Scottish Qualifying Cup first round. Much to the chagrin of the travelling support Rovers lost by 3-1 and centre-half Lyons even missed a penalty, just to rub it in. The following Saturday Falkirk Amateurs visited Coatbridge in a friendly but due to a major life-boat procession and spectacular taking place in central Coatbridge, there were very few spectators to watch Rovers win 4-1.

Left-back Cain from Sheffield United made his debut in the home victory by 2-1 over Queen's Park Strollers in the Combination before Royal Albert were also defeated by three clear goals in the same competition. The Cameronians were then played in a friendly in the fourth game on the trot at the Meadow and soundly defeated by 7-0.

The Lanarkshire Cup first round match against Airdrieonians took place at Broomfield in front of three thousand spectators and Rovers with six old Diamonds in the team, fought out a no-scoring draw. This was the first time there had been no goals scored in a match between these great rivals. The 'Onians had the last laugh at the Meadow winning by 1-0 but Rovers protested, the L.F.A. agreed with them and ordered the match to be replayed. Airdrie were incensed with this decision and scratched from the competition.

Old rivals Cartvale then visited Coatbridge and, in a match played during torrential rain, were defeated by 2-1 before, at last, Wishaw Thistle had to give best by 3-1 at the Old Public Park in the second round of the Lanarkshire Cup. Third Lanark 'A' won 3-0 in Glasgow in the Combination before Longriggend were defeated, in the Lanarkshire Cup semi final, by 4-0 leaving Rovers to face Royal Albert in the final. Two further defeats then took place away from home in the Combination — 3-2 to Thornlienbank and 4-1 against Arthurlie. This latter match was a disaster for Rovers, as only six players turned up at the station and the Committee had to make up the team. The Committee were also shattered with the news that the Devlin brothers had joined the Volunteers during the week and had gone away to the War in South Africa.

The Lanarkshire League popped its head up again and the opening game against Royal Albert at Coatbridge ended in a 2-1 victory in front of one hundred spectators and was followed by a 1-1 draw against Wishaw Thistle in a game which finished in semi darkness. Thistle scored in the ninetieth minute and there was a break-in by the Wishaw fans onto the pitch when Rovers scored their goal.

Back on Combination business for the next three games the sequence started with a 3-0 defeat at home against Thornliebank before Third Lanark 'A' won 1-0 in Glasgow. The match against Wishaw Thistle was on a very muddy day and when the referee didn't turn up, Dan Dickson of Wishaw Thistle was pressed into service and it is perhaps a measure of his impartiality that Rovers won this one by 3-0.

Excitement in the Iron Burgh was at high pitch the following week when at Fir Park, Motherwell, the Lanarkshire Cup final between Rovers and Royal Albert was due to take place. The first game ended up a no-scoring draw in front of two thousand spectators and a gate of £40.1.11d. On the third of March the replay took place at Broomfield with Rovers making one change from the previous match—Frame taking over from Dobbins at right half. A crowd of four thousand and gate receipts of £73.16.0d saw Rovers run out winners by 2-1 with Dave Smellie scoring both goals in the second half. Rombach missed a penalty at the end but Rovers were well worthy of the win. Thus Jock Frame won a medal with his first game for the Club. Rovers team was Martin, Boag, Rombach, Frame, Lyons, O'Brien, W. Scott, O'Rorke, Smellie, Conway and Diamond.

The impetus of this victory was carried on to the next match against Combination leaders Arthurlie at Coatbridge when bottom of the table Rovers soundly defeated them 3-1 and at Raploch Park the following week a 3-3 draw was secured against Royal Albert. However, Kilbarchan halted this winning sequence with a 3-0 victory down in Renfrewshire. With Jimmy Marshall being married on the Friday night, Rovers celebrated in the Lanarkshire League match against Carfin Emmet by winning by 3-0. Rovers again slumped to the bottom of the table in the Combination by losing 3-1 at home to Johnstone. The Emmet gained a 3-1 revenge in the return match in the Lanarkshire League at Carfin before Royal Albert also exacted a 2-1 defeat at Larkhall. The match against Wishaw Thistle was a 1-1 draw at Wishaw only for Rovers to win the return match at Coatbridge by 2-0. The Combination finished with matches against Wishaw Thistle, Thornliebank and St. Mirren to finish off a poor season with the sole high-point being the winning of the Lanarkshire Cup.

Season 1900/01
A clear out took place during the close season and when the Combination programme opened on Wednesday the 15th of August against Clyde, the team was represented by Palmer, Boag, Harding, McDonald, Lyon, McGinn, Brodigan, Tinto, Dow, Slaven and McGinn. It was obvious with so many new faces in the team that it would take time for the new mix to gel and it was no surprise when Clyde won by 3-1 and rather more convincingly that the score would suggest. The following Saturday a 2-2 draw was gained at Stirling against King's Park and the same score against Wishaw United at Coatbridge.

The Scottish Qualifying Cup first round saw the Accies chalk up a 2-0 score at Hamilton and Rovers protested against the Douglas Park right back which was upheld by the S.F.A. This did little good for Rovers as the following week Hamilton won by an even more emphatic 3-0 scoreline.

The next six games were all in the Combination with first of all Thornliebank losing at Coatbridge by the only goal of the game. Rovers started off with only nine men whilst McLean and Geordie Dick, the trainer, made up the numbers. Disaster was to take place the following week when the equipment hamper was lost on route to the match and Rovers lost 3-1 to Arthurlie. This was followed by a 4-0 defeat at Hampden at the hands of Queen's Park Strollers but Wishaw United were defeated 4-2 in this first visit to the new team's ground.

Third Lanark 'A' were next to come to Coatbridge and Rovers played new signing Archie McFarlane from Lincoln City, who had been advised by doctors to cease playing earlier in the year due to knee problems. Rovers played for the day in white jerseys and eventually won 1-0 but this was only due to the referee disallowing a goal in favour of a penalty which the Thirds team subsequently missed. With the news that Alex Boag was retiring his full-back position, Paddy McWilliams was signed from St. Mirren and played in the match with St.Mirren at the Meadow which ended in a 2-2 draw. This game was remarkable in that referee McInnes of Thornliebank blew his whistle ten minutes early and had to recall the teams from their early baths but no further goals were scored in the final period although the players finished the match in sartorial disarray—some without stockings and others without jerseys. Against Ayr Parkhouse the following Saturday, in a friendly, the long trip 'doon the watter' ended up with a 4-0 defeat.

At the beginning of December, Royal Albert drew 1-1 at Coatbridge but this game was marred when Diamond was ordered off along with Smith of the Royalists. There was considerable concern in Whifflet over reports at this time that the Club was likely to fold but the players took it all in their stride winning 3-2 at Love Street against St. Mirren.

Three straight defeats then took place starting with Queen's Park Strollers winning 6-2 at Coatbridge in a game which started thirty minutes late and a crowd of under one hundred paid £2 gate money. Rovers 'lucky' white shirts let them down on this occasion. Royal Albert inflicted a 7-1 defeat at Larkhall and there followed a break of several weeks due to bad weather and the funeral of Queen Victoria on the second of February. When football re-started on the ninth of February a visit to Kilbarchan found Rovers wanting and it was an easy win for the home team by 4-2. A fortnight later the green shirted Emmett acted as hosts in the Lanarkshire Cup when a 3-1 defeat was inflicted at Carfin.

Two Combination away games then took place, first of all with Thornliebank winning 2-1 then Johnstone winning 4-3. There were many complaints around this time regarding the organisation of the Combination structure with games starting late and referees not turning up. Also Rovers were concerned regarding the condition of the Meadow which tended to be very uneven and prone to waterlogging.

The Committee enquired about the advisability of returning to Cowheath but after some discussion with the owners it was subsequently not available.

In the opening Lanarkshire League match Airdrieonians fought out a 1-1 draw at Broomfield with Airdrie equalising in the second half. Back in the Combination, Johnstone came to the Meadow but the refereee, Mr. Robertson arrived late and substiutute referee Brown had already started the game which ended up as a 3-0 victory for Rovers. At the beginning of April, Airdrieonians, in their familar red stripes, came to Coatbridge and lost 2-1. Wishaw United were next defeated at Wishaw by 3-1, both matches being Lanarkshire League fixtures. In a friendly Carfin Emmett were defeated 3-1 in front of 1,000 fans.

A bit of a revolt took place the next week in the Lanarkshire League match against Motherwell when McWilliams and Brodigan tried to get an increase in wages for the professionals and they did not strip. Due to the carry-on in the pavilion, the game started fifteen minutes late, with Rovers in their white change strip because of Motherwell's blue strip. Rovers saw their 2-0 half time score sufficient to win the match but the next week in the Combination, Arthurlie were the visitors and whilst the game started eighteen minutes late, it was a disaster for Rovers who lost 4-0 and had McWilliams ordered off.

The return visit to Motherwell, in the Lanarkshire League, ended in a 1-1 draw and the season finished with the Scottish Qualifying Cup holders, Stenhousemuir, visiting Coatbridge and their superior skills won the day by 3-2.

The season had an anti-climax about it with no trophys to show for the team's efforts, concern about the condition of the playing field and thoughts on a move to pastures new.

Season 1901/02

In the close season there was the usual feverish activity by the Committee and a fair number of new faces in the line-up on the 17th August in the friendly match at home against King's Park which ended up in a no-scoring draw. Rovers started off the season with the following — Copland, McCorrie, Busk, Sergeant, Lyon, McLellan, Dale, Sneddon, Dow, Edwards and Conlin. Despite the heavy rain, an £8 gate was taken and this was followed by another friendly against Renton who played the first twenty-five minutes of the game without one player but then lost three goals in the second half without reply with a full complement.

The Scottish Combination season started the following week with a home match against Royal Albert at a time when all Coatbridge was agog with the brutal murder in neighbouring Dunbeth Park of Mary Watt on the previous Thursday. This game ended in a resounding 5-2 victory for Rovers which set them up for the first round Scottish Qualifying Cup match at Larkhall against the same team when a 3-3 draw was the result followed by a win in the replay by a Sandy Rowan goal to nil.

Next Saturday in the second round of the same cup saw an incredible situation against Wishaw United who had been formed out of the Wishaw Thistle ashes. Despite the best efforts of the Coatbridge Pipe Band and a protest, the no-scoring result stood and the match was instructed to be replayed again at Meadow Park, this time ending in a 1-1 draw with Paddy McWilliams scoring with a late penalty. Again Rovers protested and again the S.F.A. threw out the protest and the second replay took place at Wishaw resulting in a 2-2 draw after Rovers led by two Conway goals to nil at half time. The third replay, this time at Broomfield, saw Rovers again go into a 2-0 lead at half time in front of four thousand spectators and with Englsh outside-left Conlin ordered off in the tenth minute, Rovers had to hang on for a 2-2 draw after extra time.

A fourth replay took place at Motherwell where with no scoring after ninety minutes, it took a goal in the last minute of extra time by McWilliams to keep the score at one each. This was followed by the suspension for four weeks of John Conlin and he was sorely missed in the fifth replay at Hamilton which ended up at one each over ninety minutes but in extra time McWilliams missed a penalty and Rovers lost the only goal scored to lose after an incredible six games in successive Saturdays against Wishaw United, a situation which was never to occur again in the history of the Club.

After eleven games Rovers had only played three different teams and due to this the team was now very much behind in the Combination. The next week St. Mirren 'A' drew at the Meadow in a 2-2 draw where John Conway missed a penalty. Royal Albert won the next match by 2-0 before Kilbarchan were beaten at Coatbridge by 4-0.

The following Saturday, down at Johnstone, the team was losing 3-2 when big Davie Haddow, who had been taking a fair bit of stick from supporters and players alike retaliated at an incident and the crowd behind Rovers' goal spilled onto the pitch seeking retribution. The players scrambled for the pavilion from where Rovers declined to return, and as darkness fell, the game was abandoned. This was a match in which only six supporters travelled and even they missed the kick-off as their train was late in arriving at the station. The Combination Committee instructed the game to be replayed and this was scheduled for a fortnight hence. In between times a friendly was fixed up at home against Vale of Leven and this turned out to be a 3-2 victory for the Rovers.

In the replayed match against Johnstone the game kicked-off at three o'clock and with Rovers winning 2-1 the game was abandoned with five minutes to go due to pressure by the police and failing light. Cup victors Wishaw United were visited in the Combination for a 1-1 draw before, in the Lanarkshire Cup, Dykehead came to the Meadow for a 5-1 trouncing. This good form continued at Cathkin the following week in the Combination by a 2-0 margin. In the return match the following week Third Lanark 'A' was defeated by 5-0 in the quagmire which was Meadow Park.

A change of competition saw the Lanarkshire Cup match at Wishaw against the inevitable United with Rovers winning easily by 5-0 and John Conlin scoring three. This was followed by a Friendly at home against Renton which was won by 6-0. These last five results were all wins with twenty-three goals for and only one against really setting Rovers up for the Lanarkshire Cup Final at Broomfield on the fifteenth of March against Hamilton Academical. This was the third final appearance in three seasons and with a crowd of more than seven thousand fans in the ground and gate receipts of £166.8/-, Rovers meekly gave up possession of the Cup by 3-0. The presentation took place in the Royal Hotel and Rovers were represented by Haddow, McWilliams, Scott, Cairns, Lyon, McLellan, Glegg, Main, O'Rorke, Conway and Conlin.

Just to show that the final result was a freak, Queen's Park Strollers were crushed 5-0 in the next Combination match before, in the Lanarkshire League, the Accies' team could only draw 2-2 in front of more than two thousand fans. A trip to Kilbarchan on Combination business gained a 2-0 victory on the second of April, which was the day of the Ibrox disaster at the Scotland v England game. The next week East Stirlingshire were the visitors in a 1-1 friendly before Johnstone were whipped in a Combination match by 5-0. This was a most surprising result as Johnstone were topping the League at the time.

The following week Wishaw United, that team again, visited Coatbridge in a match which was agreed by both the Scottish Combination and the Lanarkshire League to be played for both competitions. The match ended up with Rovers winning by 3-1 which made them proud winners of the Lanarkshire League and put them well on the way to winning the Combination as well. Queen's Park Strollers lost 1-2 at Hampden before two Conway goals were sufficient the following week to defeat Johnstone to make Rovers clear winners of the Combination in a match which started off thirty minutes late at 4.30 and drew £34. Johnstone sitting top of the League could willingly have thrown away their striped shirts at the end of the match, as Rovers still had two games to play in the Competition.

Motherwell visited the Meadow in a Benefit Match for the Coatbridge Brass Band who were playing at most home games and ended up winners in a close 2-1 game. Hamilton Accies won the following Saturday in the Lanarkshire Cup by 3-1 and the season finished with a 2-1 victory at Paisley over St. Mirren 'A' in the Combination giving Rovers the title by five clear points from second placed

Johnstone.

The last game of the season was in the Coatbridge Express Cup when Airdrieonians won easily by 3-0.

The season therefore had ended up on a very successful note with the winning of the Lanarkshire League and the Scottish Combination and during the close season the good work was kept up with the team winning the five-a-side tournament in the Motherwell Annual Sports with a team of Glover, Main, Cairns, Conlin and O'Rorke.

Season 1902/03

Despite the successes of the previous season the team for the first day of the season showed changes in all departments and when the new term opened on the 17th August at the Meadow against Royal Albert at a game at which the Combination championship winning flag was unfurled, Rovers won 3-0 in front of a crowd of fifteen hundred. Rovers were represented by Glover, M. Scott, Morrison, McCorrie, Grozier, Watson, Lynn, Boyd, O'Rorke, Main and Brodigan. The good form was continued in the next game, also at home, when Johnstone were beaten 4-0. This game was thirty minutes late in kicking off due to the visitors baggage being lost in transit by the Railway Company. Kilbarchan was the venue of the first away match when a 3-0 score made it three wins in a row and ten goals without reply.

September saw the Scottish Qualifying Cup first round match when a special train took the Support to Larkhall for a 1-0 victory over Royal Albert. Vale of Leven were defeated at Coatbridge in the Combination by 4-2, this result putting Rovers top of the ten team League table.

The inevitable first defeat of the season came at Motherwell in the second round of the Qualifying Cup when, in front of four thousand fans, who paid £110, Motherwell won 7-1 and Rovers were hampered by Conway being off for a considerable period. A second defeat was inflicted at the hands of Renton by 5-1 before Rovers got back on the goal trail against Falkirk Amateurs at home in a Friendly winning by the same score.

A considerable effort had been put in during the close season to improve the pitch and a horse-drawn mower was employed on the sward which made it fairly trim. Seven straight Combination games then took place with the first at Wishaw seeing Rovers win 4-0 followed by home draws of 2-2 against Kilbarchan and 1-1 against Renton. An away draw at Johnstone of 3-3 saw Rovers consolidate their position at the top of the Combination.

Third Lanark 'A' were next to play at Whifflet and lost 2-0 for their trouble followed by Thornliebank who lost by 6-0 and Frank O'Rorke missed the chance of a hat-trick when he thumped a penalty kick over the bar. Vale of Leven then were visited with the score 2-0 in favour of the Rovers.

At Falkirk in a Friendly, Rovers won by 4-2 before a visit down to Thornliebank saw a 5-0 victory. This was immediately nullified by a defeat of 5-1 in a game where another penalty was missed by Rovers. St. Mirren 'A' team was defeated by 4-1 at Paisley before the Lanarkshire Cup match against Carfin Emmett was transferred to Coatbridge as the Carfin team had no ground at the time. Rovers won 6-0 on a very frosty January morning.

In the Combination match, on the 14th January, Renton were the visitors in a stormy match in which Rovers were leading by 3-2 when at half time fights broke out between the rival fans and the stand was emptied. The game, whilst being finished ended up being declared void by the Combination Committee and was required to be replayed later in the season at a neutral ground. This was followed by a home victory of 2-0 over St. Mirren 'A' and with no game the following week a friendly was quickly fixed up with Clyde at Coatbridge giving a £7 guarantee to the visitors. In heavy rain Rovers won 3-0 and the second half was restricted to only thirty minutes.

In the Lanarkshire Cup match at Coatbridge against Airdrieonians a 3-1 defeat was inflicted but the problems started for Rovers at the kick-in when McCorrie was injured and the game started with Rovers playing with only nine men. Great concern was being expressed at the playing condition of Meadow Park and moves were seriously being made to find a new ground at Coatdyke, but in the Combination, Third Lanark 'A' drew 2-2 before St. Bernard's won well by 2-1 in a Friendly. Rovers submitted a request to the Scottish League for Second League status and this was considered by the Scottish League. The next week Lanark, who had taken over Wishaw United fixtures following this team's demise, were defeated 8-1 with Peel scoring four and Conlin a treble. In the midst of a blizzard on the 11th of April, Royal Albert on their own patch won by the only goal of the match, putting a spoke in Rovers' Championship winning hopes.

The next week a Friendly was fixed up with Partick Thistle with the usual £7 guarantee being dangled and a 2-2 draw was played out with Rovers taking the opportunity of freshening up the team with some trialists. The last game in the Combination took place when the re-scheduled match against Renton was fixed for Broomfield and four thousand fans, who had paid £87, saw Rovers win easily by 4-2 with O'Rorke scoring three and thus the Combination championship was retained. This is the only time the Rovers have won a trophy in successive seasons. The Champions finished three points ahead of Renton in second place.

On this high note a couple of Friendlies finished the season with Rovers winning 8-0 at home against Royal Albert and at Broomfield, in a Benefit match for the Old Union Brass Band, by a score of 2-0 against Airdrieonians.

MR. ALBION ROVERS No. 1

SIMON SCOTT

A founder member of Albion Rovers when the Club was set-up in 1882. In his career at Meadow Park and Cliftonhill he was Player, Committee Member, Match Secretary and Director over a period of fifty-seven years.

He was a Partner in the family business known as the Athletic Warehouse in Main Street, where the family were well-known in the sports goods field.

Sime came from a famous footballing Coatbridge family and his brothers John, Adam and Willie, all played for Albion Rovers. John, with Sunderland, and Adam, with Notts. County, crossed the Border and gave great service to their English clubs, whilst Sime and Willie finished their days at Meadow Park.

He served Rovers faithfully from October 1882 until September 1939, when he retired on account of ill-health. He was an outstanding cricketer starting with Albion and afterwards with Drumpellier. Eventually he acted as Professional with Stenhousemuir when for twenty-one successive seasons he topped that Club's batting averages.

As a player he occupied every position in the team over the years and often acted as captain. His unswerving devotion to Rovers caused him to turn down several offers to play for leading English Clubs over the years and when his playing career was over, he devoted himself to the task of Match Secretary which he first took up in 1894 at the age of 28.

Represented the Lanarkshire County team on several occasions, he also acted as captain at this level. As a Committee man he even played in emergencies up to 1913 and his last appearance in the first team was against Paisley Academicals in the Scottish Cup when he was the tender age of 47.

When the Club moved to Cliftonhill, Sime became one of the first Board of Directors, a position which he retained until 1939.

He retired in 1939 and had devoted a lifetime of unstinting service to the Club. Mr. Scott died at home in Dunbeth Road in January, 1941 aged 75.

CHAPTER THREE

A SEARCH FOR STATUS

Season 1903/04
Rovers were successful in their request for inclusion in the Second League and the push was on to sign suitable players for this higher grade of football. The non-league days were at last at an end.

The first game in full League status in the Second Division took place at Meadow Park on the 15th of August against Leith Athletic. Despite the interest locally in this game, only a crowd of two thousand paid £45.1.1d. to see a 2-2 draw with O'Rorke scoring both goals. Rovers team was Muir, Morrison, Murphy, Chalmers, Ramsay, Boyd, Peel, Cameron, O'Rorke, McKillop and Conlin. The English left-winger was to have a field day the next week at Ayr against the local Parkhouse, scoring four goals in the 5-2 victory. The third game against St. Bernard's at the Gymnasium saw the first defeat of the season by 2-1.

The Scottish Qualifying Cup first round was next in line and a fine 5-0 victory was logged against Carfin Emmett. The return match at Logie Green against Leith Athletic ended with the Edinburgh team winning 3-2 but worse than that Rovers were fined two points by the Scottish League for playing Clark and Murphy two unregistered players.

In the second round of the Qualifying Cup saw Wishaw Amateurs routed by 6-2 before St. Bernard's came to Coatbridge to lose 2-0 in a League match. This game saw the opening of the Pavilion complete with hot water and baths. Conlin was top marksman with nine and O'Rorke on six, after seven matches.

Next in line in the Qualifying Cup was the home match against Hamilton Academical which ended up at 1-1 in a match where Conlin missed a penalty. In the replay the following week two train-loads of supporters helped to swell the fifteen hundred crowd for a £170 gate and goals by Main and O'Rorke were enough to see Rovers win through in the end by 2-1. In the League next week Falkirk fought out a 1-1 draw in a match where goalkeeper Muir saved a penalty and Willie Main scored with his penalty attempt but then after being ordered to re-take missed at the second attempt. The next week the fourth round Qualifying Cup match saw a journey to Shawfield against Clyde and a resounding 7-2 victory which was controversial in that the referee whistled for half time when the game was less than forty-three minutes old. Despite Clyde protests the S.F.A. allowed the result to stand. This was followed by a fifth round match against Maxwelltown Volunteers at Palmerston when five hundred fans travelled by special train to see a 4-1 victory for Rovers. Back to League football the following week a visit to Kirkcaldy found a 2-2 draw again Raith Rovers coming back to equalise in the second half.

With cup tie fever riding high in the town the semi-final of the Scottish Qualifying Cup arrived with an away draw at Ayr where one thousand supporters travelled down to Ayr in two special trains to add to the seven thousand crowd and £150 gate. A fighting no scoring draw was achieved to bring the tie back to Coatbridge the next week. The replay saw six thousand pay £144.6/- to stand in a gale and watch an O'Rorke goal be sufficient to take the team into the ninth final of the Scottish Qualifying Cup at Dens Park on the 28th November.

In very heavy rain an eight thousand crowd paid £158.17/- and Rovers were represented by Muir, Smith, Morrison, W. Chalmers, Ramsay, Boyd, W. Scott, Main, O'Rorke, McKillop and Conlin. Arbroath fielded Strachan, Clark, Ferguson, Johnstone, Murray, Petrie, Black, Middleton, Willocks, Guild and Neave. The referee was W. McArthur (Stirling).

A support of something like five hundred left Coatbridge in a special train from the Caledonian Station for Dundee in ample time for the 2.45 kick-off. High spirits were tempered with the news that little Conway had fallen from a thirty foot high scaffold in Langloan Iron Works the previous Monday and would be missing. Willie Scott was to take his place. However there was consternation on the platform at Dundee when it leaked out that Chalmers, Smith, Ramsay and McKillop had all lost their train connection and were missing. They finally made it with thirty-five minutes to go and so all was set for the big match. The ground was soft, rain was falling heavily and there was a raw North-Westerly wind chilling the fans to the marrow. Rovers won the toss putting Arbroath to face the elements and Mr. McArthur of Stirling set the game in motion. The game was not the expected classic with Arbroath playing the long ball whilst Rovers played their usual close passing. Five minutes from the Interval Arbroath got first blood when 'keeper Muir was bundled over the line from a corner. Immediately from the kick-off Main had his shot palmed out to O'Rorke who poked in an equaliser for the game to end all square at half time.

The game re-started in an absolute deluge with good football being out of the question and the ball sticking in vast pools of water. On the hour Arbroath again scored but Rovers stuck to their guns and ten minutes later fair-haired Willie Main took a fine Scott pass to ram the ball home with the finest shot of the day. Disaster followed with right back Smith being caught in two minds leaving the Arbroath left winger an easy task to rob him and go unchallenged to put his team into the lead. This virtually finished the game as a contest but in the midst of a heavy Arbroath attack a whistle was heard causing the Rovers defenders to hesitate. As it had not been the referee Arbroath played on and left winger Neave scored his second goal so snuffing out Rovers' challenge.

Thus finished the first appearance of the team in a National Cup Final and in their first-ever game against Arbroath they were unfortunate to have lost by such a heavy score. The return journey home was in good humour despite the defeat and there was a large crowd of supporters at the station waiting for the team. Nevertheless, the Scottish Cup was now on the horizon where there were thirty-two contestants—the sixteen clubs in the quarter finals of the Qualifying Cup together with the sixteen exempt clubs. For that season the exempt teams were Airdrieonians, Celtic, Dundee, Heart of Midlothian, Hibernian, Kilmarnock, Leith Athletic, Motherwell, Morton, Partick Thistle, Port Glasgow Athletic, Queen's Park, Rangers, St. Bernard's, St. Mirren, Third Lanark and the qualifiers were Abercorn, Aberdeen, Albion Rovers, Alloa, Arbroath, Ayr, Clyde, Hearts of Beath, Kilwinning Eglinton, Maxwelltown Volunteers, Newton Stewart, Nithsdale Wanderers, 6th G.R.V. Stanley, St. Johnstone and West Calder.

The next week it was back to League business at Ralston Park playing Abercorn but the team lost 2-1 and the same result took place, seven days later at home, against Clyde before Falkirk were beaten by the one and only goal away from home. Centre half Ramsay had to be fielded in goal in the return match against Clyde but was unable to stop a 2-1 defeat. With a trialist in goal, who was untroubled by Abercorn, a 3-0 victory at Coatbridge was achieved.

ALBION ROVERS SEASON 1903/4 QUALIFYING CUP FINALISTS GROUP

On the 9th of January, Hamilton Accies were visited but Johnny Conlin dislocated his arm in a 2-1 defeat which was disappointing as "Kiltie" Cameron had put Rovers in the lead at half time. In an attempt to inject some punch, Prowdfoot, an inside left from Lincoln City, was fielded and he scored the first goal in a 3-3 draw against Arthurlie before the Scottish Cup proper tie which paired Rovers with Kilwinning Eglinton. These fellow qualifiers had advantage of home venue but Rovers bought this out and the Ayrshire team came to Coatbridge where Rovers won comfortably enough by 2-1.

The third home game in a row was next against Hamilton Accies in a 1-1 draw in front of an enthusiastic three thousand crowd. Raith Rovers came to visit on a day when the Meadow was very heavy following wet weather. There were many complaints by all and sundry but Rovers still pocketed the points by 3-2. Kilmarnock were the next opponents in the second round of the Scottish Cup when new left winger McGill scored both goals in a 2-2 draw bringing the play back the following week to Coatbridge. Rovers lost this one by the only goal of the game. There was a change in cups in the next game with Motherwell being the opposition in the Lanarkshire Variety. For the day Rovers played in maroon with Motherwell in their usual blue and in front of five thousand fans, Rovers won 3-2. The visit the following week to Larkhall saw a fine 4-2 victory over the Royalists, again in the Lanarkshire Cup.

Next to visit Coatbridge was the amateur team Ayr Parkhouse on League business and they were soundly defeated by 5-1 but this run of three victories on the trot came to an abrupt end at Hamilton in the Lanarkshire Cup semi-final against the Accies who won easily by 2-0.

The other team from the Honest Town came in search of League points and Ayr won 3-2. On the second of April, East Stirlingshire were visited in the League which, with Rovers winning 4-0, was abandoned in the sixtieth minute due to the gale and rain conditions. The same day at the Meadow a team of reserves were on the field in a friendly match against Darlington as the Scottish League would not allow the postponement of the East Stirlingshire match and Rovers had to field two teams on the day.

On return to play down at Ayr, again in gale conditions, in a match which Rovers lost 2-1 and an unusual feature of this game was that not one foul was given against Rovers during the entire game. It was back to winning ways against Arthurlie by 3-1 and then in the East Stirlingshire home match which Rovers also won by 2-0. This was followed by the replayed 'Shire match at Falkirk when Rovers were sunk without trace by 4-2. The season finished in a friendly which Rovers won by the only goal against Partick Thistle.

So finished the first season in the League with Rovers finishing in a creditable seventh position and the great excitement of the almost successful Qualifying Cup run earlier in the season.

Season 1904/5
At the end of the close season when the trainers called up the players for action most of the previous season's players were available with a smattering of new faces. A friendly match was set up with Hamilton Accies prior to the League Programme commencing, as a Benefit for the Coatbridge Brass Band. Airdrie had refused the invitation to provide the opposition and Rovers lost 2-0.

The League proper opened on the 20th of August at Shawfield against Clyde and despite considerable effort the team was unlucky to lose by the narrow margin of 2-1. Rovers were represented by Muir, Smith, Mitchell, Chalmers, Ramsay, Boyd, Darroch, Main, O'Rorke, Conway and McGill. It was good to see John Conway back in a Rovers' shirt following his serious accident a year earlier. On the following Monday a friendly match was arranged against Motherwell for the Janet Hamilton Memorial Fund.

Ayr were then visited and a Willie Main goal was sufficient to see Rovers pocket both points before the Scottish Qualifying Cup first round match at Renton was due. A special train-load of fans travelled with great expectations but with new forwards, Dillet from Cambuslang Hibs and Donachie from Morton, the team fell at the first hurdle this time instead of the last hurdle and Renton won out by the close margin of 3-2. Back on League business the next week against Abercorn who, in front of a two thousand crowd, were hammered by 5-1 at Coatbridge. When Raith Rovers came to contest a well merited 1-1 draw, Rovers climbed to the top position in the League.

However, this heady position was too much for the team who lost four successive matches losing 3-1 at Falkirk and 1-0 at Raith Rovers before Hamilton Accies and Arthurlie won 1-0 and 2-1 respectively at the Meadow. Left to pick up the pieces the team was freshened up for the home match against St. Bernard's when a 3-2 victory was the outcome. This was followed by the same score at Coatbridge against Ayr. The return match at the Gymnasium saw a 2-1 victory against St. Bernard's before a 4-4 draw at East Stirlingshire took the unbeaten run to four games.

A hiccup occurred against Abercorn away from home with a 3-0 defeat before the game against Clyde, which started ten minutes late, and with Rovers winning by 2-1, Mr. Riddell the referee stopped the game in the seventy-ninth minute due to crowd interference. Subsequently the points were awarded to Rovers with the score standing. Leith Athletic were the next visitors and on a snow-covered pitch a fine 5-3 victory was the result. The match against East Stirlingshire at Falkirk turned out to be horrific because, not only was the team beaten by 5-2, but goalkeeper Muir was injured in the sixtieth minute. Duguid was ordered off and O'Rorke arrived late causing the Rovers to commence the game with ten men.

Again around this time there was more talk about the old, well-vented subject of a new ground and there was a Meeting held on the 16th December to have this yet again thrashed out. After a rest of a week the team had two away matches at Arthurlie in a 2-2 draw and Hamilton, on the last day of the year to lose 3-0.

On Monday the 1st of January the short journey was made to Broomfield to play a Friendly for former player Davie Rombach. There was much misgiving by many of the Rovers' fans who remembered that Airdrie had refused to play in the Benefit Match, earlier in the season, for the Coatbridge Brass Band. However, the game took place and in front of a two thousand gate the 'Man of the Moment' scored the winning goal in a 3-2 defeat for Rovers. A £30 gate was the result the following week against Falkirk in a 2-2 draw but when Aberdeen came to visit on the 14th of January an O'Rorke goal was enough to win the points against the Qualifying Cup finalists of the previous season.

Leith Athletic had an amazing 7-0 victory in Edinburgh before three friendlies followed in which Rovers took the opportunity of trying out several new players. All three games were played at Coatbridge and firstly Abercorn shared two goals and Hamilton Accies eight. Falkirk brought this parity to an end winning by 3-0. In this game full-back Smith was injured and Falkirk agreed for Duguid to substitute for the crippled back.

The first ever visit to the Granite City followed and a 7-2 defeat recorded before the Inter-County Competition commenced. Ayr visited Coatbridge to lose 3-2 with ex-Strathclyde centre O'Hara scoring all three goals. The referee failed to turn up for this match which kicked off half an hour late. The 18th of March found Rovers struggling to field a team at home against Abercorn. With all three signed goalkeepers injured, Ramsay was in goal and Committee man Willie Thomson played outside left. Ramsay himself was injured with Tom Smith taking over in the second half.

In the Lanarkshire Cup at Motherwell the Fates were with Rovers for with the score at 5-0 for Motherwell the game was abandoned in seventy minutes. In a friendly East Stirlingshire fought for a well deserved 2-2 draw before the replayed Motherwell Cup tie found the teams still level on 3-3 at full time and the replay also all-square at 1-1 a week later. The third game was taken to Broomfield where Motherwell won by 3-2.

The season finished with an Inter-County match down at Ayr which was lost by 3-1 and a third defeat on the trot took place at Coatbridge in a Charity Match against Rangers by 2-1.

A slight improvement had taken place with one place, eighth, higher than the previous season and one point more at twenty. There was still much to be done to the team, the playing surface and more thoughts of pastures new.

Season 1905/06
There was a considerable influx of new players for the new season. A new Rule in all matches was that goalkeepers must stand on the line at penalty kicks and would no longer be allowed to rush out to the kicker and this decision was controversial. The build-up to the season commenced with a couple of Friendlies, the first being against Wishaw Amateurs for a 1-1 draw. This was followed by a home match against Airdrieonians when a single goal saw the laurels go to Airdrie.

The season proper started in the League with an away match at the Royal Gymnasium in Edinburgh against St. Bernard's when Rovers won 2-1 being represented by McBean, Ramsay, Duguid, Chalmers, Dooey, McAuley, White, Main, Stevenson, Hamilton, and Donald. The following game saw the Ayr team in their chocolate and yellow stripes visit Coatbridge to win 4-2 immediately before the special A.G.M. convened to consider the floating of the Club into a Limited Company. Unfortunately the intention to raise £3,000 by Share subscription fell at the final hurdle and the Club lost a considerable sum of money in the attempt.

Raith Rovers were then visited in Kirkcaldy for a famous 3-2 victory but this good result was tempered by Cowdenbeath's visit to Coatbridge the following week and winning easily by 3-0. Rovers were continuing to build up their team for the coming Qualifying Cup matches and McNab was signed from Hamilton, Govan from Hearts and Garret from Airdrieonians all in time to meet Vale of Leven at Coatbridge. New boy Duguid scored the only goal of the match to put Rovers into the hat for the second round. This success however was short lived and the Accies. won easily at Hamilton by the only goal of the game in the next round.

With nothing to trammel their thoughts other than League business six straight victories were then recorded, the first two being at Clyde where new right winger Shaw scored a hat-trick immediately following his signing from Glasgow Rangers. The same score was noted against East Stirlingshire when centre Quinn had a hat-trick. Four straight home matches then saw a 3-1 victory over Raith Rovers and the following week the 4-0 victory over the blue shirted St. Bernard's saw Rovers go top of the League. New inside right Clark from Carluke added some zip to the forward line and firstly Arthurlie were defeated 2-0, then Vale of Leven participated in a ding-dong battle which at 4-1 at half time looked to be easy for Rovers. Two quick goals by the Vale closed the gap but Rovers came back with a late rush to finish off winners by 5-3.

Much effort was being done to bring the pitch up to a satisfactory standard for League play. A new fence had been fitted in front of the pavilion and further banking fitted at the terracing just in time for the friendly match against English Leaguers Blackpool, who had been given a £35 guarantee which on the day was justified as the gate proceeds were £45 for the two thousand crowd. However, the recent good results came to an end and the North of England team were good winners by 3-2.

A 2-2 draw at Abercorn the following week saw Rovers still at the top of the League Table with John Quinn scoring the two goals. In another 2-2 draw against Vale of Leven the same man scored another goal in his last appearance for Rovers before signing for Everton for a reputed £150 fee. The player received a £10 signing-on fee and a guarantee of £4 a week in wages.

Back at Coatbridge, Rovers lost to an improving Clyde team by 2-1 but Abercorn were beaten the following week by the only goal of the game before another friendly match was fixed up at home against Broxburn. Unfortunately this time the gamble of giving a £6 guarantee to the visitors was not covered by the gate receipts. However all was not lost as the score was a 3-1 victory for the homesters.

On New Year's Day, as a Benefit for Matt Scott, Airdrieonians were visited and Rovers ran out winners by 4-0. Rovers showed great courage by playing goalkeeper Glover of Wishaw Amateurs at centre-forward. He justified the Committee's perception by scoring the second goal. The following day, a 1-1 draw was fought out down at Ayr and, despite losing 3-0 at Arthurlie the following week, Rovers remained at the top of the League with hopes high for the Championship. The success of the local club was catching on with the home contingent and Mr. Forrest, the local butcher offered ten pounds of prime roast for three goals at the next home match against Leith Athletic. On the day, however, the match was played in atrocious conditions with a water-logged pitch and Mr. Phillips of Glasgow the referee abandoned the match, with Rovers winning by four Duguid goals to nil. There were stormy scenes by the crowd, who were incensed at the referee's decision.

East Stirling were the next visitors in the League and they lost 5-1 before a 2-1 defeat at Cowdenbeath saw Clyde edge ahead at the top of the League. There were feverish activities going on behind the scenes at this time with news of a new grandstand and the development of Meadow Park now that a move to a central situation seemed to have been discarded. Hamilton Accies were next to fall, by 2-0, before Royal Albert came on Lanarkshire Cup business only to lose by 4-1; all goals again being scored by Jim Duguid, who also missed a penalty. The new stand was already being erected, following approval by the Dean of Guild Court.

The re-scheduled Leith Athletic match next took place with the incredible reverse score of 1-0 for the men from the Capital and this situation was continued in the second round of the Lanarkshire Cup against Hamilton Accies by 4-1. It was no better the following week against Clyde, when a 1-0 defeat was inflicted at Glasgow.

Jim Duguid said his farewells in the next League game at Leith when he scored

Rovers' only goal in a 3-1 defeat before being transferred to Hibernian for £100 plus the promise of a Friendly match. The new stand was completed in time for the visit of the London amateur club West Norwood, who participated in a no scoring draw. The grandstand cost £165.0.0d. and was erected by Mr. Spittal, joiner, from Whifflet.

The A.G.M. took place in the Eagle Inn on the 6th April and Hugh C. Watterson of the North British Iron Works was elected President. At this Meeting, Tom Mowatt was granted Life Membership for his outstanding services to the Club. This was quite a stormy Meeting, with Members passing a resolution that the Committee was not to spend more than £30 without Club Members' approval, and also Mr. Kyle's proposal that all A.G.M.'s in future take place before the 15th March was carried without difficulty. The Club ended the year with a Credit balance of £22.0.1d.

Rovers just failed election to the First Division at the League A.G.M., following the relegation of Kilmarnock and Queen's Park. The first ballot saw Hamilton elected with ten votes, whilst Clyde and Rovers had seven, Leith six and Raith Rovers three. Eventually after a third ballot, Clyde took the other place by nine votes to Rovers' six.

With these disappointments behind them, Abercorn were visitors in an Inter-County match, losing 2-1 and the season frittered out with three friendly matches. The first of which at Coatbridge saw Rangers win by 4-0 with Menzies injured and off in the second half when the score was 0-0 and Rangers running through the depleted Rovers' team. Airdrieonians were then visited and, despite 'keeper Allan saving a penalty, the homesters won by 4-3 and the final game of the season was a 2-2 draw at Coatbridge against Motherwell.

So did the curtain fall down on a disappointing season with Rovers being runners-up in the League but failing miserably at early hurdles in the various Cups. The loss of star players Quinn and Duguid did nothing to endear the Committee to the Support. There was quite a clear-out during the close season leaving many new faces to be knitted together for the coming season.

Season 1906/07

Two faces among the newcomers included two of Rovers' all-time legends in wee Robbie Ralston from Kirkintilloch Rob Roy, who was to play for many years for the Coatbridge club, and Peter Boyle, the Irishman, who was subsequently to play for his country. The season started with a pre-season friendly against Wishaw Thistle, which was successfully negotiated by 2-0 before on the 18th August, Arthurlie visited Coatbridge to be soundly trounced by 3-0. Rovers were represented by Higgins, Carmichael, Boyle, Chalmers, McPherson, Menzies, Low, Main, D. Wilson, Ralston and Donald. This was followed by a visit to the Old Gymnasiun ground to play Leith Athletic, who the previous season had won the Scottish Qualifying Cup and had become Second Division Champions. Before the match the Championship flag was unfurled and the home team's Cup was full to overflowing with a 2-1 vicory by the end of the day.

The Scottish Qualifying Cup Campaign started with a match at Wishaw against the local Thistle. At 2-1 for Rovers the match was abandoned with two Wishaw players being ordered to the pavilion. The S.F.A. ruled that the result was to stand due to the misdemeanours of the Wishaw club. This was followed by a 1-0 victory at Kirkcaldy against Raith Rovers in a rather rough game, when Rovers missed a penalty, whilst goalkeeper Higgins saved one at the other end. With Cup fever

Leith v Albion Rovers 1906

gripping the town, Hamilton Accies were visited with two special trains full of local supporters who were gratified by a 2-1 victory before Ayr Parkhouse were defeated at Coatbridge by 2-1. In this match centre half Menzies missed two penalties although he scored one goal from his second attempt in a rebound from the goalkeeper.

Tontine Park, Renton was the venue of the third round of the Qualifying Cup when a 1-1 draw was the result and the following week at Coatbridge in a game that started ten minutes early in front of four thousand fans, a 3-3 draw was the result. Five thousand fans paid £116 at Ibrox in the second replay to see Renton lead 3-0 at half time and although Donald knocked one back this turned out to be a simple victory for the Dunbartonshire village team.

Back in the League Abercorn were defeated 4-0 at Coatbridge before visits to Dumbarton and East Stirlinshire saw firstly a 1-0 reverse followed by a 2-0 defeat. Better stuff, however, was round the corner and in heavy rain the next match at Coatbridge against Dumbarton was a 2-2 draw. Next result was an amazing 3-2 victory at Abercorn in a match where Rovers were really toiling when Ralston was ordered off for fighting in five minutes and lost a penalty goal in ten minutes. The good form continued with another fine victory over Vale of Leven at Coatbridge by 3-1 with custodian Higgins saving a penalty. This was followed by a 4-1 victory at home over Cowdenbeath.

This fine form made the team perhaps over-confident for their visit to the amateurs of Ayr Parkhouse. They were languishing at the foot of the Second Division but an away goal in the second half was enough for the amateurs to pocket the points whilst Rovers' disappointed and Jimmy Donald missed a penalty.

In the wake of this result, the local press gave notice of the setting-up of a new team in Coatbridge with a strong Irish bias but despite this possible competition Rovers took on Leith Athletic, soundly defeating them by 6-2 before Hibernian visited the Meadow, in the friendly match promised at the time of the Duguid transfer, and on a snow-covered pitch, Rovers won 3-0 although Rovers' bad form with penalties continued when Menzies missed again from the spot.

Vale of Leven won very convincingly by six goals to no reply down at Dunbartonshire before the Qualifying Cup holders, Raith Rovers, visited Coatbridge to be soundly whipped by 4-1. Again another missed Menzies penalty found Rovers losing 3-1 in Edinburgh against St. Bernard's before the League game against East Stirlingshire was cancelled at the last minute and a friendly arranged to defray expenses of both teams. The pitch was very icy and Mr. Smith of Third Lanark the referee had no other decision to take on the day. However, the teams played two thirty-five minute halves in a 2-2 draw.

The visit to Ayr on the 2nd of February saw a 1-0 defeat before East Stirlingshire were thrashed by 7-3 assisted by a Robbie Ralston hat-trick. Added excitement was caused at one stage by a drunken spectator falling down the Railway embankment onto the line amidst heavy rain and mud. A train which was on the up-line managed to stop in time and the culprit got away, the hoots of the spectators sounding in his ears.

At Cowdenbeath the following week the Fifers won 4-0 before Dykehead were trounced 6-0 at Coatbridge in a Lanarkshire Cup first round match. Back in the League the next week Ayr won 2-1 in a match played in driving snow with the lines being continuously obliterated. The referee mercifully blew his whistle three minutes early in this game.

The A.G.M. was held on Friday, 15th March and it proved to be very stormy, with members very unhappy with the general play of the team and the League position. Also the condition of the pitch caused considerable concern to members.

Two draws followed next with a 1-1 draw at Arthurlie followed by a no-scoring draw against St. Bernard's at Coatbridge before the first of the Inter-County Shield matches surfaced with Royal Albert losing 3-0 at Coatbridge. Airdrie were the visitors in a Benefit match for Willie Main, who scored Rovers' goal in a 2-1 defeat.

Back in the Inter-County Shield the following week Royal Albert were again defeated 1-0, this time at Larkhall, before Arthurlie lost 5-2 at Coatbridge only to win 1-0 in the return the following week. The season finished with a Lanarkshire Cup semi-final match against Airdrieonians at home which finished up all square at full time but Airdrie won 3-2 after extra time.

The season had again been most disappointing and the fans were looking for much more in the season to come. Again many changes were to be made in personnel during the close season and it was hoped that the new combination would gel better than the earlier mix.

Season 1907/08
It was straight into League business in an away match against Arthurlie on 17th August when in a narrow 1-0 victory Rovers were represented by Dickie, Tomlin, McSkimming, MacArthur, Ramsay, Menzies, Collins, Main, McCormack, Young and Donald.

In their first home match in the League the red and white shirted Ayr team managed a 1-1 draw but in the two thousand crowd there were two bad fights among fans and several arrests by the local constabulary before a visit to North End Park, Cowdenbeath saw the home team win comfortably by 5-0. The Scottish Qualifying first round match arrived this time against Royal Albert away from home and a Robbie Ralston hat-trick was enough, with only one in reply, to see the team through to the next round. The next week in the League at Bainsford a 1-1 draw was fought out against East Stirlingshire before Dykehead were dismissed from the Qualifying Cup second round by 3-0 at the Meadow.

The Leith Athletic match ended up a shambles when the referee came late and, with the game starting well after the scheduled time for commencement, thick fog rolled in at 4.20 p.m. with Rovers losing out by 5-4. The match was classed as a friendly and the reserve Leith goalkeeper became Mr. Laing—Referee. The following week Dumbarton came to Coatbridge undefeated in the League and with fifteen minutes to go were losing by 3-0 but the match ended all square, which was most disappointing for Rovers. The long journey down to play Ayr Parkhouse was then on schedule and an easy 3-0 victory was the result. Non-leaguers Galston next appeared at Coatbridge in the third round of the Qualifying Cup and shocked Rovers with a 5-1 victory.

Abercorn, who were currently topping the League, were next hosts and Rovers returned home with a 2-1 victory with Bob McSkimming scoring his first goal for Rovers. The following week the East Stirlingshire game started with a late kick-off due to the Falkirk team missing their train connection. The referee Mr. McPherson of Kilmarnock, abandoned the match due to darkness with Rovers losing 3-0. It was Rovers turn to miss their train connection the following week down to Somerset Park to play Ayr and, although the game started fifteen minutes late, it managed to finish this time with Rovers scoring a late penalty but still losing 4-1.

Leith Athletic next appeared at Coatbridge to win 2-0 and a further defeat came at the hands of Vale of Leven away from home by 4-1. Rovers reshuffled their team and introduced outside-right Mackenzie from Douglas Park, who scored the winning goal in a 2-1 victory at Kirkcaldy against Raith Rovers. The following week, at Logie Green, Leith Athletic were easy winners by 5-3. Two other away games saw Dumbarton share the points with a 1-1 score but St. Bernard's won by 5-2. That man Main scored his tenth goal to put him top scorer.

Ayr Parkhouse came to Coatbridge with Rovers winning 3-2 and Rovers' goalie Hutchison saving a penalty at the close to deny the Ayr team a point. The next week was the Scottish Cup proper first round at Pittodrie against Aberdeen, resplendent in their black and gold strip, but Rovers lost by three second-half goals to nil. The losing ways continued at Coatbridge the next week when Raith Rovers scored the only goal of the match, before bottom dogs Arthurlie came to the Meadow to be trounced easily by 5-2.

Vale of Leven visited Coatbridge in a 1-1 draw before St. Bernard's, the Qualifying Cup holders, won 3-1 in a match which started twenty minutes late and was played in a rain-storm and gale. Rovers played in Lord Rosebery's colours of red and yellow in opposition to the Edinburgh team's blue strip.

Three home games on the trot saw three defeats; the first being a 3-1 score against Wishaw Thistle in the Lanarkshire Cup before Abercorn were successful by 3-2. Menzies missed this one by being married and Rovers lost Tomlins for five minutes and Donald for fifteen, finishing the match with only nine men with East Stirlingshire winning 2-1. The night after a very stormy A.G.M. was held in the Royal Hotel when, after much discussion, Willie Kyle resigned his membership of Rovers after many years' faithful service.

The last League game took place against Cowdenbeath with two Robbie Ralston goals to one, giving the homesters a 2-1 victory but the last game of the season was a 5-1 drubbing at the hands of Airdrieonians in a friendly match.

The season had been disappointing with the ignomy of losing to non-league Galston in the Qualifying Cup and elimination at the hands of Aberdeen and Wishaw in the first matches of the Scottish and Lanarkshire Cups respectively. The League position was much worse than the previous season with three places and four points worse off. The Supporters were disenchanted to say the least.

Season 1908/09
Again changes were wrung by the Committee with feverish close season signings and when Arthurlie appeared on the 15th August for the opening League clash, a 3-3 draw was the result, only possible by 'keeper Hutchison saving a penalty. Rovers were represented by Hutchison, Cook, Brown, Lindsay, Robertson, Chalmers, Watson, Barr, Ferguson, Reynolds and Farr.

On the following Thursday Motherwell visited Coatbridge for a Benefit for Wattie Chalmers and the visitors won by 4-1 and on the following Saturday Abercorn easily crushed the Rovers' opposition by 3-0, down in Paisley. Leith Athletic slumped to a 1-0 defeat at Coatbridge in front of two thousand fans and Wishaw Thistle were crushed 4-1 at Wishaw in a match which started thirty minutes late because again the referee missed his train connection.

Raith Rovers were next to visit the Meadow to lose 1-0 in a match which had as much going for it off the field as on, with the Coatbridge Instrumental Band playing before the kick-off and at half-time and Mr. McGuire plus two pupils giving an exhibition of Indian club swinging. The gate didn't seem to have been particularly swelled because of these attractions however.

Rovers fell at the first major hurdle of the season in the Scottish Qualifying Cup first round at Coatbridge losing by the only goal of the game to Clyde. The following week second top Dumbarton came to Coatbridge to win by 4-2 in a rough match in which Ralston and McCulloch of Dumbarton were ordered off for fighting.

High drama came about at Cowdenbeath, on the 3rd of December, when a Sheriff Officer arrived before the game with a Writ from Cowdenbeath for Rovers' share of the gate for alleged non-payment for the match held at Coatbridge earlier in the year. The Rovers' Officials simply ignored the Officer and the team promptly defeated the Fifers by 4-1. The other Fifers, Raith Rovers, took ample revenge the next week with a 3-1 victory and it was left to a home victory over St. Bernard's to save Rovers slipping to the bottom of the League.

Next was a visit to Ayr Parkhouse where the amateurs won rather easily by 4-0 before Cowdenbeath returned to Coatbridge losing this time by 3-1. Again that Sheriff Officer accompanied the Cowdenbeath team looking for £25 compensation for gate money. Former President Tom Mowatt was at the match after a bad bout of incipient consumption but looking quite fragile.

Down at Dumbarton, the following week, the first home defeat of the season was inflicted by Rovers at 3-1. This was a match which was very violent and after a spectator struck a Rovers' player, a riot broke out which was only controlled by a baton charge by police. Perhaps this affected Rovers more than they would like to admit because they promptly lost 1-0 the following week at home to East Stirlingshire.

Two new faces were introduced, outside left Tennant from Airdrie and Cook at inside right, and the first named scored the Rovers' goal in a 1-1 draw at St. Bernard's and also scored in the 2-1 defeat at home against Abercorn. Ayr were next on the agenda and they won easily 5-1 down the coast but the following week the return match went 2-0 in favour of Rovers with Tennant scoring his third goal in four appearances. In the last game of 1908, in a sea of mud, Ayr Parkhouse visited Coatbridge to win by 2-1. The New Year started disastrously with a 6-2 defeat against Leith Athletic and another by 5-0 against Vale of Leven, both as away matches, and Arthurlie being defeated away from home 2-1 before East Stirlingshire won 4-1 at Falkirk.

There was now a respite of some five weeks due to very inclement weather but, at the end of March, Royal Albert fought back to a 1-1 draw in the Lanarkshire Cup, at Coatbridge, with Rovers handicapped by McNab being off for more than an hour. In the replay at Larkhall, Rovers ran out winners with a Tennant goal to no score but in the semi-final Airdrieonians easily won 3-1 in a downpour at Broomfield. The last League game took place on the 24th of April when Rovers soundly defeated Vale of Leven by 5-0.

The season had been very mediocre and it was clear that a shake up was needed from the top downwards. At the A.G.M., Tom Mowatt retired and Andrew Jeff became the new President.

Season 1909/10

Again the close season saw the changes being rung, and the pre-season Friendly at Dykehead, which was lost 2-1 saw six new faces in the team. When the team lined up at Ayr, in the first League match, on the 21st of August, there was little cohesion to be seen and a 4-3 defeat was recorded. Rovers team was Hutchison, Brown, McSkimming, Smith, Jones, Chalmers, Allan, Dickie, Turnbull, Ralston and Hutton.

Cowdenbeath were first visitors at Coatbridge in a 1-1 draw and at this match there was a very strong demonstration by Supporters at the very disappointing results. This spilled over into the next match when the Scottish Qualifying Cup first round was an emphatic 3-0 victory for Dykehead, which also saw a missed penalty and also the introduction of Hemphill from Maryhill and Turnbull from Morton to the forward line.

Changes were certainly being rung and in the no-scoring draw at Coatbridge against Raith Rovers, Charlie Wyse, a centre-forward from Darlington St. Augustines, was played but he had to wait until his second game, at Dunterlie Park, Barrhead, to score in the 2-2 draw against Arthurlie. The visit to Cowdenbeath, who were currently League leaders, was not looked on with much confidence and this was confirmed in the 1-0 reverse which greatly flattered Rovers.

The fans were beside themselves when Ayr Parkhouse came and won very easily by 3-1 when Jones and goalkeeper Hutchison, of the Ayr team, were ordered off but the final humiliation arrived against Vale of Leven when, on Melbourne Park, Rovers lost 4-1 to slump to the bottom of the League. St. Bernard's came to Coatbridge with the unenviable record of the last pointless team in Scotland and lost by 3-2 with Charlie Wyse scoring a double.

Raith Rovers were visited but a 3-0 defeat was the outcome and against Dumbarton the following week, in a match which kicked-off ten minutes early, a Hemphill hat-trick to one in return was enough to see Dumbarton sent back down the Clyde pointless. A visit was made to Abercorn but a 3-2 defeat was the result.

Following this the Half Yearly Meeting of Members took place where much consideration was given once more to the floating of a Limited Liability Company by the Membership. A Wyse hat-trick contributed to a 4-1 victory over Arthurlie before a 2-2 draw was secured at Ayr Parkhouse.

The Consolation Cup was next on the cards and Abercorn visited Coatbridge only to lose by 4-2 in a match which was abandoned at sixty minutes due to bad snow and fog. In this match Jimmy Lang of Benburb made his debut. The Cup organisers agreed the match score should stand and Rovers went into the next round which was scheduled against Wishaw Thistle.

However, it was back to League business the next week with a no-scoring draw at Dumbarton which was remarkable if for no other reason than goalkeeper Hutchison could not strip and wing half Smith took his place in goal. Ayr were the next visitors to lose 2-0 before a single goal defeat at Leith saw the last of Charlie Wyse, who was transferred to Clyde.

New Year's Day match at Coatbridge against East Stirlingshire was a 2-1 victory before the Consolation Cup match, at Bellhaven Park, against Wishaw Thistle ended up with no score. This was the same result as the following week at Coatbridge before the second replay at Broomfield saw Rovers bundled out by 2-1 after extra time.

The Meadow was a quagmire with continuous rain for the next match against Abercorn but Rovers managed to win by 5-2 in what turned out to be Bob McSkimming's last match before being transferred to Sheffield Wednesday. Members were furious at this latest act of treachery in their eyes and a series of meetings took place during the week following with a tremendous display and demonstration before the match against St. Bernard's in Edinburgh which was lost by 4-0 and their demeanour was no better the next week when Leith came to Coatbridge and won 2-1 with Smith even missing a penalty in the last minute.

March commenced more satisfactorily with a 2-1 victory over Vale of Leven and then goalkeeper Sanderson and right half Paton were signed in time to strip for the home Lanarkshire Cup match against Dykehead. The game was only saved in the last minute with Jimmy Lang scrambling the ball home for a 1-1 draw. The replay at Dykehead saw no goals and on the following Monday a Coatbridge Express Cup match was played at Hamilton against the Accies who won easily by 3-0.

Back to the Dykehead saga and the second replay of the Dykehead Cup Tie was due to be played at Broomfield but this was cancelled due to heavy snow. As a protest the players played a seventy minute friendly which ended at 3-3. The following Wednesday saw the second replay at Broomfield which Rovers finally won by 3-1.

East Stirlingshire won 1-0 at Falkirk in the League and it was made known that Rovers received £175 for Wyse and McSkimming and that the playing staff were each currently paid £4 a week. The balance sheet showed a £79 profit. Again there were efforts made regarding the floating of a Limited Company and yet another Committee was set up to pursue this end.

The season fizzled out on Tuesday and Wednesday the 26th and 27th of April when Wishaw Thistle played in the Lanarkshire Cup firstly at Coatbridge for a 1-1 draw and the next day at Wishaw for a no-scoring draw. The Lanarkshire F.A. decided that the tie should not be decided this season but be replayed the following season.

This was the last straw in a season of great disappointment for the fans. The team had finished nowhere in the League and had gone out of the Qualifying Cup in the first round. Worthy players had been lost and the ground was in need of considerable improvement.

The A.G.M. was extremely difficult for the Committee but as happens in such circumstances a new Committee was appointed and they set to work with a will to organise for the new season.

Season 1910/11
Again much activity had taken place to produce the first team of the season which played in the uncompleted Lanarkshire Cup tie of the previous season. This was played at Motherwell and Wishaw Thistle ran out winners by 1-0. Rovers were represented by Sanderson, Brown, McCrossan, Waterson, Diamond, Lindsay, Turnbull, Devlin, Chalmers, Andrews and Ralston. Abercorn opened the League season and promptly lost 2-1 before the trip to Cowdenbeath saw another victory chalked up, this time by 1-0.

The first round of the Scottish Qualifying Cup took place, again against Abercorn who this time lost 4-0, before a friendly match at Coatbridge against Dumbarton Harp ended with no score. The good crowd of more than six thousand saw Morton beat the homesters 3-2 in the second round of the Qualifying Cup and Dundee Hibs made their first visit to Coatbridge and gained a no-scoring draw. Arthurlie were played at Barrhead in a 1-1 draw whilst a missed penalty by Menzies proved expensive when Port Glasgow Athletic ran off winners by 1-0 at Coatbridge.

Things took a turn for the better with a 2-1 victory against Vale of Leven away from home to hoist Rovers third top in the League. This was followed the next week with a 3-0 home victory over Dumbarton. Notices were displayed around the ground prohibiting swearing by spectators which had become an annoyance in recent times. The good form continued with a trip down to Ayr where a 2-1 victory sent the team to the top of the Second Division.

Leith Athletic struggled for a 2-2 draw at Coatbridge but the victory in Edinburgh against St. Bernard's of 3-0 the following week saw Rovers go three points clear from Dumbarton Harp at the top of the League Table. Vale of Leven were held to a 1-1 draw in a snow storm. Before the next game centre-forward Duncan claimed he had been 'tapped' by one of the big English teams, thus causing a ripple in Scottish football circles. Perhaps this put Rovers off their stride because the result was expensive with a 3-1 defeat against Port Glasgow Athletic.

The next home match against Arthurlie saw Mr. Pringle, the prospective Tory candidate for the General Election kicking-off and he saw a return to the winning ways with a 3-2 victory. Despite losing 3-0 at Dumbarton the next week, the team remained League leaders.

Another point was dropped in a no score match against Cowdenbeath at home but then a narrow 1-0 victory was scraped against East Stirlingshire. Armadale were defeated 3-0 and only a disputed penalty goal allowed Dundee Hibs victory in the return fixture in Dundee. The Consolation Cup first round match against Port Glasgow Athletic ended in a 2-1 victory for Rovers but, as the referee only allowed eighty-eight minutes, the Port protested. This was thrown out by the Committee and the following week the amateur Dumbarton Harp were visited but the best Rovers could muster was a 2-1 defeat.

The next week, in the Lanarkshire Cup, Mr. Nisbet from Cowdenbeath, the referee, came up with some very individual time-keeping when Dykehead won 1-0 at Shotts. The referee allowed only a forty minute first half and forty-five minutes in the second half then with a five minute change of ends to make up the ninety minutes. Rovers made a protest in this respect which the L.F.A. threw out after much consideration, as the letter of protest came to late. It is an interesting fact that in those days there were four letter deliveries in the day and often it was dependent on which train the mail was transported in as to whether the letter which you received in the morning could be replied to and even that letter delivered during the same day. Rovers' letter went on the wrong train and arrived a day late causing great consternation with Rovers' fans and Secretary Sime Scott was hauled over the coals for this state of affairs.

Ayr United were next to come to Coatbridge and their 2-1 victory dropped Rovers into second place in the League. St. Bernard's the following week lost by the same score but Leith Athletic, on their own Logie Green, won by the only goal of the game. A fighting win of 1-0 then took place in Falkirk against East Stirlingshire before Airdrieonians won 2-1 in a Friendly match at Broomfield and Royal Albert drew no scoring in the Coatbridge Express Cup first round.

Whilst Rovers had been playing these matches other teams had been amassing points in the League and when Rovers took up their League Programme in the visit to Abercorn, Rovers lost 1-0 and at the same time they slumped to fourth position. The replay of the Coatbridge Express Cup against Royal Albert took place but again the score was nothing each at Larkhall whilst the second replay was only played again at Meadow Park thanks to the toss of a coin. Gerry McCrossan scored what proved to be the only goal of the game with an own goal. The season finally finished with a Friendly played against Bedlay Juniors which allowed Rovers to experiment with their team whilst losing 2-1 to the minor team.

The Members were absolutely livid at this inept performance where the team which promised so much early in the season failed to do anything in the League and the Cup challenges had been snuffed out before they had even started.

Season 1911/12

A clear-out of players once more took place and when Leith Athletic were visited, on the 19th of August on League business, a narrow 1-0 defeat was suffered with the team reading as follows: Graham, McKinnon, McCrossan, Smith, Diamond, Brown, Mitchell, Chalmers, Plunkett, Stevenson and Hutton.

On the Monday, Motherwell were visited in the Lanarkshire Cup first round to share two goals and then back on League business St. Johnstone made their debut at Coatbridge by winning 1-0 in heavy driving rain with a second-half goal. Motherwell won the replayed Lanarkshire Cup tie at the Meadow by 2-1 in a remarkable match, played throughout in a thunder storm, with the players having to be taken from the field on several occasions due to the heavy rain.

The Scottish Qualifying Cup first round challenge ended quickly against old rivals Royal Albert at Larkhall with Rovers losing 4-2. Three of the Royalists goals were penalties and Rovers protested on the grounds of crowd encroachment but this was turned down.

And so, once again, it was left to the League Programme for any success where there had already been two 1-0 defeats chalked up. The worst possible start was achieved at Paisley against Abercorn losing by 3-1 but the green shirted Dundee Hibs were defeated 1-0 at Coatbridge with a Plunkett penalty. After a no-scoring draw at Falkirk against East Stirlingshire two 1-0 victories were achieved at Coatbridge against Vale of Leven and away over Dundee Hibs. The season so far had produced some dreary fare with seven games of either no goals or a single goal out of ten played.

Vale of Leven brought this modest run of success to an end by a 2-1 victory before Arthurlie came to Coatbridge to win by the only goal of the game — that score again.

Despite new goalie Monteith saving a penalty, Rovers slumped to a 2-1 defeat at Cowdenbeath. When Ayr United won 2-0 at Coatbridge, Rovers slid to the bottom of the League which position was confirmed with the emphatic 5-0 victory by Arthurlie at Barrhead in the next game.

With a crowd of well under four figures Rovers played new boys Hudson, from Rob Roy at full-back, and Goodridge, a soldier boy on leave, against East Stirlingshire in a 4-1 home victory. This score proved to be a veritable island in a sea of deep despair with seven defeats on the trot which started with a 3-1 score at St. Johnstone with the Saints even missing a penalty in the first half after Rovers had led at half time. Cowdenbeath won 5-2 at Coatbridge and the visitors next week St. Bernard's after a half time deficit won 3-2. The return match against St. Bernard's the next week ended at 1-0 and Abercorn came to Coatbridge for a 4-1 victory before the last League defeat in this sequence took place at Dumbarton by 2-0. However, another defeat was on the cards on the 2nd January at home, against Motherwell in a Benefit match for Robbie Ralston, which was won by the 'Steelmen' by 7-1.

The home Members were disgusted and needless to say the Committee weren't exactly overjoyed either. Gates had plummetted to an all-time low and there was again much talk of moving to a more central position in Coatbridge. Wonders will never cease and Leith Athletic were defeated 1-0 in the League before a draw in the Consolation Cup first round at Port Glasgow saw a victory in the replay against the Athletic at Coatbridge by 4-1. In the next round Wishaw Thistle won easily on their home ground by 2-1 in a match where Rovers showed little backbone or interest.

Ayr United then won easily by 4-0 down at the seaside before the last game in the League saw Dumbarton beaten 2-1 at Coatbridge. However, this victory was not enough to stop Rovers finishing at the bottom of the League. Things were so bad and the heads were so far down that when the Coatbridge Express tie against Airdrie was due Rovers scratched for the first time ever from any competition.

The talk was rife in Whifflet that the Club was ready to fold and it was quite in keeping with the air of doom and despondency in Coatbridge that the news of the sinking of the White Star liner, Titanic, came on the 15th of April with the loss of 1635 lives.

Rovers had to apply for re-election along with Vale of Leven and, whilst they were both successful, also elected were Dunfermline Athletic and Johnstone being admitted to the Second Division for the first time.

Season 1912/13

Again a clear-out took place and when the opening game against new Leaguers Johnstone arrived on the 17th of August two thousand fans keenly watched a 3-1 victory for the rejuvenated team who played as follows: Monteith, McCrossan, Brown, Rennie, McAteer, Toye, McEwan, Thorburn, Plunkett, Fitton and Hannah. The following Monday the Lanarkshire Cup match at Shotts found the teams deadlocked at no score when the game was stopped in the seventy-fifth minute due to darkness. At Melbourne Park, Vale of Leven won 1-0 and during their home match against Cowdenbeath which was lost by 3-0 black arm bands were worn and the flag flown at half mast in memory of former player John Conway who had died following an accident at work.

The Scottish Qualifying Cup first round was scheduled for Coatbridge against Dykehead with a 2-0 score for Rovers. A visit was then due to 'New Boys' Dunfermline Athletic, who ran out easy winners by 5-2. Wishaw Thistle, that old bogey team, were drawn in the second round of the 'Qually' and a 1-1 draw was the result at Coatbridge with no score at Wishaw in the replay. The second replay at Broomfield saw a single goal enough to take the tie to the 'Jags'. Rovers' consolation being the share of the three gates.

Leith Athletic were kept to a no-scoring draw at Logie Green but Ayr United won 1-0 at Coatbridge before Dundee Hibs were defeated 5-1 at the Meadow. Ayr United won 3-0 at home then a friendly against Royal Albert took place with half hour halves ending no score.

Back in the League fray St. Johnstone won convincingly at Perth by 2-1 with Archibald taking over in goal from Monteith. Another trip to Edinburgh saw St. Bernard's win 3-2 before Rovers return visit to Johnstone met with a 3-0 defeat and the team slumped to the foot of the League.

A 3-0 victory was achieved over Leith Athletic at Coatbridge inspired by a Johnny Archibald penalty save. The following week at Dumbarton the team went down by 3-2 and Alec Brown's brother was signed from Armadale in time to play in the return game against the 'Sons of the Rock'. This was a game at which the Portsmouth Directors were present to cast an eye over forward Plunkett, who then went down to Pompey on a month's trial. Tobin scored the only goal of this match in the first half but a last minute goal down at Abercorn lost the points in frustrating fashion.

In the midst of a snow storm, St. Johnstone came to Coatbridge and, with the assistance of Gallacher from Coatdyke All Saints, Rovers won 2-1. The following week Dunfermline were defeated by the same score with old boy Hemphill playing with the 'Pars'. The third home match in a row ended up a no-scoring draw despite Plunkett returning from his month down south. Bobby Archibald, an outside-left from Rutherglen Glencairn and a brother of goalkeeper Johnny, was signed in time to play in the match against St. Bernard's. On his debut he scored two fine goals and Plunkett scored the other with St. Bernard's only able to score two in reply. Both players were again on target in the next game at home against Arthurlie in the 4-2 victory. Plunkett scored two and Archibald a single in the 5-0 home victory againt Vale of Leven in the best result of the season.

Unfortunately this run of good fortune ended at Cowdenbeath. Plunkett and White were off injured during the last twenty minutes and the team lost by 2-0 and up at Dundee, against the Hibs, the next match was a 2-1 defeat. At Bainsford against East Stirlingshire a Bobby Archibald goal was sufficient to win the game and the frustrated Shire fans, who had seen their team second top in the League, attacked the Rovers' players leaving the pitch. The S.F.A. closed their ground for one month and banned them from playing within five miles plus a £5 fine.

In the Coatbridge Express first round, Motherwell came to the Meadow on the Monday and earned a 2-2 draw and, as Fir Park was engaged the following Saturday, the Meadow was used for the Rovers to go through to the second round by 3-1.

The Abercorn home game saw the largest gate of the season but a disappointing no scoring draw was the result. A disappointing season ended with the Express Cup game at Fir Park against Royal Albert which ended up a 1-1 draw thanks to a McAteer penalty, but this was only by courtesy of the referee who allowed the first kick, which was missed, to be retaken. On the following Wednesday, again at Fir Park, Rovers won by 3-2. Only ninth League place with twenty-three points had been attained. On the Monday, Archibald was guesting with Edinburgh Hibernian against Hamilton Accies and he scored a fine goal in the 3-1 Hibs' win.

There were several changes in personnel during the close season and when trainer Miller brought the players together for the new season, the Archibalds had gone, Plunkett, McLay, McAteer and McCrossan were no longer available and the new blood were not to languish on the sidelines for long.

Season 1913/14
The opening game of the League season was a home match against Arthurlie which, thanks to a Bell penalty, ended up one goal each. Rovers were represented by Harrigan, Trainor, D. Ewing, Ralston, R. Ewing, Weir, Chalmers, R. Martin, Bell, Collins and Brown. Another draw, this time no scoring, was the result at Johnstone before Dykehead came to Coatbridge in the Lanarkshire Cup to win by a mammoth five goals without reply. An understandable start to the season with so many new faces in the team.

In the League the next week at Coatbridge, St. Bernard's were defeated by two Guy Watson goals to one in the local boy's debut. Sime Scott made an appearance at left-back which meant he was stripping for his thirty-first season in senior football. With Paisley Accies waiving their home rights in the first round of the Scottish Qualifying Cup, Rovers had an easy 6-1 victory with Sime Scott retaining his place. The Johnstone home game saw Dave Ewing return to his left-back spot following a turn at centre-forward the previous game and Captain Robbie Ralston's team went to the top of the League with a clear-cut 5-1 victory.

The second round of the Qualifying Cup saw Dumbarton Harp fight out a no-scoring draw, although a Martin goal had been disallowed in the fifth minute. For the replay a special train took the Coatbridge contingent 'doon the watter' to witness a fine 4-1 victory. In the next round at Shotts against Dykehead, two special trains took a good Coatbridge support and three thousand fans saw Rovers win by a solitary Watson goal.

Dundee Hibs then visited Coatbridge in the League and with Rovers losing Chalmers with a broken bone in his foot, played the last half hour with only nine men but still managed to win by 2-1. The next week the fourth round of the Qualifying Cup, at Warner Park, Stevenston, over one thousand adults and two hundred children in two special trains welcomed back winger Bobbie Archibald to the fold from Third Lanark. He scored the only goal of the match against Stevenston United to put Rovers in the next round. Johnny Archibald made a fleeting appearance in goal in the home match against Vale of Leven which Rovers won 2-1. Another away Qualifying Cup match, in the fifth round, took place at Castle Holm Park, Sanquhar against Nithsdale Wanderers and six hundred fans cheered on Rovers to a famous 3-0 victory.

Cowdenbeath were visited for a no-scoring draw before the sem-final of the Qualifying Cup arrived with cup fever high in the Iron Burgh. It was a home match this time against Arthurlie and Captain Robbie Ralston, who had been married the previous night, was so keen to play that he postponed his honeymoon and the Meadow was in raptures over the 3-0 victory. The team then awaited their opponents in the final which was due to be played in four weeks' time.

The previous season's Qualifying Cup winners, Abercorn, then visited the Meadow to lose by 4-1 with a Martin hat-trick scuttling them in the second half. Dunfermline Athletic won 3-2 on their own ground in a match which, with Watson injured, Rovers were over-stretched. The following week, on a frost bound pitch, St. Johnstone came to Whifflet and Rovers had to fight back from being behind in the first half to be all square at 2-2 at the finish.

The town was agog at the end of the year with the appearance of the team against Dundee Hibs in the Scottish Qualifying Cup Final. On the 13th December, Tynecastle was the venue and in front of a 10,000 crowd and complete with the Rosehall Pipe Band, Rovers were represented by Harrigan, Trainor, D. Ewing, Ralston, R. Ewing, Weir, Galbraith, Archibald, Martin, Watson and Prentice and Dundee Hibs by McPhilips, Hannan, Forbes, Whyte, Henderson, Boland, Brown, E. MacDonald, Martin, Linn and Stoessel. In a hard fought match, despite leading by 1-0 at half time through centre-forward Martin, Hibs equalised in the second half to put the match into a replay. Seven days later, again in Edinburgh but this time at Easter Road, Tom Robertson of Glasgow was again the referee but the match once more ended up a 1-1 score with outside-left Prentice doing the needful. However, on the 27th December a second replay was held back at Tynecastle. There was a change of referee this time, Tom Dougray of Nitshill, and with a 1.45 kick-off in case of extra time, the match commenced in a snow blizzard. The same teams had played in all three final matches but the attendances had reduced in each game, with only receipts of £20.7.1d. for this third match.

The support thought back to the earlier Cup Final played in similar conditions, when Arbroath had won by 4-2 and hoped that lightning was not going to strike twice in the same place. When the game started the conditions favoured the 'Brig club and for the first fifteen minutes it was all Rovers. There was controversy when Davie Ewing accidentally handled inside the penalty box but the referee allowed the game to continue and the Rovers' contingent breathed a sigh of relief. The self same man then went off on a brilliant solo run before being brought down outside the penalty line quite cynically by a Hibs' defender. However, the Rovers bonnets were in the air in the twenty-sixth minute when Galbraith sent forward a fine pass to centre-forward Martin, who from short range drew first blood for the Coatbridge team. Rovers continued to monopolise the play and first Robbie Ewing and then Prentice all but got a second goal. With five minutes before the interval, the goal, which was long overdue, came from a free kick. This was taken by Robbie Ewing and Martin's shot was only partially cleared leaving Guy Watson an easy opportunity to rattle the back of the net. Half time was piped with Rovers leading 2-0.

The second half did not reach the same high standard and feeling crept into the game with Bobby Archibald suffering much from the attentions of the Hibs' defenders so much so that he had to leave the field on two occasions for attention. In the fifty-fifth minute Martin took on the entire defence and set up a chance for Watson who shot a magnificent third goal for his side. With something like thirty minutes still to run, Galbraith missed a fine opportunity to add to Rovers' score when, from an open goal position, he shot weakly past.

The Hibs came more into the game in the last quarter and with five minutes to go only the post prevented Stoeffel scoring with a rocket shot, whilst with the last kick of the game Galbraith shot again into the capable hands of McPhilip. Full time came with Rovers in front by 3-0. Harrigan had had little to do and Trainor and

Ewing were steady whilst Ralston was the best of a good half-back trio. Of the forwards, Watson, Martin and Archibald were the men who mattered.

Despite this tremendous victory in the National Competition, Rovers made a financial loss of almost £100.0.0d. At the close of the match, Mr. Campbell, the Vice President of the S.F.A. who had acted as one of the linesmen, presented the Cup to Rovers in the absence of the S.F.A. President. President Hugh Thom accepted the Cup and the return journey was on back to the Iron Burgh.

Meanwhile, back at Coatbridge, the news had reached an expectant population and, when the train containing the players, officials and supporters arrived at Sunnyside North British Station, they were met by a crowd numbering several thousands. The Coatbridge & Airdrie Tramway Company had sent along one of their 'char-a-bangs' to convey the players around the town and the Coatbridge Instrumental Band struck up "The Conquering Heroes" as soon as the train pulled into the station. The players were mobbed and many were carried shoulder-high right along Main Street. After the players and officials were seated in the bus, the Coatbridge Instrumental Band led a torchlight procession numbering many thousands by way of Sunnyside Road, Bank Street, Dundyvan Road, round by Whifflet, Coatbank Street along Main Street to where the players, officials and members all assembled in the Royal Hotel hall and drank from the Cup in honour of the great victory. The celebrations continued long into the morning and merged into the New Year's celebrations for many.

On Thursday, New Year's Day dawned and a Coatbridge Express Cup match was due for the Meadow against Wishaw Thistle with the 'Jags' losing by 4-1 and on the Saturday, Cowdenbeath, sitting as League leaders, visited but there was no chance of them getting a result as the adrenalin was still flowing in the Rovers' veins. Cup heroes Martin and Watson again scored the goals in a 3-1 victory. It looked a different story the next week when East Stirlingshire scored with only five minutes to go, in a match which was played in very patchy fog, but Rovers managed to equalise in the last minute to share the goals and the points.

In the first away match since the winning of the Cup, Arthurlie were hosts and they exacted full revenge for their semi-final defeat in the Qualifying Cup by winning 3-0. At Leith the following week in gale force conditions, Trainor and Hyde of Leith were ordered off before other injuries ended up with both teams playing with only nine men during the second half. Justice was seen to be done with the match ending all square with a score of 1-1.

St. Johnstone were played at Perth, again in gale conditions, the following week but the homesters won easily by 5-0. The Scottish Cup proper was next on the agenda and First Leaguers Aberdeen were drawn as opponents but despite a hard fight by Rovers the Dons won quite easily by 4-1. Dundee Hibs were hosts in the League the following week with Robbie Ewing scoring two goals in the first half but he failed to complete his hat-trick by missing a penalty in the second period and the game finished all square at 2-2. The following week at Abercorn, despite Harrigan saving a penalty, the team went down to the only goal of the game scored in the first half. Dunfermline lost at Coatbridge when Archibald scored the only goal of the game and amidst considerable pressure by the Support for a move to a new pitch, East Stirlingshire were visited and a 2-0 defeat was the result.

Amidst heavy rain, Leith Athletic came to Coatbridge and they lost comprehensively by 6-4 before Wishaw Thistle gave up their ground rights in the Coatbridge Express Cup to lose 8-1 at Coatbridge, with Bell scoring a hat-trick. At the Gymnasium in Edinburgh, St. Bernard's were defeated by 1-0 and the last

ALBION ROVERS QUALIFYING CUP WINNERS 1913/14

Back: R. Boag, W. Smith, E. McLaren, W. Johnstone, W. Gibb.
Centre: S. Trainor, W. Smith, A. Bell, R. Ewing, D. Harrigan, H. Thom, D. Ewing, J. Grant, T. Muir.
Front: S. Scott, R. Archibald, J. Weir, D. Galbraith, G. Watson, R. Ralston, R. Martin, C. Prentice, J. Chambers, D. Millar.

game in the League Programme saw a 3-2 victory against Vale of Leven away from home put Rovers, four points behind Cowdenbeath, in second position.

The Coatbridge Express final took place at Fir Park on the 25th April and despite a hard battle the Shotts team ran out narrow winners by 2-1 with Rovers' team being Harrigan, Trainor, D. Ewing, Ralston, R. Ewing, Weir, Galbraith, Martin, Bell, Wallace and Archibald.

Thus ended the most successful season so far in the thirty-odd year history of the Club. A major national trophy had been won in the Qualifying Cup and the team had finished second top of the Second Division championship. There was the making of a fine team with the Ewing brothers, Robbie Ralston, Duncan Harrigan, Bobby Archibald and not least the recent debutante Joe Wallace signed from Bedlay Juniors. However, the threat of war hung heavy in the air during the summer of 1914. Many of the young men of the town volunteered for army service and whilst most were kept in reserve, many were immediately mobilised and went on training. Rovers were luckier than some in that most of their conscripts remained in the area and were available for duty on the football pitch in the new season.

Season 1914/15
With great expectations the season opened with an away match at Melbourne Park, Alexandria against Vale of Leven. In front of two thousand enthusiastic fans Rovers won by a first half goal by inside forward Murray. Rovers were represented by Smith, Watson, D. Ewing, Ralston, R. Ewing, Blue, Boylan, Murray, Smith, Denholm and Forester. The following Wednesday a Benefit for R. Mackie took place up at Broomfield with the homesters winning by 3-2.

A second away match in the League took place against East Stirlingshire with no score before, on the Wednesday, a Lanarkshire Cup match saw Motherwell win on their own patch by 4-0. The first home League match of the season was against Johnstone and with two Guy Watson goals in the first half it looked like a second win was on the cards but it was not to be and the game finished all square at 2-2. There was a collection taken for the War Relief Benefit by the Boy Scouts and this raised £2.17.6d. The Burgh was excited with the prospect of the Qualifying Cup match away from home against Vale of Leven. A special train took the Supporters of the Cup Holders but, despite the teams drawing at half time, Vale of Leven won rather too easily by 3-1. This was Willie Harris's last game before going off to war. Everyone with the Club was absolutely dejected at this dramatic turn in fortunes and the heads were still down the next week when Abercorn won more clearly than the 1-0 score would suggest with Charlie Watson, brother of Guy, making his debut in place of Harris. However the team got back on the rails in their second home match in eight games against Dunfermline Athletic, winning 3-0 with Watson scoring two of them. Clydebank were then visited in a 1-1 draw with goalie Harrigan saving a penalty and the blushes.

Two reverses were to follow, the first at home against Leith Athletic, who had a sweeping 4-0 victory, before the first visit through to Fife to play Lochgelly United. They were lying adrift at the bottom of the League but the team slumped to new depths to lose by 1-0 causing much valid protest from the fans. Murray became top scorer with five goals in the 2-0 victory at home over Arthurlie before League leaders Cowdenbeath came up trumps with a reverse of that score. Dundee Hibs were then defeated 3-0 at the Meadow with Guy Watson enjoying the luxury of missing a penalty.

Guy Watson
1913-15, 1919-20

Robbie Ewing
1913-18

Davie Ewing
1913-18

Bobby Archibald
1913-14, 1918-19

77

President Hugh Thom and Match Secretary Simon Scott with the Qualifying Cup at Tynecastle Park, Edinburgh, December 1913

ALBION ROVERS SEASON 1914/15. MINOR TEAM GROUP AT MEADOW.

A 2-2 draw at Johnstone was followed by a home no-scoring draw against Abercorn which was all the more praiseworthy as Bob Murray broke his leg in two places in the tenth minute. Further bad luck followed in fog-shrouded Edinburgh the following week when St. Bernard's won 3-1 and Smith, after equalising a first half deficit, broke two ribs. Two home matches followed with first of all Clydebank drawing 2-2 but Cowdenbeath scored the only goal of the game in the next match.

Due to injuries the Committee were stretched to field a team for the visit to Dundee against the local Hibs and the team selection showed many changes but that didn't stop the Hibs winning by 6-1 with centre-forward Martin scoring five of them. The next match against St. Bernard's, at Coatbridge, saw centre-forward Curle from Abercorn fielded in the 1-1 draw. With Bob Martin, signed from Belfast Distillery, making his debut and with the return of many of the regulars this was all too much for East Stirlingshire who were swamped by 4-2.

The following Monday, Dykehead were the opponents in the Coatbridge Express Cup first round first leg and a Guy Watson goal was enough to take the leg, which captain Robbie Ralston missed due to missing his train connection. The trip through to Fife against Dunfermline on the Saturday produced a 4-0 defeat. Revenge came the following week when Lochgelly United were defeated 2-1, on the day when local rivals Dykehead lost 3-0 to St. Bernard's in the Scottish Qualifying Cup Final.

St. Johnstone did their usual competent job at Perth winning 4-1 before Arthurlie were defeated by three clear goals at Barrhead. This score was reversed the following week against Leith Athletic before, in the middle of a blizzard, St. Johnstone were defeated 4-1 giving sweet revenge for the earlier reverse. Vale of Leven were the next visitors and they also lost by 4-1. This was a game in which three balls were used due to various mishaps. Inside forward Boylan was married the night before and had been presented with a clock by Players and Committee and Club linesman Willie Kyle also got hitched and he had received a gift of cutlery. However even without this duo the once mighty Vale of Leven were easily crushed.

Abercorn came to visit Coatbridge in a Benefit match for broken leg victim Bob Murray. The game started thirty minutes late and was played in a blizzard with Referee Andrew Peace from Shotts abandoning the match after sixty-five minutes ending all square at 1-1 and the visitors had to borrow two Rovers to make up their numbers. A visit against all-conquering Dykehead in the Coatbridge Express Cup first round second leg saw the homesters win 1-0, thus tying the match over both legs. The match was replayed at Wishaw the following Saturday when the teams again were tied at the end of the ninety minutes by sharing two goals and in extra time Dykehead won by one corner to nil. Ninth position had been achieved in the League which was a comedown from the record of the previous season.

The season came to an end with a Friendly at Broomfield which also ended all square at 1-1.

All during this past season with the Great War lumbering on inexorably over on the Continent there had been an air of unreality in the football scene. It therefore was no surprise when news came from the Scottish League that there would only be a First Division operating for the duration. With no relegation or promotion that year this was particularly hard on Cowdenbeath who had tied with Leith Athletic and St. Bernard's at the top of the Second League all with fifty-seven goals. The three clubs played each other in a series of test matches and Cowdenbeath defeated the other pair. At the end of this unfortunately for them there was no place in the higher Division.

Rovers organised themselves in a Western League, which meant a return to matches against non-league old friends of the far and distant past. The Scottish Cup was also cancelled for the duration. Many of the players were in reserved occupations and there was little change in the personnel of the playing staff for the new season, whereas in other clubs wholesale volunteering for the Forces was the rule.

CHAPTER FOUR

MARKING TIME

Season 1915/16
Accordingly, on the 21st of August the season opened at home against Dykehead in the Western League, the only new face was inside-forward Sloan and Bob Murray was welcomed back following his leg break. He celebrated by scoring Rovers' first goal of the season for the second successive year in the 2-1 victory when Rovers were represented by Harrigan, Trainor, D. Ewing, Ralston, R. Ewing, Wallace, Galbraith, Murray, Martin, Sloan and Campbell. The away match the next Saturday against Dumbarton Harp was going well enough until goalkeeper Harrigan got injured with five minutes to go before half time with no scoring. Even with the irrepressible Dave Ewing in goal in the second half he could do nothing to stop four second half goals for the Harp.

Two new faces who stripped for the home match against Johnstone were goalkeeper Eden from Tottenham Hotspur and outside-left Gifford from Partick Thistle. The winger scored the only goal of the match but these signings could do nothing the next week against Vale of Leven when the team lost by 2-0.

The trip down to Dunterlie Park saw a fighting 2-2 draw against Arthurlie with Harrigan making a welcome return in goal. Rovers were lucky the next week when second top Stevenston United visited. The only goal of the match was a controversial penalty which referee Curran from Larkhall gave despite the foul having occurred outside the box, according to all eye witnesses. The trip to Wishaw found the 'Jags' in fine form winning 4-1 and then Vale of Leven came to Coatbridge and in a bad tempered 0-0 draw there was considerable crowd trouble which required police intervention.

Renton, sitting bottom of the League, were then hosts to the team from the 'Brig and they surprised their visitors by a fine 2-1 victory. Worse was to follow at home against Clydebank the following Saturday when despite introducing inside-forward McConnachie from Queen's Park, the team lost by the only goal of the match. Non-success continued with two draws at 1-1 at Larkhall against Royal Albert and a home 2-2 draw against Dumbarton Harp before Royal Albert were defeated 2-1 in the Coatbridge Express Cup first round first leg at Larkhall. New signing centre-forward MacGregor was proving a find but the fans were stunned when they arrived at Ardrossan to play League leaders Stevenston United to see the young centre in goal, due to Duncan Harrigan failing to appear and the seasiders won 1-0. Despite a hat-trick the following Saturday by inside-forward Frew the team lost 4-3 at home in the return Express Cup match against Royal Albert. Before the replay could take place two away defeats were experienced at 3-1 against Johnstone and 3-2 against Clydebank.

In the replayed Express Cup Tie against Royal Albert at Hamilton the Royalists took a 3-0 lead just after half time. Despite a spirited fight back by Rovers they could only amass two goals which was not sufficient to stop the Larkhall Club going into the next round.

Four straight home wins in the League then came about with first of all Abercorn losing 5-2 in a match which turned out to be Charlie Watson's last game before signing for Clyde. Dykehead then lost 4-2 and Arthurlie and Wishaw Thistle were both defeated by 2-1 before a Friendly match in Falkirk against East Stirlingshire

81

found Rovers six men short but two soldiers were picked up in Falkirk to make up the numbers and there was even an appearance for Sime Scott in this match which the home team won by 2-1. Down at Ralston Street the next week in the League, Abercorn won 4-3 before the Lanarkshire Cup match against Wishaw Thistle saw the 'Jags' win 4-0 in the first leg.

Back in the League, Royal Albert were defeated by a fine goal from left-back Dave Ewing with Dave Galbraith missing a penalty. The return match against Wishaw Thistle in the Lanarkshire Cup saw Rovers win 2-0 and at this match President Hugh Thom who was Band Master to both Coatbridge Brass Band and the Coatbridge B.B. Band, brought both sets of muscians to regale the fans. They were obviously a tremendous success because they appeared again the following week in the last League game of the season against Renton with Rovers winning by 3-0 helped by two goals by trialist Murphy from Croy Celtic.

Thus a very dull season finished, a season where there had been no highlights. Fifth position in the League with twenty-two points was thirteen less than champions Vale of Leven. However, there were more important things on everyone's mind at this time other than football. The War which was to have lasted just a few months was still rumbling on with no sign of an end in sight. For the coming season the Committee got down to finding new talent in very difficuult circumstances.

Season 1916/17
Rovers continued in the Western League and when the season opened on the 19th of August at home against Wishaw Thistle, Davie Galbraith was playing with the 'Jags' and there was an 'unofficial' crowd standing on the railway embankment having a free view of things. However new boy Willie Watson got them off to a good start with two goals and by half time Rovers were four clear goals up with the game eventually ending 4-1. Rovers' team was Harrigan, Crossan, D. Ewing, Duncan, R. Ewing, Wallace, Boylan, Dickson, Brown, W. Watson and Welsh. The first away match was also a victory by a Dickson goal to nothing.

There were two reverses next with firstly Clydebank winning 4-0 on Clydeside and then Dumbarton Harp winning 2-1 at Coatbridge. On the 16th of September when the team visited Johnstone to lose by the only goal of the match there was a grand Carnival being held in Coatbridge in aid of War funds. Provost Davie who was Chairman of the Carnival Committee arranged for Dr. Murray and Willie Kyle to take charge of the Meadow where there was a five-a-side tournament, which Kyle refereed, as a preliminary for the week long Carnival in Dunbeth Park. During this period an aeroplane landed, £1700 was uplifted and there were thirteen entrance gates. The Red Cross and Volunteers were on parade, as were many limbless soldiers, broken products of the war on the Continent.

The following week Abercorn equalised with only a minute to go to snatch a point they didn't deserve in a 1-1 draw, and with Crossan missing his train connection, yet another Watson — Dave from Clyde, made his home debut. Against Arthurlie left winger Bennett was signed from Motherwell to add some punch but the team still lost 3-2 and at Royal Albert there was another 1-1 draw. Tom Dunsmore, ex-Partick Thistle and Dunfermline, made his debut at left back in an attempt to plug the leaky defence. Back at Whifflet the whole place was incensed at the increased prices in the local chippies of fish suppers for 4d. or 6d. It was considered a gross case of profiteering in the austerity of the War days.

However, on more serious matters, the 14th of October arrived with very inclement weather and, when the Wishaw Thistle match commenced, a hurricane wind added to the torrential rain and gave the referee no option other than to abandon the match after only a few minutes. The first of the Lanarkshire Cup matches was next on the agenda with a home game against Dykehead, who were defeated by 2-0, and in the second leg the next week the Shotts men ran out easy winners by 4-1 thus taking the tie despite Charlie Watson being re-engaged from Clyde for what turned out to be a three game spell.

The second of these was a home draw against Stevenston United at 2-2 before Arthurlie fought out another 1-1 draw down in Barrhead. Hugh Thom, son of President Hugh, played in this match at left back signing from Renton earlier in the week. His home debut was in a League game against Clydebank which started twenty minutes late and had to be abandoned in seventy five minutes due to darkness. There was no scoring but the game was very expensive in manpower with firstly Crossan off and then Harrigan off to hospital.

A new goalkeeper had to be found for the visit to Dykehead and Airdrie lad Joe Hudson was signed from Queen's Park in time but he was unable to save defeat in a 1-0 scoreline. With no League match scheduled a Friendly was set up with Queen's Park Strollers but with poor weather there was a loss made on the guarantee given to the Amateurs. It was clear from this match that the days of friendlies as a crowd pulling feature were over. For the record Rovers lost by the only goal of the game.

Back in the League at Paisley, Abercorn won 2-0 whilst at home the following week a no-scoring draw with Vale of Leven continued the team's miserable form. The next week, the sixth game in a row without the forwards hitting the net, saw Dumbarton Harp win easily by 2-0. As a final gesture, on the second last day of the year, Johnstone were trounced by 3-1 at Whifflet.

The New Year saw the start of the Inter-County Championship with a visit to Glasgow against Queen's Park Strollers when a second half Hugh Thom goal culled the points for Rovers. In the return match at Coatbridge the following week the Strollers were beaten by 3-1 in a match which was played with two forty minute halves. There were problems with other teams in the competition and Dykehead, Royal Albert and Wishaw Thistle all resigned due to transport difficulties.

Back on Western League business a trip down to Alexandria saw Vale of Leven win 1-0 before again in the Inter County competition Queen's Park Strollers were hosts. This time the Amateurs were successful by 2-1 and, in the same competition the following week, Renton, whilst missing a second-half penalty, shared in a 2-2 score.

Clydebank came to Coatbridge in the Western League for a 1-1 draw and after the match left-winger Tom Welsh was presented with a clock to commemorate his marriage. His adrenalin was obviously flowing because he scored Rovers' goal on the day. Dumbarton Harp then came in the Inter-County Championship to win 1-0 in a match which started half an hour late and in deplorable ground conditions. Renton in the Western League visited the Meadow, this time to lose 5-1, again missing a penalty in this game.

Duncan Harrigan made a welcome return to goal, after his long spell off, in the visit to Stevenston United in the Inter-County Competition but the homesters won by 2-0 and the Committee were by this time quite concerned at the lack of punch up front. In the Friendly at home against Royal Albert goalkeeper Harrigan was given the job of centre-forward and though by no means a failure and scoring the second Rovers' goal in a 3-0 victory, the experiment was never repeated.

There then followed a gargantuan fixture muddle with Renton scheduled to play in two different competitions on the same day. The first team played Vale of Leven in a Renfrewshire Cup game and sent their second team to Coatbridge in the Inter-County Competition where they lost 4-0 for their pains. Airdrieonians were then played in a Friendly where two Dave Galbraith goals were sufficient to see the local rivals beaten once more. Galbraith had a penalty effort saved but followed up to score Rovers' second goal before more than two thousand fans. The last game of the season was played away against Dumbarton Harp where the amateurs won by 4-0.

Another inauspicious season had taken place as far as the matters on the field were concerned, with Rovers finishing seventh in the League with fourteen points—nineteen behind Clydebank as Champions. There were moves afoot for Rovers to change their ground and the Committee were seriously looking for alternative sites in a more central position in the hope that when this War eventually finished the move could be completed and in the happier days which were longed for by all and sundry in the future the Club's fortunes would take a decided turn for the better.

Season 1917/18
With admittance again in the Western League the season kicked off with an away match at Johnstone where a 2-2 draw was the disappointing result. Rovers were represented by Hudson, Crossan, Thom, Sloan, Ewing, Wallace, Galbraith, Gallogley, Trialist, McAlpine and Bennet. However, smiles returned to the Coatbridge faces when Abercorn were beaten by 4-0 at home and then Arthurlie by 2-0 at Barrhead.

A 3-2 victory at home over Renton saw the team zoom to the top of the Western League. However, before they got too cocky, Stevenston defeated them by three goals to no reply down in Ayrshire and in the return match against Johnstone, Rovers narrowly won by 2-1.

Abercorn managed a 0-0 draw when with a flurry of transfer business, Duncan Harrigan was despatched to Arthurlie and forwards Dowds of Third Lanark and Anderson from Airdrie joined Bob Penman, who was to become one of Rovers' all-time greats, signing from Motherwell. The Arthurlie team came to Coatbridge and were beaten by 3-1 which result saw Rovers consolidate their position at the top of the League and Hugh Thom, who had been called up for War Service, played his last match against Vale of Leven in a 1-0 victory in which Davie Galbraith missed a penalty.

Despite losing 3-2 at Renton, Penman and Ralston both missed their train connections for this match but Dave Ewing made a welcome return from the Army. Dumbarton Harp were defeated 2-0 with Pat Corcoran making a scoring debut leaning heavily on his experience gained with Clyde and Hamilton Accies. In the return match the next week at Dumbarton a reverse by 3-2 was the disappointing result but, nevertheless, Rovers were still at the top of the League table.

The Western League Cup then fell to be played and it was arranged that this would be played on a league basis. In a match where there was tremendous crowd trouble and stand-up fights between players, Arthurlie won 2-0. Stevenson United visited Coatbridge to end up with an 8-1 thrashing despite having old Rovers Dave and Charlie Watson in their ranks. Vale of Leven fought a hard won draw of 1-1 down in Dunbartonshire before, in the Western League, the same team visited Coatbridge to be trounced by a mammoth 8-0 score helped greatly by a Dowds hat-trick and Gallogley's double. This result was sufficient to win the Western League Championship for the Coatbridge team by one point from Renton.

Back to Cup business the following week and a visit to Johnstone brought a no scoring draw made worse by Joe Wallace missing a penalty. Penalties were to continue to be headline material the following week in the match at Coatbridge between the same two teams, when, with the referee failing to turn up, Willie Kyle was given the job of being referee and in controversial manner gave two penalties to Rovers, one of which was scored by the redoubtable Wallace which turned out to be the only goal of the game.

For the match against Renton, Rovers' train was held up at Carmyle Station due to a derailed mineral train, and this meant that the Team and Supporters got to their destination with it being virtually impossible for the game to finish in daylight. The game was finally abandoned with Renton winning 1-0. In the last game of the year, Vale of Leven visited Coatbridge to lose again by 8-0 thanks to an Anderson hat-trick and Dowds and Gallogley scoring two each before Captain Ralston put the icing on the cake in a match which was too one-sided to be interesting.

On Wednesday, 2nd January, Motherwell came to Coatbridge in the Lanarkshire Cup and were trounced by 4-0. Due to a family bereavement outside-left Bennett did not play against his old team with Robbie Ralston filling-in on the left wing. Motherwell were unhappy with the state of the pitch and appealed for the match to be designated a friendly, which was subsequently upheld by the Cup Committee. At a pleasant ceremony before the game kicked off, the Western League Championship flag was unfurled by Mrs. Thom, wife of the President.

Abercorn were defeated 1-0 at the Meadow in the Cup before Dumbarton Harp came and won 4-3 in a match where debutant ex-Hamilton Accies, Dave Wilson, an outside-left scored Rovers' third goal. The return match saw a reversal of fortunes and Rovers winning this time by 2-0. Queen's Park Strollers then came to Coatbridge but thanks to Paddy Corcoran scoring four goals, one of which was from the penalty spot, they went home with a 5-1 defeat under their belts.

In an astonishing match down in Ayrshire on the 16th February, a Cup Tie against Stevenston United saw the game start in dreadful wind and rain conditions. Rovers were winning 3-0 at half-time but Jones and Corcoran were on the point of collapse with the result that when the game restarted, Rovers only fielded eight men. This made little difference in the circumstances and the referee eventually abandoned the match in the sixty-third minute. The game was replayed the following week with Rovers winning easily by 5-2. Hugh Thom was welcomed home on leave and he played at centre-half in this match. Arthurlie were then despatched home with a 3-1 defeat but this good result was tempered by the news that Robbie Ewing had been taking to the Royal Infirmary and had undergone a serious operation. Abercorn were then visited in the Cup but this time it was Rovers' turn to lose by 3-1.

When the A.G.M. took place on the 15th March, Sime Scott was congratulated on his 21 years as Match Secretary.

The rescheduled match from New Year time in the Lanarkshire Cup against Motherwell took place at the Meadow on the 22nd March with Rovers winning by 2-1. An unusual situation took place at the end of the game with Joe Wallace apparently scoring a goal but the referee blew his whistle as the ball was crossing the line and deemed the game was finished before the ball eventually reached the back of the net. You can imagine the whistler was not top of the popularity stakes at the end of the match. A Friendly against Abercorn was the second of a series of home matches and this one ended up a win for Rovers by 5-1 to be followed by a 0-0 draw in the Cup against Renton and a 1-1 draw in another Friendly against Queen's Park Strollers.

Hugh Thom was again home on leave and able to take up the left-back position in the Lanarkshire Cup match against Hamilton Accies in the 3-0 victory but the following week in the Final, despite a record gate for Meadow Park of over 8,000 with receipts of £185.11.0d., Airdrieonians were victors by 2-0. Both goals came within a minute of each other and Rovers only real chance came when Bobby Young playing at outside-left, hit the post. Rovers' team was Hudson, Penman, Thom, Sloan, Duncan, Wallace, Corcoran, Gallogley, Dowds, Anderson and Young.

On the following Saturday a Charity Match for War Funds was played, as a seventh home match on the trot, against a Lanarkshire Select which Rovers won by 3-1. Rovers' player Jones appeared at left-back, whilst ex-Rovers Galbraith, now of Airdrie, and Bennett, now of Motherwell, played for the Select team. This was the first of a group of games in a little competition and Rovers met Motherwell the following week in the Final. In front of a 5,000 crowd which drew £100.0.0d at the gate and with Gillette razors as prizes, the Motherwell team ran out victors by 1-0. Rovers' team was Hudson, Penman, Caffrey, Sloan, Duncan, Wallace, Corcoran, Gallogley, Charlie Watson, Anderson and Spiers.

The season had consequently finished with some success in the winning of the Western League Championship but again the Club had been the bridesmaid and not the bride when it came to Cup Finals. The Committee who had been slaving away for months past in arrangements for a new ground, had still nothing to show for their labours. When the new season approached several new players had been signed on but it was obvious that at least for the foreseeable future the home ground would still be in Whifflet.

Season 1918/19
The first match of the new season was an away fixture against Dumbarton Harp and a defeat of 1-0. With changes in all departments the result was perhaps not unexpected. Rovers team was Harrigan, Penman, Caffrey, Jones, Daly, Wallace, Monoghan, McNeillage, Noble, Dowds and Creighton.

In the first home game against Renton another reverse, to the tune of 2-1, was the result. Willie Hillhouse, who was to be one of Rovers memorable great characters, made his debut from Motherwell at outside-left in this match. Signs of better things to come at Barrhead the following week with a 4-2 victory over Arthurlie followed by 1-0 victories at home against Johnstone and away against Renton before Dumbarton Harp brought the winning streak to a close at Coatbridge by 2-1.

The following week, despite Corcoran missing a penalty which would have given him his hat-trick, Rovers still won by 3-1 over Arthurlie. The next Saturday again a missed penalty—Hillhouse this time—stopped him achieving a hat-trick in the 4-0 victory over Stevenston United, the team he played for before joining Motherwell.

Current good form and free scoring continued in the away match at Stevenston with Rovers winning 6-0 with Creighton scoring four goals and, thankfully, one of them from the penalty spot. This good win was tempered by the sad news that Willie Kyle, who had been a prime mover in Rovers circles over many years and the Club's official linesman, had died quite suddenly. The Club was further saddened when news came of the death of left-back Caffrey's wife and he missed the match against Vale of Leven which Rovers won by 3-2. In the eleventh straight League game in a row Rovers won happily enough by the only goal of the game down at Johnstone before, in the Lanarkshire Cup at the Meadow, Wishaw Thistle were trounced by 11-0, with Creighton scoring three, Corcoran and Young two each, and singles from Hillhouse, McNeillage, Penman and Duncan. The team was Harrigan, Penman, Caffrey, Noble, Duncan, Wallace, Corcoran, McNeillage, Creighton, Hillhouse and Young.

Back to League business and a visit to Abercorn found a fighting draw at 1-1 and the next week the Western Cup, which was to be run on league lines, surfaced with a 5-0 victory over Johnstone at Coatbridge. Vale of Leven, in a League match, were defeated 1-0, a score aided greatly by Harrigan saving a penalty. Rovers' goal in this match was scored by Joe Wallace and was also from the penalty spot. Another high-scoring game in the League came the following week when Abercorn were trounced by 8-1 with Creighton scoring another hat-trick. This completed the League competition with Rovers ending up as runners-up on nineteen points — one short of Dumbarton Harp.

In the Western Cup an away match at Barrhead was abandoned in the seventy-eighth minute with the score at 1-1 and at the end of the year, the last home match was played with Rovers winning by 2-1 against Vale of Leven. On Tuesday, 2nd of January, a no-scoring draw was fought out at Broomfield against Airdrieonians in the Lanarkshire Cup before Arthurlie were beaten in the Western Cup 2-0 at Coatbridge.

Johnstone were then visited with the honours going to the Coatbridge men by the only goal of the game and the following week, in a Friendly, the match against Queen's Park Strollers started one hour late due to the Amateurs baggage being lost by the Railway Company en route. Rovers won this game by 3-1. It is amazing that not only could the equipment be found and returned but that the fans were prepared to wait for the match to commence.

There were now very serious moves afoot to transfer the Club to another ground and for the Club itself to become a Limited Company. There was serious talk of a move to a more central position nearer the Tramway Depot and close to the tramway lines, although there was a strong body of opinion among Members that the present ground could be improved far more economically and it was also close to the main railway lines which criss-crossed the country.

However, when Dumbarton Harp came in the Western Cup, they managed a creditable 3-3 draw and the following week, in the same competition, the same clubs met in a roughhouse where Corcoran was sent off and the Harp won by three clear goals. There was more trouble for Rovers in the next game at home against Renton, for despite winning 3-0 another player was sent off in Willie Anderson. The following week Stevenston United were defeated by the only goal of the game at Coatbridge with the town fairly buzzing about the imminent move by Albion Rovers to the grounds of Cliftonhill House between the Town Centre and Coatdyke.

A Meeting was held of Club members in the Back Temperance Hall on Friday the 14th of February at which there was a large attendance. President Hugh Thom occupied the chair and the motion calling for the dissolution of the Club and the forming of the concern into a Limited Company was immediately moved, seconded and unanimously agreed. This was a momentous decision indeed and so simply and swiftly arrived at.

President Thom reported that at the previous attempt to form a Limited Company the Club had incurred a large debt but at this time the Club could not be in a better position, both from the financial and the playing point of view. He thought that if this venture failed the Club would lose any chance of further advancement in footballing circles and that election to full League status would be a priority. If the Powers-that-Be were to allow the Coatbridge Club League status a new ground would be essential. The Meadow pitch at Whifflet was small, particularly boggy despite several attempts at drainage and would need to be provided with a fence round the field and a barricade round the playing pitch instead of the customary ropes. Also this ground was presently held on a three month's let from both the Caledonian Railway Company and the North British Railway Company.

There were snags apparently on the Cliftonhill site as the Scottish Tube Company had recently taken out a lease of the area for recreational purposes for their newly-formed Welfare Club.

A motion was agreed that negotiations be entered immediately with a view to securing the new playing pitch on the Main Street. Mr McAndrew Glasgow, was appointed the Law Agent and the tumultous evening then concluded with calls for a Public Meeting and an influential committee to be appointed. President Thom offended several people by taking a different view, feeling that only Albion Rovers Supporters be involved in these meetings and the influential people should be kept out.

Accordingly, on Saturday, 8th March, two Meetings took place in the Co-operative Hall, Dunbeth Road. The first was confined to Members and President Thom confirmed that after considerable discussion the Tube Company were prepared to waive their use of the Cliftonhill Ground on condition that their Welfare Club got certain privileges at Meadow Park, which had been agreed to. Rovers would have full rights to the field and the pitch would be laid out from east to west and the general thought was that the proposal would make for an ideal football field and could become a miniature Hampden. A prospectus was read over and the agreed capital of the Limited Company was fixed at £4,000.

Immediately following there was a Meeting of Supporters at which standing room was the order of the day. President Thom welcomed all present and outlined the progress to date. He pointed out that it had been agreed to extend the Scottish League by one club and from the information he had it looked like Rovers had very definite prospects of being elected. He stated that the Club had a good Bank Account and he confirmed that six acres of ground at Cliftonhill had been successfully negotiated as a lease.

At the close of an enthusiastic and good-hearted Meeting, all present were asked to take up the £1 Shares by 5/- on application, 5/- on allotment and the remainder to be called as the Directors determined. Mr. Hugh McMath was the first to hand over his hard-earned cash to such an effect that in fifteen minutes the President was able to announce that almost £1,500 had been promised as the first instalment towards the £4,000 capital. The die was now cast and all waited with bated breath for the outcome of the League A.G.M. which was due to be held on Thursday, 3rd April.

Meanwhile, back on the field, the Victory Cup had now appeared and the Club were drawn away from home at Kilmarnock. The game finished at no score at ninety minutes and in extra time Joe Wallace scored Rovers' goal in a 1-1 draw but the team were decidedly lucky as Killie missed one penalty whilst scoring with another.

The replay the following Wednesday, found Kilmarnock wanting and a Corcoran goal was sufficient to give Rovers the tie in which Duncan Harrigan was a hero saving yet another penalty. On the Saturday following the winning ways continued in a 4-0 home victory over Vale of Leven which was a perfect build-up for the Victory Cup tie against Celtic.

With the highest crowd of the day, over twenty thousand and gate receipts of £546 of which sum 5% was siphoned off for War Funds, Celtic went into a 2-0 lead at half-time and despite Celtic having only ten men in the second half, the result ended in a disappointing 3-1 victory for the 'Bhoys'. In the Western Cup, two 2-1 defeats were suffered away from home against Renton and Vale of Leven, but these paled into insignificance whilst the Iron Burgh waited with bated breath for the outcome of the League A.G.M. on Thursday, 3rd April and the answer to the question of whether Rovers would be elected to full League status and so join the 'Big Boys' of Scottish Football.

The night turned out to be memorable as the single vacant position for election to the First Division was up for grabs and Albion Rovers and Cowdenbeath were both proposed for election. The warring parties carried their own support with Cowdenbeath having solidly the East faction from Aberdeen, Edinburgh, Dundee and Raith Rovers but Rovers scooped the West side of the country with support coming from virtually all the Glasgow and Lanarkshire contingent and the final tally ended up at ten votes each.

It was only by the use of the casting vote by the Chairman of the League, Mr. Tom Hart of St. Mirren, that Rovers were elected. It was just as well that the Chairman was from the West otherwise Cowdenbeath could well have been elected.

Joy was unbounded and when the news reached Coatbridge, the Town was in a tizzy of excitement. It was only now that the immensity of the future possibilities really sunk in. This was the butterfly coming from the chrysalis and every Member, Shareholder and Supporter would need to look to their laurels and redouble their efforts to ensure the furtherance of the new Limited Company. It was also important that too much would not be expected too soon and that the honeymoon period of a reasonable length of time would be given.

Just to keep things in perspective the following Saturday, while Scotland were drawing with England 2-2 in the International, Rovers were burying their chances of winning the Western Cup by losing 2-1 to Vale of Leven and further defeat followed the next Saturday against Airdrieonians in the Lanarkshire Cup to the tune of 3-2. At this game was Mr. Alex Davidson Junior, Partner of the Coatbridge Architectural firm of James Davidson & Son, who was "casing the joint" at Broomfield in his design of the new Cliftonhill and obviously was taking in many of the existing grounds and current design features.

On the 15th April, news was announced that the Abercorn home game was taking on a more than normal importance as there would be only this one game between the clubs and therefore four points were at stake. Rovers won easily by 3-0 and this continued good fortune spread into the next match against Stevenston United with a 4-1 victory with Hillhouse scoring a double against his old mates.

Off the field, back at Cliftonhill, work was proceeding on apace and by the 26th April, word was out that a contract had been placed and a start would probably be made at the ground within the next few days with the Main Contractor, R. Provan of Rutherglen, who was very experienced in Sportsgrounds. This firm had been responsible for laying out the grounds of Hampden, Celtic Park, Ibrox, Firhill, Fir Park and the grounds at Clydebank, Chelsea, Woolwich and Queens Park Rangers.

The initial word was that the ground would be fit for play come the opening of the League Programme in August although this was to prove optimistic in the extreme. The newly elected M.P. for the constituency, Col. Buchanan, came to the rescue and agreed to provide turf for the playing field of his own resources.

As a taste of the team's quality against class opposition, a Friendly match was set up at Aberdeen, where in front of a 7,000 crowd, on the day England defeated Scotland by 4-3, an exciting game was played which Aberdeen won by 2-1.

Rovers recent good form in the Western Cup had again given them another fleeting chance to lift the Cup and, whilst work was continuing at the new ground, Rovers played a final and fateful game at Celtic Park to decide its destination. In front of a good attendance, Dumbarton Harp ran out convincing winners by 4-1 and thus lifted the Cup by finishing two clear points ahead of Rovers who were once more runners-up.

So the season closed and the long hot summer was ahead in which to build the ground, lick the wounds and prepare for the stirring battles to come.

MR. ALBION ROVERS No. 2

HUGH THOM

Hugh Thom was a man of many parts. He was in turn Firemaster of the former Voluntary Coatbridge Fire Brigade, a group with which he was connected for forty-one years. The Brass Band movement in Scotland was another group whom he served well and faithfully.

The name Thom and Coatbridge Town Band are synonymous. Hugh was Band Master for 35 years, to be succeeded by his sons, Charles and Hugh, and was Secretary for an astonishing 65 years. He was a leading official for many years with the Scottish Amateur Brass Band Association.

His football connection started in the Meadow days, when he joined the old Committee in 1903. He became Treasurer in 1908 and President from 1910, in which position he was the guiding light in Rovers changeover from the Meadow in Whifflet to Limited Company status and first League place at Cliftonhill. The first Chairman of the Limited Company, he stood down in 1922, having been supremo for twelve years.

Hugh was a Life Member of the Lanarkshire Football Association and of the Scottish Football Association, during which time he was a Member of the International Selection Committee. He was an administrator who gave freely of his time and energies for the benefit of Albion Rovers in particular and football locally in general. His son, Hugh, also played for Rovers and went on to a career abroad where he represented Jamaica eleven times.

His enthusiasm for football administration waned after Rovers were relegated

91

from the First Division in 1923. After a lengthy spell of non-attendance at Board Meetings, he was removed as a Director in May 1925. This allowed him to devote more time to his Brass Band activities but he continued to attend Albion Rovers matches with his Town Band or Boys Brigade Band for many years.

The family Slater and Plasterers business was a great source of employment for many Albion Rovers players at a time of major unemployment, although there was never any serious intention of any of these lads taking up a Trade as a Slaterer or a Plasterer. Hugh Thom died at home in Reid Street aged 85 in December, 1957.

CHAPTER FIVE

GREAT EXPECTATIONS

Season 1919/20
In the build up to the new season, the Directors, whilst involved with the new ground, were busy in fixing up players and preparing for the actual games. They were also active in promoting the Limited Company side of affairs and on Saturday 15th July, a Meeting held in the Lesser Town Hall was chaired by John Waddell with several of the Town Fathers in support led by Provost Lavelle. The First Citizen of the Town, on addressing the audience, pointed out that the current climate was not the best time to be looking for money, with costs of materials being at their highest and that almost everything was abnormal as a result of the recent War. Any spare cash, which could be put towards Shares in Albion Rovers Limited was being requested at a time when the Government was floating their Loan Scheme and when the Local Victory Loan was being launched.

Despite people going on holiday, it was hoped that the thousands of supporters Rovers had in the town would rally round and produce the necessary capital. Other speakers at the Meeting were Dean of Guild Wilson and Chairman Hugh Thom, who gave the resumé of progress to date regarding Cliftonhill, team building prospects and also a vote of thanks to the Speakers.

A call had been made from the Platform for Councillor Hugh Martin and Mr. Hugh Waterston to join the Board of Directors and it was agreed that this matter should be decided at the earliest constitutional moment. However, this does not appear to have taken place because the first Board of Directors were the following: — Chairman—Hugh Thom; Secretary—Simon Scott and Messrs. William Faulds, Edward McLaren, John Pettigrew, John Waddell and Andrew Wilson.

The subscription list taking up Shares continued throughout the summer and on the playing side, it became more and more obvious that the new ground could not possibly be ready in time for the new season kick-off. The Club was grateful for the generosity of near neighbours Airdrieonians in arranging for all Rovers' home games to be played at Broomfield Park, Airdrie, until the new ground at Cliftonhill was ready for play. At the same time a new Trainer and Groundsman was appointed. He was Charlie Couts, a professional runner and had just recently been demobilised from France. Charlie had previous football experience as trainer with Raith Rovers and Kilmarnock.

Season tickets were put on sale but due to Excise Authorities restrictions, these tickets would not be available for games played at Broomfield. However, Qualifying Cup and Lanarkshire Cup Ties were to be run off at Meadow Park and the tickets would be available for these and for subsequent games played later that season at Cliftonhill. Andrew Wilson and Simon Scott were dealing with the briefs which were priced at 15/- (75p) for all parts and 10/- (50p) for ground only.

The first game was due to be played at Pittodrie and the new season also heralded an increased gate charge of 1/-. As a preliminary, a Charity Friendly Match was played at Motherwell with Rovers losing 5-1 but with five new faces in the team, the result was hardly surprising. The great new venture got off to a proper start on a sour note with Aberdeen winning quite clearly by 2-0. The team was represented in the First Division for the first time by the following players: Roney, Penman, Ford, Wilson, Duncan, Wallace, Ribchester, Hillhouse, Wilson, Gray and

Young.

The following Saturday in a Lanarkshire Cup Tie at the Meadow, Royal Albert were well beaten by 4-1 in front of a 3,000 crowd and this was followed by the first "home" match played at Broomfield against Partick Thistle which Rovers won by 2-0 with a goal in either half.

Mighty Rangers were next opponents at Ibrox but the New Leaguers were too inexperienced and the 'Gers won this one by 3-0. This was followed by a match against old rivals Kilmarnock, down in Ayrshire, in which the team again failed to score for the third time in four outings in the League and Kilmarnock won by the only goal of the match.

Former Rover, Guy Watson, signed on again in time to play in the home Qualifying Cup Match against Paisley Grammar F.P., in a game where Rovers' superiority was always in evidence and a 3-1 victory was the eventual outcome. In a bid to add more punch up front, John Hart was signed from Rangers and he had a scoring debut against Clydebank at home in a 2-1 victory and also scored both Rovers' goals at Love Street in the 2-1 win over St. Mirren. An unusual situation occurred for the trip down to Ayrshire to play Ayr United on the Wednesday, 17th September, when Rovers allowed themselves to be talked into a 10.45 a.m. kick-off. Not surprisingly, with some of the players still feeling as though they should be doing something other than chasing a football at that unearthly hour, the home team won very easily by four clear goals. On the Saturday a Second Round Qualifying Cup match was scheduled for Renton and ended a no scoring draw and the following week good business was done at the turnstiles with £148 being taken in gate receipts at the Meadow in a Lanarkshire Cup Tie which Rovers won by a Johnny Hart goal to nothing against Motherwell.

The following Saturday saw the replay against Renton at the Meadow and with an 8d. admission, 6,000 fans paid £176 to see Rovers win convincingly by 2-0. On the following Monday, Hibernians ran out narrow winners by 2-1 at Broomfield before Clydebank had a crushing 5-2 victory which clearly underlined the fact that Life at the Top was proving to be as difficult as had been anticipated. With only three wins as against six defeats in the first nine matches, it was clear that the only way to go was up.

Joe Shortt, a goalkeeper from Shettleston Juniors, was signed and he made his debut the following Saturday at Tynecastle and managed to put up the shutters but this proved to be the first draw in the League as the forwards could not score any goals either. There was no doubt the crowds were there for First Division football as a 14,000 crowd witnessed this game. A further 8,000 saw Motherwell fight out a 1-1 draw at Broomfield before a tousy game at Falkirk saw the third draw in a row, again 1-1, end in a fracas with fighting on the terracing between the rival factions.

November opened with Rovers scratching to Royal Albert in the 5th round of the Qualifying Cup and instead defeated Ayr United in the return match by 2-1 before Third Lanark won by the only goal of the game in Glasgow. In the game against Queen's Park at Hampden, Rovers started this one with only nine men as Ribchester, Young and Duncan failed to appear by kick-off. Despite a delayed start, Rovers committee feverishly hounded up reserves and eventually the eleven jerseys were filled. Queens could not take advantage of the lack of numbers in the blue jerseyed ranks and Rovers won by 2-0 with the goals being scored in the first half. Twelve thousand saw Rovers lose 3-2 at Dens Park against Dundee and a further 16,000 witnessed Rangers' 4-0 victory at Broomfield.

Albion Rovers v Dundee 22nd November 1919

Left to right: C. Thomas, D. Melville, G. Watson, D. Duncan, W. Ribchester, A. Ford, J. Blue, J. Wallace (Captain), J. Shortt, J. Hart, R. Penman and W. Hillhouse.

The Contractors were now well advanced with works at the new ground and feverish activity made sure that the first match to be played at the new ground would be the game against St. Mirren on Christmas Day. A visit to Dumbarton saw a 2-1 defeat but Hamilton Accies were defeated 2-0 at Broomfield before the last 'home' game at Broomfield took place on the 20th December against Falkirk when two Willie Hillhouse goals were sufficient to see Rovers end up winners by 2-1.

All was set up for 'the Big Day' the following Thursday, and although the ground was by no means complete, the pitch and terracings were in excellent condition and the grandstand was well on the way. Huts were hastily erected and fitted with baths for temporary dressing accommodation, whilst the old stand from Meadow Park was re-erected on the North/West corner of the field. The opening ceremony was presided over by Chairman Hugh Thom and the opening ceremony was performed by Provost Lavelle.

The hierarchy of Scottish Football were present, together with a representation of the various Clubs, and there is no doubt the groundsman at Airdrie was pleased that his beloved Broomfield would now get a bit of a rest and a chance to recuperate from the extra playing which had taken its toll over the ground during the past four months. The team chosen for the big day was — Shortt, Bell, Penman, Wilson, Duncan, Ford, Ribchester, Blue, Hart, Gray and Hillhouse. St. Mirren rather spoilt the celebrations by winning by 2-0 but at least the sun shone on the 8,000 fans who witnessed the homecoming of the 'Wee Rovers'.

Further disappointment was to follow with the same score occurring in the return match against Partick Thistle before on Wednesday, New Year's Day, a further trip up to Broomfield where Airdrieonians won an exciting game by 2-1.

All was not well, however, and there was a considerable faction of Shareholders who felt all was not right with the Club. Whilst it was realised that the new ground was not totally finished and that the team was only being built-up, they were impatient for success and wanted the Club to turn away from their old Committee-orientated outlook. They wanted a full-time Manager like the big clubs and displayed an eagerness, which bordered on fanaticism, for people with a background of business training to be added to the Board. The situation drew to a head after the next home match against Dundee, watched by 8,000 fans, and which was lost by 2-1 when a petition signed by a number of Shareholders was handed to the Secretary requesting a Special Meeting for the purpose of appointing a Club Manager.

There had also been rumours that players were ready to go on strike unless an increase in their wages was forthcoming. This allegation was denied by the Directors but it then leaked out that there had indeed been an impromptu Meeting of the players at which a 30% increase in wages had been requested, as well as other matters relating to presentations. This situation certainly brought it home to the Directors, if they had not been aware beforehand, that all was not going to be plain sailing. However, Board, players and fans alike all pitched-in and the differences were papered over for many reasons. Firstly, there was too much to do to the ground, grandstands and terracing. Secondly, the team was sitting in a very lowly league position, and thirdly, the Shares had not all been taken up and it was difficult to keep the momentum going whilst trying to work on all of these fronts at the same time.

One very important event occurred following the Dundee match and that was the signing of John White from Bedlay Juniors. John was to become one of the all-time greats of Albion Rovers and the following week at home against Clyde, he and

Charlie Emmerson, an outside right from Shotts United, made their debuts but were unable to add that extra bite that was required to secure that first elusive win at Cliftonhill with Clyde winning 2-0.

'Jock' White got off the goal scoring mark the following week at Greenock against Morton in a 1-1 draw before the first round of the Scottish Cup was due against Dykehead at Coatbridge. Another gate of 8,000 attended this match but were once more disappointed with no win. All was not lost as, with a no scoring draw the match required a replay which took place the following Wednesday at Shotts.

Special trains with 1,500 fans left Coatbridge in the hope that a good Cup run was in the offing. Hundreds of others arrived by ordinary train and motor buses but hundreds were left behind in Coatbridge when the special trains left half an hour before the advertised time. Rovers drew first blood when John Black first timed the ball past the helpless Eden but Rovers were lucky when Geddes beat Shortt only to see the post come to the rescue. In the second half Jock White scored from a Ribchester corner and, with the pitch now resembling a quagmire, the Dykehead team encamped in Rovers' half. In a breakaway, Ribchester scored direct from a corner but in those days the score was disallowed, as the ball had to be touched by another player. Pandemonium broke loose when Dykehead scored with ten minutes to go but the Coatbridge club hung on grimly for a 2-1 victory.

Huntingtower were next in line for Cup business but they scratched from the Second Round match leaving Rovers to get on with League business in the meantime. The grandstand had now started and its skeleton rose rapidly from the brick base. Success was still to be elusive at home when Dumbarton were the next visitors winning by 2-1 thanks to Joe Wallace missing a penalty kick.

20,000 saw Rovers' first visit to Celtic Park on League business where the 'Bhoys' won rather too easily by 3-0 before the Third Round Cup tie was due against St. Bernard's at Powderhall in Edinburgh. The gate money was £770 and Rovers' team was Shortt, Penman, Bell, Noble, Duncan, Ford, Ribchester, Black, White, Watson and Hillhouse. Play was even at the beginning of the match but Shortt in goal put the cat among the pigeons by dropping a cross at Saint's centre's feet and that was the first goal. Rovers took up the play thereafter but the old failing of not accepting chances was evident for all to see. Willie Hillhouse missed enough chances to win the League Championship but he ended up the hero of the day by scoring a very controversial goal. After gaining possession of the ball in midfield, he shot weakly for goal but the goalkeeper allowed it to slip through his legs, managed to stop it with his feet and then after a struggle scooped it away. The referee however was right on the spot and he immediately signalled a goal much to the consternation of the Saint's team who strongly contested the decision. However, a draw it was and back to Coatbridge the following Wednesday for the replay.

Rovers introduced John Hart to centre with White in place of Black at inside right and Young on the left wing instead of Hillhouse and lo and behold the changes worked. Hart scored a hat-trick and Andy Ford got the other in a famous 4-1 victory which was the first home success at Cliftonhill in six outings. Not only that the team moved into the quarter finals of the National Cup. On the Saturday, Motherwell won 2-0 in a League match on their own patch. But the Cup was the thing and Aberdeen were next for shaving. 13,000 fans paid £503 for this home tie with Rovers represented by Shortt, Penman, Bell, Noble, Duncan, Ford, Ribchester, Black, White, Watson and Young.

The game had a sensational start when Bobby Young had the ball in the net in the first minute. Aberdeen kicked off but lost possession at once and Young went on a mazy run eventually belting the ball past the Dons' goalkeeper. Aberdeen were astonished and, when Ribchester crashed the ball against the crossbar a few minutes later, it showed the way the game was going. In the twentieth minute Cliftonhill went delirious when John Black fastened on to a loose ball in the penalty box and slotted in number two. The fans were now considering that the stiff breeze which Rovers had in the first half could work against them in the second half. Facing the elements did not affect Rovers' play, and although Aberdeen were more in the picture and scored in the fifty-first minute, the tide turned again in Rovers' favour and the boys in blue more than held their own to the end.

The new stand was still unfinished although the press box was used for the first time. It was clear that sizeable sums of money were being lost through the slow progress of the stand. The view from the grandstand must have been quite something with the west end jam-packed and the old stand filled to capacity. Immediately above the area was the former Cliftonhill House in its Scottish Baronial Architectural style looking something like a castle in its partly demolished state. However great excitement gripped the Town as the team were in the semi-final of the Cup. It was no surprise that Hibernian were defeated 1-0 through at Edinburgh in the League but Raith Rovers took some of the shine off the euphoria with a 3-0 victory through at Fife.

Mighty Rangers had been drawn in the semi-final and on the 17th March at Parkhead, 30,000 people paid £1,100 to see the new League minnows take on the Rangers' team who were currently seven points ahead of Celtic at the top of the Scottish League and carrying all before them. The only people who thought Rovers had a chance came from Coatbridge and again a strong wind favoured the Coatbridge lads in the first half. Rangers scored first with a fine header that Shortt got his hands to but could not stop. Then Ribchester again scored direct from a corner, only to have it disallowed, leaving Rangers in the lead at half time. It was quite clear to the Rangers' fans in the crowd that with the wind behind them the wee Rovers would soon be crushed. They were soon to be disillusioned, for Rovers set about the Glasgow team as though they had never heard of their reputation and eventually, in the course of a melee around goalkeeper Locks, Bowie gave away a penalty kick which Ribchester rifled behind the Rangers' custodian with cool precision. This was the first goal Rangers had lost in the entire Cup competition and the game ended all square at 1-1. Rovers' team was Shortt, Penman, Bell, Noble, Duncan, Ford, Ribchester, Black, White, Watson and Young. Mr. Tom Dougray of Bellshill was the referee.

The following Wednesday evening saw the replay, again at Parkhead, with a 6.15 p.m. kick-off, Rovers fielded the same team. This time 40,000 spectators paid £1,407 to view this further opportunity of seeing Rangers humble these upstarts from Coatbridge. It was not to be however and the game again ended all square this time with no goals.

Meanwhile back in the League, Heart of Midlothian came through from Edinburgh to be trounced by 6-2, making it first things first at Cliftonhill on the first Saturday of April. It was the first day of the new stand, first time the Rovers had scored more than two goals in a First League match at Cliftonhill, the first home League win for the team on their new ground and the first of many hat-tricks by John White. The following Monday, Aberdeen visited Cliftonhill in a fighting and spirited 1-1 draw but on the Wednesday evening the match all Scotland had been waiting for, the second replay of the Scottish Cup semi-final, again at Parkhead, saw Rovers make nine changes in personnel from the Monday game to field the following team— Shortt, Penman, Bell, Wallace, Duncan, Ford, Ribchester, Black, White, Watson and Hillhouse. All of Glasgow expected the wee Rovers to be annihilated this time, if for no other reason their extreme impertinence in taking the top team in Scottish football to a third match was quite unheard of. But on the night the better team turned out to be Rovers. First of all Willie Hillhouse scored a wonderful solo goal before Guy Watson put Rovers in a commanding 2-0 lead at half time. Try as they might in the second half, Rangers could not improve on the scoreline, and when the ninety minutes were up, Rangers were out and it was Rovers in the Scottish Cup Final. Heady days indeed!

The number of cup ties meant that the League programme was running behind schedule. The League made no allowances for a Cup Final appearance and on the following Saturday, Clyde fought out a 2-2 draw in Glasgow before Rovers were forced to play a League match against Celtic at Cliftonhill, on the Wednesday before Cup Final Day. Rovers rested five of their Cup Final team and in front of 11,000 spectators the Celtic team ran off easy winners by 5-0.

Saturday, 14th April, 1920 however was the big day. Since beating Rangers ten days earlier, three games had been played and serious injuries had occurred to key players. First Noble had been lost and then the key-stone of the defence Davie Duncan, thus breaking the back of Rovers' half-back line. John White's brother James, who had recently been signed from the Junior ranks, made his fourth senior appearance in the Cup Final team as Rovers struggled to make up the deficit in numbers of the established players. Wilson was also drafted in to right half and Black moved back to centre half. Killie's men were all fit and the teams turned out as follows:

Kilmarnock: Blair, Hamilton, Gibson, Bagan, Shortt, Neave, McNaught, M. Smith, J.R. Smith, Culley and McPhail.

Albion Rovers: Shortt, Penman, Bell, Wilson, Black, Ford, Ribchester, James White, John White, Watson and Hillhouse.

The Referee was Mr. Willie Bell of Hamilton.

Rovers lost the toss and Killie kicked off but Rovers started well and John White had hard lines when his well-placed shot was pushed onto the crossbar and over for the first corner. However, the Coatbridge bunnets were up in the air in five minutes when James White sent Ribchester away down the right and his cross was behind keeper Blair in a twinkling by Watson. 'The Coatbridge gong' which was a huge metal plate with the inscription 'The Death Nell', had been carried by a group of Coatbridge youngsters which was used as a musical instrument and could be heard above the terrific cheering. Slackness by Penman almost cost a goal but Joe Shortt managed to clear the ball away with difficulty. In sixteen minutes the equaliser came when Culley scored with a strong shot which gave Shortt no chance of saving. There were chances at both ends but try as they might there was no further score and the Interval arrived with the score at 1-1.

A weak clearance by Penman two minutes into the second half was picked up by Matthew Shortt who flipped the ball into the nett past his namesake, Joe, in the Rovers goal, who was busy claiming offside.

Kilmarnock fairly piled the pressure on after that and Rovers' goal was in danger on several occasions but Ribchester, who had been starved of the ball for much of the second half, lobbed a fine cross in from the right, finding Wilson who pushed the ball out to the left. There was a race between Hamilton and Hillhouse but it was the Rover who got to the ball first and he equalised with a great shot. Willie himself was so overjoyed that he danced a horn-pipe in the penalty box.

Kilmarnock were lasting better and Culley eventually carved his way through Rovers' defence on the hour mark and passed to former Rover J.R. Smith who gave Kilmarnock the lead for the second time with an unsavable shot. The game continued ding-dong to the end but no more goals were scored and Rovers' big chance had gone.

The team was by no means disgraced, especially when it was considered that of the eleven players on the field, three had been playing as Juniors at the start of the present season. Shortt was not at his best, Bell was the better of the two full-backs, and Andy Ford the pick of the half-back line. Up front Watson and Hillhouse were tops. Killie were stronger on the day but neither side reached the standard they had set up in the earlier rounds.

The official attendance was 95,600 and the gate money of £4,521.0.0d., was the highest other than for an International match up to that time. It was also intriguing that two provincial teams could produce this kind of gate. Thousands were also turned away when the gates were shut, which was most amazing considering that in the earlier International match between Scotland and England, accommodation was found for 127,000 spectators. As far as attendances were concerned the Rovers—Rangers third cup match also constituted a record for an evening game up to that time.

The presentation of the Cup took place in the Reading Room of the Queen's Park Pavilion at the close of the game. Mr. Tom White, President of the Scottish Football Association, handed the Cup over to Mr. Cunningham the Vice-President of Kilmarnock Football Club. Chairman Hugh Thom led the Coatbridge delegation in this the forty-second Cup Final.

On the Monday, Morton visited Cliftonhill and, although they brought in Kiernan and Melville to freshen-up the rather leg-weary Cup Final team, Morton won 4-2 whilst on the Wednesday evening with six new faces on display, Queen's Park won 2-1 at Hampden. Airdrieonians were next to visit Coatbridge and 11,000 fans saw the 'Diamonds' win by two clear goals before on the Monday, Raith Rovers fought out a no scoring draw at Coatbridge. Hamilton Accies arrived on the Wednesday to fight out a League match at Cliftonhill at a creditable 1-1 scoreline.

The same team was the opposition on the Friday in the forty-first Final of the Lanarkshire Cup. It was another Final in which Rovers fell at the last hurdle. Accies won this one by 2-1 and Rovers were represented by Shortt, Penman, Bell, Wilson, Duncan, Ford, Ribchester, Blue, John White, Watson and Hillhouse. With the team falling about with exhaustion, Kilmarnock visited Coatbridge the next day winning by 2-0 in the League which was Jack Bell's last game before returning to Motherwell following his period of loan.

Finally, on Wednesday 5th May, Third Lanark visited Coatbridge and despite Rovers winning by 3-2 they finished in bottom place in the League with twenty-eight points, which was one behind Hamilton and three behind Falkirk. Rangers won the League in a canter on seventy-one points, three ahead of Celtic and fourteen ahead of third-placed Motherwell.

The first season in the big League had been quite hectic with fifty-eight matches played throughout the season and in a hectic forty days at the end of the season a prodigous sixteen games were played with an amazing five played within an eight day period at the death. There was a great sense of achievement, what with a newly-floated Limited Company, a new ground, League status, an appearance in the County Cup Final but, above all else, an appearance in the National Cup Final. The euphoria was tinged with regret that again Rovers had been bested at the final hurdle but there was always next year..........

Season 1920/21

The close season was no rest for the Directors, who were busily putting the final touches to the ground and surrounds at Cliftonhill. All attention was not directed to the pitch however as on Monday the 25th June the Directors' appointed Archie Montgomery as Secretary/Manager. Mr. Montgomery took up his duties immediately having had long experience in football management. He had kept goal with Rangers before joining Bury at which club he was eventually appointed Player/Manager and subsequently Secretary/Manager, a position which he held for 10 years. He vacated that position during the War and he came highly commended.

The appointment took place two nights before the first A.G.M. of the Limited Company, which was held in the Town Hall, at which the Board of Directors were confirmed unanimously.

On the playing front, the cream of the previous season's staff had been retained but some much required experienced was also signed on in the shape of Willie Reid ex-Rangers and Scotland, Alec Bennett ex-Celtic, Rangers, Dumbarton and Scotland and old friend Bob McSkimming back from Sheffield Wednesday. Other lesser known new faces were Gordon Kerr from Ayr United, George Greenshields from Plean, John McColgan from Vale of Clyde, Willie Young from Kilsyth Rangers, Bobby Gray from Airdrieonians and Douglas Henderson from Queen's Park.

The opening game of the season was a charity match against Motherwell which ended up at 2-2 but the season proper opened on the 16th August at home against Raith Rovers and that was lost by 1-0, the goal being scored by ex-Rover Bobby Archibald. Rovers' team was— Kerr, Penman, McColgan, Noble, Duncan, Ford, John White, James White, Reid, Bennett and Gray.

The following Saturday, Celtic visited the 'Brig when, in front of 17,000 fans, the new Grandstand was formally opened. The score was the same as the previous week with the away team winning by the only goal of the game. The next Monday saw the fourth home game on the trot and Hearts drawing 1-1. On the following Saturday, Airdrieonians won very easily by 5-1 in front of 15,000 fans at Broomfield, whilst again Rovers' inability to score manifested itself on the following Monday against Partick Thistle at home in a no-scoring draw.

This blight continued when Aberdeen came to visit Coatbridge and won more easily than the 2-0 score would indicate. That meant that just two goals had been scored in six League matches, and despite two draws that elusive first win was proving as difficult as ever. Manager Montgomery's baptism was proving difficult and the following Monday the visit to Ibrox saw Rovers score once but Rangers scored a double to take the points.

Presumably the Manager was happy with the display because the same team was retained for the visit down to Dumbarton, when quite unexpectedly Rovers won by four clear goals, all scored in the second half. The good form continued next week at home against Falkirk when a 3-1 score was the result but on the Monday, Third Lanark visited Cliftonhill to win 2-1 before the return match on the following Saturday saw a 2-2 draw in Glasgow.

Willie Reid was finding goals difficult to come with only three out of nine outings. A fighting draw of 1-1 was played when Motherwell visited with Rovers'

101

Albion Rovers v Motherwell 7th August, 1920
Standing left to right: C. Couts, D. Duncan, R. Noble, J. McColgan, G. Kerr, R. Penman, A. Ford.
Seated left to right: John White, James White, W. Reid, A. Bennett, W. Hillhouse.

scorer being Willie Hillhouse against his old team before 9,000 fans saw Kilmarnock beaten by 2-0 at Coatbridge. A good Edinburgh crowd of 16,000 saw Rovers snatch a draw with John White, so impressing the Hearts' Management that they offered £2,000 for his transfer. This was turned down by the Board and was seen by the Support as a grand vote of confidence.

The poor home form continued when Ayr United won 2-1 but the first League victory over Celtic took place at Parkhead by two Hillhouse goals to nothing before Clydebank defeated the boys in blue by 4-1. This result was followed by another away defeat against Hibernians by 5-2. St. Mirren, who the previous season had played the inaugural match at Cliftonhill, again visited Coatbridge, this time winning by 2-1. Both goals came in the second half after George Greenshields had given Rovers a first half lead. Queen's Park were visited for a 1-1 draw and the following week a new ground record was hoisted when over 21,000 watched Rangers win by 2-1 and Rangers' winning goal came in the second half.

At the beginning of December, Morton came to Coatbridge to lose 3-2 but the journey up to Dundee saw the home team win by 3-0 before the best result of the season came in the home match against Clyde in a 5-2 victory. Another important signing was made during the week when Murdoch Walls was signed from Vale of Clyde. 'Murdie', from Baillieston, was a younger brother of 'Fister' of Rangers fame and was to become a Rovers' giant in the years to come.

Rovers' good form continued with a 4-2 victory in Kirkcaldy and on New Year's Day a 1-1 draw was the happy conclusion against Airdrieonians with a crowd of over 17,000 in the ground. On Tuesday, 4th January, Royal Albert visited Coatbridge on Lanarkshire Cup business and two John White goals were sufficient to defeat the Royalists who could only score one in return. Whilst Rovers were sharing two goals at Motherwell, James (Tec) White broke his leg in an Alliance match at Parkhead. Another draw the following week at home at the same score against Clydebank came before Morton were defeated 3-1 at the Tail of the Bank.

There was much activity on the transfer front around this time with Jimmy Geddes a centre half with experience with St. Mirren and Dykehead, and Jimmy Davidson, an inside left from St. Bernard's coming onto the payroll and old friend Joe Wallace leaving for Renton.

A no scoring draw was fought out at Firhill and at the close of the game, Rovers players, accompanied by Director John Waddell, travelled to Portobello where the players—in view of the Scottish Cup Second Round Match—undertook a course of spray baths and did a lot of walking exercises. Mr. Montgomery, who had been in Edinburgh with the Alliance team, joined the party along with four of the reserve team and all sixteen returned to Coatbridge on Monday hale and hearty. It was clear the Directors meant to take no chances against Mid-Annandale in the second round of the Cup and indeed the end result was a pleasing 3-1 victory with old Rangers, Bennett and Reid, sharing the goals.

The following Wednesday, Kilmarnock exacted full revenge for their earlier defeat at Coatbridge in a 3-1 scoreline before Hibernian won 2-0 at Cliftonhill. Rovers' erratic form continued when they bested St. Mirren by 2-1 at Love Street the following Tuesday. The Third Round of the National Cup found an away draw at Armadale and the home team, with a whirlwind start, crossed over at half time two goals in the lead. A fine fight back in the second half saw first Hillhouse score and then John White equalise to take the game back to Coatbridge the following Saturday, where in front of 12,600 fans, and despite extra time, a no scoring draw was the result.

The displaced League match against Hamilton was then played on the Monday and, despite a Hillhouse hat-trick, Hamilton won by 4-3 before the Third Round second replay against Armadale took place on neutral ground at Hampden on Wednesday, 3rd March. 7,000 fans followed on and the game ended all square at full time with no goals being scored with much of the credit for that going to former Rover Joe Shortt in goal for the 'Dale but Greenshields and John White eventually broke the deadlock for the Coatbridge team to win 2-0 after extra time. The next match was the quarter finals of the Cup at Dundee and the 'Brig men were cock-a-hoop with two second half goals from Young and Ford to bring a successful conclusion to the tie. Cup tie fever was again gripping the Town with visions of the team going one better than in the previous season. But before the big day could dawn, there were two League matches to fight out and first of all Queen's Park were defeated 2-1 at Coatbridge and a no scoring draw played out at Hamilton.

On the 26th March, Rangers were again the opponents in the semi-final match coincidently again played at Parkhead. 63,000 people paid £3,200 for the pleasure and wondered if this time Rangers would surmount the hurdle of their bogy team of the previous season. In a fast, rousing match, Rovers hopes were to be dashed when Rangers moved into a 3-0 lead at half-time, and although John White knocked one back in the second half, the perfect ending was not to be and Rangers ran off with the match by a comfortable 4-1 margin. Rovers were represented by — Kerr, Penman, McColgan, Greenshields, Duncan, Ford, Bennett, White, Young, Dawson and Hillhouse.

The team was despondent after this reverse and two successive home defeats occurred, firstly with Dundee winning 3-2 and Clyde scored two without reply on

Left to Right: G. Greenshields, J. McColgan, W. Reid, R. McSkimming, J. White.

the following Monday. The visit to Falkirk saw a no scoring draw before the visit down to Ayr produced a 3-0 victory for United. The team got back on an even keel against Dumbarton at home winning 3-0 which set the team up for another Cup Final appearance, this time in the Lanarkshire Cup, on Wednesday, 13th April, against Hamilton Academical at Motherwell.

Rovers were pressed to provide a team on the left flank with both Hillhouse and Gray injured. Rovers solved the problem by introducing Noble at centre and providing a new left wing. The replacement centre made the most of his introduction and scored the only goal of the first half and a penalty by John White in the second period enabled Rovers to receive some satisfaction at the end of the season. Rovers' team was— Kerr, Penman, McColgan, Greenshields, McSkimming, Ford, Bennett, White, Noble, Young and Craig.

The last League game was a visit up to the Granite City where Aberdeen won 1-0 leaving Rovers in fifth bottom position with thirty-four points, ten points higher than Dumbarton in bottom place with Rangers again winning the League with seventy-six points—ten more than Celtic.

Royal Albert were soundly defeated by 5-0 in the Coatbridge Express Cup giving another final appearance on the 22nd February against Motherwell, when a no scoring draw was fought out.

The final game of the season was the replayed Express Cup match against Motherwell which the 'Steelmen' won by 2-1. Rovers team was— Britton, Penman, McSkimming, Noble, Geddes, Walls, Bennie, White, Kiernan, Young and Gray.

Season 1921/22

During the close season, despite feverish activity, few players were added to those who had been retained from the previous season. Kirk from Clydebank Juniors, Chambers from Dunipace, Campbell from Parkhead and Abrines from Parkhead were added to the retained players. Before the season started, Alex. Bennett, who had given good service, decided he had reached the end of his playing career and the former Scottish Internationalist left with the best wishes of Directors and players to take up the post of Secretary/Manager with Third Lanark.

The season opened on Monday, 15th August with a home match against Kilmarnock which drew a commendable 9,000 crowd and resulted in a 4-0 victory for Rovers, with Willie Reid picking up where he left off the previous season scoring a second half double. The team which opened the seasons campaign was— Kerr, Penman and McColgan, Greenshields, McSkimming and Ford, Bennie, John White, Reid, Tec White and Kirk.

The next match was a fighting 2-2 draw at Tynecastle against the mighty Hearts. In front of a crowd of 25,000 on Tuesday 23rd August, despite a valiant Rovers' display against Rangers, a first taste of defeat for the season was experienced at 3-1. The team bounced back against Clydebank at home in the next game winning easily 2-0 with two first half goals, John White scoring his third goal of the season.

As an aftermath to the Rangers game, Rovers' Directors met and in all future games banned bus parties who carried "banners, bugles or ricketties" and there was great consternation by the provincial clubs at the noise generated by supporters of the bigger city teams. This was considered as unsporting and attempts were made by various clubs to curb this expression of noisy support.

Back on the field a John White goal was enough to secure a 1-1 away draw against Kilmarnock and on Monday, 5th September a 2-0 victory was gained against Raith Rovers.

The first meeting of the season against Airdrieonians was at Cliftonhill and the team was now really getting into its stride, as was proved by the 2-0 victory in front of an 11,000 crowd. This was followed in quick succession with away victories of 1-0 over Falkirk and a swingeing 4-0 over Queen's Park which put our swashbuckling Rovers' team in second top position in the League. The all-conquering Rovers' top scorer was Willie Reid with eight goals, John White closely following at five goals.

Lanarkshire neighbours Motherwell were next to visit Cliftonhill and in front of a 13,000 crowd a no-scoring draw was secured with all the credit going to Rovers, who played a considerable part of the second half with ten men as goalie Gordon Kerr was off injured.

On Monday, 26th September the Lanarkshire Cup campaign was commenced against Dykehead and a 2-0 victory was notched. The twelfth game of the season, an away defeat at Love Street, was recorded by the tight margin of 2-1 and this was followed by a home defeat of 1-0 by Partick Thistle and 3-1 at Celtic. This disastrous run of three games without a single point was temporarily stopped at home against Queen's Park when 'Tec' White scored a late goal in a 1-1 draw. Despite an early goal in the away game against Morton a further 2-1 defeat was recorded with a slump down the League.

Meanwhile the Reserve Eleven was doing very well and an appearance in the second eleven final home and away against Airdrieonians recorded a 3-0 victory at Cliftonhill for the wee Rovers, but Airdrie won the second game with an incredible 5-0 score in which they nullified Rovers' first leg lead by half time, running out easy winners by 5-3 which was caused by the cream of the Reserves playing in the first team. Despite this shambles the first team had their pride severely dented with a 2-0 defeat at Aberdeen but a Willie Reid goal in the first half was enough to grab the points against Hamilton Accies at Cliftonhill.

In the next game Dundee had a comfortable 2-0 victory at Dundee but a rather fortunate draw was secured at Shawfield with Young scoring his first goal for the League side. Ayr United were the next visitors at Cliftonhill and despite goals by John White and Bobby Kirk, a 3-2 defeat was noted. But this depressing blow was softened by a courageous late goal by Andy Ford to convincingly defeat Hibernians although it turned out to be the only goal of the game.

As the next game was at home against Rangers, the team took the opportunity of training at Portobello during the week but either they overdid the training or it did not agree with them because Rangers had an extremely easy 5-0 victory in front of a 12,000 gate. The ban by Rovers' Directors on supporters turned out to be of little avail, and although a 1-0 victory over Dumbarton was next noted for the Record Book, the last game of 1921 resulted in a lack-lustre display and a deserved 3-0 victory for Raith Rovers.

1922 started with high hopes and the game against Airdrieonians on 2nd January, with 13,000 fans in attendance, saw a rousing 1-1 draw giving Rovers three points out of four over their near neighbours for the season. However, the good work was not continued at home the next day against Morton, who recorded their second 2-1 victory of the season over the Blues. The death was announced the next day of Manager, Archie Montgomery, after a short illness. His short period in charge had not been blessed with success but all the Club were saddened by the news. Saturday, 7th January was quite an occasion for the sporting White family

John White

for, whilst Jock and Tec scored two of Rovers' three goals, their brother Willie, playing in goal for Hamilton, put up the shutters to enable the points to remain at Hamilton, with the final result at 5-3 against Rovers.

The next two results were draws with Willie Reid scoring both goals and Jock Britton saving a penalty at Third Lanark. After this game, Rovers signed John McBeth from Pollok Juniors and in the next match Clyde scuttled home after sharing two goals at Coatbridge.

During the next week an event which was to have a major contribution to the fate of Rovers over the next few years was to take place, when Willie Reid agreed to become Player/Manager in place of Archie Montgomery, and in his first game as Supremo, Mr. Reid led his team to a 1-1 draw at home against Clyde with Willie Ribchester scoring his first goal of the season.

The quest for Scottish Cup glory commenced when Rovers rattled Johnstone to the tune of 6-0 with Willie Reid scoring four and the White brothers one each. Was this to be Rovers' year in the Cup? Hopes were high in the 'Brig with a semi-final place the previous season and losing finalists in 1919/20.

On 4th February the next game saw the team at Ayr losing 2-1. Rovers had to do without the services of Jock White in this game, as he was playing for Scotland against Wales to record the only time a serving Albion Rovers' player has received a Full Cap for Scotland. Unfortunately, Scotland also went down 2-1 in this game. The reports of the time indicate that the Rovers' player was skilful and courageous but an injury midway through the first half reduced his effectiveness.

During the next week the team were once again at Portobello in preparation for their Cup Tie at home in the second round of the Scottish Cup once more against

Rangers. Brave men these Directors; superstition was a word obviously unknown to them. The game was an outstanding success for Rovers in all but the score and Rangers were apparently lucky to troop off at the end of the day with a 1-1 draw although they scored the first goal. Willie Reid scored in the second half against his old club to lead his men into a replay at Ibrox on the following Wednesday night when the superior fitness and strength of the Glasgow team provided a 4-0 victory. The gate was 30,000 in the replay and the receipts were £1,200 which was good business for a midweek match. The Saturday game at Cliftonhill had attracted 23,000 people.

A 3-0 victory against Clydebank away from home was the start of seven successive wins by Rovers and it was clear that defeat at the hands of Rangers had not caused any permanent damage. Hibs were next to lose at Cliftonhill 2-1 and then their fellow travellers Hearts were defeated forcibly 2-0.

Despite the big gates and the big crowds that were available for League football at this time Rovers were still having difficulties in the transfer from the Meadow to Cliftonhill and the added expense of League wages, together with the building-up of the ground. Paying all the bills involved with that led them to serious cash flow problems, and immediately after the Dundee game when Tec White's goal turned out to be the only scoring shot of the game, the Directors announced that they were willing to receive offers for Jock and Tec White, Greenshields, Ford and Telfer. This news caused grave consternation amongst Rovers' fans and much heated argument stemmed from this announcement. Despite their financial troubles, Rovers continued apace on their winning ways beating at home firstly, Falkirk by 4-0 and then Third Lanark by a John White goal in the last win after an impressive run of success lasting almost two months. Rovers' first taste of defeat came at the hands of Aberdeen at Pittodrie by a 2-0 score and another win at Dumbarton by 2-1 in which Murdy Walls scored both goals. Jock White continued to impress the Scottish Selectors and he was included in a game on Wednesday, 22nd March with the Home Scots playing against a team of Anglos.

In the Lanarkshire Cup Motherwell, in front of 5,000 fans, fought out a rousing 1-1 draw at Cliftonhill but lost the match at Fir Park to a Willie Reid goal. Before Rovers could meet Airdrie in the final they played Partick Thistle at Firhill in the League and again a Willie Reid goal was enough for Rovers to snaffle the two points. On Wednesday, 12th April in the Lanarkshire Cup Final a disappointing Rovers' team never got to grips with the opposition and Airdrie recorded one of their easiest victories over Rovers by a score of 3-0. Rovers' team was Britton, Penman, McColgan, Greenshields, McLaurin, Walls, Bennie, John White, Reid, James White and Kirk.

Celtic were next to visit Cliftonhill and they recorded another 3-0 victory in front of 10,000 fans. Rovers squeezed their last League point out of St. Mirren at Cliftonhill in a no scoring, uninspiring game, which was followed on the Monday night by a game against Royal Albert in the Coatbridge Express Cup. For the record Rovers won 2-1 and Bob Penman was forced to play in goal as Gordon Kerr did not turn up. He must have cherished memories of this game as a stop-gap for he even saved a penalty. The second leg ended 2-0 for Rovers, Airdrie scratched from the final and the Cup was awarded to Rovers.

As the curtain was wound down on the season the team slumped to an away defeat at Motherwell to the tune of 2-1.

Out of a twenty-two team League a creditable eleventh position was obtained. A position which has never been bettered to this date in the First League. Top

ALBION ROVERS SEASON 1921/22

Back Row: J. Ross (Pay Attendant). Directors—Messrs. Hugh Martin, John Waddell, J. B. Pettigrew, H. Goldie, E. McLaren, A. Wilson, D. McPhail (Asst. Trainer).

Middle Row: C. Coutts (Trainer), G. Kerr, R. Noble, M. Walls, A. Ford, J. McColgan, J. Britton, W. Young, R. McSkimming, J. Geddes, J. McLaurin, R. Penman.

Front Row: H. Thom (Chairman), P. Bennie, G. Greenshields, John White, W. Reid, W. Chalmers, R. Kirk, R. Telfer, S. Scott (Director), James White.

scorer for the season was Willie Reid with twenty-five goals. John White was the only other player to reach double figures with thirteen.

Season 1922/23
Progress since the move to Limited Company status and to Cliftonhill, had been favourable in all respects apart from finance. The first season had seen an appearance in the Final of the Premier Cup and the second season an appearance in the semi-final of the same trophy. The third season had seen a vast improvement in the League position to a very comfortable mid-league status. To the dismay of the faithful, the very heart of this promising team was ripped out when Jock White was transferred on the 18th May to Hearts, followed two weeks' later with his brother Tec who went to non-league Maidstone. This was bad enough but when Geordie Greenshields was transferred to Dundee in exchange for John Bell a centre-forward with a big reputation, Telfer returned from whence he had come to Dykehead and Ribchester was loaned to St. Johnstone, it was clear that new faces were desperately necessary. On top of all that Willie Reid decided to hang up his boots to concentrate on Management.

When Trainer, Charlie Coutts, called the players to the starting line for the build-up to the new season, Johnnie Bell from Dundee was joined by Jack Sharp from Hearts, Tom McQuade from St. Anthony's and new goalie local boy D.L. Smith.

The first game was against Airdrieonians in the Lanarkshire Cup at Cliftonhill on Wednesday, 16th August, which ended up in a 0-0 draw in front of an exuberant crowd of 9,000. The boys in blue were represented by Britton, Penman, McColgan, McBeth, McSkimming, Walls, Bennie, McQuade, Bell, Sharp and Kirk.

This was immediately followed with another home match against Kilmarnock in the opening game of the League Programme, when new man Sharp scored a late goal in a 1-1 each draw.

A third home game on the trot was next for the record book against Hamilton and a 2-0 victory was the happy result which was a great build-up for another tilt at near neighbours Airdrieonians at Broomfield in the League but alas a 2-0 defeat was the disappointing result. And the same result was the best that could be achieved against Aberdeen at home in the next League match.

The sixth game of the season was the second leg of the Lanarkshire Cup set at Broomfield as a third meeting between the near neighbours. In front of a 6,000 crowd the Waysiders again turned up trumps with the only goal of the game. This made an extremely disappointing start to the season, with only three goals scored in six games, whilst in three games against Airdrieonians no goals were scored with three lost. To say the least the natives were restless! . . . . . .

Big time Hearts were next to act as hosts and a shake-up in the team resulted in a new approach by the players. After leading 2-1 at half time, a 2-2 draw was the final result. The gate was 21,000 and one of the highlights of the game was the display of John White against his former colleagues which display was marred latterly when both he and Jack McColgan were ordered off for butting each other. At home the next week Falkirk were the visitors and in front of 8,000 points-starved fans a 2-1 defeat was the end result of a hard afternoon's work.

Spirits slumped even further after the next game against Clyde at Shawfield when again no goals were scored and three lost. The situation was becoming desperate and Borland, a centre forward from Kirkintilloch and Fleming an inside right from Clyde were both signed. The team was obviously feeling the loss of the White brothers and also the decision to retire from an active playing position by

Willie Reid, was proving quite embarrassing.

At the home game against Dundee the fans rolled up expecting fireworks but in a poor game no goals were scored by either side. A further point was picked up though in the next game at Love Street when two goals were shared in an exciting match with Sam Fleming notching his first goal for the Club.

The Referees' Committee dealt leniently with Jack McColgan for his earlier ordering off offence and he was only severely censured thus enabling him to turn out against Third Lanark at home, but he must have felt sick in a one goal defeat as he missed a penalty at a crucial stage in the game.

After twelve games, seven of which ended in blanks for Rovers, a disappointing seven goals had been scored and Rangers were next due to be visited at Ibrox. Spirits were low but it's amazing how a big name and a big crowd will lift even a mediocre team and a well-merited 2-2 draw was achieved and a welcome point gained. Partick Thistle then won 3-0 before the second win of the season in the League was chalked up at 2-1 against Alloa Athletic at home with both new boys Moreland and Fleming on the score sheet. The local derby against Motherwell at home in the next game in front of a 10,000 crowd ended up 1-1 with Jack Sharp lifting his total for the season to five making him clearly the top scorer at this stage. At Ayr a 2-2 draw was the last point to come Rovers' way for the next seven games which was to prove disastrous in Rovers' attempts to retain First League status.

First of all Hibs had an easy 3-0 victory at Easter Road followed with a 3-2 victory for Celtic at Cliftonhill after which game wing-half McKnight of Bo'ness, a former Celtic and St. Anthony's player, was signed. This made no difference to the result against Morton at Cappielow when Rovers tumbled 3-0 or the next game against Raith Rovers at Cliftonhill where a 2-1 defeat was noted. However, one bright note came from this game for the future as Jim Cameron, a strong running centre half from Dykehead and Airdrie played his first game and he was to prove a strong pivot over the next eight seasons and become one of Rovers' best club servants of all time.

1922 which had started so promisingly, finished very disappointingly with a 2-1 defeat at home at the hands of Hearts and a comprehensive 4-0 drubbing at Dundee. The New Year started off on Monday, 1st with Airdrieonians as First Foots but they proved uncharitable visitors by taking away the points in a 2-1 defeat. This was the last defeat of a very lean spell as, on the Tuesday, Third Lanark were visited and a 2-2 draw achieved. Clyde were next visitors to Cliftonhill to be beaten by three clear goals.

The Scottish Cup next gave a touch of relief from the more serious League business and the first round tie saw a visit to Hamilton where the Accies' won 1-0 and to rub salt in to the wound, Jimmy Geddes missed a penalty. With nothing now to side-track their fight for survival and collection of League points, an encouraging start was made when St. Mirren visited the 'Brig and were defeated 2-0 but this good work was immediately nullified by a loss at Alloa by the same score.

A Wednesday away game against Hamilton Accies resulted in a similar score as for the cup tie but the team really got down to it in the next few weeks and started off on a 3-0 victory at home against Morton. This was followed by a well won point in a 1-1 draw at Parkhead the following Wednesday. New signing Christie from Arbroath Athletic scored the valuable goal from the centre forward position and followed this up at Starks' Park on the Saturday in a 1-1 draw against Raith Rovers with former Rover Archibald scoring the goal for the homesters.

Willie Reid
1920-23.   Manager 1923-29

Bob Penman
1917-24

Peter Bennie
1920-23

Bob McSkimming
1907-10, 1920-23

Young Christie was again on the mark in the next game at home against Ayr United when Rovers won 2-1 but Motherwell easily lifted the points by scoring the only goal of the game at Fir Park and Hibs came to Cliftonhill and won easier than the 2-1 score suggests.

The following day a young lad of slight build was signed from Cambuslang Rangers who was to prove a veritable giant in the history of the Club. He was Harry Brant, will-o-the-whisp inside left with a penchant for scoring goals. His debut game against Kilmarnock away from home did not give any indication of the promise and could have put a more resolute laddie off as Kilmarnock romped home to the tune of 7-0, with Murdie Walls being ordered off. Hamilton Garrison then lost 5-1 in the Express Cup at Coatbridge.

Incredibly high-flying Rangers were defeated 2-1 at Cliftonhill and a result the other way round would have clinched the League title for Rangers at this stage in the season from Airdrieonians but this only put off the inevitable for one further game.

The League status situation was now desperate and the ball was up on the slates in the third last game of the season at Brockville when a 1-0 defeat was inflicted. Despite a 2-1 victory at Aberdeen, the League campaign ended with relegation to the Second Division by a 1-0 defeat at home against Partick Thistle in a disappointing game where Jim Geddes was ordered off for arguing with the referee over an "obvious" handling in the penalty box.

Rovers thus ended second bottom team three points adrift of the next lowest, Hamilton Accies, and accompanied Alloa Athletic into the lower echelons of the Scottish League. The grand new adventure had turned sour. The great ideals had crumbled. Now, amidst the financial problems was relegation and a period, which was to last for eleven years, commenced before First League status was to be regained.

A big clear-out of well known faces now took place and such stalwarts as Rankin Noble went to pastures new and Eddie McLaine was freed amongst several other players who eventually emigrated to America and played for Car Steel Club, Montreal and ended up top scorer in the Canadian League of 1925/26 and played for Canada against U.S.A.

CHAPTER SIX

THE LONG WAY BACK

Season 1923/24

In the build-up to the first Second Division campaign, new Chairman Hugh Martin and his Directors transferred Peter Bennie to Burnley and Tec White, who had been retained throughout his non-league appearances in England over the previous season, was transferred to Motherwell on the eve of the new season. Only two new players were signed in readiness for the kick-off. Centre forward Mackie from Baillieston and outside right McCornish from Barclay Curle.

The opening game of the league campaign was at Dumbarton and a successful start was made with Sam Fleming scoring the only goal of the game. The team was Britton, Penman, McColgan, Geddes, Cameron, Walls, McCornish, Fleming, Mackie, Brant and Kirk.

St. Johnstone were the first opposition to be seen at Cliftonhill when a 0-0 each draw was the result. A visit on Wednesday, 29th August up the road to Broomfield in the Lanarkshire Cup resulted in a victory for the First Leaguers by 3-0 and this was followed by a defeat by Dundee Hibs at Dundee to the tune of 2-0.

This was a repeat of the previous season with a disastrous start and only one goal scored in four games, even if only one of which had been at home. The next game at home against Dunfermline did not improve the position with a 2-1 defeat. At Forfar the following Saturday a 3-1 defeat was jotted in the history books and the game is only memorable by the presence of the Duke and Duchess of York who were interested spectators.

At Edinburgh, St. Bernard's were defeated 2-1 for only the second win of the season and an injured Sam Fleming took the post of Rovers' Linesman from Tom Griffen who was ill and this success was followed by a 1-0 victory at Alloa. The good run was continued at home against Armadale the next week to the tune of 4-0. Broxburn brought the team and Support firmly back to earth with a 4-2 victory at Broxburn but Lochgelly, who visited Cliftonhill for the first time, were well and truly trounced 5-0 with Harry Brant scoring the first of very many hat-tricks for the Club.

A 1-1 draw was secured in the next game at Larbert and then B'ness were trounced 4-0 at home. Middle of the table Johnstone shared six goals in the next game away from home which was followed up with a 2-1 victory at Methil.

Around this time there was considerable talk of the Second Division being split into two sections on a regional basis, due to the considerable distances involved, as the expense involved was not inconsiderable and for a reduced gate in the lower Division.

A 4,000 gate saw Cowdenbeath visit Coatbridge and go home pointless after a 2-1 result and a visit was then made the following week to Vale of Leven but no goals were scored. A new record score for Cliftonhill was notched on the 8th December when Arbroath lost 7-1 when Harry Brant scored another hat-trick and Jimmy Geddes notched two. Rovers then transferred their reserve player Abrines to Barrow.

The next match was at home against Bathgate and ended up 2-2 whilst further draws of 1-1 at Stirling against King's Park and 1-1 at Bo'ness were then recorded. A fourth draw on the trot was averted by St. Johnstone easily winning 6-1 at Perth on New Year's Day, whilst on the 2nd the run-up to the season commenced with another 1-0 victory over Dumbarton at Cliftonhill.

King's Park were next visitors at Cliftonhill and went home defeated to the tune of 3-0 but the seesaw existence continued with a 2-0 defeat at Bathgate. This was followed by a 3-1 victory at home against Johnstone which result was reversed in the Scottish Cup first round at Ayr when only centre-forward Mackie could break through a strong Ayr defence.

The Arbroath game away from home on the 2nd February resulted in a 1-1 draw but old Rover, Charlie Watson, returned to the fold and scored Rovers' only goal. This was Jack McColgan's last game when, following three years good service, he was transferred to Portsmouth.

Another draw at 1-1 against Dunfermline away from home was forerunner to a sound thrashing at Cowdenbeath to the tune of four goals without reply in front of a 5,000 gate. Two home draws at 2-2 against Stenhousemuir and 1-1 agnast East Fife were notable only for all the Rovers' goals being scored by Murdie Walls.

Rab Bernard was signed from Airdrieonians and played in goal against Vale of Leven when an easy 5-0 score was notched followed by an incredible 1-0 defeat away from home against Lochgelly United who were destined to finish bottom of the League with a meagre twelve points from thirty-eight games. The only goal in a one-sided match was scored against the run of play in the last minute.

A 2-0 victory over Alloa was next which was all the more commendable as Kirk was ordered off and missed a considerable part of the game. For this misdemeanour he suffered a two week suspension. A visit to Logie Green the following week against St. Bernard's produced a 1-1 draw.

A disappointing end to the season commenced with a 2-1 defeat by Dundee Hibs at Cliftonhill followed by a 3-1 defeat at Armadale. On the day Airdrieonians were winning the Scottish Cup against Hibernians by 2-0, on the 19th April, a crowd of 1,500 were at Cliftonhill watching a 3-1 victory over Forfar Athletic. Broxburn Athletic came to Cliftonhill in the final game of the season and won by 3-1 thus ending a most disappointing first spell in the Second Division with fifth place attained out of twenty and forty-two points from thirty-eight matches. St. Johnstone and Cowdenbeath were promoted and Clyde and Clydebank were relegated from the First Division.

Top scorers for the season were Brant and Mackie, who was freed for his trouble to be immediately snapped up by Dundee United. Also leaving Cliftonhill was popular Bob Penman who was given a free transfer in lieu of benefit and was gratefully picked up by St. Johnstone who saw many years' excellent service in the sound full-back.

Season 1924/25
Four days before the curtain went up in the new season manager Willie Reid sold his star goalkeeper Jock Britton to Dundee but, as former Rover Lammie Smith had been re-signed from Mid Annandale, this position was well covered. Other new-comers were 'Puck' Ure from Bellshill and Jimmy Dougan from Baillieston to cover the fullback positions, Matt Cornock an inside right from Stenhousemuir, old Rover Tom Gallogley from Exeter, Jimmy Liddell from Preston North End, and Willie McKenna, an outside right from Bo'ness and all played in the opening game against Clyde at Shawfield. In the 1-0 defeat Rovers were represented by— Smith, Ure, Dougan, Geddes, Cameron, Walls, Gallogley, Liddell, Cornock, Brant and McKenna. The first home game of the season saw St Bernard's defeated 2-1 with

3,000 faithful fans in attendance to see Matt Cornock score the first goal of the season.

In the Lanarkshire Cup the following Tuesday, the soldiers of Hamilton Garrison were annihilated 10-0. McNally made a scoring debut at left back with Jimmy Geddes notching a hat-trick in setting up a record score for Cliftonhill and Rovers' highest score since the 11-0 victory over Wishaw Thistle, also in the Lanarkshire Cup, in November 1918. Up at Forfar the next week a good fight back from a losing score at half time resulted in a 2-2 draw in a game at which the Earl of Strathmore was present. This was followed by another draw at home against King's Park, both teams sharing two goals. Despite Matt Cornock's second half goal at Bo'ness, the two goal deficit at half time was not bested and left winger Callaghan from Hibs had a scoring home debut in the 3-2 victory over Bathgate in the next game. Centre forward Mackie was put on the transfer list and at Arthurlie an easy 3-0 victory over the home team took place. In an attempt to improve the goals-for column, the former Arthurlie inside forward Forrest was signed on his homecoming from American football and he made a scoring debut in a 5-2 victory at home against East Fife where Rovers eased off in the second half after leading 4-0 at half time. A further 2-1 victory at Johnstone took place next and Bob Mason from Shettleston played the first of three trial games in goal. During the next week long serving player Murdie Walls who was still unsigned appealed for a transfer which was turned down by the Directors.

Broxburn United came as visitors to Cliftonhill where they won clearly by 2-1, all three goals in the game being scored by Broxburn players.

East Stirlingshire were next to visit Cliftonhill and due to an excellent display by Mason in goal a 3-0 victory resulted. The following week Bobby Mason played his first game as a fully fledged Rovers' player at Arbroath in a 4-1 victory and whilst one player arrived another left, when centre forward Mackie was transferred to Dundee United.

The first game in November saw Stenhousemuir as visitors and a 4-1 victory was the result, with Matt Cornock scoring a hat-trick against his old clubmates. Near neighbours Clydebank and Dumbarton, who then received Rovers in the following two games, both ended up winners at 3-0 and 2-0 respectively, with Rovers never even looking like scoring.

November ended with League leaders Dundee Hibs visiting Cliftonhill and in front of a 5,000 gate the newly re-signed Murdie Walls led his team to a 1-0 victory. This pleasing result was followed with a further 3-1 victory against Armadale with all goals being scored by trialist Reid of Yoker, who obviously considered his future lay elsewhere, as he only signed on the dotted line in the following summer.

At Alloa the next week a single penalty goal defeat was a bitter pill, especially as Jimmy Geddes himself missed from the penalty spot, but it was back to the victory trail the next week again at Dunfermline with a 2-1 score and for the third week running a trialist centre had been given an outing.

The game with St. Bernard's proved pointless with a 2-0 defeat and on Thursday, 31st December, Arbroath were the visitors. This ended in a 1-1 draw in a game when every one of the twenty-two was a hero in the gale and mud, leaving the 3,000 faithful to go home to their First Footing in readiness for the initial game of 1925 at Larbert. In front of 1,600 spectators the 'Warriors' won 1-0 and Lammy Smith was transferred to Queen of the South. King's Park won 2-1 at Stirling in the next match, whilst as a preview of the forthcoming Scottish Cup match, newly relegated Clyde, who had won on the opening day of the season, were at Cliftonhill and succeeded in securing a point in a 1-1 draw. This good result was clouded for Rovers by 'Puck' Ure suffering a double fracture of his right leg. This match was watched by the Marquis of Clydesdale and Provost Kirk.

In an attempt to solve their centre forward problem, King's Park striker Scullion was signed prior to the East Stirlingshire game. The only goal went to the Falkirk side and then the way was clear for the cup tie. Scullion hadn't long to wait for his first goal. It came in the first half much to the Cliftonhill Supporters' delight, but despite Bobby Mason saving a penalty, Clyde equalised in the second half and on the following Wednesday evening the replay at Shawfield was a disappointing 3-1 to Clyde but again all the credit was due to the losers. Mason was injured and stretchered off when there was no score in a tackle with Clyde's Wallace. The latter then got involved with O'Neil who had been substituting in goal, and both were ordered off when the score was 2-0 for Clyde. Rovers then played out the game with nine men with Jimmy Dougan in goal but despite a tremendous effort the first half deficit could not be undone and Clyde won by 3-1.

Back to League business and the next week Bo'ness were defeated 2-1 at home with Rovers even enjoying the luxury of Walls missing with a penalty. An away visit to Dundee saw the Hibs win 3-2 and in the next match against Arthurlie, Rovers won 3-1 with deputy keeper Hodge saving a penalty.

Referee Neil McMillan of Glasgow had a handful at Cliftonhill the next week at an all-action match against Johnstone in the 3-1 victory for Rovers. Walls scored two goals and then missed a penalty, and again trialist keeper Hodge saved a penalty proving he was some deputy. The visit to Bathgate for the next game resulted in a 3-1 defeat but another away match, this time to Armadale, resulted in a 1-0 victory with George Stewart, newly signed inside right from Bridgeton Waverley, making his debut.

Alloa were next for Cliftonhill and picked up the points with a resounding 6-3 victory. On Friday, 20th March, Broxburn was the venue but due to heavy snow, the referee abandoned the game and when it was replayed a week later, Broxburn won by 2-1.

At Methil the next week, East Fife had an easy 5-0 win doing all the damage in the first half and easing up to score only one further goal in the second. An improvement was achieved the next week at Cliftonhill in a 0-0 draw against Clydebank which at least stopped the run of defeats. In the semi-final of the Lanarkshire Cup the following week, Royal Albert were defeated 2-1 leaving the way open to play Airdrieonians in the Final.

Back on League business, a home victory by 3-1 over Dumbarton was followed by an away defeat at Dunfermline with a 3-0 scoreline and the season finished disappointingly with a 3-1 defeat at home against Falkirk. This was followed by a defeat at the hands of Airdrieonians, once again in the Lanarkshire Cup Final at Broomfield, when new-signing Dick from Rangers scored Rovers' only goal in the first half. Airdrie proved quite a handful in this match.

The season had ended even more disappointingly than the previous one, with only thirty-five points gained and fifteenth position. Top scorer again was Harry Brant for the second season running with twelve goals. At the end of the season no regulars were freed with the single exception of old favourite Tom Gallogley.

Season 1925/26

New faces for the new season were Cornock from Stenhousemuir and McCulloch from Bathgate, and when, on the 15th August, Arbroath opened the Second Division Championship at Cliftonhill, before four thousand expectant fans, there were two new Rules to contend with. For the first time a 'throw in' had to be from behind the touch-line and two and not three players were now required for an offside decision. Rovers won the first game with a Stewart goal in each half without reply and were represented by — Mason, Cornock, Dougan, Geddes, Cameron, Walls, McKenna, Stewart, Reid, Brant and McCulloch. The same team visited Shawfield the next Saturday to lose by a single first half goal.

On the Monday, Hamilton Accies were hosts in the Lanarkshire Cup with Rovers making four changes in personnel and introducing McLure from Airdrie Crusaders and Ferguson from Third Lanark. David Hutchison, an outside right from Dykehead, made his debut at home against Ayr in a no scoring draw and scored in the 3-3 home draw in the Express Cup the following Wednesday against Airdrieonians.

At Arthurlie he scored a further two goals in the second half but the home team ran out winners by 4-2. The new man continued at centre forward at home against East Fife and scored the second goal in a 2-0 victory.

The Express Cup away leg at Broomfield on the following Wednesday was a disaster with the team losing by two clear goals, causing the Management to make seven positional changes for the visit to Bathgate. These were all to no avail and the team was sunk without trace by 3-1. Stewart scored a double and Jim Cameron missed a penalty in the 4-2 home defeat against St. Bernard's with Hutchison now playing in his fourth position wearing the No. 8 jersey. Worse was to come the following week against Nithsdale Wanderers by a 3-0 scoreline, all the goals coming in the first half, at Sanquhar.

For the visit by King's Park the entire forward line was changed around and two other positional changes took place. Willie McKenna celebrated his first appearance of the season at centre forward with a hat-trick, his first score in eight appearances, in the 4-1 victory. The team continued in the high-scoring vein against Stenhousemuir at Coatbridge and raced to a 3-0 half time scoreline but were lucky to hang on in the end for a 4-4 draw.

At Bo'ness the following week, Jim Cameron scored a solitary goal from the, unaccustomed for him, inside right position, but the East Coast team rattled in four in reply. Bobby Mason missed his first game of the season in goal and young Ellwood from Gartsherrie was given a run. Even with Jim Cameron back in the central pivot position and the Walls brothers appearing together for the first time, Queen of the South ran out narrow winners at Coatbridge by 4-3. However two Willie McKenna goals were enough to win 2-1 at Alloa with Joe Kirk making his debut on the left wing signing from Johnstone. The next match was also away at Cathkin with Third Lanark winning 3-2. There was great controversy the following week with the visit by Armadale. Rovers were winning 2-1 and with only four minutes left the referee abandoned the match due to heavy fog. The match was re-scheduled for the following Wednesday, only for Armadale to win by the only goal of the match scored in the second half.

Two single goal victories both away from home took place, the first at Bainsford against East Stirlingshire and then Dumbarton with the 'Sons' missing a penalty when there was no score. Despite these successes the Management were still unhappy with the performances of the side and Reid was reinstated at centre with Dick on the right wing in the home fixture against Broxburn United which Rovers won very comfortably by 5-2.

The following home match against Bo'ness saw a battle to have the ground cleared of snow for the kick-off and the hard work put in by the ground staff and supporters was rewarded by a 2-0 victory. A fifth victory on the trot came against King's Park at Stirling by 2-1, thanks to a McKenna brace. However at Ayr the United team fought out a hard won point in a 2-2 draw on Friday, New Year's Day. The following day Dunfermline came to Coatbridge as League leaders and a first half McKenna goal was enough to give the Coatbridge club the points, much to the satisfaction of their support. The same team took the field against St. Bernard's on the Monday in Edinburgh but a 3-1 defeat was the result and Murdie Walls contributed to the miserable result by missing from the penalty spot.

Three positional changes were made for the visit by Clyde but another 3-1 defeat resulted before Stenhousemuir went one better at Larbert to win by 3-0, helped greatly by old Rover Joe Shortt in goal. The following Saturday ample revenge was gained for the earlier defeat by the South of Scotland team. Nithsdale Wanderers were defeated 6-1 at Coatbridge in the Cup with McKenna scoring a hat-trick. For the visit by Dumbarton on the 30th January, Rovers introduced two new wingers, Walker from Bo'ness on the right and Wood from Overton on the left. Rovers were in top gear from the start and 5-1 up at half time with the eventual scoreline finishing up 11-1 in favour of the Coatbridge team. McKenna scored five and Brant and Walker two each. Rovers' team was — Mason, Cornock, Dougan, Geddes, Cameron, Walls, Walker, Hutchison, McKenna, Brant and Wood. This is the record score by Rovers in the Second Division.

The Scottish Cup was next with a home tie against Peebles Rovers and three thousand five hundred spectators paid £126. The home support was confident when Walker gave Rovers a half time lead. Even when Murdie Walls missed yet another penalty, the fans weren't too worried but the Rovers from Peebles equalised and hung on for a draw at full time causing a visit down to the Borders the following Wednesday. The same team was given the job of redeeming their tarnished reputation and they made no mistake with two goals in each half without reply.

The following Saturday Broxburn, who were sitting bottom of the League, had a fighting 4-3 victory over Rovers and on the Wednesday Nithsdale Wanderers suffered for the team's lapse with a 3-0 defeat on the rebound. This was an ideal pick-me-up for the Cup Tie at Greenock but despite this Manager Reid made five positional changes. This seemed to unsettle the rhythm of the team and in an exciting game watched by more than ten thousand fans, Morton won by the only goal of the game, scored late in the second half. With only the League to consider from now on, Rovers made a hash of the next match which was at Arbroath, losing 4-2. Against Arthurlie at home Rovers won 3-2 but there was a stormy finish to the game with the visitors being awarded a penalty in the last minute which Mason saved. There was a vigorous demonstration against referee Holborn at the end. The visit through to Methil saw Rovers win by 3-1 to inflict the first home defeat of the season for the Fifers and the winning ways continued at home against Bathgate by 3-2 in the next match.

Down at Dumfries a 3-3 draw was fought out before Alloa won 2-1 at Coatbridge. In the last away game Armadale won 3-1 whilst the season finished with three home matches, the first against East Stirlingshire, which Rovers won by 3-1 with McKenna scoring all Rovers' goals. Third Lanark then fought out a no-scoring draw and Champions Dunfermline finished the season in a 1-1 draw with

119

Hutchison equalising in the second half and a good crowd of over four thousand in attendance.

At the season's end ninth place was achieved on thirty-eight points with Dunfermline champions on fifty-nine, promoted with Clyde and Broxburn on the bottom rung of the ladder. Raith Rovers and Clydebank were demoted from the First Division. There had been no high points of the season, only an improvement of six places in the League table which was always something.

Season 1926/27
The close season found Manager Willie Reid scouting about for new talent and Joe Whyte from Blantyre Vics, Stuart McIntosh from Mid Annandale and Willie Clark from Gartsherrie Athletic were all signed and sealed before Tom McArthur called the players for training for the lead-up to the first game of the season.

The season opened with Dumbarton the visitors and Joe Whyte capping his debut with a hat-trick in a 4-0 victory with Willie McKenna getting off the mark early with his usual counter. Rovers' team was — Mason, Clark, Dougan, McIntosh, Cameron, Walls, T. Dick, Whyte, McKenna, Brant and Wood.

On the following Monday, Hamilton Garrison were visitors in the Lanarkshire Cup and were trounced a convincing 7-1 with Harry Brant getting a hat-trick and Willie McKenna the other four goals.

This was a more satisfactory start to a season and hopes were high for a return to the First League but these were dashed by Ayr United at Ayr by 3-0 in the next match. Willie Clark, the new promising full back, was injured in fifteen minutes and this didn't help the team's prospects. A 3,000 gate then witnessed a 1-1 draw against Forfar at Cliftonhill with Forfar players scoring both goals and a further own goal was recorded by an Athletic player at Alloa but a 4-3 defeat was inflicted.

On Wednesday, 8th September, Airdrieonians were at last defeated in the Lanarkshire Cup by the score of 3-1 with many of the support saying "not before time". McKenna with a brace and Harry Brant were the scorers. This improvement was not continued in the League when Armadale visited the 'Brig and, despite a Harry Brant penalty, a 3-1 defeat was logged. However, at Palmerston in the next game, with James Rae of Baillieston at right half putting in some sterling work, a 5-3 defeat was noted which was followed by the bold James being signed. A third defeat in a row at the hands of Stenhousemuir then followed at Cliftonhill to the tune of 3-1.

The rot was stopped at Cathkin the following week when six goals were shared with Third Lanark and Johnnie Dick scoring a fine hat-trick. This result was more impressive when it is noted that McKenna was injured in the tenth minute and was a passenger for the rest of the game. Another draw was gained the following week against East Stirlingshire despite a gale-force wind with Jim Cameron scoring a late goal in the 2-2 draw. Jimmy Rae was married and missed this game by being on honeymoon.

Raith Rovers were then visited and the Coatbridge side was annihilated to the tune of 7-1 and slumped to the foot of the table with five points out of a possible eighteen. There was much despondency in the town and also talk of relegation to Division Three.

However, in the next game at home against Arthurlie, a devastating six minute period in which all the goals were scored, a 3-0 victory gave cause for hope, but strong going Bo'ness easily thrust aside the Coatbridge challenge by 5-3 and went to the top of the League. McKenna and Brant hit the goal trail at Arbroath in a stirring 2-1 victory and in each of the next three games Willie McKenna hit a brace of goals with mixed fortunes for his team. In the first game against Clydebank at home in front of a 3,000 gate and during continuous, heavy rain, Clydebank won 3-2 and Harry Brant and Murdie Walls both missed penalties. This result caused the frustrated fans to demonstrate at the end of the game and there were several meetings of Supporters throughout the town at this time to discuss the lack of success by the Club. Against Nithsdale Wanderers in the next game, despite a 2-2 draw, Rovers slumped to the foot of the Second Division table. The next game at home against East Fife was an improvement when the visitors were soundly beaten by 4-2 but St. Bernard's nullified this by a 4-1 victory at the Royal Gymnasium. On St. Andrew's night the Supporters' Club was formed.

December dawned with the news that the Club was £2,000 in debt and that £1,100 in addition to that was owed to the Directors. This news, together with the general depression in the town, came as no surprise to the Support. Attendances had been very poor and for instance the £33.5.0d. weekly wage bill was paid out of an average income of £50.6.0d., which, when viewed against the guarantee of £50 to the opposing clubs, looked a clear case of financial suicide in continuing the battle. Meetings were held throughout the town by Supporters and friends and the team came up with a Harry Brant goal victory over Bathgate at home but then lost 4-1 at Stirling against King's Park and followed that up by a 3-0 defeat at Dumbarton on Christmas Day.

With the knowledge that the Scottish Cup draw earlier that week had paired the team with Elgin City of the Highland League, a more disastrous draw could hardly have been imagined. Rovers would only have the guarantee of fifteen weekend third class railway fares and £3 extra because the distance was over one hundred miles. There was the hope that City would not feel up to footing the bill and then Rovers would get the opportunity of the tie being transferred to Cliftonhill but Elgin, as was their right, insisted that the game be played at Elgin.

On New Year's Day a strong Ayr United, who were third top of the League, came with the lump of coal and the bottle but were swept out of sight by a very decisive 5-1 victory and at Forfar on the Monday a goal in the last thirty seconds for the homesters saw the long journey back to Coatbridge guaranteed not to be a happy occasion.

The Lanarkshire Cup game against Motherwell, who were sitting top of the First Division by two clear points, provided some seasonal fare away from the serious business of points collecting in the League and again Willie McKenna scored two goals in the 2-2 draw in front of 2,000 festive fans and left it all to be played for on another day. Two 1-1 draws, against Alloa at home and away against Armadale were next as a prelude to the visit to Elgin on the 22nd.

A special train pulled out from Coatbridge with 200 loyal fans to travel the 389 mile round journey. Spirits were very low as the team was not playing well but worse than that weather conditions, whilst not good at Coatbridge, were not expected to be any better in the North. When the team and support arrived, it was clear to all that the pitch was unplayable with snow and ice, despite the valiant efforts by the locals to have the ground declared playable.

The game commenced however and Rovers lost a goal in the first half much to the glee of the home support, who were roaring on their local heroes. Rovers never looked like scoring and that's how the game finished. All Rovers had to show for their efforts and long journey was £81.10.0d., as their share of the gate. The team and fans limped back quietly to Coatbridge and their loved-ones.

At home against Queen of the South, newly signed Andrew Hamill, a centre forward from Duntocher Hibs, scored a couple of goals which, added to Harry Brant's goal, secured a 3-2 victory. Andrew, a handy scorer, had scored the goal in the earlier draw against Alloa and it was looked to him to provide missing punch. Snow was a problem at this game and it cost a reputed £3 to clear the pitch prior to the game taking place.

A measly 500 crowd watched Hamill notch Rovers' goal at Larbert in a 1-1 draw but at Cliftonhill against Third Lanark in the next game, not even Andrew could continue with his record of a goal a game and, when Jim Cameron missed a penalty, it was not surprising that Third Lanark scraped off home with a 1-0 victory. An away draw at 4-4 against East Stirlingshire didn't look on at the start of the second half with the score 4-0 for the homesters but Hamill, Dick and Brant squared things by the end of the ninety minutes. In the next game, against Raith Rovers, Hamill again scored in the 1-1 draw. The following Tuesday at Arthurlie, Hamill two, Brant and Cameron scored in the fine 4-1 victory.

Attempts were made for the next home game against Bo'ness to encourage the attendance and it was well advertised that ex-Chairman Hugh Thom and his B.B. Band would be at the game to lead community singing by the Supporters' Club with R. Smellie as leader. There were "Evening Times" Song Sheets provided and 5,000 fans rolled up, which was well over the odds of the average gate at that time, to see a first half Jim Cameron penalty goal be enough to send the Bo'ness team home pointless. Despite this defeat the Bo'ness team was well in line to run away with the Second Division title at the end of the season.

Arbroath next visited Cliftonhill and shared four goals and the points and Andrew Hamill got back on the goal trail at Clydebank in the 3-1 defeat. However he again, along with Jock Wood, scored at home against Nithsdale Wanderers in the 2-2 draw. East Fife was then visited, fresh from their 2-1 victory over Partick Thistle in the semi-final of the Scottish Cup, and looking towards their Cup Final appearance against Celtic, which they subsequently lost 3-1, but were far superior to Rovers. Despite Hamill scoring two goals, the Fifers were outright winners by 8-2.

In the forty-seventh final of the Lanarkshire Cup against Motherwell at Broomfield, Rovers' team could not cope with the atrocious weather conditions and Motherwell had a comfortable 2-0 victory. This was not as bad a result as would appear, as Motherwell were finishing second to Rangers in the Scottish First Division. Harry Brant scored a pair of goals against St. Bernard's at home after being a goal behind at half time and during the next week Chairman Hugh Martin and Director A.C. Brown both resigned, which was not a good climate for the Club to visit Bathgate where they promptly lost by the only goal of the game.

In the last game of the season at home against King's Park, a resounding 6-1 victory was chalked up with Hamill scoring four lovely goals and immediately after this game Willie Clark, the enterprising young left back, and Jock Wood the swashbuckling outside left, were both transferred to near-neighbours Airdrie. It is just as well this game was won as it hoisted Rovers to sixteenth position in the League with thirty-three points. Five points separated eleven teams from second bottom place up to ninth top. Willie McKenna was top scorer with twenty-three goals and Harry Brant and Andy Hamill runners-up with seventeen each.

Season 1927/28

With only ten players signed it was clear that Manager Willie Reid and his Directors were going to be busy on the signing front and it was not long before Bobby Fraser, right half of Law Scotia, Alf Dickson a right back from Mid Annandale, Willie Crichton an inside right from Strathclyde, and John Quin an outside left from Croy Athletic, had signed on the dotted line. Nearer the kick-off for the season, Willie Upton was signed from N.B. Athletic and for a bit of experience Harry Preston an outside right was signed from Torquay United.

For the first game of the season against East Fife at Methil a disappointing 2-0 defeat was marked up for the record books. The team was — Mason, Dickson, Dougan, Rae, Cameron, Walls, Preston, Fraser, McKenna, Brant and Quin. Leith Athletic were the first visitors of the season to Cliftonhill and 3,000 fans were entertained to a no-scoring game in which Harry Brant missed a penalty. The following Wednesday the first round match of the Lanarkshire Cup against Motherwell took place at Cliftonhill with John Quin scoring his first goal in the 1-1 draw. Arbroath was then visited but a 4-2 defeat was the result to be followed by a 2-0 defeat in the Lanarkshire Cup Replay at Motherwell.

The first victory in the League for the season was against Armadale at Cliftonhill to the tune of 3-1 with last season's hot shots Brant, Hamill and McKenna, all scoring singles but at Ayr the following week Rovers went down 5-3 with Jimmy Smith, centre forward of Ayr United, scoring all their goals in the first half. There followed three successive defeats all the same score of 3-2. The first was at home against Dumbarton before which game Alex Marshall, centre half of Law Scotia, was signed. The second up at Dundee against the Hibs, Tom Crosskeys was signed from Crystal Palace as goalkeeper but he was unable to stem the run of defeats against East Stirlingshire at home where Willie McKenna notched both Rovers' goals and were leading by 2-0 at half-time.

David Rae, an outside right from Dunblane Rovers, was then signed prior to the 2-2 draw at Cathkin and Jim Cameron, who had been considering emigrating to the U.S.A. to take up golf and had been in dispute with the Club, re-signed in time to play against Stenhousemuir. Willie McKenna scored a fine hat-trick in what turned out to be his last game for the Club, as he was transferred to Airdrieonians for a reported £400. This meant that the Waysiders had signed three of Rovers' most promising players in a period of four months.

Despite continuing on the goal standard with another four goals, the team went down 4-6 at Arthurlie and followed that with a 1-0 defeat at the hands of King's Park at Cliftonhill. Bobby Mason who had given a good three years' service to the Club, was freed prior to the game against Alloa, when two goals by Brant and one by Rae were enough to record a 3-1 victory.

There was much talk of the Clydebank team folding and of Dog Racing taking over, but nevertheless the game at Clydebank took place. Rovers won easily by 2-0 in a game in which Tom Crosskeys even saved a penalty. John Hogan a left back from N.B. Thistle was signed and played in the no-scoring draw against Morton at Cliftonhill but St. Bernard's easily won at home to the tune of 3-1 with a solitary Brant goal being the sum total of the forwards' efforts for the afternoon. The Coatbridge War Memorial was unveiled the same day, nine years after cessation of hostilities.

In an effort to produce some punch in the forward line Alex Marshall was drafted-in to centre forward and, against Queen of the South at home, he knocked in two goals with Harry Brant scoring the third in a comfortable 3-1 victory. After this game Bury were quoted as having offered £1,000 for wee Harry. But at Bathgate 3-1 against was the score which would have been worse if Crosskeys had not saved a penalty. Crichton tore a muscle in his shoulder in this match and this hindered the forwards' efforts to score. A 2-1 defeat at the hands of Forfar at Cliftonhill was the last time for seven matches that Rovers were to lose.

An Alec Marshall hat-trick without reply was enough to defeat East Fife at Cliftonhill and Armadale were then defeated on the last day of the year by 3-2 with Marshall scoring another brace. On Monday 2nd January, at the Stenhousemuir ground, Supporters, who had travelled by special train, came back in rampant mood with their team's 3-0 victory which was followed on the following day with the third away match on the trot at Ayr with Alec Marshall scoring in the 1-1 draw.

Arbroath next first footed their way to a 3-1 defeat at Cliftonhill and then the Fans in their special train returning from the 1-0 victory at Dumbarton were in optimistic mood. The team was now on the crest of the wave and just in the right frame of mind to tackle Glasgow University in the Scottish Cup first round at Cliftonhill. The Students were summarily dismissed to the tune of 5-1, helped by a Harry Brant hat-trick, but Third Lanark next came to Cliftonhill and walked away with three goals for no reply, to break Rovers' good run. East Stirlingshire gained the points with a 3-1 victory at Firs Park when the controversial second goal, which turned out to be crucial, was granted when Rovers' goalie grabbed the ball and turned round on the goal-line with the ever-alert referee confirming that he had taken the ball over the goal-line.

The next game was in the second round of the Scottish Cup against Brechin up in Angus and the special train carried an optimistic support to help swell the 1,300 crowd. The team did them proud with a 4-1 victory with Harry Brant notching a couple. The old adage of there being "gold in the cup" was once again disproved with £53 being the sum total of the gate. But at least there was hope of a bumper gate in the next round when it was known that Airdrieonians had been drawn at home. Before this game was due Dundee United visited Cliftonhill and Marshall's two goals were good enough to take the points on the day. The Monklands was agog with Cup Fever as Saturday, 18th February and the Third Round Cup Tie between the two local clubs drew near.

There was much hope that the ground record would be broken but this was not to be when only half that number, 12,275 in fact, paid £487 to see Rovers win a famous victory by 3-1 with Marshall, Brant and Crichton all scoring. The Airdrie team were unfortunate to lose their centre shortly after they had opened the score but despite this the better team won on the day.

This game was followed by a 4-0 victory against King's Park, at Stirling, but a surprise 1-0 defeat at home was next on the cards against Arthurlie. Fresh from their victory in the Cup against Airdrie, another home game was their lot against Rangers and this time a new record gate for Cliftonhill was recorded when 25,000 paid £1,164.9.0d. to see what turned out to be a thrilling game which ended as a 1-0 defeat at the hands of the Glasgow team. In an effort to strengthen the team, Willie Wishart, an outside right from Third Lanark, had been signed on the eve of the match but his experience was to no avail and Rovers' further interests in the trophy immediately ceased.

Leith Athletic were then visited but much of the steam had been taken out of the team and the adrenalin had stopped flowing. Only Alec Marshall was equal to the task in the 4-1 defeat. Despite getting on the goal standard for the next game at Alloa the homesters won by 4-3.

Albion Rovers v Kings Park 22nd February 1928

Standing left to right: J. Cameron, J. Creighton, R. Fraser, M. Walls, A. Dickson, T. Crosskeys, J. Dougan. Sitting left to right: W. Rae, W. Upton, A. Marshall, H. Brant, J. Quinn.

125

The next match against Clydebank at Cliftonhill was a game Jim Cameron was not likely to forget in a hurry. The final score was 4-2 for Rovers and Jim gave away three penalties, the second of which was saved by keeper Crosskeys and the third missed. The bold Jim even finished up by scoring Rovers' fourth goal.

Alec Marshall scored two goals to lift the points against Morton at Cappielow and then St. Bernard's visited Cliftonhill to be thrashed 6-2 with Harry Brant scoring a hat-trick. At Palmerston, Rovers won 4-2 and were 0-2 at one stage. The last victory for the season was notched against Bathgate by 2-1 on a day when Harry Brant was playing in the Scotland versus the Anglos game which ended up with a 7-2 defeat for the Home Scots. The last defeat for the season came at Forfar to the tune of 4-1 with Alf Dickson off for the entire second half.

The last game of the season was a friendly arranged for Cliftonhill against Airdrieonians, who were smarting after the Scottish Cup defeat earlier in the season, but this fizzled out to be a poor no-scoring draw.

A great improvement had taken place in the League placing but it was still only a disappointing eighth top with thirty-eight points from the same number of games. Harry Brant was top scorer with twenty-four goals and Alec Marshall hard on his heels with nineteen.

Season 1928/29
As the opening to the season approached, Chairman Eddie McLaren and his Directors were in optimistic mood for the season ahead and, despite feverish activity, no signings were made prior to the first game against Dunfermline Atheltic although hints were that signings were just around the corner. Only the continued refusal by Crosskeys to resign posed a problem from the otherwise settled team and Willie Moyes, Rangers Reserve goalkeeper, was signed on loan. The visit was made to Dunfermline for the opening game of the season and a resounding 5-1 victory was secured with Harry Brant scoring a quick two goals. Rovers team was — Moyes, Dickson, Dougan, Fraser, Cameron, Walls, Rae, Upton, Marshall, Brant and Quin.

On the following Monday at Hamilton in the Lanarkshire Cup first round, a special L.M.S. train took 270 fans to cheer Harry Brant's two goals in a 2-1 victory. The news that Johnnie Archibald had been signed from Darlington to appear in goal bolstered spirits for the first home game of the season against St. Bernard's which resulted in a 3-2 victory with Brant, Quin and Upton all scoring.

Back to League business, a visit to Alloa saw a no score draw and then Arthurlie came to Coatbridge where, complete with new signings Robert Weir a centre from Alloa Athletic and Andrew Rae a right half from the Juveniles, Weir became a hat-trickster on his debut and Upton scored in a 4-1 victory. Against Motherwell on the Monday night in the Lanarkshire Cup Final first leg, a vital penalty miss by Jim Cameron enabled Motherwell to win 3-2 at Cliftonhill.

John Harkins an outside left from Dalkeith Thistle was signed prior to the King's Park game, at Stirling when a 1-1 draw was a pleasing result, in front of 3,000 fans. Back home the next week Clydebank were soundly defeated by 3-0. The following week goalkeeper Crosskeys re-signed and was in position between the sticks to see Arbroath, at the Seaside, win by 5-3. In the next game after giving Leith Athletic a 2-0 lead at Cliftonhill, Weir crashed in four goals and then Brant and Quin finished the scoring to make it 6-2 for Rovers.

The second leg of the Lanarkshire Cup Final took place at Fir Park with Motherwell winning 2-0 on the night and 5-2 on aggregate. Despite this reverse

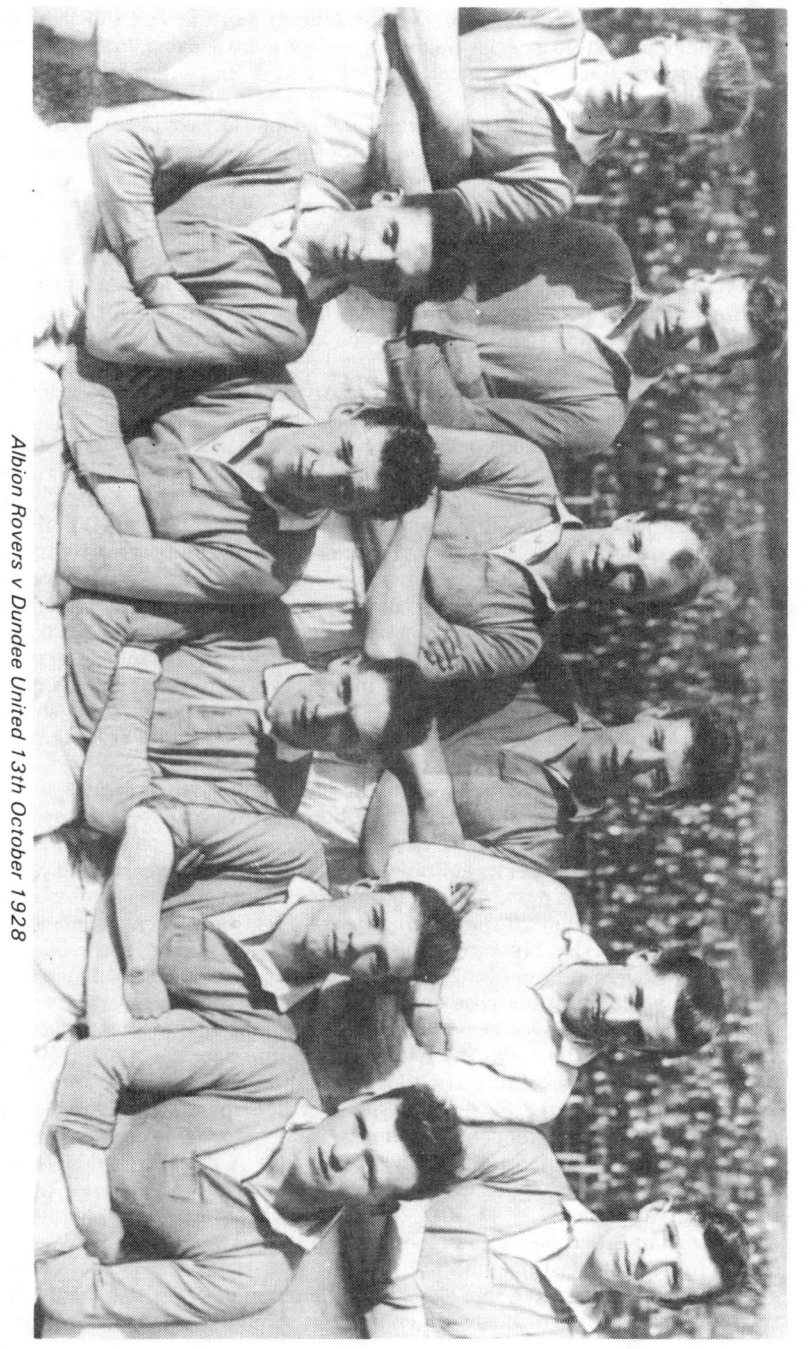

Albion Rovers v Dundee United 13th October 1928

Standing left to right: R. Fraser, J. Cameron, M. Walls, A. Marshall, T. Crosskeys, A. Dickson. Sitting left to right: W. Rae, W. Upton, R. Weir, H. Brant, J. Quinn.

spirits were high and the support was picking up. For the visit to Falkirk against East Stirlingshire two special trains were necessary leaving from Whifflet and Coatbridge for the bargain prices of 1/6d. and 1/3d. return respectively. The amazing number of 1,416 persons travelled only to be disappointed by a 5-3 reverse. However, Dundee United who were League leaders returned to Cliftonhill the next week to lose by two Willie Upton goals. During the succeeding week goalkeeper Archibald was transferred to Airdrie and at Larbert, the following Saturday, Harry Brant's goal was poor reward for all the effort and the 'Muir won easily by 3-1.

The next match at home against Bo'ness was won by 4-0, both Quin and Weir scoring two apiece, but this was much less important than the loss of Harry Brant with a fractured ankle and the fact that Upton was ordered off. Hugh Goldie, former Director of the Club, was presented after the match with a Life Members' Badge.

Five hundred souls travelled by train to Armadale to view a no score draw whilst at home Jim Cameron played a considerable part of the game with a split eye and Rae was off all of the second half with a twisted knee. Despite these misfortunes a 2-2 draw was secured but the next match at Dumbarton resulted in a 1-0 defeat.

Queen of the South then visited Cliftonhill and went home with a 2-0 defeat whilst Willie McKenna, newly signed from Airdrie, appeared for the Dumfries team. Against East Fife, 'Bunty' Weir had a hat-trick in a 4-1 victory which was followed by a further 2-1 victory again at home over Bathgate. Forfar Athletic fought out a 3-3 draw, with Weir scoring two and Bobby Fraser the third, to put Rovers third top in the League. A further draw was achieved against St. Bernard's in Edinburgh at 1-1 with new signing George Radcliffe from Dalkeith Thistle appearing at outside right. Tom Crosskeys was transferred the next week to Heart of Midlothian and Dunfermline came to Cliftonhill in the last game of December to shatter the unbeaten home record by 4-3 despite Jim Cameron and Bunty Weir, two, scoring for the home team.

Peter Taylor was signed from Bathgate and appeared in goal on Tuesday, 1st January. Stenhousemuir came to be sent home pointless with Radcliffe and Weir scoring for the homesters. Next day 'Bunty' Weir's two goals were enough to secure a division of the points at Bo'ness and at home Alloa were soundly trounced 3-1. Andrew Blyth, a right back from Motherwell Juniors, was signed before the visit to Barrhead when, despite a great second half fight back, Arthurlie won by 2-1. The Scottish Cup first round home tie against Galston gave a resounding 7-1 victory for Rovers in front of a 2,000 crowd and gate of £79.5.4d. Jim Cameron missed a penalty but otherwise scored two goals along with 'Bunty' Weir's hat-trick. The next game was also in the Cup, again at home, against Clackmannan when the score this time was 8-1 with a 2,000 attendance accruing £70 from the gate. Upton this time was the hat-trickster with Weir scoring two.

Big changes occurred for the next game at Clydebank where the Wednesday game and depleted attendance meant a total gate money of only £6.9.6d. Arbroath were the next visitors to Cliftonhill to lose by 2-1 and then it was back to the Scottish Cup with old Cup rivals Kilmarnock in the third cup tie in a row at home. An attendance of 7,000 keen fans was affected by Airdrie playing Motherwell at Broomfield also in the Cup and Rovers inglorious exit was due to a solitary goal at the last minute.

However for the next game old chums, Cameron with a penalty and Weir with two were sufficient to beat East Stirlingshire at home 3-1. At Dundee the following

Wednesday an 8-1 defeat was recorded and continuing with the see-saw form of recent times Armadale came to the 'Brig the following Saturday to lose 9-1 with 'Bunty' Weir scoring four and Willie Upton two. It was good to note that this was Harry Brant's return game and he scored number nine. This was also Upton's last game as he was transferred to Blackpool for £1,400.

The topsy-turvy scoreline persisted next week at Greenock where 10,000 fans watched the homesters win by 3-1. The following Wednesday, King's Park came to Cliftonhill, the match ending up a no-scoring draw but Dumbarton were not so lucky on the Saturday when despite winning 3-0 at half time, Harry Brant hit five and 'Bunty' Weir a single in a 6-4 win. At Palmerston the next week the half time score of 2-0 in favour of Queens was not changed in the second half.

At Methil a great fight back from 3-1 down at half time ended with Brant, Quin and a Weir double scoring in the second half for a fighting 4-3 victory. In the third match-in-a-row away from home Leith Athletic were never in trouble even with Weir scoring the only goal of the second half the team still going down by 3-1. The season finished on a high note against Forfar Athletic at Cliftonhill by a score of 6-2 and immediately after this game John Quin who opened the scoring was signed by Liverpool.

Another improvement had been achieved during the season with a creditable fourth position with forty-four points from thirty-six games in a League which lost Bathgate and Arthurlie during the season. Top scorer was 'Bunty' Weir with forty-five goals with Harry Brant in second place on seventeen and Willie Upton sixteen.

Season 1929/30
After finishing in fourth position in the League the majority of players were re-signed for the following campaign and when Forfar Athletic came on League business on the 10th August, the opening line-up was Maxwell, Marshall, Blyth, Fraser, Cameron, Walls, Radcliffe, Harkins, Weir, Anderson and Lauder. Bobby Fraser scored the first goal of the season with 'Bunty' Weir also scoring in a 2-1 victory. Armadale were then knocked out of the Lanarkshire Cup by 4-0, thanks in the main to a Weir hat-trick, before the trip through to the Marine Gardens saw Leith Athletic win 2-1 with Rovers losing a goal in the last few minutes.

A new blue and white flag, which had been donated by the Supporters Club, was unfurled by Mrs. McLaren prior to the home game against Alloa Athletic when another Weir hat-trick was sufficient to set Rovers up for a fine 4-2 victory. This was followed by a 1-0 victory at Methil against East Fife with that man Weir again doing the needful. King's Park were drubbed 6-1 at Coatbridge with Harkins top dog with two goals. The following Monday, Celtic sent a representative team to play a benefit match for Murdie Walls which ended at 4-4 in front of 2,000 benevolent sporting fans on a glorious autumn evening. Murdie was the richer by £50 by the end of the night.

The long journey up to Links Park, Montrose, ended up a wasted journey with the East coast team winning by 2-1 but in the next round of the Lanarkshire Cup, Royal Albert were routed 6-2 and 'Bunty' Weir scored five of them. The bustling centre forward scored the first goal of a 2-1 victory against East Stirlingshire before Third Lanark, in the third home game in a row, were soundly defeated 4-2. This time Willie Anderson took on the mantle of goal-scorer with a brace.

Arbroath was the next venue with a 3-3 draw being the outcome before Brechin came to Coatbridge in their first season in the League to lose 7-1 for their pains. That man Weir again scored another five with Johnny Harkins the remainder. A 1-1 draw away at Bo'ness was the forerunner of a series of fine victories, the first of which was a 5-2 hammering of Stenhousemuir before Clydebank went down 3-1. In the next match at Dunfermline an Anderson hat-trick was one better than Dunfermline could muster before Armadale were narrowly defeated by 2-1 at the 'Brig.

The Supporters Club donated a red strip as a change strip instead of the black and white jerseys which had been the alternative colours for many years. This was used for the first time at Dumfries against Queen of the South in a 1-1 draw before two victories, both at 2-1, were secured firstly over Dumbarton down the river and St. Bernard's at home.

There was considerable disappointment at this time with the gates. A fifteen hundred crowd had witnessed the St. Bernard's match but often the crowds had bordered on or just under the one thousand mark. The Directors made it clear that this was not a paying proposition and that unless gates increased dramatically it would be all the more difficult to put a winning team on the field and certainly one which could gain promotion into the First Division.

As if the players had decided to take the matters into their own hands they played attractive, open football and two hat-tricks from Messrs. Weir and Harkins added to a single by Lindsay thoroughly demoralised a Raith Rovers team. Just to put icing on the cake, Maxwell even saved a penalty. The support heartened by this result visited Forfar the following week in a special train but the homesters won easily enough by 4-0. In the last match of 1929, League leaders Leith Athletic visited Coatbridge and, in front of a nine thousand crowd, a rousing game took place with Rovers moving into an early lead and eventually running out winners by 3-1.

On New Year's Day the customary visit took place to Stenhousemuir and although a 3-0 victory was the result and Weir scored two goals, the support were despondent with their smart centre being taken off the field with a suspected broken arm. Eventually after a check-up in hospital the limb was found to be only badly staved. He did however miss the next two matches which were a 6-1 home victory over Bo'ness and a no-scoring draw at Alloa.

The local hero made his welcome return in the home match against East Fife, which was played on a snow covered pitch, and it was so cold that the referee, Mr. Seath of Glasgow, made the players immediately change round at the Interval without a stoppage of any length. 'Bunty' scored two goals in a 3-0 victory. The following week in the first round of the Scottish Cup, Rovers had drawn Alloa at home whilst Airdrie had drawn Dunfermline at Broomfield. The Rovers' game appeared the better crowd puller as the gate at Coatbridge was £140 as opposed to £122 at Broomfield. Rovers won easily enough by 4-2 moving into the second round and another home tie against Beith.

Before the second round match however a visit to King's Park saw Rovers bundled out of their second top League position by a 4-0 scoreline but the following week Beith were defeated 2-1 with Rovers badly handicapped in the game with goalkeeper Maxwell first of all off the field and then playing at outside right during the first half.

Another big score this time against East Stirlingshire, at Falkirk by 6-2, set the team up for the third round cup match at home against Montrose. With Maxwell unavailable, Willie Moyes was signed from Rangers, and despite 'Bunty' Weir scoring two goals, the game stood 2-2 at half time with no further goals scored in the second half despite constant pressure by Rovers. The prospect of the replay, the following Wednesday up in Angus on a wintry day, was not relished by team or support alike and Rovers' fans were stunned when Montrose went into a 3-0 lead before the struggling visitors were awarded a penalty. Unfortunately Marshall slammed the ball past and it was left to Weir to score a solitary consolation goal in a shock cup exit. Montrose drew Rangers in the next round at Ibrox and were soundly defeated by 3-1 but it was they who laughed all the way to the bank.

With no little disappointment the team returned to League business the following week with Arbroath the visitors and helped by two Anderson goals Rovers ran out winners by 3-2. As an amazing coincidence the next match was again in Angus against Brechin City, who were currently bottom of the League, thus making four games on the trot against Angus clubs. Rovers fared no better than their previous visit to the East coast and lost by the only goal of the match scored in the first half.

The team got back on the goal-scoring waggon in the next three matches scoring three goals in each game but with varying results. The first game at home against Clydebank was a 3-0 victory but Dunfermline Athletic won 5-3 through in Fife, although Rovers remained third top despite this reverse. At Volunteer Park, Armadale, Weir scored a couple with Jim Cameron scoring from the spot in a 3-1 victory.

Rovers were hovering just behind the leaders in the race for promotion. Leith Athletic and East Fife were neck and neck and it was anyone's guess who was going to lift the title with Rovers in the wings waiting any mistakes. Queen of the South came to Coatbridge and gave the home team no favours in a 1-1 draw. Rovers signed Willie Cox, an outside right from Falkirk, and he added much penetration to the forward line for the home match against Dumbarton which Rovers won by two second half goals to nil.

Another debutant in the next match, against St. Bernard's through in Edinburgh, was Duncan Mackenzie who signed from Milton Parish and he took over from Jim Cameron in the centre of the defence. Saints fought out a hard won draw at 1-1 but matches the following week finally scuppered Rovers' promotion aspirations. On the Monday, Third Lanark won easily by 4-0 at Cathkin before Raith Rovers exacted revenge for the earlier trouncing at Coatbridge, by winning 6-2 through in Fife. With only one game to play in the League, Rovers' chance had gone.

On Monday, 28th April, the Lanarkshire Cup Final came on the scene with Motherwell the opponents at Broomfield but, despite a close match, there was to be more cup disappointment for the wee Rovers who lost by 1-0. Rovers' team was Maxwell, Marshall, Dickson, Rae, Cameron, Walls, Cox, Hart, Weir, Harkins and Radcliffe. On the last day of the season Montrose were the visitors and the goals came in this match when they had been more needed in the earlier cup tie. Rovers were winning 4-0 by half time and eventually ran out easy winners by 5-2.

The season now completed had therefore had its moments with some high-scoring games, twice scoring seven goals and on four other times scoring six. The eventual League position was third, three points behind both Leith Athletic and East Fife and two above Third Lanark. However all that good work had been ruined by the nightmare of the Montrose cup defeat and the further disappointment in the Lanarkshire Cup Final defeat. But there was nothing for it but to buckle down through the close season and build on the very reasonable foundation in the annual attempt to climb out of Second Division.

Season 1930/31

The season opened through at Kirkcaldy against Raith Rovers when, in front of five thousand fans, a 3-3 draw was the upshot. Rovers' team was — Maxwell, Blyth, Dickson, Fraser, McKenzie, Walls, Radcliffe, Hart, Weir, Harkins and Lindsay.

Forfar Athletic were the opposition in the opening home match which Rovers won 4-2. Their County neighbours Montrose again put the dampers on things up in Angus winning by 3-2 before, on the following Wednesday, Armadale were defeated 2-1 in the Lanarkshire Cup.

The home match against East Stirlingshire was debut-day for Alec Scott from Dennistoun Parish and Jim McPherson from Rangers and they both played their part in the 3-1 victory before, in yet another Lanarkshire Cup Final, Airdrieonians were played at Broomfield on the 1st September. Again unfortunately Rovers fell at the final hurdle and lost by 2-1. This was the first of a two leg final arrangement so there was still some hope that the team would be successful on their own patch.

The visit to Cathkin saw a 2-2 draw against Third Lanark before the second leg of the County Cup Final arrived. This proved to be a disaster for Rovers as they tumbled to a 4-1 defeat only scoring from a penalty by Anderson. There was some consolation in the gate money which amounted to £182.0.0d. which was good by the standards of the day. The heads were down and it was going to take a lot of effort by the Management to lift the team. St. Johnstone were next to visit Coatbridge and they won very easily by 3-1 before two no-scoring draws against Stenhousemuir away and Alloa at home finished September.

For the third game running Rovers' forwards failed to find the net at Armadale at the start of October but the Armadale forwards had no such trouble and banged four into the back of the Rovers' net. Prior to the next match Jimmy Liddell was signed from Dumbarton and, with fifteen hundred fans roaring them on, Rovers defeated Clydebank in a rousing match by 5-2 with the trialist goalkeeper even saving a penalty. At the Gymnasium, St. Bernard's were beaten soundly by 4-2 before Brechin received a lesson in the art of goal-scoring by 3-0 at Cliftonhill.

The boot was on the other foot with a vengeance the following week at Dunfermline when the 'Pars' won on their home patch by six goals without reply. Queen of the South then came to Coatbridge and Rovers put on a competent performance to win 4-2 whilst a Hart hat-trick at Bo'ness in the following week set the team up for a 4-1 win. Down at Dumbarton goalkeeper Maxwell was unable to get to the game due to fog in Glasgow and Rovers had to field mid-fielder Rae in goal. Despite this handicap Dumbarton were only able to score a solitary goal but it was sufficient to lift the points.

At Forthbank, at the beginning of December, King's Park had a convincing 5-3 victory but Rovers finished the year with a flourish having successive wins at Coatbridge over Bo'ness by 4-0 and Raith Rovers by 2-0 before finishing at Forfar in a 4-4 draw.

Coatbridge boy 'Bunty' Weir was married on Hogmanay and Rovers had to do without his services on New Year's Day against Stenhousemuir at Cliftonhill in the 2-2 draw and at Alloa on the Friday in the 3-3 draw a match which saw an Anderson hat-trick.

The next three months witnessed the most remarkable see-saw form with Rovers winning one week only to lose the following week, a situation which lasted for virtually twelve weeks. The sequence started at home against Montrose with a fine win aided and abetted by two Anderson goals but the following week a 3-0 reverse occurred against East Stirlingshire. The Scottish Cup first round now surfaced with Vale of Atholl visiting Coatbridge and Rovers winning 6-0 thanks to four goals by Anderson. The gate was sixteen hundred and the takings £48. Despite a home no-scoring draw against Third Lanark, the next round of the cup at Motherwell saw a 4-1 defeat but a share of a £240 gate.

It was back to winning form the next week against Armadale at home by 5-2 but it was vile luck at Clydebank the following week when goalkeeper Maxwell had to remain in the pavilion during the second half. In the circumstances Clydebank put in three goals to run out easy winners by 4-1. With the news that Millwall had tabled a bid for Johnny Harkins, Rovers took the field against St. Bernard's and with ten minutes to go were losing 4-2 with two men off injured. The players came storming back with two late goals to make it a great fight back against the odds at 4-4. The next week the visit to Brechin was worthwhile with two Lindsay goals in the second half being sufficient to overhaul Brechin's 1-0 lead at half time for a good fighting victory and in the first match in March Lindsay again had a double in a snow storm in the 3-0 victory over Dunfermline.

Although on the injured list, Harkins signed for Millwall and the Club visited Queen of the South to gain a 3-3 draw. Remarkably Lindsay scored another double in this match which made six goals in three games to be added to the two he had scored in the rest of the season. A disastrous four defeats in a row then occurred starting at home against Dundee United who won all too easily by five clear goals before three away matches found Arbroath winning 3-2, Dundee United winning 4-0 and, on the following Monday St. Johnstone also winning by four clear goals.

With three games to go and only a mid-table position possible three home games finished the season in mixed fortunes. Dumbarton were first in a 1-1 draw which saw Bobby Fraser score his fifth goal in four seasons before King's Park won 4-2 in front of fifteen hundred fans in a match when all the goals came in the second half. Finally Arbroath were beaten by 3-1 on Wednesday the 29th April to complete the season's fixtures.

This left Rovers in ninth position with thirty-nine points, twenty-two behind Third Lanark and eleven behind Dundee United, both of whom were promoted but seventeen above Bo'ness who ended up bottom of the pile. Another blow to the moral of the supporters came on the fifth of May when Bobby Fraser was transferred to Aberdeen for £950. He was to have a long and illustrious career with the 'Dons' and all at Coatbridge were sad to see him go. Both he and Johnny Harkins were two quality players who would be hard to replace.

Willie Reid, who had been Secretary/Manager since January 1922, resigned to take up a similar post with Dundee United and Chairman Eddie McLaren and his Board of Directors were unanimous in offering the positions to one of their own members, William Webber Lees, and he buckled down to arranging the signed list of players for the new season.

Season 1931/32
Only four players were retained from the previous season — Walls, Anderson, McKenzie and Scott — and before the season kicked-off nine other players were signed all of whom, plus a trialist, made their debut in the opening game against Montrose on the 8th August. It was really too much to expect a satisfactory result with such wholesale changes and disappointingly for the local support the only goal of the game went Montrose's way but it was clear that several of the players signed were fair prospects. Rovers' team was — Keegans, Seath, Gilroy, Faulds, McKenzie, Wood, Davidson, Lee, Anderson, Joyce and Trialist.

The second game was a visit to East Stirlingshire where a 5-1 drubbing was received. The team was left unchanged apart from changing over the inside forwards but it was clear that more would be required. During the intervening week, Alex Browning was signed from Tranent and J.T.R. Jessiman from Clyde and much was expected of this pair. Their inclusion in the team against St. Bernard's at home seemed to have the desired effect but it was left to trialist Willie Wilson from Third Lanark to score both Rovers' goals with his signing being a logical subsequence a day or two later. The following Wednesday the trip to Dunfermline saw a goal lost in each half without reply.

St. Johnstone had their usual victory at Perth this time by a swingeing 7-0 and with Murdy Walls re-signing for the new season, his inclusion in the team for the Wednesday home match against King's Park gave the fans new hope. This however wasn't enough and the team was sunk without trace by 3-0 which then made three matches in a row with no goals scored and only three goals scored in six games so far this season. Manager Lees was aware that goalscorers were required and it was clear that the top men of the previous season, Weir and Anderson, were sadly missed. In an unchanged team against Stenhousemuir at home, on the day that Celtic's John Thompson died in the Old Firm match in Glasgow, a single goal by Wilson was all Rovers could do against the three scored by the 'Muir.

Manager Lees decided that desperate situations required desperate measures and moved Duncan McKenzie up from centre half to centre forward for the trip to Alloa and he scored in the first half. Despite Alex Browning also scoring his first goal for the Club, Alloa won by 4-2. On the Wednesday afternoon a visit to Broomfield saw debuts by Duncan Connolly and Dan McColgan but despite McKenzie scoring two goals, Airdrie ran out clear winners by 5-2. The Directors agreed for boys under the age of ten to be admitted free if accompanied by their parents and also a request was made by Mr. Beattie for Cliftonhill to be used for Greyhound Racing.

With Willie Anderson now re-signed, the team looked more composed and when Armadale came to visit McKenzie went one better with a hat-trick and the team turned in their best performance of the season to win by 5-3.

The amateurs of Edinburgh City acted as hosts but Rovers won easily by 4-1 with McKenzie again on the score sheet and Willie Anderson scoring his first goal of the season. For the next match at home against Raith Rovers, Jimmy Gray who had acted as Rovers' linesman for over one hundred successive matches became ill and Tom Griffen took his place. Despite Anderson scoring with a penalty, Rovers lost this one 3-1 and the following two matches were also defeats, at Forfar by 4-3 and at home against Bo'ness by 3-1. During this game McKenzie was swapped over with McColgan who scored Rovers' only goal in the 3-1 defeat.

Further disappointment happened the following week at Brechin with a point dropped at 1-1 but for the following game another of Rovers' all-time greats was signed on in John Renwick, centre forward from East Stirlingshire, who was unable to command a place in the promotion-seeking Falkirk team. Dumbarton were the visitors at Coatbridge and Renwick got off to an explosive start with three goals in the first half and the team winning 5-0 on the day.

Despite this good result the good work was undone at Palmerston with Queen of the South winning 4-0 before a visit through to Edinburgh saw the Hibernian win by 4-1 in front of four thousand fans. During the week Hugh S. Munro, Managing Director of R.K. Wallace Limited was co-opted a Director in place of Willie

Albion Rovers v Kings Park 2nd September 1931

Standing left to right: D. McKenzie, T. Faulds, W. Keegan, J. C. Seith, T. Gilroy, M. Walls.
Sitting left to right: J. Gray (Club linesman), Kilpatrick, A. Browning, W. Wilson, P. Lee, G. P. R. Jessiman.

Thomson, who had resigned some time ago in time for Rovers to win a home match against East Fife by 2-1. This was followed by another home match against Arbroath which ended up 2-2. The success continued at Stirling where King's Park were defeated by 2-1. This score was reversed in favour of Dunfermline at Cliftonhill.

After approval by the Town Council, greyhound racing commenced and in the match just prior to Christmas, Montrose was visited and an Alex Browning hat-trick without reply made it a happy Christmas for Rovers' fans. When on Boxing Day League leaders East Stirlingshire came to Coatbridge, Rovers pulled out all the stops to win in an enthralling match by 3-2 making it a fine end to the year.

On Friday, New Year's Day, the visit through to Larbert found the 'Warriors' win by 5-3, much to the disappointment of the supporters who had travelled by special train from the 'Brig. The following day Alloa first footed at Coatbridge and Rovers had a fine 6-2 victory with both Renwick and Anderson scoring two goals each. Through in Edinburgh the following week in a closely fought match, St. Bernard's won 3-2.

On the 16th January the Scottish Cup first round match against Leith Athletic was played in a hurricane at the Marine Gardens and an Alex Browning goal in the second half equalised Leith's half time lead and Rovers received a paltry £24 for their half share of the gate but more importantly, the right to replay back at Coatbridge the following Wednesday. In this match Leith drew first blood and were leading 2-1 at half time but Browning equalised before ninety minutes to put the game into exrta time. Rovers rolled up their sleeves and gave the First Leaguers a hard match and first of all Wood and then Renwick scored two goals with Rovers running out winners by 4-2. St. Johnstone were next visitors at Cliftonhill but in a tight match Rovers lost by the odd goal in seven. The following week saw the second round of the Scottish Cup with an away match at Kilmarnock when 7,600 paid £307 to witness Kilmarnock win by 2-0 in a disappointing match.

The following week Edinburgh City came to Coatbridge and, although Walls missed a penalty, Rovers won easily by 5-2. Raith Rovers won 4-0 up at Kirkcaldy and the following week Forfar won 4-1 in a match which Rovers were hampered by McColgan being off for the entire second half and the 'Loons' eventually overran the ten-men Rovers by 4-1. At Bo'ness in a closely fought game the home team won 4-3 and this was followed by Brechin City visiting Coatbridge but Rovers won this one by 4-1. Willie Anderson missed a penalty but it didn't really matter. Unfortunately the next penalty did matter but the same man missed from the spot in the match at Dumbarton which was eventually lost by 3-1. Two home games in a row saw victories first of all Queen of the South by 4-0 and then Hibernian by the only goal of the match scored by John Renwick.

The season finished with three away matches all of which were defeats starting at Methil, against East Fife, by 6-2, then at Arbroath by 6-4 in a gale force wind and finally at Armadale by 3-2 due to a last minute winner.

This had been a disappointing season over the piece and Messrs. McLaren and Lees had a lot of work to do to lift Rovers from the fifth bottom position in the Second Division. East Stirlingshire and St. Johnstone had been promoted with Dundee United and Leith Athletic being relegated. Six players were re-engaged but before the season could start, Duncan McKenzie was transferred to Brentford and was a drain on the Rovers' limited playing resources. Two all-time greats were signed in Bobby Beath and Andy Waddell, who were to form an outstanding full-back partnership over the next ten years, and also fixed up were Johnny Barclay,

Johnny McPhee, Joe Kirk, Matt Hailstones and Willie Bruce.

Many of the Clubs in the Scottish League had made a concerted effort to get away from the continual loss and Bank overdraft arrangement and more players than normal were freed at the end of the season. Those players who had been retained were convinced that a reduction in wages would not be in their best interests, refused to re-sign thus received no money at all during the close season.

The Scottish League considered £156 per year as a reasonable wage for the First Division and £78 for the Second Division but most regular players in either Division received considerably more than these sums. The overall industrial depression prevalent at the time was mirrored in football, with the result the provincial clubs were generally carrying on with an annual loss.

Rovers were no exception to this situation and both Board and Players treated each other at the time very carefully. Meanwhile, Eddie McLaren was unanimously re-elected President of the Lanarkshire Football Association with automatic inclusion in the Scottish Football Association where he was appointed to the Referee's Committee. During the close season the Board Room, Dressing Rooms and Bathroom were re-varnished by members of the Supporters Club and part of the field was re-turfed.

Season 1932/33
When the opening game was played on the 13th August at the Royal Gymnasium Ground, Edinburgh, against St. Bernard's, Rovers' team again showed tremendous changes from the previous season and seven new faces were evident in all departments. The game was a great disappointment to those who travelled by special train and the Saints ran out easy winners by 4-1. Rovers' opening goal of the season was scored by Johnny Renwick. Rovers were represented by Connolly, Waddell, Beath, Hailstones, Bruce, Walls, McPhee, Kirk, Renwick, Browning and Barclay.

On the following Wednesday Armadale visited Coatbridge in a Lanarkshire Cup Tie and ex-Dale players Barclay and Hailstones were prominent in the 2-0 victory. The same score for Rovers saw Hibernian sent back to Edinburgh pointless and a further victory at Arbroath by 2-1 saw the good start to the season maintained. This was continued in the next match at Armadale where Rovers won 3-2 with John Renwick scoring the first goal but missing the second half by being in the pavilion due to concussion.

The centre missed the next match which was the Lanarkshire Cup second round tie at home against Airdrieonians and the team missed his scoring flair with a no-scoring draw being the result. The following week Forfar Athletic visited Coatbridge and with John back in his customary centre forward position, he scored two fine goals in the comprehensive 4-1 victory over the Angus side. The next Wednesday he was again on target with another brace and with Barclay scoring a hat-trick in the even more emphatic score of 5-0 over Dunfermline Athletic in front of a 2,500 crowd.

The visit to Dumbarton brought the good results to a halt with a 3-0 defeat but Renwick got back on the goal standard at home against East Fife the following Wednesday in a 3-2 victory. With the Directors aware of the defence's deficiencies, Joe Buchanan, a right half, was signed from Celtic. Joe made his debut the following week in the home match against Alloa, which, with Renwick in rampant form scoring four goals, Rovers ran out winners by 5-2. The following match at Larbert against Stenhousemuir was a no-scoring draw before the second leg of the Airdrieonians Lanarkshire Cup match at Broomfield on the Monday. Five thousand fans paid £84 for the privilege of watching Airdrieonians thump four fine goals behind Rovers' keeper. Rovers' bad luck continued and, despite leading 1-0 at half time through a McGillvary goal, Willie Bruce was taken off with a broken ankle which caused the defence to crumble in the second half and Raith came from behind to win by the odd goal in three.

Joe Buchanan was drafted into centre half in place of Bruce and the long trip to Montrose saw a successful conclusion in a 3-2 victory with Renwick getting back on the scoring lists with a double after a three week gap. Rovers were top of the League and confidently faced up to Queen of the South at Coatbridge in front of a four thousand crowd who were surprised at the strength of the challenge by the 'Doonhammers' who won more easily than the 3-0 result would indicate. Newly relegated Leith Athletic entertained Rovers at Marine Gardens and the Coatbridge team held on to their 2-0 half time score to run out narrow winners over the ninety minutes by 2-1. Edinburgh amateurs, the City, came to Coatbridge and lost by a solitary second half goal. Arbroath were defeated by four clear goals at Coatbridge before East Fife thrashed Rovers by 6-1 through in Fife.

The next match was scheduled to be against Bo'ness but this team had gone defunct. There was an application in front of the Scottish League by Newcastle United to take up the fixtures of the defunct club which was considered by the Management Committee of the League in Glasgow on the 16th November, when it was decided not to entertain the application. The Committee however agreed to allow the players of Bo'ness to go on trial to any club desiring their services. Rovers therefore had no game that week but they seemed none the worse of their lay-off when Brechin City came to Coatbridge with a John Renwick hat-trick leading Rovers on the a fine 5-1 victory. The next match was at Tannadice where Dundee United won easily by 2-0 before King's Park were defeated in Stirling by 3-2, a victory which kept Rovers in contention at the top of the League table. A Renwick goal made him second-top scorer on twenty-one.

Next was a re-arranged match with Dundee United, brought forward because United had been due to play Bo'ness and this took place in Coatbridge with an emphatic 4-2 victory by Rovers with the home team leading 2-0 at half time. United came back with a spirited fight in the second half but the early lead stood Rovers in good stead. On Christmas Eve, St. Bernard's were defeated 3-1 at Coatbridge and John Barclay missed a penalty but Renwick had a double which more than made up for this bloomer. On Hogmanay a special trainload of fans went through to Edinburgh where in a close match the half time score was unchanged at full time and Hibs won 2-1.

On the Monday, Dumbarton were defeated 3-1 at Coatbridge and on Tuesday the 3rd Alloa were defeated at Recreation Park by 2-0. Renwick missed this game and his trialist replacement scored both Rovers' goals. The next game was scheduled to have been a home match against Armadale but this team had also gone defunct and Rovers had another holiday. The following Saturday the visit to Station Park, Forfar, saw a 1-1 draw and the draw for the Scottish Cup first round match paired Rovers with Inverness Thistle and the match was scheduled for Coatbridge. The Inverness team made an approach to Rovers to reverse the venue which was turned down by the Board of Directors. The Highland League team proved a hard nut to crack and it took two Alex Browning goals in the second half to take the team into the second round. Stenhousemuir came to Coatbridge and stole away the points by the only goal of the match before Dumbarton were hosts in the second round of the Cup. There were three thousand five hundred of a crowd giving a gate of £130 and two Johnny McPhee goals one in each half, were sufficient to achieve a win by 2-1. The bonus for this victory was a bye in the third round.

Newly signed Peter Duke from Hamiltonhill S.C. had a scoring debut against Raith Rovers in Fife but the other Rovers won 2-1 before Montrose were defeated by 5-1 at home. Queen of the South won 4-1 at Dumfries but the big match atmosphere was reserved for the 25th February against Celtic at home in the Scottish Cup fourth round. It was anticipated that Rovers' record gate would fall and the team would go on to the semi-final in the cup. On the day only fourteen thousand turned up, which was very disappointing, and a sum of £569 was shared in a game which was graced by the presence of Sir Harry Lauder. However, on the park there was great excitement when John Renwick scored his usual goal but this was equalised by Celtic and the match went into a replay, at Parkhead, the following Wednesday with the gate 23,810 paying £747. The Glasgow team ran out convincing winners by 3-1 although Renwick had a goal disallowed at a crucial time, much to the disgust of the Rovers' support. On the Saturday, Leith Athletic sallied forth to Coatbridge to receive full vent of Rovers' vengeance in a 5-1 victory for the homesters led by a fine Renwick hat-trick. Edinburgh City were even worse off the following week with Renwick again scoring a treble in the 7-0 victory for the Coatbridge team. Oh! for some of these goals in the cup tie!

Dunfermline Athletic won 3-1 at East End Park before Brechin City were defeated 4-1 with Renwick scoring three of the goals and going top-scorer in the Second Division. The last game of the season was at home against King's Park but despite another Renwick hat-trick, the Stirling team ran out winners by a narrow 4-3 score.

Rovers ended the season in fifth place on forty points which was fourteen adrift of Hibernian who won the League and nine behind Queen of the South in second position. Renwick set up a record for League goals of forty-two which is unbeaten to this day. He also ended the season by scoring eighteen goals in the last nine games and four hat-tricks in the last five games.

In the close season the A.G.M. confirmed the Board of Directors to remain en masse and Chairman McLaren as retiring director was re-elected to be subsequently reconfirmed as Chairman. The year was generally financially satisfactory although there was a loss overall of £310.1.2½d.

Twelve players were retained for the coming season and before the players were called for action at the dawn of the new season, Joe Lindsay, John Donnelly, Jimmy Liddell, were all signed with several others in the pipeline.

Season 1933/34

Montrose opened the season at Cliftonhill and Rovers got off to a fine start with a 6-2 victory thanks to a hat-trick by McPhee and a double by Renwick, although Kirk scored the first goal of the season. Rovers team was — Connolly, Waddell, Beath, Donnelly, Bruce, Liddell, McPhee, Kirk, Renwick, Browning and Barclay.

Forfar Athletic were visited the next week and in the tight confines of Station Park, Rovers were sunk without trace by 3-1. Murdy Walls was drafted into the team in place of Liddell for the visit by East Stirlingshire and as a result Rovers' performance was more fluent, reversing the previous score for a fine home victory. At Alloa a 1-1 draw was due to a second half Renwick penalty equalising a first half Alloa score.

M. Walls

R. Beath

J. Donnelly

A. Browning

Dumbarton at Coatbridge were defeated by two clear goals with David Miller from Falkirk making a scoring debut at inside left. Morton won by the only goal of the game down at Greenock before on Wednesday the 30th September, Airdrieonians were defeated 3-1 at Cliftonhill in the Lanarkshire Cup with Donnelly, the professional runner, scoring his first goal for the Club and Renwick scoring a double. St. Bernard's had a fighting 1-1 draw at Coatbridge before Rovers visited Stenhousemuir and came back from behind to share four goals. A third draw in a row took place at Coatbridge against East Fife when Renwick, who scored Rovers' goal, was injured and was to miss the next four matches.

For the visit of Edinburgh City, Rovers signed John Beath from Raith Rovers and brother of left back Bobby. He was drafted into the team at right half and from that position scored two goals with deputy centre Miller scoring a hat-trick. 5-0 was the half time score with the score at time up being 8-1. The next week in the third consecutive game at home, Leith Athletic were defeated 2-0 although McPhee missed a penalty in this one. The visit to Arbroath the next week found Rovers wanting with the Gayfield team winning easily by 4-1. Dundee United then visited Coatbridge and were 3-2 ahead at half time but, when their goalkeeper was taken to hospital with a badly bruised kidney, Rovers eventually ran out winners by the narrow margin of 4-3. The following week a disappointing display at Stirling saw King's Park win easily by 2-0.

During the next week former goalkeeper Tom Crosskeys was signed from Cowdenbeath following his spell with Hearts, and he made his debut in goal against Raith Rovers. This was a match which centre Renwick missed through injury and without his goalscoring abilities the Fifers ran away with the match scoring a goal in each half without reply. Willie Upton was also re-signed during the week from Chester, after his spell at Blackpool, and made his debut at Brechin in the 3-1 defeat but he was not quite match fit. Peter Duke displaced Miller at centre for the home game against Forfar and he scored two goals in a 3-2 victory. East Fife were then beaten 2-0 at Methil before St. Bernard's came to Coatbridge to win by the same score.

Prior to Christmas, Director Hugh Munro gifted a handsome sideboard to add to the Board Room furnishings and in the draw for the Scottish Cup first round, Rovers were paired with Vale Ocoba, which caused great discussion among all the pundits as to who this team was. It turned out that the name was really an abbreviation for Vale Old Church Old Boys Association. Originally the club was composed of ex-members of the Second Alexandria Company of the Boys' Brigade who were now in their fourth season and present champions of the West of Scotland Amateur League playing at Melbourne Park, the old Vale of Leven pitch. This game was due to take place in January.

Meanwhile the last match of the year was a visit by Morton who were defeated soundly by 3-1 and the New Year started on the Monday with a visit to Dumbarton with Rovers sitting in eighth position in the League. The Sons' won this one easily enough by 2-0 and, on the Wednesday, Alloa visited Coatbridge but after the teams drawing one each at half time, a Bobby Beath penalty was enough to lift the points.

Young brother John was promoted to centre forward on the Saturday against Stenhousemuir at Coatbridge and Rovers won by 4-0. Bobby Beath scored two goals, one from the penalty spot, whilst brother John scored a single and Joe Kirk made up the scoreline. The following week against Dunfermline at Coatbridge three John Beath goals were sufficient to beat the Fifers 3-2 and he had another hat-trick the following week in the first round cup match against Vale Ocoba. The gate here was 1,500 giving £24 in a match in which Bobby Beath missed a penalty kick in the 4-1 victory.

Back in the League, Leith Athletic were defeated by the only goal of the game scored by John Beath before the team returned home the following week in the second round of the Cup against old Cup adversaries, Kilmarnock. Hero of the hour was again John Beath who scored the winning goal at 2-1 with all goals being scored in the second half. In a tough match, Jimmy Liddell was ordered off and Crosskeys saved a penalty. The gate was 11,665 and the proceeds were £404 which was the ninth highest of the cup matches. News came that David Miller had been loaned to East Stirlingshire and the following week Raith Rovers visited Coatbridge where Johnny Beath scored the first goal against his former mates before brother Bobby missed a penalty making Rovers have to fight back with a Willie Bruce penalty in the second half to tie the game at 2-2. Liddell was suspended for one month for his misdemeanour. Ross County were the opponents in the third round of the cup in a match where Walls took Liddell's place and John Beath was outside right with John Renwick making a welcome return after injury. Rovers ran out clear winners at 6-1 with Renwick scoring five and Browning the other in what was the worst attendance of all six ties.

With no League game the following week, due to Dundee United tendering their resignation from the League, Motherwell were the opposition in the fourth round of the Cup at home, when again the worst attendance of the four ties in this quarter final saw 16,155 fans pay £640, but a 1-1 draw was the best that could be mustered. On the following Wednesday, Rovers got into all kinds of bother with Crosskeys injured and Bobby Beath having to play in goal. The final result was a crushing 6-0 victory for the 'Steelmen'.

Rovers bounced back in the League the following Saturday with a 4-0 victory over Arbroath. Sir Harry Lauder attended the match at Dunfermline when, with Athletic at the top of the League, Rovers surprised friend and foe alike by winning by 2-1.

Eight hundred faithful Coatbridge fans in a special train wended their way to Falkirk for the match against East Stirlingshire to be rewarded by a fine 3-1 victory and the following Wednesday, another away match against Edinburgh City, saw Rovers win by 1-0. The team went top of the League with forty-one points from thirty-one games by means of a victory by 4-2 over King's Park but the away match at Montrose was made all the more difficult when, after scoring Rovers' goal from a penalty, Willie Bruce was injured and off for half an hour. This sufficiently disorganised Rovers' team at Montrose for the homesters to win by a narrow 2-1 margin. Brechin City came to Coatbridge in the last home match of the season and in front of two thousand enthusiastic Coatbridge fans the Angus side were soundly defeated by three clear goals.

This made the position at the top of the Second Division very intriguing with Rovers, Dunfermline and Arbroath all very close. Rovers had no game on the 21st April and Dunfermline were sitting with their programme complete on forty-four points with Rovers in second place with forty-three and Arbroath at home to play St. Bernard's on forty-two. A clear win for Rovers at Tannadice would gain Rovers promotion and a draw would only make them equal in points with Dunfermline and Arbroath but that would not be sufficient as their goal average was much worse than either of these teams.

The Supporters Club arranged a special train leaving Coatbridge L.M.S. at 1.00

ALBION ROVERS
2nd DIVISION CHAMPIONS — SEASON 1933-34

Back Row: Directors—T. J. Griffin, J. Wilson, G. Wilson J. Waddell, S. Scott.

Middle Row: D. Ellis (Trainer), A. Waddell, J. Kirk, W. Bruce, T. Crosskeys, J. Donnelly, J. Renwick, M. Walls, A. Birrell (Asst. Trainer).

Front Row: J. MacPhee, A. Browning, J. Beath, E. McLaren, (Chairman), R. Beath, J. Liddell, J. Barclay, W. W. Lees, (Secretary).

Inset left: H. Martin, Director

Inset right: H. S. Munro, Director.

p.m. and returning from Dundee West at 8.15 p.m. at a cost of 4/6d. return. The game was exciting and after a goal-less, including a disallowed Walls' goal, first half Jimmy Liddell scored the first counter but in a very physical match he was ordered off shortly afterwards. Johnny Beath and Murdie Walls both scored to make it 3-0 for Rovers but with the legs failing and the ten men holding on grimly, United scored with two penalty kicks in the last six minutes. There was great drama with the second one when Crosskeys firstly saved the penalty but the referee ordered it to be re-taken and the keeper was unable to repeat his earlier feat. However, in a desperate rear guard action, time was piped with Rovers winning 3-2 and thus the Championship was won for the first time in the Club history. This feat has not yet been repeated.

When word reached the 'Brig, the town went wild. Arrangements were made for the team and supporters to be met and when the team arrived there were thousands waiting led by Past Chairman Hugh Thom and his band. The celebrations went on for many hours.

It was quite a day for the Monklands because Airdrieonians required to gain a point from Ayr United at home in the last game of the season—a feat they managed to do, thus both teams from the Monklands being in the First Division for the first time in many years.

The following Monday at Hamilton in the Lanarkshire Cup the same team was fielded, except for Kirk in place of McPhee on the right wing and the game ended 2-2. The following Saturday Rovers received an invitation to play St. Mirren at Love Street for the Paisley Charity Cup and this was a game which Rovers won resoundingly putting a 3-1 deficit in the first half into a 4-3 victory. McPhee made a welcome return to the outside right position and his two goals in the second half were sufficient to bring the Cup to Coatbridge, the first time it had left Renfrewshire in fifty-two years.

Rovers' team was Keenan (St. Bernard's), Waddell, R. Beath, Donnelly, Bruce, Walls, McPhee, Browning, J. Beath, Liddell and Barclay.

Thus was a most successful season concluded. Never before had a major League Championship been won and all efforts were now towards consolidating the Club and playing staff but before that the Town Council gave a Civic Reception in the Lesser Town Hall on Friday, 11th May to honour the Second Division Champions. Provost Riddell presided and extended a hearty welcome to the Directors, Players, Officials, Supporters and friends of the Club. There were several notable dignatories from the football world present and he finished his remarks by encouraging the team to go forward and win the Senior Championship Flag the next season. Baillie Kirk, the Senior Magistrate, proposed 'Our Guests' toast in which he reviewed the History of the Club and Chairman Edward McLaren replied also in reminiscent vein. Dr. Murray Snr. and the Provost did other speechifying before a musical programme was carried out by Mr. Jack Brownlie and Mr. Tom Griffen with Patrick O'Neil, the Burgh Organist, presiding at the piano.

The Supporters were not forgotten and a Victory Dance was arranged for the Town Hall the following Friday. During this, the players displayed the newly won Second Division Championship Trophy.

All was not entirely rosy as Rovers' trainer, ex-Airdrie and St. Johnstone outside right David Ellis, resigned to take up the appointment of trainer with Manchester United. However, on Wednesday, 30th May, after a testimonial match, a Meeting was held in the Club gymnasium with the purpose of re-organising the Supporters Club. There was a large and enthusiastic attendance presided over by Tom Griffen,

SIGNATURES

1934 Civic Reception Programme

BURGH OF COATBRIDGE.

Complimentary Dinner

TO

The Directors, Officials and Players
OF
Albion Rovers Football Club

Lesser Town Hall, Coatbridge,
On FRIDAY, 11th MAY, 1934.

Chairman
Provost ANDREW RIDDELL, J.P.

MENU

Hors D'Oeuvres d'Eddie.
Crosskey Cocktail.

Cream a la Waddell.   Bob's Kidney.

Sole—Bruce's Best.

Lamb du Donnelly.   Murdy Mint.
Roast Sirloin.   Yorkshire Pudding.
New Potatoes.   Sugar Peas.

Kirk's Kreems.   Beath's Bon-Bons.   Liddell's Lumps.
Browning's Bouchées.   Barclay's Baps.

Savourie
Webber's Wonderful.

Salted Almonds.   Griffin Mints.

Coffee.   (First Division).

Cigarettes.
Rover's Players Please.

WM. AUSTIN, LTD.   CATERERS.

TOAST LIST

The King.

Our Guests, ... Bailie JOHN A. W. KIRK.

Reply, ... Mr. EDWARD McLAREN,
Chairman of Albion Rovers F.C.

The Provost, Magistrates
and Councillors of the   Dr. WM. MURRAY, Sen.
Burgh of Coatbridge,

Reply, ... Provost RIDDELL.

The Chairman, ... Bailie FELIX McCANN.

Reply, ... CHAIRMAN.

Vocal Music

SONGS "Bonnie Wee Thing," ... ... Fox
       "Afton Water," ... ... Hume
       Mr. THOS. J. GRIFFEN.

SONGS "The Gay Highway," ... ... Drummond
       "The Border Ballad," ... ... Cowen
       Mr. JACK BROWNLIE.

Accompanist—Mr. PATRICK O'NEILL, A.R.C.O.

Chairman McLaren, Secretary Webber Lees, Director John Waddell and Mr. Tom Moffat, Secretary of the Supporters Club. Tom Griffen gave a resume of the history of the Supporters Club from its commencement on the 30th November 1926, and in due course the officials were unanimously re-elected and it was also agreed that members should pay 3d. per week per Member. Many other suggestions were made with a view to helping Rovers.

During the close season, the Supporters were at the ground until it was dark and six or seven even sacrificed their Fair Holidays to give their services voluntarily to assist in making the enclosure fit for the First League. One hundred and fifty cart-loads of ashes had been placed on the North side of the ground where several steps of terracing had been completed, while on the West side similar work had been accomplished. The main stand had been painted and work was now afoot to paint No. 1 Stand.

Special fencing had been erected by the Coatbridge Co-operative Society to obscure the view of the Cliftonhill side of the ground and for this the Co-op Directors were granted the privilege of using the No. 1 Stand for advertising purposes.

At the A.G.M. on Monday, 17th June, Chairman McLaren was re-elected, along with Secretary Lees. The Directors also decided to institute a Victory Fund and a thousand circulars were issued appealing for subscriptions and also others for prominent Citizens to rally round the Club and buy Season Tickets.

MR. ALBION ROVERS No. 3

EDDIE McLAREN

Eddie McLaren was connected with Albion Rovers from the Meadow days when he was first elected to the Committee in 1912. He served the Club well in those days and was elected to the first Board of Directors of the Limited Company in 1919 and eventually made Chairman in April, 1927.

The days of Second Division status were numbered when Eddie and his Directors worked hard to win the Championship in 1933/34. He spent much of his spare time on Club business and was instrumental in having many of the players of the mid-War years sign on for Rovers.

He had thirteen consecutive years in the Chair retiring to continue as a Director until May 1952, having contributed forty continuous years of service to the Club.

He also represented Albion Rovers on the S.F.A. Council, acting on the Referee's and the Emergency and Finance Committees and also with Lanarkshire Football Association where he was Chairman for several years.

A Partner in the local Engineering and Brass Foundry business of Burgess & McLaren, he left the district in the mid Fifties and died in Largs in November 1970.

CHAPTER SEVEN

IT'S TOUGH AT THE TOP

Season 1934/35
For the start of the season, private telephone lines were installed at the ground by the three Glasgow evening papers — The Times, News and Citizen — but the first game was scheduled for Dens Park against Dundee. The home team went into a 2-0 lead at half time and, despite a spirited fight back in the second half, Rovers finally went down by 3-2. The wearers of the colours in this first match in the second spell in the First Division were Crosskeys, Waddell, R. Breath, Donnelly, Bruce, Browning, McPhee, Kirk, J. Beath, Liddell and Barclay.

The following Wednesday for the Lanarkshire Cup Final the new telephone lines were used for the first time at Cliftonhill against Hamilton Accies. A 5,000 gate saw Rovers go behind before half time and, in a match in which they never really got to grips with the opposition, finally a 5-1 score for Hamilton was the result. Rovers team was Crosskeys, Waddell, R. Beath, Donnelly, Bruce, Browning, McPhee, Liddell, J. Beath, Renwick and Barclay. On the 18th August prior to the Partick Thistle League match, Mrs. McLaren unfurled the Second Division championship flag and Provost Riddell presented Mrs. McLaren with a dinner gong as a memento of the occasion.

Next Wednesday a home League match against Queen's Park ended up with no scoring but the visit to Ayr was more profitable on the Saturday, when a John Beath goal was enough for Rovers to lift the points and a share in the £248 gate. Motherwell were next visitors to Cliftonhill and the 9,000 fans were pleased to have a new large Exit gate erected near the No. 1 Grandstand, which assisted greatly in relieving the crushing experienced on leaving the ground up to then. Motherwell won by 3-2 but the following Saturday saw the first encounter of the season against Airdrieonians, at Broomfield, which Airdrie won by 3-0, and an unusual feature was the choice of referee, Peter Craigmyle from Aberdeen, who had refereed the previous match against Motherwell.

The Directors were concerned about the lack of goal scoring and for the visit to Tynecastle the following Wednesday, Willie Anderson, ex-Falkirk and Morton, was signed and made his debut. Unfortunately, the team lost 4-0 and was in deep relegation trouble. Nothing was improved on the Saturday when St. Mirren came to Coatbridge winning 3-2, leaving Rovers high and dry at the foot of the League with only five points from a possible sixteen. Encouragement was taken from the fact that Anderson scored his first goal and Renwick got back onto the scoring lists. Bobby Beath missed this game, his first, since joining Rovers.

A trip through to Fife against Dunfermline Athletic saw a change in Rovers' fortunes with a Renwick hat-trick revitalising the team, which won convincingly by 3-1. During the following week Tom Lyon from Yoker Athletic was signed and he found a place in the team at inside right for the visit by Celtic, when another two Renwick goals were sufficent to defeat the 'Bhoys' by 2-1. The next game at Falkirk was a disaster with both Bobby Beath and John Renwick missing with penalty kick attempts and Willie Bruce scoring an own goal in a 3-0 defeat. Hibs then visited Cliftonhill to see Tommy Lyon's first goal for Rovers, which along with Anderson's, made Rovers' score 2-0. This score was reversed the following week at Perth against St. Johnstone before Aberdeen visited Coatbridge in a 1-1 draw

ALBION ROVERS SEASON 1934/35

Top left to right: A. Browning, J. Liddell, T. Crosskeys, J. Renwick, T. Donnelly, J. Lindsay.
Bottom left to right: J. Beath, J. Waddell, R. Beath, A. Kirk, W. Bruce, J. Barclay.

with Lyons equalising in the second half.

Hamilton had a fine 4-2 victory at Hamilton before Rangers had a runaway victory at Ibrox by 5-1. Willie Turnbull from Yoker Athletic was signed in time to play against Clyde in Glasgow, when a Browning score was enough to see a share of the points at 1-1. A Lyon's goal in the second half was enough to defeat Queen of the South 3-2 at Cliftonhill and the following week, again at home, a Renwick goal was enough for the points to stay at Coatbridge against Kilmarnock.

With John Renwick back on the goal scoring trail, the Board of Directors agreed to release John Beath on loan to Leith Athletic, as it was considered there was now ample cover for the goal scoring forward positions. The visit to Hampden saw Rovers gain a 1-1 draw, thanks to a Bruce penalty in the second half, but the same Willie was not so lucky when Hearts visited Cliftonhill. In a towsey second half, Rovers, after equalising at 2-2, scored what appeared to them to be the winner only to have referee Hutton chalk Liddell's goal off. For his protestation Bruce was ordered from the field and was, in due course, fined £5 by the S.F.A. Referee's Committee. Bruce again became the hero the following week by scoring a penalty but this was not enough to stop the Dundee team having a Merry Christmas at Cliftonhill by a 2-1 scoreline. Partick Thistle also had a Happy New Year, thanks to Rovers, with a 1-0 score.

The gloom continued on Tuesday, New Year's Day, when Airdrieonians visited Cliftonhill and in front of 12,000 fans repeated their earlier score of 3-0. The following day at Motherwell, Motherwell won 5-2 and Bruce was injured in the second half.

Despite these five defeats in a row, Ayr United came to visit on the 5th January and hat-tricks by Renwick and Lyon, coupled with a double by Barclay, ran up Rovers' highest-ever score in the First Division by a mammoth 8-0 with Jimmy Liddell playing superbly in Bruce's place at centre half. Another high scoring match took place at Love Street when St. Mirren won by 5-4 and Dunfermline exacted ample revenge for their earlier defeat by winning 2-1 at Cliftonhill.

This was hardly the ideal preview to the Scottish Cup, which was the next match at Cliftonhill against Paisley Accies. in the first round. 2,381 fans paid £38 to see Rovers win 7-0 with Renwick scoring four and Lyons three goals. But in the following League match at Parkhead, Celtic won very easily by 5-1 with Renwick getting only a consolation goal in the second half. Disappointment was to follow, in the second round of the cup, at Pittodrie against Aberdeen, where in front of a bumper crowd of 19,359 and a payroll of £880, the Dons won clearly by 4-0.

For the next match George Dudley, a left winger signed from Twechar, made his debut at home against Falkirk in a no-scoring draw before the visit to Easter Road produced a fighting 3-3 draw coming back from a 3-1 deficit at half time. The following midweek, St. Johnstone were the visitors but the forwards shot-shy manner continued allowing the Perth team to win by 3-2.

The Directors were conscious of their lowly League position, being fifth from the foot with only 23 points from thirty-two games. Ayr United were bottom with 19 points and St. Mirren above them with one point more. A visit was made to Broomfield and the transfer on loan to the end of the season saw Johnny Connor, centre forward from Airdrieonians, find a peg in Rovers' dressing room. He turned out in the visit to Pittodrie against Aberdeen and scored Rovers' goal in a fighting 1-1 draw in which right half Donnelly fractured his nose. Connor scored a further two goals in the next match against Hamilton Accies at Cliftonhill with Rovers winning easily 4-1, although in fairness the Accies ended up with nine men due to injuries.

Clyde were next visitors at Coatbridge with Connor this time scoring a hat-trick in a 4-1 victory before Queen of the South burst the bubble at Palmerston by the only goal of the match. The following Wednesday the mighty Rangers were visited at Ibrox and goals from Lyons and Connor were sufficient to give Rovers a share of the points at 2-2. The third away match in eight days took the team to Kilmarnock in the last match of the League programme with Killie winning 2-1. The completed League table showed Rovers as fifth bottom on 29 points, same as the two teams immediately underneath them, with the relegated teams being St. Mirren with 27 points and Falkirk with 24. Thus the team had achieved its initial objective which was to retain First League status. The effort was now channelled into ensuring that the team could build on this good start.

To finish the season the Lanarkshire Cup had to be decided. The LFA considered that this Fifty-fifth Final should be on a home-and-away basis. Rovers were drawn against Motherwell but they withdrew and on Monday the 29th April, Airdrieonians came to Coatbridge and in front of 4,500 fans, strolled home by 2-0. They held on to this lead by drawing the second leg at Broomfield on the following evening by 3-3 to lift the Cup. Rovers were represented by — Crosskeys, Lindsay, Walls, Donnelly, Liddell, Browning, Turnbull, Gilmour, Lyon, Anderson and McPhee. The second game was obviously considered by the fans as being a foregone conclusion and only 2,500 turned up to pay drawings of £45.

During the close season Rovers decided that the team now in the First League should have a Team Manager and when the Directors advertised for the post, they were literally swamped by applications. The candidates were whittled down to a short leet of four — John Weir, one time member of Airdrieonians' Board of Directors and a well-known Scout in Scotland for English Clubs; Bob Bennie, formerly of Airdrieonians and Hearts and latterly Manager of Raith Rovers; Willie Moffat a Hibernian player and John Kerr, a former Director of Hamilton Academical and a Scout in Scotland for Preston North End.

Whilst all this action was taking place at the Club Jimmy Liddell, Rovers' popular half back, met with a serious accident at the end of May. He was employed with the Central Electricity Company as a Linesman and was working down in the Borders when he fell from a pylon some 20 metres onto barbed wire fencing surrounding the base of the pylon which broke his fall. Nonetheless, he was severely injured and taken to Carlisle Infirmary where it was thought initially he would not be able to walk again. Happily this was to prove inaccurate and, after a long period of convalescence, he was again to don a first team jersey and play senior football at the highest level.

Meanwhile, back at the Club the Directors met on Monday, 6th June, and chose John Weir to be the fourth Manager of the Club. This appointment allowed Webber Lees to continue with the Secretaryship without having to worry about team management. At the end of June the A.G.M. took place and showed that the Club had a loss for the year of £389.3.9d. Edward McLaren the retiring Director was re-elected.

The new season dawned with Jimmy Liddell still being in hospital, although now transferred to the Victoria in Glasgow, but Alec Browning was removed to hospital for an appendix operation. This was not the best of starts for new Manager, Johnny Weir.

J. Renwick

W. Bruce

J. Barclay

A. Waddell.

Season 1935/36
When the season dawned on the 10th August, Dunfermline were the visitors to Coatbridge and Mr. Weir's first introduction to team management ended on a sour note with the 'Pars' winning 3-1. Rovers' first goal of the season was scored by new centre forward Rice, and Rovers were represented by Shevlin, Waddell, Beath, Lyon, Bruce, Anderson, McPhee, Gilmour, Rice, Graham and Grant.

Despite signing Robert Whitelaw from Celtic and Hugh McFarlane from Hibs and playing them on the following Wednesday night against Raith Rovers, another defeat, this time by 2-1, was the end result. However, the long visit to Arbroath saw a Rice double sufficient to defeat the "Red Lichties" by 2-1 before the Lanarkshire Cup first round match against Airdrieonians was played at Broomfield the following Monday. 6,000 fans paying £139.8.9d. saw Rovers come back from a deficit at half time to a fighting 2-2 draw with centre Rice again scoring making his tally for the season four goals in four games.

The centre was again on target in the 5-1 home victory over Ayr United before the visit to Hamilton on the following Wednesday saw the Accies win by an emphatic 7-2 margin although Rice scored both Rovers' goals. County neighbours Motherwell had an easy 2-0 victory in the League before Third Lanark were defeated by the same score at Cliftonhill. Celtic were the next victors over the 'Blues' by a 4-0 margin at Parkhead.

Airdrieonians came to Cliftonhill and two goals apiece by Rice and McPhee helped the team to win 4-1 but the following week Partick Thistle were too good for the Coatbridge boys by a 5-3 margin. After eleven games new centre Rice had scored a creditable twelve goals but the rest of the forwards were not keeping pace with the new lad and, although McPhee had four goals, centre half Bruce was breathing down his neck with three.

After the Partick Thistle game, inside left Graham was transferred to Cowdenbeath and Dundee were the next visitors in a 1-1 draw. Johnny Harkins was signed from Millwall and took his place at inside left for the match at Easter Road which Hibs won by 3-0. Queen of the South were then defeated 2-0 at Coatbridge before Hearts were visited in Edinburgh. In front of a 12,000 crowd the 'Jam Tarts' won convincingly by 4-2 in what was the start of five successive defeats. The first of these was at home against Kilmarnock by 3-2 before Clyde were hosts in a 5-2 reverse. Aberdeen came to Coatbridge and won 3-1 with St. Johnstone doing likewise the following week at 2-1.

The run of defeats came to an end on St. Andrews Day, when Queen's Park lost to a last minute goal by Miller, who had been drafted into centre in place of Rice, and he was first on the score sheet the following week at Coatbridge against Hamilton in a 4-0 victory. Johnny Harkins also scored his first goal for the Club since his re-joining them earlier in the season.

Rangers won easily by 5-1 in Glasgow before an incredible 5-5 scoreline at East End Park in Dunfermline enthralled the 4,000 spectators with seven goals coming in the second period. The forwards continued in this high scoring vein the following week with an emphatic win over Arbroath by 5-2. Outside right Grant was taken off in this match with a dislocated elbow which caused him to miss the next three matches.

On Wednesday, New Year's Day, Broomfield was the venue with Rovers winning narrowly in the end by a 2-1 margin, whilst on the following day Motherwell were visited with a coincidence being referee D.F. Reilly from Port Glasgow in charge of both games against the County rivals. Already one ahead at

153

half time, Motherwell scored the only goal of the second half and Rovers were hampered when Tom Crosskeys had to leave the field in the fifty-eighth minute with Lyon taking up the goalkeeper's jersey.

The Manager played Dunlop from Hamilton as last line of defence in the next match down at Ayr but the 'Honest Men' won by 4-1. Archie Gourlay was then signed from Partick Thistle and made his debut in the match against Third Lanark at Cathkin when a Tommy Lyon second half goal was sufficient to lift the points. Celtic visited Coatbridge on the 18th of January and in front of 17,000 enthusiastic fans the 'Bhoys' won by an emphatic 3-0 scoreline. This was again poor preparation for the forthcoming Scottish Cup tie against Wigton, the kick-off of which was delayed by a two minute silence in memory of the late King George V. When the game did get underway, Rovers were soon in ecstasy with a 5-0 scoreline at half time and soon this was changed into seventh heaven when the match finished a massive 7-1. The 'Brig was in high excitement during the following week when the Cup Draw paired Rovers and old Cup rivals Rangers at Cliftonhill. Before that game however a warm-up against Partick Thistle at Cliftonhill saw Rovers win 5-2 and thus all was set for the big day on the 8th of February.

There was great interest in the West of Scotland in this match and much talk that the ground record would be increased, in fact there was thought that a crowd in the region of 40,000 might attend. The Club employed a squad of workmen during the intervening period to terrace and step the ground opposite the grandstand. A special car parking facility was secured in the field opposite the grandstand with capacity for holding five hundred cars. When the referee Mr. J.M. Martin of Ladybank got the game started on a frost-bound pitch, 27,500 had paid £1,096.14.6d. which was indeed a record which stands to this day. Rovers playing in black and white vertical stripes for the day, got off to an explosive start in six minutes when they were awarded a penalty. Willie Bruce stepped up for his sixth conversion of the season but missed for the first time in his career at Coatbridge. However, he made amends with ten minutes of the first half to go with a lob tailor-made for Rice to head strongly past Jerry Dawson in the Rangers' goal and at half time tha air was buzzing with a sensation in the offing. Unfortunately it was not to be and the mighty 'Gers came out in the second half to win by 3-1, much to the disappointment of the Coatbridge contingent.

Rovers were represented by Gourlay, Waddell, Beath, Anderson, Bruce, McFarlane, Grant, Lyon, Rice, Browning and Dudley.

On a snowy, foggy day the trip to Dundee the following week saw another defeat, this time by 2-0, in a match which was Tommy Lyon's last game before being transferred to Airdrieonians on loan to the end of the season. Without his assistance Hibernian were winners by the only goal of the game at Cliftonhill and the team lost at Queen of the South by the same scoreline. The other team from the Capital, Hearts, came to Coatbridge and also won by a single goal margin, this time by 2-1, before a fighting 2-2 draw was achieved at Kilmarnock. Rovers were 2-0 down at half time and were further handicapped by Harkins being injured but eventually reached parity in the second half.

The following Wednesday saw another draw, this time by 4-4, against Clyde with Rice scoring two goals and Bruce scoring two penalties before Aberdeen won by a convincing 6-1 at Pittrodie.

The League season finished with two victories, 3-2 at Perth when McPhee nullified a first half goal for the Saints direct from a corner and in the last game of

Cartoon from "News of the World"

the season Queen's Park were defeated 2-1 at Coatbridge. The final match of the season took place on Tuesday the 28th April in the second leg of the Lanarkshire Cup against Airdrieonians. The earlier game had finished 2-2 at Broomfield and after ninety minutes finished 3-3 at Cliftonhill and a further goal by both teams in extra time left the match still undecided as the season came to an end.

The Club remained in the First Division and although the A.G.M. in July showed another loss of £2,218.0.0. on the year's working, Manager Weir was confident that the Club would be well up in the League during the next season.

Season 1936/37

When the season opened, Rovers were again in trouble in the goalkeeping department. New signing John Ferguson from Shettleston was quickly promoted to meet St. Mirren at Love Street on the opening day of the season. He had an inauspicious start in a 3-0 defeat in the following line-up — Ferguson, Waddell, Beath, Anderson, Bruce, McFarlane, Grant, Lyon, Rice, Holland and Dudley.

George McMillan was signed during the week from Bradford and the former Rangers' player was drafted into the side for the Tuesday night match against Airdrieonians in the replay of the Lanarkshire Cup carried forward from the previous season. Although McMillan scored in the second half, Rovers lost this one by 3-1. It took to the following Saturday and the third game of the season before Rovers came good with 'keeper Ferguson having a shut-out and the forwards scoring four goals.

The return match against St. Mirren took place on the Wednesday and McMillan got himself ordered off in the towsey 6-2 victory for the Paisley side. Inside right Knox scored five of the visitors' goals. A no scoring draw was next at Cathkin before Celtic came to Coatbridge winning 3-1. The Manager was most disappointed with the display of his team and on the following Monday the Lanarkshire Cup Tie against Motherwell was used for experimentation. With ex-

ALBION ROVERS SEASON 1936/37

Back left to right: Anderson, Miller, Morrison, Beath, McFarlane, Bruce.
Front left to right: Stark, Lyon, Dudley, Connor, Blackwood.

Airdrie 'keeper Morrison in between the sticks, the opportunity was taken to play goalkeeper Ferguson at centre forward. Tommy Lyon was also tried at left back in place of Bobby Beath. Neither experiments were a success and Motherwell won very easily by 6-1.

Dundee then won by the only goal of the game before a fight back in Edinburgh saw Holland equalise a first half goal from Hibs. Arbroath were defeated by 2-0 at Coatbridge and before the next match at Falkirk the S.F.A. Referee Committee fined McMillan £5 and severely censored him for his earlier ordering off. This was fortunate for Rovers as he was then able to take his place at Falkirk but despite two goals by centre forward Holland, the 'Bairns' won by 3-2. Partick Thistle won the next week at Coatbridge by 4-2 and Blackwood from Bridgeton Waverley and James Connor from Shawfield Juniors were signed in readiness for the visit to Dunfermline. Connor was a brother of John who had assisted the Club two seasons earlier on loan from Airdrie and he came with a reputation as a goal-scorer. It was left however to Blackwood, who had a double on the day, to extract a point from the 'Pars' at 3-3. The next match at home against Motherwell was the stage for Connor's first goal for the Club but the game ended in defeat for the team by 4-1 in a match when two balls burst causing much consternation to the officials and embarrassment to the Club.

Troubles continued to heap themselves upon the 'Wee Rovers' and when Kilmarnock were visited the best the team could do was a 3-1 defeat. Worse was to follow with the news that Johnny Harkins was in hospital requiring an operation to his knee and George McMillan was freed to immediately sign for East Stirlingshire. Alec Trotter, a forward from Arsenal and Ashfield, was signed and he helped the team to a 1-1 draw against Clyde at Cliftonhill and in a match which should never have been lost. Aberdeen then won 4-1 at Pittodrie with 'keeper Ferguson being stretchered off before half time in his return to the team. George Grant was also transferred during the following week to St. Bernard's, as he had lost his place to Stark and Blackwood and the Directors felt they were well covered for wingers with Dudley and Trotter also available.

Ferguson was fit for the trip to Perth but couldn't stop St. Johnstone winning 4-0. Another new signing took place during the week — John Murray, an inside forward from Newcastle, Rangers and Saltcoats Vics being fixed up and made up a left wing with Blackwood for the home match against Queen's Park. The 'Spiders' won this one 3-2 and so it was back to the drawing board for the Manager. He lashed out the following week and signed Alec McLennan a centre forward from Partick Thistle who had a scoring debut the following day against Hamilton Accies by a double in the 3-2 victory. The other new man, Murray, also got on the score list in this match. Rangers were the next visitors at Coatbridge and ran out winners by 3-2. Rovers were 2-0 up in this match but lost right half Jimmy Waddell before half time and eventually lost to a last minute goal. Centre half Willie Bruce scored Rovers' first goal which made him top goal scorer of the team with five goals.

Following that bit of bad luck, the long journey to Dumfries saw Rovers lose 5-2 and Waddell returned in the next match in time to be injured again and with Hearts winning 3-1 at Coatbridge into the bargain. Rovers' position was now perilous and this defeat was a shattering blow to the faithful, as was the news the previous Thursday that King Edward VIII had renounced his Throne to his brother the Duke of York after a short reign of less than eleven months.

The Supporters' Club had recently been reformed taking up the name of The Albion Rovers Supporters Social Club with Willie Wood being President, T.D.

Supporters Club Committee

Back left to right: Tom Kerr, Geo. Hamson, A. Birrell (Asst. Trainer), J. Gordon, J. McMillan.
Front left to right: Webber Lees, Tom Griffen (President), Tom Moffat.

Moffat Vice-President and John McMillan, Secretary. Treasurer was John Russell and the Committee comprised Messrs. T. & J. Harkness, Crozier, Wardrobe, Baillie, Thomson, Hay and Miller. They buckled to the hard task of providing funds for the beleaguered team.

On Tuesday the 15th, Provost Chassels read the proclamation of Accession of King George VI at the Fountain and the following Saturday a 4-0 scoreline saw Celtic pocket the points at Parkhead. Centre forward McLennan was freed and Alec Hyslop, a right back from Huddersfield, was signed and he took up his place in defence against Falkirk at Cliftonhill on New Year's Day but the visitors were not in a benevolent mood winning by 4-1. Worse was to come the following day at Motherwell when a record 9-1 score was run up by the 'Steelmen' in what is still today the top score against Rovers in the First League.

The following Monday saw changes in all departments of the team and a change in fortunes with new signing Hugh McMahon from Doncaster Rovers injecting much needed backbone to the defence and also getting on the scoreline in a 4-0 victory over Queen of the South. Former Rover, John Renwick, missed from the penalty spot for Queens immediately after half time. It was Rovers' turn to miss a penalty the following week when Willie Bruce was the culprit and this enabled Dundee to share the points in a 1-1 draw. The trip to Arbroath the next week saw the East Coast team win 4-2 and despite a 4-0 victory at home against Dunfermline, a very disgruntled and disillusioned Willie Bruce asked to be put on the Open-to-Transfer List and immediately the Directors agreed to this request.

On the Saturday the Cup Tie against Leith Athletic was postponed due to ground conditions and the match was eventually played the following Wednesday at Meadowbank. With heavy rain throughout, the pitch cut up very badly but with the second top attendance of the day at 6,714, Rovers managed a 4-4 draw with Tommy Lyon notching a hat-trick. Sandwiched between the replay was a League match against Partick Thistle at Glasgow in which the 'Jags' ran out easy winners by 6-1. It was with little real heart the disillusioned team lined up against the Edinburgh side on a day not conducive to good football. The match was played much of the time in a blinding snowstorm with an attendance of only about 3,000. But Rovers won 5-3 against all expectations and were drawn against Celtic at home in the next round.

This was the fourth time the teams had met in the Cup; the first time being at Parkhead in 1888 when the Celts won by 4-1. A second round visit in 1893 saw Rovers lose 7-0 before in 1933 after a 1-1 draw at Coatbridge the Glasgow team won by 3-1. Again there was great excitement in the town with the hope that the ground record would again be exceeded. In the event only 19,000 fans paying £725 witnessed the match which saw Celtic overtake a 2-1 deficit at half time to run out clear cut winners at 5-2.

It was then back to League business with Kilmarnock being the next visitors to Coatbridge. A 3-1 defeat resulted followed by a 4-1 defeat in Glasgow against Clyde saw the team at the foot of the table and great pressure building up on Manager Weir. This pressure proved too much and the manager, having thought things out over the weekend, tendered his resignation on Monday the 8th March. This was immediately accepted by the Directors.

With Rovers practically assured of relegation, there were rumours in the town of the new aspirants for the Board of Directors, even although the Annual General Meeting was not until June. The two retiring Directors who are eligible for re-election were Messrs. Simon Scott and Tom Griffen.

The support was further stunned with the news that Tommy Lyon was transferred to Blackpool and, with their heads down, the team meekly went through the motions and gave up the points in a 4-0 defeat at home against St. Johnstone. The following midweek Aberdeen came to Coatbridge and ran out easy winners by 5-1 before another defeat this time by 3-2 was inflicted by Hamilton Academical.

Although the relegation issue was critical a fighting 3-3 draw at Hampden didn't really improve the situation as it left Rovers with only sixteen points from thirty-six games with Dunfermline at twenty points from thirty-five games and Queen of the South twenty-three points from thirty-six games. Rangers were visited at Ibrox and only a first half penalty goal saw the points stay at Ibrox whilst the last game of the season saw Hearts score five without reply at Tynecastle. Thus Rovers were relegated once more to the lower reaches of the Scottish League along with Dunfermline and seven points behind next placed Queen of the South, to join Airdrieonians in the Second Division. Lack of goal scorers was the main problem and when the centre half could end up as the top equal scorer with nine goals this showed the poverty of scoring skills by the other players.

At the A.G.M. came a loss for the year of £1,622.18.1d. and at this Meeting Webber Lee was confirmed as Secretary and once more took up the mantle as manager. New faces were signed for the new season in Robertson and Corrance from Falkirk, Bell from Queen of the South and Douglas from Clyde with smart juniors in Burke from Kirkintilloch and Love from Clydebank Juniors. On the debit side though, Willie Bruce was transferred to Queen of the South.

Johnny Bell being welcomed to Coatbridge by Eddie McLaren and Webber Lees.

The Supporters' Club were very busy in the close season making many improvements at Cliftonhill, especially lavatory accommodation within the grounds. Captain Andy Waddell spent several nights assisting the Supporters in the plasterwork. The turnstiles at Stewart Street had been dispensed with, a wall erected and much paintwork had been carried out around the ground, making the place look spick and span for the new season.

Season 1937/38

The opening game in the Second Division programme on the 14th August was in Falkirk against East Stirlingshire when a fine 4-1 victory was recorded with new centre forward Love scoring two fine goals and all the new men showing up well. It was good to see Jimmy Liddell make his reappearance at left half after being missing for the entire previous season. Rovers' team was — Robertson, Waddell, Beath, Corrance, Miller, Liddell, Burke, Trotter, Love, Bell and Douglas.

First home match was against Forfar Athletic and again Love scored a couple in the 3-0 victory. East Fife became the third scalp for the First Division aspirants at 2-1 before a fourth victory on the trot over Cowdenbeath by 4-3 got the team off to the best possible start in the League Programme. With Miller unfit, Taylor from Dumbarton fitted-in at centre half as Hugh McFarlane had been transferred to Dunfermline. The following Saturday came the first of the local derbies against Airdrieonians but with the score at 1-1 in the first half, Bell was injured and Airdrie went on to win 2-1. Old pal Alec Browning was at right half for Airdrie.

With the threat of world war in the air, a Peace Week had been arranged by the Burgh of Airdrie involving all walks of life and a peace procession was organised for the 18th September for Dunbeth Park to the War Memorial in West End Park and then back to Dunbeth Park led by ex-Baillie John Kirk, Chairman of the Coatbridge Branch of the League of Nations. This was in direct opposition to the home match against Dundee United and the poor crowds which had been present at Rovers' earlier matches were not assisted by this opposition, despite Rovers making arrangements to have all unemployed admitted for 6d. on production of the Yellow Card supplied by the Labour Exchange. Irrespective, Rovers won 4-1 and the fans who did turn up were happy enough.

A sixth win in seven outings at Brechin by 4-1 was followed by a 1-1 draw with Stenhousemuir which was only possible by goalkeeper Robertson saving two penalties. The visit to Leith Athletic found Rovers losing by an 85th minute goal but remaining in the second top position in the League. But for centre half Miller missing a penalty, Rovers would have done better than draw 2-2 at home against Dunfermline before St. Bernard's were soundly cuffed 5-0 at Coatbridge with keeper Robertson again the hero saving a penalty kick.

Former player Tom Crosskeys, now with Montrose, defied all Rovers' efforts until the 80th minute when the only goal of the game by Jackie Burke was enough to give Rovers the points. Recently signed George (Cock) Loudon played at centre in this match. Despite Burke scoring two further goals at Dumbarton the following week, the team went down 3-2 before the amateurs from Edinburgh, the City, came to Coatbridge to be beaten 5-3 with Willie Love scoring four of the goals. The trip to Stirling saw King's Park defeated 2-0 despite Waddell missing a penalty and the crunch match in the Division came on the 27th November when Raith Rovers came to Coatbridge sitting top of the League with Rovers breathing down their neck. The battle of the Rovers ended with the Kirkcaldy team winning 5-1.

Smarting from this defeat, Rovers lined up against Alloa at Coatbridge the

ALBION ROVERS SEASON 1937/38

Standing: R. Corrance, A. Waddell, J. Robertson, H. Miller, J. Liddell, R. Beath.
Seated: J. Burke, A. Trotter, W. Love, W. Cameron and A. Douglas.

following week with trialist Alec McLetchie at inside left. Although he didn't score, he did sufficient in the 7-1 victory to be signed immediately after the match. Cowdenbeath were defeated 3-2 in Fife before, on New Year's Day, Airdrieonians took the short journey down to Coatbridge to win their second match over their rivals this time by 2-0. On the Monday the long trip to Forfar saw another all-time great make his appearance on trial at inside right, Coatbridge boy Tommy Kiernan from Clydebank Juniors. He had an outstanding match in the 2-2 draw and was signed on the bus on the journey home. He scored his first goal for the Club the following week at Dunfermline in a match where Rovers were three goals up at one stage but eventually only drew by 3-3. Rovers had slumped to fourth position in the League table.

On the 15th January, Brechin City came to Coatbridge and in a match of devastating scoring power, Rovers were seven up at half time eventually running out easy winners at 10-0 which remains today the record score for Rovers in the Second Division. New signing Kiernan scored a hat-trick in five minutes and Love, Beath and Burke all scored doubles with Cameron making up the final scoreline. This was a tremendous fillip for the Scottish Cup match the following week against Dundee at Coatbridge and it was no surprise when Rovers ran out easy winners by 4-2 against their First Division opposition with Kiernan scoring in this one to give him five goals in four outings. The adrenalin was flowing again.

St. Bernard's then fought out a 1-1 draw in Edinburgh before Rovers went to Alloa to win 2-1 which again was a good build up for the second round cup tie away to Highland League, Ross County. There was a special train taking 145 fans north and the 3,500 crowd saw Kiernan score another hat-trick in the 5-2 victory. Two home matches then saw East Fife draw 2-2 and Leith Athletic were beaten 2-1 setting the team up nicely for the third round cup tie at Falkirk. Despite a special train and a goodly crowd, Rovers surprisingly lost this one without much fight and Falkirk won just as easily on the day as the 4-0 score would suggest.

High-fliers Raith Rovers then did the double over the Coatbridge Rovers by 4-1 but a 3-0 victory the following week at home against Dumbarton sent Rovers back up to third top position and this was confirmed the following week with a 2-0 victory over Edinburgh City. The team took time off from the League campaign to play Hamilton in the Lanarkshire Cup but the Accies were too strong winning 2-0. With promotion excitement growing as the season neared its climax King's Park fought out an exhilarating 3-3 draw at Coatbridge before Stenhousemuir were defeated 3-2 at Larbert and East Stirlingshire routed by 7-0 the following Wednesday.

With two games to go it was neck and neck at the top and Rovers and Airdrie were both in with a shout. As Rovers won their second last match at Dundee United by 4-1 they only needed to draw their last home match to accompany Raith Rovers upstairs and this they comfortably did against Montrose by 1-1, the scoring hero of the day being again Tommy Kiernan. Everybody connected with the Club was elated that they had amassed forty-eight points to Raith Rovers fifty-nine with near neighbours Airdrieonians one point behind. A pleasing aspect was in the influx of new players with new star Tommy Kiernan a hero with sixteen goals in his first nineteen games. Great credit was also due to new boys Louden, McLetchie, Love and Burke.

The Supporters Club organised a Promotion Dance in the Town Hall on the 23rd of May and the A.G.M. was held on the 9th of July. With the team in the First League again, season tickets were expected to go well at £2.2s for ground and

Promotion winning officials, players and supporters at Coatbridge Town Hall

A happy group taken at the Promotion Dance

164

reserve stand (£1.10s for ladies) ground and No. 1 stand £1.5s, ground only 15/-, O.A.P. 10/- and boys up to fourteen 3/-. It was also agreed that Rovers were to run a reserve team in the new League Combination composed of First League clubs which took the place of the old Scottish Alliance. This meant that there would be football every Saturday at Cliftonhill Park during the season. Chairman Eddie McLaren and Secretary/Manager, Webber Lees and their co-Directors then buckled to the signing of suitable players for the First League programme.

Season 1938/39
The opening First League game was scheduled for Arbroath and this turned out to be no pushover with the 'Red Lichties' winning by 3-2. Tommy Kiernan and Willie Love showed that they had not lost their scoring touch but this was not enough and it was obvious that the months ahead would require much effort. Rovers were represented by Robertson, Waddell, Beath, Sharp, Miller, McLetchie, Burke, Kiernan, Love, Bell and Loudon.

For the first home League game of the season against St. Johnstone, the Supporters' Club presented a St. Andrew's Cross flag and it was unfurled before the game which resulted in a 3-2 defeat. On the following Wednesday, Arbroath visited Coatbridge in the return match which also ended up 3-2 but this time in favour of Rovers. A trip down to Ayr found the points shared in a 1-1 draw before news came of the retiral of the Grand Old Man of the Club, Simon Scott, as a Director. He was one of the Founders of the Club in 1882 and had served the team as player, match secretary, honorary secretary, committee man and Director for an amazing fifty-six years almost to the day. He was also a noted cricketer first with Drumpellier and latterly with Stenhousemuir and acted as Professional for the latter club for a period. He also won the 'Muir batting average for twenty-one successive years. The Club was the lesser for his going although he was still to take a lively interest in the affairs of the Club for the remainder of his life.

Partick Thistle were next visitors at Coatbridge and in front of an enthusiastic 8,000 crowd the home team won 3-1 whilst Falkirk were visited the following week but the 'Bairns' won by the odd goal in seven. Things were no better the following week with a 4-0 reverse at Perth against St. Johnstone and it was clear that Jocky Robertson was being missed in goal. At the same time the forwards were finding goal scoring in the upper League more difficult than in the Second Division. Tom Kiernan was top scorer with five out of seven games. Things looked bleak on the following Saturday when Johnny Bell was declared unfit with Dempsey taking his place in an otherwise unchanged team. Hibs won by the only goal of the match, thus plunging Rovers to the foot of the table.

Bell was to return for the next match against St. Mirren at Love Street and in this game, drawn 1-1, Kiernan was next to be injured and unavailable for the home match against Celtic. This was lost by 8-1, firmly planting Rovers at the bottom of the League.

The disasters appeared to be piling up and 17,000 fans saw the hapless team lose captain Waddell in the first ten minutes of the match at Cathkin which eventually Thirds won by 4-0 before Motherwell confirmed Rovers' bottom place in the League by winning 4-3 at Coatbridge. Queen's Park were visitors the following week and won by 3-1 leaving the Committee wringing their hands in despair at the ineptitude of their team.

For the trip over to Hamilton, Rovers' bad luck continued with Waddell incapacitated in the first half and limping as a passenger on the wing for the remainder of the game which Hamilton eventually won 2-1 and the return of Robertson in goal wasn't favoured with good fortune. He had even worse luck the following week at Cliftonhill when Rangers ran out easy winners by 7-2, although it was good to see Tommy Kiernan getting back among the goal scorers. This ended a six defeats-in-a-row sequence, making the Club's position at the foot of the First Division very serious.

In an attempt to stem the tide, Alan McClory, the erstwhile Motherwell goalkeeper, was signed in time to make his debut against Queen of the South at Coatbridge along with Jimmy McClure, on loan from Kilmarnock, taking Liddell's place at centre half. This seemed to do the trick for the team ran out good winners in an entertaining match by 2-1 and the following week also at home the team were most unfortunate to lose by the narrowest possible margin against the Hearts who won by dint of a first half goal. The next match was a trip down to Kilmarnock — never a happy hunting ground — and so it again proved with Killie winning 4-2.

The 'Bully Wee' were next visitors for Coatbridge and, after a sticky first half when no goals were scored, Rovers stepped up a gear to win in the end by 3-0 showing that there was a glimmer of fight left in the team. A narrow 2-1 defeat was the result at Aberdeen the following week and the team continued their spirited fight back with a fighting, well-earned draw at Stark's Park against Raith Rovers by 1-1 to move up to second bottom place. Another draw, this time at home by 3-3 against Ayr United, retained that position and the upturn in fortunes continued in Glasgow against Partick Thistle in a 3-1 victory. In icy conditions against Falkirk in the first match of the New Year, the 'Bairns' won out the park by three clear goals which dropped Rovers back to the bottom rung of the ladder.

The following day at Motherwell saw the home team win rather easily by 3-1 and the following Wednesday the players, battling for survival in the upper League,

The Directors Box 1936.

defeated St. Mirren in a rip-roaring game by 2-1. The Scottish Cup Tie at Pittodrie against Aberdeen was lost only by a second half goal in a match which was alway interesting and close, even up to the final whistle. The following Wednesday the return match against Celtic at Parkhead found Rovers wanting once again by a 4-1 margin.

The defence kept losing goals as if they didn't matter in the next game at Coatbridge against Third Lanark and ended up 4-2 down but in Edinburgh, Hibernians found the team with more spirit and the half time score of 2-1 was well defended in the second half to become the final result. Despite this good result and a similar score at Hampden against Queen's Park the following week, the team were still anchored at the bottom of the League but a resounding 5-0 victory over County rivals Hamilton Accies, when all goals were scored in the first half, was enough to move Rovers into the heady position of third bottom due to the results by the other teams in similar difficulties.

Despite three victories on the trot, which was by far the best performance of the entire season so far, the visit to Ibrox against Rangers ended up hopelessly. An unchanged team, playing in black and white stripes for the day, lost equally convincingly by 5-0 to Rangers. Try as they might Queen of the South couldn't gain revenge for their earlier defeat but fought back to a creditable 3-3 draw at Palmerston.

The Wednesday match at Tynecastle against Hearts had a 5.15 p.m. kick-off and the 4,000 fans were treated to a fine display by the home team who ran out winners by 2-0. But glory be! Rovers bounced back the following week against Kilmarnock at Coatbridge by 6-1 with Tommy Kiernan scoring the first hat-trick of the season and the team looking to climb higher in the League. This they did the following week against Clyde in a no scoring draw and fourth bottom place was attained with only two matches to go.

A bit of light relief in the shape of the Lanarkshire Cup saw the 'Diamonds' win very easily with three second half goals and it was all down to a fighting finish to retain First League status. These games were both at home and both won. The first was against Aberdeen where a Tommy Kiernan goal with only four minutes to go was sufficient to keep the points at Coatbridge, which virtually assured Rovers of remaining 'upstairs' for the following season. The final match against already relegated Raith Rovers was played to a nail-biting finish with a nervous 2-1 scoreline for the home team who ended up fourth bottom on thirty points, one ahead of St. Mirren, Queen of the South gained twenty-seven and Raith Rovers twenty-two, being the relegated teams.

However, a bit of good fortune followed when the League Management Committee met and awarded Rovers £50 compensation for the loss of revenue owing to their game on the 25th March with Heart of Midlothian at Tynecastle being postponed, as it was the venue for the Clyde -v- Hibernian Cup Semi Final.

And so into the summer and the close season during which several important League decisions were taken to discuss reconstruction of the First and Second Divisions. Both Leagues were to continue under the present system but a Special Meeting was to be arranged before the 1939/40 season started to suspend the rules relating to Relegation and Promotion.

A temporary rule was to be made whereby the two bottom clubs in the Second Division were not to be re-elected at the end of that season whilst the top Second Division club was to be promoted and the three bottom First Division clubs relegated. This would give two leagues of eighteen clubs each, whereupon relegation and promotion was to be reintroduced as under the then current system.

Alan McClory was signed as a fully fledged Rover after his period on loan and Albert Degnan was to add considerably to the scoring potential of the forward line.

At the A.G.M. Eddie McLaren was re-elected Chairman and the two vacancies in the Directorate caused by the retiral of Simon Scott and Hugh Munro were left vacant meanwhile. The Club also splashed out £500 to Hibernian for the signature of centre half Jimmy Miller and so the players and staff went on holiday looking forward to the new season despite the current, rather unreal atmosphere with continual talk of War in Europe.

CHAPTER EIGHT

THE LOST FORTIES

Season 1939/40
On the 12th August, Ayr United opened the season at Coatbridge and Rovers immediately got on the scoreline by 5-0 with Jackie Burke scoring a hat-trick. Fans and players alike were delighted with such a good start by the following team — McClory, Waddell, Beath, Sharp, Miller, McLetchie, Degnan, Kiernan, Burke, Bell and Loudon. Two succeeding away defeats both by 2-1 took some of the shine off that good start however. First of all Partick Thistle and then Ayr United succeeded in lowering Rovers' standard before 7,000 fans saw St. Mirren fight out a dour no-scoring draw at Coatbridge. During the week ex-Baillie John Kirk was co-opted a Director and his considerable business experience was viewed to be greatly in Rovers' favour. On the 2nd September, Mr. Kirk saw his new team win confidently by 5-3 against Hibs in Edinburgh overcoming a 2-1 deficit at half time. With new signing George Campbell from Partick Thistle making a scoring debut, this result placed Rovers in a comfortable mid-league position.

On Sunday, 3rd September, Prime Minister Chamberlain announced to a disbelieving nation that Britain was at war with Germany and on the 6th September the S.F.A. cancelled all competitions. It was left to the Scottish League to arrange friendlies to take place from the 13th onwards. The Government ordered that all entertainments, both indoor and outdoor, should cease and that functions which gathered people together in confined spaces such as football matches, should be banned. All players' contracts were suspended as from the outbreak of war and the S.F.A. interests were to be looked after by two specially appointed Committees called the 'Finance and Insurance' and the 'Emergency' Committees.

Opinions were varied as to whether friendly football would be viable. Rovers' Board were of the opinion that the country would be better without friendly matches and were not satisfied that the public would attend such games in sufficient numbers to meet with the expense in players' insurance and all the other expenses necessary. Secretary of the S.F.A., George Graham, did not agree with this view and he felt that the restrictions on outdoor entertainment would be modified and that league and cup football would be permitted.

There was then a welter of Meetings of the various Committees and Clubs in conjunction with the Government. Eventually, after the dust had settled, it was proposed that league football in Scotland be conducted under two competitions embracing sixteen clubs in each. Rovers were to be involved with Airdrieonians, Ayr United, Celtic, Clyde, Dumbarton, Hamilton, Kilmarnock, Motherwell, Morton, Partick Thistle, Queen of the South, Queen's Park, Rangers, St. Mirren and Third Lanark and temporary rules were to take the place of the then current rules for the carrying-on of the two competitions.

In the east of the country a league comprising Aberdeen, Alloa, Arbroath, Cowdenbeath, Dundee United, Dundee, Dunfermline Athletic, East Fife, Falkirk, Heart of Midlothian, Hibernian, King's Park, Leith Athletic or St. Bernards, Raith Rovers, Stenhousemuir and St. Johnstone was arranged.

With the phoney war well advanced and the anticipated invasion looking less likely by the day, it was clear that the initial restrictions could be amended. The

Home Office was satisfied with the arrangements and had relaxed the earlier stringent conditions on travel so far as local and district groups were concerned on the basis that the Clubs concerned should be able to travel and return home on the same day. There was also talk of players being temporarily transferred to assist those players who were at work or residing some distance from the Club. To reduce the strain already thrown on the Post Office by the War, Football Pools transactions were suspended.

The new League arrangements were scheduled to take place from the 21st of October and, although there was a threat that a sufficient number of clubs, particularly from the East, would vote against the plan to ensure that it did not receive the necessary two-thirds majority, the eventual vote was thirty-one to seven for the two-league plan to be put in hand. The only clubs who voted against the proposals were those who were to be left out of the competition, namely, Brechin City, East Stirlingshire, Edinburgh City, Forfar Athletic, Leith Athletic or St. Bernard's and Montrose.

New rules were drawn up and they were to provide that in any football competition in which any Club took part no Club was to allow its interests to interfere with the work of 'National Importance'. Clubs were not able to pay players more than £2 per week plus actual travelling expenses. Players were not to be compensated for loss of wages other than football wages caused through injury while playing. Gate drawings after expenses were to be divided equally between the competing clubs and a guarantee of £50 to be given to the visiting club, which was half the previous season. Matches should only be played on Saturdays or on holidays recognised in towns in which both competing clubs were located. At the end of the competition no Club was to be considered as Winners or regarded as Champions for the season.

Regarding registration of players, clubs were also able to register the player of another club without procuring a transfer assuming the club concerned consented. Such players' registration was to automatically cease at the close of each season unless sooner cancelled. This was a system geared to suit some clubs more than others. Rovers were destined to have their share of 'guest' players in the next few years.

To enable players and teams to play themselves back into fitness, various games were fixed up for the 14th of October, Rovers playing at Motherwell in the Lanarkshire Cup but the 'Steelmen' were too good by a 4-1 margin. The new Western League kicked-off on the 21st of October as arranged and Rovers visited St. Mirren to win by 2-1. The Saints were assisted by three Anglo Scots — Wilson, Milne and Caskie, and their goal was scored from the penalty spot in the second half. The first match at home in the new competition was also a 2-1 victory for Rovers with a Bobby Beath penalty kick being sufficient to see Rovers go top of the League.

The left back was not so happy the following week at Dumbarton when he missed a penalty and Miller was also off for 20 minutes. Neither of these facts were helpful to Rovers who eventually lost by a 4-1 margin. However, it was back to winning ways the next week at home against Third Lanark by two Tommy Kiernan goals to nothing and the same player scored the only goal of the match at Firhill to see Rovers third top of the new set-up.

Better was to follow with Celtic being defeated 3-2 in an exciting game at Cliftonhill and the high-flying Queen of the South were next on the fixture list. They were currently hovering at the top of the League and in a hard fought match

Queens were worthy winners by 4-2. Not to be outdone, Rovers came back with a bang against Queen's Park at home the next week thanks to two Beath penalties, eventually winning comfortably enough by 5-2.

The trip into Ibrox to table-topping Rangers was billed as a "clash of the two teams in form" and a worthy gate of 13,000 saw a contested match, with all the goals being scored in the second half. Rangers won 2-1 but with Rovers the more impressive side on the day. Third spot in the League table was confirmed the following week when Morton were soundly thrashed by 3-1. Hopes of finishing the year on a high note were dashed when despite two Burke goals Kilmarnock won 3-2 in a very close contest which Rovers really should have won.

New Year's Day match on the Monday against Airdrieonians saw old pal Willie Bruce playing with the 'Diamonds' and 10,000 fans saw Rovers comprehensively defeat their close neighbours by a 4-1 margin and the team giving one of their finest displays of the season. This good form continued the following day when Motherwell were First Foots and the strong running Rovers' team overwhelmed the Motherwell men by four clear goals consolidating their position as fourth top and overhauling Motherwell in the process.

Captain Waddell was not fit for the visit to Shawfield against Clyde who routed the Cliftonhillers by five goals without reply. More suffering was to follow at Douglas Park the following week where Hamilton won a close match by 2-1.

All teams at this time were suffering loss of players as they were called-up or volunteered for Service in the Army. Immediately after the Hamilton match, Albert Degnan signed up with R.A.O.C. and Tommy Kiernan took to the Royal Engineers and their availability from now on would be dependent on where they were trained and their eventual posting. After a meeting of the Scottish League and the Scottish Football Association, it was agreed that a Regional Cup Competition would be run as a substitute for the Scottish Cup. There was much controversy about this competition and within a week this idea was scrapped.

Whilst these deliberations by the Ruling Bodies were taking place the visit to Cathkin found a 2-2 draw before a Degnan hat-trick assisted in a fine victory over Partick Thistle by 4-2. Eventually agreement was reached between the League and S.F.A. to promote a cup competition and to provide a trophy and medals. There was to be a condition that 2½% was to be deducted from the semi-final and final gates as a fund to compensate the six clubs excluded from this competition.

Rovers were drawn at home against Aberdeen. This game turned out to be an old-fashioned Cup tie with the fans on the edge of their seats to the last minute. The match eventually ended up all square at 3-3 and the following week at Aberdeen a Johnny Bell goal in the first half was enough to take Rovers through to the second round. Old cup foes Kilmarnock were the opponents in the second round in another away match and Rovers, who never recovered from losing the first goal, ended up 2-1 down.

Back in the League the following week and League leaders Rangers' visit to Coatbridge found them in rampant form, racing to a 3-0 lead in 20 minutes. Not to be outdone Rovers rolled up their sleeves and in a pulsating first 45 minutes, pulled back to a share of six goals when referee Scott blew half time. The fans sat back awaiting another avalanche of goals in the second half but despite the game being well contested, there was no further scoring and fans and players alike went home happy after a good display. This good form was continued at the Tail of the Bank against Morton with a 3-2 victory but again old bogey team Kilmarnock ran up their third win of the season this time by 6-2. Immediately following this game,

1940 "Evening Times" Propaganda Cartoon for D.O.R.A.(Defence of the Realm Act)

Kilmarnock centre half Jimmy McClure was signed on loan for his second spell with the Club.

April started with a visit on the first Wednesday by St. Mirren and new boy McClure got off to a fine start with a goal in the first half and the team winning 2-1. The following Saturday, Airdrieonians gained revenge for their earlier defeat by winning by the only goal of the match. The following two Wednesdays were of mixed fortune with first of all Ayr United winning at Ayr by 2-0 before Dumbarton were defeated 3-1 at Coatbridge. The Clyde team had done so well against the Rovers' team earlier in the season that they came confidently to Cliftonhill but goals by Burke and Bell in the first half were sufficient to send them home pointless.

The following Tuesday Celtic visited Coatbridge and in a close match Rovers were handicapped by the loss of right back Waddell for more than half an hour with concussion. His absence was enough to account for the 3-1 victory by the Celts.

A further defeat took place at the hands of Hamilton Accies by 2-1 before, on the last day of April, Queen's Park were defeated 3-1 at Hampden. There were great hopes that the team would finish in the top four of the League with only two games to go, but unfortunately both were lost by 3-2 to Queen of the South at home and 2-1 at Motherwell in the last game of the season. This left Rovers in sixth position out of the sixteen team league.

With the War continuing in Europe and the mobilisation of all able-bodied manpower the Football Authorities in Scotland decreed that League football would be suspended during the following season. This decision was reached at the

A.G.M. in June but it was emphasised that there would be no bar to Clubs forming local competitions. The Office Bearers would retain office until the first Annual General Meeting following the termination of hostilities and the temporary Rules, adopted the previous year for the running of the Regional League Competition, were recinded. The registration of all players, as at 30th April 1940, would remain in operation until further notice and further discussions then took place throughout the summer to come to some arrangement for senior football. This was unpopular with clubs and fans alike.

In July, a decision was made to invite Heart of Midlothian, Hibernian and Falkirk to take part in a Competition which would include the leading Clubs in the West of Scotland. The Meeting was called by James Brown of Rangers F.C. and attended by Chairmen of all First Division Clubs, which took part in the Western Section of the Regional Competition, with the exception of Queen of the South. It was agreed to limit the Competition to sixteen clubs, namely, Albion Rovers, Ayr United, Celtic, Clyde, Falkirk, Hamilton Academical, Hearts, Hibernians, Morton, Motherwell, Partick Thistle, Queen's Park, Kilmarnock, Rangers, St. Mirren and Third Lanark.

Football matches were to be harder hit by Entertainment Tax. From now on the 6d. admission would be taxed by 2d. and 1/- admission which was presently taxed at 2d. would be 4d. and Stand prices were to be increased in proportion. This Tax, which had first been introduced during the First World War, was viewed with some dismay by Club Treasurers.

The August Meeting of Coatbridge Town Council endorsed the Licences of Cinemas in the Town with the order that admittance would be refused without patrons carrying their gas mask. The Chief Constable extended this to cover football and this ruling spread to all other centres of population. This decision was taken in time to be effective at Rovers' first home game in the new season.

Season 1940/41
The season opened on the 10th August in the Western Regional League with St. Mirren the opponents the match being played at Ibrox. The Rovers' team came home kicking themselves for only drawing 1-1 and innumerable chances were missed by the forwards and even Bobby Beath missed a penalty kick. Local boy, Charlie Gavin, made his debut at centre half and ex-Celt Carruth at inside forward. Rovers were represented by — McClory, Waddell, Beath, Sharp, Gavin, McLetchie, Taggart, Carruth, Burke, Bell and Degnan. Goalkeeper George Hunter from Kilmarnock who had played so well against Rovers in previous seasons was fixed up for goal and Johnnie Gould was signed from Arbroath to play at inside forward against Third Lanark in the match when gas masks became a necessary part of a football fan's apparel. Rovers won this one by 6-1 and new boy Gould celebrated his signing for the Coatbridge Club with a second half hat-trick.

Tommy Kiernan was temporarily transferred to Chelsea and Bob Johnstone to Third Lanark, but Jimmy McClure was again signed on from Kilmarnock and was the only change in the team to meet Celtic at Cliftonhill. Ex-Celt Carruth scored in the first half but Celtic won convincingly in the end by 3-1. McClory was re-introduced in goal for the match against Airdrie at Broomfield but all Rovers could put up were two penalty goals by Sharp, which were not enough to stop Airdrie winning 3-2. The following week all was forgiven when the team raced to a 5-1 lead at half time over Falkirk at home but this was very much a game of two parts, with Falkirk coming out in the second half and scoring freely to make the game an astonishing 5-5 at full time. A more normal sized scoreline took place the following week against Hibs at 1-1 before Motherwell were soundly defeated by 3-1 at Coatbridge.

Neilly Dewar, centre forward of Third Lanark and Scotland, was signed on the dotted line and appeared at centre against Morton for the trip to Cappielow. This was not a happy introduction, the forward line was very disjointed and the team eventually lost 4-0 with the heads well down. They remained down over the next two games with a 1-0 defeat at home against Clyde and then a 2-0 defeat away against Rangers. Charlie Gavin was transferred to Clyde but on the credit side, former 'keeper David Hanson — who had returned to the Club after being discharged from the Forces with war wounds — took his place between the sticks on the 2nd November against Dumbarton. There was considerable bad language from the partisan Dumbarton support and eventually police were called to this match. Referee Horsborough from Midlothian eventually abandoned the game in the fifty-eighth minute with Rovers winning by dint of a Johnny Bell goal. Hamilton Accies ran up a 4-1 scoreline at Coatbridge in the first of three defeats on the trot with Hearts winning the following week 3-1 in Edinburgh and St. Mirren 2-0 at Coatbridge despite the introduction of Alec Miller, ex-Preston North End and Celtic in the half back line.

St. Andrew's Day saw Third Lanark beaten 3-0 on their own patch by a second half flurry of activity by Rovers, when all goals were scored, and the following week Peter Blane from Dennistoun Waverley had a scoring debut in the 1-1 draw against Partick Thistle. Celtic won 2-0 at Parkhead before Hibernian visited Coatbridge to go 2-1 up at half time only to find a spirited fight back by Rovers' players keeping the points at Coatbridge by 4-3.

The Scottish League Management Committee made arrangements for a League Cup Competition to commence on the 1st March on a home-and-home principle with four sections of four teams each. The second section in which Rovers were drawn included Hamilton, Morton and St. Mirren.

The last game of 1940 was played at Falkirk with the home team winning 2-0 against a feckless Rovers' bunch. Due to bad weather conditions the first game played in the New Year was away from home on the 18th January against Clyde. The team showed all signs of rustiness with Sharp even missing a penalty in the 4-2 defeat.

All Coatbridge was saddened on the 25th January with the news of the death of one of the Founders of the Club. Simon Scott, that great servant of the Club as player, Committee man, Director and mentor, passed away at his home in Dunbeth Road and the further bad news was that his brother also a former Rover, was taken seriously ill on the same day and removed to hospital. At the home match that day against Rangers both teams wore black arm-bands and the Town Band played 'Abide with Me' prior to the commencement of the game. Rangers were too good for Rovers in this one in a resounding 7-2 victory.

A third heavy defeat in a row was handed out by Queen's Park by 6-1 at Hampden and the cup of woe was overflowing at Dumbarton with another loss, this time by 4-1. The team were struggling and Davie Hanson must have wished he had stayed away at the War, losing seventeen goals in three matches. Once more the team was shaken up with no fewer than eight positional changes from the previous match and also the introduction of inside forward Farrelly from Northampton saw an improvement in a 2-0 victory at Hamilton but both goals, including one from the new signing, were scored in the last five minutes.

The 1st March duly arrived and the League Cup Competition got under way. As in the League earlier, the inaugural match was against St. Mirren away from home and with Willie Bruce back at centre half in an otherwise unchanged team, the Saints ran out winners by 4-1. Joe Curruth's moment of glory arrived in the next match against Morton when he scored four goals in the 5-2 victory but for the rest of the League Cup Competition it was all downhill. At Hamilton a 1-1 draw was the last point to be gained from the Competition with defeats following at the hands of St. Mirren, by 2-1, Morton, 5-1 and finally Hamilton by 3-0 saw Rovers finish bottom of the section. Waddell missed the Hamilton game, as his mother had died, but he was back for the Hearts' visit in their 3-0 victory at Coatbridge. Willie Bruce's father, Jimmy, himself an old Rover, died the following week with the result that the big centre half was missing for the home game against Morton. This ended up with both teams sharing six goals. The next day news came that Adam Scott had died making it a very bleak 1941 so far for Rovers and their Support.

This mood was not lightened at all by Airdrie's 4-2 victory at Coatbridge and eventually the replayed match against Dumbarton saw the Sons walking off with victory at 2-1. When the earlier match had been abandoned, Rovers had been winning by the only goal of the game. The team missed Alec Sharp's bite in midfield following his transfer to Partick Thistle and the season ended with three very heavy defeats, starting with 6-0 against Motherwell in the last League match before Third Lanark won 5-2 in Glasgow and 4-1 at Coatbridge in the Summer Cup.

Thus another season came to its conclusion. There was none of the euphoria connected with the previous season and at the end of the day fans and players alike couldn't play the last game quickly enough.

There was now considerable concern regarding the financial stability of the present match arrangements and several Meetings were held to discuss the future of the Club. At the A.G.M., it was noted that the Club had made a loss of £885 over the previous season and there was a large overdraft at the bank. Eddie McLaren stood down as Chairman and John Wilson took over for the new season. The Directors agreed to continue despite the difficult circumstances and several new signings were made for the new season, including Tom McConnell as Trainer.

Season 1941/42
The League Competition was renamed the Southern Regional League and the first shock came before the season even started when long-serving Andy Waddell announced his retirement, thus breaking a partnership with Bobby Beath, which had lasted since 1932 virtually uninterrupted. Young trialist, Alec 'Chic' Muir from Burnbank Athletic lined up in Waddell's place for the opening match against Partick Thistle and also making his debut was Jock Calder, high-scoring centre forward from Greenock Morton. Otherwise the team was as the previous season and the campaign opened with a fiercely contested 2-2 draw in which the new centre scored on his debut. Rovers' team was — Hanson, Muir, Beath, Blane, Trialist, McLetchie, Burke, Kiernan, Calder, Loudon and Degnan.

Corporal Tommy Kiernan was unavailable for team duty for the visit to Celtic Park and Johnny Bell was drafted in his place with another newcomer, Lang from Queen of the South, taking up the left wing position. With Celtic going into a strong position at half time leading 2-0, the Rovers' fight-back in the second half was to no avail and the green and whites ran out winners by 4-2. After his successful trial games, 'Chic' Muir was signed in time to line up in the second home match against

Hibernians, together with centre half McNeil from Armadale Thistle. The inexperience of these boys, however, was exploited to the full by the Edinburgh team and, despite the score being 2-2 at half time, Hibs swamped the homesters to an 8-3 drubbing.

Tom Dunsmore from Luton Town was signed during the following week and he set about attaining fitness but was not considered for the Falkirk game when, with an unchanged team, the Committee showed great strength of character and the players responded with a fine 4-2 victory at Brockville. Centre forward Calder showing his reputation as a goal scorer, was well founded by a double in this match which gave him five goals in his first four games.

The Airdrieonians next visited Cliftonhill but the unchanged team this time lost by 3-2 whereupon the Directors considered some new faces were necessary. John Thomson was signed from Hamilton and for the trip to Motherwell played at right half in a match in which Dunsmore made his debut at outside right and Joe Burke was re-introduced at inside right. This change in personnel seemed to have done the trick at half time with Rovers leading 2-0 but Motherwell took a grip of the game in the second half and eventually ran out winners by 5-3.

Changes were the order of the day for the St. Mirren visit to Coatbridge. Blane was introduced at inside right, Burke going to the wing, and Dunsmore was slotted into Bobby Beath's position in what for him was a rare absence. The new formation clicked at once and three goals were scored without reply. This good form was continued in the next game against Third Lanark, although the team lines showed six positional changes from the previous game, the most notable of which being the introduction of Johnny Black, signed from Third Lanark, at centre half. Rovers were 3-1 up at half time and another Calder goal in the second half made the eventual score 4-3 for Rovers in what was a very exciting and exhilarating match. This was Calder's tenth goal in eight matches and he was the new hero of the fans.

For the Rangers visit, George Loudon was re-introduced on the left wing in place of Lang, otherwise the team was unchanged but Rangers won this one by the only goal of the match. Queen's Park scored two without reply at Hampden before the team was again re-vamped for the visit to Dumbarton. New signing Kirkwood from Ayr United was introduced and Dunsmore, showing his versatility, popped up in a number 11 jersey. Perhaps because of all these changes the team rhythm was nowhere in sight and the 'Sons' won easily by 5-2. The visit to Hamilton the following week was not looked on with any great hopes and five changes in personnel again did not augur well. But as often happens in these circumstances the new formation clicked at once. A 3-0 lead at half time was not flattering and even the missing of a penalty by Bobby Beath didn't stop the team scoring a resounding 6-1 victory with Calder notching a hat-trick, Bell scoring a double and Beath converting from the penalty spot.

The visit by Hearts the following week saw the Edinburgh team steal the points by 2-1 in a match which Rovers should have won by a barrowload. This time the sinner was Jock Calder who missed a penalty at a crucial stage and worse was to follow with three successive defeats starting with Morton winning 5-1 at Coatbridge before two visits to Glasgow saw first of all, Clyde win 4-2 and Partick Thistle 5-1. Calder was now on sixteen goals from the same number of games but he was to miss the visit by Celtic with Burke taking his place. The lads from Parkhead were shocked by Rovers going into a 2-1 lead at half time and further shocked when the score stood at 4-1 for Rovers in the 70th minute with the fans yelling for more but in a hectic finish the Celts equalised making the final score 4-4.

For the trip to Edinburgh the following week against Hibernian, Rovers introduced trialist Willie Findlay from Blantyre Victoria and had a new outside left in Carter from Derby. Both debutants scored in this match but Hibs ran out 5-2 winners. Their task was made much easier as Rovers had to play Johnny Black in goal as keeper Hanson missed his train connection and did not arrive before kick-off. The goalkeeper was back for duty the next week against Falkirk at home in a match which saw Findlay play his first game as a signed player and both he and Carter again got on the scoreline in a 3-1 victory.

The return match against St. Mirren found Saints winning 4-2 and the last match in 1941 saw the defenders do a Santa Claus act to the Third Lanark forwards who rattled in three goals to Rovers' solitary counter by Findlay. This match saw the introduction of Johnny McIlhatton from Ardeer Recreation and his signing allowed Joe Burke to be granted a free transfer. For the New Year Day match at Broomfield, new scoring star Findlay and new boy McIlhatton formed the right wing. However it was Airdrie who first showed their aptitude and the Broomfield boys quickly rattled in three goals which was the half time score. The half time cuppa must have had some Ne'er Day spirit in it as Rovers came out to swamp the opposition to win the fiercely contested match by 4-3. Willie Findlay's winner in this match gave him five goals in his five senior matches and soon the fans were not missing their absent soldier star Tommy Kiernan.

Two days later Motherwell were First Foots and won by 5-1 the only point of note for Rovers being McIlhatton's first goal for the Coatbridge Club. Jock Calder got back on the goal standard against Queen's Park in the 4-1 victory. His hat-trick gave him nineteen goals from twenty matches. There was then a break of some three weeks due to bad weather conditions before the next match at Greenock on the 14th February found Rovers completely out of match practice and the Morton scored eight goals without reply. Their cause was not helped any by Blane injuring his elbow and being off for a period and to cap a black day for the Coatbridge Club, Johnny Black was ordered off.

The League Cup competition now re-surfaced and again Hanson didn't appear for duty and Clyde loaned their reserve goalkeeper, Fraser, for the day but despite this the team got off to a good start with a 4-3 victory. During the next week, Bobby Johnstone was signed from St. Mirren and he took his place between the sticks in the away match against Airdrieonians but the second match of the Cup competition went Airdrie's way by a 3-1 margin. Partick Thistle had an easy 5-2 victory in Glasgow before the second leg matches turned out hopelessly for the Coatbridge Club. Airdrie drew 1-1 at Coatbridge but Clyde comprehensively won 7-3 in Glasgow and the Competition ended for Rovers with another 1-1 draw at home against Partick Thistle leaving them once more bottom of their Section.

Back on League business the following week revenge was gained over Clyde by 4-3 at Coatbridge after which centre forward Calder was transferred back to his first love Morton. Two draws of 2-2 in Edinburgh against Hearts and 4-4 against Hamilton at home saw the visit to Ibrox and the playing of two trialists in the inside forward positions. This was not good enough against the mighty Rangers and in a close match the score was 2-1 for the Govan team.

The final game in the League took place on the 2nd May with Dumbarton playing out a no scoring draw in a typical end-of-season fixture. There was then a break of some three weeks before the Summer Cup Competition played on a home-and-away basis. Queen's Park were the first round opponents and in an excellent Cup tie Rovers won convincingly by 2-0 which was just enough to take them through to the next round on a 5-4 aggregate as they lost the return match at Hampden by 4-3. In the second round Hearts were the opponents and the luck of the draw saw Rovers have ground advantage first and they took full use of this to lead 3-0 which was just as well as the return match in Edinburgh ended up 2-0 for Hearts.

It was then on to the semi-final match against Rangers at Hampden but a place in the final against Hibs was not to be as Rangers won this one after a strongly contested match, by 3-2. This Competition was a late financial bonanza with £1,200 each being shared by finalists Rangers and Hibs. Rovers' share of the semi-final was £292 whilst Hibs and Motherwell, the other semi-finalists, shared £287. A total of £934 each went to Rangers and Hibs as a result of their final tie and the pool produced £90.6.4d. for each of the sixteen Clubs in the Contest. Thus the curtain fell on the season and with many of the players in uniform and no sign of a cessation of hostilities it was obvious that the next season would be much as before.

Season 1942/43
Most of the previous season's stalwarts were fixed up for the beginning of the season and a smattering of new faces led by George Mudie, who had made three appearances in the Summer Cup, and new centre George Wilkie from Queen's Park from whom much was looked. A notable 'new boy' was ex-Celtic and Scotland outside left Frank Murphy, a Coatbridge boy with a grand reputation. When the opening day arrived on the 8th August, the visit to Hibernians saw Rovers represented by Hanson, Dunsmore, Beath, Blane, Sharp, McLetchie, McIlhatton, Mudie, Wilkie, Bell and Loudon, and despite scoring a first half goal through 'Cock' Loudon, Hibs scored three in the second half to make the final score 3-1. For the first home match against Falkirk, Murphy made his debut with Mudie being dropped, but the Bairns proved to be too strong winning 4-1 in what turned out to be Davie Hanson's last match for the Club. The new goalkeeper was Anderson, signed from Arbroath but also with experience at Broomfield, and he put up the shutters in a no scoring draw at Love Street before Tommy Kiernan made his first appearance of the season and scored against Motherwell in the 2-1 defeat at home.

Against Airdrieonians at Broomfield, Airdrie, two up at half time went to 3-0 and it looked all over bar the shouting but, ably led by Murphy who scored two goals, Rovers fought back and in a rousing finish the match ended up all square with a share of eight goals. Another division of the points at 2-2 with Third Lanark was the disappointing outcome the following week at Cliftonhill with Murphy again scoring a double. Willie Kilpatrick was signed from Chelsea during the week and the ex-Ranger lined up against his old team-mates at Ibrox with Dunsmore donning the No. 5 jersey. These changes were unsuccessful in producing the desired result and Rangers won easily by 3-0. Queen's Park then lost 3-1 at the 'Brig with ex-Spider Wilkie scoring the final goal.

In a much changed team the following week at home against Dumbarton and despite leading 3-2 at half time, the 'Sons' overran the Rovers in the second half to win 4-3 but the next match against Hamilton saw McIlhatton get on the scoreline for the first time this season with a double and Wilkie scoring his third goal in three matches to assist Rovers to a 3-1 win. That good score was immediately nullified by the 5-1 defeat through at Edinburgh against Hearts and the 2-1 defeat against Morton at Greenock.

There was a distinct lack of fight by the players and led by a Dougie Wallace hat-trick, Clyde crushed the Coatbridge challenge 5-1 and Partick Thistle continued to pile on the goals against the struggling Rovers by 6-2 in Glasgow before Celtic were due their annual visit to Coatbridge. The Glasgow team quickly ran up a 3-0 scoreline but McIlhatton cut one back before half time. In a stirring second half captain Bell led a tremendous revival to square the match at four each at the end of ninety minutes. Willie Picken was signed from Bradford and he found a place at left back in place of Dunsmore for the visit of Hibernian who won too easily by 4-1 thus completing the double over the Coatbridge side.

Falkirk did likewise the following week winning 7-2 and despite being overwhelmed, the young trialist centre half was signed to take his place the following week in the game against St. Mirren. Jock Stein from Blantyre Victoria helped to put a backbone in the defence and with the leaks plugged at the back, the forwards came on to something like their old form and Tommy Kiernan in only his fourth match of the season scored two goals but missed a penalty which would have given him his hat-trick in the 5-1 victory. Motherwell won the next match by the only goal of the game and in the Rangers match the Glasgow club won 4-0 in a match which was more memorable for the £16 collection taken in aid of Coatbridge Churches than for the football. The Third Lanark defence must have thought it was Christmas courtesy to give out League points as their defence was all at sea in Rovers 3-1 victory.

On New Year's Day, Airdrieonians were trounced 5-3 with Loudon scoring four goals but on the Monday Dumbarton pocketed the points in a 6-1 victory. Rovers played Alec Sharp at centre forward and goalkeeper Waugh from Hearts at Hampden and this scratch lineup clicked from the outset to defeat Queen's Park by 4-1. Tom Kiernan, now based in the south of England, had changed his allegiance from Chelsea to Brentford on loan and he was not to take any further part in the season ahead.

For the match against Hamilton which Rovers lost 3-2 with Loudon scoring Rovers goals, one from a penalty after Frank Murphy missed a penalty earlier on. This was the first of six defeats on the trot in a disappointing run which started when Hearts won 3-1 at Coatbridge despite former player Tommy Lyon returning from Chesterfield and scoring in his debut, Morton won 5-0. Clyde moved into double figures over Rovers this season in a 5-1 victory in which Dougie Wallace scored his second hat-trick of the season against the boys in blue.

The defence lost another five goals against Partick Thistle at Coatbridge the following week with only one in reply before Celtic finished the losing sequence in a 4-0 victory. The Board were having difficulty in fielding a recognised team and with eighteen players on the payroll of H.M. Forces, it was only with the use of many trialists, players on loan or the assistance of Commanding Officers allowing players leave, resulting in teams being fielded. There was no hope of continuity of team selection and when the League Cup matches arrived at the end of February, only Stein retained his position and five others played in different positions from the previous week in a lineup which showed ten positional changes, including new signing Bobby Keyes from Falkirk.

Despite this handicap the 'Sons' were defeated by two Tommy Lyon goals to one and Tom Mooney was signed to take over the outside left position against Falkirk with Bobby Beath making a welcome re-appearance but the Bairns won this one by 1-0. A good point at Greenock in a 1-1 draw was the prelude to wins over Dumbarton by 2-1 and Falkirk by 5-1. This latter game was a personal triumph for centre forward Lyon who scored all Rovers five goals. The last game in the League Cup was a 1-1 draw against Morton when dead-ball expert Mooney scored his first goal for Rovers from the penalty spot.

That ended the season apart from the Summer Cup which again took place at the end of May. This time Rovers went out at the first hurdle losing 1-0 at Coatbridge and 4-0 at Falkirk:

Thus the season came to a swift conclusion but the difficulties of team selection, player availability, coupled with all the war-time restrictions, had made the past year more of a trial than a pleasure. The new season ahead was to be dearer bringing the basic admission charge up from 1/3d to 1/6d and just to underline the difficulty clubs were finding, Manager Webber Lees appealed to supporters to hand over any spare clothing coupons they had to provide stockings and pads for the players. The A.G.M. showed a profit for the year of £128.6.0d. but it was reckoned by Chairman John Wilson and his Board that the season ahead would again be a very difficult one for the Club.

Season 1943/44

The season kicked off on the 14th August against Third Lanark in a home match which Rovers lost 3-1 in a disappointing start with the only goal for the Coatbridge side coming from wing half Sharp. Davie Hanson had been re-signed from Blantyre Victoria and he made his debut in this match which turned out to be his only one of the season. Rovers' team was — Hanson, Dunsmore, Picken, Sharp, Stein, McLetchie, McIlhatton, Sloss, Loudon, Stevenson and Moonie.

Last season's custodian Anderson was re-engaged and was between the sticks to visit Hibernian but couldn't stop the Edinburgh forwards scoring three goals without reply. The third match of the season saw the first victory and Falkirk being defeated 2-1 with trialist McDonald scoring Rovers' first goal. Coatbridge boy Tommy Brady was signed from St. Mirren and played at inside forward for the visit to Motherwell which resulted in a 2-1 defeat but Airdrieonians were defeated at Cliftonhill 2-1 before Partick Thistle inflicted the heaviest defeat so far by 4-0. Centre forward Park was signed from Newcastle and he made an immediate impact by scoring two goals against St. Mirren in a match which ended up disappointingly. Rovers were leading 3-0 at half time but at the end of the match could only achieve a 3-3 draw.

The match at Parkhead saw the Celts win 3-2 before Hamilton ran up a mammoth 7-1 scoreline on their home ground in a match in which Muir made his first appearance of the season, new inside forward McInally from Motherwell made his debut and full back Kilpatrick drafted to fill the No. 10 jersey. Stein, who had been injured in the Hamilton game, missed his first match since signing for Rovers in the visit to Clyde. A goal in each half was sufficient for Rovers to pocket the points with Alec Sharp doing well as deputy centre half.

This was to be an isolated bright point as the next eight matches were all to be lost. The first of these was at home against Dumbarton by 1-0 before Queen's Park won 3-1 at Hampden. Peter Smith from Saltcoats Victoria made his debut in the Rangers visit and 5-1 victory at Coatbridge. The new lad scored Rovers' goal and even Stein's return in this match couldn't stem the tide. The result was closer against Hearts at 2-1 but only because Anderson saved a penalty then Morton had a high scoring 6-2 victory at Greenock. The next game also away from home ended 3-2 in favour of Third Lanark.

An English amateur soldier stationed in Scotland, Freddy Keeble, was introduced at centre forward against Hibs at home and scored both Rovers' goals in the 4-2 defeat. Also introduced in this match was Willie Savage, right back, on loan from Queen of the South. The last of this miserable run of defeats took place at Falkirk by a 4-1 margin with Tom Kiernan making a welcome return to the team at inside forward.

Coming up to Christmas, Motherwell visited Coatbridge and saw Rovers lift their first point in a fighting 2-2 draw which would have been a win but for Kiernan missing from the penalty spot. On Christmas Day, Partick Thistle came to Coatbridge but found Rovers in an uncharitable mood over the piece although they did have a 1-0 lead at half time. However, in the second half McIlhatton started the revival by scoring direct from a corner before Keeble got the winner. Airdrieonians got their own back for the earlier defeat by winning 4-2 at Broomfield and on the Saturday Morton were defeated 4-1 at Coatbridge in a match in which the homesters were never troubled.

A defeat at Love Street by the same 4-1 margin saw Rovers slide to the bottom place in the League. Bottom dogs or not, Celtic knew they were in a match the following week at Coatbridge and after an evenly contested first half, Rovers pushed ahead in the second period and a McInally score ensured the points would stay at Coatbridge by a 2-1 margin. The same team was favoured the following week against Hamilton but the County rivals won 4-2 before Clyde were beaten 2-0 in the third home match on the trot and Jock Stein scored his first goal for Rovers in the first half. The visit to Dumbarton saw a well-earned point at 2-2 before Queen's Park came to Coatbridge to win 5-0 and it was the same score the following week with Rangers winning at Ibrox. The third match in a row when Rovers failed to score saw Hearts pocket the points by the only goal of the match. Young trialist Willie Hannah from Polkemmet Juniors was signed following his display in this game.

With the arrival of March came the League Cup matches and new boy Hannah celebrated his signing by scoring Rovers' first goal in the 3-3 draw at Greenock from the outside left position. Hibernian won 2-1 at Edinburgh before a second point was picked up against Third Lanark in Glasgow by virtue of a 2-2 draw. The return match against Greenock Morton ended up 4-1 for the Clyde coast team and with Hibs winning 2-0 Rovers had no chance of going any further in the Competition. The last game against Third Lanark at Cliftonhill was purely academic although Rovers won this one by 4-2.

Motherwell were the opposition in a 3-3 draw where just under 2,000 fans saw this tame affair bring the season to a close. It was three weeks before the usual Summer Cup Competition saw Rovers paired with Hearts in the first round but there was to be no glory in this Cup run with Hearts winning 5-1 in Edinburgh and 3-2 at Coatbridge.

It had been another difficult season maintaining a good standard and it was not easy to fix-up Juniors as they generally were called-up to H.M. Services soon after signing. Nevertheless, the Directors and scouts were continually looking for suitable prospects and one top Junior, Lachie McInnes of Blantyre Victoria had already been signed and he had been the star of the season 1944/45 Junior Cup Final.

Season 1944/45
The opening match of the Southern League Programme was at Paisley on the 10th August and McIlhatton opened the team's account in the first half and after an

181

equaliser by the Saints, Hannah scored the winner in the second half to set the team off to the best of all possible starts. Rovers were represented by Henderson (Larkhall Thistle), McInnes, Savage, Blane, Stein, McLetchie, McIlhatton, Smith, Hunter (Polkemmet Juniors), McDonald and Hannah. After his good performance, Jimmy Hunter was signed and played in the opening home game against Celtic the following week, when Anderson made a re-appearance in goal. Before the match there was a one minute silence for former player John Thomson who had been killed in action in France and, in what turned out to be a rough match, Celtic won by a late penalty in the second half. Hannah was ordered off which made the team's job more difficult. The visit to Falkirk was a waste of time with the 'Bairns' winning 7-1 and further bad news came when Partick Thistle romped to a 3-0 lead at half time. When McInnes missed a penalty in the second half, Rovers couldn't come back and that ended up the final score.

A fourth defeat in a row then came at the hand of Airdrieonians, at Broomfield by 4-0, in a match where Joe Henderson of Larkhall Thistle was given a second trial and a trialist centre was also tried out. Henderson spurned Rovers' signing offer and opted for Hibernian. Anderson returned to goal against Motherwell when two Mudie goals in the first half were enough to beat the County rivals. Again a mid-season run of defeats was to come starting the following week at Cathkin by 2-1 before Hibernian won 5-0 at Coatbridge. At Hamilton the fans must have thought the team was on the way to a victory when Rovers went into a 2-0 lead in twenty-three minutes but Accies raced to a 6-2 lead at half time and despite trialist Black from Annbank United scoring two in the second half, Hamilton ended up 8-4 winners.

Clyde next won by 3-1 before Rangers were faced at Ibrox with new-signing Johnny Black at centre but the forwards could do nothing against the Rangers defence and Rangers ran out winners at 3-0. Luck was still against the wee Rovers the following week against Dumbarton and whilst two McIlhatton goals saw them leading 2-1 at half time, Dumbarton thumped in three goals in the second half to win by 4-2.

John Waddell retired after forty years as a Director and Committee man and troubles just continued to heap on Rovers' misery. The visit to Hampden ended disastrously in an 8-1 defeat before Hearts came to Coatbridge the following week and perpetrated a withering 10-3 defeat on the hapless team. Archie Kelly at centre forward scored seven of the goals and his opposite number, trialist Bobby Kerr from Burnbank Athletic, must have thought that was the end of his senior career prospects. Also goalkeeper Bob Forsyth had lost eighteen goals in two games and his third and last match for Rovers was at home the following week against Morton where he lost another three goals, giving him the worst goalkeeping record of any goalkeeper in Rovers' history. Consolation for him was that the game against Morton was a victory at 4-3. Also introduced in this game was Harry Beaton the former Clyde captain at right half.

For the game against St. Mirren, Jack Gillespie appeared in goal and Tommy Kiernan made his first appearance of the season in a no scoring draw before Celtic won 5-0 in Glasgow with Rovers still struggling in the goalkeeping position.

Bobby Kerr of Burnbank Athletic made another attempt to join the senior ranks against Falkirk in a 3-1 victory and after a fine display was promptly signed as a senior player. Partick Thistle had a convincing 4-1 victory in Glasgow and during the week Rovers went to Falkirk and signed goalkeeper Jim Pidgeon. He put up the shutters against Third Lanark at Cliftonhill the following week when a first half

ALBION ROVERS SEASON 1944/45

Standing: W. Savage, P. Blane, J. Stein, J. Pidgeon, R. Kerr, A. McLetchie.
Seated: J. McIlhatton, T. Kiernan, J. Black, W. Hannah, G. Louden.

McIlhatton goal was enough to give Rovers the points. There was also great satisfaction in the new full back partnership of Savage and Kerr. Unfortunately, the euphoria lasted only one match and it was back to heavy defeats, this time by Motherwell at 7-2 leaving Mr. Pidgeon with thoughts as to why he had inflicted this on himself. All was forgiven the following Monday, New Year's Day, when Airdrieonians were defeated 3-2 with Hannah, Kiernan and McIlhatton all scoring.

Two away defeats on the trot at 3-0 to Morton and 4-1 to Hibs led to keeper Pidgeon being freed, having lost sixteen goals in five matches. Gillespie was given another chance in goal against Hamilton at Coatbridge in a 2-2 draw which was disappointing considering Rovers were 2-0 up at half time. But better was to follow against Clyde when a good second half performance saw Rovers come from behind to win 3-2. The third home match in a row welcomed Rangers with trialist Mackie of St. Anthony's in goal. He had a good match although the team lost 4-0 and he signed on the dotted line to take his place against Dumbarton but despite two Willie Hannah goals the team went down 3-2. Bobby Kerr took Stein's place at centre half in this the big defender's first absence of the season. The deputy centre half retained his position for the home match against Queen's Park which the Amateurs won 3-2 and the last League match in Edinburgh against Hearts ended up again in defeat by a 2-1 margin.

The League Cup Tournament saw Rovers drawn against Rangers, Third Lanark and Hibernian and was to be a particularly barren period with only two draws and four defeats, making depressing history. The opening match was at Ibrox and despite Rovers leading at half time by a Dougie Gray own goal, Rangers scored two in the second half to lift the points and Corporal Jimmy Hunter made a welcome reappearance in this match. Third Lanark won 3-2 at Coatbridge before the first point came Rovers' way in a 1-1 draw in Edinburgh against Hibs where the team should have done better after opening the scoring with a Mudie goal. The return match against Rangers was lost by 3-1 before a fighting draw was gained at Cathkin at 3-3. Hibernian finished the season at Coatbridge with a swingeing 8-1 victory.

Five weeks later the Summer Cup Tournament opened with Rovers against Celtic in the first round and, with ex-Morton Archie Leven at outside left, the first leg ended up 1-1 but the return in Glasgow found Celtic clear winners by 4-2. This turned out to be Tommy Kiernan's last game before being transferred to Celtic, thus ending several months of speculation as to his eventual billet.

With the War now over in Europe, the League Management Committee agreed to recommence League football for the new season with two Leagues of sixteen teams each. Rovers and near neighbours Airdrieonians were "relegated" to Division 'B' much to the consternation of both clubs, who felt that as they were First League members at the outbreak of War, they should have retained that position at the formation of the new Leagues.

By the time of the A.G.M., Rovers showed a profit of £400 on the year's working plus the money for Kiernan's transfer. John Kirk was appointed Chairman in succession to John Wilson, Tom Griffen became Vice Chairman and apart from those players who were available for the beginning of the season, Rovers still had Muir, Beath, Sharp, Taggart, Degnan, Findlay, Keeble, Hunter and Bell in His Majesty's Services.

MR. ALBION ROVERS No. 4

WILLIAM WEBBER LEES

Webber Lees was a legend in his own time as an astute spotter of young football talent. His career with the Club started as a Supporter, following a career as a navy man during the First World War in H.M.S. Gloucester where he fought at the Battle of Jutland.

He was Secretary/Treasurer of the Supporters' Club at its inception in 1926 until Mr. Willie Reid, the former International centre-forward, resigned the position of Secretary/Manager of Albion Rovers to become Manager of Dundee United at the end of season 1928/29.

Mr. Lees took over the joint office in an Honorary capacity and the team he built won the Second Division Championship in season 1933/34, the only time in the history of the Club that a major League Championship has been won.

He made way, for a short period, when Johnny Weir was appointed Manager, but after relegation of the Club at the end of season 1936/37, he again took up the reins as Manager taking the Club back into the First Division in a single season.

At the end of World War II in 1946, he left his full-time employment with the Clyde Valley Electric Company to become full-time Secretary/Manager; as well as continuing as a Director of the Club, and again was instrumental in promotion from Division 'B' at the end of season 1947/48. The short stay of a single season in the upper Division virtually ended his career at Cliftonhill.

At the Board Meeting on the 9th of June 1949, he failed to retain his seat on the Board of Directors, although still holding the posts of Secretary and Manager. Always a man of principle, Mr. Lees resigned and one week later took up the reins at Dunfermline Athletic as Secretary/Manager, where he took over from ex-referee Bobby Calder.

The stay at East End Park lasted less than a year and he ended his footballing career as Manager with Alloa Athletic. His last years were spent outwith football, allowing him to take a more active interest in his Sports Outfitting business in Coatbridge. He died in 1963.

Among the many stars who owed their introduction to senior football to him were Bobby Beath, Andy Waddell, Tom Lyon, Tommy Kiernan, Jock Stein, Willie Findlay, Johnny McIlhatton and Willie Hannah. All made their mark with Rovers and other teams.

CHAPTER NINE

THE FIGHT BACK TO THE TOP

Season 1945/46
On the opening day of the season the campaign to gain promotion to Division 'A' took off with a home match against Alloa when McIlhatton scored a hat-trick. Rovers' team was Mackie, McInnes, Kerr, Beaton, Stein, McLetchie, McIlhatton, Martin, Black, Hannah and Murphy and they were satisfied in a fine 6-2 win.

As part of the celebrations of the 'Victory in Europe', Provost Gray of Airdrie gifted a Trophy to be played for by Rovers and Airdrieonians with the proceeds to be in aid of the Coatbridge Victory Fund and the Airdrie Welcome Home Fund. The first leg took place at Cliftonhill and with Joe Burke re-signed and leading the attack, Rovers went into a 4-0 lead but Airdrie came back with a late rush to make the final score 4-3. The first away League match was at Dumbarton where the Sons won 4-0. In the second leg of the Provost Gray Cup, at Broomfield in front of 5,000 fans, Rovers were down 4-1 at half time and with no further goals, Airdrie picked up the Cup on a 7-5 aggregate.

Back in the League a Willie Hannah goal in the second half was sufficient to defeat Dundee United at Coatbridge but on the visit to Cowdenbeath, Rovers lost by the only goal of the game and had centre half Stein ordered off. Airdrieonians made the short trip down to Coatbridge and Rovers went into a straight 3-0 lead at half time. Again Airdrie came back with a rush in an exciting game with the final score 3-2 in favour of Rovers. Stein, due to suspension, then missed the next two matches, both of which ended up in defeats by 1-0 at Arbroath, when McIlhatton missed a penalty, and 3-1 at Ayr.

With Stein back in the team and included in six positional changes, East Fife were beaten in a close match by 3-2 and in another home match a no scoring draw was fought out with Stenhousemuir which showed the wisdom in bringing back goalkeeper Mackie. At Dunfermline 'Joker' Black scored both Rovers' goals in the 5-2 defeat before League leaders Dundee visited Coatbridge. Rovers failed to knock them off their pedestal and the Dark Blues left with the points in a competent display by a 2-0 victory. St. Johnstone were next guests at Cliftonhill but they were too strong for Rovers on the day and, with a fine second half display, ran out winners by 6-1.

For the following trip to Kirkcaldy with Tommy Coats from Burnbank Athletic making his debut at left half, Alec McGregor of Polkemmet in goal, Alec Browning from Liverpool and with Freddie Keeble making his first appearance of the season at centre, the Englishman scored the only goal of the game to start a run of six straight victories. Willie Findlay returned temporarily from the Forces and celebrated with a double and with Alistair McLellan from Shettleston introduced at inside left, Dumbarton were overrun in a free-flowing display by a 3-0 scoreline. Alloa was defeated 2-0 and next Dundee United 3-2 in away victories. Peter Blane was freed to sign for Airdrie and Browning, who had taken his place, scored in the 4-0 victory over Cowdenbeath but his month's trial period ended and he left to join Cowdenbeath.

In the game against Ayr United, Rovers were in trouble at the start and the game kicked off with Rovers only fielding nine men. Sharp and Kerr stripped and joined their pals but it was a struggle to contain the lively Ayr team to 2-2 at half time,

187

Willie Hannah scored the winner in the second half for a good result. Arbroath fought well for a share of the points in a 1-1 draw at Coatbridge before East Fife won by the only goal of the game through ex Methil. The last game of 1945 saw a Keeble goal sufficient to send Stenhousemuir home pointless.

On New Year's day, Broomfield was the setting for the usual Local Derby and 8,000 fans saw Airdrie go into a deserved 2-1 lead at half time but Rovers came away with a tremendous display in the second half and completely overcame their opponents by banging in four goals without reply, running out easy winners by 5 goals to 2.

The following day Raith Rovers visited Coatbridge and, even with McIlhatton missing a penalty, Rovers still ran out easy winners by 3-0. With only one defeat in eleven matches, Rovers had climbed up the League and when Dunfermline were defeated by two Willie Hannah goals to nil at Coatbridge, Rovers moved into second top position in the League. This set up the clash of the top two at Dens Park but Dundee again showed their class winning this one in a one-sided game by 2-0. The final game in the League was a 3-0 victory for St. Johnstone at Perth.

The 'B' Division Cup paired local rivals Rovers and Airdrieonians together, with the first round being played at Cliftonhill which Rovers won 2-1 in front of 9,000 delirious fans. For the return match the following week, the gate was boosted to 11,000 but Airdrie won 4-3 and keeper McGregor was handicapped with a broken bone in his hand. As the teams were locked at 5-5, a play-off was fixed for Hampden on Wednesday the 7th February, and attracted about 30,000 spectators which stands as the record gate for a match between both teams and saw Airdrie win by one goal and eight corners to one goal and five corners. McLetchie equalised Watson's first half goal and it was only due to the good display by Moodie in Airdrie's goal that the game ended all square at the end of ninety minutes with Rovers rueing the missed chances in the first half.

Newly formed Stirling Albion were then fixed up for a friendly at Annfield Park and Rovers completely changed their forward line in the comfortable 2-2 draw played at the new ground. Dunfermline Athletic then won 3-1 before Airdrieonians were defeated in the 'B' Division Cup Section C by a Freddie Keeble goal to nothing with new signing Davie Martin from Rutherglen playing a fine match at inside right. St. Johnstone had a rampaging 9-0 victory at Muirton in a match which saw Willie McClure, signed from Douglasdale, make his debut. The return match against Dunfermline saw Freddie Keeble hit a hat-trick in the second half for the home team to win by 3-0. Airdrieonians gained ample revenge for their earlier defeat by winning 5-1 at Broomfield in front of 10,000 fans. 'Joker' Black was freed and promptly joined Stirling Albion and there was to be no revenge for Rovers in the return match against St. Johnstone which ended up with no scoring.

After a three week lay-off, the Victory Cup first leg at Shawfield saw McClure hit his first goals for Rovers in a double but Clyde won by 4-2. They were assisted in this by Stein being off injured in the second half and he missed the return game at Cliftonhill the following week which Clyde won by 2-1. Johnny McIlhatton scored in this match which was his last appearance for Rovers before his transfer to Everton, much to the disgust of the fans who were convinced that Rovers did not want promotion.

The close season was one of consolidation and, despite the loss of star man McIlhatton, there was keen interest among the support with the return of the Forces players Hunter and Taggart who would be available along with Bell and Beath. 'Chic' Muir was expected to be back in time for the new season but Findlay

'Cigarette' Cards: Jock Stein, Johnny McIlhatton, Willie Hannah, Tommy Kiernan, Willie Findlay.

189

would not be available until September. Season tickets were competitively priced at £2.10/- for ground and reserve stand, £1.15/- for ground and No. 1 stand with ground only being 17/-. Old age pensioners were 12/6d. and boys at 4/6d. Hard work was put in on the ground as usual by the Supporters Club. Webber Lees was appointed full-time Manager and resigned from his appointment with the Clyde Valley Electrical Power Company and he set about signings for the new season ahead.

Season 1946/47
The 'B' Division campaign opened on the 10th August at Alloa with a 2-2 draw and trainer Tommy McKenna was disappointed that some of the players did not display a greater keenness for the match. Rovers were represented by — McGregor, McInnes, Kerr, Martin, Stein, Coats, Wallace, Hannah, Keeble, Stephenson and Hunter.

The following Wednesday saw the 'B' Division Supplementary Cup first leg at Methil which the home team won 2-1. In the third game of the season the home campaign was opened with another disappointing result at 1-1 against Cowdenbeath. A feature of this game was the first loud-speaker announcements at Cliftonhill. The second leg of the Supplementary Cup took place with an emphatic victory for East Fife by a score of 4-1 and thus early in the season Rovers' interest in a Cup was at an end.

The first victory of the season was reserved for Airdrieonians at Broomfield when, after a no scoring first half both teams came out fighting and Rovers just edged out as winners by 2-1. After having waited so long for a win the next match saw Dumbarton overwhelmed 3-0 at Cliftonhill and the trip to Dundee saw the local United losing 3-0 at half time and despite a fight back in the second half 3-1 was the final score in a match which placed Rovers firmly at the top of the League. Fred Keeble scored his last goal for Rovers in this game as he was now released from the Forces and was returning to England to be signed by Grimsby Town. Rovers' fans were sorry to see the back of the popular amateur.

Rovers filled his place by drafting in Stephenson at centre and another competent display saw Arbroath defeated 3-1 at Coatbridge. The centre moved over to inside right to make space for Tom Doonan from Forth Wanderers in the League Cup at home against Ayr United and the new signing scored a couple in a pulsating cup tie which found the Ayr team leading 3-2 at half time but Rovers ran out eventual winners by 5-4. The next match in the Cup was at Broomfield where the Diamonds gained revenge for their earlier defeat by winning 6-1. The return match at Ayr found United winning 4-3 but there was to be no revenge for Rovers in the re-match against Airdrie who again won comprehensively by 5-1.

Part of the McIlhatton transfer deal to Everton was for a match to be played at Goodison Park and the party went south on Wednesday, 23rd October, for a match which the English side won by 6-3. The long journey South seemed to have taken the zoomph out of the team for East Fife came to Coatbridge on the Saturday and won very easily by 4-1. Jimmy McClure was signed for the third time from Kilmarnock and played at centre half in place of Stein in the visit to Ayr where a good 3-1 victory was chalked up.

Joe Henderson was finally signed from Hibs and made his debut in goal in the 2-1 home victory over Raith Rovers which was followed by a 1-1 draw against St. Johnstone at Coatbridge. High flying Dundee chalked up four goals without reply at half time and finally ran out winners by 6-2 before Findlay, celebrating his demob, scored the first goal in a fine 5-1 victory at Coatbridge over Dunfermline. The next home game was against Stenhousemuir when, despite going ahead with a Wilkie goal in the first half, the advantage was thrown away with the Larbert team allowed to equalise in the second half.

A satisfactory replacement for Johnny McIlhatton had not yet been found and four players had been tried throughout the season without success. Rovers dipped into the transfer market and bought local boy Neil McKinnon from Dundee United and the ex-Rangers' player was drafted in against Alloa but, in the third home game on the trot, Alloa won easily by 6-1 and Willie Findlay capped Rovers' day of woe by missing a penalty. Another penalty was missed, this time by Stein, at Central Park but Cowdenbeath were still defeated by 4-2 and the news was released that popular veteran Johnny Bell had been appointed full time coach. The New Year's Day match saw Airdrieonians come to Cliftonhill and win by the only goal of the game, notched in the second half.

Manager Lees was shocked when Johnny McMullen, Secretary of the Supporters Club, sent to the local newspaper a copy of an open letter addressed to the Directors of the Football Club. The Supporters asked if the Board had noticed during the past few weeks the number of Coatbridge football fans who were leaving the town by the various transport services for other teams in Glasgow and district on Saturday afternoons. They went on to ask the apparent reason for this and they answered their own question by suggesting that these fans, disgusted by the results of Rovers' own games over the past few months, were fully convinced that the Cliftonhill Board were content to remain in 'B' Division football. The letter went on to claim certain positions in the team had been very weak and that little had been done to strengthen these positions other than switch players from one position to another.

Bristling under this criticism the visit to Dumbarton on the 2nd January saw Bobby Beath welcomed back to the fold with Kerr moved to left half and the introduction of McInnes at right half in an otherwise unchanged team but the best that could be achieved was a 1-1 draw. On the Saturday, the visit to Kirkcaldy found Raith Rovers too good winning by 2-0.

Langloan boy, Adam McLean, was signed from Baillieston Juniors to take his place at centre forward against Ayr United in a home match which Rovers won by 2-1 and the local boy scored the winning goal. On sale at this match were ground and enclosure tickets for the forthcoming first round Scottish Cup tie against Airdrieonians. The preparation for the match, as far as Rovers were concerned, was a disaster with a 5-1 drubbing through at Dunfermline whereas Airdrie were up on cloud nine having defeated Cowdenbeath 7-2 at Airdrie. However, it was a different story in the cup tie which Rovers won easily by 3-0. All the goals came in the first 13 minutes of the match and try as they might, Airdrie were unable to cut back on that deficit with much of the credit going to Stein snuffing out the menace of centre forward Bobby Flavell. 14,500 fans paid receipts totalling £850 for the local derby.

The following week Dundee were the visitors in a League match and the League leaders were held to a 2-2 draw in an exciting game.

Off the field, meetings were being held with Shareholders to consider a new scheme of financial arrangements for the Limited Company and Chairman, John Kirk, received the unanimous approval of Shareholders to proceed for the reduction and re-organisation of the Share capital.

Another friendly match against Stirling Albion was fixed up which ended 2-0 in

Leaving on Cup business at Dundee 1947.

favour of Rovers. This was intended as ideal preparation for the awaited Cup tie at Dundee the following week but Rovers were never in the hunt and Dundee won very easily by a 3-0 scoreline with Rovers having very few successes.

The fans were suitably unimpressed with this display and it was just as well the next match against Stenhousemuir was postponed because of fourteen inches of snow to allow tempers to cool. The long trip to Arbroath saw Rovers romp to a 3-0 lead at half time but carelessness in defence allowed the home team to square the match at 3-3 by full time. When St. Johnstone were three up at half time in the next match the fans looked to a revival from Rovers to emulate the previous fixture but this was not on and the Saints ran out winners with no change in the scoreline.

A friendly at Alloa saw McLean score four out of a 5-0 victory. At Larbert with the score 1-1 Referee Duthie abandoned the game at half time. This turned out to be Willie Findlay's last game for Rovers before signing for Rangers.

High scoring East Fife were visited with Rovers, despite a late rally, losing 2-1 before the Stenhousemuir match was finally played in midweek with the scoreline 4-1 in favour of the 'Muir. Rovers, now with no chance of promotion and at best a fourth or fifth position in the League, visited Dumfries for a friendly match against Queen of the South which ended with the teams sharing six goals before the final League game against Dundee United at Cliftonhill ended up with a resounding 5-1 scoreline for the Cliftonhillers enabling them to attain fourth position on goal average over Alloa. The promoted two were Dundee as Champions and Airdrieonians.

The season ended with a Monklands Charity Cup match against the newly promoted Airdrieonians and two goals from corner kicks converted by McKinnon and Stephenson put Rovers ahead before the Interval but with five minutes to go, first of all Dalgleish and then Flavell equalised before the ninety minutes. A head count of corners was taken and it was announced that Rovers had won the match by the margin of six corners to four. This was in the days before a penalty kick play-off. Thus Rovers' sideboard was adorned by a Cup for the first time in many years. £306 was taken at the gate at this match; the money being distributed to various charities in the area.

Now with Airdrieonians being promoted, there was even less sense in Rovers being in Division 'B'. During the close season all efforts were put into the provision of a team capable of promotion. The summer saw tremendous work by the supporters in altering the terracing and re-painting the stand. At the A.G.M. all the Directors were re-appointed and the Balance Sheet showed a profit of £1,727. Former player, Jock Robertson, was signed on as trainer and he had the players fit and raring to go for the opening games.

Season 1947/48
The opening match in the League Cup on the 9th August found Dundee United the visitors and a convincing 3-0 victory was possible thanks to two penalties by 'Chic' Muir. New signing Willie Dickson from Junior Cup Holders Bo'ness had a promising debut and Captain Stein was well pleased with the display of his team, which was Henderson, Muir, Kerr, Martin, Stein, Coats, McKinnon, Dickson, McLean, Hannah and McClure. Five away matches were next on the cards with Ayr United being defeated 2-0 in the League and Cowdenbeath defeated 3-2 in the League Cup before Leith Athletic at New Meadowbank came back from behind to square the match at 2-2.

Back on League business, Dundee United were again defeated, this time by 1-0, and the following Saturday the East coast team gained revenge by 2-1 in the return Cup match. Tommy Coats was played in his third position for the season, at centre forward, for the home match against Cowdenbeath and scored a hat-trick in the 4-1 victory. In the last League Cup match, Leith Athletic managed another draw this time at 1-1 with Rovers having to come back from behind in this one.

For the away League match at Hamilton, Dougie Wallace was signed from Dunfermline and took up position at centre forward but despite or perhaps because of five positional changes, there was no rhythm in the team and Accies ran out easy winners by 3-0. The South African centre forward retained his position against his former club, Dunfermline, and scored the second goal in a 2-0 victory before he scored a double in the 3-1 victory over Leith Athletic at Edinburgh.

Rovers were now hovering at the top of the League and the team was showing a bit of style. Raith Rovers, who were also table topping, scored a second half equaliser in a 1-1 share of the points. In the match at Larbert against Stenhousemuir, Tommy Doonan made a welcome reappearance from Service duty and scored the first two goals in a 3-3 draw. St. Johnstone were next visitors to Coatbridge and Joe Devlin was introduced from Clelland Juniors to partner Wallace with Coats again at centre. The Coatbridge team won 3-2 having to come back from behind by 2-1 at half time. The victory by 2-1 over Arbroath the following week saw Rovers top the League but a point was dropped at Dumbarton in the 1-1 draw in a match where Willie McClure was ordered off.

East Fife put a spoke in the promotion plans with an emphatic 3-0 victory at Bayview. Alistair McKillop was signed from Morton to play at centre for the visit of Kilmarnock and he did his bit in the 2-1 victory, retaining his place for the visit to Stirling which the local Albion won clearly by 7-0 with centre George Henderson scoring four goals. This was a terrible result against the babes of the Scottish League and the first victory by this club over Rovers in three matches.

At Cowdenbeath the following week Rovers got back on the rails with a 3-1 victory, with all Rovers' goals scored in the second half, to overcome a 1-0 deficit. Bobby Beath made a welcome reappearance at left back in this match, fifteen years after signing for the Club, with Kerr taking up the left half position. New signing John Craig from Bridgeton Waverley made his second appearance at outside left and gave a pleasing display. The following week Alloa were defeated 3-1 in a match where Rovers missed many chances, including a penalty by Muir, and Ayr United were also defeated in the last home game of the year by 2-0 before another hiccough in the promotion surge came at the hands of Dundee United by 3-0.

The promotion hopes were further dashed on New Year's Day when Hamilton came to Coatbridge and pocketed the points in a 2-1 victory. This was made all the more annoying as the home team had led by a McKillop goal in the first half. Worse was to follow on the Monday when the trip to Dunfermline found the 'Pars' in tremendous form giving Rovers their third defeat in a row by 4-0.

Leith Athletic came to Coatbridge but, with one goal in each half, Rovers ran out easy winners by 2-0 to stop the rot. During the following week Lachie McInnes was exchanged for centre forward Arthur Carrie from Arbroath and the new boy lined up at centre in the visit to Fife against Raith Rovers and scored two goals in the second half to overcome a 2-1 deficit at half time to record a famous 3-2 victory. After this game full-time coach and long time servant of the Club Johnny Bell retired to Blackpool to take up hotel management with the best wishes of the Club and fans.

ALBION ROVERS SEASON 1947/48

Standing left to right: A. Muir, D. Martin, J. Henderson, J. Stein, R. Beath, J. Hunter.
Seated left to right: J. Craig, N. MacKinnon, A. Carrie, J. Love and D. Wallace.

Lindsay Cartoon of Hibs Cup match.

Johnny Love signing for Albion Rovers on 13th February 1948.

This victory had been a perfect preview for the first round Cup match against Hibernian at Coatbridge. The stand and enclosure were all-ticket at 5/- and 3/-respectively and a crowd of 15,000 turned up on the day to see Rovers miss several chances in the first half, notably from winger Craig who even ran the ball past an open goal before Hibs scored in the first half. Try as they might in the second half the lads could not stem the tide from the green and white shirted team who ran out eventual winners by 2-0.

Following this game Adam McLean was transferred on loan to Leith Athletic and two McKinnon goals in the first half were enough to secure a 2-2 draw at home against Stenhousemuir. Johnny Love was signed from Leith Athletic to make his debut in the match at Perth which Rovers won by the only goal of the game. The winning ways continued at Arbroath with a 3-1 scoreline and when Dumbarton came to Coatbridge the following week a high-scoring match saw the home team win 5-3 to remain in the promotion stakes.

A rest from League business came with a friendly at Hampden when a Stein penalty equalised a first half goal for the Queens. The following week at Kilmarnock Rovers went in at half time 2-1 up thanks to own goals by defenders Hood and Thyne, whilst a penalty by Stein and a final goal by Dougie Wallace saw the Coatbridge team return home with a fine 4-1 victory under their belt. Stirling Albion came to Coatbridge looking to emulate their earlier result but the 5,000 fans saw Rovers completely in command to win by two McKinnon goals. This result put Rovers in second top position to Hamilton Accies on goal average. Two 3-1 victories were next recorded, the first at home against Cowdenbeath and the second at Alloa, and with Rovers favourites for promotion there was only one game left in the League.

The first match of April saw the 'B' Division Supplementary Cup matches commence with Rovers drawn against Raith Rovers. The teams were tied at one each when Bobby Kerr scored in the last minute to take Rovers into the next round. On the Friday of the same week, Ayr United, in the second round, fought out a hard-won draw at 2-2, in which Stein missed a penalty, but in the replay the following Wednesday Rovers won 2-0. Promotion rivals East Fife put paid to their further advancement in the tournament by winning at Methil in the third round by a massive 9-1. This match, on the Thursday evening, did not augur well for the match at Cliftonhill against East Fife in the last League game of the season. Despite trying all they knew, the best Rovers could achieve was a 4-1 defeat and East Fife were accordingly promoted as Champions with Rovers Runners-up. Hamilton were in third spot two points behind. As a run up to the First Division, Celtic were played in a friendly match at Coatbridge but the Glasgow east-enders proved too strong and Rovers finished the season with a 7-2 defeat.

So promotion had at long last been achieved. At the same time it was disappointingly noted that Airdrieonians had been relegated along with Queen's Park and there would be no local derby's again during the following season. The Directors set about signing new players as two teams would be required each week, in the First Division and the Alliance League. At the A.G.M. in August, a profit of £1,412.5.3d. was declared and a dividend of 5% was recommended on the Preference Shares which was the first time in the Club's history that such a Dividend had been made.

Trainer Jocky Robertson laying it on the line to the squad for 1948/49 season.

ALBION ROVERS SEASON 1948/49

Standing: Trainer J. Robertson, D. Martin, J. Paterson, A. McGregor, S. English, J. Hunter, J. Stein.
Seated: J. Craig, J. Love, D. Wallace, P. Smith and J. Smith.

Season 1948/49
The opening game in this fourth spell in the First Division was in Glasgow against Partick Thistle and when the teams ran out on the day the fans were greatly intrigued to see the blue shirts were carrying numbers for the first time. Newcomers Paterson, English, McLeod and Smith all made their debut in a disappointing match which ended up in favour of the 'Jags' by 3-0. Nothing that ex-Thistle player Smith did could change the result. Rovers' team was McGregor, Paterson, English, Hunter, Stein, McLeod, Craig, McKinnon, Doonan, Love and Smith.

The first home match took place the following Wednesday but St. Mirren won this one by the odd goal in three before Motherwell took their County neighbours to the cleaners by a 5-1 margin. Three defeats in a row did not bode well but some hope was gleaned from the Falkirk visit to Coatbridge. They found Rovers better prepared and who equalised their total score for the season so far in the 2-0 victory over the Bairns.

For the trip through to Easter Road, Rovers equalised an early goal by Hibs but Laurie Reilly scored just before half time and again just after half time to make it 3-1. When Cuthbertson scored the fourth Edinburgh goal it looked all up for Rovers but with 12 minutes to go Love and Smith made it 4-3. When Jock Govan, in desperation, floored Smith, Jock Stein gave Kerr no chance with the penalty kick making the teams all square at four each. On the Saturday, Celtic came to Cliftonhill and in front of 25,000 fans a cup-tie of a match was played out. Celtic were 3-1 in the lead with ten minutes to go with Jock Weir twice and Tully scoring for Celtic and Wallace for Rovers. The Bhoys well deserved their lead at that stage

1948 Old Crocks Match v Airdrionians.

Standing left to right: Andy Waddell, John Donnelly, Jock Britton, Murdy Walls, Bobby Beath, Jimmy Liddell.
Seated: Jock Robertson, John McPhee, Charlie Cannon, Jimmy Connor, Harry Brant, Willie Hillhouse.

but when Love scored and then Wallace rushed in an equaliser with five minutes to go, the odds were on Rovers taking the points. Indeed the Celtic goalkeeper was well beaten by a shot which was punched over the bar by left back Mallon when incredulously, with the referee in good position, he indicated a corner. He was the only person in the ground who wasn't convinced that the decision should have been a penalty. Celtic thus limped away with a most fortunate point and from there on in for the rest of the season it was obvious that Rovers were going to find survival very difficult.

The League Cup Competition now took over and the visit to Dundee saw Rovers forced to make a change in goal, with Fraser making his debut, but the men from Dens Park ran out winners by 2-1. Four of Rovers' regulars, McGregor, Stein, Hunter and Craig, were absent through injuries and illness and Rovers' team was rather makeshift. But new keeper Fraser did particularly well in goal. Motherwell came to Coatbridge and won by the only goal of the game with Falkirk also winning by the odd goal at Brockville this time by 2-1. The following Monday, Hamilton Accies drew 1-1 in a Lanarkshire Cup tie at Coatbridge when Rovers took the opportunity of trying some positional changes, notably with Jimmy Smith at centre forward and new signing McMaster making his debut on the left wing. More trouble for Rovers was the 3-2 defeat by Dundee at Cliftonhill in a match which Rovers should have won. Full back Bobby Kerr broke his leg playing for the Reserves at Dens Park to add to Rovers' troubles.

At Motherwell the return match against the 'Steelmen' proved to be disastrous with an 8-3 defeat being recorded before Falkirk were defeated in the last match of the Cup at Coatbridge by a 2-1 margin.

Back in the League Morton visited Coatbridge and the stalemate was broken when Johnny Paterson, the chunky right back, took a free kick from just over the half way line and thanks to a dummy by Rovers' forwards the ball thundered into the back of the Morton net giving Rovers the first goal. Doonan scored another goal to give Rovers only their second League win out of nine outings at 2-1. The current bogey team, Dundee, came to Coatbridge and with Rovers handicapped by Jock Stein injured and off for much of the game, Dundee ran out easy winners by 6-0. The visit to Cathkin ended in a disappointing and feckless 4-1 defeat. Sam English took Stein's position at centre half and with Rovers losing 1-0 Hunter missed a penalty and from that moment the 'Hi-Hi' never looked back being 3-1 up at half time and having another goal in the second half.

At the end of November John McMullen, who had recently retired from the Secretaryship of the Supporters Club, was the recipient of a suitably inscribed wrist watch from the members of the Club at a social function held in the British Legion Hall. Archie Fleming, Chairman of the Supporters Club, handed over a fountain pen to Manager Webber Lees, Trainer Jock Robertson and each of the players. The Supporters Club totalled over 300 at the time and Mr. Fleming confirmed that a Branch had now been opened in Shotts.

At the beginning of December Queen of the South came to Coatbridge on League business and in a disappointing match the players simply didn't contest the game and Queens had an easy 3-1 victory virtually without breaking sweat. The following week a first half goal by Clyde at Shawfield was enough to give them the points. In a spirited fight back the Coatbridge team tried hard in the second half, especially in the latter stages, but another odd goal defeat was the result.

All Supporters were most unhappy with the team's performances and, when it was made known that the players had been making heavy financial demands on

Jock Stein
1942-50

Bobby Kerr
1944-53

Alec 'Chic' Muir
1941-53

Johnny Craig
1947-53

the Club, there was much consternation in the Town. The obvious disharmony spread to the field in no uncertain terms and in the visit by Hearts there was a distinct lack of fight about the team in the 5-1 defeat by the Edinburgh side. On Christmas Day Love Street was visited and yet another odd goal defeat was the result with Rovers losing this time by 3-2. News came from Ibrox that former player Willie Findlay had broken his leg during the afternoon which did nothing to lift the gloom from Coatbridge and the team's position confirmed at the bottom place.

The New Year's Day match saw Motherwell visit Coatbridge and set themselves up for a win by going into an early lead eventually running out winners by 3-1. The home supporters were incensed at the lack of spirit by the players but worse was to happen at Falkirk on the following Monday when Archie Aikman, the 'Bairns' centre forward rattled in six goals in a 7-1 drubbing with Johnny Love gaining a consolation goal in the second half. McGregor was brought back into goal for the visit by Partick Thistle but he was unable to prevent the 'Jags' winning by 3-2 in a match when all goals were scored in the second half. Bad luck continued to dog Rovers and in the next match at Parkhead they had to play with nine men for over sixty minutes when Coats was injured with a dislocated shoulder and McGregor and McKinnon were also incapacitated. Jimmy Hunter had to don the goalkeeper's red jersey and Celtic strolled home to a 3-0 victory.

Henderson was back in goal for the Scottish Cup tie against Hamilton at Douglas Park. 12,000 fans paid £840 to see Jimmy Smith put Rovers into the lead at half time and although Walter Rothera both scored and missed with penalties, it was Johnny Love who sent Rovers into the second round with a 2-1 victory. Back in the League the following week Hibernian came to Coatbridge but found the team with no fight and the final score was 3-0 in favour of the Edinburgh team when it could have been many more.

Next Saturday the second round cup tie at Larbert was postponed due to fog, much to the disgust of the travelling support, but the following Wednesday when the match was eventually played there was a considerable players' revolt prior to the game. They were not in the right frame of mind to take on the Second Division team who had an easy, if unexpected, 5-1 victory. There were wholesale changes for the next game with nine positional changes but fellow promotion team East Fife, who were in the upper half of the League, took complete command to win 3-0.

Dundee scored their fourth victory of the season against the luckless Rovers at Dundee winning 5-0, which totalled sixteen goals against and only three for, in a match when Rovers were never at the races. This was Johnny Love's last appearance before signing for Nottingham Forest for a reputed £9,000, 10 per cent of which went to his former club Leith Athletic. The fans' First League aspirations finally disappeared in the 5-1 lashing at home by Third Lanark in a disastrous run which had seen fifteen defeats and only one victory out of sixteen games. The Monthly Meeting of the Supporters Club passed a Resolution of No Confidence on the Directors and there were accusations that it was the players and not the Directors who were running the Club and another Meeting was set up for later in the month.

The players were aware of the fans' discontent and when Aberdeen came to Coatbridge at the beginning of March, on a water-logged pitch, only 1,000 fans were there to see the Dons go into a 1-0 lead at half time. Two goals in the last ten minutes from McKinnon and Kerr from a penalty kept the points at Coatbridge for the relegation-doomed team. The following week saw the return match at Pittodrie and the Dons gained ample revenge by a 4-0 margin.

This was the last straw for the supporters and more than 300 supporters and shareholders met in the Mutual Service Hall, Coatbridge, on the following Thursday to unanimously pass a vote of No Confidence in the Club's Directors, although they excluded Andrew Beattie from this as he had only been appointed to the Board in the past few months. They also excluded the full-time staff. Lamie Smith, former goalkeeper, was appointed Chairman and he and Alec Brown, who was appointed Secretary, said that the Directors had done nothing to save the team from relegation although it was obvious months ago that the team was doomed to relegation. The Meeting ended with members looking for candidates to contest election to the Board at the forthcoming A.G.M.

On the field the team took the trip down to Dumfries the following Saturday, but found no improvement, and another heavy defeat by 4-0 was the outcome. The following week with no match scheduled, a friendly was set up against Stranraer and Adam McLean scored a hat-trick in the 5-2 victory in which game Joe Henderson saved a penalty before there was any score. This turned out to be the last victory of the season with the final six League matches all ending in defeat. Goalkeeper Henderson had no answer to the Heart's forwards at Tynecastle in a 7-1 defeat, one of the goals being scored by his own defender Jimmy Hunter. On the day revered by all fans as Jimmy Cowan's Wembley International when Scotland were winning 3-1, new boy Johnny Coutts made his sole appearance of the season in goal but the Cowan-less Morton ran out easy winners by three clear goals with the forwards never seriously testing the Morton goalkeeper. The following Friday saw a Dougie Wallace goal in the first half, against his old team Clyde, overtaken by the Shawfield team, who ran out winners by 2-1.

On Monday, 18th April, the visit to Ibrox found Rovers up against a Rangers' team poised to lift the First Division Championship and the 'Gers' made no mistakes winning 3-1 although Rovers were unlucky in this one where a draw would have been a fairer result. On the Saturday the last away match took place at Methil and East Fife rattled up a 5-1 scoreline at half time but fortunately for Rovers they eased up in the second half for the score to be unchanged at full time. The season ended with Rangers' return visit to Coatbridge. The team needed one point to clinch the Championship and they went one better by building on their 2-0 half time lead to finish clear champions by one point from Dundee with a 4-1 victory. Rovers were relegated with a paltry eight points from thirty matches to be joined in 'B' Division by Morton on twenty-two.

So ended the most horrific season in modern times. Great upheavals were imminent and the first break came when Councillor Tom Griffen resigned from the Board, reportedly not wanting to have anything more to do with the Club, after having been actively associated with it for more than twenty years. Further Meetings were held by interested supporters and shareholders prior to the A.G.M. and another surprise was Andrew Beattie succeeding John Kirk as the Lanarkshire Football Association's Representative at the S.F.A. Council. He had only joined the Board relatively recently and such a rise to legislative council powers had caused much surprise in football circles.

Mr. Beattie also received permission from the Burgh Planning Department to lay down an ash speedway track at Cliftonhill. This was to take the place of the existing greyhound racing track while Mr. Beattie was actively engaged in laying down a new Greyhound Stadium on the old Cowheath site. The A.G.M. arrived, held in the YMCA Institute in Bank Street on the 9th June. There was a record attendance for such a Meeting and great local interest that the Board was about to receive a massive transfusion of new blood. Despite the knowledge that both Chairman John Kirk and Eddie McLaren had indicated their intention to retire, it turned out that both were re-elected by an overwhelming majority. Andrew Beattie was also re-appointed and two new Directors, John Rankin and Ralph Wright were appointed. Unsuccessful were Webber Lees, James Jarvie and old players Guy Watson and Lamie Smith.

The Club's Solicitor, Mr. McGill George read out a prepared statement prior to the Meeting, referring to the vote of No Confidence by Shareholders and Supporters and he depreciated the slur cast on Directors Kirk and McLaren and asked for them both to stand for election. There was great controversy over 7,000 votes which did not feature in the voting tallies and Mr. Jarvie protested, which was subsequently satisfactorily explained to the Meeting.

Quite a number of supporters had turned up with proxy cards but were not admitted to the Meeting because the votes had not been satisfactorily lodged. Also a large number of non-shareholders had to remain outside the Meeting awaiting the result.

Manager Lees, who had been unsuccessful in being re-appointed to the Board at the A.G.M., tendered his resignation on the 16th June, thus severing his connections with the Club after eighteen years' service as Secretary/Manager, and over the past three seasons this on a full-time basis. Eddie Wilkie took over as Interim Secretary and the appointment of a Manager was left to be considered meanwhile. Events moved swiftly for Mr. Lees after that and within seven days he took over at Dunfermline Athletic, who had been without a Manager for some eighteen months.

Towards the end of a tumultuous close season the members of the Supporters Club decided to 'bury the hatchet' and offered to carry out minor repairs to the stand and do paintwork at the ground.

A big clean out of players took place with only sixteen players being retained. The fight back to 'A' Division was considered not to be beyond the scope of the current players and the half dozen or so signed on prior to the new season commencing, notably Willie Jack, Tommy Anderson, Willie Black and Jimmy Wilson. Airdrie were also still in 'B' Division and at least the fans looked forward to some of the local rivalries to liven up the season ahead.

CHAPTER TEN

IN THE WILDERNESS

Season 1949/50
The season opened on the 13th of August with a League Cup Tournament on a sectional basis with four teams in each section. Rovers were drawn with Stenhousemuir, Hamilton and Forfar, and the opening day saw the visit to Larbert with the Club being represented by Boyd, Muir, English, Martin, Stein, Kerr, Craig, P. Smith, Jack, Devlin and J. Smith. As if to underline the difficulty of the promotion bid it was only a penalty in the second half by Jimmy Smith which saw the points come home to Cliftonhill. However, the start was a win, which was always something. On the following Wednesday, Hamilton Accies were beaten by 1-0 in the opening match at Cliftonhill. The long trip up to Forfar saw Rovers lose their first goal of the season and indeed were 3-1 down at half-time. Despite a Willie Dickson goal in the second half a 3-2 defeat was the end result.

The following Monday, further disaster struck Cliftonhill, in the shape of a fire, which destroyed the West wing of the grandstand. The seating available for the following match was reduced to 200 and these would all be confined to Reserve Stand ticket holders. The blaze occurred somewhat after eleven o'clock when Margaret McDade of Albion Street was walking home along Main Street when she noticed the stand ablaze. She hurried along to the Clyde Tube Works office where she met the Night Watchman and the Fire Brigade were contacted. However, by the time the detachment had arrived, the flames had got such a strong hold that auxiliary appliances had to be called in from Motherwell, Hamilton and Bellshill.

Within twenty minutes, six pumps were pouring thousands of gallons of water into the blazing building with Firemaster Nesbit directing the operation himself. With the flames shooting upwards, the asbestos sheeting comprising the roof ignited, cracked and exploded into the air to be scattered over a wide area. It took the firemen more than an hour to get the blaze under control but by that time the entire West wing had been reduced to a skeleton. One of the firemen received an injury when part of the stand flooring collapsed on him and he was treated at Alexander Hospital. Although the West portion was gutted, the area of the stand where the Board Room and Office are situated as well as the Dressing Rooms and training quarters escaped damage other than water penetration.

It had been the biggest fire in Coatbridge since the early '40's when the Middle Church in Church Street had been destroyed. Even Hitler and his bombers in the recent war hadn't managed so much destruction to Coatbridge.

The debris was cleared away and the ground staff and players prepared for the Saturday match against Stenhousemuir. Despite losing a first half goal Rovers fought back to a 2-2 draw and ended up the remainder of the campaign with draws at Hamilton by 1-1 and at home against Forfar in the last game of the section by 2-2.

The opening game of the League Campaign was against old foes Kilmarnock and, after a spirited match, a 3-1 victory was recorded. Three draws were next noted, the first being at Hamilton by 1-1 before the Lanarkshire Cup Tie against the Accies, also at Hamilton on the following midweek, gave Rovers the opportunity to do some experimentation and introduce George Cockburn in goal, Don Cornock at right half and re-introduce Willie Jack to the inside left position. The changes didn't

Albion Rovers v Stenhousemuir 27 August 1949

Standing: A. Muir, R. Kerr, J. Stein, A. Sinclair, W. Black, S. English.
Seated: W. Dickson, W. Jack, J. Boyd, J. Craig, J. Smith

seem to do any harm and the game ended all square at 2-2.

Back to League matters on the Saturday, Airdrieonians came to Coatbridge and centre forward Wilson doubled his score for the season with two goals in the 2-2 draw and this made four goals in five games for him. By having won a Lanarkshire Cup final place by means of a toss of the coin against Hamilton Accies, Rovers were down to play Airdrieonians on September weekend Monday at Broomfield in the Final. Willie Webb from Glasgow had an extremely exciting match to referee and the 6,000 fans received full value for their entrance money. After a well contested first half, Airdrie went into a deserved lead at half time but in a spirited fight back in the second half two goals, first of all by Wilson and then Smith, were sufficient to land the Cup for only the fourth time to Coatbridge which made up in some way for the disappointments of the previous season. Rovers' victorious team was Boyd, Muir, Kerr, Black, Stein, Murphy, Craig, Sinclair, Wilson, Jack and Smith.

It was again League business the following Saturday and back to a defeat with Dunfermline winning 4-1 through in Fife. Wing half Jimmy Hunter was transferred to Morton following his long period of refusing to sign and so a new phase in 'Sanddancer's' career was about to take off.

Forfar Athletic were next visitors at Coatbridge and they were soundly defeated by 6-1, the most notable feature of which was four goals by centre forward Wilson. This made ten goals in eight matches, making him top pin-up for the time being. The two Smiths scored the other two goals in this match. The visit to Alloa saw a no-scoring draw before Stenhousemuir had a resounding 6-0 victory at Larbert. With Jimmy Hunter at left half, Morton came to Coatbridge for a no-scoring draw before the visit to St. Johnstone saw new signing Jimmy Maxwell from Maryhill being introduced at centre forward but the team failed to score for the fourth match on the trot, this time losing 5-0.

The new centre retained his position and Cockburn was re-introduced in goal for the visit by Dumbarton. Maxwell scored his first goal for the Club and Jimmy Smith the winner in what turned out a 2-1 victory. Two further away matches found victories over Cowdenbeath by 3-1 and Dundee United 5-2 before Queen's Park called a halt to this run by winning 1-0 at Hampden. The team slipped up in the home match against Arbroath, allowing the Angus team to win 1-0 and for the trip to Ayr United, Cornock was re-introduced at right half in what turned out to be a no-scoring draw. Just before Christmas, Kilmarnock visited but the home team won 2-1 before, on the second last day of the year, Hamilton won 3-1 with Smith missing from the penalty spot at an important stage of the game.

15,000 turned up to see the Monday match against Airdrieonians and Jimmy Paterson made his first appearance of the season at right back in place of Muir with Wilson re-introduced at centre forward. Despite the latter scoring Rovers' goal, the Airdrie team, in top gear, won easily enough by 4-1 and the following day Dunfermline first-footed the Coatbridge team but despite Smith's penalty in the first half, the Fifers ran out winner by 3-1.

Polish amateur Joe Zangrande from Rutherglen Glencairn was signed and appeared in goal for the away match against Forfar Athletic with Muir at right back, Anderson at left half and Maxwell re-introduced at centre. This formation proved to be disastrous and the Angus team ran out convincing winners by 6-1. Cockburn returned in goal, Martin to left half and outside right Stewart from Larkhall was tried out against Alloa at Coatbridge when three Willie Jack goals in the first half were enough to fend off a fight back by the Alloa team in the second half ending up 3-2

209

winners. Stenhousemuir came to Coatbridge and again Willie Jack with a second half goal equalised a first half effort by the 'Muir, the game ending all square at 1-1.

In the Scottish Cup the following week Alloa were the visitors and Rovers were again victorious in this one, winning by a second half Dickson goal. Back in the League Morton won 2-0 at Greenock before the second round cup match with Dunfermline. In very soft conditions after a heavy snowfall, Rovers were edged out by 2-1. This result was particularly disappointing as the previous Thursday the Rovers' players had been the guests of the Directors in A.B. Brown's Tea Rooms when the Lanarkshire Cup Medals were presented. These were handed over by Mrs. Kirk with Bobby Beath, on behalf of the players, thanking the Directors and Eddie McLaren replying for the Board.

The following week the trip to Dumbarton ended up with the team being victorious by 3-0 but with a tragic leg break to right half Willie Black, who was in his first season from Junior Benburb and showing tremendous promise as a player for the future. It was a bad break and there were fears that the lad would not play football again. The following week the result was reversed at Cowdenbeath and then Dundee United visited Coatbridge to lose by 2-0. The second Rovers' goal was a penalty kick converted by Muir, but the kick was ordered to be retaken by Referee Davidson and, cool as you like, big "Chic" slotted the ball home for the second time.

Queen's Park came to Coatbridge and drew 3-3, with Muir again being on target from the penalty spot, and Arbroath received a real roasting up in Angus with Rovers winning 3-1. Ayr United had the best of a high scoring game at Somerset Park winning 5-3. The final League game found Rovers winning easily by 3-0 at home with all the goals coming in the first half. Despite this fine victory Rovers could only amass 27 points and 11th position whilst Airdrieonians were promoted on 44 points as runners-up to Morton who had 47 points.

The month of April saw, first of all, the Lanarkshire Cup semi final against Hamilton which Rovers won again at Douglas Park by 3-1 and on the following Monday Morton were defeated 3-1 in the first round of the 'B' Division Supplementary Cup. The second leg of the Lanarkshire Cup took place at Coatbridge with Hamilton fighting hard for a place in the Final and leading 1-0 at half time, but a Jimmy Smith goal in the second half was enough to share the points for Rovers to take them through on a 4-2 aggregate to meet Motherwell. The second round 'B' Division Supplementary Cup was an away tie at St. Johnstone which the Saints won by 4-2 despite valiant efforts by Cockburn, who also saved a penalty when the score was 3-2 in favour of the Saints.

The Final of the Lanarkshire Cup took place at Motherwell on the 13th May and Rovers were doing quite well up to half time but then ex-Motherwell player Tommy Anderson injured an eye and was off for the entire second half. The handicap was too great for Rovers to overcome and eventually the more experienced Motherwell side won by 4-0. Rovers' team was Cockburn, Paterson, Kerr, Cornock, English, Anderson, Jack, Dickson, Maxwell, Sinclair and J. Smith.

Five floodlights were erected during the summer for practice and training during the winter months provided by the Supporters Club. With money at a premium various avenues were pursued to raise finance. One of these was the coming of the Don Cossack Riders, a troup of Russian horsemen who performed on Cliftonhill's turf in the middle of May. The crowds entertained were not great but appreciative. Unfortunately the pounding of the horses' hoofs did nothing for the drainage at Cliftonhill and it was many years before the football ground recovered from the damage.

At this time came the first grumblings by players who were dissatisfied with their lot and several international players from Britain moved to South America to play at Bogota or the less fortunate went non-League, especially in Wales. Rovers found themselves involved in such a situation when former skipper, Jock Stein, signed for the Welsh non-League club Llanelly. Rovers would lose financially from the situation which was particularly galling as they had refused an offer for him from Kilmarnock earlier in the year.

Prior to the opening of the season Bobby Beath, who had been recently acting as a Scout for the Club and who had served as a player since 1932, was appointed part-time Manager, taking over the position made vacant when Webber Lees resigned.

At the A.G.M. at the end of July, Chairman Kirk reported a loss of £2,687:5:5d and retiring Directors, Ralph Wright and John Rankin were duly re-elected. With some hard work put in by groundsman Alec Birrell and his staff, the pitch was in fine shape and, as the supporters had properly terraced the enclosure in front of the stand and carried out their usual paint job, all was ready for the year ahead off the field. On the field it was a different matter and the rebels who were refusing terms—Muir, Sinclair and Anderson, had not put pen to paper as the last week before the new season dawned.

Trainer Jocky Robertson in full song 1950.

R. Kerr, J. Craig, D. Cornock, G. Cockburn, S. English, J. Creelman, W. Jack, W. Clark and T. Coats.

Season 1950/51

When the season opened on the 12th August, only 'Chic' Muir was holding out for better terms and the first team of the year was Cockburn, Paterson, Kerr, Cornock, Coats, Anderson, Craig, Dickson, Maxwell, Sinclair and Smith. Bobby Beath's first match as Manager saw the team start in whirlwind fashion with Andy Sinclair scoring in the first minute with the quickest goal of the Scottish season.

Maxwell and Craig also got in on the act and the scoreline at the end of the 90 minutes was 3-2. The new Manager also signed Archie McFeat from Torquay, who had been Jimmy Cowan's understudy at Greenock, and the former Polkemmet Junior took up his position in goal for the midweek match at Forfar which ended up with a 2-0 victory.

Regrettably that was the last win in the League Cup section with three straight defeats in a row coming first of all with Alloa Athletic at home by 3-1 and then Arbroath gaining revenge at the East coast by 1-0 despite Sam English making a welcome return at centre half in place of Tommy Coats who moved over to right half for the injured Cornock. A Tommy Anderson goal was not enough against Forfar at home who, despite Rovers' pressure, ran off winners at 2-1. The final game of the League Cup saw the visit to Alloa and a special train, organised with the bargain rate of 3/5d return, saw Rovers go into a 2-1 lead at half time but Alloa came back in the second half to square things at 2-2. Thus once again the League Cup campaign was unsuccessful and it was now up to the League.

The opening game in Division 'B' for this season started up at Forfar with the homesters winning by the only goal of the match before Stirling Albion appeared at Coatbridge to win in a very one-sided match by 3-1. Worse was to come the following week at Hamilton with the Accies winning 5-1 and Coatbridge boy Charlie McMullen scoring two of the Hamilton goals. Webber Lees brought his Dunfermline Athletic team to Coatbridge and went home smiling as a result of the 2-1 victory over his old love. For this match 'Chic' Muir had re-signed and made his first appearance of the season with Cornock and Craig also reappearing following injury but to no avail. The fifth defeat in a row came at Kilmarnock with Killie winning 3-2 and much grumbling from the fans who were looking for new faces.

Against Stenhousemuir at home Dick Cumming, brother of Scottish International George, was signed on a month's trial and he played at centre forward. Muir got the team off to a good start with a first half penalty and the first League win was recorded when Creelman made it 2-0 in the second half. The trip to Hampden saw a Creelman hat-trick in a fighting 3-2 victory when all the goals were scored in the second half but the other Queens, from Dumfries, put the Rovers' gas at a peep by winning 2-0 at Dumfries with Scotland centre forward Billy Houliston scoring the second goal.

The home match against St. Johnstone saw an exhilarating 4-4 draw fought out with Dick Cumming scoring a goal at last on the final day of his month's trial before being released. The next player to score a hat-trick was Jimmy Maxwell in the 5-1 victory over Dumbarton but the following week saw Cowdenbeath win 1-0 through in Fife. Dundee United won 4-0 at Coatbridge, even although Archie McFeat saved a penalty in this one and Tommy Anderson even scored a goal through his own keeper in this match which is best forgotten. At Alloa the next week the team came back from a 2-1 half time deficit to tie the match with a 'Chic' Muir penalty at 3-3. The next match was at Arbroath where three second half goals by Maxwell and Creelman saw the home team defeated 3-0.

During the next week Andy Dolan was signed from Accrington Stanley and he

Cliftonhill 1951 after stand blaze.

Cliftonhill 1985 same view.

Cliftonhill 1951 general view to east.

Cliftonhill 1985 same view.

214

lined up in place of Craig against Forfar Athletic in his home debut. Maxwell scored a double in his second successive match in the 3-2 victory. The new winger also scored the winner. There was some controversy about Dolan's signing and it was to be several weeks before he again donned a Rovers' jersey.

For the next match a visit to Annfield found Stirling Albion again winning 3-2 with wingers Craig and Creelman scoring the Coatbridge goals. On a rain soaked New Year's Day, Hamilton Accies were defeated 3-1 in a match which Hamilton right back Muir started Rovers off on the right foot by passing the ball beyond his own keeper's reach in the first half. There was then a closedown due to snow and ice until the 20th January when Queen's Park were visited and top scorer Jimmy Maxwell scored his 10th goal in 16 matches in the first few minutes. He was badly injured in the 10th minute and removed to hospital for treatment and with 10 men Rovers held on valiantly for a point, even though Queen's equalised in the first half. Maxwell was not to play again until the third last match of the season which was to be a severe blow for the team.

The Scottish Cup saw Stenhousemuir drawn at Larbert in the first round and with the fans thinking of the disastrous last trip there in 1948, they were quite relieved when a Johnny Craig goal was enough to share the points and bring the tie back to Coatbridge the following midweek. The smallest Cup attendance of the day of 3,300 paid £233 to see Rovers win by 2-1. The result was much better than the score would suggest, as both wingers Craig and Creelman had to leave the field suffering from dislocated shoulders. The experiment of playing Tommy Coats at centre forward was not a success but the crippled team did well to hang on to go into the hat for the second round.

Captain Tommy Anderson leading out the team against Clyde in the 2nd Round Cup Match 1950/51.

215

Snow cancelled the next game and a fortnight later League leaders Clyde visited Coatbridge in the second round of the cup where 9,500 fans paid £576 looking for their scalp. The Manager made a bold experiment by playing Bobby Kerr at centre forward. He had not played for several weeks due to the excellence of Willie Clark at left back and it was soon obvious that he was a misfit at centre. It was only when Rovers were two goals down that Captain Anderson and he changed places to give the team a much more balanced look. However, the remedy was too late and the tie was lost. Rovers were further handicapped with Creelman again suffering from a dislocated shoulder and being off for a considerable part of the second half.

Back on League business the following week saw Anderson continue at centre with Kerr at left half and Jimmy Smith re-introduced at outside left. This lineup seemed to click and assisted by two goals from right back Muir, one from the penalty spot, a 3-1 victory was recorded.

Rovers were kicking themselves the following week when Cowdenbeath came to Coatbridge as Airdrie had been drawn at home against Clyde in the next round Cup and the Broomfielders beat the Glasgow team by four clear goals. Back at Cliftonhill a Jimmy Smith goal in the last minute was enough to keep the points at Coatbridge. Dundee United were the next opponents but they won quite easily by 2-1 at Tannadice.

The next home match was again played in opposition to a Cup Tie, at Broomfield, where Hibs won 3-1, and two penalties from Muir and a double from Craig were enough to defeat Alloa 4-2. Muir was on the mark once more against Arbroath in a 4-0 win and for the match at Ayr, Clark was missing through injury and Bobby Kerr was reintroduced at left back but no goals were scored. In the Lanarkshire Cup, at home against Hamilton Accies, Rovers were 4-2 up with ten minutes to go but Hamilton with a spirited fight back squared the game at 4-4. On the last day of March, St. Johnstone received a jolt when the strong Rovers' team banged in three goals in the first half and, try as they might, neither team could add to the score.

Despite the team going well the visit through to East End Park and Webber Lees' Dunfermline Athletic ended up a tense affair, and Rovers scoring the only goal of the match through Andy Dolan. Kilmarnock did the double over the Coatbridge team the following week when Sam English got them off to a good start with an own goal in the first half and the Ayrshire team ran out easy winners at 3-1.

With no match scheduled for the next week, the team travelled to take on Leeds United, complete with John Charles and Derek Iggledon. The Yorkshire team won 2-0 with Clark being unfortunate and scoring the first goal for the Englishmen. On the Wednesday, Queen of the South came to Coatbridge and Scotland centre Houliston had the first goal in their 4-1 victory.

The team, which had played unchanged for five matches, was freshened up with Kerr in place of Clark at left back, Coats deputising for the injured English at centre half and Willie Jack was given another run at inside left in place of Andy Sinclair. Again this seemed to work and a 2-1 victory over Ayr at home took place the following Saturday. This was followed by a 1-0 victory at Larbert in the last League game of the season. An improvement over the previous season showed with eighth place being attained and five more points scored.

It was now on to the Hamilton Accies second leg Lanarkshire Cup Tie at Douglas Park when another 1-1 draw was fought out. Hamilton won the toss of the coin for the venue for the replay and when the match was played Walter Rothera was both saint and sinner scoring an own goal for the opening goal for Rovers in the first half and then equalising from the penalty spot in the second. Jimmy Maxwell in his second game back since return from injury scored the all-important winner in a match where Charlie McMullen broke his leg in a clash with goalkeeper McFeat and left the Hamilton team a man short for much of the second half. It was then on to the final which was played at Cliftonhill on the 19th May against Motherwell. Rovers fielded a completely revised forward line led by Jimmy Orr, signed during the week following a free transfer from Airdrieonians, and the tall bustling centre forward was flanked by Sinclair and Jack with Dickson taking up the right wing and Craig crossing over to the left. Orr, whilst he did not score in this match, played a vital part with his non-stop display which left the other players some room. Craig opened the scoring after 15 minutes with a raging shot from the left wing but keeper McFeat blotted his copybook by dropping a simple shot from Watson to put the game into extra time. The First Division team played a very frustrating game using the offside trap, but the eager Rovers' forwards were not to be denied and with only a few minutes to go, Willie Jack first timed a great shot into the roof of the net to lift the Trophy for only the fifth time. Rovers' team was McFeat, Muir, Kerr, Cornock, English, Anderson, Dickson, Sinclair, Orr, Jack and Craig.

Bobby Beath could look back with reasonable satisfaction at his first attempt at Management. A Trophy had been won and, although promotion had not been achieved, an improvement in the League position augured well for the season ahead. The display of the team in the latter half of the season was enough to suggest that better things were just around the corner.

During the close season it was confirmed that Willie Black would be unlikely to play football again following his leg break the previous season. A silver plate had been fitted in the damaged leg but it would be a long way back for the young wing half.

The Festival of Britain was held in the summer months and the Scottish Football Association agreed to hold a Tournament for a Festival Quaich. Rovers were drawn against Dunfermline Athletic away from home and Manager Beath set-to to organise a team for this match.

At the A.G.M. it was reported that Rovers had incurred a record loss of £3,373 during the previous season, and it was another unwanted record that more than once it was possible to count the spectators on the terracing in what must have been new low attendance records even for a 'B' Division Club. However, John Kirk and his beleaguered Board agreed to carry on for yet another year.

Season 1951/52
The Festival Cup game at Dunfermline saw new hero, Jimmy Orr from Airdrieonians, emerge a four goal scorer in a rousing 5-4 victory with 'Chic' Muir scoring a penalty to win the match. Great hope was now placed on the team who had drawn Airdrieonians at Broomfield in the second round. Rovers' men at Dunfermline were McFeat, Muir, Kerr, Cornock, English, Anderson, Dickson, Sinclair, Orr, Jack and Craig. Captain Anderson led his men out at Broomfield but the Airdrie team roared into a 3-0 lead at half time. Victory was beyond the Rovers' players and, despite contesting the match better in the second half, the Diamonds won 4-2.

For the start of the League Cup campaign, the match against St. Johnstone at Coatbridge saw Clark introduced at left back, Dickson moved to right half for the injured Cornock and Creelman introduced at outside left with Craig moving over to the right wing. Again a terrible first half saw the visitors 3-0 up and, despite equalising this score in the second half, the Saints popped in one more to lift the points by 4-3. Another defeat took place on the following Wednesday at Shawfield when Clyde ran out easy winners by 4-0.

Jimmy Orr was again the hero scoring the only goal of the match at Arbroath in a game where goalkeeper McFeat was injured and Cornock had to play in goal. Again Orr scored the only goal of the match up at Perth in revenge for the opening game defeat. The first half score was made all the easier when St. Johnstone had to play the second half with ten men, a player having broken his leg.

High-flying Clyde came to Coatbridge and again a first half lapse was enough to lose the points for the Cliftonhillers, with Clyde going into a 2-0 lead, and although no goals were scored in the second half, Rovers had given up long before the end of the game. Cockburn continued in goal for the injured McFeat and had to look lively in a high scoring match against Arbroath at home which looked all over bar the shouting at half time, when Rovers were leading 4-0, but a fight back in the second half by the Angus team eventually made the final score 5-4. Coatbridge was stunned when Tommy Anderson, who was in his third season with the Club since signing from Motherwell, was transferred to Clyde following this match.

Bobby Kerr took over the Captaincy for the home game against Queen's Park in the first League match at Coatbridge, with Tommy Coats taking Anderson's place. Jimmy Maxwell made his first appearance in the season at outside right and scored the equalising goal in the second half to share the points at 1-1. McFeat came back to play in goal with Alf Reid, from St. Mirren, at left half to welcome former Captain Anderson and his new team mates from Clyde in a match where Billy McPhail ran riot scoring four goals in their 5-1 victory. McFeat must have wished he had stayed on the injured list. Things were no better for him in the second half and Hamilton Accies won at Coatbridge by the only goal of the match and during the holiday week D.L. Smith, former goalkeeper and Shareholder, accepted an invitation to join the Board of Directors.

For the match at Kilmarnock, Rovers signed Amateur International J. Lindsay Hodge and played him at outside right. The team lost 3-1 with all the goals coming in the second half. Trialist Reid was also released after this match. The high-flying Falkirk team came to Coatbridge, where Willie Robb signed from Aberdeen, took up the left half position which had not been satisfactorily covered by three different players following Anderson's transfer, and he had a fine display. The match ended up 1-1 thanks only to a horrific mis-kick in mid-field by centre half Sam English which allowed ex-Hibs centre Angus Plumb on his own to beat McFeat with a strong drive. An unchanged team travelled through to Cowdenbeath to receive a 3-1 drubbing, whilst the following week lost a 3-0 half time lead to a poor Stenhousemuir outfit, the match ending all square at 3-3. Kerr was injured in this match and Muir took over the mantle of Captaincy with Clark appearing at left back and Maxwell taking Orr's place at centre forward, as the big centre had rather dried up from a goalscoring point of view. Against Dumbarton at home Maxwell scored Rovers' goal in the 1-1 draw, whilst Rovers' fans were again stunned with the news that wing half Don Cornock had been transferred, joining his old club captain with Clyde. Muir was appointed Captain and Willie Smith was signed from Arthurlie to take Cornock's place. The 22 year old P.T. Instructor was hoped to be as good an investment as the signing of Robb had been. Captain Muir scored with a second half penalty but it was not enough to overcome the Alloa 2-0 half time lead.

Willie Clark was reintroduced at left back and Jimmy Orr at centre forward for the match against St. Johnstone and the big centre scored a second half goal to keep the points at Coatbridge. Working on the Twin Centre Plan, Jimmy Maxwell and Orr got on the scoring list the following week against Arbroath in the 3-1 victory. The trip down to Ayr, which saw Willie Jack take Maxwell's place at inside right, was ill-fated and despite Orr's goal giving a first half lead, the 'Honest Men' won easily enough by 3-2. This ended up as Jack's last game for the Club and he went on to sign for Kilmarnock, subsequently to score the Ayrshire Club's winning goal in the League Cup Final against Rangers the following season.

The news that Jock Stein had signed for Celtic came as a surprise to Coatbridge but, for the home match against Dunfermline, the only change was Maxwell being placed at inside right. The Fifers ran out easy winners by 3-1. It was a different story the next week with Coats taking English's place at centre half and new signing Tom Cunningham from Partick Thistle at inside left. Orr made an unusual appearance at outside left with Maxwell taking up the centre forward berth. The new boy got off to a good start in scoring the first of three goals without reply in this match and the following week a friendly was fixed up against Kilsyth Rangers who had two Rovers' provisional signings, Bobby Holmes and Willie Ferguson, in their side. Rovers won by a solitary Orr goal.

For the trip to Hampden, Alex Forsyth from Linlithgow Rose, playing his second trial on the left wing, was signed after a fine display but it was not enough to stop Rovers going down by 2-1. Forfar Athletic then visited Coatbridge with Lindsay Hodge opening the scoring for his first goal as a Rover in a very competent 5-2 victory which saw Willie Robb, advanced to inside left, scoring the fifth goal. An unchanged team saw the Rovers, dressed in their alternative red and gold strips, visit Hamilton in the first of three no scoring draws, the others being home matches against Kilmarnock and Cowdenbeath.

The following Wednesday, Falkirk were visited but in an uninspiring game 3-1 for the Bairns was the final result. On the Saturday for the trip up to Arbroath, goalkeeper McFeat was injured and Dickson deputised in goal, the remaining ten men came back from a 2-1 deficit at half time to a 2-2 draw with Lindsay Hodge doing the needful in the second half.

At a function in A.B. Brown's Tea Rooms in Main Street, the Lanarkshire Cup winners were each presented with a small suitably engraved replica cup by George Carrol, Vice-Chairman of Airdrie and President of the L.F.A. Tom Anderson was unable to be present but all the other winners were in the company.

Just before the Scottish Cup second round match against Stranraer, it was announced that Tom Griffen had died. The former Director had in his time been official linesman and Director and as Vice-Chairman he played a major role during the Second World War on behalf of charity and raised large sums of money for the Coatbridge Provost's War Fund, the Red Cross and other organisations. Lammie Smith resigned from the Board, disillusioned at the poor running of the Club's affairs thus making a dramatic week in Club affairs.

King George VI died on the Wednesday before the Cup Tie, at which all players wore black armbands, and the non-league team shocked Rovers going into a first half lead. It was left to recent signing Alex Forsyth to score a goal in the last minute to take the match into a replay in the deep south the following Wednesday. For his pains the left winger was dropped and Cunningham introduced at inside left with Sinclair moving over to the left wing. Despite Rovers leading 2-1 at half time, Stranraer again squared the match in the second half and in extra time Rovers scored two to one from Stranraer to win 4-3 on the night in front of 3,500 ecstatic, if disappointed, locals. Ex-Rovers, Hanson and Stephenson, played for the non-leaguers.

On the following Saturday, Rovers ventured up to Perth and were handicapped with goalkeeper McFeat breaking his collar bone and the team eventually going down by 3-0. With no reserve team this gave Rovers a problem for the coming Cup tie against Third Lanark as the other goalkeeper in the books, George Cockburn, was nothing like match fit. However, he duly took his place between the sticks with Smith being introduced to the half back line and Hodge back at outside right. The 'Hi-Hi' stormed to a 2-0 lead at half time and although centre half Forsyth scored an own goal for Rovers, the Coatbridge team were unable to cut the deficit any more and Thirds won by 3-1.

Six positional changes were made for the visit by Ayr United and two of the wee men, Craig and Creelman, scored the second half goals in a 2-0 victory but the following week a point was dropped at home against Alloa at 1-1 before Dunfermline won easily on their own patch by 5-1. The second-last League match found a no-scoring draw up at Tannadice and Clyde, pushing for promotion to Division 'A', made their point by coming to Coatbridge and sweeping the Rovers aside by 3-0. A bitter pill for Rovers' supporters to swallow was the fine display by both Clyde wing halves, former Rovers' players Cornock and Anderson. In the 'B' Division Supplementary Cup, St. Johnstone came to Cliftonhill and for the second successive week Rovers lost 3-0.

There was a two week lapse before the next League match was played against Stenhousemuir at home. With a trialist in goal, Rovers were overwhelmed by 6-2 with four coming in a second half collapse against their fellow basement dwellers. Forfar, who were also at the bottom of the League, won convincingly by 2-0 up in Angus before the last game of the League programme saw Dunfermline routed 4-1 in a fine away victory with Jimmy Orr scoring a hat-trick.

The Lanarkshire Cup was left to round up the season and in the first leg at Cliftonhill, Rovers were trailing 2-1 at half time but fought back to parity at 3-3 over the ninety minutes. The following Wednesday at Douglas Park the 2-0 deficit at half time was too great a hurdle to overcome and Accies went through by 2-1.

The season thus came to an end with Rovers losing the only trophy they held and a slump from mid-table in the League down to third bottom with ten points less accumulated than the previous campaign.

At the A.G.M. at the end of May, Chairman John Kirk, Director Edward McLaren and Manager Bobby Beath, all resigned. The filling of the two vacancies on the Board, as well as the vacancy resulting from the earlier resignation by Lammie Smith, were left in the hands of the remaining two Directors, Andrew Beattie and Ralph Wright.

Eddie McLaren thus severed a connection which went back to Meadow Park days. The Balance Sheet showed a profit for the year of £104:3:5d. which was solely attributable to the transfer fees gained for Cornock and Anderson.

Further misfortune was to befall Rovers in the middle of July, when Jock Robertson left Coatbridge to become trainer to English Third Division Club Bradford Park Avenue. The trainer had been a popular figure in his dual role as trainer to Rovers and also the Paisley Pirates Ice Hockey Team. In the middle of June an Appeal was launched to keep senior football going in Coatbridge. The subscribers to the Appeal were Ian A. Dickson, Walter Loudon, Angus Mackay, William Purdie, T. D. Storrar, Dr. James Sweeney, ex-Provost James Tennent, Dr. James Thomson and ex-Provost John Pirie. The Supporters' Club were one of the first to come forward with a donation of £100 immediately and the promise of another hundred, which meant that the Club had to abandon meantime the furnishing of their new premises at Cliftonhill.

Long-serving supporter and local businessman, Tom Fagan, was appointed to the Board and Hugh Good was appointed trainer.

Season 1952/53

The opening game of the season was in the League Cup at Cliftonhill with Queen's Park as the visitors. Rovers, continuing without a Manager meanwhile, and with five new faces in the team, scored a goal in each half to beat the Amateurs 2-0 and get off to a successful start in their campaign. It was to be a prophetic victory as the only other point to be gathered in the section was in the last match as a draw. Captain Joe Johnstone from Motherwell, who had been appointed as Player/Coach after serving fifteen years at Fir Park, had vast experience to put at Rovers' disposal. Rovers' team was McFeat, McNellis, Clark, Dickson, McLean, Robb, Craig, Goldie, Orr, W. Johnstone and J. Johnstone. The remainder of the League Cup Campaign was to be a disaster with three away matches in a row, all ending in defeat. St. Johnstone first of all won by 6-3 and Stenhousemuir scoring the only goal of the match late in the second half with Eddie Dowdalls ex-Celtic, making his debut at right back. Queen's Park then won easily by 2-0 at Hampden before St. Johnstone came to Coatbridge and, despite two Robb penalties, Saints won by a clear cut 4-2 margin. Dowdalls was released after this match and McNellis resumed at right back for the home match against Stenhousemuir where Hamilton Sturgeon scored a hat-trick in the 4-4 draw which turned out to be Johnny Craig's last match before signing for Alloa.

A first League match was at Dumbarton saw the welcome reappearance of Lindsay Hodge at outside right and Captain Willie Robb at centre half. The 'Sons' won by a second half goal before the first League point was gained at home against Cowdenbeath with both the Johnstones' scoring in the first half in the 2-2 draw. Rovers introduced their 16 year old signing Bobby Thomson at inside right in this match along with centre half Eddie Curran, newly signed from New Brighton.

Rovers' fans were shocked at Hamilton when new man Curran was fielded in place of Thomson and Jimmy Orr was tried at centre half. The experiments were not a success, with Rovers losing 3-2. 'Chic' Muir resolved his differences with the Club and resigned in time to take his place at right back against Stenhousemuir. He was immediately made skipper but centre forward Jimmy Silcock scored the only goal of the game. The Lanarkshire Cup Tie against Airdrieonians at Broomfield took place at September Weekend with Rovers experimenting in the forward line with only Hodge retaining his position. Hugh Goldie at centre forward for the day scored a glorious double in the 3-2 victory over the local rivals. Former player Tom Kiernan, who had returned to the fold signing from St. Mirren played inside left in this match.

The following week the away match against Kilmarnock was postponed because they were playing Rangers in the League Cup Final to win by a Willie Jack goal to nothing, and a friendly match was fixed for Cliftonhill against a Rangers XI. Tommy Kiernan, making his home debut, scored a hat-trick in the first half but the more experienced Rangers' team came back from a 3-2 deficit at half time to win 5-3 with Archie Aikman the former Falkirk centre who had already scored five against Rovers in the ill-fated Division 'A' sojourn in 1947/48 season scoring a double.

Sam English made his first appearance of the season in the home match against St. Johnstone which Rovers won by 3-0 but Arbroath brought the recently improved form to an abrupt halt by winning 3-0 through in Angus. The visit by Stirling Albion found the youngest team in Scottish football winning by the only goal of the match with Willie Johnstone making his last appearance before being released. The support were sorry to see the tall, gangling forward leave. The trip to Forfar found Rovers wanting in all departments and this also marked Joe Johnstone's last game for the team before also being released. This was a 4-2 defeat.

Dundee United came to Cliftonhill and won by 4-2 with centre forward Mackay having a hat-trick against Sam English who, despite this difficult match, was signed after the game by United and thus another Rovers' player of some years standing had gone. Rovers tried two trialists in this match but although they played subsequent games, they were not signed.

For the match at Alloa trialist Beverage got Rovers' two goals in a 4-2 defeat and Mike Quigley from Dunfermline Athletic took English's place at centre half. The next match through in Fife against Dunfermline saw Jimmy Fullarton from Arbroath and Jimmy Lang from Middlesborough take their places in the forward line but despite a good first half Rovers went down 2-1. After this match 'keeper Archie McFeat was transferred to Falkirk.

The following week at Coatbridge, Ayr United were the visitors but with the Ayr team winning by 1-0, the game was abandoned after 21 minutes due to torrential rain and flooding of the pitch. When operations were continued the following week against Morton, George Taylor from Hamilton Accies was given a trial in goal with a junior winger at outside left but the formation was not a success and the Greenock team won easily by five without reply. For the home match against Queen's Park, Jim Burns of Bellshill Athletic had a try out in goal with Jim McCarthy from Airdrie at centre half and new signing Dave Tennant from Ipswich at outside left. The entire forward line was changed around and with Tennant scoring in the first half, Rovers managed a 1-1 draw. The following week, again at home to Dumbarton, Walter Anderson made his debut from St. Mirren at right half in the 3-1 victory. Burns was signed for the visit to Cowdenbeath and with Dickson taking Hodge's place at outside right the team was otherwise unchanged but the Fifers won by 3-2 despite a second half fight back by Rovers.

New Year's Day against Hamilton Accies at Coatbridge was a disaster with the County rivals winning easily by 6-0 and there were wholesale changes on the Saturday for the visit to Stenhousemuir with Archie Bannon from Lesmahagow at outside right and a junior centre half on trial. The new forward scored Rovers' only goal in the 3-1 defeat but was signed after the game and made his home debut, in his own position of centre forward, against Kilmarnock along with former Killie centre half Bobby Caldwell who had also played with Airdrie and Queen's Park and was currently Scotland's Amateur International Captain. Despite Killie being one up at half time, Rovers fought back through goals by Tennant and Goldie to lift the points at 2-1.

Playing an unchanged team against St. Johnstone at Perth, Rovers again were one behind at half time but goals by Hodge, Goldie and Bannon saw a fine, fighting victory. The following week in the replayed match against Ayr United the same players scored with Bannon securing a hat-trick, but in an incredible match Rovers lost 6-5.

The next home match was against Arbroath which Rovers lost 2-1 despite

Albion Rovers v Dunfermline 21st March 1953

Standing: W. Dickson, A. Muir, W. Robb, J. Burns, R. K. Caldwell, J. McNellis.
Seated: J. L. Hodge, T. Kiernan, J. Orr, H. Goldie, A. Bannon.

getting off to a fine first minute goal scored by Bannon in a match which was played in gale force conditions. The next week saw a Scottish Cup second round match at Coatbridge against 'C' Division, East Stirlingshire and, although Rovers toiled in the first half mainly due to a fine display by the minnows, goals by Goldie and Orr, who was playing at outside left for the day, were sufficient to see Rovers into the next round. This was against Queen of the South at Palmerston and a goal in each half by the Queens saw them usher Rovers out of the Cup.

Back in the League at Dundee, United won 2-1 and the same score saw Alloa pick up the points at Coatbridge the following week. In another home match, Lindsay Hodge scored the only goal of the first half direct from a corner but victory was denied by Dunfermline sharing the points at 2-2 with Rovers trying six positional changes in this match. For the trip down to Ayr, Rovers got a 4-3 defeat for their trouble. Six different positional changes were tried out against Morton and this time they worked for the Greenock team were defeated 4-1 due very much to the leadership shown by new captain Bobby Caldwell.

The centre half played against his former team at Kilmarnock but the Ayrshire team won easily by four clear goals. The last point of a poor League performance was gained at home at 1-1 against Forfar before the League season finished with heavy defeats by 4-0 against Queen's Park and 3-0 against Stirling Albion, both away from home, leaving Rovers very clear wooden spoonists with a paltry 14 points from the 30 games played. Forfar were second bottom with 20 points and Stirling Albion and Hamilton Accies were promoted. Stirling clinched their promotion in the last game of the season with their victory over Rovers.

Burns and Muir played their last matches for Rovers in the Stirling Albion game. Some hope of success at the end of the season came in the fine 4-2 victory over Airdrieonians at home which made a 7-4 aggregate over the two games with Whifflet boy Jim McCracken in goal, having been signed the previous night from Hibernian. After six seasons at Cliftonhill this was Willie Dickson's last game before the team moved on to the last game of the season against Motherwell in the Lanarkshire Cup Final at Fir Park. This game turned out to be an absolute disaster for Rovers, who were down at one stage to only eight men. Johnny McNellis in his last match for the Club was ordered off, whilst Robb and Lamont were both unfit to continue for a period although both returned to the fray before the end. In the circumstances it's surprising Motherwell did not win by a more flattering score than 3-0. Hugh Goldie and Jimmy Orr also played their last match for Rovers in this tie. Rovers' team was—McCracken, Lamont, Clark, McNellis, R. K. Caldwell, Robb, J. L. Hodge, Kiernan, Bannon, Goldie and Orr. New Manager, Jackie Hutton, was most disappointed with his team and with a large shedding of players the rush was on to sign fresh talent. He also had to arrange a new trainer as Andy Aitken resigned. John Walters of Kilsyth was duly appointed.

In July, Eddie Wilkie, who had been carrying on the post of part-time Secretary since Webber Lees left, resigned. At the A.G.M. a loss of £1,491:3:7d was reported and Chairman Beattie and Directors Johnny McMillan, Tommy Fagan, Davie Shanks and Ralph Wright would have a hard job to consolidate the team in the months ahead.

Raids were made on the Junior ranks and several players were fixed up, although many of them had to prove themselves in the Senior sphere.

Season 1953/54

The season opened with a team comprising seven players new to Rovers, three of whom were straight from the Junior ranks and the supporters did not have particularly high hopes in the opening League Cup match at Hampden. Their worst fears were realised when Queen's scored two goals in each half without reply. Rovers' team was—McCracken, Kerr, Clark, Boyce, R. K. Caldwell, Robb, Crawford, T. Kiernan, F. Kiernan, O'Donnell and Clifford.

Joe McLaughlan, the former Celtic and Raith Rovers defender, was signed to play at right back in the opening home match of the season against Ayr United. The full-back scored Rovers' goal in the first half but an avalanche of goals in the second half saw Ayr run out easy winners by 4-1.

The following Saturday further disaster befell the Coatbridge team, with Stenhousemuir winning 4-0 on tiny Ochilview. Sam Dunn from Clyde was fielded at left back and Dick Cumming from Motherwell took up the outside right position. The first point of the season came in a fighting 1-1 draw against Queen's Park at Coatbridge, but Ayr United, the following Wednesday, confirmed their superiority winning 3-0 at Ayr, a result which left Rovers firmly at the foot of their Section. This was a position which was not changed by the 2-2 draw against Stenhousemuir at Cliftonhill in the sixth and last game. Ayr easily won the Section to proceed to the quarter finals. Although there was not much success on the field in the way of points, the team was shaping up with Sam Dunn now performing at centre half with Bobby Caldwell at right back. New signing John Docherty from Maryhill Harp was now at outside left to be nursed along as one for the future.

For the opening League game against Third Lanark at Coatbridge, Arthur Nugent from Arthurlie at left back and John McPhail from Ashfield at right half were introduced in a very inexperienced team and it was firmly expected that Third Lanark would win without much exertion. This was not to be and, assisted by fine work from Dunn and tremendous long goal kicking from McCracken, they kept the Third Lanark defence under pressure. It was no surprise when Felix Kiernan scored his first goal for Rovers in the first half which turned out to be the only goal of the match. The turning point of the game was when finally McCracken was beaten with a shot from the Thirds' forwards but Dunn raced back to scoop the ball off the line just prior to Rovers opening the scoring. Following the game the two junior trialists were signed but less good news was the refusal of ex-Clyde Dunn to sign following his very successful month's trial and for the next game in the away match against Dumbarton. Bob Sommerville, another former Clyde player, was signed to fill the vacancy. The player had originally decided to hang up his boots but Rovers were very persuasive in their arguments and the player turned out in place of Dunn for the match which turned out badly with Rovers losing by 5-1.

In the next match against county rivals Motherwell, a good stroke of business was done by persuading Celtic to transfer Johnny McGrory on loan until the end of the season, and the versatile player teamed up at centre forward with Nugent reverting to right back, his junior position. Clark was at left back and Sam Dunn, persuaded to sign, took up his position at centre half. This allowed Sommerville to be released from his contract and the Motherwell team found themselves in quite a game. McGrory scored the first goal but this was equalised by half time and in a tremendously exciting match, Docherty scored with a grand header from a McGrory cross but the more experienced Motherwell team were too strong and they eventually won in the end by 3-2. Not to be disheartened the team was unchanged, apart from Lindsay Hodge, now available after holidaying in Spain,

Albion Rovers v St. Johnstone 3rd October 1953

Standing: A. Nugent, W. Clark, J. McCracken, J. McPhail, S. Dunn, W. Robb.
Seated: J. L. Hodge, T. Kiernan, J. McGrory, F. Kiernan, J. Docherty.

taking the place of Archie Bannon at outside right and this formation immediately clicked with Felix Kiernan and McGrory scoring in the first half before McGrory got a third goal in a famous 3-0 victory which was marred by Captain Bobby Caldwell breaking his leg to such an extent that he had to spend three weeks in Kilmarnock Infirmary until the limb was properly set.

Willie Robb took Caldwell's place at left half for the visit by St. Johnstone and Rovers held on to a 2-0 score line, despite a spirited fight back by Saints in the second half, by winning 3-2, thanks, in the main, to a fine defensive display by new Captain Dunn. At Cowdenbeath the following week the Fifers won 4-3 despite Rovers leading 2-0 at half time and what for them was a most disappointing result.

Stenhousemuir came to Coatbridge and a Felix Kiernan goal in the second half saw the points remain at Coatbridge. It was the same player who scored again the next week at Arbroath but the Angus team ran out winners by 3-1 and a 2-2 draw at Alloa was next. Andy Batton ex-Morton played against his old mates at Coatbridge at right back and a tremendous fight back in the second half saw Rovers overcome a 2-0 deficit into a fine 3-2 victory. So much so that Phil Cole, the local publican and ardent fan, presented all the players with shaving mugs in commemoration of the event. At Hampden the following week another fight back was called for with again a 2-0 deficit at half time and this time the team managed to draw level but couldn't get the all-important winner.

Thanks to Director Davie Shanks's help, the grandstand had been rebuilt following the fire in 1949 and was available for paying spectators for the home match against Ayr United. This ended up as a triumph for Rovers at 4-2 and another good result was the 3-1 victory in front of 9,000 fans against Dunfermline Athletic. Forfar were defeated up at Angus by 2-1 before Dundee United fought out a hard one point at 3-3 at Coatbridge, although they must have been kicking themselves as Rovers had another fight back from a two goal deficit at half time, this time 3-1 in favour of United.

Third Lanark gained revenge for their earlier defeat winning by a second half goal to nothing at Cathkin and the following Wednesday, prior to Christmas, Rovers inaugurated the new floodlights at Saracen Park against Junior Ashfield. Rovers changed their formation from the team which had played in the previous seven matches and fielded three juniors and ex-Celt Pat McAuley at left back. The Junior team won 4-3 and to complete Rovers' night of misery, John McGrory missed a penalty, not only kicking it over the bar but straight out of the park.

On Christmas Day, Dumbarton were the visitors and went into a half time lead but, as was now expected of them, Rovers charged back in a tremendous second half revival to win 4-1. The following Friday, on New Year's Day, Motherwell inflicted a 6-0 defeat on Rovers in a match where nothing came off for the Coatbridge men and the Motherwell team were intent on ensuring there was no fight back this time. With Dunn still missing through injury, Captain McGrory led a spirited forward line against Kilmarnock and Archie Bannon equalised a first half goal by Killie to share the points in a match during which goalkeeper McCracken complained of feeling unwell. On the Sunday he was taken to hospital and operated on for appendicitis. The following Wednesday another friendly against Junior opposition took place with Maryhill visiting Coatbridge and again Rovers took the opportunity of playing many trialists with John Docherty appointed captain for the day. Rovers won 2-1 and several promising boys were noted.

Come the following Saturday, Ken Brodie, Junior Scotland's International keeper from Duntocher Hibs, was introduced in goal and Sam Hadcroft to left half from the Junior Shettleston team. Despite playing at centre half against St. Johnstone, Captain McGrory scored a double in the 3-3 draw. He welcomed back Sam Dunn, who resumed the Captaincy, and, most surprisingly, appendix victim McCracken back to goal for the match at Cliftonhill against Cowdenbeath. Rovers romped to a 3-1 lead at half time and eventually ran out winners by 3-2 with McCracken acquitting himself excellently in goal.

At Larbert the following week Stenhousemuir won rather easily by 3-0 and Pat McAuley was signed from Luton Town in time to play at left half at home against Forfar which the Athletic team won by 2-1. McAuley was played at right half, in place of McPhail, against Arbroath at Coatbridge in the 1-1 draw and for the Scottish Cup first round match against Dundee the following week played at right back — his third position in three games for the Club. Rovers were in trouble for this match, with Dunn being unavailable, and man-of-many-clubs George Henderson was signed from Dunfermline Athletic in the 'wee sma hoors' on the Saturday morning to line up at centre forward. Dundee were disappointed that Billy Steel their international forward would not be available for the forward line but the First Division team were bristling with personalities and they were quite confident in winning this one.

There were many games off that day, especially the Falkirk/Celtic Tie and such was the interest generally in the match that the players from Falkirk came through in the Celtic bus to view the thrills. Thrills and spills there were to spare in what turned out to be a real old-fashioned Cup Tie. The first half was all Rovers but no goals were scored. Bill Brown was the busiest man on the park in the Dundee goal but when, after all the Coatbridge pressure, centre half-cum-centre forward George Merchant scored, you could have heard a pin drop. Then, when the ball was at the other end of the pitch, Danny Malloy the Dundee centre half made a rash foul in the penalty box on Henderson to give away a stupid penalty and skipper McGrory ordered Pat McAuley to take the important kick. Unfortunately the experienced ex-Celt was not up to the occasion and his pathetic effort from the spot was easily saved by Bill Brown, much to the dejection of the Rovers' fans. Then Rovers thought they had got it right when Brown saved, fell, dropped the ball and Felix Kiernan banged it into the back of the net. For some inexplicable reason the referee chalked off the goal, but Rovers were not to be outdone and in due course justice was done when new centre George Henderson scored, the ground erupted and Dundee hung on grimly for a draw over the remainder of the ninety minutes.

The following Wednesday up at Dundee the replay was again one-sided, this time in favour of Dundee who ran out easy winners by four George Merchant goals to nil and Rovers were once more out of the Scottish Cup. The following Saturday, Rovers were, not unexpectedly, rather jaded and when Alloa came to Coatbridge, despite Henderson scoring his second goal for the Club, the 'Wasps' ran out winners by 3-1.

A friendly was fixed up against Berwick Rangers as the Queen's Park match was postponed because of the Amateur International and both teams were affected by players appearing in the match. The Berwick game ended up 1-1 before the following Saturday at Ayr, the 'Honest Men' equalised a first half deficit in a 2-2 draw. Dunfermline was the next team to be visited and two McKinlay goals were enough to keep the points in Fife before Dundee United had an overwhelming 6-2 victory over Rovers with centre forward Mackay hitting a hat-trick. The fifth away match in a row saw a Johnny McGrory goal sufficient to take the points to

Coatbridge from Greenock.

On the next week Motherwell visited for a 1-1 Lanarkshire Cup Tie before the last Division 'B' match saw two McGrory goals sufficient to beat the Queen's Park team in the re-arranged match and, although Rovers' League position was much improved from the previous year, they could only attain seventh place with 31 points which was 12 off promoted Kilmarnock with Motherwell clinching the Championship with 45 points.

The League winners visited Coatbridge the following Saturday and again drew in the Lanarkshire Cup, this time by 1-1. In extra time there was no scoring and Motherwell won the toss of the coin to take the replayed match to Motherwell and John McGrory scored his last goal for Rovers before signing for St. Mirren, much to the disappointment of the Rovers' fans. Motherwell won the tie by 4-1.

In the close season there was a clear-out of players, including George Henderson and Tommy Kiernan to Alloa. Young inside forward Bobby Thomson was signed by local rival Airdrieonians on an amateur form but most of the stars of the past season were available when new trainer Tom Kearney prepared the players during the close season. Manager Hutton signed centre forward Sammy Hemple from Celtic, Tony Reilly from Falkirk, Tommy Quigley from Airdrieonians and Walter Auld from Middlesborough in an effort to install more punch in the forward line.

Season 1954/55
For the opening League Cup section tie, Morton were the visitors. Felix Kiernan scored the only goal in the second half to get Rovers off to a promising start. The team was — McCracken, Nugent, Clark, McPhail, Dunn, Robb, Quigley, Crawford, Hemple, Kiernan and Auld. The following midweek match at Alloa was no scoring but Arbroath won 3-1 on the following Saturday at Angus.

Morton also won convincingly by 3-0 in the third away game in a row before Alloa fought out a real ding-dong cup tie 2-2 draw at Coatbridge. Revenge was gained over Arbroath by a 3-1 margin but once again Rovers were unsuccessful in proceeding further in the League Cup.

Against Ayr United in the opening 'B' Division match at Coatbridge, despite a 3-2 first half lead, Rovers lost the game by 5-4 and followed this up with a fighting draw at 3-3 against Airdrieonians at Broomfield, having trailed 2-1 at half time. Rovers fielded Charlie Higgins at left back, Dan Stillie at inside right and Willie Graham at centre forward against the 'Diamonds' and this seemed the impetus needed by Rovers. On September Monday, Broomfield was again the venue for the Lanarkshire Cup tie at the holiday weekend, which Airdrie this time ran out easy winners by 6-1 in front of 6,000 fans.

A fight back in the second half saw Tony Reilly equalise a first half goal from Stenhousemuir in a match which saw Willie Robb play his last game before being transferred to Bradford City. The team would miss his strong forceful play but wished him well in his career. During the week amateur internationals Bobby Caldwell and Lindsay Hodge re-signed and they took up the right back and outside right positions respectively in the home match against Arbroath with John McPhail taking Robb's place at left half. The forward line was re-cast but the first half didn't show much promise with the score at 3-1 for the Angus team. There was better to come in the second half with the match ending all square at 4-4. The trip to Brechin City saw the disappointment of a half-time lead lost to a second half equaliser. It was the same score the following week against Third Lanark at Coatbridge. In both of these matches new signing Ken Maxwell from Northampton showed fine form at right back.

Trialist Maguire from Ashfield at outside left scored a fine goal in the first half to defeat St. Johnstone by the only goal of the match at Perth and Dundee United came back in the second half to equalise a Reilly goal for a 1-1 draw. The Forfar match was another 1-1 draw but the visit to Dunfermline turned out to be a disaster losing by an emphatic 7-0 margin with O'Brien scoring a hat-trick. There was to be no quick bouncing back from that defeat when Queen's Park were victorious at Hampden by 2-0. When Morton visited Coatbridge the following week, a fine 3-3 draw was played out with a fight back from a 2-0 deficit at half time saving the day.

Rovers A.G.M. held on Tuesday, 30th November, showed a profit of £896:18:7d and found Tom Fagan succeeding Andrew Beattie as Chairman. Mr. Beattie was re-elected to the Board and Jackie Hutton, who had been part-time Manager up to this time, was voted on to the Board in place of Johnny McMillan who had retired.

With Rovers struggling with injuries, captain Sam Dunn was unavailable and McPhail occupied his position with Caldwell taking over the Captaincy. Junior players Ure at left back and Delaney at outside right, were given a trial but the Hamilton team showed no compassion and romped to a 5-0 victory. During the next week, old chum Willie Findlay was re-signed on a free transfer from Rangers and Johnny Farquhar ex-Queen's Park, Cowdenbeath and others, was signed to make up the right wing with Findlay. Johnny Hannah from Stranraer was fixed up for left half and with Dunn back at centre half, the team showed nine positional changes from the previous lineup. Against Ayr United, in a thrilling 2-2 match, which was a respectable scoreline with so many players new to each others' play.

On New Year's Day, 13,000 fans first-footed Cliftonhill for the visit by Airdrieonians. Despite winning 2-1 at half time, the 'Diamonds' equalised through top-scorer Hugh Baird to make the final scoreline 2-2. Captain Dunn scored Airdrie's other goal. The visit to Cowdenbeath found the Fifers winning 4-2 but Willie Findlay scored his first goal following his return to the team. The same player also scored in the next match at home against Stenhousemuir but the Warriors won this one by 3-2 overcoming a 2-1 lead by the homesters at half time.

The next match saw Rovers visit Cathkin to win 2-1 thanks to an own goal by Thirds left back McCreadie, with Findlay having opened the score for Rovers. The big lanky inside forward could do nothing in the Scottish Cup Tie at Shawfield the following week when three goals by the First Leaguers in the first half were enough to sink Rovers from this competition. The following week, Findlay got back on the goal scoring waggon with a double in the 4-2 victory over St. Johnstone at Coatbridge and another home victory was secured, this time over Dunfermline by 2-1 thanks to a Sam Dunn penalty. All goals were scored in the second half in this match.

Johnny Farrell, that versatile pint-sized player from Alloa, was signed during the week and he took up the left half position against Queen's Park at home but the Amateurs ran out easy winners by 3-1. Young John Docherty asked for and received a free transfer after this match, which was only his eleventh appearance of the season.

Rovers played Hannah in Docherty's place, moved Farrell to centre half and Dunn to left back for the injured Clark against Morton at Greenock. But a goal in each half saw the points stay 'doon the watter'. Rovers switched inside forwards

S. & J. FAGAN
DEMOLITION CONTRACTORS
26 CALDER STREET
COATBRIDGE
Phone — 735
SECTIONAL HUTS and GARAGES

Coatbridge Stadium
RACING MONDAY AND FRIDAY AT 7.30
Scotland's Finest Greyhound Track
Tel. Coatbridge 88

Tel. Coatbridge 825
WEBBER LEES (SPORTS) LTD.
"THE SPORTS SHOP"
160 MAIN STREET, COATBRIDGE

HUGH DOUGLAS
ELECTRICAL ENGINEER
BLAIR ROAD
COATBRIDGE
ESTIMATES GIVEN FREE

Telephone — Coatbridge 19
THE HILTON BUILDING & FIREPLACE Co., Ltd.
SLATERS & PLASTERERS
201 MAIN STREET   COATBRIDGE

FIXTURES

1954
		Goals		
		For Agst	Pts	
Aug. 14 — AYR UNITED | 4 | 5 | 0
     18 — AIRDRIEONIANS | 3 | 3 | 1
Oct. 2 — STENHOUSEMUIR | 1 | 1 | 1
      9 — AIRDRIEONIANS | 4 | 4 | 1
     16 — BRECHIN CITY | 1 | 1 | 1
     23 — THIRD LANARK | 1 | 1 | 1
     30 — ST. JOHNSTONE | 1 | 2 | 1
Nov. 6 — DUNDEE UNITED | 1 | 1 | 1
     13 — FORFAR ATH. | 1 | 7 | 3
     20 — DUNFERMLINE ATH | 0 | 2 | 3
     27 — QUEEN'S PARK | 0 | 2 | 0
Dec. 4 — MORTON | 4 | 3 | 3
     11 — HAMILTON ACAS. | 1 | 1 | 1
     25 — AYR UNITED | 2 | 2 | 1
1955
Jan. 1 — AIRDRIEONIANS | 2 | 1 | 0
      3 — COWDENBEATH | 2 | 4 | 0
      8 — STENHOUSEMUIR | 1 | 1 | 0
     29 — THIRD LANARK | 0 | 2 | 0
Feb. 12 — ST. JOHNSTONE | 4 | 2 | 2
Mar. 12 — DUNFERMLINE ATH | 1 | 2 | 2
     19 — QUEEN'S PARK   Home
     26 — MORTON   Away
Apr. 2 — HAMILTON ACAS. Home
      9 — ALLOA   Away

POSTPONED GAMES.
Cowdenbeath (h); Alloa (h).
Brechin City (h); Arbroath (a).
Dundee United (h); Forfar Athletic (a).

No. 132

Remember—Your Programme may have the Lucky Number—
If so, collect your prize at the Office.

Albion Rovers F.C.

Saturday
19th March
VERSUS

QUEEN'S PARK
KICK-OFF 3 p.m.

OFFICIAL PROGRAMME   3d.

ROBERT REILLY
SECTIONAL BUILDER and TIMBER MERCHANT
BUSINESS ADDRESS:—   Tel. COATBRIDGE 906
47 DUNDYVAN ROAD   ::   COATBRIDGE

ANGUS MACKAY
MEAT PURVEYOR
Corned Beef and Pickled Tongue
SAUSAGES A SPECIALITY
88 WHIFFLET ST., COATBRIDGE
Phone: Coatbridge 340

E. & R. WRIGHT
Fishmonger and Poulterer
125 MAIN ST. and 111 BANK ST.
COATBRIDGE
Tel. Coatbridge 482

WM. GORMAN
DUNDYVAN ROAD
COATBRIDGE
Private Parties Catered for
at Keenest Prices

TEAS   ::   ICES
ARTHUR RUSSO, LTD.
RAINBOW CAFE
MAIN STREET :: COATBRIDGE
HAVE YOUR MORNING COFFEE

Printed by Wm. Craig & Sons, 45 Main Street, Coatbridge

Albion Rovers v Queen's Park Programme Saturday 19th March 1955

WM. NICOL
(Haulage Contractors) Ltd.
BROWN STREET
WHIFFLET
COATBRIDGE
Phone — 288

SHOP AT THE
**COATBRIDGE
CO-OPERATIVE
SOCIETY, LTD.**
Who can supply
YOUR REQUIREMENTS
IN QUALITY GOODS
AT THE RIGHT PRICE
WITH A
HANDSOME DIVIDEND
EACH HALF-YEAR

Donald McLaren, Ltd.
Motor Hirers
THE CROSS :: COATBRIDGE
Telephone—132

James Davidson
M.P.S.
PHARMACIST
57 SUNNYSIDE ROAD
and
125 GARTSHERRIE ROAD
COATBRIDGE

J. PEEL
SALOON BAR
290 MAIN STREET, COATBRIDGE
DISCUSS THE GAME IN COMFORT • TWO MINUTES' WALK FROM GROUND

Esso and Tecalemit Service
ANGUS & POTTS, LTD.
CLIFTONHILL GARAGE, COATBRIDGE
Telephone 534

TEAMS
ALBION ROVERS
McCRACKEN ✓
MAXWELL ✓   CLARK ✓
          (2)   (3)
McPHAIL ✓   DUNN ✓   FARRELL ✓
   (4)   (5)   (6)
FARQUHAR ✓ FINDLAY ✓ KEIRNAN ✓ CRAWFORD ✓ DOCHERTY ✓
    (7)   (8)   (9)   (10)   (11)

READ THE REPORT ON THIS GAME   — IN TOMORROW'S
AND ALL THE OTHERS IN   NEWS of the WORLD

W. OMAND ✓   R. DALZIEL ✓   M. MURRAY ✓   R. McCANN ✓   J. REID ✓
    11
   J. ROBB ✓   J. VALENTINE ✓   R. CROMAR ✓
      W. HASTIE ✓   I. G. HARNETT ✓
              F. CRAMPSEY ✓
QUEEN'S PARK
Referee—J. JACKSON (Glasgow)
Linesmen—A. P. GOW (Edinburgh), H. G. RUTHERFORD (Edinburgh)

After the Match, Visit
THE CENTRAL BAR
(Prop. D. McDONALD)
509 MAIN STREET
COATDYKE

ALEX. STARK
DAIRYMAN
BURNSIDE DAIRY, COATDYKE
Tel. COATBRIDGE 909
"Dairy Maid" Ices

JACK HASTINGS
WHOLESALE AND RETAIL
IRONMONGERS AND TOOL
MERCHANTS
8 SUNNYSIDE ROAD
COATBRIDGE
Telephone: Coatbridge 813

JAMES REID
PAINTER :: DECORATOR
— and GLAZIER —
21 ELLIS STREET
COATBRIDGE
ESTIMATES
Phone: — Coatbridge 978

H. Campbell & Co. Ltd.
45 BANK STREET
COATBRIDGE
We Specialise in Delivery of Orders
Telephone   185

THE
**NIGHT STAR
FISH RESTAURANT**
AT
90 WHIFFLET STREET
TRY OUR FISH SUPPERS
Always at Your Service

Robert Irvine & Sons
Ladies and Gent's Tailors, Clothiers,
Outfitters and General Warehousemen
6 CHURCH STREET
COATBRIDGE
Tel. 26   Estb. 1899

WM. CRAIG & SONS
Printers, Bookbinders and Stationers
45 MAIN STREET   ★   COATBRIDGE
Telephone COATBRIDGE 172
Manufacturing Stationers and Printers for
Social and Sports Programmes, Members'
Cards, etc.

231

Crawford and Findlay and reinstated Clark at left back with Caldwell at centre half against Alloa Athletic and this was enough to secure the points in this away match by a 2-1 scoreline.

Recently married Felix Kiernan scored a double in the 3-2 victory over Hamilton Accies before the long journey through to Angus found Forfar Athletic winning easily by 4-1 in a rearranged match, the original match having been postponed due to frost. The following week saw Rovers without a match and a friendly was arranged at Cliftonhill against Baillieston Juniors. The Coatbridge team took the opportunity of trying out several youngsters and a 1-1 draw was the result.

Alloa regained ample revenge for their earlier defeat by a 2-0 victory at Coatbridge and a second half goal was enough to keep the points at Arbroath the following week.

To end a very disappointing season, Brechin City visited Coatbridge on a Wednesday at the end of April in a torrential downpour. Goals by Crawford and Findlay gave Rovers a win by 2-0. Rovers had tried to have the game postponed in view of the Scottish Cup Final replay being played the same night at Hampden, but Brechin insisted that the match go ahead. Only 172 paying spectators provided £10:18:3d, leaving Rovers 13/7d to meet the £150 guarantee to the Angus Club after having paid for the match officials. An interesting feature of the Cup Final was both captains were former Rovers' captains — Tommy Anderson (Clyde) and Jock Stein (Celtic).

The following Saturday Cowdenbeath came to Coatbridge, but despite leading 2-0 at half time, Rovers lost 3-2. The last game, again at home, against Dundee United was won by a 3-2 scoreline with Rovers this time fighting back from a 2-1 deficit at half time.

A final game of the season was played at Cliftonhill against Airdrieonians in the Lanarkshire Cup and, with Rovers introducing three new players, the 'B' Division Champions won fairly comfortably by 3-2. There was a big rush of free transfers from Cliftonhill, notably Willie Findlay, but also Arthur Nugent, Archie Bannon and Johnny Farquhar, who all went to pastures new. Despite a generally poor season, as far as results were concerned, the fans generally were satisfied that the new regime had brought with it an air of promise for the future and that it was only a matter of time before the team would fight its way out of Division 'B' and join Airdrieonians in Division 'A'. The League position was eleventh with 26 points from 30 games and Airdrieonians as Champions with 46 points from Dunfermline's 42. Brechin, who had been promoted from 'C' Division the previous season at the expense of Dumbarton, were wooden spoonists on 19 points.

In the close season the Scottish League agreed to admit the five teams which had been languishing in Division 'C' playing the reserve teams of predominantly 'A' Division sides. These were Berwick Rangers, Dumbarton, East Stirlingshire, Stranraer and Montrose. The Scottish League Division 'A' was also increased to 18 clubs with the bottom two teams — Motherwell and Stirling Albion — remaining in the upper Division although Stirling had amassed a paltry 6 points from 30 matches and Motherwell 22.

Season 1955/56
New trainer, Jim Rodger, had his players in fine trim for the opening match at Dundee against the local United when four new players were fielded in a satisfying 3-1 victory. Rovers' team was — McCracken, Maxwell, Clark, McPhail, Dunn, Wilson, McKinstry, Crawford, Kiernan, Carr and Gibson. There was a good crowd

at the first home match again caused in part by Rovers' season tickets which were a bargain costing the same as the previous season but for six matches more. This was against Forfar Athletic and ended up a single goal victory thanks to a first half goal by inside left Carr who had now got off to an explosive start with three goals in two games. Veteran Peter Rice, former Raith Rovers and St. Mirren right winger, took McKinstry's place at outside right and Johnny Farrell made his first appearance of the season at outside left against Motherwell but a goal in either half by the 'Steelmen' saw Rovers receive their first defeat of the season.

For the midweek League match against Cowdenbeath at home, the current rave of Junior football, Pat Quinn of Bridgeton Waverley, was given a trial with new signing Alec Paterson from St. Mirren at left half in place of Wilson and Farrell being played at right back in place of Maxwell. The Quinn-inspired team won 5-1 with the Junior scoring two magnificent goals. Despite all efforts, Quinn refused to sign much to the disappointment of the Management and supporters. On the following Saturday against Dundee United, in the return League Cup match, Carr was re-introduced to inside forward making up the right wing with McKinstry, a 3-3 draw was fought out. This season's League Cup Section ended in disarray with the final two games ending in away defeats. First of all, Forfar won 2-1 and then Motherwell by a 4-0 margin.

Joe McGowan, from Baillieston Juniors, made his debut in the Motherwell match and another newcomer Bob Wyllie, from Dalry Thistle, took up the outside right position for the next match against Stranraer. Jimmy McCracken failed to pass a fitness test and trialist McCulloch from Bridgeton Waverley was given a run in goal. This game was a bit of a disaster for Rovers with centre half Dunn being ordered off and Rovers eventually losing 5-1. The following week East Stirlingshire came to Cliftonhill and, with McCracken back in goal and Maxwell at right back, trialist Quinn played his third and last match for Rovers, in a game which started well with Rovers 2-1 up at half time but the match was squared at the end of 90 minutes at 2-2.

For the match at Hampden, Felix Kiernan appeared at left half and Farrell at inside right which for both was their fourth position of the season but the Amateurs won by 2-0. The following Wednesday, Forfar came to Cliftonhill with Andy McColl from Clyde fielded at left half. He immediately tightened up the defence and the forwards had a field day winning 4-0 over the piece. Hamilton Accies were next visitors to Coatbridge and new boy Reilly scored his first goal in a 3-2 win.

Next Monday Airdrieonians were the third visitors in a row at Coatbridge in a Lanarkshire Cup tie with high-scoring centre forward Hugh Baird playing his 60th consecutive game for the 'Diamonds'. Rovers with a re-cast left wing were out of it in the first half going in at half time 2-0 down and despite a fight back in the second half when centre forward Wilson scored, Airdrie regained control of the game to end up winners by 2-1.

Back on League business the following Wednesday, East Stirlingshire demolished the boys from Coatbridge in a 4-1 defeat with Rovers playing new signing Pat Glancy from Blackburn Rovers at inside left. For the Saturday match at Stenhousemuir, Glancy was played at left half and Kiernan now at inside left scored the equaliser in a 1-1 draw. The next match saw Ayr United visit Cliftonhill with Kiernan, now at centre forward and Glancy back at inside left. Despite having the handicap of goalkeeper McCracken being off and inside right Crawford in goal, both forwards scored two goals each for a clear 4-2 win. With a virtually unchanged team, the following week found St. Johnstone 3-0 up at half time and,

233

despite Kiernan scoring two goals in the second half, the Saints ran out easy winners at 7-2.

Three days later was the Scottish Cup first round match against Alloa, managed by old friend Webber Lees, and with former players Bobby Kerr and Jimmy Hunter playing with the opposition. Rovers were struggling in the first half and it was only a second half goal from Felix Kiernan which squared the match into a replay the following Wednesday at Alloa. In front of a 2,700 gate, Alloa took full use of the home advantage to win by 4-0.

Seven positional changes the following week at Dumbarton was no improvement and despite two goals by Pat Glancy the Sons won 3-2. Alloa were played for the third time in four matches this time at Cliftonhill and in a tousey match with Rovers, losing 1-0 at half-time, had right half McColl ordered off and only equalised through Crawford via the penalty spot. Two away games followed with Rovers losing 1-0 at Brechin before two Kiernan goals in the second half equalised a 2-0 half time score at Arbroath.

At the A.G.M. on Thursday, 24th November, Chairman Fagan reported a loss of £87:15:6½d and that the total debit balance of the Club was £5,070:0:0d. Another innovation was the laying of an electrical cable across the playing field for training lights to be fitted on the far side of the ground.

The home game against Dundee United saw recent signing Joe McGowan score his first goal in the first half although United equalised in the second half. After an absence of seven weeks Sam Dunn returned to centre half and McColl after suspension, but despite leading by a solitary goal at half time, Berwick Rangers ran out victors by 2-1.

In an attempt to inject some punch to the attack, high-scoring centre forward of many clubs, Jimmy Inglis was signed on a month's trial and was fielded against Morton at Greenock with Campbell Dunn signed from Dunfermline occupying the right back position. The new centre had a satisfactory debut and scored Rovers' two goals in the 2-2 draw. In a clear out at the Club, Farrell, Maxwell, McColl and Wilson, all defenders, were released from their Contracts. The fans then thought the Directors had got it right this time when the Montrose team came to Coatbridge and were beaten by four clear goals with Inglis scoring another double. Stranraer were next to visit Coatbridge, with former player Dave Tennant in their ranks, and he scored one of the goals in a 3-2 win by the South of Scotland team.

There were rumours that long-serving left back Willie Clark was about to join Kenny Maxwell in Canada but meanwhile Clark took his place at Hamilton on Monday, 2nd January, with inside left Carr scoring Rovers' goals in a 2-2 draw. The team went to pieces the following Saturday against Queen's Park when the Amateurs won easily by 6-0 at Cliftonhill. The Manager obviously considered that things were desperate and eight positional changes saw Felix Kiernan being played at centre half and trialists Moffat, McGuffog and Hill in an all-change line up which saw the Rovers win at home by 3-1. Ayr United won 3-2 the following week in what proved to be Willie Clark's last game before finally emigrating to Canada but he was unable to have a happy farewell with the team losing 3-2.

Hamilton Accies were then approached for players and they transferred on loan Ian Jeffries, George Falconer and Gavin Kerr, the first two of whom played in the home match against St. Johnstone. Falconer playing at outside right scored both Rovers' goals in the 2-2 draw. Kerr was introduced against Forfar Athletic but it was new boy Jeffries who got his first goal for the Club in another all-change selection.

Five positional changes were made for the visit to Cathkin against Third Lanark, the most notable being the appearance of high-scoring Matt Carson from the local amateur league and John McPhail playing at right back with Jeffries in McPhail's position at right half. This was a match in which Rovers were never in it and the new centre was given few chances to shine other than viewing the opposing centre forward Dobbie's skill in the art of goalscoring with four clever examples. The big centre kept his position the following week against Dumbarton which saw Bryce Houston from Ashfield play a trial at left back and new signing Willie Hardie from Third Lanark took up the other fullback position and his fellow ex-Thirds player Joe Muir at left half. Needless to say with all this change in personnel Dumbarton won by a second half goal in a team which featured former player Don Cornock.

Ayr United were the next benefactors transferring Gordon Finnie and Charlie McNulty in time to play at Alloa. The team was never in the hunt and Houston's first game as a signed player showed how difficult the transition to senior football was to be with the Alloa team winning by 5-1 in a rough match in which John McPhail and Felix Kiernan were both ordered off.

Finnie missed the next match at home against Brechin City and the team was much altered with six positional changes. These didn't work either and despite Kiernan scoring from the penalty spot in the second half, Brechin ran out winners by 3-1. For the next match, at home against Arbroath, "Bunny" Houston got married and was missing but with ten positional changes the team put in a better performance and a Charlie McNulty goal in the first half was enough to keep the points at Coatbridge. Jimmy Cannon, ex-St. Johnstone and Coatbridge boy, was signed and made his debut against Third Lanark at inside right the following midweek and scored the first goal in a 2-1 victory. Flushed with success following these two games, the same team was played against Dundee United but the black-and-whites won by two clear goals.

At the beginning of the week Rovers made one of their most profitable signings of the season when they fixed former Airdrieonians' Captain and centre half Jim Rodgers as Trainer/Coach. The ex-pivot, whose last club was Morton, was a qualified SFA Coach and his first view of his team was that defeat at Dundee which gave him an insight to the job ahead of him. For the away match at Berwick, Carson was re-introduced at centre with Houston at centre half and local boy John McGuinness from Hozier Thistle at left back. A fight back saw a Falconer goal equalise a first half score by the Berwick team in a 1-1 draw. In the last three matches only one point was to be gained and the sequence started when Morton won 2-0 at Coatbridge, a 2-2 draw was fought out at Montrose before the season ended at Cowdenbeath with the Fifers winning 3-1.

Big centre forward Carson had found the transition from local juvenile to senior football overmuch for him and eight games later he had still to score his first goal. Again there was a large clear out of the playing staff with only nine players being retained including Willie Clark who was now in Canada. The team had also slumped back to the foot of the league table in third bottom position with 27 points out of 36 games. Montrose were bottom with 11 points. Queen's Park won the Championship with 54 points from Ayr United with 51. This time Stirling Albion were indeed relegated with 13 points from their 18 matches and joining them downstairs would be Clyde.

Season 1956/57

The new season opened with a new batch of signings, many of them with a local flavour. Coatbridge boys McCracken, McGuinness, Kiernan and Carson, gave the team a real local flavour and the home match against Arbroath saw the fans keenly anticipating a vast change in fortunes from the recent mediocrity. The team for the opening game was McCracken, D. Bell, McGuinness, Finnie, Kiernan, McPhail, T. Bell, Smith, Carson, Harper and McKenna. The big, keen centre at last got on the goal-scoring waggon with a first half goal and new signing Alec Harper scored the winner in an exciting opener of the season for Rovers to win 2-1. The second match in the League Cup was at Forfar and, although Carson again got on the score list and Rovers were leading 2-1 at half time, the home team won well in the end by 4-2.

When East Stirlingshire came to Coatbridge on the 18th August, they could hardly have contemplated the disaster which was to befall them and even at half time when they were losing 3-1, they were not quite ready for the avalanche which hit them in the second half. Rovers ran out winners by a prodigious 9-2 score with Carson scoring four and outside left McKenna three. Rovers only failed to go into double figures for the first time in 20 years by Alec Harper missing from the penalty spot. The trip up to Montrose on the following Wednesday on League business saw Rovers draw their first blank of the season and with the "Gable Enders" scoring three first half goals saw the first League points of the season stay at Links Park. By a strange quirk of fixture planning, Rovers had to return to Links Park the following Saturday on League Cup business and were in no mood to make mistakes the second time around and quickly a 3-2 scoreline was set up which was improved in the second half for Rovers to win by 5-3. The inclusion of Gordon Finnie at inside forward and wee Dunky Smith at outside right, did much in improving Rovers' sharpness in front of goal.

The following week saw a home first round Scottish Cup draw against Vale of Athol and the homesters swamped the non-league team by a fine 8-2 scoreline with Gordon Finnie clocking-up a hat-trick. Again the scoreline could have been greater but for McPhail missing a penalty. The following midweek Stirling Albion visited Coatbridge and, despite Rovers leading at half time by a McKenna goal, the men from Stirling equalised in the second half, the game finishing 1-1.

East Stirlingshire could not have viewed the coming of Albion Rovers with much joy the following week and when Carson set the Coatbridge team off in the lead in the first half, the team moved smoothly into gear to win in the end by 5-1. The return match against Stirling Albion also ended up all square at 1-1 and Matt Carson scored his 11th goal in nine matches for the season to keep the fans happy. Before the impending second round Scottish Cup match there were two home League matches to play and first of all Stranraer were defeated 2-1 which was a very creditable score considering the South of Scotland team were League leaders at the time and revenge was gained over Montrose by 6-1 for the earlier defeat in Angus. A feature of this game was two goals each being scored by Finnie, McKenna and Carson. Rovers tried out Peter Hannoway from Ashfield at outside right in this match. Felix Kiernan was also transferred to Dumbarton who were reputed to also be after goalkeeper McCracken. It was reported that Rovers sold Kiernan for £500 but that Swindon Town and Rochdale had both been prepared to offer £1,000 for the player. Rovers allowed him to go to Dumbarton as he wanted to stay in Scotland.

For the second round cup tie at Peebles, Rovers and the 2-2 result must have come as a shock to many supporters back in Coatbridge but the goal-happy Rovers really were not so hard pressed in this game as the score would suggest. If a little care had been taken in front of goal in the second half, a replay would have been unnecessary. The small sloping Peebles ground was very bumpy and there was a real shock in the offing when Rovers were two behind which was a reasonable reflection on play at half time. However, two goals from Rovers in the second period ensured a replay back at Coatbridge. Before this could be played a Lanarkshire Cup match took place the following Monday at Broomfield and Rovers used this game as a good workout for the replayed cup tie to win by 3-1 thanks to a fine second half display. On the following Saturday, Peebles Rovers turned up at Coatbridge looking for a cup shock but their own defender Blyth scored the first goal before Rovers took command and scored three goals in each half without reply to show the vast difference between the two teams.

The draw for the third round of the cup made the Rovers' Treasurer hang his head in disgust with another non-league tie, this time down at Innerleithan, which is next door to Peebles. The team and support duly went back down to the Borders the following Saturday and, in the neat little ground tucked behind the houses off the Main Street, a goal in each half was sufficient to see Rovers win this one by 2-0 to go into the next round draw. On the following Monday the Lanarkshire Cup Final was played at Fir Park against Motherwell and Rovers played an unchanged team against the First Leaguers but the match was an absolute drubbing for the Club with another high score but this time for the opposition. The Motherwell team were 3-0 up at half time and gave the Second Division opposition no chance of a fight back in the second half, eventually winning by a mammoth 7-1 scoreline.

For the next match against St. Johnstone at home, John McIntyre was signed from Motherwell and he made his debut in goal. This was a game in which Johnny Hill made his first appearance of the season, on leave from the Services in Egypt, and goalkeeper McCracken was put up for transfer. The team got off to a great start with Carson scoring in the first half and eventually completed his hat-trick with Finnie scoring the final goal in a 4-1 romp. This was an excellent preview for the fourth round Scottish Cup tie which was again an away draw, this time against Highland League Forres Mechanics. The only change in the team was Dunky Smith back at outside right for Hill who was on his way back to his billet. The Highland League team shocked Rovers by going into a 1-0 lead at half time and the portents were bleak when Smith was taken off injured early in the second half. Ten man Rovers could do nothing against the stonewall defence and it was no surprise when the home team rattled on a further two goals to bundle Rovers out of the Cup after a ruinously financial cup run.

The tailpiece to the trip up to the Highlands was the party of 28 set out for Fraserburgh after the match to the Hotel, owned by Mr. Andrew Beattie, the former Chairman, where they were to spend the night. Mr. Beattie had arranged a Dance in the Hotel which was joined by the locals. Next morning the players had a round of golf then lunch before setting off on their long drive home. The former Chairman came up trumps by footing the bill for this hospitality which helped to assuage the pain of defeat.

Brechin City came to Coatbridge in the League in a match where McCracken was recalled to goal and Tommy Bell to outside right with Smith being replaced by Harper and a real tussle ensued with the Angus side running out narrow winners at 3-2. The following Sunday saw the last tram from Airdrie to Glasgow pass by Cliftonhill amid much pomp and ceremony on 4th November at 1.30 a.m., thus

Matt Carson

John McGuinness

John McPhail

Jim McCracken

ending a tradition of the followers of football at Cliftonhill taking the tram up the Main Street. The following Wednesday the second leg of the Lanarkshire Cup match was due at Broomfield and, with the only change in the team being McIntyre in goal for McCracken, a rousing game saw Rovers win handsomely by 6-4 with all forwards and right back Houston scoring the goals. The next away match was at Alloa where in front of 3,000 fans Rovers had to come back from a 2-0 half time deficit but could only muster a Tommy Bell goal to lose 2-1. New signing Davie Duncan, ex-Stirling and Stranraer, made his debut in this match.

Although losing, the Manager was satisfied with the team's display and the same players were sent out the following week against Stenhousemuir at Coatbridge and despite going one behind at half time the boys responded to the Manager's faith in them and rattled in six goals in the second half without further reply. Four positional changes were made from this high-scoring team to face Clyde at Coatbridge and it took a Matt Carson goal in the second half to equalise the lead taken by Clyde in the first half to share the points.

After an absence of four games, George Crawford was reintroduced at centre half for the away match at Tannadice but with his immediate opposite number, centre forward Coyle scoring four goals in the 7-0 defeat. He was immediately relieved of duties for the following match, also away from home this time at Forfar, with John McPhail fitting-in at centre half. This one ended up a close encounter with the final score being 3-3. The same squad turned out for the visit by Berwick Rangers. Rovers got back on the goal scoring waggon with a 6-3 victory, which could hardly have been guessed at by half time with a poor performance by both Clubs which ended up at one goal apiece.

Not unreasonably, the same team took the field at Boghead but this time McPhail got the run-around against Hughie Gallacher who scored a rollicking five goals in an 8-1 trouncing. Shocked by this score, the Manager re-introduced McCracken in goal, McPhail to his own position of right half and fielded a junior trialist in the problem position of centre half and things seemed to click immediately against Cowdenbeath with the team slipping into a smooth 5-1 victory at half time, with Carson having a hat-trick and Finnie a double. There were no further goals in the match and the fans hoped that this was surely now a more settled formation and were looking forward to the new year, especially as Cowdenbeath were sitting top of the League and had been defeated so convincingly by the Rovers' team, who had played fast, exciting, scoring football.

On Tuesday, New Year's Day, two Gordon Finnie goals were enough to defeat Hamilton Accies 2-1 and on the following day the trip down to Stranraer was well justified. With the strong running Finnie in tremendous form scoring a hat-trick, the team won with a second half two-goal burst by 5-3. More was to come and luckless East Stirlingshire were fairly trounced by 7-1 on the following Saturday at Coatbridge, with Alec Stewart scoring Rovers' hundreth goal in all matches for the season. Young Jim Forsyth in the East Stirlingshire goal must have hated the sight of the Rovers' forwards, having picked the ball out of the net on twenty-one occasions this season in matches between the two teams. This goal scoring feat was all the more satisfactory with an all-scoring forwardline. Although getting the opening goal, Gordon Finnie blotted his copybook by missing from the penalty spot before Carson made it 2-0 for Rovers at half time. The team failed to make it five wins-in-a-row in a 1-1 draw up at Brechin before getting back onto the winning trail at 2-0 in a home match against Arbroath. All this time Rovers were still experimenting in the number 5 shirt and Crawford became the eighth pivot in a row in an otherwise unchanged team for the visit to Perth which turned out to be a close-fought match ending at 1-1.

Due to cup tie matches the following Saturday, Rovers contacted Third Lanark as both teams had been eliminated, suggesting they should bring forward the following week's match by one week. However, the Thirds' Board turned down the offer and left Rovers with a blank Saturday which they filled in with a friendly against the Junior Ashfield. They took the opportunity of slotting in some juniors into the usual formation, which although the boys from the lower league won 3-2, the result didn't really matter. Following the game Dennis Leary from Bellshill Athletic was signed provisionally as a centre half of the future.

The following week when Third Lanark eventually came to Coatbridge there had developed a bit of needle to the game, as all Coatbridge felt Thirds' decision not to forward the match to the previous Saturday was ill-conceived and cost both teams money. Rovers immediately set about their promotion rivals who were fresh from a 7-0 beating of Dumbarton. This game was really a four pointer with both teams hovering in 3rd and 4th position in the League and going hard for promotion. It took Carson half an hour to open the scoring but in the second half Rovers scored a further four goals without reply to systematically demolish their promotion rivals to the delight of the 6,500 crowd. Carson scored Rovers' 100th goal covering League, League Cup and Scottish Cup matches in this game. They were definitely looking the better promotion prospect. Dunky Smith made a reappearance after a long spell off injured at outside right in the visit to Arbroath but the recent good displays by Rovers were of no avail. The "Red Lichties" steam-rollered the high flyers by 5-3 with inside forward Fernie scoring four goals. Just to show they were not totally out of steam Rovers defeated Forfar Athletic 3-1 and, in the home match against Alloa, it was a tale of two centre forwards with Carson scoring Rovers' goal in the first half but Dignam counting with two in the second half for the points to go East. A chance of a share of the points was scorned when McKenna missed from the penalty spot.

Two away defeats followed, firstly a high-scoring 4-3 defeat at the hands of Stenhousemuir before League leaders Clyde showed their class in a 5-0 demolition job at Shawfield. The versatile Frank Pattison made his debut at outside left in this match but was slotted in at left half for the visit by Dundee United which Rovers won by 5-1 thus regaining some of their respect after the earlier seven goal drubbing. Pattison then was played at right half against the strong-going Morton team, which had gone 13 games without defeat, and were confident of winning on their own patch. But new boy George Ryan led the way with a couple in Rovers' fine 5-2 victory before another close match this time down at Berwick, when Rovers squeezed through by 2-1, although they could have made things easier for themselves if Houston had not missed from yet another penalty.

Dumbarton were soundly defeated 3-1 at Coatbridge before the following midweek Hamilton Accies scraped through by 2-1 to make virtually certain that Rovers would remain once again in the Second Division. Such talk in any case was 'pie in the sky' when Third Lanark, at Cathkin the following week, clinched promotion with champions Clyde in a 4-0 redress over the Coatbridge men. A third defeat in a row found third placed Cowdenbeath win 5-2 but the last game of the season saw Rovers redeem themselves somewhat beating Morton by 3-2, although it was a close thing, with Morton almost catching Rovers, following their 3-0 half time lead.

So ended the most exciting League chase for many a long day, the team finished in fifth position although they were nine points adrift from runners-up Third Lanark with poor East Stirlingshire in bottom slot with a mammoth 121 goals scored against. There was a big clear-out at the end of the season and much was looked for with the high scoring combination of Carson and Finnie and the versatile Pattison who had played in four different positions in nine games.

Season 1957/58

It was all change for the opening League Cup match at Cliftonhill against St. Johnstone. With the ground looking spick and span and in bright sunshine Rovers fielded five new signings amongst the pick of the previous season's players. In an all-change lineup Rovers fielded Selkirk, Houston, McGuinness, McPhail, Sievewright, Glancy, Hannoway, Finnie, Carson, Harper and Neil. The problem position of centre half was hopefully solved by the inclusion of Junior Scotland centre half, Jimmy Sievewright, but he and his fellow defenders could do nothing against the strong running Saints who ran out good winners at 4-2.

The following Wednesday, Rovers fared little better losing 3-2 at Hamilton before the first victory of the season saw Arbroath defeated 2-0 at Coatbridge. Tragedy was to strike the following Wednesday at Coatbridge in the first League match against Dumbarton in a match which Rovers won 3-1 but key player Gordon Finnie had the misfortune to suffer a bad leg break. This was to turn out to be bad luck for both player and Club and Gordon was destined not to return to the team until April.

Back on League Cup business the following Saturday, and with Alec Harper taking Finnie's position, the team put in a very disjointed performance and were never in contention in the 6-2 drubbing by St. Johnstone. On the Wednesday, Hamilton made it three points out of four for them with a 1-1 draw before Arbroath, on the day Scottish Television commenced in Scotland, were far superior in all departments to run out easy winners by 4-1 leaving Rovers once again at the bottom of their League Cup Section. This Cup had now been run in this fashion for 10 years and Rovers had yet to win their Section. Also, big Matt Carson was missing his partner in the goal scoring stakes and had only managed five goals in ten games which was under half his rate for the previous season.

The League Programme now swung into action and Rovers fielded Bobby Herbert, newly signed from Doncaster Rovers, with McPhail continuing at centre half for the injury-prone Sievewright. But the Ayr team had an easy 4-0 victory on their own pitch before Brechin City fought back from a half time deficit to square the next League match at 2-2.

Frank Pattison made his first appearance of the season at outside left at Dumbarton but the team, with goalkeeper Selkirk lame for much of the match, had no answer to the strong running homesters who ran out easy winners by 6-0. Stirling Albion compounded this misery the following week at Stirling with a 4-0 scoreline, despite Rovers fielding ex-Celt Andy Bell in goal, and the team list showed seven positional changes. With such a leaky defence, drastic measures were called for and new signing Herbert was drafted in at centre half with McPhail and Glancy flanking him in the half back line and Whifflet boy Jim Bingham from Shawfield Juniors was given a run at outside left. With big centre Carson looking more like himself, a double from him was enough to keep the points at Coatbridge by 2-1.

The Lanarkshire Cup second leg against Airdrieonians at Coatbridge saw soldier boy Johnny Hill making a welcome reappearance at inside left and even getting on

ALBION ROVERS SEASON 1957/58

Standing: J. Sievewright, J. McGuinness, A. Bell, J. McPhail, R. Herbert, P. Glancy.
Seated: A. Harper, W. Murray, M. Carson, J. Hill, F. Pattison.

the scoreline but the stronger Airdrie team won by 4-2. This squared the goals at 8-8 and a replay would be required. The following Saturday John McPhail scored a penalty in his second successive match and this was enough to share the points in the 1-1 draw against Hamilton but Stenhousemuir taking a tight grip of the game in the first half to go two up, found Rovers unable to do anything about it, and the points stayed at Larbert thanks to a 2-1 victory.

Handy-man Pattison scored his first goal for Rovers in the 3-1 victory over East Stirlingshire and on the following Monday the Airdrieonians replayed Lanarkshire Cup Tie took place at Broomfield in a match where Rovers could never get their noses in front and the 'Diamonds' won by 3-2.

At Cowdenbeath on the following Saturday, Rovers were winning 1-0 at half time but, shortly after scoring a second goal, right back Sievewright was stretchered off and the Cowdenbeath team bounced back off the ropes to steal the points with a 3-2 scoreline. This match was John McPhail's last for the Club before being transferred up the road to Airdrieonians. His place was immediately covered by the signing of Alec Devanney from St. Anthonys and also Jim Bingham was signed from Shawfield. The visitors from Berwick found the Rovers' defence a hard nut to crack and Peter Hannoway scored his fifth goal of the season in Rovers 1-0 victory. Sievewright made a reappearance wearing the No. 11 jersey for the trip to Montrose in a no scoring draw, but the experiment was not a success and was not continued with for the Alloa match at Coatbridge. Billy Thomson was signed from Hamilton Accies but a terrible first half performance saw Rovers 2-0 down at half time and, although they improved in the second half, Alloa won in the end by 3-2.

Fellow strugglers Morton were visited the following week with a team showing six positional changes and this had a very unsettling effect on the team with the 'Tail of the Bank' men winning by four clear goals. Billy Thomson scored the only goal of the match in a home victory over Dunfermline before a 1-1 draw and a welcome point was gained at Perth.

When December arrived a marked change in fortunes was to take place and with the benefit of two home matches, Matt Carson scored his first goal in nine matches, making it a double into the bargain, with Bingham also getting on the score sheet for the first time in the 3-0 victory. More good stuff was to follow the next Saturday against Dundee United, with Carson scoring directly from the kick-off in under nine seconds and making it a double in the 3-1 victory over United. The big centre was also on the mark at Forfar scoring the only goal of the game in a match where trialist McFarlane put up the shutters for the second week running in goal.

With the news that the Club's first Chairman, Hugh Thom had died the previous day and with the team wearing black armbands, Peter Hannoway scored a fine hat-trick at Arbroath in the 3-1 victory. Bell returned to goal and McGuinness to left back following his first absence since making his debut in the opening game of the previous season.

New Year's Day saw Hamilton Accies hosts to Rovers as First Foots and they were exemplary hosts allowing Rovers to win by a 4-1 margin but Stirling Albion repeated this example the following day at Coatbridge winning by two first half goals to nil.

On the Saturday the trip to Brechin was a bit of a disaster with the team bus being involved in two smashes and arriving at the ground after the scheduled kick-off time. This being winter and pre-floodlight days, meant that the game eventually finished in darkness, but with Rovers always trailing the City won by 2-1, leaving

Rovers to limp home in more ways than one.

After the team being unchanged for four matches, goalkeeper McFarlane from Thornliewood United was signed and took up his position against Stenhousemuir with Junior team-mate Willie Howley having a run at right back and four other positional changes in the team. They played as though they had played with each other all season and in a well-drilled, well-oiled exercise, the Warriors were comprehensively defeated by 6-1, with Matt Carson back on the goal-scoring band-waggon with four goals. This was his 21st goal of the season in 32 outings but he also missed his first outing for two seasons in the next match against East Stirlingshire and Devanney took the trialist's position at right back and Thomson donned the No. 7 jersey but it was 'Shire who won this one by 2-1.

The following week at Coatbridge, Berwick Rangers were visitors in a Scottish Cup first round match and Rovers went into top gear immediately. The 3-1 scoreline at half time ended up being the final result. Long time serving Director Andrew Wilson, who had been a constant follower of Rovers since his retiral from the Board, was at this game but took ill in the Directors' Box and died before assistance could be summoned. Rovers' next match was postponed but the Town was agog with the news of their opponents in the second round — Hearts, through in Edinburgh. There were more than 2,000 Rovers' fans in special trains going through to the Capital in a crowd of 23,451 paying £2,712. Before the match kicked off there was one minute's silence for the Manchester United Munich disaster. When Referee Mr. Massey of Dundee eventually got the ball rolling, it was the First Division team who scored first and well led by Internationalist Alec Young, were never really in trouble against the plucky Second Division team for whom Bobby Herbert scored from a free kick in the second half. The eventual final scoreline was 4-1.

Back on League business, Montrose found Rovers in a very generous mood at Coatbridge and the Angus side ran out easy winners by 3-0. Alloa then had a clear-cut 4-1 victory at Recreation Park with the only current bright spot for Rovers being news of the return of Johnny Hill from the Forces and back in training.

In the first of three home matches Morton, in a dour game, drew 2-2 before Dunfermline gave the boys in blue a drubbing by 8-1 which was Hill's return to the first team. Smarting under this reverse, eight positional changes were made for the visit by St. Johnstone and after a goalless first half two Carson goals were enough to keep the points at Coatbridge by a 2-1 margin.

Three away matches now took place, all ending up as defeats, the first being to Stranraer which threw up Danny McCulloch as the man of the match. Stranraer were 4-0 up at half time with McCulloch pulling back two quick goals but when the trialist goalkeeper was injured, McCulloch had to go in goal leaving the score at 4-2. Dundee United won 2-1 before Airdrieonians ran out winners by 3-1 thanks to a fine first half performance in the Lanarkshire Cup.

With four matches left in the League, three of which were at home, Rovers were hoping for a mid-league position, but even with Gordon Finnie back in the team following his leg break, Forfar Athletic won comfortably by 3-1 before the last away match of the season saw Berwick Rangers squeeze home by 2-1. With Rovers sliding down the League, the home match against Arbroath got off to a fine start with a goal in 20 seconds by Bingham but by half time the Angus team were 3-2 in the lead and the 750 fans saw the only goal of the second half go to the maroon-shirted team who were going strong in the League and were to finish in third place. The final game in the League Programme was at Cliftonhill on Monday,

28th April, with Cowdenbeath as the visitors but after being all square by 1-1 at half time, the Fifers won by 3-1, thus confirming Rovers' position as third bottom from Stenhousemuir and East Stirlingshire, who were on the same points total but with inferior goal averages.

Stirling Albion won the Championship with Dunfermline also promoted and Berwick were wooden spoonists on 15 points. East Fife and Queen's Park were relegated.

At the A.G.M. on 26th March, Chairman Fagan stated a loss of £1,949 over the year making the team £7,020 in the red. Retiring Director, David Shanks was returned, leaving the Directorate at three, along with Director/Manager Jackie Hutton.

An abnormally heavy free list saw Gordon Finnie, Bryce Houston, Frank Pattison and Alec Harper all move on but with Matt Carson taking a fortnight off his work at Stewarts & Lloyds Calder Works to attend the S.F.A.'s Summer Coaching Course, hoping this would put him back among the goal scoring leaders for the new season. Jimmy McCracken, ex-Rovers goalkeeper, was also in attendance at the Coaching Course in Largs and took over as Rovers Coach, mainly to take over the second eleven which Rovers intended running during the next season.

Season 1958/59
Prior to the new season getting underway, Rovers re-signed John McPhail from Airdrieonians and captain Glancy with seven new players in the team for the League Cup match against Stranraer down in the South of Scotland, found the opening game of the season too much for him by being ordered off. Goalkeeper Hamilton was also injured and the match ended disastrously for Rovers by a 4-1 defeat. The game had got off to a reasonable start but the roof caved in in the second half with Stranraer rattling in three goals. Rovers' team — Hamilton, Campbell, Gallacher, McPhail, Herbert, Glancy, Mulhall, Carmichael, Carson, Kiernan and Duncan.

Trainer/Coach McCracken stepped into the goalkeeping breach for the home tie against Stenhousemuir but 1,500 horrified fans saw Rovers' team put in one of the most inept displays of the decade to deservedly lose 4-0. For the first League match at Cliftonhill against East Fife, Felix Kiernan, who had scored Rovers' only goal so far this season, was posted to left half and Willie Howley made his first appearance at right back. After a poor first half, where no goals were scored, one apiece was the end result of the second half but still no improvement in the team's play. Back in the League Cup the following Saturday, East Stirlingshire were beaten by a 4-1 margin, the only change in personnel being Bingham replacing Duncan at outside left. The final game in the League Cup saw the long visit to Berwick rewarded by a tremendous second half fight-back, which saw a 2-0 deficit at half time equalised at 2-2 by full time.

Once the League Programme proper got started, 3,000 fans at Hamilton saw an exhilarating local derby with a point apiece being fair doings at 2-2, although it was Hamilton's turn to come back from a 2-0 half time deficit. The long trip to Forfar saw the third away match in a row but this time a poor second half result found Forfar winning 4-1. Centre forward Joe Shaw from Armadale took Carson's place at centre in the home match against St. Johnstone which Rovers won 3-2 and in midweek a no scoring draw was fought out down at Stranraer.

Pat Glancy scored four goals in the 6-2 defeat of Stenhousemuir which was a perfect pick-me-up for the Lanarkshire Cup second leg match against Airdrieonians also at Coatbridge the following Monday. Rovers were never in trouble in this one and won at the end of the day by 3-2. Unfortunately, it was not enough and with a 5-4 aggregate Airdrie went on to contest the Final.

After an absence of nine matches, Bobby Herbert was played at centre forward and scored Rovers' first half goal which was equalised in the second half by Arbroath. An unchanged team at Cliftonhill saw Ayr United consolidate their position at the top of the Second Division and ruining Rovers' unbeaten home record at the same time with a 4-1 victory. In a rough, tough, spine-tingling second half in which two Rovers players were booked and McCracken carried off unconscious, the Coatbridge sides' resistance crumbled before Ayr superiority. Despite heroics by Herbert in place of McCracken in goal, the Ayr team won easily enough. The big 'keeper was fit for the visit to Berwick and with Kiernan making has first appearance of the season at centre forward and scoring Rovers' first goal, it was not until late in the second half that Berwick took control to win by 3-2.

Brechin City were next to visit Coatbridge and, although winning 1-0 at half time, were always inferior to Rovers who eventually won 4-3. This score could have been greater had McPhail not missed from the penalty spot. Cowdenbeath had a clear-cut victory by 4-0 through in Fife. New goalkeeper George Torrance signed from Leicester City made his debut at home against East Stirlingshire with nine positional changes including Teddy Hammond being introduced at centre half from Queen of the South. Once again the team from Falkirk had no answer to Rovers strong running and Pat Glancy with four goals leading the way to a fine 8-0 victory.

This turned out to be Matt Carson's last match as a Rover as he moved on to English non-league team Cheltenham. This was an incredible ending to Carson's career with Rovers as he had risen from obscurity to national fame and fortune in less than a year and then plummeted back to obscurity playing for Rovers in their Reserve side. The fee, although never disclosed, was reckoned to be well under half what could have been achieved just twelve months earlier. Signed to take his place was David Fagan from Coltness United, son of the Chairman. There were many who said that this was an unenviable position for the youngster but in his debut against Montrose at Cliftonhill three goals by captain Glancy in nine minutes late in the game were sufficient to take the pressure off the new centre, although he was unlucky when a raging first time shot in the first half cracked off the Montrose post. Rovers were sitting seventh in the League with Ayr at that stage leading all comers by six points. In the next match at Greenock, Glancy scored another two goals taking his tally in three games to nine, but this was not enough to stop Rovers going down by the odd goal in seven.

On a foggy November day at Dumbarton 2,000 fans saw young Fagan score his first goal for the Club but the home fans were disappointed with the overall display and the team went down by 2-1. Worse was to follow at Alloa the following week when the 'Wasps' won out the park by 5-2. The following Tuesday Morton were played in a friendly down at Greenock in a floodlit match which the Greenock side won by 6-2.

Back in the League, on the Saturday, a 4-3 victory for Rovers over Dundee United underlined their superiority against the Black and Whites with centre forward Fagan scoring the winner. Queen's Park were next for the hammer at Coatbridge and Paddy Glancy hit a hat-trick in the 5-2 victory. McCracken had to play in goal as goalkeeper Torrance took ill travelling up in the team bus but the team was unable to hold the strong going Fifers who won easily by 5-1.

For the visit to Perth, John Kerr the young Coatbridge full back was signed from Queen's Park and he kept his end up in the 1-1 draw before young reserve goalkeeper Bill McIlraith was fielded in goal for the home game against Stenhousemuir. A fine hat-trick by Fagan assisted Rovers to a 6-2 victory but following this came the resignation of Jim McCracken as Team Coach. Former player Tom Kiernan, now retired from Alloa, was appointed Coach and was in charge of the team for the home match against Arbroath which was intended to be a pre-Scottish Cup match warm-up for the game against Celtic. Torrance returned to goal but the home team who were 3-0 up at half time fell to pieces in the second half and the "Red Lichties" fought back so well that by the end of 90 minutes they had overtaken the Rovers' score and won by 4-3.

This was not an ideal preparation for a Cup Tie and Bobby Herbert was reinstated at centre half in place of Hammond with Jimmy Duncan taking Mulhall's place at right half for the game.

Rovers came away from Parkhead after losing by 4-0 but with a cheque for more than £1,000 and the knowledge that the present team could well be the basis of a promotion bid next season. Celtic with experienced Internationalists — Bobby Evans, Bertie Peacock, Charlie Tully and new boys Mackay, Colraine and Auld in their ranks, were well held in the first half and Rovers were only one down over the first period. Rovers didn't enjoy the best of luck and in the the early minutes goalkeeper Torrance was in the wars with blood pouring from a gash in his hand caused by the bone hard, rutted field. He had to have stitches at half time and Bingham played the first five minutes of the second half in goal. Goalkeeper Haffey should have been beaten on several occasions but it was not to be and even John Kerr scored his second own goal in two games to complete the Coatbridge misery.

McCracken made a surprise return to goal for the visit to Ayr against the local United and Rovers' challenge was swept aside by a competent Ayr display; the final result being 6-2. Wing half Shields, another product of the Reserves, made his debut in the third away game in a row to Brechin and the team looked like heading for a good result with a 2-1 lead at half time but the City players put it all together in the second half to run out winners by 3-2.

Kiernan took Shields' place for the visit by Cowdenbeath but it was another defeat this time by 3-1 much to the disgust of the fans. East Stirlingshire made it six defeats in a row with a 1-0 victory at Falkirk before Montrose yielded a point in the 1-1 draw at Links Park. Morton scored the double over Rovers by 5-2 when they visited Coatbridge and McPhail even missed a penalty. Bill Lamont of Bellshill Athletic signed in time to take his place in goal against Dumbarton but in a much changed team, with nine positional changes, there was no cohesion and two second half goals saw the points remain at Boghead.

The following Monday the Lanarkshire Cup first leg took place against Airdrieonians with Fagan taking McPhail's place at right half and Bingham at inside right. But the Broomfielders won 2-1 with all the goals coming in the second half. Jock Wallace in Airdrie's goal was not greatly troubled and the 3,000 Easter Monday crowd were bored out of their skulls at the poor fare provided by both teams. The following week the second leg took place at Broomfield and this time Airdrie ran out winners by 3-1 thus qualifying again for the Final by a 5-2 aggregate.

Full back Tommy Campbell who had missed four games, and was feeling unhappy about standing on the terracing watching, commented to Chairman Fagan that it would be better playing him at centre than the Chairman's son. In a moment of inspiration, the Chairman agreed to this request, Campbell promptly donned the No. 9 jersey and scored both goals in the 2-0 defeat of Alloa Athletic at Cliftonhill the following Saturday. He scored another two in the 3-1 victory over Dundee United at Coatbridge before two away matches saw Rovers win 2-1 at Hampden and draw 2-2 at Berwick with Campbell scoring a goal in each game.

The big centre went off the boil in the first of three home League matches but the new goal scoring hero of the Second Division was so well policed by the Forfar Athletic defence that three of his mates were able to score goals without reply before Big Tam came up with the second goal in the 2-0 victory over Hamilton Accies.

A last game of the season saw young Fagan as Campbell's feed at inside right and Mulhall swapping to right half. This combination was an immediate success with the big centre scoring all of Rovers' four goals in the 4-0 defeat of Stranraer. Rovers finished in tenth position with 35 points from 36 games and Montrose wooden spoonists with 18. Only eight players were retained and so it was goodbye to John McPhail, Felix Kiernan, Joe Gallacher and the others who had served Rovers well.

Season 1959/60
When the season opened on the 8th August, the first game played at Coatbridge was against Stenhousemuir in the League Cup with only two new signings forming the left wing and, despite Jim Bingham opening Rovers' account for the season, the 'Warriors' ran out winners by 2-1. Rovers team was — Lamont, Howley, McGuinness, Mulhall, Herbert, Glancy, Bingham, Fagan, Campbell, McGill and Neilson. Much had been expected of goal scorer Campbell but Tommy was not able to come up with the goals in this match. However, it was a different story at Boghead when a hat-trick saw the big centre off the mark for the season scoring all Rovers' goals in a 3-3 draw. Captain Glancy had to force his men on from a 3-2 half time deficit.

Jimmy Duncan re-signed in time to take up the outside right position against Arbroath. Rovers won by 3-0 in a match where goalkeeper Lamont was injured and Bingham had to be fielded in goal. Campbell again came good with a couple in this match. In the opening League match at Larbert, Campbell again scored twice in the 3-3 draw and the same venue, but this time in the League Cup the following Saturday, saw the Larbert team gain ample revenge by 3-0, thus completing the double over Rovers in the Cup. The League Cup Section was completed with victories over Dumbarton, by a solitary Campbell goal, and 4-1 over Arbroath; both matches being played at home. This took Campbell's goal scoring exploits to ten in seven appearances but he was not on the score sheet in the 2-2 draw at Brechin, when the League proper got underway the following Wednesday. He also missed scoring, as did all the rest of the team, at Hamilton when Accies scored three.

The following Wednesday, Montrose won 4-1 and then on the Saturday Forfar won by the only goal of the match, giving the longest spell that Campbell had not found the net since being promoted to goal scorer. All was forgiven, however, when Brechin City visited Coatbridge and strikers Campbell and Glancy each scored a pair in the 6-3 victory and in the next match the captain managed Rovers' first half goal in the 1-1 draw against East Fife. The third home match running found Glancy opening the scoring and centre Campbell scoring a double in a 5-1 victory over Montrose.

East Stirlingshire caused an unexpected shock with a 3-0 score at Falkirk before, on September Weekend Monday, at home against Hamilton Accies two Jim Bingham goals in five minutes of the first half were sufficient to give Rovers a commanding lead in the tie. Berwick Rangers set up a 3-0 lead at half time and, despite Campbell knocking one back, try as they might, Rovers were unable to better the situation.

Glancy was pushed forward to inside right for the home match against Stranraer but Rovers footered to a 6-1 defeat and worse, the talented captain was transferred to Stirling Albion to take the place of Ian Spence who was presently at loggerheads with his club for refusing to train at Stirling. It was a bad week for the Monklands as another personality player — Jock Wallace — left Airdrie to join West Bromwich Albion.

For the fourth home match running against Falkirk, Harry Oliver was signed to take Glancy's place. Two Dunky McGill goals in the first half almost made the fans forget their former skipper but a fighting comeback by the Bairns saw the points shared in a 2-2 draw.

Dundee United in a poor match shared the points but no goals before St. Johnstone won 4-1 at Perth in a match where new signing Eddie McLeod made his debut. The following week saw a visit to English North East non-league Ashington take place but Rovers were well beaten in this one by 5-2. Back on League business in the first home match in three games, Morton were the opponents but Rovers' stronger play was sufficient to take the points at 3-2 before the 'Blues' found the 'Doonhammers' too strong in a 4-1 drubbing.

Two Junior trialists were tried out the following week at home against Dumbarton and only the missing of a penalty by Bobby Herbert stopped Rovers from lifting the points, the match finishing all square with no score. At Cowdenbeath the following week Campbell rattled in a couple of goals for a 6-2 victory with Lamont back between the sticks whilst Alloa were lucky to scrape a 2-2 draw the following week. Willie Howley's brother John was fielded at outside right at Hampden and contributed to a fine 2-0 victory by the Coatbridge side. This result was repeated at home on Boxing Day against Stenhousemuir and following this match the youngster was fixed up to make his debut as a signed player in the New Year match at Hamilton. This was a rousing match with Tommy Campbell scoring a hat-trick and Rovers winning by 3-0. The following day Forfar came to Coatbridge and another Campbell hat-trick saw Rovers win 7-1 but East Fife put a stop to the current good results with a 4-1 victory which would have been worse had Lamont not made a great save from a penalty. This was Rovers' first defeat in eight matches.

It was back to winning ways the following week with a 2-1 victory over East Stirlingshire but Berwick Rangers were value for their 4-1 victory down the Borders the following week.

On a freezing cold, icy blizzard type of a day, Rovers had a home match against Tarff Rovers in the Scottish Cup and a goal in each half by Tommy Campbell was just sufficient to take Rovers through by 2-1. There was further good news with the presentation of a £1,000 cheque by the Scottish League for Football Pools Handout Money. All other matches were postponed due to bad weather conditions until the second round of the Cup saw Rovers travel to Eyemouth and with an excuse of bad road conditions prolonging the journey, the team only arrived in Eyemouth after two o'clock to have a meal and then take the field with barely any time to spare. It was not the ideal preparation for a cup tie. The ill-prepared Rovers went one down in the first half and try all they could and driven on by captain

Martin Mulhall, there was never any likelihood of the team drawing level, never mind winning the tie. The gate receipts were only £67 which was more than the £50 uplifted in the previous round but both were financial disasters and with Rovers well down the League there was no likelihood of promotion from the lower League.

The following Saturday saw Dundee United visit Coatbridge, complete with new signing outside left Gibby Ormond fixed up during the week from Airdrieonians. He was instrumental in the 4-1 victory by the East of Scotland team and as they had done when signing Sam English several years earlier, United left Coatbridge with a new centre forward — Top scoring Tommy Campbell much to the great disappointment of all Rovers fans for a reputed paltry £1,000.

For the next match against table-topping St. Johnstone at Cliftonhill, Mulhall took Campbell's place at centre and new signings Fraser and Grant were also introduced. Putting the disappointment of losing the effervescent Campbell behind them, the team buckled down to the job at hand and were 2-0 up at half time. Despite Saints pulling one back a do-or-die effort by the defence ensured a 2-1 victory. The good work done on the previous match was ruined the following week at Dumbarton with the 'Sons' winning 6-0 thanks to five goals being scored in a tremendous second half display.

The following day former player Jock Stein was confirmed as Manager of Dunfermline Athletic following his period as Coach with Celtic. As though to rub salt in the wounds, Tommy Campbell was chosen as the Second Division centre forward in their select match.

Morton, who had been having an indifferent season so far, went into a 1-0 lead at half time down at Greenock but a spirited fight back by Rovers in the second half saw them run out winners by 3-1. Queen of the South made it a double with a comprehensive 3-0 victory at Coatbridge when Rovers tried out two juniors in the forward line. Falkirk won narrowly by 2-1 on the following Wednesday in hurricane conditions and then Cowdenbeath fought out a typical end of the season match in a 1-1 draw.

The campaign finished on a brighter note with three victories starting with a 3-2 win at Alloa and on the following Wednesday, Stranraer lost 3-1 at Coatbridge. In the final match Queen's Park were soundly defeated by 4-1 but despite this flurry at the finish, the best position Rovers could attain was tenth on 36 points. Cowdenbeath were bottom dog whilst St. Johnstone won the Championship followed upstairs by Tommy Campbell and his Dundee United mates. Another disappointment only less sad was the news that the "Garden" or Whifflet Picture House was to close. Another Whifflet institution was to be no more.

Season 1960/61
The season started off as usual with a fair clutch of new signings and the 13th August saw a goodly number of them in the team for the opening match against Queen of the South at Coatbridge. The team got off to the worst possible start with a 3-0 defeat. Rovers' team was — Lamont, W. Howley, McLuckie, McGuinness, Herbert, Beecham, Stevenson, Mulhall, Reilly, J. Howley and Murphy. The midweek match at Montrose was no better with the Angus team winning 3-1. Mulhall opened Rovers' account for the season and was also first scorer in the home match against Queen's Park which Rovers won 3-1.

The following midweek saw the same venue and opposition in a Second Division match with a McLuckie goal sufficient to keep the points at Cliftonhill. The other Queens, from Dumfries, in the return League Cup match the following Saturday had another victory by three clear goals this time by a 5-2 margin.

Archie Kerr, ex-Motherwell and St. Mirren, signed and was played at inside forward against Montrose and he helped to lay on the two Herbert goals which gave Rovers a 2-1 victory. Although married the previous day, John McGuinness was in his usual position on Saturday to assist in Rovers' 1-0 victory over Queen's Park at Hampden. This match saw Charlie McInally from Bradford play at left half in the last of the League Cup matches.

The League programme proper got off to a fine start against East Fife the following Wednesday with a 2-0 victory over East Fife with McLuckie taking McGuiness' place whilst the latter went abroad on honeymoon. The match at Douglas Park was full of incident with goalkeeper Lamont breaking his nose in a clash with his own centre half Beecham and Rovers going down 4-3. The return match against East Fife in midweek ended in a 4-2 victory for the Fifers. Arbroath scored the only goal of the game at Cliftonhill before the long trip to Brechin found Rovers winning 6-2 aided hugely by a fine hat-trick from Mulhall.

A usual September Weekend Monday Lanarkshire Cup Tie, this time against Airdrieonians, was played at Cliftonhill but the 1,500 fans found Airdrie too strong on this occasion and after leading 1-0 at half time, Airdrie put on the pressure to run out easy winners by 5-0.

Surprisingly, the same players were given an immediate vote of confidence and there were no changes for the visit to Cowdenbeath. Unfortunately there was no improvement in the result with the Fifers winning 2-1. Still, the selectors considered they were on the right lines and once more the same team lined up, this time to be smashed 3-0 by Montrose with further humiliation by Beecham being sent off after scoring had been completed.

At last the penny dropped that the team would not do in its present form and wholesale changes were made for the home match against East Stirlingshire. But another defeat was inflicted this time by 4-2 and Rovers ended up with ten men as the unfortunate Scott McLuckie was carried off with a broken ankle.

For the journey up to Forfar in heavy rain, local boy Danny Hegan was tried out along with Jack Gilroy signed from Forfar. A McGuinness penalty was good enough to share the points at 2-2. New boy Hegan signed and changed over to inside left for the home match against Morton but with Rovers winning 3-2 at half time, a fight back by the Greenock team saw the match end all square at 3-3.

On the day the electrified train system to Glasgow was inaugurated (the Blue Trains), the 5th November, Rovers went in the other direction to Alloa but despite leading by a Murphy goal at half time, the 1,000 present witnessed a fine second half display by the homesters and the final score ended up 4-1 in favour of the 'Wasps'. A surprise return to the team saw McLuckie make a remarkable recovery from his broken ankle bone to play at right back in the team which appeared at Stranraer. The team display was too disjointed and they fully deserved their 4-0 defeat.

During the following week, Rovers said farewell meanwhile to Andy Murphy who was off on his two years National Service. Jim Kelly from Shettleston Juniors was given another try-out in Murphy's position for the home match against Stirling Albion with full back Willie Howley taking up the right wing. All that seemed to do was upset the rhythm and the team crashed to a 4-2 defeat. Kelly was signed however and celebrated on the following Saturday, again at home, against Dumbarton by scoring two goals in the 5-0 victory and it was no surprise when the same team was sent out the following week against Stenhousemuir at Larbert. The team immediately got off on the wrong foot, being two down at half time, which was increased to 3-0 at full time. Falkirk fought out a no scoring draw at Coatbridge then a 1-1 draw at Berwick found Queen's Park visiting Cliftonhill on the last day of the year as the bottom of the league team. Stevenson was dropped and McLuckie was fielded at right half. Despite a fine start, and leading by a Mulhall goal at half time, Rovers fell to pieces in the second half and Queen's deserved their 2-1 victory. After this game, left back John McGuinness was transferred to Stirling Albion to have a long career with the Annfield club.

On Monday, 2nd January, Hamilton visited Coatbridge and 2,000 Ne'erday fans saw Rovers hit top form in a 5-3 victory romp with Herbert enjoying the luxury of missing a penalty. The following Saturday the trip to Arbroath found the Angus team win 1-0 then Brechin wreaked full revenge for their earlier hammering by winning 2-0 at Coatbridge, when there was another penalty miss this time by Mulhall.

Against Cowdenbeath the following week, Rovers played in yellow jerseys and had a fine 4-2 victory, especially as goalkeeper Lamont broke a bone in his hand and Willie Howley had to play much of the match in goal. This was serious for Rovers as there was no other goalkeeper available with the Scottish Cup tie due the following week at Montrose. Rovers signed Willie Goldie ex-Airdrie and Celtic to take Lamont's place but the SFA refused to allow him to play as he was not signed on for the necessary number of days prior to the Cup match. Chairman Fagan solved this problem by signing Ian McLaughlin, an amateur, from Stonehouse Violet and he duly took his place between the sticks along with new signing Donald McLure from Stirling Albion. Despite the promptings of the new power-house, Rovers slumped to a 3-1 defeat and were never really in contention.

Salt was rubbed in the wound the following week at the same venue when Montrose again won, this time by 2-1 despite Rovers having seven positional changes. Yet another defeat took place, this time at home, at the hands of Berwick Rangers by 2-1 despite leading at half time through a Kerr goal. But the position was much improved the following week through at East Stirlingshire when a Dunky McGill hat-trick helped Rovers to a fine 4-0 victory with all the goals being scored in the second half. McLure collected his fourth booking of the season in this match, was suspended for fourteen days and so failed to line up against his old mates at Stirling where Rovers turned in a very slipshod display in a 6-0 defeat.

More wholesale changes took place the following week for the match at Greenock which the home team won without looking round at 4-0. For the next match against Stranraer at Cliftonhill, Rovers clad in maroon, played in monsoon conditions. It was a terrible day to welcome back goalkeeper Lamont and with the score standing 1-1 at half time, the referee shortened the Interval due to bad light. The teams returned to the pitch after only a couple of minutes to finish with a 2-2 draw in a match that was lucky to finish. Dumbarton visited Coatbridge the following week and their 2-0 lead at half time was sufficient to lift the points with no further goals being scored.

Queen of the South visited the following week and in another waterlogged match when two trialists were fielded in nine positional changes once again. There was no cohesion in their play resulting in a 4-1 defeat. Rovers slumped to the foot of the League with their third defeat in a row at home at the hands of Stenhousemuir by 5-2 in a match which saw Danny Hegan score his first goal for the Club. But an unexpected victory occurred at Palmerston when Rovers fielded a makeshift team with full back John Kerr at outside right but the former Queen's Parker scored both goals in a 2-1 victory. With three games to go the home match against Forfar looked like giving Rovers two points after Mulhall scored in the first half and Forfar missed a penalty but the Angus team scored in the last minute to force a 1-1 draw. The new floodlights had been erected and were an indication that thoughts were for the future and not the current disasters.

A last Saturday of the League programme saw Falkirk hosts in a match which if won by the home team would ensure promotion. They certainly had a whirlwind start racing to a 5-2 lead at half time and it was only academic that they added three more in the second half without reply to make sure Stenhousemuir could not catch them in the League Table. The final game was at Cliftonhill with Alloa Athletic as visitors and Rovers' support was astounded to find goalkeeper Lamont playing at outside left and could have been excused for thinking Rovers were pushed to field fit outfield players. Nothing could be further from the truth as the bold William had been pressing Tom Fagan for many weeks for a chance to display his talents in the outfield. The 'new' winger had a good display and the team went on to record a fine 3-1 victory with youngster Hegan scoring an encouraging double. This match was played on the same evening as the Stein-led Dunfermline Athletic defeated Celtic 2-0 in the replayed Scottish Cup Final and a telegram of congratulations was sent to the former player and his team from the Board.

The League season had thus ended with third bottom place achieved and that only on goal average scoring 24 points with Morton bottom dogs on 21. Stirling were Champions with 55 and Falkirk one behind. Clyde and Ayr United being relegated from the First Division. Only one game was left to be played, that being the second leg of the Lanarkshire Cup match against Airdrieonians at Broomfield. Despite Danny Hegan scoring another double and Rovers leading 3-1 at half time, the Broomfield boys bounced back in the second half to take the match by 5-4 and go into the Final on a 10-4 aggregate.

Only seven players were retained and two of these were goalkeepers — Lamont and McLaughlin. Hegan, McLuckie, McLure and Murphy were also re-signed along with Dunky McGill who was signed on as Player/Manager. After many years of rumours the decision to change the team colours from Royal Blue to Primrose and Red was taken and the new strip was registered with the Scottish Football Association in time for the new season. The Club had played for 79 years in the blue shirts but from now on the colours would be quite different with two reasons being given for this. Firstly, there were eleven other clubs in the Scottish League whose official colours were blue and white and in the Second Division alone seven out of the current complement of eighteen teams meant that there were many necessary alternative strip changes required during the season. The other reason was that many neutral spectators were kept away from supporting because of the religious undertones of the blue colour. Of the two reasons, the first was valid although it could have been argued that if anyone should have been changing it should have been the seven teams who were younger than Albion Rovers. But the reason for changing because of neutrality was completely unfounded, as the support didn't change in any meaningful way following the change of colours. However, the search was on for new players and the Board gave the clear statement that new players would mainly be outstanding juniors and the man in charge of them was a new trainer — Frank Hasson — who was a qualified physiotherapist. A football pools was also set up on similar lines to that run by Dundee United.

MR. ALBION ROVERS No. 5

TOM FAGAN

Tom Fagan has spent a lifetime as a Rovers fan. After many years of following on from the terracing, he was co-opted to the Board of Directors in August, 1952. Within two years he took over as Chairman from Andrew Beattie, a position he has held until the present day, apart from two short spells. These were in 1959/60 and in 1967 when David Shanks and Johnny Lees respectively took over the helm.

His entire spell on the Board has been spent in the Second Division in Rovers' longest spell outwith the top League. This is despite much ingenuity and effort from him over the years, which has seen the introduction of stock car racing, speedway (twice), greyhound racing, Sunday football matches and floodlit football.

A shrewd talent spotter, he has been responsible for many young lads being given their first step on the ladder of football fortune. Tony Green, Jim Brown, Mike Green, Matt Carson, Andy McQuarrie, John McGuinness and Phil McGovern, all of whom moved on to successful careers elsewhere.

Another great feature of Tom has been his ability to see potential of a player in a position other than the one with which he has been signed on. The most notable example of this was Tommy Campbell, but Felix Kiernan, Sam Dunn and Peter Dickson are other good examples of Defenders being made Forwards or vice versa.

David, his son by his first marriage, took on the No. 9 jersey from Matt Carson in 1958 before moving on to a career elsewhere, including Australia. His son by his second marriage, Anton, also looks like keeping up the Fagan footballing tradition.

Tom is a man of many parts, being in turn a Demolition Contractor, Car Dealer and Publican in his native Coatbridge. He is a respected elder statesman in footballing circles and has served on the S.F.A. Council in varying capacities over the years, including a stint as an International Selector in the late '60s and early '70s. The Lanarkshire F.A. has also seen sterling service from this man whose consuming love is football.

Tom died in Monklands District Hospital Airdrie on Monday 29th September, 1986.

CHAPTER ELEVEN

THE NEW DEAL

Season 1961/62

The 12th of August was the great day when the curtain was lifted on the new season and a bigger than average crowd came to see what was on offer under the New Deal promised by the Management. East Stirlingshire were the opposition and Rovers, led by their Player/Manager, launched a blistering attack from the whistle. But as so often happens on these occasions, from outright attack a breakaway caught the defence flat-footed and centre forward Ritchie opened the scoring for the Falkirk side. Two goals by Andy McQuarrie in his debut made the score more respectable at half time and, in a dreadful display of bad temper, left half Frickleton brought down McGill in the penalty box to be promptly ordered off. Hegan unfortunately popped the ball over the crossbar from the kick but Rovers, against the ten men, were not to be denied. Firstly McGill and then Hegan twice scored before Pearson added a second goal for the opposition on full time to make the score final 5-2. Rovers' team was Lamont, McLuckie, Burns, Harvey, Leary, McLure, Livingstone, McQuarrie, McGill, Hegan and Bryceland.

Man of the match on the Wednesday at Hampden was Andy McQuarrie with the former Junior International scoring a fine hat-trick in the 3-1 victory. The team were then measured for blazers to be supplied by the local Outfitters, John Hunter & Son, and with Rovers at the top of their Section, there were high hopes, for the first time, of reaching the quarter finals. Then at Forfar it was Captain McGill's turn to hit a hat-trick in the 5-3 victory which had the whole town buzzing. When the temporary change from League Cup to League took place the following Wednesday, there were more than 4,000 in the crowd to witness a match against Ayr United, one of the relegated teams, and in this match, Rovers fielded Eddie Gray at inside left for his experience. It was this player who scored in the second half to equalise the lead gained by the Ayr team in the first half. Although the smoother moving outfit, Ayr were happy to leave Coatbridge with a point following Rovers' never-say-die attitude.

The following Saturday, Morton visited Coatbridge in the last game in the League Cup Section and another four thousand plus gate saw Rovers again in devastating form and newcomer McQuarrie scoring another two goals, giving him eight goals in five appearances, in the 3-1 victory. Unfortunately, the winning of the Section was not to be enough and to the disappointment of the players it was realised that by being in Section Nine, which always included the bottom five teams of the previous season's Second Division, there had to be a play-off against one of the other sections to enable eight teams to go forward to the quarter finals. East Fife, who had come out tops in their section, were the opponents and the matches were set for the Monday and the Wednesday of the following week. Before that and for some inexplicable reason Rovers decided to play a friendly against Largs Thistle and this decision rebounded on them when the match developed into a rough house and several Rovers players were injured. Donald McLure, Rovers' left half, was ordered off and whilst losing 3-2 the team decided defeat was better than several badly injured players.

This was not the best of preparations for a cup tie but the following Monday saw the first leg of the play-off take place at Bayview. All seemed to be going to

Albion Rovers v Ayr United 23rd August 1961

Standing: S. McLuckie, A. Burns, W. Lamont, S. McCorquodale, D. Leary and D. McLure.
Seated: I. Livingstone, A. McQuarrie, D. McGill, E. Gray and H. Bryceland.

plan when Ian Livingstone scored the only goal of the first half. The Fifers came back with a bang in the second period and scored four goals without reply which was to prove a damning lead. On the Wednesday it was like Carnival Day all over again with T.V. cameras even appearing at Coatbridge for the first time and the second leg got off to a whirlwind start with Player/Manager McGill scoring in the first few minutes to give Rovers the chance of making a fight of it and, with the aggregate then at 4-2, Rovers set about the opposition in no uncertain manner. However, the man writing the script seemed to forget that Rovers were supposed to win and the more organised Fifers squared the match before half-time and then went into the lead in the second half putting the result beyond question. Disappointingly the team and support trouped home 2-1 down on the night and 6-2 on aggregate.

There was much disappointment about the League Cup position and this showed the following week at Hampden when, leading from a first half goal by McQuarrie, Queen's came back to square the match at 1-1. A third defeat of the season was next experienced at Greenock with the 'Tail of the Bank' team winning by 2-0.

A fighting victory at Hamilton the following Saturday by 2-1 saw a double blow for Rovers. New young star Danny Hegan was transferred to Sunderland for a reported £5,000 but more importantly Player/Manager and Captain Duncan McGill was carted off to hospital for a cartilage operation and would be out of commission for several weeks.

Immediately from being a swashbuckling carry-all-before-them type team, Rovers became overnight withdrawn and hesitant and for the trip to Montrose the introduction of the two junior players in the forward line did nothing to improve the situation. The Montrose team had an easy 3-0 victory which was followed by a visit to old rivals East Fife who again showed their superiority, also by 3-0.

It was back to winning ways, though, the following Wednesday, in the return match with Montrose and good to see young McQuarrie back on the goal standard with two goals. Montrose started well and were one up at half-time but four straight goals in the second half ensured the points would remain at Coatbridge. In the home match against Stranraer, the first half had a whirlwind period of three goals in three minutes giving Stranraer a 2-1 lead at half-time, but Rovers fought back to square the match at 2-2 by the end of the game. For the game at Arbroath the team was never in trouble and eventually ran out winners by 3-1. Brechin City, together with former Rovers' Captain Martin Mulhall, visited Coatbridge and the former Rover scored the goals in the 2-0 City victory. Berwick Rangers were always in control in their journey to the West and, despite all efforts by Captain Burns, the English team won by four clear goals. Later the same day former Chairman John Kirk died after a short illness.

In an attempt to break the losing sequence, McQuarrie was placed at centre forward and Alec Stewart, from Airdrieonians, was tried out at outside left against Stenhousemuir at Larbert but the 'Warriors' still won 3-1. Despite introducing John Blair, also from Airdrieonians, at inside forward for the visit to Central Park, Cowdenbeath were leading 1-0 before Livingstone was switched to centre which improved Rovers performance but didn't add any goals. Andy Rolland scored a couple for the Fifers and McIntosh made it three shortly afterwards. Table-topping Clyde came to Coatbridge the following week and as usual Rovers put up a better display against the classier opposition but were 3-0 down at half time. Captain Burns, playing against his former team-mates, led a tremendous revival in the second half with Rovers just failing to equalise thanks to a stout Shawfield defence the final score was 3-2. Wing-half McCorquodale was tried out at centre forward for the visit by Queen of the South but this proved not to be a success and Queens won easily by 3-0.

East Stirlingshire were 1-0 in the lead at half time but with McLaughlin in goal putting up the shutters in the second half and the forwards getting amongst the goals, Rovers ran out winners by 2-1. For the next game against Alloa, McLaughlin kept his place and Billy Lamont was fielded at centre forward. The move was not a success but despite a second half comeback, a narrow defeat was the result at 2-1. The goallie-come-centre retained his position but the same result found Rovers floundering again in the lower reaches of the League. Andy McQuarrie, who had not scored for seven matches, got a double in the 2-1 victory over Dumbarton at Coatbridge before Dunky McGill made a welcome re-appearance following his cartilage operation. The Player/Manager and his team found the going too hot for them at Forfar with the local Athletic winning emphatically by 5-1.

Ayr United, who were not finding the return to the First Division in a single season easy, were nevertheless confident of beating lowly Albion Rovers in the first match of 1962. They were surprised with the quality of the Rovers' play and Lamont scored the first goal in a fighting 3-1 victory in which goalkeeper McLaughlin even saved a penalty. Hugh Bryceland was also welcomed back, after an absence of twelve matches following an operation, and Lamont scored the only goal of the game in the second half against East Fife.

For the long trip to Stranraer, McGill was at centre with Stewart at outside right but the men from the far South won 2-1 in this warm-up for the Scottish Cup tie at East Fife. This was to be the fifth meeting of the two clubs with three victories to the Fifers and one to Rovers so far. The portents were not good for a Coatbridge victory even although the outside right berth would be filled by new signing, junior Perthshire forward John Flanagan. With Lamont back in goal, the travelling Supporters were satisfied with a reasonable display in the first half and the thought that one goal down was not beyond them but, despite an all-out effort in the second half, only a cruel stroke of fate kept the new winger from scoring in the last few minutes. Rovers chance was gone for another year and the Fifers went through by the only goal of the game.

Down in the dumps the team welcomed Arbroath, who went promptly 2-0 into the lead in the first half, and again, despite a good second half, the game had been lost early on when the final score of 3-2 for the Angus team did not flatter them. Two away matches were then scheduled for far flung Brechin and Berwick and in the Cathedral City, old pal Mulhall scored the only goal of the first half for Brechin but two goals by John Flanagan in the second half brought the points back to Coatbridge.

In was the other way round at Berwick with Livingstone scoring the only goal of the first half and Berwick this time making the recovery, but Rovers fought them off to secure a fighting draw.

Hugh Bryceland scored the double in the 3-2 victory at home against Stenhousemuir but, in front of only three hundred and fifty fans, Cowdenbeath came the following week to win by 4-0. Nothing would go right for Captain Burns and his not so merry men and it was decided to give Lamont another try at centre and re-introduce McLaughlin at goal for the visit to table-topping Clyde at Shawfield. Rovers got off to a good start with Stewart scoring the only goal of the first half but Clyde showing their class went up a couple of gears in the second half to win 2-1. Two trialists were given a run at forward and with Leary suspended for fourteen days, Burns took up the centre half role but East Stirlingshire easily won by 2-1. Eight positional changes were the order of the day for the following game, the most notable of which being the placing of Alec Stewart at left back. Despite his all-action display the team went down, for the third time in a row by 2-1, in this home match to Alloa.

A third home match in a row saw Gus McLeod of Gourock Juniors make his debut at centre half and in an uninspiring game a 1-1 draw was the outcome. With interest at a low ebb and crowds at rock bottom, the visit to Dumbarton saw yet another 2-1 defeat but, on the following Friday, a Flanagan goal was enough to defeat Morton at Coatbridge. On the next Tuesday, Airdrieonians were defeated 3-2 in a Lanarkshire Cup tie with Captain McGill scoring a double and Flanagan the goal which proved to be the winner being 3-0 up at half-time but brought back to 3-2 with a tremendous second half revival by the Diamonds. Forfar were defeated in the last home match by a Flanagan goal to nothing, which was scored in the first half. In the final League match at Hamilton, Willie Telfer the former St. Mirren, Rangers and Scotland centre half was played in the forward line and eventually got himself on the scoreline in the resounding 5-1 victory for the Accies which saw Rovers slump to second bottom place thirteen points ahead of Brechin on twenty-five but far adrift of Clyde the Champions on fifty-four or runners-up Queen of the South on fifty-three. The demoted pair this season were St. Johnstone and Stirling Albion.

The last game of the season was the Lanarkshire Cup tie at Broomfield when an Eddie McLeod goal in the first half was first of all equalised before half time and then overcome in the 2-1 defeat thus squaring the tie at four goals each. Referee Rodger of Stonehouse ordered off Player/Manager McGill in this one which was a sad ending to his career as a player and subsequently Player/Manager with the Club.

The New Deal as promised by the Board had not materialised. The strip had certainly been changed but the efforts on the field were if anything worse than the year gone by despite the very early promise of improvements.

During the close season Willie Telfer, now at the end of his playing career, was offered the post of Manager and he accepted this challenge with great optimism before the start of the new season. Several new players were signed up for the kick-off but it was clear that it was to be much as before with the vast majority of the players retained from the previous season forming the new playing staff.

The A.G.M. was held on the 20th March and was the first for three years. The accounts for the 31st March 1959 were presented and there was great controversy as to why the accounts should be three years behind but few answers were given by the Board to those who were concerned.

Season 1962/63
A new era Mark 2 was about to take place, with Willie Telfer firmly in charge when Dumbarton came to Coatbridge in the first League Cup Match on the 11th August. The team only showed three changes from the previous season and immediately got off to a disastrous start. Dumbarton, who had only managed to finish one place above Rovers in the Second Division the previous season, with a paltry three points more over the thirty-six games, had obviously done their homework better during the close season than the Coatbridge team. They were already in fighting mood from the off and quickly built up a 3-0 lead by half time. Rovers managed to

emulate this in the second half but the Dumbarton team produced another two goals to end up winners by 5-3. Manager Telfer realised thus early that his job would not be a sinecure. Rovers' team was Renucci, McCorquodale, Stewart, Harvey, McLeod, McLure, Flanagan, McQuarrie, Price, O'Hara and Bryceland. For the second match, Billy Sneddon from Cumnock took the injured Renucci's place in goal and managed to keep a blank score sheet in the no-scoring draw at Forfar.

The following midweek East Fife visited Coatbridge in the first League match and Joe Walters, that swashbuckling player from Clyde, was fielded at left half. His enthusiasm spilled over to the other players and dragged them from a mediocre 1-1 draw at half time to a resounding 4-2 result at the finish. This good performance was continued into the visit to Brechin in the League Cup, and a fine 4-0 victory was clocked up with new centre John Taylor playing a predominant part and giving Rovers their first win. The final game in the Section was against Stenhousemuir at Coatbridge but the visitors won 2-1 and Rovers only managed to score from the penalty spot through McLeod.

In the League proper against St. Johnstone at Perth, Bobby Park from St. Mirren took Sneddon's place in goal, Stewart was repositioned at outside left with McLure filling the left back slot. The changes were not helpful because the team lost convincingly by 7-1 to be followed on the Saturday by a 4-2 reverse at Hamilton.

Gerry Hood, from St. Rochs, was introduced on trial against Arbroath and, although the forward was not Rovers original choice from St. Rochs he showed abundant opportunism by scoring a goal in either half in the 2-0 victory to be promptly signed by the Cliftonhill Club. At Stranraer the following midweek, Dunky McGill playing for the South of Scotland team scored the first goal in their 2-1 victory before Dumbarton were visited and a fine John Taylor treble proved Rovers to be the better team by 3-1.

A return match against Stranraer found right winger John Shearer from Clyde scoring the only goal of the match and the brother of the Rangers full back was well pleased with his display. McLeod missed a penalty in this match, which would have made Rovers win more emphatic. A couple of thousand rolled up to see Ayr United win 3-0 at Cliftonhill in a match where Rovers showed all the wrong attributes and it was no surprise the following week when East Stirlingshire won 4-2 at Falkirk. Stirling Albion came to Coatbridge to lose 3-2 with yet another penalty miss for Rovers, this time by O'Hara, but Rovers outside left Hugh Bryceland, brother of Tommy of St. Mirren, had the last laugh in a game of mixed fortunes scoring the winning goal.

The next two matches away from home proved disastrous with first of all Forfar winning 4-1 and then Alloa winning 4-2. The Berwick Rangers game at Coatbridge found Rovers move into a smooth 2-0 lead at half time, thanks to goals by Price and McQuarrie, whilst Hood slotted in a third goal in the second half in the 3-1 win which was McQuarrie's last game for Rovers before being transferred to Chesterfield for £3,000. Yet another missed penalty in this match, by Hood, meant that Rovers had now missed three penalties and scored with only two.

Rovers went into a fine 2-0 lead and were not too perturbed when Morton knocked one back before half time but it was a different game in the second half, however, and the Greenock men came out with their sleeves up to eventually win 4-2. John Freebairn was signed on a free transfer from Partick Thistle and took his place in goal for the visit of Stenhousemuir in a match which Rovers won well by 4-1. The final goal here was scored by very experienced and prolific scorer of yesteryear, Peter Price, who had not shown any of his goal scoring ability at

Coatbridge, this being only his third goal of the season. In an unchanged team the big goalkeeper was unable to stop Cowdenbeath winning through in Fife by 4-1 with a defence which was mainly static. The next match at Brechin saw Joe Walters become the fourth player to miss a penalty in an otherwise competent performance in Rovers' 3-2 victory. But the following week a goal in each half was enough to down Montrose by 2-1 to finish a very medocre year.

On Tuesday, New Year's Day, Hamilton were the visitors and amidst very snowy conditions, the County rivals ran out winners by 2-0. The Saturday saw a McLeod goal in the second half enough to keep the points at Coatbridge.

Arctic weather conditions then prevailed, calling off all football until the Scottish Cup tie at the end of the month at Dundee against the local United. The ground was virtually unplayable but the referee allowed the match to proceed and twelve thousand, which was the top attendance of the day, paid £1,582 to see the players skate about in most unlikely conditions and go in at half time with a blank scoresheet. In the second half the black and white hooped jerseys mastered the conditions more satisfactorily and rattled in three goals to no reply, thus ending Rovers interest in the Cup for yet another year.

On the 2nd March, referee Willie Brittle abandoned Rovers' game with Alloa Athletic with only half an hour to go, much to the annoyance of the Coatbridge Officials, who then tabled a Protest to the Referee Committee. But the following week down at Berwick the team showed much more flair and application, winning by 5-1.

At Stirling on the Wednesday, a hard, tough match ended up all square at 3-3 although Hugh Bryceland had been ordered off with Rovers 3-2 down and Johnny Lawlor of Stirling carried to the Pavilion due to Bryceland's attentions. At Coatbridge Morton were soundly defeated 3-0 despite being good promotion contenders and three Flanagan goals at Hampden saw Rovers win 3-1. Rovers failed to make it five without defeat when visiting East Fife, losing by 2-0 and the return game in midweek against Queen's Park found Rovers doing the double on the Amateurs by 4-2.

The team which had been unchanged for seven matches now showed six positional changes against Cowdenbeath, the most important of which being the reappearance of Denis Leary at left back. He had been missing for almost a year following a foot operation. Also welcomed back to the fold in this match was Tommy Campbell who had been around a bit following his earlier spell at Coatbridge, having been at Dundee United, Carlisle and Dumbarton. The Fifers started very well and moved into an early lead but Campbell showed he had lost none of his flair for goal-scoring by hitting the equaliser in the second half in a 3-3 draw.

A Wednesday visit to Arbroath found the homesters win 3-0 and, before a desultory two hundred and fifty gate, Brechin City were trounced 5-2 with Campbell hitting a double before the see-saw continued the following Wednesday at Ayr losing 5-0. This poor form continued at Montrose, losing this time by 2-0. In an attempt to plug the leaks, Andy Brown, St. Anthony's goalkeeper, was tried out against St. Johnstone on the last Monday of April in a match which found Rovers winning by a Gus McLeod goal to nil.

The goalkeeper was duly signed and on the Wednesday evening two Flanagan goals in the first half were enough to give Rovers the points over East Stirlingshire. The match against Forfar the following Saturday saw Rovers play their fourth game in eight days and winning it well by a 4-1 margin.

A last League match, and the fourth on a trot at home, found Alloa as opposition and referee Brittle taking charge of the match which he had earlier abandoned. Rovers needed to win to have any chance of finishing in the top six but lost 2-0 to finish seventh with thirty-eight points. St. Johnstone won the Championship with East Stirlingshire being runners-up on fifty-five and forty-nine points respectively, with Brechin bottom of the pile with only nine.

Then there was a bombshell — Hibernian floated the idea of a 22-League First Division whilst Rangers and Celtic suggested a reduction of League Clubs. A statement put out on who might suffer stated that those to be axed were the ones with the lowest aggregate home support for the preceding season which would include Albion Rovers. The suggestion was that Rovers, Berwick, Brechin, Forfar and Stenhousemuir, would all be excluded from the Scottish League. This was serious indeed for the future of Rovers and counter moves were put in hand immediately to ensure that this suggestion would not be approved at the League A.G.M. on the 17th of June.

In the midst of all this furore, there were the Lanarkshire Cup matches to be played and the two-leg tie against Airdrieonians was played in the second last week in May, on the Monday and Wednesday, both games were refereed by Bobby Davidson of Airdrie. The first was at Cliftonhill and, with Rovers always behind, the Waysiders won this one by 2-1 and held on to their overall lead in the second leg on the Wednesday evening, when at Broomfield, the best Rovers could do was a 2-2 draw. Thus the Diamonds once more moved into the Lanarkshire Cup Final and left Rovers to battle on with their fight for survival.

As it happened at the League A.G.M. there was little support for the Edinburgh Club's initiative and, in fact, the motion was overwhelmingly defeated, receiving a mere 5 votes whilst 25 were needed for adoption. This was an unusual stance by the Hibernians who had consistently in the past pressed for a reduction in the number of clubs in the First Division. In this attempt they were supported by Clyde and Raith Rovers who hoped to avoid a relegation drop, Morton who had looked to earn themselves quick promotion and Kilmarnock. However, the subject was not to go away and, as it happened, the result was only to provide breathing space of less than twelve months before the fight would be on again in earnest.

Season 1963/64
Before the season even got started, there were more shocks for the Rovers' support just getting over the traumatic events of the long hot summer. Star outside right Johnny Flanagan was transferred to St. Johnstone for a reputed £10,000 but the usual new handful of signings found Rovers ready to tackle Cowdenbeath on the opening day of the season on the tenth of August through in Fife with Brown, Plunkett, Stewart, Walters, McLeod, Cooper, Henderson, Campbell, Taylor, Hood and Murphy, flying the flag. Manager Telfer's boys got off to a fine start with a tremendous fight back from a 2-0 half time deficit turning this into a 3-2 victory. The support were further overjoyed the following Wednesday when Stirling Albion were defeated at Cliftonhill by the same margin and, when Alloa came to call the following Saturday, a third win was notched by 2-0.

The usual intervening first League match appeared the following Wednesday and the first set-back occurred when Queen's Park at Hampden chalked up a 4-2 victory but it was back to Cup smiles when Cowdenbeath were defeated at Coatbridge by 2-0. In another physical match against Stirling Albion, with McLeod missing a penalty when his team were losing 2-0 in the second half, the spirit and the points deserted the players and it was left to a home match against Alloa on the last Saturday of the Sectional matches when Alloa in front of two hundred success-starved, expectant fans awaited Rovers' entry into the Quarter Finals. The game was in its very last stages and at a satisfactory no score when in extra time a corner taken at the Coatbridge end saw goalkeeper Brown fumble the simplest of crosses quite unchallenged. Alloa had won 1-0 and Rovers had failed once again. The fans couldn't believe it for with the first four games out of six being straight wins for Rovers, it had seemed a formality to win the Section but once again Rovers were to stumble at the last hurdle.

All that was left was success in the League but a bad start was achieved at Kirkcaldy in the second League match when Raith Rovers won 3-0. Two home games amassed three points with Hamilton Accies getting off with a 3-1 "doing" but being held 3-3 over the ninety minutes and, in the midweek return match against Raith Rovers a Gordon Haig own goal in the first half being sufficient to give Rovers the points. This was a match remembered mainly by the strip which was donated by the Supporters' Club and was an incredible crimson shirt with tangerine sleeves. Talk about brighter football!

The winning ways in the League continued with a 5-1 victory over Stranraer and at Dumbarton Norrie Innes was injured in the second half after scoring Rovers' second goal in the 2-0 victory whilst Brechin City were defeated at Cliftonhill 3-1. Dumbarton, in the return match, gave a tremendous battling display and fought out a well-merited draw at 3-3. A third match at home in a row saw Arbroath share two goals and the points.

It was then a case of two away matches, the first being against East Fife where two penalties were scored, one in each half, by the Fifers making referee McConville of Wishaw an unpopular man with the Coatbridge fans and the Fifers winning 2-0. At Shawfield Clyde were leading 2-0 when Joe Henderson opened Rovers' account direct from a corner but despite a spirited second half the 'Bully Wee' won by 3-2. A 3-1 victory at home against Ayr United was made all the easier with the Ayr goalkeeper being off with concussion during the second half, but it was Rovers who ended up with ten men the following week at Stirling when Leary was ordered off for Rovers to lose 2-1.

Dunky McGill played at centre in this match following his re-signing from Stranraer but he was moved to inside left for the visit by Stenhousemuir. In a match where all the goals were scored in the second half, Captain McLeod and his boys couldn't stop the Larbert men winning 2-1.

This was a season which was becoming dominated by penalty kicks and the visit of Cowdenbeath saw Andy Matthews give the Fifers the lead with two penalties before Andy Murphy missed one for Rovers. Gus McLeod then scored two minutes later with a penalty and centre forward Taylor finished the scoring to make the final score 2-2. However, the Alloa game at Cliftonhill gave the fans something different to shout about when after an insipid non-scoring first half Rovers went three up and then Alloa pulled them back to 3-3 and it was only in a late rush that Rovers managed to win by the odd goal in seven. Tommy Campbell scored a hat-trick in this one.

At Berwick the following week, four goals were shared before Morton, showing no consideration whatsoever for new goalkeeper Duncan Wilson, slammed three goals past him to win 3-1. Manager Telfer, who was a great strategist, introduced Rovers to the current "in system" the 4-2-4 and a second half goal by Innes was enough to produce both points for Rovers in another uninspiring game. Forfar put paid to such niceties with a 3-0 victory at Station Park and the year finished with a win at home over Queen's Park leaving Rovers in a mid-table position.

The New Year started ominously at Hamilton with the red and white hoops winning 5-2 but there was consolation in the display at centre forward of trialist Les Sneddon from Bailieston Juniors. He had another trial the following day at home against Stranraer and scored in the 4-1 victory, with Rovers missing yet another penalty, the culprit this time being McLeod.

The following Saturday, making four games in eight days, Rovers put on another sterling performance at Brechin to win decisively by 4-2 after a tremendous second half fight back. With bad weather putting off many games, a match was fixed up against English Non-League team Ashington as a warm-up for the coming Scottish Cup tie against Arbroath. As a trial this was hopeless with the Englishmen winning 3-0.

Next week when Arbroath travelled down to Coatbridge two thousand five hundred fans witnessed an old-fashioned cup tie with the match swinging backwards and forwards before Rovers eventually won by 4-3. Referee Webster got a roasting from the fans when he disallowed a Murphy goal at a crucial stage in the match but all was right on the night and Rovers went through to the next round. The Angus team got ample revenge the following week with a 2-0 victory. For the next match against East Fife Dave Brown was signed from Stirling and the right back took his place to line-up with Joe Walters in an uncompromising 1-1 draw.

All roads then led to old Cup rivals Kilmarnock the next week for the Cup tie. They were well prepared for Rovers having had a decisive 9-2 victory over Falkirk the previous week and were looking to the match against Rovers as being a stroll in the sunshine. Almost ten thousand fans paid £1,282 and saw Rovers fighting hard but losing the first goal in injury time in the first half and, despite a courageous fight of it in the second half, a second and clinching goal in the third minute of injury time in the second half saw Rovers once more out of the Cup, this time by 2-0.

The following week at Ayr, Davie Brown reappeared, having been ineligible for the cup tie, and Rovers' fans were astounded when big 6'3" centre half Tommy Loughran turned out at centre forward. It looked early on as though Rovers might spring a surprise when the big centre scored the first goal but eventually Rovers ran out of steam and the 'Honest Men' won 4-3. For the visit of Stirling Albion, Rovers introduced their two provisional signings on the extreme wings, Eddie Rutherford and Bobby MacCallum from Kirkintilloch Rob Roy, and both were instrumental in many fine moves, with MacCallum being especially impressive and scoring Rovers' second goal in the 2-2 draw. With both lads back with the junior club the next week, Henderson and Murphy took up the wing positions and helped to achieve a fine 2-1 victory at Larbert.

Two draws were next on the cards, 1-1 at home against Cowdenbeath and 2-2 at Alloa with the second being all the more creditable as Rovers finished with ten men when Hood, who had scored the first goal, was ordered off. In the week when the twinning of the Burgh of Coatbridge with the Paris suburb of St. Denis was announced, Berwick Rangers came to visit and won 2-1 whilst Morton, who were running away with the Championship, came to Coatbridge as Champions and were held to a no-scoring draw.

Despite this good result, Rovers were struggling to maintain a mid-table position and the fine 4-3 victory over Montrose at Links Park helped their cause when two of the Montrose goals were from the penalty spot. This left two matches to be played in the Second Division programme.

But first of all the Lanarkshire Cup found Rovers at Douglas Park. Despite leading 2-0 at half time they were held to a 2-2 draw on the Wednesday, Forfar came to Coatbridge on the Friday and shared two goals in a League match. On the Monday the Academical came to Coatbridge in the Lanarkshire Cup second-leg and another draw was the order of the day with Rovers losing out once again, this time by a toss of a coin to put Hamilton through into the Final. The season finished with yet another draw on the Wednesday by 2-2 against Clyde, a result which put Rovers in ninth position with thirty-six points from the same number of games. Morton were Champions with sixty-seven points and Clyde runners-up with fifty-three. This time Stirling Albion were bottom with twenty on goal average from Forfar. Davie Fagan made another reappearance in this match at right half.

With the end of the season came the world-shattering news that Rovers were to be axed from the Scottish League along with Berwick, Brechin, Stranraer and Stenhousemuir and being considered as minnows in the Scottish football scene. Oh! the disgrace for a Club whose chequered career had seen service at the highest level but whose present form left much to be desired!

This would be an almighty upheaval for the Monklands. Under the new proposals, Airdrieonians would end up in the Second Division whilst Rovers would be out in the cold. It would need the support of eleven other clubs to join with the Monklands Clubs to overrule a decision made at Ibrox in an informal meeting, when it was confirmed that both local teams' worst thoughts were to be realised.

Tom Fagan was a leading light in the fight to gain support and, apart from the five threatened teams, support was confidently expected to come also from Celtic, Third Lanark, East Stirling, Kilmarnock, Queen of the South, Ayr United and Hamilton Academical. Although the League A.G.M. was not until the 28th May, Rovers were already confident by the tenth of May that they had at least the thirteen votes required in their pocket. Threat of legal action by the five plus Third Lanark and Airdrieonians was mooted and the S.F.A. gave the Clubs permission to take this course of action if the proposal suggested by Rangers was adopted. The Scottish League Management Committee agreed to call a Special General Meeting on behalf of the seven affected clubs immediately before the A.G.M., when they would be given the opportunity of appealing against the Committee's decision that there were no grounds for an Inquiry into the Meeting held at Ibrox at which the twenty-seven clubs voted to reform the League into two Divisions each of sixteen clubs. Third Lanark put up a motion for the status quo to remain for another season and the other by Rangers was to wind up the League.

When the big day came, the showdown ended in stalemate with no firm decision being taken. The following week at the Court of Session in Edinburgh, Lord Cameron confirmed that his Interim Interdict banning a Rangers proposal to reconstruct the Leagues should become permanent. So the battle was won, at least for the moment, and thoughts could now turn to providing a team for the new season.

Season 1964/65
Rovers daily sweepstake was providing some much needed revenue for the Club and the calling up of the provisionally signed laddies added to several exciting signings gave Rovers' Supporters the chance to dream that this, at long last, was to be their season. The opening game of the League took place in shirt-sleeved weather on the 8th August up at Arbroath where, in holiday mood, Rovers' fans,

who took the trouble to travel, were treated to a fine display of fast, accurate, strong-running football, with Rovers winning by 3-1. Goalkeeper Madden was not troubled and Rovers with four ex-Kirkintilloch Rob Roy players in the side found Coatbridge boy John Dillon revelling in the service and the portents did indeed look good for the season ahead. Rovers' team was Madden, Brown, Stewart, Cooper, Loughran, Murphy, Rutherford, Dillon, Sneddon, McIlwraith and MacCallum. A great goal by Queen's Park two minutes before the interval was enough to bring Rovers back to reality in the first home match with Rovers lack of punch being dreadfully exposed. This ineffectuality was underlined when Clyde came to Coatbridge on the Saturday and went nap. The Rovers cause was not helped by young winger MacCallum breaking a small bone in his arm. The Club also were fielding a second eleven under the guidance of Bobby Park in an attempt to bring on young players.

A glimmer of hope for the future came in the mid-week League match against Ayr United, again at Cliftonhill, when with Denis Leary re-signed, after having been previously freed, and taking up the centre half position, he tightened up Rovers' leaky ship and the forwards rattled in two second half goals to pocket the points. Arbroath took revenge for the opening day defeat by reversing the earlier score whilst Rovers went one better the following Wednesday against Queen's Park at Hampden when two Sneddon goals were enough to win the points. The visit to Shawfield found the Clyde team again scoring five goals but Rovers at least managing this time to score once in the first half. Another season had gone with Rovers failing once more to win their Section in the League Cup.

The League Programme started again at Hampden with the third Wednesday match out of four against Queen's Park since the season began and this time a solitary goal in the second half was enough to make it two wins out of three for the Amateurs. On the following Saturday, at Hamilton, a fine fight back by the Accies saw them come back from a 2-0 deficit at half time to square the match at 2-2 before Stirling Albion were soundly defeated by 3-1 at Coatbridge in front of a measly five hundred fans on the Wednesday evening.

It was a different story on the Saturday with E.S. Clydebank. This was the old East Stirlingshire team which had been moved lock-stock and barrel to Clydebank and amalgamated with the former Junior Club of that name, and had been admitted to the Scottish League this season under the guidance of the Steedman brothers. This was the first game against the new team and with a good travelling support, two and a half thousand witnessed Rovers' decisive victory. The enlarged gate was not all due to the League "New Babes" because, after five matches, Rovers were sitting sharing the lead at the top of the League Table. This was the Clydebank team's first defeat of the League season. The following Wednesday Queen's Park came to Coatbridge in the fourth match between the teams and this time a twelve hundred gate saw a match which Rovers should have won by three or four goals ending up with the Amateurs winning by 2-1. Bobby Clark in Queen's goal was in unbeatable form and Mr. Callaghan of Glasgow the referee was the butt of the fans when he disallowed a goal by Sneddon. With twenty minutes to go when Rutherford did score a goal which actually counted, it was considered to be only a matter of time before Rovers won. But Clark and his Airdrie centre half Willie Neil put paid to such thoughts.

The match at Stirling was a further setback with a 3-0 defeat but worse Leary was injured and off at half time and was to miss the next eight matches. Berwick visited Coatbridge and Rovers introduced Mike Fascione from the successful

ALBION ROVERS SEASON 1964/65

Standing: J. Dillon, J. Cooper, D. Leary, R. Madden, A. Murphy, A. Stewart.
Seated: E. Rutherford, A. Jones, D. Brown, S. McIlwraith, R. MacCallum.

second eleven at inside right and he scored the first goal in a 2-1 victory. Arbroath won 2-1 up in Angus in a match which saw centre Sneddon being tried out at right half. With Sneddon back at centre for the visit by Stranraer, a much more recognisable Rovers' team had an easy 5-0 romp and this was followed by a fine 2-1 victory up at Kirkcaldy against Raith Rovers. The defeat the following week against East Fife at Methil was a bitter pill to swallow when, with the game tied at no score with three minutes to go, Rovers' defence finally crumbled and the Fifers scored two late goals to pick up the points.

Eddie Rutherford was missing for the home match against Brechin City with his former junior clubmate MacCallum taking his place and Stewart on the left wing. This combine seemed to click and it was no surprise when a 4-2 result was the satisfactory outcome. During the week E.S. Clydebank made an offer for both wing starlets — Teenagers Rutherford and MacCallum — but this was turned down. There was also a suggestion, floated by Chairman Fagan, that with dwindling attendances at Cliftonhill and also Broomfield and with many locals going to the Rangers and Celtic games, that Saturday evening matches could well be the salvation for Scotland's smaller clubs. Whilst Rovers did not have floodlights at this stage, it was a point worth considering, especially as the smaller English clubs had adopted the idea playing either on Friday or Saturday evenings and leaving the Saturday afternoons free for the bigger clubs.

Rovers' next match was the long journey to Forfar where the 'Loons' won 4-0 and for the visit by Stenhousemuir a gritty 1-1 draw was next with the 'Warriors' goal coming from former player Billy Howie. Another long trip, this time to Dumfries, saw Jim Mallon of Johnstone Burgh given a try out at centre but Queens were always in command and ran out winners by 2-1. Rovers had Stewart at centre for the home match against Dumbarton but it was the defence who let the side down with the 'Sons' winning 3-0.

A third defeat in a row came at the hands of Cowdenbeath by 3-1 despite heroics by Madden in goal, including a penalty save. Montrose were then soundly beaten 3-0 at Coatbridge, Rovers getting back on their winning ways and with Mallon, now signed, the forward-line was looking more goal hungry by the minute. The big centre scored his first goal for Rovers down at Ayr in a 3-1 victory which was an incredible result considering the Ayr team had at least eighty per cent of the play. With relatively few chances Rovers scored with virtually every attempt they had at the Ayr goal leaving the Ayr players and fans alike thoroughly deflated and disillusioned.

On the following Friday, New Year's Day, Hamilton Accies were First Foots and the good form continued with Rovers at one stage 3-0 up. Hamilton eventually got a consolation goal but Rovers were never in any difficulty in this one. The following day found the visit to E.S. Clydebank particularly unfortunate. The final score was 2-1 for the 'Bankies' but Rovers had the excuse of Murphy being off all of the second half with an eye injury and also Cooper failed to finish the match minus a tooth requiring dental treatment after a head knock.

Brechin was the venue for the Scottish Cup first round match when a £66 gate was shared by both teams. Four goals were shared by Sneddon and MacCallum with a 4-3 victory putting Rovers into the next round. The League match at Berwick found the Rangers too strong by 3-0 and all hopes were pinned on the home draw against Queen's Park in the Cup at Hampden. There was no scoring in this game, on a day when the whole programme of football was overshadowed by the funeral of Sir Winston Churchill, and the replay was scheduled for a week come

Wednesday. Another disaster took place in-between times down at Stranraer, losing 4-0 in a League game but then it was back to the Cup.

The Supporters Club were greatly to be praised for their outstanding efforts in getting Cliftonhill fit for this Cup tie. Fans joined with Officials on Sunday and had the snow off the field in the hopes of a Monday game. Local referee Bobby Davidson ruled the ground unplayable and it was back to work for the workers dumping many tons of sand on top of the hard surface until it looked more like the Sahara Desert than a football ground. Both teams wearing baseball boots found the going surprisingly good and the match was played out on Wednesday afternoon, in these pre-floodlit days, with all the local schoolboys taking the afternoon off and many workers admitting to a tremendous number of "Granny funerals".

The match itself was a bit of a let-down, with the teams very well matched and Rovers struggling to get back from a goal scored in the second half by the Amateurs. They succeeded in the last minute when full-back Davie Brown headed the ball in from a high cross and the match went into extra time but no further goals were scored. The second replay took place the following evening at Firhill and on a fog-bound pitch Queen's were through by dint of a solitary first half goal. It had taken three hundred minutes to score three goals to separate the teams. All Rovers were left with now was the League. Not unexpectedly Manager Willie Telfer tendered his resignation on the following Friday which was accepted by the Directors.

For the match against Raith Rovers local boy and provisional signing John Boyle was given a run at inside left. The youngster scored the third goal in the 3-0 victory. Bobby Flavell was offered and accepted the post of Manager and took up the position in time for the home match against Arbroath which ended up a no scoring draw. Another home draw took place the following week this time at 2-2 against East Fife.

Once again a proposal to reorganise the Scottish Leagues was floated by the League Management Committee this time proposing three Leagues of fourteen, twelve and twelve. Promotion and relegation was to be continued on the present two up two down basis and guarantees would be £500 in the First Division, £200 in the Second Division and £150 in the Third. To compensate for loss of fixtures a new Spring Cup was to be organised. It was a prospect with which Rovers were not happy. Always on the look out for money-making ventures, Chairman Fagan entered into negotiations for Stock Car Racing to be held at Cliftonhill during the Summer.

The visit to Stenhousemuir was rather an anti-climax against all this off-field activity but to the players credit a 3-2 victory was chalked up. Queen of the South dampened the team's ardour at Coatbridge in coming back from a 1-0 deficit at half-time to take the match by 2-1. Sandy Jones left the club to emigrate to Australia with the best wishes of players and fans alike and the following day the trip to Dumbarton found the 'Sons' narrowly winning by 2-1. Madden saved Rovers' bacon in this one including a fine penalty save but even he could not stop the surge by the homesters.

A jaunt to Alloa found another depressing 3-2 defeat. Cowdenbeath also won 3-0 through in Fife, a match in which Andy Murphy missed a penalty but was really only notable because it was Leary's last match being freed and also the match in which Tony Green made his debut at inside left. Young Green held his place for the visit to Brechin and Loughran took Leary's place at centre-half. It was left to Rovers to raise the tempo of their game in this end-of-season match to lift the points with a solitary McIlwraith goal.

The fifth away match in a row was controversial to say the least at Montrose finishing up no scoring but the four hundred and fifty fans were amazed when, after Montrose forward Kemp shot into the side net, the referee initially gave a goal to Montrose. After great protestations by the whole Rovers' team, he altered his decision to a goal kick. The season finished on an even more dismal note at home against Alloa with the 'Wasps' winning 3-2 leaving Rovers in eleventh position on thirty-three points with Stirling being promoted as Champions, on fifty-nine and Hamilton accompanying them with fifty. Brechin were again bottom with nineteen points.

Stock Car racing started on Easter Monday and was run by Mr. and Mrs Cecil, who comprised Spedeworth Limited, and their Formula II stock car racing. The intention was for meetings to be held on Sundays at two-weekly intervals throughout the Summer and as five thousand enthusiasts had visited the ground for the inaugural meeting, who would say that this would not be the making of Albion Rovers in terms of finance.

Big changes were also mooted in other spheres locally with Whifflet, originally the home of Albion Rovers, scheduled for redevelopment, the new S.T.D. Telephone Exchange coming into operation during the Glasgow Fair holiday and the Planning Quinquennial Review for the redevelopment of Central Coatbridge being published. On the football field the Glasgow Corporation five-a-side tournament in their Annual Sports invited Celtic, Partick Thistle, Queen's Park and Albion Rovers to take part. In the first round Rovers beat Celtic 2-1 and in the final defeated Partick Thistle by the only goal of the match. Rovers' team was youngsters Rutherford, Green and Dillon with experience coming from Murphy and captain Brown.

At the beginning of June a new set-up was announced by Chairman Fagan when the three-man Board, Messrs. Fagan, Moffat Millar and William Higgins, was augmented by local business men John Lees, Tom Timpson, Ernest Capocci and Bobby Flavell. The last named was going to carry on the dual role of manager and Director and by the time Ivor Llewellyn, the new trainer, called the players forward for training a whole complement of new players had been fixed up.

Season 1965/66

The annual resurgence of optimism swept the town but with more reason than for many a season as this young Rovers' team with experience in the form of Jimmy Harrower, Andy Murphy and Davie Brown looked, on paper at least, as though it was capable of giving all the others a good run for their money. The season opened at Cliftonhill with a League Cup sectional match against Queen of the South and seven hundred fans witnessed a hard, fast game with Rovers showing much authority and good football and at the end of the day unfortunate in sharing the points and two goals. Rovers' team was Madden, Brown, A. Murphy, Cooper, Jamieson, Wilson, Rutherford, Green, Dillon, Harrower and MacCallum.

Airdrie, who had been relegated the previous season along with Third Lanark, were in the same Section and the Monklands was buzzing with the prospects of at least four matches between the local rivals. On the Wednesday night, four thousand fans saw Airdrie demolish the young Rovers' team, unchanged from the previous match, by a 6-1 margin. This was a game in which Rovers never got to grips with the opposition and new centre half Jamieson found particularly trying. The visit to Stranraer saw Cooper take Jamieson's place, John McTurk at right

ALBION ROVERS SEASON 1965/66

Standing: D. Brown, A. Murphy, R. Madden, J. Jamieson, J. Cooper, A. Wilson.
Seated: E. Rutherford, A. Green, J. Dillon, J. Harrower, R. MacCallum.

back, following his signing from Stirling Albion, and coloured wing half Dougie Johnston were introduced. Despite seven positional changes the line-up was not considered a success despite the 0-0 scoreline. It was particularly galling in the return match at Dumfries with the Queens scoring two goals in the last two minutes to put Rovers firmly at the foot of the Section table.

Two draws and two defeats in the first four matches were hardly adequate preparation for the return match on the 1st September against Airdrieonians. The 6.45 kick-off found the re-arranged Rovers' team start off in whirlwind fashion with John Dillon scoring the opening goal in the first minute. Rutherford made it 2-0 in the twenty-third minute and several other chances were missed of adding to Rovers' tally. Airdrie's chance to get back into the game came when McTurk handled a Black drive and Jonquin, normally so safe with penalties, shot straight into Madden's arms but two minutes before the interval outside right Ferguson scored a cute goal. What had transpired gave no indication of what was to happen in the second half. In a terrific four minute spell immediately after the re-start Rovers added a further three goals with Dillon, MacCallum and Wilson putting Rovers 5-1 up in fifty-three minutes. The Airdrie team folded after this and Dillon scored another before Madden butterfingered a Gardner long range effort over his head. McTurk rubbed it in by showing how a penalty should be taken after Hannah had made a brilliant save from an overhead kick by Green. 8-2 was the final score but the difference between the two teams was so marked Rovers could easily have scored double figures on the night. So excited were Rovers' delighted young fans that there was a pitch invasion at the end, for which the local team were reported to the League by Mr. Stewart, the referee, and reprimanded. Not surprisingly the team was on a high at Cliftonhill in the last game of the Section which was purely academic, with Airdrie already qualified, but for the record Rovers won 2-1 against Stranraer.

The League programme opened at Dumfries with the third meeting of the two teams out of seven matches which was won by the Dumfries side with the only goal of the game. East Fife were next to be visited and a fighting Rovers were rewarded by a 2-1 win which was all the more meritorious as Tony Green was injured and hobbled at outside left for most of the second half. The winning goal was scored by Dixie Deans, a junior trialist from Neilston. Revenge was sweet against Queen of the South where a Rutherford goal in the second half was sufficient to beat the 'Doonhammers' in a match where Murphy was stretchered off in the last minute.

Murphy was sufficiently recovered to take up the centre forward position for the League match at Coatbridge against Airdrieonians. The Airdrie team came determined to wipe out the memory of their earlier heavy defeat and the match was played at some pace. There were no goals in the first half but Rovers were always in command. In the second period goals by McCallum and Wilson were sufficient to confirm a 2-1 win and make it two to one in victories over their old rivals so far this season.

Four Brazilian professional footballers arrived at Cliftonhill. They had been in this country with their Portuguese agent looking for transfers to Scottish Clubs as the Brazilian F.A. were desperately short of money. These lads had been training with Celtic but when their business was done they were offered training facilities at Cliftonhill until such times as they could get fixed up. There was no chance of Rovers meeting the kind of fees which would be required by their Brazilian Clubs and there was also the problem of the players themselves receiving work permits, a task which their agent was working on. However, Rovers took them with the squad up to Forfar the following Wednesday where on tight Station Park trialist Reilly from Dalry Thistle scored the winner in a 2-1 victory. The following Saturday at Ayr, with Murphy again at centre, the 'Honest Men' ran out winners by 2-0.

With Forfar bottom of the League their visit on the following Wednesday prompted Rovers to play one of their Brazilian guests and Ayrton Inacio was handed the number eight jersey. Also making his debut at left back in this match was Joe Gallacher from Lochend Amateurs. The dusky, stocky inside forward was prominent early on with neat touches and indeed scored with a fine daisycutter for the first goal. The Forfar defence decided to cut him out of the play and he received some fairly rough treatment and fell out of the game. With the Rovers' team being rather lopsided thereafter it was no surprise when Forfar, with something to prove against foreign players, ran out winners by 3-2.

On the 2nd of October, East Stirlingshire were the visitors at Cliftonhill in a fine 4-1 victory for the Boys of the 'Brig. The news also came through that the Brazilian players had moved on and it was left to Rovers other coloured player Dougie Johnstone to take up the running which he did at Cathkin the following week scoring in the 2-1 defeat. There was talk during the week that John Flanagan was to return to Cliftonhill but at the last minute negotiations broke down and the popular winger was transferred to Partick Thistle.

Brechin City, complete with former Rovers Loughran, McIlwraith and Sneddon came to Coatbridge but former Brechin player Johnstone scored two goals in Rovers' 4-0 victory. The following week Angus neighbours Arbroath ran up a 2-0 scoreline in the first ten minutes and it took Rovers all their time to level the scores at 2-2 over the piece. The visit to Alloa found Rovers winning 3-1 in this one amidst gale and rain but their job was made much easier by Alloa having only ten men in the second half. A no-scoring draw at home against Berwick was coupled with the news that Jimmy Harrower had been suspended for six weeks for field misdemeanours.

For the game at Cowdenbeath Joe Reilly was signed on and played at centre forward. With snow lying on the pitch Rovers won this one 2-1 with Madden, again showing his prowess at penalties, making a fine save. The match against Dumbarton at Coatbridge was nothing each when referee Rodge of Stonehouse abandoned the match in the eighty-third minute in the midst of a hailstorm.

John McMullen, long time Secetary of the Supporters' Club, died and the team wore black armbands in his memory at Montrose. On an icy-hard pitch, Rovers could make nothing of the surface and the home team won 4-0. Two home victories then occurred, the first by 1-0 against Raith Rovers and then 2-0 against Stranraer, a result which put Rovers third top in the League. Despite the success on the field there were signs of disharmony between the Football Club and the Supporters' Club. The Supporters were asked to vacate their club rooms in Bank Street and there was also concern regarding the Development Pool. 1985 ended with a 4-3 victory at Hampden on Christmas Day which was all the more creditable as Rovers were down 3-2 at half time.

The following Saturday, the New Year's Day clash at Broomfield, was long awaited and four thousand five hundred fans saw Rovers, who were fourth top, go into a 2-0 lead in the first ten minutes. Airdrie fought back to square the match at half time and powered into a 4-2 lead in the second half before the referee dealt rather harshly with John Cooper, who was ordered to the pavilion for an over robust challenge on an Airdrie forward. Airdrie took this opportunity to emulate

Rovers high scoring in the earlier part of the season but try as they might the match only finished 7-2 with the honours pretty even and the Diamonds failing to score that elusive eighth goal. On the Monday, East Fife won by the only goal of the match at Coatbridge whilst the third defeat in a row came again at Coatbridge against Ayr United by 2-0 in a match which saw Walter Zimmerman make his debut at outside left.

In between these matches came the 41st A.G.M. covering seasons 1959-64. This showed the Club had made a profit in three of these and the overall debit was reduced to £5,520.14.5.

Rumours flooded the town that Rovers were leaving Coatbridge for a new home in East Kilbride. This was strenuously denied by Chairman Fagan and East Kilbride officials would only confirm that Third Lanark were considering the move together with another un-named team.

The Scottish Cup had come round again and Rovers had an away draw against Berwick Rangers. On a pitch which was barely playable and heavily sanded over the icy surface, fourteen hundred fans saw Rovers dice with death when referee Webster from Falkirk disallowed a last minute goal for Berwick, the match finishing all square with no scoring. The following Wednesday a thousand fans saw the replay with Rovers moving swiftly to a 3-0 half time lead. The players eased up in the second half and Berwick even missed a penalty for Rovers to move into the second round.

The Supporters' Club fixed up a new pools organiser in George Walker and the daily winnings were increased in a completely new set-up. Third Lanark visited Coatbridge and shared the points in a 1-1 draw before Rovers visited Queen of the South in the Scottish Cup. Rovers did not seem to learn from their previous four matches against Queens and the dangerman of the previous games, right winger Jimmy Davison, especially ripped Rovers' defence apart time after time and it was no surprise when Queens won by 3-0.

Rovers' heads went down and it showed in the next match at Cliftonhill against Alloa when opposing centre St. John broke his leg in the fifth minute but his team still won by 4-0 in what was an absolutely wretched display by the Rovers' team. Ample revenge was gained by Berwick over the Border in the next match by 4-1. The team showed some sign of fight when Cowdenbeath were the visitors as, after being one down at half time, Rovers fought back to win 2-1.

During the next week Chairman Fagan stepped down as supremo and John Lees became the new Chairman, an appointment which coincided with the launching of an ambitious plan to put the Coatbridge Club back on the football map. Mr. Lees announced that the property to the rear of Cliftonhill was to be redeveloped to include a social club. The Football Club were also to take over the Supporters' Club Development Pool and run it for the sole financial assistance of the Football Club. Unimpressed with all this talk of revival at Coatbridge, Dumbarton acting as hosts, handed out a 2-0 defeat. For the next match at Larbert young trialist Kenny Jenkins from Johnstone Burgh was tried at centre and he scored the only goal of the match and put in an overall fine performance.

The journey to Brechin the following mid-week was a nightmare with the team bus being held up due to road accidents and the kick-off was delayed by half an hour. This did not seem to put off Rovers who ran out winners by 4-1 and on the Friday the good form continued with a third win in seven days over East Stirlingshire by 4-2, with trialist Jenkins again making a goal-scoring appearance this time with a double. The fourth win in a row at home saw Montrose dumped by

3-0 and fellow Angus side, Arbroath, on the Wednesday fight out a 1-1 draw in a match which saw new forwards Mike Murphy, brother of Andy, and Kenny Jenkins play their first game as signed players. Jenkins got Rovers' goal in this match.

Another 1-1 draw was fought out at Kirkcaldy whilst the following Monday saw Hamilton Accies win 1-0 at Coatbridge in the Lanarkshire Cup. A spurt in the last four League matches saw Rovers end the season undefeated with first of all Stenhousemuir drawing 2-2 at Coatbridge before three Kenny Jenkins goals in the first half were enough to beat Stranraer 3-2 at Stair Park. In the replay of the abandoned match against Dumbarton there were still no goals scored and Jenkins finished a successful start to his career by scoring the only goal of the match against Queen's Park at Coatbridge.

Rovers finished seventh in the League which was an improvement of four places over the previous season with forty-three points. Ayr lifted the Championship with ten more and Airdrieonians accompanying them upstairs on fifty points. Forfar were bottom dogs with seventeen.

The new Daily Sweepstake was taking off and George Walker was now full-time Area agent and his four District agents plus ten part-timers were doing a grand job. Prizes were £75, £15 and £10 drawn weekly instead of daily as before. During the close season much effort was put into the signing of players and the playing surface was brought up to a condition not seen at Cliftonhill for many a day. The terracing was also given the once over and much of the credit was being given to Ivor Llewellyn who was recently appointed as full-time Trainer/Groundsman.

An innovation for the start of the new season was the introduction of a substitute who could be played at any time during the ninety minutes. The original idea was to be in reserve in case of injury but very quickly became employed as a tactical manoeuvre.

Season 1966/67

On what turned out to be the wettest day for thirty-four years, Scunthorpe United, complete with Ray Clemence in goal, turned out at Cliftonhill on the sixth of August in a pre-season friendly. Rovers were given the old one-two-three in no uncertain terms with the English team, who had finished fourth in the Third Division the previous season, too strong in all departments. Rovers were represented by Madden, McMurray, Gallacher, Dillon, Jamieson, A. Murphy, Rutherford, (M. Murphy), Green, Jenkins, Wilson (Halliday) and McCallum.

With that bad start behind them, the Support wended their way for the opening League Cup match of the season at Alloa but the result ended even worse with the home team winning by 4-0. The Wednesday evening match at Coatbridge ended up a no-scoring draw against Hamilton Academical as did the Saturday match at home against Montrose.

A mid-week match against Queen's Park was the opening home League fixture and Tony Green had the honour of scoring Rovers first goal of the season which turned out to be the only goal of the game in the fifty-fourth minute. It had thus taken Rovers four hundred and fourteen minutes to score a goal which was disappointing given the promise of new centre Jenkins and the quality of Rutherford, Dillon, Green and Wilson. Queen's forward Mackay was ordered off in this match which made it all the easier for Rovers. A second 1-0 victory in succession came in the return League Cup match against Alloa and at Hamilton, despite a disappointing 3-0 defeat, diminutive winger Willie Callaghan made his debut and was promptly signed for the season. The trip to Montrose found Rovers sharing four goals and the points but a bombshell was to burst during the week with both Rovers' Manager Bobby Flavell and Trainer/Groundsman Ivor Llewellyn resigning. It was quickly pointed out by the Board that Flavell was only giving up the Managerial duties and that he would remain as a Director but with Llewellyn it was a case of accepting a better post outside football. Rovers immediately advertised for a Manager and were completely inundated with applications.

The Wednesday match against Queen of the South at Palmerston was memorable for two reasons. Firstly, a whopping 7-4 defeat was logged in front of three thousand fans but more importantly Rovers first substitute took the field in this match when Joe Gallacher came on for John Jamieson. It was the same Gallacher who was in the wars the following game at Hamilton when he got injured in the second half, with Rovers only able to field eleven fit men, the injured Jamieson was on the substitute bench in the hope that he would not be required. With Rovers winning 1-0 but rather lopsided with Jamieson's inclusion after Gallacher had gone, two penalty kicks by Accies finished the match in a very unsatisfactory 2-1 defeat for the Coatbridge team. For the visit by Queen of the South Rovers introduced Ian Moffat from Forth Wanderers in goal and he put up a fine display in the 2-0 victory. On the following Saturday Stenhousemuir came to Coatbridge and were easily defeated 4-1 with Dillon scoring a hat-trick. Immediately following this game Jackie Stewart, who had been coaching at Broomfield and who was a former Dundee and Airdrieonian wing-half was fixed up as Manager.

Jackie got a dismal baptism at Hampden the following week when the Amateurs over-ran the men from Coatbridge by 5-1 and it was then underlined to the new Manager that he had a difficult job on his hands. But at Arbroath the following week he saw a fighting draw, despite the fact that Arbroath missed a penalty and found Rovers sharing two goals, their own being from the penalty spot in the second half.

The first win under the new Management had Kenny Jenkins getting back on the score sheet but he suffered concussion in the second half and didn't return to the field. However, in torrential rain Rovers were not to be denied and it looked the same thing the next week at Clydebank when Jenkins scored a hat-trick and McMurray scored twice from the penalty spot in the first half to make it look all too easy against Clydebank. The new League 'Babes' came out with a vengeance in the second half and Rovers were lucky to hold on to a 5-3 lead. Airdrieonians reportedly made a half-hearted bid for Tony Green but this was turned down by the Board.

It was just as well as the young inside forward had a fine display against Brechin at Coatbridge scoring two goals with McMurray being the saint and sinner at the same time. Billy scored a first half penalty and then succeeded in missing two further penalty attempts hitting the post with the first one and belting the next one over the bar. This would have been a unique Rovers' hat-trick for him had all three been netted. Nothing daunted McMurray scored from the spot in the first half against Morton, at Greenock, but the home team came back in the second half to win 2-1 in front of six thousand fans. Raith Rovers took the lead in the first half at Coatbridge but a Jenkins goal in the second half squared it at 1-1 before Rovers went to Cathkin. With the score at 1-0 for Thirds and twenty minutes gone, left half Andy Murphy went to take a shy but found no Rovers' player within thirty yards of him. When he gave his mates some vocal encouragement to come a bit closer he used some language with which the referee took exception and promptly ordered the bold Andrew for an early bath. The team soldiered on but it was a lost cause and Thirds scored another goal to run out winners by 2-0.

The following week at Alloa, in a mud bath of a pitch, referee Kelly of Motherwell made three bookings but could not stop rampant Rovers winning 4-1 helped by hat-trickster Kenny Jenkins. New signings Johnny Sorley from Greenock Juniors and Tommy Anderson from Stirling made their debuts in this match. Both new signings kept their places for Forfar's visit and this time the Rovers forwards were sadly lacking in front of goal and it was left to full back McMurray to score the only goal in the second half.

Berwick Rangers were next visitors at Coatbridge with new signing former Airdrie goalkeeper Jock Wallace in goal, and he put on a sterling display to help Rangers to a 3-2 victory. The visit to Dumbarton the following week had a disappointing result with the 'Sons' winning 3-0. Following the match John Lees resigned as Chairman, although he would remain as a Director. Tom Fagan returned to the Chairmanship and set himself to a further stint in the hot seat.

The Referees' Committee fined Andy Murphy £7 for his ordering off earlier in the season and he was lucky not to have been more severely dealt with. At Montrose a narrow 2-1 victory found trialist centre half Bernard Fagan from Ballieston Juniors turning in a fine performance and he was given another try out in the home match against Stranraer which ended up 1-1. The last home game of the year was played in most unpromising circumstances with an ice rutted field covered with snow. The ground staff did a great job in preparing the pitch into a condition suitable for the referee to agree play should commence. Rovers got off to a blistering start when right back Cunningham ran from his own half to lash the ball into the roof of the net and Rovers quickly went into a 5-1 lead. Snow started to fall around half time and, with the lines beginning to be obliterated, thoughts were that Rovers' best score for a long while would be erased when the match was abandoned. However, the match did finish with the score unchanged. On the last day of the year, Rovers visited Cowdenbeath and wingers Murphy and Callaghan scored the only goals of the game in the first half to clinch victory.

Hamilton Accies hanselled in the New Year at Coatbridge on Monday, 2nd January, and a Dillon goal in the first half won the points for Rovers. At that match the Development Fund First Annual Draw tickets were sold before a two thousand crowd. Mrs. Lees, wife of the former Club Chairman, pulled the eight lucky winners from the drum. The first prize was a Singer Chamois motor car taxed for one year or £500 cash and was won by a Mossend man, whilst the second prize — a two week holiday for two in Palma went to Tomintoul. The rest of the prizes went to local people and Rovers were reputed to have made a modest profit on the deal. The match next day at Stenhousemuir proved to be expensive for Rovers when Tony Green, who received very close attention from the Muir defence, was bundled to the ice covered pitch so often that he broke a bone in his hand and would be missing for the next eight games.

This, together with an injury to Kenny Jenkins, was a severe blow to the Scottish Cup aspirations in the home match against Cowdenbeath. Dillon was fielded at centre and Callaghan at inside right but the team display was quite without real effort or enthusiasm. Cowdenbeath's newcomer Donaldson at outside left scored with five minutes to go in the first half and it was left to goalkeeper Madden to keep Rovers in with a chance. Cowdenbeath deserved more but had done enough to enjoy an attractive first round proper tie against St. Mirren.

Andy Murphy played most of the match with a broken jaw which added to Rovers' growing injury list. This result once more acted as a depressant for Rovers and they lost their next two matches both by a 2-0 scoreline, firstly against East Stirlingshire and then Clydebank.

Andy Murphy and Rovers got their due revenge over Third Lanark in a 1-0 victory before Brechin City were defeated 3-2 at Glebe Park but the following week Morton came as League leaders and a ding-dong battle ensued. Two thousand fans were enthralled with the fare but also incensed when, in front of the enclosure John Dillon was knocked cold with a fine upper cut which any self-respecting boxer would have been proud of. Referee Elliot from Barrhead missed it but justice was done shortly after when Joe Harper missed a penalty. Rovers went down in the end by 1-0.

Arbroath won convincingly 4-0 at Coatbridge and Rovers slumped into sixth top and more gloom was perpetrated with the 2-1 defeat at Kirkcaldy and the news locally that the Stewarts & Lloyds Works of Coats and Waverley were to close. Tony Green made a reappearance in the home match against Alloa but was obviously not match fit and the team went down once more this time by 2-0. Two further away defeats followed, by 4-2 at Forfar and 2-1 at Berwick, making six defeats in a row before the slide was stopped in a 2-2 draw at home against Dumbarton. Moffat, who had been reintroduced in goal, was working extra hard but he had an easier time against Montrose with Rovers winning 4-1 in front of their own fans.

With only three League matches to go, Rovers were again chasing hard to end up in the top six teams and two fine victories away from home by 2-0 against Stranraer and 2-1 against East Fife left a home match against Cowdenbeath to clinch the matter. The game turned out to be an anti-climax, being a no-scoring draw, and Rovers ended up in seventh place by one goal of a goal difference. Much to the consternation of the Coatbridge fans, this was Tony Green's last game, being transferred to Blackpool for a reputed £13,500.

The last game of the season was a Lanarkshire Cup Tie at Coatbridge against arch rivals Airdrieonians and with Charlie Oliphant on trial at right half and John Dillon taking Green's place at inside left, a well contested share of four goals was the result. As it had been decided that there would be only one leg in Lanarkshire Cup ties from now on the match ended with a toss of a coin deciding who should go through to the Final. Airdrie were lucky in this instance and Rovers once more were out in the cold.

Three less points than in the previous season had been attained and one place lower in the League Table. Morton were promoted as Champions with a record sixty-nine points, with Raith Rovers joining them on fifty-eight. Brechin were bottom on twenty-three and, despite having picked up an extra team in Clydebank, Third Lanark resigned from the League at the end of the season after a year of turmoil. The usual lengthy list of players were freed with the promise by the Board and hope by the Supporters that the newcomers would give that added impetus to a serious promotion bid.

In May, Celtic had their moment of glory in Lisbon defeating Inter Milan 2-1 in the European Cup Final and on a more parochial note, Rovers were again Champions for the third year in a row at the Glasgow Corporation Sports five-a-side Tournament. They beat Falkirk and then Airdrie with the following team—the Murphy brothers, Charlie Oliphant, Jim Cunningham and Kenny Jenkins with Tommy Dunn as reserve.

At the end of June, Rovers were contacted by two South American players who had been playing with the French side Rouen and a twenty-four year old Argentinian, Louis Fullone, was signed to fill Tony Green's boots and the Argentinian was joined by a Brazilian, Roberto Farria, at Cliftonhill with training facilities. Both players had been recommended by the Brazilian Inacio who had played with Rovers two seasons earlier and they wished to break into British football.

The sale of effects at Cathkin did not attract much attention, other than to Albion Rovers and Forfar Athletic and Chairman Fagan picked up the stand tip-up seats which were fitted to Cliftonhill. Other items purchased were a lawnmower, nets, corner flags, dressing room electrical equipment, treatment tables as well as upholstered chairs and a sideboard for the Board Room.

Glasgow Fair weekend arrived with bombshell news of the resignation of Director John Lees pointing to Board Room differences. Part of the reason for the resignation was the freeing of the Argentianian Fullone without him officially kicking a ball for Rovers. Two weeks later, further disquiet with the Board saw the resignation of Ernie Capocci. However, back on the pitch Manager Stewart and Trainer Bobby Holmes were working hard to prepare the players for the new season and a pre-season match against European Champions Celtic, who fielded virtually their Cup-winning side, Rovers won by 2-1.

Season 1967/68
It didn't seem like Summer when East Fife came to open the League Cup campaign on the 12th August to be greeted by a waterlogged pitch and when Tom Wharton got the season going Rovers were immediately toiling against their old League Cup foes. The Fifers were 2-1 up at half time and ran out winners by 4-2. Rovers' team was Moffat, Cunningham, McMurray, Oliphant, Fagan, A. Murphy, M. Murphy, Dunn, Jenkins, Gallagher and Dillon with Jamieson as substitute.

There was better fare on the Wednesday when Arbroath suffered their first defeat at home in over eighteen months. In front of two and a half thousand fans Rovers came away in the second half to win by 3-1 and in an unchanged team the following Saturday Alloa were defeated 4-1.

Queen of the South became the third away match in a row on the Wednesday first League contest but Rovers again failed their Palmerston hurdle, losing to a solitary second half goal. Undeterred the same team went out to East Fife at Methil but again a single goal defeat was the result for Captain Andy Murphy and his boys. Showing more than reasonable faith in the players, the same team was played for the fifth match in a row against Arbroath and the rot was stopped with a 1-1 draw.

However, enough was enough for the final cup match against Alloa and Alec Smith, who had given up football some eighteen months earlier to devote more time to his glazing business with David Catanach of Celtic made his debut in the number eleven jersey. He helped to steady the midfield in a 4-3 victory, due to a fine fight back in the second half after being down 2-1 at half time. Alloa also made it difficult for themselves by missing a penalty.

Back on League business, Hamilton Accies were the opposition for the first home match which saw young trialist Mick Green from Benburb given a run at inside right. Two first half goals were enough to get Rovers off to a good start. The following Wednesday Rovers gained ample revenge over Queen of the South with young Green retaining his position and scoring the third of Rovers three goals to no reply.

At Alloa a Jenkins goal was disallowed in the final minute by referee Henderson which meant that the points were shared in a 1-1 draw and, with excitement running high in the town that this might just be the team to gain promotion, East Fife appeared for the third time this season. The big crowd was disappointed to see Rovers go down 2-1 although new boy Green was quickly making Rovers supporters forget about his namesake, who was now doing great things in the Blackpool team.

Rovers brought forward their match against Alloa scheduled for the Wednesday night to Monday and fielded yet another Benburb player Bobby Graham in the forward line. In the match which kicked off at 5.30, young Green scored both Rovers goals in the 2-0 victory giving him four goals in five matches. Come the Saturday, Clydebank were visited and the usual close game was the result. Dick Madden was in goal for the Bankies and Jenkins scored both Rovers' goals in the 2-2 draw. The match was fiercely contested and the referee considered that Dillon's part was too much so and he was ordered off leaving his mates to fight out the match shorthanded.

If the fans thought that match was volatile they hadn't seen anything yet when Ayr United came to Coatbridge the following week. With the stand bustling with various Club Officials and Scouts headed by Sir Stanley Matthews of Port Vale, Harry Johnstone of Everton, Neil McBain of Leeds United, together with representatives of Portsmouth and Fulham. All were disappointed, especially with Rovers players, as none of the young starlets lived up to their reputations and with fifteen minutes to go, Ayr had a man ordered off. With Rovers losing 2-0 in the eightyth minute. Jamieson was also given his marching orders and Ayr won the battle of the ten men by 2-0. Andy Murphy and Jamieson swapped places with Mike Murphy taking Dillon's place on the right wing against Forfar. This lineup seemed to immediately click and Rovers won in the end by 4-1. The Referee's Committee gave Dillon a fourteen day suspension for his ordering off and he was again missing for the visit to Hampden where with Blackburn representatives watching Tommy Dunn, a Green goal in the second half helped to share four goals in an otherwise unimpressive display by both teams. Montrose were next visitors in a match which Rovers won by a goal in each half but they were not so lucky the next week at Falkirk when they could only share four goals with East Stirlingshire. At Arbroath the following week, in a gale force wind when it was difficult to even stand upright, the Angus team won by a second half goal due more to their ability to weather such conditions rather than any football skill.

For the Lanarkshire Cup Semi Final at Fir Park, Rovers recast their team against Motherwell with Dillon at right half, Green and Dunn forming the right wing and A. Murphy and Smith the left wing and the floodlit match found Rovers quickly on the ascendancy and it was no surprise to the two thousand five hundred fans when Rovers went 2-0 up in the first half. Goalkeeper McCloy was the culprit allowing a prodigious free kick from left back McMurray from the half way line to drop over his head. Kenny Jenkins scored the other three in Rovers 4-1 victory. The adrenalin was still flowing on the Saturday when Berwick were the visitors for Rovers steam-rollered their way to a 5-2 victory with Dunn scoring a double.

Two defeats were next on the cards with the first by 1-0 at Dumbarton but more disappointingly, 2-0 at home against Cowdenbeath. Charlie Kelly of Greenock Juniors was signed after his display in this match. He took his place on the left wing for the trip to Stranraer with Jim Graham, signed from Dunfermline, at centre at the end of the week which heralded the announcement of Edinburgh

Monarchs Speedway team coming to Cliftonhill in the Autumn.

Rovers' stuffy performance and second half fightback was enough for them to share the points at 2-2 down at Stranraer, which was considered fair preparation for their journey to the other end of Scotland in the Scottish Cup against Elgin City at Burroughbriggs. A special train was arranged by the Supporters' Club at the special fare of £1.10/- for adults and 15/- for children. Team and support travelled in style on the Saturday morning and arrived to find the Elgin area covered by heavy snow. The home fans had been busy and the ground was in fine trim for the match and Rovers were confident of doing well. Manager Stewart schemed for a twin centre attack with centre Jenkins playing with the number eleven jersey and new boy Graham in the centre of the park. Rovers went one down but were not too perturbed as Manager Stewart's thinking seemed to be working when Jenkins equalised to put the teams in at half time all square. Unfortunately, the move was never repeated in the match and Elgin scored twice more to make it a rapturous evening for the home fans. It was a very dispirited Coatbridge squad who returned by the special train. Elgin moved on to Tarff Rovers in the next round and were eventually eliminated by Airdrieonians at Broomfield.

Tuesday the 19th of December was a black day for the Burgh when the Town Hall section of the Municipal Buildings was burned down. Only the heroics of Provost Dowdalls and staff saved the Provosts' portraits and other valuables.

Brechin City were last visitors for the year at Cliftonhill complete with ex-Rovers Cooper and Sneddon but were no match for the boys still smarting from their Elgin result and Rovers won this one by 3-1 with Green scoring a fine double.

On Monday, New Year's Day, the short trip to Hamilton found another two Green goals sufficient to beat Accies 2-1 in a match which was no place for the weak-hearted. Both goalkeepers were in excellent form with ex-Rovers' Lamont in the Hamilton goal outstanding. On the Saturday the long journey up to Methil saw the first reverse of the year with East Fife winning by a second half goal to nothing on a rutted, bone-hard pitch.

It was two weeks into January before Rovers had their own First Foots in the shape of the Clydebank team, complete with ex-Rovers players Madden and Rutherford. With slippery conditions, there were plenty of unintentional mistakes and chances galore but at the end of the game no goals. During the following week disaster hit Cliftonhill on the Monday when gale force winds hit Coatbridge. The covered enclosure collapsed and the floodlighting on top of it was also demolished. The stand was also battered and torn and a large section of a retaining wall was toppled. The plans by the Club for the arrival of Edinburgh Monarchs were at a very advanced stage and this was seen as a major setback to the setting-up of speedway in Coatbridge. Fortunately the next two matches were scheduled to be away from home which would give the Club time to clear away the debris.

Trailing eighteen points behind League leaders St. Mirren, Rovers travelled to Ayr but found no comfort from that quarter with the 'Honest Men' winning by 5-2. For the match at Forfar Peter Coleman from Cambuslang Rangers was tried out on the right wing in a match which Rovers lost 2-1. The trialist's play was promising and he was promptly signed to retain his position against Queen's Park but another heavy defeat, this time by 5-3, showed that Rovers were not yet happy with their formation.

The trip to Montrose was traumatic, both from a playing sense, with the team losing 3-0, but also Alec Smith being ordered off. This was Billy McMurray's last game as he was freed only to sign for Dumbarton the following week. Two home

ALBION ROVERS SEASON 1967/68

Standing: J. Cunningham, W. McMurray, I. Moffat, C. Oliphant, B. Fagan, J. Jamieson.
Seated: T. Dunn, A. Smith, M. Green, K. Jenkins, J. Dillon, J. Kelly.

matches provided better fare, the first against East Stirlingshire with a 3-2 victory found Peter Coleman scoring his first goal for the Club. With Blackpool representatives watching Mike Green, the player responded in the first half with a goal in the 1-1 draw against Arbroath.

Two away victories found Rovers win, thanks to an Andy Murphy penalty, at Berwick and the same player scored the winner, again from the spot, in the 3-2 victory over Cowdenbeath. Mike Green was absent for this game being in London with the S.F.A. Professional Youth Team in preparation for their visit to Portugal. Against Stranraer at Coatbridge Rovers won 3-0 in what turned out to be Ian Moffat's last match before emigrating to Canada. The newspapers were full of praise for Mike Green in Portugal, coming on as substitute in one match and scoring a great goal for Scotland in another, in the Youth Tournament.

Saturday the 6th of April was the big day on the Speedway front and history was made when Coatbridge Monarchs met Glasgow Tigers in a special match introducing First Division Speedway for the first time to Lanarkshire. There was earlier speedway at Motherwell in the 50s but this was in the Second Division. Over ten thousand fans queued up, the Clan McGregor pipe band provided pre-match entertainment and Provost and Mrs. Edward Dowdalls performed the official opening. The Monarchs were trailing 45-51 from the first leg of the Championship Derby at White City the night before and they won on the night to the overall score of 99-93. New names now ringing about Cliftonhill were Dougie Templeton, Bernie Persson, Bert Harkins, Reider Eide, Lars Jansson and Bill McMillan.

Meanwhile, back at the fitba' . . . . . On the next Wednesday, Dumbarton were on the receiving end of one of Rovers' best performances of the season and although the score was only 3-1 in favour of the Coatbridge team, it could have been many more. A fighting draw at Love Street against League leaders St. Mirren found Rovers equal to the table toppers and the points were shared at 2-2. With decimalisation now having taken place and 5p and 10p coins taking the place of shillings and two-shilling pieces, the away game against Stenhousemuir found another sharing of the points this time by 1-1. The return game saw Rovers again in rampant form scoring three goals in each half without reply.

A second last League game found Champions St. Mirren much too strong at Coatbridge and Rovers were humbled by 5-0, with Tommy Dunn bidding farewell to Cliftonhill following his transfer to Dundee United. Thus the last League game of the season was set for Brechin and Rovers only needed one point to make the top six which would exempt them from the early rounds of the Scottish Cup. It looked a banker with Brechin eleven points behind in the League and in third bottom slot but again it was not to be, as one of the most insipid performances of the season saw Rovers fritter to a 2-0 defeat. New signing Phil McGovern from St. Anthony's took Dunn's position and made a promising debut but he was let down by the more experienced players all around him. In fact, Rovers finally finished in eighth position on thirty-seven points with St. Mirren Champions on sixty-two and Arbroath runners-up on fifty-three. Stranraer were bottom of the League on twenty.

The season finally ended with a Lanarkshire Cup Final match against Airdrieonians at Broomfield. The match proved to be an exciting encounter with the score see-sawing. Smith and Jenkins scored for Rovers and the match required extra time. Airdrie scored their third goal with two minutes of extra time to go and so won the Cup by 3-2. Rovers' team was Gray, Fagan, A. Murphy, Dillon, Jamieson, Oliphant, Coleman, Green, Jenkins, McGovern and Smith with Graham as substitute.

Jackie Stewart in his attempts to build a promotion-winning team was still well away from his target and much would be required of the new signings. Meanwhile the Speedway was continuing to satisfy its fans.

The Supporters' Club were pleased with the response that had been achieved with their Appeal Fund to repair the damage done at Cliftonhill. This had been most heartening and local rivals, Airdrieonians, had been one of the first donors. Appreciation was acknowledged for the fine effort and the evidence of the repair work carried out was there for all to see.

Season 1968/69

The season opened with a Friendly against York City, who had finished fourth bottom in the English Fourth Division the previous season. They proved to be a big, strong, hard team and there was little studied football in the game which started off as though York City would strike up a cricket score. But the game eventually finished 4-3 in favour of the Englishmen. Rovers' new goalkeeper was Ted McFeat, son of Archie, who had been Rovers' custodian eighteen years earlier. Rovers' team was McFeat, Gemmell, Murphy, Dillon, Fagan, Oliphant, Smith, Green, Jenkins, McGovern (Graham) and Colman. Mike Green got the first goal of the season in this Friday night match.

A week later the season proper started on the 10th of August with an away match at Dumbarton. Rovers had something of a crisis in goal as McFeat was declared unfit, Frank Connor was signed from Celtic. The new goalie was injured after only half an hour with Rovers leading 1-0 and Kenny Jenkins donned the goalkeeper's jersey to prove during the match to be no mean keeper. Perhaps the fact that his father had kept goal for Rangers twenty years earlier contributed to his skill in this department. The lad did so well that Rovers with Smith now on as substitute ended up winners by a resounding 4-0. With neither signed goalkeeper being fit for the visit by Queen's Park on the following Wednesday, young Gray, who had played in the Lanarkshire Cup Final at the end of the previous season, again donned the goalkeeper's jersey and played his part in a 3-2 victory with all the goals coming in the first half. Peter Coleman made it four goals in four games by opening the scoring for the visit by Forfar but the 'Loons' soon took control and Rovers were well defeated in the end by 4-2.

For the first League match at Motherwell, Rovers introduced Willie Batchelor at inside right but Rovers were no match for the Fir Parkers, who even missed a penalty, in their 7-0 romp in the sun. Back in the League Cup the following Saturday, Rovers went top of the section by doing the double over Dumbarton, this time by 5-0, with Mike Green making a hat-trick. The same player made it five in two games in the 3-2 victory at Hampden where Andy Murphy made it all the more difficult at the end by missing a penalty with only eight minutes to go. However, the winning of the Section was confirmed by a 2-2 draw at Forfar in a match where Manager Stewart took the opportunity to field some of his new signings and Fagan, Batchelor and Paterson were given a run.

Having won their Section for only the second time in the history of the League Cup the Fates decreed that Rovers should again be paired in a play-off with another Section. When it was known that their opponents would be Stranraer, there was considerable optimism at Cliftonhill of further advancement. This seemed to be borne out when, at Stranraer in the play-off, Rovers were 3-1 up but were shocked by the home team squaring the match at the end of ninety minutes by 3-3.

However, with the home leg still to come, Rovers were quite confident. This confidence was entirely misplaced with the most ineffectual display for many a season in which Rovers appeared to think that goals would come without any great effort on their part. At the end of the day, Stranraer were worthy winners by 2-0 and yet again, Rovers had failed to proceed further in this Trophy.

For the League match at Hamilton, Connor was re-introduced in goal and eight positional changes saw a much more workmanlike performance by the team and a fine 5-3 victory was recorded over their County rivals. The visit to Montrose was worthwhile and the Jenkins' inspired forward line were on the ball to win by 3-1.

Two home victories, both of them against Angus clubs were recorded, the first by 2-1 against Forfar and the second 5-4 over Montrose, although in this latter match, a Kenny Jenkins hat-trick helped to thwart a tremendous fight back by Montrose who almost overtook the home team but ran out of time. In this match all-action Whitburn wing half Russell Halliday was given a trial. The fourth match in a row against Angus opposition saw the team visit Brechin with Murphy taking Halliday's place in a fine 4-1 victory, this result putting Rovers third top of the League and optimism now high with the Fans that here at last was the team blend which would win promotion. The team were playing very fluently with a lot of skill and for once, the luck seemed to be going their way.

September weekend found Rovers through at Cowdenbeath and two goals in the second half were sufficient to win the match for Rovers and put them joint top of Division Two, which was the first time they had been in that position for twenty-two years. On the Monday, Broomfield was the venue for the Lanarkshire Cup First Leg when a 2-2 draw was fought out but Rovers could not get back quickly enough to League football. All at Cliftonhill were disappointed in the no-scoring draw against Queen's Park at home before Dumbarton put a spoke in the promotion aspirations by winning 3-1 down at Boghead. Big Drew Rodgerson had been signed from Stirling Albion to take up the central defensive position in this match but this was a mistake and cost Rovers dear as the lad was obviously not match fit. It took a Kenny Jenkins goal in the second half to equalise an earlier goal by Stranraer in the home match which kept Rovers in touch with the top teams in the League.

The return match against Airdrieonians in the Lanarkshire Cup took place on Tuesday the 22nd October which was the first official floodlit match at Cliftonhill. True to form, in firsts relating to Albion Rovers, the match was lost by 2-1, all the damage being done in the second half as Rovers had been leading by a Mike Green goal at half time. During the week, Alec Smith and Bobby Graham were transferred to Stenhousemuir and were in their places against their former mates the following week in Rovers' 3-2 victory at Larbert.

An unchanged team saw two successive home victories with, first of all, East Stirlingshire losing 2-1 and then Queen of the South 1-0. A fine away victory at Alloa set up the promotion clash at Stirling the following week and this turned out to be a tremendous match with Rovers displaying all the attributes of a promotion winning side in the 1-1 draw. On St. Andrew's Day, Clydebank came to Coatbridge to be soundly beaten by 3-1 and putting Rovers back to the top of the League. But it was not to be, and all Coatbridge was stunned to read in the Sunday papers that Jackie Stewart had resigned to take up a full-time appointment with Dumbarton, their fellow Second Division club. The Fans couldn't believe that Jackie, who had worked so hard to get the blend right and just as it looked as though he had succeeeded, should up and leave his proteges and go to Dumbarton where he would have to do it all over again from scratch.

However, that was the way it was, and with no match the following week, Rovers fixed up a game against a Hearts XI and promptly lost 4-0. In the next match at Berwick they failed to score again but as the Rangers were in a similar position it did not matter too much. The managerless team then welcomed East Fife to Coatbridge and, on a frost-bound pitch, assisted by the Fifers missing a penalty, won by 4-1 and on the last day of the year the trip down to Ayr United proved disappointing with a 3-0 defeat.

Wednesday was New Year's Day and Hamilton Accies were the visitors with Rovers going nap against them for the second time this season. This time the score was 5-0 but the following day the journey to Forfar proved fruitless with Dillon scoring Rovers' goal in the first half but being ordered off with the score at 2-1. Ten man Rovers were no match for the home team who ran out eventual winners by 4-1.

The Second Preliminary Scottish Cup round was due and third top Rovers were confident of going through to meet Airdrie at home in the next round as 'Muir were bottom dogs. Ex-Rovers Smith and Graham were playing and the match was probably lost before the kick-off when Kenny Jenkins was fielded although obviously not fit and with a leg heavily strapped. The fans couldn't understand why Rovers didn't use their substitute early on when it was obvious that Jenkins was not mobile but despite continuous pressure there was no real concern that the match was in any danger—that was until Graham passed a fine ball to the outside left who beat McFeat but right back Gemmell punched the ball off the line. Inside left Ritchie had no trouble in scoring from the penalty and from then on it was a succession of misses by Rovers until eventually with seventeen minutes to go Oliphant was brought on but again incredibly the management kept the limping Jenkins on the pitch and took off the extremely mobile Halliday.

For the home match against Cowdenbeath the team was much changed with Jenkins replaced by McGovern and the makeshift centre was the hero with the only goal of the match. Trainer Bobby Holmes left to join Jackie Stewart at Dumbarton and Frank Connor, the reserve goalkeeper, was appointed Coach on a temporary basis. The 'Sons' also made an offer for Charlie Oliphant which was turned down. Jenkins returned for the Queen's Park match at Hampden and scored Rovers' goal in the 1-1 draw and Dillon made his last appearance, prior to starting his fourteen day suspension, when Brechin City were defeated 2-1 at Coatbridge.

Jackie Stewart and his new Dumbarton team came to Coatbridge and received a noisy reception from the Coatbridge fans. With the Dumbarton team were Stewart, trainer Holmes and Billy McMurray and things looked good for Rovers when McGovern gave them an early lead but Dumbarton slowly wore the Coatbridge team down and by the end of the day, Stewart had the last laugh taking the points in a 2-1 victory. On the Monday a Friendly was arranged at Coatbridge with a Celtic XI which gave Rovers the opportunity to play Bobby Tuddenham, on trial from Camelon Juniors, in a match which ended with no scoring.

John Jamieson went to Texas on business for his firm, but due to bad weather throughout the month of February, all matches were postponed and he arrived back in Scotland not having missed any games. Also a request for Rovers to run Sunday Speedway was rejected by Coatbridge Town Council and there was also talk of Rovers being sued by a local Quantity Surveying firm in respect of unpaid fees for the Social Club, which had now foundered.

When football re-started again on the 1st March, the trip down to Palmerston to play Queen of the South found the pitch icy and snow-covered. Rovers' team could make nothing of the going and the Queen's men ran out easy winners by 3-0. Tuddenham made his debut as a signed player against Alloa at home with Rodgerson pushed to centre forward and the big man scored Rovers' two goals against his former team in the 2-0 victory. He did likewise the following week at Coatbridge against another former team of his, Stirling Albion, in the 2-1 victory where another provisional signing Jim Brown from Bargeddie Amateurs had a try-out in goal.

Down at Clydebank Rovers found Madden in inspired form in goal for the homesters who ran out winners by 2-0 then Berwick Rangers were defeated 2-1 at Coatbridge on the day the Speedway season restarted. Two heavy defeats away from home were next on the cards the first being at the hands of East Fife by 2-0 and then Stranraer by 3-0. There was a players' revolt for this Monday match with several players unhappy about the re-scheduled midweek match and concern regarding loss of wages. By the time the team bus left Dillon, Jamieson, Jenkins, Murphy and Rodgerson had not appeared and there was a rush to pick up players to make up a team. Jim Brown was fielded in goal, Sammy Ferris made his debut in the number eleven jersey, Eddie Halliday from Blantyre Celtic was given a trial and Peter Dickson filled the substitute's jersey. Despite Stranraer having a player ordered off after fifteen minutes with the score 1-0 in their favour, it was no real surprise that the South of Scotland team won in the end by 3-0.

On the Wednesday of that week a touring Cypriot side, Anothosis Famagusta, were fixed up to play a Friendly and Chairman Fagan put up a cup for the winners. Rovers repayed him handsomely by winning 2-0 with Halliday making his debut as a signed player at right back.

The season was to end disappointingly despite there being three home games left and Ayr United started off the rot by winning 1-0 at Coatbridge. East Stirlingshire emulated that score via a penalty goal at Falkirk before at Stenhousemuir, Alec Smith and Bobby Graham and all, Rovers managed to make a last win of the season at 4-2, although an over-weight and out-of-match-practice Bobby Graham scored both the 'Muir goals. Ted McFeat was on his honeymoon and Connor was in goal for this game. The final game of the season saw Rovers line up to applaud the Motherwell team onto the pitch as Second Division Champions having won the title the previous week. Rovers with Jim Brown in goal put up a creditable display but the champions were worthy winners by 1-0.

This had been the most frustrating season for many years and Rovers attained only seventh place with forty-three points which was twenty-one less than promoted Motherwell who themselves were eleven points ahead of Ayr United. Stenhousemuir were last with eighteen points. Jackie Stewart's Dumbarton ended up only fourteenth with twenty-seven points and there were still many who were to say that had Stewart not left Rovers would have taken one of the two promotion places. Long-serving Andy Murphy and John Dillon were both freed among the ten free transfers and the lookout now was for suitable replacements.

During the close season Jimmy Harrower was engaged to manage team affairs coming from Sauchie Juniors with a wealth of experience behind him. Frank Connor was confirmed as trainer and Chairman Fagan was elected to Scotland's International Selection Committee as a member of the S.F.A.

Season 1969/70
There were no pre-season Friendlies this year and it was straight into the League Cup Tournament with a home tie against Montrose on the 9th of August. The only new face in the first team was Willie Currie from Rutherglen Glencairn who was an amateur. The game was very poor stuff with Rovers going down to a second half goal, certainly not the best of starts for new Manager Harrower. Rovers' team was Brown, E. Halliday, Gemmell, Oliphant, W. Currie, Jamieson, Coleman, Green, Rodgerson, R. Halliday and McGovern.

Two away matches were next on the cards and at East Fife a 1-1 draw was fought out with Eugene McDonald of Pollok making his debut when he replaced Coleman but centre forward Rodgerson got Rovers' first goal of the season in this one. Motherwell were all over Rovers in the 5-1 defeat with big Tom Forsyth scoring Rovers goal past his own goalkeeper. For the match at Methil, which Rovers won 2-1, Rodgerson replaced Oliphant in the number four shirt with McDonald up front at number nine. The bustling centre scored his first goal in Senior Football and Mike Green the winner. The Section ended with two home matches, the first a 1-1 draw against Montrose and the final one a 4-2 defeat at the hands of Motherwell.

Scotland was enjoying an Indian Summer and when East Fife opened the League Programme at Cliftonhill amongst intense heat the six hundred shirt sleeved fans saw Rovers get off to a winning start thanks to a Peter Coleman penalty in the second half. On the Wednesday Forfar won 3-2 in Angus and Stenhousemuir were defeated 3-0 at Larbert. In the home match against Stirling Albion, which ended up 1-1, Coleman missed a penalty and, although the same player scored Rovers' goal in the home match against Berwick, the Englishman scored two goals in the last six minutes to win 3-1.

The trip to Stranraer on the Wednesday found Rovers winning 4-0 but the shorter journey to Falkirk on the following Saturday found the 'Shire winning 2-1 whilst Clydebank came to Coatbridge and overwhelmed Rovers by a 4-1 margin. The Autumn holiday weekend saw Hamilton Accies fight out a no-scoring draw and on the Monday Rovers travelled to Brechin for a 5-0 hammering.

October found Rovers hosts to Falkirk and in a rough-house Rovers lost 4-0 and had defender Currie ordered off into the bargain. The following Tuesday, Airdrieonians took the short journey down to Coatbridge on Lanarkshire Cup business and won by 2-1.

For the away match at Alloa, Rovers re-signed Billy Lamont who took his place in goal and with John Jamieson freed, and subsequently signed by Dumbarton, the hunt was on for defenders. Rovers lost this one by the only goal of the match scored in the second half, a result which put them in sixth bottom place. A Friendly was fixed up the following week at Broomfield and with Rovers leading 2-0 Airdrie applied tremendous pressure to end up winners by 7-2. Rovers introduced Tony Hanlon from Queen's Park at left back and Ian Thomson from Hamilton Accies at inside left. They also tried Peter Coleman at right back but as an experiment this was not a success. League leaders Cowdenbeath were next hosts and Rovers, against all the odds, came away from this one with a creditable 1-1 score. Jackie Stewart and his Dumbarton team of Coatbridge ex-patriots visited Coatbridge when a dour no-scoring draw was fought out.

Immediately following this match Manager Harrower was sacked and there was talk that the Speedway may go elsewhere. At Hampden the Amateurs, on a cold, windy day, were too good for Rovers winning by 2-1 with Thomson scoring his first goal for the Club.

J. Moffat Miller Director and sometime Club Secretary died on the 14th November having served Rovers well and capably.

Currie was suspended for seven days by the Disciplinary Committee and he missed the visit by Montrose. Again Coleman was at right back and again Rovers were soundly beaten by 3-1. Only Lamont and McGovern retained their places for the visit to Arbroath when another disappointing 3-1 defeat was the outcome.

Prior to the match at Clydebank news came that Bobby Flavell, one-time manager of St. Mirren and Ayr United, presently a Director at Cliftonhill, had accepted the Managerial post with Frank Connor continuing as trainer and Billy Lamont and Jim Kennedy doing the coaching. Rovers also appointed a Physiotherapist in Bobby Smith. This new line-up faired no better with Clydebank winning 3-0 leaving Rovers firmly in second bottom place with nine defeats and three draws since their last win 'way back in mid-September.

Against Forfar at home eight positional changes were made and it looked at half time as though Mr. Flavell had waved his magic wand with Rovers two up. The defence resisted a spirited second half fight back by the Forfar team to ride out the day winners by 3-2. Twelve hundred fans were at Methil to see Rovers win 4-2, thanks to McGovern's hat-trick in the second half, and these two wins were a fine boost for Rovers' chance of success in the following Second Preliminary Round Scottish Cup match against Berwick. The game was a fast exciting tie but it looked to be heading for a no-scoring stalemate when young Sam Ferris wearing the number seven jersey first timed a headed clearance on the twenty yard mark to smash the ball high into the net past goalkeeper Wilson and Rovers were through to another home match against Dundee in the First Round proper. The annual pilgrimage to play Queen of the South took place again on a pitch more suitable for ice skating than for football and found Rovers unable to come to grips with the playing surface and losing by the only goal of the match.

It was a different story on New Year's day at Hamilton when Rovers gave Hamilton a lesson in the art of goalscoring with Coleman and Green scoring hat-tricks in the 6-2 victory. Billy Lamont also thwarted his former team mates by saving a penalty.

Bad weather intervened once again and there was no football for a couple of weeks. Rovers, on their third away match in a row, visited Berwick, who were thirsting for revenge, for that Cup exit. Two second half goals were enough to give the points to Rovers and as a prelude to the Cup tie, news was released that the Coatbridge Monarchs would be leaving Cliftonhill for Wembley to be known in future as Wembley Lions. Mr. Hoskins, an Australian who was the Promoter of Monarchs and who had promoted Speedway in Scotland since the Second World War, revealed that the move to Coatbridge had been due to the Commonwealth Games Development but that the attendances had been disappointing in Coatbridge and when Glasgow Tigers had moved out to Hampden it had not been a paying concern for either club.

The big day appeared and Dundee arrived for the cup tie. Three thousand fans were in the ground and there was another Cup match at Broomfield against Hamilton which Airdrie won 2-0. Rovers were immediately at their First Division opponents but it was Dundee who scored first through Coatbridge boy Alec Bryce in eight minutes and they made it 2-0 with three minutes to go in the first half. Rovers re-doubled their efforts in the second period and McGovern smashed the ball into the net from fifteen yards. However, Dundee slipped into top gear and

Rovers had no answer to their skill and aggressiveness and in the end the better team won 2-1.

Back on League business, on the last day in January, Stenhousemuir were given the run-around and Rovers won by 2-0, the goals being scored by McGovern and Ferris. This was McGovern's last match as a Rover before being transferred to Newcastle United for a reputed £15,000 sum.

There was virtually no football played in February with Rovers' first game being on the last day of the month at home against Alloa when a Peter Coleman goal was enough to keep the points at Coatbridge. The following week Falkirk won very easily by 4-1, confirming their position at the top of the League. A Friendly during the week against a Hearts XI allowed Rovers to try out several trialists with the match ending 2-1 for Rovers. On the Saturday Cowdenbeath came through to win 2-0 and take their place at the top of the League, whilst Rovers next travelled to Dumbarton to lose 2-0 in a poor match.

Queen's Park visited Cliftonhill where Rovers introduced Bert Rice from Blantyre Celtic in the midfield. This youngster had a fine game in Rovers' 4-1 victory and was promptly signed to take his place against Stranraer on the following Tuesday. Thanks to an own goal by centre half Heap, Rovers won 2-1. The recent good form came to a halt at Montrose when the team lost 1-0 but returned to the winning ways the following Tuesday at home against East Stirlingshire when Stewart Liddell from Petershill scored the winning goal in Rovers 2-0 victory and was signed at the end of the match.

Rovers swapped Coleman and Ferris in the forward line and played Gemmell and Hanlon at the back for the visit to Stirling but this was to no avail with the Albion winning 6-0. With three games left all at home Rovers were looking to maintain their mid-table position. They started off with a 3-2 victory over Brechin City with Angus Peden, a South African of Scottish parentage, given a try-out at centre and the new boy did well enough scoring a goal in his debut. In the match against Arbroath it looked all up in the first five minutes when the visitors went into a 2-0 lead. Coleman chopped one back in the first half before Jim Lynn from Blantyre Victoria, who had been provisionally signed earlier in the season, scored the equaliser and the season finished with Peden scoring two goals in the 3-1 victory over Queen of the South.

Rovers ended in a poor eleventh position with thirty-three points with Falkirk winning the Championship on fifty-six points and Cowdenbeath followed them upstairs on fifty-five. Hamilton were bottom dogs on twenty points.

Charlie Oliphant and Peter Coleman were surprise frees with Billy Lamont also seeking pastures new. The fans viewed the new signings with great expectancy hoping that this would be the year of the big climb out of the Second Division and all reported ready for the opening gamee.

Season 1970/71

When the new season dawned a pre-season Friendly was arranged with mighty Rangers. Complete with Peter McCloy and Colin Jackson, the Ibrox team was a mixture of experience and youth. Rangers were first to score but Stewart Liddell equalised in the second half, the match ending all square at 1-1. Rovers' team was Brown, Gallacher, W. Currie, Rice, Rodgerson, R. Halliday, Tuddenham (Ferris), Green, Johnstone, Liddell and Lynn.

An opening League Cup tie was at Falkirk and proved to be calamitous with the Bairns winning 5-0. In the first home Cup tie Liddell was ordered off in the first half leaving his team-mates to fight out a 2-2 draw against Clydebank. On the Saturday, Arbroath were defeated 2-1 but at Clydebank, with newly signed Jim Thorburn in goal, the former St. Mirren and Raith Rovers player could do nothing to save the avalanche of five goals thumped past him by a rampant Bankies team in a match in which Rovers scored the first goal in the 5-1 defeat.

The team selection was shuffled around a bit for the return home tie against Falkirk but the fifteen hundred Fans were disappointed with another defeat, this time by 3-0. All the goals came in the first half with no fight in the second period from Rovers' team. The last Cup match of the section at Arbroath was no improvement on what had gone before and Rovers failed to do the double with the home team winning 5-3. This put Rovers firmly at the bottom of their Section with only one win out of six.

The League Campaign didn't start any more promisingly with East Fife at Coatbridge. The crowd had by this time dwindled to only three hundred and with East Fife coasting to a 2-0 victory with two minutes to go, the game suddenly came alive when Rovers were granted a penalty. In the incident goalkeeper Gorman was injured and substituted and after all this had taken place, Green scored with the penalty. All was set for a grand finale but it was not to be and the Fife team scored a third goal in injury time. The away match on the following Wednesday was a dour tussle against Dumbarton which ended up 1-1 and for the Saturday game at Hamilton, Rovers had to do without the services of Liddell who was suspended for seven days following his ordering off. Rovers dipped into the junior market and signed centre half Sid Sage from Shotts Bon Accord and left half Roddy Smith from Cumbernauld United. With Ferris taking Liddell's place the two new men in the half back line only Gallacher and Lynn retained their places from the previous match and Rovers with a fine second half burst ran out worthy winners by 3-1.

Not unnaturally, the same team was fielded at Coatbridge for the visit by Queen of the South which saw Ferris hit a first half hat-trick within ten minutes and Rovers won out of the park by 4-0 with all the goals coming in the first half. With ample cover for the central defending positions with Sage and Currie, Drew Rodgerson was freed. For the match against Stranraer, Liddell was available and returned to the forward line with the exclusion of Gibby Kerr and he celebrated by scoring the winner in the 2-1 home victory. On the following Wednesday he also scored in the 1-1 draw at Palmerston against Queen of the South, a result which put Rovers into second top position.

For the home match against Stenhousemuir, complete with recent signing Rodgerson, six goals were shared. Stirling Albion made it three draws in a row the following Saturday with the visitors equalising a counter by Smith in the second half. At the beginning of October, East Stirlingshire were defeated 2-1 at Falkirk, whilst for the visit by Brechin Jim Brown was reinstated to goal and the six hundred fans were treated to a 4-1 home victory with Green and Ferris scoring a double apiece. Stewart Liddell had a bad double leg fracture in the opening minutes down at Berwick but, with Kerr on as substitute, Rovers put up a good fight to run out winners by 2-1. Raith Rovers equalised in the last minute to disappoint the Coatbridge Rovers who, up to that point were leading 2-1 and looking favourites to pocket both points. Former Chairman Eddie McLaren died in retirement down in Largs thus severing the last link with Meadow days.

The match against Clydebank at Cliftonhill was abandoned by referee Wilson in the fifty-fifth minute due to flooding when the score was 1-1. The annual trip to

Hampden saw Rovers come back from 2-1 behind at half time to win 3-2 and Angus Peden from South Africa made his first appearance of the season as a substitute when he came on for Smith. The new man was again substitute for the home match against Partick Thistle when four thousand fans were entertained to a real cup tie match. There was great excitement in Coatbridge when Mike Green scored in the first half as Alan Rough in goal fumbled a cross from the left and the young forward was in position to score what turned out to be the only goal of the match.

Rovers were now rampant and looking a good bet for promotion but the trip up to Forfar saw them lose to the only goal of the match which ended a best ever run of thirteen games without defeat. Another reverse, at home this time, by Arbroath came due to an incredible refereeing blunder by referee Anderson of Glasgow. Rovers were losing 1-0 at the time and an Arbroath defender was lying injured on the ground some twenty yards out from the goal-line. The ball came quickly from Rovers' defence to Jim Johnstone, standing on his own a couple of yards inside the Arbroath half. The ex-Rangers player ran on and blasted the ball into the net for a fine solo effort only to find the referee blowing for off-side, a decision not agreed with by his linesman. Needless to say, Rovers were incensed at this decision but the referee had made up his mind and, although the fairest decision would have been for the game to have been stopped once he noticed the prostrate player, this acted as the turning point in the game which Arbroath went on to win by 2-1.

A First Round Preliminary Scottish Cup Tie found Rovers drawn at Forfar but the team again slumped to defeat for the second time in two weeks at Station Park. Forfar got off to a dream start when centre forward McInnes headed past goalkeeper Brown with only two minutes clocked. Thereafter it was mostly Forfar but the Coatbridge team's fate was finally sealed ten minutes from time with a penalty decision which saw the entire Rovers' team surround the referee protesting against the decision. During the melee Halliday became involved with left winger Stewart, who was knocked to the ground and, after consulting the linesman, referee Crawford sent Halliday to the Pavilion. When the referee had cleared the penalty area and cooled things down, defender McNicol slammed the ball past Brown putting the tie beyond Rovers for whom goalkeeper Brown was their best player.

The following week at Coatbridge the game against Alloa was equally controversial with Alloa forward Willie Allan scoring a fine goal past Brown in the twenty-fourth minute. However, before referee Mullen could get the teams to line up, Rovers' defenders pointed out to him that the ball was not lying snugly in the back of the net but on the track behind the goal. After a lengthy inspection of the net by referee, linesmen, groundsmen and players, no-one could find a hole big enough for the ball to go through the net and the goal was promptly disallowed, much to the Alloa team's disgust. Further excitement was caused when, on the hour, referee Mullen himself collapsed and had to leave the pitch to be replaced by the senior linesman. To crown all, with only a few minutes left, Sid Sage, who had been put up in front for the day, scored what proved to be the only goal of the match to the utter disgust of the Alloa team and Support. Rovers played new man Corrigan from Stirling Albion at centre half in this match.

On Boxing Day, Rovers were at Methill to have full back Gallacher stretchered off in the seventieth minute but the game was lost in any case by this time, East Fife running out winners by 3-0. This was also the day of the Ibrox disaster at the Rangers/Celtic match which was a black day for Scottish football with the

ALBION ROVERS SEASON 1970/71

Standing: A. Rice, W. Currie, R. Smith, J. Brown, S. Sage, R. Halliday, Sub. G. Gallacher.
Seated: M. Green, S. Ferris, R. Skippen, Trialist, J. Lynn.

Monklands suffering death and injury to several spectators.

The Friday New Year's Day match found Hamilton Accies at Coatbridge with Bobby Skippen from Arthurlie being tried out in the forward line and Corrigan taking Gallacher's place at full back. This was a game in which Rovers were always in control and the 3-0 result did not flatter them one bit. Bert Rice took Skippen's place in an otherwise unchanged team for the trip to Stranraer the following day but the South of Scotland team won well by 3-1. Stenhousemuir came to Coatbridge, complete with former Rovers, Rodgerson and Jamieson, and proved too good for Rovers on the day winning 2-0. Halliday was suspended for seven days following his earlier ordering off and five changes were made for the visit to Stirling for a 1-1 draw whilst at Montrose the following week a similar score was the best Rovers could come up with.

The team did get back on the winning way against East Stirlingshire in the home match winning 4-2 with Stewart Liddell an interested spectator with his plaster off for the first time. The young forward had a cruel stroke of luck five days later when he slipped and broke his leg once again to the dismay of his colleagues. The trip to Brechin found Rovers winning 2-0 but Clydebank then won by the only goal of the match at Coatbridge. A Friendly match was fixed up with a Celtic XI complete with Kenny Dalglish in midfield which ended up a 1-0 victory for the 'Bhoys'. The following Saturday the 2-0 home victory over Raith Rovers deposited the Coatbridge team back in third position in the League with Bobby Skippen making his debut as a signed player. The trip to Clydebank saw the Bankies put an end to Rovers' promotion push with a 2-0 victory before Rovers got back on the winning track by 2-1 against Queen's Park. An unchanged team visited Firhill but did not see much in the way of thrills from a Rovers' point of view as the 'Jags' won easily by 3-0.

Goalkeeper Thorburn was recalled for the visit by Forfar and it took a second half goal by Corrigan to equalise an earlier score by the 'Loons' for a share of the points. Staying with Angus clubs, Arbroath won easily by 2-0 on a day when Willie Currie played for Amateur Scotland against Bulgaria. Goalkeeper Eddie Pryde from Kirkintilloch Rob Roy was in goal against Montrose at Coatbridge and found the going hot although he saved a penalty. He later had to admit defeat for the only goal of the game which was again from the penalty spot.

March had proved to be a ruinous month with only three points scored out of a possible eight and April, having started with the defeats by the Angus teams, finished Rovers' chances of challenging for promotion. With three League games still to go Berwick Rangers lost at Coatbridge by a Sid Sage goal to nothing and a fighting draw at Alloa at 1-1 left Rovers a final match against Jackie Stewart and his Dumbarton team at Coatbridge. Even if Rovers won this one Dumbarton would stay one point ahead of Rovers. Peter Coleman was playing for the 'Sons' and in the end Rovers had to give best to a superior Dumbarton team who ran out winners by 6-2. This left Rovers in seventh position with thirty-nine points, Dumbarton in fourth. Partick Thistle were Champions with fifty-six points, runners-up East Fife on fifty-one and Brechin were bottom dogs on nineteen. Despite some of the best football seen for many a long day, Rovers again fell badly in the run-in to the Championship and were bitterly disappointed with their final placing.

A final match of the season saw Airdrieonians come to Cliftonhill where they won by 2-0. A bigger than usual clean-out saw only nine players retained including Stewart Liddell and the loss of Billy Currie to Queen's Park. Rovers again made forays into the Junior ranks and several players were engaged for the season ahead. Just prior to the season opening the news all Coatbridge had been waiting for was announced—Mike Green's transfer to Blackpool. Ironically he was signed to cover for Tony Green who had been transferred from Blackpool to Newcastle United.

Season 1971/72
The opening game of this season was another pre-season Friendly with mighty Rangers which boosted the first gate of the season to over three thousand. Captain Tuddenham and his boys put up a fine display with Rovers' star being Ray Franchetti of Baillieston who scored two goals. The match was not played in any friendly spirit, so much so that Rovers' new centre Gus McLeod and Rangers' goalkeeper Gerry Neef were ordered off for fighting. The match finished 3-3 and Rovers' fans looked forward expectantly to a promising season. Rovers were represented by Brown, Halpin, Halliday, McKinder, Sage, Tuddenham, Ferris, Franchetti, McLeod, Smith and Ness.

Following three years of no accounts, the Directors submitted their Report and audited statement at the 42nd A.G.M. at Cliftonhill on the 11th August covering the three years up to 1967. Just why the accounts were still four years behind was not explained. The Report itself made dismal reading showing a loss in each of the three years adding up to an aggregate net loss of £7,485.00 which made the Club now £13,006.00 in debt.

For the opening League Cup tie Stranraer were the visitors and, as Franchetti had refused to sign, Tommy Martin was in one of the inside forward positions to score what turned out to be the winner. At Montrose in midweek Charlie Potts scored Rovers' goal in a 1-1 draw but another rough-house took place at Love Street against St. Mirren, where referee Callaghan of Glasgow was the busiest man on the field and Rovers lost 1-0. Another defeat, this time at home, found the "Gable-Enders" winning 2-0 and at Stranraer Rovers introduced Stewart Burgess in goal. It was an unhappy debut for the new lad with Stranraer winning 2-1 in a match which saw Sam Ferris ordered off. The League Cup campaign came to an end with St. Mirren's visit to Coatbridge. Big Gus McLeod scored both Rovers' goals in the 2-1 victory and Rovers looked quite promising on this display.

When the League programme opened, Hamilton Accies were the visitors, complete with Willie Lamont in goal, but a first half Ness goal was enough to keep the points at Coatbridge. Berwick Rangers were next visitors proving too strong for Rovers and winning 3-1. In this match Roddy Smith made his return from the substitutes' bench replacing Martin and working himself into match fitness. Another defeat by the same score, this time against Raith Rovers, saw Rovers 'way down the League but a fine away midweek win by 2-0 at Forfar lifted the spirits for the Saturday match against Stranraer at Coatbridge. This third meeting of the season ended up with Rovers sweeping aside the opposition to the tune of 4-0. The following week Forfar lost by 2-0 at Coatbridge but two away defeats followed by 2-0 at Stirling and 3-1 at Berwick kept Rovers low down in the League table.

Clydebank were beaten 2-0 at Coatbridge before Stenhousemuir reversed this score at Larbert. Rovers, with two trialists on display were very uninspiring in the 1-1 draw at Coatbridge against East Stirlingshire but a fighting 2-2 draw at Brechin was a better all-round performance with Smith scoring his sixth goal of the season.

Value Added Tax arrived and Rovers and Airdrieonians, along with all the other football clubs, were greatly concerned that this would be a financial disaster for them. The local Member of Parliament, James Dempsey, was contacted and he raised the matter in Parliament with Chancellor Anthony Barbour who confirmed that no final percentage of tax had yet been fixed.

Back on the football field Queen of the South won by 1-0 at Coatbridge and then at Dumbarton the 'Sons won 3-0 in a match where Jim Brown saved a penalty and Stewart Liddell made his return to the team since his double leg break of the previous season. There were very icy conditions to contend with in the home match against Montrose when Tom Rutherford of St. Roch's made a scoring debut in the 4-1 victory. The youngster was fielded on the right hand side of midfield for the visit to Hampden which ended 2-2 and only the missing of a penalty award by Brian Ness stopped Rovers lifting both points.

Alloa were next visitors at Coatbridge and won by the only goal of the match scored in the first half, with Rutherford in this match pushed up in to the forward line and Billy Simpson ex-Falkirk and Hibs taking his place in midfield. Despite a fine display by the newcomer, Rovers were woeful in front of goal but it turned out that they were even worse the following week against St. Mirren at Paisley losing by 4-0 in front of three thousand three hundred fans.

Arbroath won 3-0 at Coatbridge and Stewart Liddell was freed, signing for Sligo Rovers the following week, whilst several teams were showing an interest in Bert Rice. On Christmas Day against Cowdenbeath, Rovers showed the best traditional feature acting as Santa Claus and gifting the game to the Fifers by 1-0 and on New Year's Day at Hamilton the same score saw Accies, who were at the bottom of the League, win in a roughhouse in which Billy Simpson was ordered off. The following Monday Raith Rovers were defeated 3-1 with new signing Jim Daly and trialist Andy Gray scoring the first of many senior goals at centre.

As a preview to the Scottish Cup Preliminary round against Queen's Park, Rovers visited Stranraer and came away with a 2-2 draw. For the Cup tie Billy McGrannaghan of Blantyre Celtic was signed and promptly took his place on the left wing. The eighteen year old had a vital debut for, with Queen's leading by a fiftieth minute goal, the wee winger grabbed the equaliser then hit a corner to perfection for Smith to head in at the near post, after only being on the pitch for two minutes substituting for Rutherford. Rovers' lead lasted precisely two minutes with Queen's equalising but with five minutes to go McGrannaghan popped up on the goal line to slot the ball past 'keeper Purvis giving Rovers an away tie against Celtic in the next round.

Clydebank won convincingly 3-1 with Rovers putting in a very inept away performance and were further uninspiring at home against Stenhousemuir. The score finishing at 1-1 with Ness again missing a vital penalty. The match at Parkhead duly arrived on the 5th February but this was one game in which David had no chance of overcoming Goliath. Celtic were in their ascendancy and all Rovers got out of the match was a 5-0 drubbing and a share of the £5,510 gate receipts. Dalglish missed a penalty and Martin was ordered off in the last minute. Rovers slipped to fifth bottom with a 4-1 defeat at East Stirlingshire and Brechin, who were having a better season, gained a point at Coatbridge. Sam Ferris was transferred to Chesterfield for £5,000 and Rovers fielded two trialists at Dumfries but the combination was not successful and Queens' won by the only goal of the match.

Table topping Dumbarton came to Coatbridge with Kenny Jenkins and Peter Coleman playing, and they powered to a 1-0 victory thanks to ex-Rover Jenkins scoring in the second half. Rovers, in the middle of a real form slump, lost at

Montrose by 2-0 where in a poor Rovers' team Peter Dickson made his debut following his signing from Baillieston Juniors. The League Management Committee meted out heavy sentences to Rovers' players with Tuddenham suspended for twenty-one days, Martin fourteen days and Rutherford fourteen days plus £5. As a consequence it was a makeshift Rovers team at Alloa which the 'Wasps' won 3-1 and two home defeats in a row both by 2-1 with Rovers' only bright spots being the scoring of both goals by newcomer Peter Dickson.

The team was now second bottom of the League, one place up from County neighbours Hamilton who had been in this department all season, and in the 2-0 defeat at Arbroath the homesters clinched promotion leaving Rovers with two home matches. Both of these were lost with Stirling winning by 1-0 before, on the last day of the season Cowdenbeath won by 2-1 making it a sad nine defeats in a row and leaving Rovers with only two points from thirteen matches. Second bottom place was the end result of this disastrous form with a paltry twenty points scored with Jackie Stewart taking Dumbarton up to the First Division in their Centenary Year with fifty-two points on goal difference from Arbroath.

Rovers retained ten players and surprisingly freed Russell Halliday, Gus McLeod and Billy Simpson. The Management approached John Cushley, the former Celtic centre half who had been unsettled at Dunfermline, but were turned down in their quest of the red haired player as player/coach. He felt that at twenty-eight he still had a year or two to offer as a player. With Frank Connor also away, Rovers were looking to the future. Former Kilmarnock wing half and Player of the Year, Frank Beattie, who had retired at the end of the previous season, was appointed as the next Manager at the beginning of July. Bobby Flavell took over as General Manager and the big man came with much goodwill from the Scottish footballing public.

Season 1972/73

There were to be no pre-season friendlies this season and it was straight into the League Cup campaign at Alloa on the 12th August. Rovers were always struggling in this one and it was no surprise when the stronger Alloa team ran out winners by 4-3. Rovers' team was Brown, Rice, Sunderland, Wilson, Sage, Tuddenham, Daly, Wylie, Dickson, Martin and Ness. In midweek, Brechin City came to Coatbridge and Rovers introduced their latest signing, Tom Balanowski, and he added sufficient strength to the forward line for Rovers to win by 3-0.

However, it was back to a 4-3 defeat in Rovers' second away match of the season at Hamilton with the best crowd of the season so far, of fourteen hundred, engrossed in a thriller of a game with Rovers just losing out. After a fine first half performance when they were leading by 2-1 Rovers had no answer to the strong-moving Hamilton team. The fourth Cup match found Rovers deservedly losing 1-0 at Cliftonhill against Forfar but a fine second half performance saw Rovers pick the points up at 2-1. Referee Alistair McKenzie from Larbert caused a real rumpus when, with only fifty minutes on the clock, he rejected the ball, which had been behaving rather erratically, but worse he also rejected the replacement ball. There was much scurrying around until a third ball was produced which finally satisfied both referee and players. The eight minute stoppage caused by this interlude put both teams off any rhythm but eventually it turned out all right on the night. By this match Rovers won their Section, moving into a play-off with Motherwell.

Before this could be played there was a League match to contend with against Raith Rovers and the team was again greatly revised from the previous match. Coatbridge Rovers lost a goal in each half without reply and for the next match new signings Jimmy Casserly, from St. Roch's, and Jim Graham from Dunfermline, made their debut in the Cup tie at Motherwell. Two thousand fans saw Rovers offer little opposition to the First Division side, going down eventually by 4-1. Two nights later, on the Wednesday, the home match at Cliftonhill saw Motherwell continue in the same vein and even with Rovers making five changes from the previous game, the result was even worse with 4-0 being chalked up.

In the League campaign, when it properly got underway at Hamilton, a Peter Dickson hat-trick enabled Rovers to share the points at 3-3 in what was, surprisingly enough, an unchanged team from the previous match, but four changes were made for the visit by East Stirlingshire and a Tommy Martin penalty in the second half was enough to beat his old team-mates 3-2 before Brechin lost 2-1 at Coatbridge, thanks to goals by Dickson and Balanowski. A third win in a row was noted at Falkirk by 2-0 against East Stirlingshire in a match where Peter Dickson was ordered off just prior to half time.

At Shawfield, Clyde won 3-1 and worse was to follow at home against Dunfermline with the Fifers winning 5-1. The disasters continued the following week at Montrose with a 4-0 drubbing to be followed by a 2-1 defeat at the hands of Queen of the South at Coatbridge.

The team had been running for some time virtually Managerless, as Frank Beattie had proved to be a very poor leader of men off the field which was in direct contrast to his tremendous abilities of leadership from the front on the field. Rovers appointed Ralph Brand former Rangers and Scotland inside forward as trainer/coach and he quickly set about trying to improve the fortunes of the ailing Albion Rovers. He got off to a poor start against Queen of the South at Coatbridge for, despite leading by a Peter Dickson goal at half time, Queen's eventually ran out winners by 2-1. This was followed by a defeat at the hands of Berwick Rangers by 2-0, in a match which saw Billy Pirie, ex-Rangers make his debut. Billy was an ex-colleague of Ralph at Ibrox who had been playing abroad and his signing for Rovers was seen as a way to keep himself fit before rejoining his club, a move which suited the Coatbridge club. Alloa were visited on he day that Danny Hegan played for Northern Ireland against Bulgaria but back home Rovers could only muster a 4-0 defeat.

With Jim Brown back in goal for the visit by Clydebank, Rovers produced their best performance of the season to date winning 4-1, despite the loss of top scoring Peter Dickson, who was serving a seven day suspension. He came back the following week at Love Street as the only change in the team in place of Frank Denholm but Rovers were sunk without trace by 4-0. Jim Graham scored in the 1-1 draw against Queen's Park at home before the same player scored Rovers' only goal in the 2-1 defeat at Cowdenbeath. Two home games had mixed fortunes for Rovers with first of all Forfar drawing 2-2 and then Stranraer winning 2-0 as a poor prelude to the Scottish Cup tie at Montrose. In the Cup match Rovers lost a goal in each half without too much effort and Rovers' Cup of woe was full to overflowing when Pirie was ordered off. This turned out to be Jim Brown's last game for the Club, being transferred to Chesterfield.

Trying to pick-up the pieces was hopeless the following week against Stenhousemuir, with ex-Rovers Jamieson, Halliday and Lynn in their ranks, who tore holes in the Rovers defence and ran out winners by 2-0 at Cliftonhill. Another trialist goalkeeper was tried out against Raith Rovers at Kirkcaldy but he was even more unfortunate losing four goals without reply. In this match Jeff King, recently signed from Fauldhouse United made his debut in midfield. The New Year's Day match on the Monday saw Hamilton come to Cliftonhill and Rovers, losing 2-1 at half time, had centre half Sage ordered off. The team for once got it together and Jim Graham equalised in the second half for the ten men to square the match at 2-2. The following Saturday the trip to Brechin found Rovers losing their fifth match in six outings to finish bottom of the League and, to boot Charlie Wylie was ordered off by referee Thompson. This match saw young centre forward John Brogan of Blantyre Celtic make his appearance and he retained his place on the following week for the home match against Clyde but despite all his efforts Rovers went down in this one by 3-0.

Montrose made it seven defeats in eight matches by a 3-1 scoreline but despite these depressing results, all Rovers' Support was talking about was the potential of Brogan, Dickson and King. In an attempt to instill some stability in defence, Pat Delaney, son of the illustrious Jimmy, was signed from Clydebank and by the time he had found his feet, in his second match against Queen of the South, the defence seemed to be more stable. The result at Dumfries was no score. However, at Dunfermline the following mid-week the 'Pars' won easily by 4-0 to be followed by a 1-0 defeat down at Berwick. At last it happened against Alloa with Brogan scoring his first of very many goals in Scottish senior football and Charlie Wylie also scoring a wonderful goal by chipping over the goalkeeper's head from some forty yards, following a bad kick out from hand, in a 2-2 draw at Coatbridge.

The double was effected over Clydebank by Rovers winning 2-1 off their own patch, but it was a different story at Love Street the next week with St. Mirren winning 3-1. This match saw Charlie Wylie being the fourth Rovers player ordered off this season, in the tenth minute. The Queen's Park team won convincingly 3-2 at Hampden before Rovers managed a fighting second half recovery to a 2-2 home draw against Cowdenbeath.

Off the football field Coatbridge, the original Iron Burgh much renowned for its industry based predominantly in the centre of the Town and generally considered as being a dirty industrial area, made a little bit of history by becoming the first Industrial Burgh in Scotland to become smokeless.

In two away matches Stirling Albion won emphatically enough at 3-0 and Forfar won 1-0 in convincing style. The previous evening Glasgow Tigers' Speedway drew eight thousand against Halifax at Cliftonhill in the start of the Summer season. A third away defeat in a row came at the hands of Stranraer with goalkeeper Ricky Gray bringing off some heroic saves and keeping Rovers in with a chance but with only ten minutes remaining the South of Scotland team scored the only goal of the match keeping Rovers firmly entrenched at the bottom of the League table.

A Lanarkshire Cup tie against Airdrieonians, at Broomfield, brought the fourth away match in a row and the third 1-0 defeat in a row, suggesting perhaps that Rovers were not just as bad as they were being painted. In fact, Airdrie's goal came from a penalty in the sixty-sixth minute, otherwise the First Division team could exact little pleasure in the victory. Only two League games remained and the first was at home against Stirling Albion where Rovers were winning by a Jeff King goal when Stirling equalised with only a minute to go, much to the disappointment of the Rovers contingent. But the final game of the season at Larbert found Stenhousemuir winners by a clear 3-0. This confirmed Rovers again in second bottom place, the same as the previous season but with two points less. Clyde were Champions on fifty-six with Dunfermline accompanying them into the upper league on fifty-two. Rovers were above only Brechin City who could amass only a meagre fourteen points.

Despite the disappointing lowly position in the League there was considerable hope based on the young players introduced at Cliftonhill during the previous season. The enthusiasm of Ralph Brand was infectious and there was an air about Cliftonhill that something was about to happen. During the year Brown had gone to Cheltenham and Tuddenham had been swapped for Pat Delaney at Clydebank. For the new season Ralph Brand was appointed Manager with Mike Jackson as his second in command. Bobby Smith was fixed up as Physio and a whole host of new players were signed up. An innovation for the new season was to be the provision of two substitutes instead of one for Scottish football only. England were to continue with a single replacement.

Season 1973/74

With Ralph Brand very obviously in charge and being a very extrovert person, it was felt that this combination, together with the promising talent that had arrived at Cliftonhill in the latter part of the previous season that something was going to happen this year. Was it to be promotion? This was still to be seen but the optimism was certainly there and Cliftonhill was humming in a way that it hadn't done for many years. By the time the season opened on the 11th of August for the first League Cup match at Forfar, the fans saw a much changed Rovers team with top scorer Peter Dickson being fielded at right back and new signings Graham, Sermanni, Struthers and Coughlin, all finding a place. Always a difficult place to pick up points the tight little Station Park ground was no exception in this meeting but Rovers showed a great deal of character in their 1-1 draw. The first goal of the season was scored by Tommy Sermanni and Rovers were represented by Graham, Dickson, Martin, Sage, McArthur, Sunderland, Brogan, Wylie, Sermanni, Struthers and Coughlin.

Better was to follow with two home victories, the first over Clydebank by 3-1 and the second over Brechin City by 4-1. It was just as well Rovers had won their Section by this time as the last game at Stranraer proved to be a bit of a let down with the homesters winning by 4-0.

Once again Rovers, by finishing in the bottom five of the Second Division, had ensured that they would be required to be in a play-off situation should they win their Section. They were subsequently drawn against East Stirlingshire who had also won their Section. Before the play-off, however, the first League match against Berwick Rangers at Cliftonhill found the English team nipping off with the points by scoring the only goal of the match. Not to be disheartened on the following Monday, Rovers won by a Sam Malcolmson goal to nil at home before travelling to Falkirk in the second leg on the Wednesday. Despite the Falkirk team trying all they knew, a no-scoring draw was the result and Rovers passed into the next round which was a home and away tie against Airdrieonians. In the second League match at Hamilton, three thousand fans watched Hamilton confirm their superiority by scoring two goals without reply.

The following Tuesday at Cliftonhill, the first leg of the League Cup took place in front of four thousand enthusiastic fans on a night when Rovers were undoubtedly far and away the better team. Rovers had been concerned with the displays of young junior goalkeeper Hugh Graham and Ralph Brand drafted in his old buddie Willie Duff the thirty-nine year old goalkeeper who had come out of retirement and his experience proved to be invaluable during the game. Rovers took the lead after thirty-three minutes when Brogan chipped the ball over the head of goalkeeper

Albion Rovers v Kilmarnock 1973/74

Standing: J. O'Connor, P. Dickson, A. Rice, S. Sage, H. Graham, S. Malcolmson, T. Martin and D. Taggart.
Kneeling: J. Brogan, J. King, W. Struthers, T. Sermanni and J. Coughlin.

McWilliams. At that stage the tension got to Dickson who watched team-mate Struthers make a hash of a pass back. This allowed an Airdrie forward a shot in at Duff which he was lucky to smother. Dickson immediately ran over to Struthers and the pair got into a real old punch-up, so much so that Dickson was booked for his actions. McRoberts hit he bar for Airdrie with eighty minutes gone but Rovers then hit two killer blows with Rice shooting home in the eighty-sixth minute from outside the box and, with two minutes to go, Sermanni hit number three to make it a night to remember for the Rovers' fans.

By coincidence the following Wednesday was a League match to be played at Broomfield and, despite smarting from the reverse earlier in the week, try as they might the Diamonds could do nothing with their Coatbridge opponents. The game ended no scoring with Rovers picking up their first point of the season in the League but still failing to score a goal.

The first League goal when it did come at Montrose the following Saturday was an own goal by centre half D'Arcy. This was not sufficient to save Rovers losing by 3-1 in a match in which Sid Sage was ordered off. In the next League match, St. Mirren visited and whilst Rovers doubled their score in the League season to date, the team overall still lost, this time by 3-2. On the Saturday Alloa came to Coatbridge and only escaped with a share of the points at 2-2 by Dickson missing a penalty. In the seventh game of the season at last Rovers broke their duck and won by the odd goal in seven. The teams tied at 3-3 at half time but a Dickson goal in the second half clinched the points for Cliftonhill.

Then came the match all Monklands had been waiting for when, on Tuesday 9th October at Broomfield, the Airdrie fans felt confident of pulling back the 3-0 deficit and the game started in real old-fashioned Cup tie fashion. That there would be no quarter given was shown when Jeff King was ordered off in the twentieth minute leaving ten man Rovers to take on the might of the Broomfield side and it was clear that Airdrie had shot their bolt by half time. It was no surprise in the second half when Brogan ran from the half way line to slot the ball behind the Airdrie goalkeeper to win 1-0 on the night and 4-0 on aggregate over the tie, thus going into the Quarter Final of the Cup.

Friday of that week also saw the last game of the Speedway for the season but back in the League the following day, Queen of the South came to Coatbridge to defeat Rovers by 2-0. The visit to Clydebank met with better luck and a King goal in the first half was enough to take the points to Cliftonhill. A further point came Rovers way at home against Stenhousemuir with Sermanni equalising a first half 'Muir goal to share the points at 1-1.

The League Cup Quarter Final first leg match was played at Coatbridge on Tuesday, 30th October at Cliftonhill in an exciting match which Mr. Sime of Glasgow had little difficulty in refereeing. Killie started the game as if they meant to push Rovers into oblivion but gradually Rovers overcame the threat and firstly Coughlin hit the bar with Stewart beaten but pressure eventually paid off and from an inswinging corner back headed by Malcolmson, Jeff King first timed the ball from eighteen yards behind Stewart. There was no surprise in the second half when Brogan scored a second goal and Killie were lucky to be only two down.

Two victories in the League were then chalked up, first against East Stirlingshire at Falkirk by 2-1 and against Stirling Albion at home by 2-0 before Raith Rovers won 3-0 through in Kirkcaldy. The League match against Kilmarnock at Coatbridge played on the Wednesday and Rovers were 4-0 down after fifty-three minutes and absolutely struggling. However, a tremendous fight back saw goals from Coughlin,

King and Sermanni leave the fans with the distinct impression that if the game had lasted another five minutes, Rovers would have won. Irrespective of this, Rovers ineptitude should have warned them for the Second Leg Cup Tie the following Saturday at Kilmarnock.

With the fans still struggling through the turnstiles, Rovers kicked off two goals to the good and confidence simply oozing from the players. In their first move down the park, John Brogan clattered the ball off the post with Stewart nowhere and the ball was cleared upfieled where a needless free kick was given away outside the box. Full-back Robertson took it and goalkeeper Graham completely misjudged the harmless looking shot and the score was 2-1. One minute later, the young goalkeeper had a sudden rush of blood to the head when he dropped a Jeff King pass-back right at the feet of centre forward Morrison and that was 2-2. Rovers were knocked off their stride never to return due to two incredible goalkeeping errors. The inevitable happened when Kilmarnock scored from the spot after Peter Dickson had brought down winger Jim Cook in the box but Brogan got one back only to find Kilmarnock scoring a fourth goal just before half time. With O'Connor on in place of Struthers, Rovers hit the woodwork for the third time but it was Kilmarnock who increased their lead to 5-1 before Jeff King scored with a penalty with ten minutes to go and the aggregate 5-4 for Killie. Try as they might, the Coatbridge team could not do it and their first ever opportrunity to go into the semi-final of the Cup was squandered, thanks to those mad first two minutes and tragic goalkeeping errors. Everybody connected with the Club was greatly disappointed.

At Stranraer the following Saturday, the team bounced back from the ropes to win by 2-1 and at the other side of the country, on Scottish Cup business the following week, a no scoring draw was fought out against Berwick Rangers bringing the replay to Coatbridge the following Wednesday. After a no-scoring first half, Jeff King and Sam Malcolmson both scored in the mud and the rain to give the tie to the Coatbridge team by 2-0.

Rovers were on far away travels in their next two matches, firstly at Brechin, when a no-scoring draw was the result, and the following week on the last Saturday of the year, Berwick got ample revenge for their Cup defeat with a 1-0 victory. On Tuesday, New Year's Day, Hamilton Accies visited and ran out winners by 3-1 with Jeff King scoring Rovers' first goal of the New Year.

With advance notification that Second Division Speedway would be played at Cliftonhill during the summer months, Rovers once again went on their football travels, this time in the second round of the Scottish Cup to Palmerston against Queen of the South. In a match which Rovers showed few signs of their earlier Cup fighting qualities, Queen's won by a penalty scored in the seventy-fourth minute. Jeff King was allowed down to play a trial with Derby County and the Kingless team were beaten 1-0 once again, this time by Alloa in the League match. Former player Billy Simpson, playing for Alloa, was ordered off and it was all the more galling for Rovers to lose to a ten man team. On a blank Saturday, Celtic were engaged in a Friendly at Cliftonhill and won by a 3-2 margin.

The first match played on a Sunday took place on the third of February with Cowdenbeath as visitors to Cliftonhill. It was considered by the Board that it was a more likely proposition to play without the opposition of the other League teams. And to some extent it was successful with one thousand fans paying for the privilege but the football didn't match up to the promise and a dull, lifeless tussle ended up with no score. Another visit to the deep south found Queen of the South

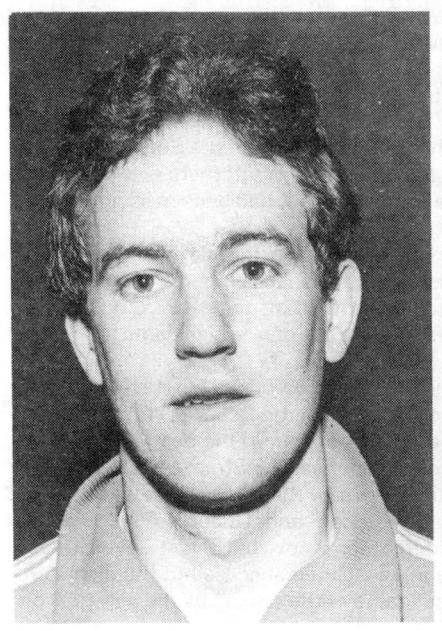

John Brogan

Tommy Sermanni

Sam Malcolmson

Albert Rice

once again too strong for Rovers, this time by 5-2, before the second home Sunday match found Rovers winning easily against Clydebank by 3-0. Following this success four hundred fans turned up the next Sunday at Larbert but Rovers lost this one by 1-0. The East Stirlingshire match at Cliftonhill saw Jeff King score with two penalties and Rovers share six goals. At the end of this match Messrs. Brand, Jackson and Smith all resigned much to the disappointment of the Support. Whilst it was clear that results had not been kind to the coaching staff there was no doubt that they had the Club humming with an expectancy that had been missing for too long.

There was an expected reaction to this situation and the players were in no mood to take on Stirling Albion at Annfield and, in a bad tempered match, poor Rovers lost 7-1. Both King and Coughlin were ordered off together with Clark of Stirling. This was just the start of an eleven defeats out of a twelve game run-up to the end of the season.

Raith Rovers won by the only goal of the match at Coatbridge before Kilmarnock beat Rovers for the third time this season by 3-1. Airdrie chalked up their first victory against Rovers by taking three points out of four in the League by a Ray Franchetti goal to nothing. Two further home matches saw Stranraer win 2-0 and Forfar 2-1 before the Forfar match at Station Park saw the Angus team win by 4-0.

Montrose were winners by 4-1 at Coatbridge and Queen's Park 3-1 at Hampden with St. Mirren making it ten defeats in a row by 3-1 at Love Street. Brechin were defeated 3-1 at Coatbridge in an isolated success but the dispirited Coatbridge side went down again in the last game of the season by the only goal of the match against Queen's Park.

A most disappointing end to what had been an unusual season. Second bottom position was the best the Club could come up with on thirty-six points. St. Mirren winning the Championship were accompanied upstairs by Airdrieonians. Peter Dickson played centre forward and Jim Coughlin at outside left against the Italian Second Division XI at Pescara in Italy with the centre scoring Scotland's goal. During the summer the Speedway continued to delight fans with gates of upwards of three thousand and by the time the new season came round, George Caldwell was appointed as Coach and Joe White as physiotherapist.

Season 1974/75

Four pre-season Friendlies took place, all at home, starting on the twenty-sixth of July against Hearts XI when Rovers won 2-1. The score was one each at half time but in the extra half hour played, O'Connor scored the winner. Rovers' first goal of the season was scored by Eric Gillespie, signed in the close season from Hamilton Accies, Crewe Alexandra were next with a 1-1 score to be followed by Nuneaton on the Monday in a match which had no goals but plenty thrills. Finally, a match against a Celtic XI found Rovers 3-2 down.

For the new season, the Second Division was augmented by the former Ferranti Thistle who were now renamed Meadowbank Thistle and whose home games were to be played at the Commonwealth Stadium. The League Cup programme was due to start on Saturday the 10th August, but the Meadowbank game against Albion Rovers was brought forward to the Friday night and thus Rovers inaugurated the Commonwealth Stadium into League football. Peter Dickson scored the first goal of the Scottish season in the second half in front of four thousand five hundred fans with the goal proving to be the only one of the game. Rovers' team was Graham, McConville, Main, Rice, Shields, Montgomery, Brogan,

Meadowbank Thistle's goalkeeper punches clear during an Albion Rovers' attack at Meadowbank Stadium, Edinburgh.

Sermanni, Dickson, O'Connor and Coughlin.

Rovers were due to play five games in their League Cup Section and each one was a victory, a situation which had never happened before nor since. The second match at Cliftonhill was against Brechin City which Rovers won by 6-1 and East Stirlingshire were then defeated at Falkirk by 2-1. Stevie Gryzka was signed from Celtic to play his first game in goal at Forfar in a fine 5-1 victory in which Dickson hit a treble. The League Cup Section was convincingly won with another 5-1 victory, this time at home against Stenhousemuir. Again, by finishing in the bottom six, Rovers had to play off with another Section winner who this time turned out to be Falkirk.

However, before this could take place, a League match at Alloa found both teams locked at 1-1 with Brogan prodding in the equaliser in the second half. In the League Cup play off, Falkirk, in the first leg at Coatbridge on the Monday, ran out winners by 2-1 despite Rovers leading at half time by yet another Dickson goal. The return leg at Brockville two days later was a run-away victory for Falkirk by 6-1 taking them through to the next round on an 8-2 aggregate.

The first home League match against Hamilton Accies ended with a victory for the Accies by 2-1 in what was a very ill-ternpered match. At one stage with Rovers awarded a penalty, substitute Smyth took the field whilst the players were lining up and got into a melee with one of the Hamilton players and was promptly ordered off the field before he had even touched the ball. None of this delay and furore did Brogan any good as he subsequently missed the penalty attempt. However, defeat against East Stirlingshire at Falkirk by 1-0 saw Graham back in goal but nothing much coming off for Rovers.

At Cowdenbeath the following Saturday a Tommy Sermanni hat-trick saw Rovers consolidate their half time lead into a 5-1 victory and the return match against East Stirlingshire saw Dickson, Sermanni and Brogan each score two goals in a 6-2 victory.

Falkirk who had gone sixteen games without defeat, came to Coatbridge and they were unlucky that there was no score at half time. However, Rovers came out in the second half with guns blazing and ran out worthy winners by 4-1. At Stirling the result was a 3-2 defeat and the following three matches ended up with Rovers failing to score. In the home match against Stenhousemuir neither team scored whilst, at Methil, East Fife won 5-0 and then Berwick won 2-0 over the border. This last result put Rovers firmly into seventh bottom place.

Graham was reinstated to goal and three other changes were made in midfield to welcome Forfar. These immediately made a difference and Rovers turned out one of their better performances winning by a 5-3 margin. On Wednesday the 23rd October, the Lanarkshire Cup Final took place at Motherwell with very few people other than ardent Rovers Fans giving the Coatbridge team any hope of success. On the night however, Rovers were the better team and two second half John Brogan goals were enough to lift the Cup for only the fifth time by a 2-1 scoreline. Rovers unchanged from the previous game were represented by Graham, McConville, Main, Rice, Shields, Gillespie, O'Connor, Sermanni, Dickson, Brogan and Coughlin.

The following Saturday at Stranraer, Coughlin equalised a first half Stranraer goal to share the points at 1-1 but Queen's Park won 2-1 at Coatbridge in a match where all the goals were scored in the first half. Airdrieonians were visited in midweek for the current season's Lanarkshire Cup and the holders won by 3-1.

Raith Rovers were defeated 2-1 at Kirkcaldy but this success was negated when Clydebank won 3-1 at Coatbridge. A fine 1-1 draw down at Palmerston saw

ALBION ROVERS LANARKSHIRE CUP WINNERS 1974/75

Standing: Jim Montgomery, David Main, Bert Rice, Steve Gryzka, Duncan Shields, John Brogan, Eric Gillespie, George Caldwell (coach).

Seated: Peter Dickson, Denis McConville, John O'Connor, Tommy Sermanni, Jim Coughlin, George Douglas.

Rovers take a point from the League leaders. The same team was given the opportunity to come up trumps against St. Mirren at Coatbridge but despite a double by Peter Dickson the Love Street men ran out easy winners by 4-2. In the return match Meadowbank played their first game at Coatbridge and despite leading by a Davie Main goal at half time, Rovers lost 3-1 thanks to two goals in the last minute for an historic result by the League Babes.

This was hardly an adequate preparation for the Scottish Cup campaign and Rovers were committed to travel to the far south of Scotland to play St. Cuthberts Wanderers in the first round., With Ian Docherty from Lanark United stiffening up the defence and Billy Paterson adding punch up front, the remainder of the team played adequately enough to win 4-1 although there was a scare when the non-league team were leading at half time by a single goal. The visit to Montrose saw the home team sitting second top of the League and this was emphasised by a 3-1 defeat for the Coatbridge men. During the next mid-week Dickson and Coughlin played for the Second Division Select at Pescara in Italy against the Itallian Second Division XI. George Caldwell also travelled as Coach to the Scottish XI.

On New Year's Day, a no-scoring draw was fought out at Hamilton in front of two thousand five hundred fans and, on the Saturday, the Second Round Cup tie at Alloa found Rovers equalising only in the last minute from Peter Dickson in a match where Gryzka saved a penalty. The replay, on the following Wednesday, found Rovers, against all the odds, winning 2-0. Dickson was suspended for fourteen days but in fact only missed the Falkirk match at Brockville which Rovers lost 3-1. In the third round of the Cup Inverness Caledonian were the opponents and over three thousand fans cheered on the local heroes who gave Rovers a very hard game for their money. A Jimmy Coughlin goal in the second half was sufficient to separate the teams. An unchanged team saw Dickson scoring a hat-trick at Coatbridge against Berwick in the 3-2 victory.

The fourth away draw in the Scottish Cup took Rovers up to Arbroath but this was a hurdle they were unable to overcome losing a goal in either half. Two and a half thousand fans paid £666.45 which was poor recompense for Rovers who had hoped to do better. Willie Muldoon was reintroduced at centre for the away visit to Forfar and he scored two goals and Peter Dickson a hat-trick in a 5-0 victory. Jimmy Coughlin got into the double scoring act the following week at Coatbridge against Stranraer in a 4-0 victory. Four goals were scored again the next week at Hampden with the final score being 4-1 for Rovers. The fifth consecutive League win came when Raith Rovers lost 2-1 at Coatbridge and Tommy Sermanni hit a double.

Clydebank stopped this good form with a 2-0 victory at Clydebank and this match saw Bert Rice return for part of the game coming on as substitute for Davie Main but it was obvious that the lad's injury had been very serious and he was only a shadow of his former self. It was back to winning ways at home against East Fife at 2-1 with a Dickson winner from the penalty spot. The same player did likewise in the 1-1 draw at Coatbridge against Queen of the South but on the following Tuesday Stenhousemuir won 6-1 at Larbert.

Speedway recommenced on Friday the fourth of April for the summer session and the next day Rovers travelled to Love Street. In front of eighteen hundred fans a Dickson goal in the second half was enough to share the points at 1-1 with Denis McConville being sent off. Cowdenbeath was the first of three home matches with this one being a victory by 2-0 but Meadowbank won 1-0 thanks to a first half goal. Rovers won the third by 3-2 against Alloa with Brogan scoring a double. At

Brechin Rovers lost 3-2 and the same opponents turning up at Coatbridge two days later with many remembered recent old scores to be settled. Brogan scored Rovers' first goal, which was the hundreth goal of the season, and was promptly sent off leaving his mates to finish up winners in a dour tussle by 3-0. Montrose came to Coatbridge requiring to win to take the championship but even with Hamish McAlpine on loan from Dundee United, he could do nothing against Rovers attacking football in a 3-0 victory. New starlet Ian McGuigan scored with a thundering free kick from twenty yards to finish the scoring. There was considerable trouble with Montrose fans at the game and police with dogs were called in. This day Airdrieonians were losing 3-1 in the Scottish Cup Final against Celtic at Hampden. The season ended in a final match at home with defeat at the hands of Stirling Albion by 4-1.

During the close season the Leagues were re-organised into Premier, First and Second Divisions. Rovers were of course in the Second Division which comprised fourteen teams the same as the First Division, with the Premier League having ten. As usual several new faces were signed up ready for the off with Ray Franchetti eventually signed for Rovers after spells with Celtic and Airdrieonians.

Season 1975/76

A pre-season match was fixed up at Coatbridge against Dunfermline Athletic and Rovers gave a hint of what they could do with a 5-0 score with Peter Dickson setting the heather on fire with a hat-trick. For the season proper, however, the Cliftonhillers played host to Morton and Rovers were disappointed when after holding the First Leaguers to no scoring with only four minutes to go the Greenock team, after taking considerable pressure from Rovers, scored the only goal of the match. Rovers were left to reflect on what might have been had Ray Franchetti scored early on when presented with a gilt-edged opportunity. Rovers' team was Gryzka, J. Docherty, Main, Paterson, (O'Connor) Shields, I. Docherty, Sermanni (Coughlin), Franchetti, Dickson, McGuigan and Muldoon.

In mid-week a no-scoring draw was fought out at Stenhousemuir and a defeat by 3-2 was suffered at the hands of Stranraer even although Dickson inspired a fight back in the second half, scoring directly from a corner kick. Another defeat by 1-0 at the hands of Stenhousemuir, made certain Rovers would not be winning this cup section and, despite a home victory by 2-1 over Stranraer, Morton insured Rovers would take bottom slot in the Section by winning 2-1 at Greenock in what was a most disappointing involvement in the League Cup.

The opening game of the League was a home match against Stenhousemuir, who had already taken three points off Rovers, and again the Coatbridge team failed to win this time the score being 2-2. The second game of the League campaign took place down at Stranraer with Rovers winning 2-1 but with centre forward Dickson sent off with two minutes to go. An unchanged team defeated East Stirlingshire 2-1 to go second top in the League but two defeats, first of all by 3-0 at Cowdenbeath and then 1-0 at home against Alloa, saw that lofty position vacated. With Gryzka back in goal at Berwick, Rovers won by a first half Muldoon goal.

Clydebank came to Coatbridge to win 4-0 with a fine display of attacking football including Sam Goodwin scoring a fine first goal from a header. Two 1-1 draws saw Stirling Albion share the points at Coatbridge before, in the match at Kirkcaldy, Rovers managed to hang on even with Ray Franchetti ordered off. Forfar Athletic were beaten 4-0 and at Hampden, Brogan was carried off with a suspected broken leg and Rovers fought back from a half-time deficit to share the points at 2-2.

Brogan's leg injury turned out only to be badly bruised but he was unable to strip for the following match at Brechin and Rovers missed his forceful play to lose 2-0. This was Peter Dickson's last game before being transferred to Queen of the South for £15,00. Meadowbank faced a completely revised forward line and the changes worked wonders for the Dicksonless team and the 'Bankies' were overwhelmed by 4-0. Pleased with the team's performance, the same players had the task of tackling strong-going Alloa but, with left back McCue becoming Rovers third player to be ordered off this sesaon, Rovers were always struggling and in the end lost 2-0.

December started with a draw at Coatbridge by 2-2 against Berwick Rangers with Big Dunky Shields scoring a fourth goal from his central defensive position. When the Scottish Cup First Round match against Hawick Royal Albert arrived it found Rovers struggling to find a team and, although the defence remained unchanged, there was still difficulty in finding a settled forward-line. The two hundred fans paid £34 and watched a drab no-scoring draw which took Rovers on a journey into dangerous country the following Thursday with a 1.45 p.m. kick-off at Hawick. Again the forward line showed four positional changes but this time they worked more satisfactorily and Rovers ran out winners by 3-0 only to draw Glasgow University in the Second Round. Rovers journeyed to play the other Albion at Stirling and were leading by an Ian Docherty penalty conversion in the first half but Stirling equalised, also from the penalty spot, to share the points at full time. Raith Rovers won 2-1 at Coatbridge but two Brogan goals were enough to keep the points at Coatbridge against Stranraer by 2-1 on New Year's Day in a match which had a 2.00 p.m. kick-off. On the Saturday against East Stirlingshire, Rovers struggled to field a team and even Coach Caldwell was called on to don one of the substitutes' track suits. Rovers struggled in this game and when O'Connor, who had gone on as a substitute, had himself to be substituted the Rovers' Coach entered the fray to tremendous cheers from Rovers' Supporters. The points were shared in this no-scoring draw only thanks to 'keeper Gryzka saving a penalty. Glasgow University were drawn at home in the Second Round Cup tie with the only change from the previous week being McGuigan in the number seven jersey with Muldoon and O'Connor as substitutes. Brogan opened the scoring but the Students equalised before half-time and this was how it finished. The following Wednesday afternoon the replay at the University playing fields found S.T.V. cameras there with presenter Arthur Montford, who was Rector at the University at the time, and the cameras showed Rovers rather fortunate winners by a single goal scored late on by Ray Franchetti. This was only his second goal of the season but an important one as it ensured another home tie in the Third Round against Partick Thistle.

Through in Edinburgh, Meadowbank, who were sitting bottom of the League, had their third win of the season by 4-1 against Rovers who seemed to be suffering from a Cup tie reaction and with new signing Donny McLean from Stenhousemuir given few chances to shine.

Partick Thistle duly arrived for the much awaited match and Rovers' Fans were quite convinced that this was to be third time lucky, and the two earlier rounds' footering displays would be put behind them and a win would be the only result. Davie Main was back at full back and Muldoon on the left wing and in fact Rovers put up one of the best performances of this season, giving the Thistle team little time to settle. All Coatbridge erupted just before half-time when newcomer McLean dispossessed a defender and hammered the ball into the net but Thistle equalised ten minutes into the second half and in sixty-three minutes Thistle were awarded a penalty but Gryzka made a fine save from Dougie Somner's effort. The goalkeeper changed from a saint to a sinner with quarter of an hour to go when he fumbled a lob giving McQuade an easy goal. Rovers did score again but the goal was disallowed and the four thousand fans had to settle for defeat.

The following week at Stenhousemuir McLean scored two first half goals against his former team mates but the 'Muir ran out winners by 4-2. In a very tousy match at Clydebank the points were shared by a 2-2 score when John O'Connor was ordered off and for Rovers, Main, Ian Docherty, Muldoon and Shields were all booked. The third away match in a row saw Rovers lose 1-0 at Forfar and this was followed by two home draws, first of all by 1-1 against Cowdenbeath and then no-scoring against Queen's Park.

This left but one game in the Second Division but meanwhile an innovation this season was the introduction of a Spring Cup with Rovers in a Section along with Dumbarton, Stenhousemuir and Arbroath. The opening match took place at Cliftonhill but Dumbarton's current wonder-boy Ian Wallace scored two goals in their 2-1 victory. At Dumbarton the score was 4-1 for the Sons but Rovers then came away strongly with two home 1-0 victories against Stenhousemuir and Arbroath. They made it three in a row by winning 3-2 at Larbert and, in the last match at Arbroath, in a gale force wind, they fought back from a 3-0 deficit to narrowly fail to reach parity finally losing 3-2. This was the end of the Spring Cup Sections and Rovers went into the Quarter Finals by means of being the highest scoring non-section winner.

Clydebank were the opponents in the Quarter Final of home and away matches and when Rovers lost 4-1 in the first leg it looked as though that was it. In the return match at Cliftonhill, Rovers immediately took up the initiative and won on the day by 2-0 with Ian Docherty scoring both Rovers' goals from penalties. Despite several near things, Rovers couldn't square the match and went out very unluckily by a 4-3 aggregate.

The last game of the season was the final League game which took place on Monday the 26th of April with Brechin City losing by 4-0 and the Coatbridge side in fine form. Rovers ended up in ninth position with twenty-four points from twenty-six games. Clydebank were promoted on goal difference from Raith Rovers with Meadowbank at the bottom of the table on sixteen points.

Airdrieonians eventually won the Spring Cup defeating Clydebank in the final and Speedway recommenced at Cliftonhill for the summer. Rovers freed five players, including Bert Rice, who had never really recovered from his injury on New Year's Day 1974. There were high hopes that this nucleus of players would do for a promotion push.

Season 1976/77

It was straight into the League Cup Sections on the 14th August with a trip down to Berwick and only a penalty equaliser goal in the second half by Jimmy Coughlin gained Rovers a point. The first team of the season was — Thomson, McConville, J. Docherty, McGuigan, Shields, Franchetti, Sermanni, Brogan, McLean (McGovern), Muldoon and Coughlin.

Phil McGovern was on from the beginning for the mid-week match against Forfar and the Fans at the first home game were pleased when Coughlin scored the

Season 1975/76 Spring Cup tie at Arbroath.

Season 1977/78 League Match at Shawfield.

only goal, this time without reply, to keep the points at Coatbridge. On the Saturday, Meadowbank fought out a no-scoring draw again at Cliftonhill. Two away victories found Rovers topping their Section with Stenhousemuir losing 3-1 and Brechin City 2-0. The last match was a very physical encounter with Franchetti ordered off and McCue, McConville and Coughlin, together with coach Caldwell, all being booked.

Following this match, George Caldwell resigned to take up a coaching appointment with Ayr United and Airdrieonians' coach and former player, Sam Goodwin, was appointed coach. The first game in Division Two was against newly-relegated Clyde who visited Coatbridge and promptly inflicted Rovers first defeat of the season by 4-1. The following Monday, the League Cup play-off at Broomfield found Rovers unlucky to lose by 3-2 in front of more than five thousand fans. The return match at Coatbridge on the Wednesday was looked on by the Airdrie contingent as being a waste of time but Rovers, playing an unchanged team, took the play to the opposition and a fine hat-trick by John Brogan ensured Rovers won on aggregate by 5-4 to go into a Quarter Final match against Celtic.

Before that however there were three League matches to be played and Rovers drew the first two at home by 2-2 against Alloa and 1-1 against Queen's Park. An away victory at Berwick by 3-1 set Rovers up for the first leg of the League Cup Quarter Final match at Cliftonhill against Celtic. Former player Jock Stein, now Manager of Celtic, led his team to a narrow victory at Cliftonhill by 1-0 and there was still all to play for at Parkhead in a fortnights time.

Three home matches followed starting with Brechin drawing 2-2 and Franchetti being ordered off. Steve Gryzka re-signed and took his place for the mid-week match against Forfar, the start of which was delayed with the Forfar bus being delayed because of torrential rain. A McGuigan goal shared the points at 1-1 before Muldoon got Rovers off to a first minute lead against Dunfermline but the Fifers ran out winners by 2-1 even missing a penalty when Gryzka made a fine save.

The return match against Celtic at Parkhead found the Glasgow League Champions taken apart by Rovers in the early stages and only daring saves by goalkeeper Connaghan saved Celtic from going three goals down. As often happens in these situations, after the initial effort by the underdogs, the big Leaguers ran out comfortable 5-0 winners on the night and 6-0 on aggregate in front of Rovers' biggest gate for years of over eight thousand.

Alan Roberts was signed from Rutherglen Glencairn and he took up his place in midfield against East Stirlingshire in a 1-1 draw and immediately following this match defender Dave McCue was freed. A disappointing home defeat by Stenhousemuir by the only goal of the match was followed by another defeat at Stirling by 2-1 in a match where Gryzka saved another penalty. League leaders Stranraer saw out October at Coatbridge and Rovers showed they were not prepared to be pushed around and a Franchetti hat-trick was a fine foundation for a 5-2 victory.

Willie Semple ex-Rangers was signed from New York Thunderers and he made his debut as substitute in the match at Shawfield against Clyde and scored Rovers' second goal in a 3-2 defeat.

In the Lanarkshire Cup Final at Fir Park, Rovers lost 3-1. Captain Shields and his men were real shadows of their earlier selves and never really gave Motherwell much of a contest in this one-sided final. Rovers' team was — Gryzka, Campbell (Franchetti), McConville, Roberts, Shields, Main, Sermanni, Muldoon, McLean, Brogan and Semple. Alloa were the visitors in a 2-2 draw the following Saturday with Alan Roberts scoring his first goal for Rovers and Thomson being reintroduced in goal. Berwick won 1-0 at Coatbridge in a poor Rovers performance but ex-Rangers Semple came into his own at Brechin scoring the first goal and laying on the others in a 3-1 victory. The same score at Edinburgh was a welcome Christmas present for Rovers against Meadowbank and League leaders Stirling fought out a thrilling 4-4 draw at Coatbridge in the last game of the year on an icy pitch with heavy snow falling. Rovers were 4-2 up at half time but lack of concentration in the second period cost them dear.

On New Year's Day, Stranraer, who had been unbeaten at home since March, were defeated at Stair Park by a Brogan goal to nothing and Rovers prepared to welcome First Division Raith Rovers in the Scottish Cup Second Round match. It looked like the Coatbridge side was up against it in the first half with the visitors winning 1-0 but in the sixty-ninth minute, John Brogan picked up a short back pass and chipped the ball over the goalkeeper from fifteen yards and it was only a matter of time before Rovers went ahead. Seven minutes later Shields had a strong header blocked by the goalkeeper but McLean followed up to hit the ball home. Due to bad weather the Berwick Rangers match was one of only four games played in the Scottish Leagues the next week and Rovers lost by the only goal of the game scored with only four minutes of the match remaining. The following week both Jim Docherty and Kenny Wilson were suspended for failing to turn up for the team bus to Berwick and Rovers made their first team change in six weeks when McGuigan took Semple's place for the Cup tie at Firs Park against East Stirlingshire. Rovers were never in trouble in this one, with Brogan and McLean with two in a fine 3-0 victory mainly due to Rovers choice of footwear, playing with training shoes due to the underfoot conditions.

Dunfermline's East End Park was the setting for the first apopearance of Hugh Hill, who came on as a substitute for McLean while the other substitute Semple took Franchetti's place. Before almost two thousand of a gate, Dunfermline won 3-1 and Rovers' job was made all the harder by Davie Main being ordered off following two bookings. Rovers served Notice to Coatbridge Tigers to quit at the end of the season and submitted an Application for a greyhound track to take over at Cliftonhill. The following week East Stirlingshire got a quick chance to gain revenge for their Cup exit at Coatbridge but Rovers were too strong. Despite 'Shire leading at half time by the only goal, Rovers came back in the second half to win 3-2. Former player Willie Upton died during the week and Rovers confirmed that players Coughlin, Holbrook, Wilson and the Docherty brothers were all suspended.

Controversy was to hit Cliftonhill prior to the Fourth Round Cup tie against East Fife when John Brogan was transferred to St. Johnstone for a reputed £8,000. There was a reaction by the Fans the following day at the home game against Stranraer, which Rovers won comfortably enough by 2-0. Hugh Hill was given the popular Brogan's jersey and he had a fine game scoring the first goal.

The following Saturday for the Cup tie two bus loads of Rovers' fans travelled through to Fife. Rovers missed several chances in the first half and Alan Roberts back to defence had a fine game but was not quite match fit. The Fifers were 2-0 up in the second half but late on Tommy Sermanni scored with a strong header to give Rovers hope. Unfortunately it was too late and Rovers' fans went home agreeing that the Brogan-less team just weren't up to it.

Davie Main played his last game before commencing a four day suspension in the 0-0 draw at Meadowbank Stadium in a match which was ruined by high winds. Stranraer were defeated 2-1 at Coatbridge and Stirling Albion fought out a no-scoring draw at Stirling. Jim Coughlin went off to Hereford United on trial. A McLean hat-trick demolished Meadowbank Thistle 3-0 at Coatbridge and then Clyde were defeated by 3-1 at home in time for Martin Ferguson to be appointed as Assistant to Sam Goodwin and move from East Kilbride Thistle. The same team took the field at Cowdenbeath with Rovers winning 4-2 and Semple scoring with two penalties. Both teams returned to the same venue the following Wednesday with Rovers this time losing 3-1 thanks to a fine display by Rovers' fan Gerry Laughlin in a Cowden jersey.

Coatbridge Tigers commenced their summer season of speedway matches on Friday, 1st April, and Rovers wended their way to Forfar the following day to lose 2-1. Davie Campbell was suspended for throwing his jersey at the dugout in disgust on being substituted by Wilson, who eventually scored Rovers' only goal. East Stirlingshire won 3-1 through at Falkirk with Gerry Laughlin on trial but five home matches in a row saw Rovers first of all beat Queen's Park 4-1 and two draws, against Dunfermline at 2-2 and Forfar at 1-1, left Rovers winning 4-0 against Brechin and finally 4-2 against Cowdenbeath to boost their points record and see them confirmed in the top half of the League. Laughlin from Shotts Bon Accord was by this time a signed player. Queen's Park won an important four pointer at Hampden winning 3-0 before Rovers won their last away match at Stenhousemuir, thanks to a McLean double, by 3-1. The last game of the season found Alloa requiring one point to achieve promotion along with Champions Stirling Albion but Rovers moved into a 2-0 lead and the home support had visions of failing in their promotion bid. It was not to be however and Alloa fought back in the second half to square the match at 2-2. Rovers ended with forty-two points and Forfar were foot of the table with twenty-four.

The usual clutch of free transfers saw Billy Semple move on to Hong Kong Rangers and Rovers retaining seventeen players. Rovers' Pools payout this year was £13,902 based on £331 per point. This gives an indication of the extent of financial input by the Pools Companies. Many teams would have gone to the wall if it hadn't been for the financial input of the Football Pools. Greyhound Racing was guaranteed to return to Cliftonhill with the Speedway having already made arrangements to move over to Blantyre and negotiations took place to smooth the change-over. Few new players were signed on for the new season with such a large retained force but the team was kitted out with new Admiral strips and new track suits for the season ahead.

Season 1977/78
Two friendly matches were arranged with the first on Friday, 5th April, against Hamilton Accies which Rovers lost by 2-1 and Danny McLean scoring the first goal of the season. Billy Leishman was signed from Motherwell and Jim McCluskey from Kirkintilloch Rob Roy and both played in the first team which was — Thomson, Docherty, McConville, Franchetti, Shields, Main, Laughlin, Leishman, McLean, Sermanni and McCluskey. The other unscheduled match was against St. Mirren which ended up with no scoring.

When the Season finally got underway on the 13th, a League game at Cliftonhill against Clyde, found both teams again failing to score and the new format League Cup saw Rovers travel to Tannadice to play Dundee United in a home and away First Round. The Premier League team were too strong and ended up winning 5-0 and Rovers, minus Duncan Shields, introduced Dave Thewliss but his rawness was fully exploited by the more experienced opponents. At Brechin City in a League match on the Saturday Rovers, with nine positional changes, won by 2-1 before Dundee United came to Coatbridge and won the return match. Gerry Gallacher, signed from Clydebank, took his place in goal but he fared no better than George Thomson in the earlier match, losing five goals. On this occasion Rovers managed to score one in reply in the second half through Tommy Sermanni. Once again Rovers' involvement in League Cup affairs had ended at the first hurdle and by a 10-1 margin at that!

Back on League business Stranraer, who were not for the first time early in the season topping the League Table, visited Coatbridge and Rovers found them too hard a nut to crack and promptly lost by 2-1. A Lanarkshire Cup tie the following week saw ex-Airdrie man Franchetti set Rovers up, after a fine performance, with a half time lead, but Airdrie came back very strongly after the interval to win by 4-3.

Not deterred, Rovers visited Meadowbank with Gallacher back in goal and won 2-1, although their second half performance left a lot to be desired. East Stirlingshire came to Coatbridge the following Tuesday and won by the only goal of the match, with Rovers giving a most inept performance. From the away game at Stenhousemuir a better all-round performance saw Rovers win 4-2 and two first half goals were enough to defeat a disappointing Forfar side at Coatbridge. For the away trip to Cowdenbeath in mid-week, Rovers, with a gale force wind to their advantage in the first half, could only go in at half time drawing 1-1 and quickly went behind to a confident Cowdenbeath team early in the second half. However, when Franchetti and Muldoon replaced Laughlin and Roberts the complexion of the game changed and Rovers ran out deserved winners by 4-3.

October started disappointingly, with Rovers' recent good form deserting them, and Berwick Rangers won easily by 2-0. Goodwin made changes in defence and reintroduced Laughlin to the forward line for the visit by Dunfermline and this reshuffle seemed to do the trick for Rovers moved smoothly into top gear to win by 3-0. The following week League leaders Falkirk came to Coatbridge and although Rovers were sitting fourth top at the time, they could not contain the Bairns who, after half time, threw off the shackles of Rovers' defence to score twice without reply.

At Kirkcaldy the following week a Dunky Shields first half goal was equalised in the second half for a share of the points. Another draw, this time against Queen's Park at 3-3 was the first of two home matches and Brechin were defeated 2-0 in the other. For the match down at Stranraer, Ray Franchetti hit a fine hat-trick in a superb 5-3 victory. An innovation this season was the whisky firm of J. & B. Rare Whisky offering cases of whisky as an incentive for hat-tricks and later in the season Franchetti was to be awarded his crate. Rovers moved third top thanks to a fine 3-2 victory over Meadowbank, with Franchetti scoring another fine double, including one from the penalty spot. Rovers then climbed into second top place on goal difference with a strong display against Stenhousemuir at Coatbridge winning 3-1.

Two away defeats in a row knocked Rovers off their high perch, the first being 3-1 against Forfar and then 2-1 against Dunfermline Athletic. It was back to winning ways at Meadowbank by 3-0 with scorers Franchetti and McLean both counting in the race to find out who between them would end up top scorer. With the news that Alan Roberts was being placed under Club suspension, high-flying Falkirk were held to a draw of 1-1 with Franchetti getting the equaliser in the second half.

ALBION ROVERS SEASON 1976/77

Standing: J. Docherty, R. Franchetti, D. Shields, G. Thomson, P. McGovern, K. Wilson, D. McLean.
Seated: Physio J. Whyte, D. McConville, D. McCue, J. Coughlin, T. Sermanni, I. McGuigan, W. Muldoon, Coach G. Caldwell.

The last day of 1977 saw Clyde win convincingly 3-0 at Shawfield with Rovers making it difficult for themselves in this one as Billy Leishman was ordered off due to his uncompromising play and a double booking. McConville and McLean were ever presents in the team at this Hogmanay match.

On the Monday, Stranraer were first foots and the Stranraer goalkeeper must have been fair sick of Franchetti who had another double in Rovers' 4-0 victory. The following Saturday saw Highland League Buckie Thistle come to Coatbridge complete with their Celtic strips of green and white hoops. All at Cliftonhill were wondering how they were going to manage to get to Buckie for the replay when Jim McCabe on his debut scored with only four minutes left, much to the relief of the Coatbridge contingent. Another late goal with two minutes to go this time came through at Falkirk with East Stirlingshire winning 1-0.

Greyhound racing commenced at Cliftonhill on Friday, 27th January at 7.30 p.m., which made a change from the speedway. This was for smaller crowds and a very different clientele. The trip down to Berwick saw a 3-3 draw, made all the more worthy when Rovers had to fight back from a 2-0 deficit at half time, but also had Dunky Shields ordered to the Pavilion. The very next day Rovers' Scottish Cup Fourth Round match was re-scheduled for Cliftonhill against table-topping Morton who had no game the previous day. Before the match Ray Franchetti was presented with his case of J. & B. whisky following his earlier hat-trick against Stranraer and three thousand five hundred fans paid £1,600 to witness a hard fought match which Rovers lost by a single goal scored from a free kick by the dead ball maestro himself, Andy Ritchie. Due to the continuing bad weather, there was no further football for three weeks but when football restarted Cowdenbeath were the visitors and a hard fought match ended up in Rovers' favour by 4-3. Tom Sermanni played his last match for Rovers in this game, being transferred to Blackpool for £15,000.

The following week at Cowdenbeath there was a very bright sun and Rovers lost the toss to kick into this obstacle. Cowdenbeath went into an early 2-0 lead and Rovers were granted a penalty and it was hoped that this would be the beginning of a fight back. Unfortunately Franchetti blasted the ball over the goal and the chance was missed. This proved disastrous as the Fifers went from strength to strength to run up a mammoth 7-1 score. Goalkeeper Gallacher who had a nightmare match was freed and went to play in Scandinavia.

At Brechin the following week a Donny McLean goal was sufficient to give the points to the Coatbridge team and he also scored Rovers' goal in the 2-1 home defeat by Raith Rovers. The visit to Hampden saw Thomson save a penalty and McLean score Rovers' goal in the 1-1 draw. Franchetti scored another two goals against Berwick in the 3-3 draw which saw Bruce Clellend score his first goal for the Club. Clyde won 4-0 at Shawfield and Raith Rovers 2-0 in Fife before a third away match claimed the third straight defeat for Rovers, this time at the hands of East Stirlingshire by 2-1.

After the three away matches, there were four home matches which started off with a no-scoring draw against Forfar and Queen's Park winning 4-3 at Coatbridge with all Rovers' goals being scored by Ray Franchetti. Rovers cause was not helped in this match by Davie Main scoring an own goal under unfortunate circumstances. Dunfermline won 1-0 in a match which saw Jim Orr and Tony Coyle play trials and the last home match found Rovers winning 2-0 against Stenhousemuir. The final game of the season was an away match at Brockville which Rovers won surprisingly easily by 2-1. Rovers had Ian Livingstone in goal on trial and McLean and Laughlin goals in the second half overcame a Falkirk half-time lead.

Rovers' record was worse than the previous season having fallen down to eighth position with only forty points gained which was thirteen less than promoted pair Clyde and Raith Rovers, whilst Brechin were again bottom of the pile with twenty points. During the close season it was disclosed that there would be a new policy for disciplinary measures based on a penalty points system.

Season 1978/79

Two English touring sides were fixed up for pre-season Friendlies and on Saturday 5th August Bradford City, who had finished third bottom in the Third Division showed Rovers a clean pair of heels winning 3-1 with Rovers goal coming from Franchetti via the penalty spot. Non-league Barrow were less fortunate the following day when, with a two o'clock start, Rovers were in the mood early and took a quick 3-1 lead to finish up winners by 4-1. Bruce Clelland playing at centre was a revelation and he scored two goals, one from a penalty.

The first serious game of the season came on the 12th August in a League match through at Methil against East Fife and a goal in each half by Clelland was sufficient for Rovers to win 2-0 the 'Brig' team being Orr, Muldoon, Main, Franchetti, Shields, Leishman, Allan, Hill, Clelland, McLean, Hart (McKee). The League Cup match on the following Wednesday saw the first of the home and away matches against Rangers and the same day Donny McLean taking his leave to go to Berwick Rangers for a fee of £5,000. Rovers were 2-0 down at half time but Clelland had three opportunities in the last five minutes in the first half to put Rovers into the lead but it was not to be and Rangers eventually ran out winners by 3-0. Back in the League on the Saturday, Falkirk were held to a 1-1 draw at Coatbridge thanks to a second half Clelland goal but in a roughhouse of a match, referee Smith ordered Shields and Clelland for early baths and also booked Muldoon.

On the following Wednesday, Cliftonhill had six and a half thousand fans in to see the mighty Rangers in the second leg of the Cup tie which eventually they won by 1-0. Alex McDonald was ordered off for a dreadful tackle on Muldoon but Rangers were through by 4-0 to the next round. Rovers introduced Jim McGregor from East Stirling at left back for this match and he had a steadying influence at the back. Three away matches then took place, the first being a 3-1 defeat in a League match at Stranraer and then a Friendly was fixed up against St. Johnstone at Perth which finished 4-4. The third match ended with Dunfermline winning 2-1 in the Second Division.

Director Sam Rogers died and the teams wore black armbands for the home match against Meadowbank which resulted in a third league defeat in a row by 2-1. Dennis McLeod from Sunderland made his debut in this match at full-back. Fortunes were reversed the following week with Forfar at Coatbridge and Rovers winning by 3-0. Berwick won 2-0 in England with Rovers hampered by Shields and Leishman both ordered off and Alloa won 2-1 at Coatbridge. East Stirlingshire saw the introduction of goalkeeper Ian Livingstone and with Leishman, Franchetti and Shields added to the defence, these alterations helped the leaky defence with the result ending up 3-3.

There was a bombshell for the support when they arrived at Hampden the following week when the news was released that top scorer Bruce Clelland had been hospitalised with a suspected collapsed lung. With young Hart substituting at centre the team were defeated by a comprehensive Spiders' performance at 2-0. A

Season 1978 Goal at Stair Park, Stranraer.

Billy Leishman double against Brechin City at Cliftonhill found Rovers winners by 3-2 with a team that showed eight positional changes. At Cowdenbeath even with a trialist at the back the Fifers were easy winners by 4-1 although goalkeeper Balavage had a fine game. Big Dunky Shields was fielded at centre forward in another all-change eleven for the visit by Stenhousemuir but a solitary goal was enough to take the points back to Larbert.

At Falkirk the game was lost in the first half and a fight back in the second period only just failed to take a share of the points in a 2-1 defeat. Hart was re-introduced at centre forward with Rovers still having difficulty in satisfactorily finding a replacement for Clelland but the youngster scored a fine double in the 2-1 victory over Stranraer. Seven weeks after his going into hospital, Bruce Clelland reappeared in the number nine jersey at Meadowbank Stadium to resume his career which a few weeks earlier had seemed to be at an end. He did not score but played himself in well in the all-change forward line where Davie Main made a welcome reappearance after injury in the number eleven jersey.

With an early kick-off, as Alloa did not have fixed floodlights, Rovers moved into an early lead through Main and, in an exhilarating display of attacking football, ran out convincing winners by 6-2 producing their best scoring performance since a similar score in 1974 against East Stirlingshire. Floodlighting again played a major part in the next game at Brechin when with Rovers losing 1-0 and only five minutes to go the lighting system failed. It took fifteen minutes to rectify the problem and the game resumed with Rovers catching City cold and Clelland equalised with a last minute penalty. The following mid-week a Lanarkshire Cup Semi-final tie was fixed for Broomfield allowing Airdrieonians to use this match to take up the one match suspension of one of their players. As a tactical measure it turned out to be a flop for the Waysiders, with Rovers leading by a Clelland goal and also having had a Laughlin goal disallowed, gave away a penalty in the last minute when goalkeeper McGarr felled Clelland with a fine uppercut. The game ended with Clelland, who was Rovers' current penalty ace, taking the award himself but shooting past the post. The other semi-final ended up as a 1-1 draw between Motherwell and Hamilton and with no other games being arranged in the tournament, the Committee decided to withhold the trophy for that season.

Director Pat Reilly died on the Friday evening whilst attending the Dog Racing at Cliftonhill and Ian Livingstone was given a free transfer but a fighting 2-2 draw in the Scottish Cup first round at Dunfermline gave Rovers another chance in a Tuesday home replay. Rovers' forward line was changed with only Clelland retaining his position and he scored both Rovers goals in a pulsating 3-2 defeat. At Stenhousemuir on the 23rd December, Rovers lost 3-2 and had Clelland stretchered off.

Bad weather had clamped down by this time and there was no further play that year, nor even in January, with the next match being a visit to Stranraer on the 18th of February, on a Sunday. Muldoon was reintroduced to the back four and newcomer Ian Gillespie introduced to the forward line in an otherwise unchanged team. A Hugh Hill goal in the second half was enough to lift the points. Rovers were bottom of the League by dint of their long lie off and had games in hand over all their immediate opponents. During the following week Rovers shed players Jackie McGillvery to New Zealand and Gordon Flavell to Australia and with five positional changes the team lost 3-1 at Cowdenbeath.

The fourth away match running, against East Fife, was very bad tempered and Rovers ran out winners by 2-1 with Muldoon ordered off and five others having their names taken. An unchanged team against Dunfermline saw a late goal by the 'Pars' square the match at 1-1. Director Willie Higgins died during the week and the Club announced that the function suite of the Casanova in central Coatbridge was to be turned into Rovers' Social Club. With Tony Taylor continuing in an unchanged team on the Tuesday night, Cowdenbeath fought out a share of the points in a 1-1 draw.

Long serving players Shields and Muldoon were transferred to Queen of the South, the latter on loan. At Berwick the team, which had played unchanged for three successive matches, was freshened up with a new midfield but these did nothing for morale and Rangers won by a 5-1 margin. On the last day of March, East Fife lost by two Clelland goals to nothing at the 'Brig and the big centre was again on the scoreline the next Tuesday against Meadowbank in another 2-0 victory. This finished a run of seven consecutive scoring matches for Big Bruce in which he scored eight goals.

A home victory, this time by 1-0 with a Hugh Hill goal, was followed with another home result of the same score with Franchetti this time doing the honours over Queen's Park. On the Monday at Forfar, a division of the points was secured by 1-1 and two days later Queen's Park came back to Coatbridge to be hammered 4-0 and Rovers welcomed back Willie Muldoon from Queen of the South.

A most unusual occurrence took place on the 12th of April when the A.G.M. took place — this one covered ELEVEN years, from 1967/68 until 1978/79. This confirmed Tom Fagan as Chairman with sole Director Bobby Flavell. David Forrester as Club Secretary confirmed the Club was £30,053 in debt and trading thanks to a sympathetic bank manager. At the A.G.M. Stephen May was appointed as a Director of the Club and he was delegated the duties of revitalising the commercial side of the Club. He was in the security business and he quickly settled down to the job in hand.

Three forward positional changes were made for the visit to Stenhousemuir and another victory was notched by a 3-2 scoreline. By now Rovers had climbed away from the bottom of the League and for the Berwick Rangers match, which was the first of four home matches on the trot, Hart took Muldoon's place in the forward line. This was unsuccessful and Rovers went down very easily by 2-0. Dunfermline Athletic then lost to a solitary Gillespie goal and, on the Tuesday, Falkirk contested a no-scoring draw. The match aganst Brechin City two days later found Rovers' players struggling for fitness but still fighting out a 2-2 draw.

The season had been extended until the tenth of May due to the earlier close-down caused by the ice and snow conditions in January and February. On the first Sunday in May a 1-1 draw was fought out at Forfar but East Stirlingshire were fortunate on the Tuesday in getting a point in a 1-1 draw, Bruce Clelland missing from the penalty spot with only two minutes to go. The following Thursday saw the last game of the season played at Cliftonhill with Rovers winning 2-1 and Bruce Clelland moving on as one of Ally McLeod's latest signings for Motherwell for a reported £40,000 thus making Clelland Rovers' highest export of all time.

This finished an eight game in thirteen days spell for the Cliftonhill team and only marginally improved their position in the Second Division table by being in seventh place with forty points. Berwick were Champions with fifty-four and Dunfermline accompanied them upstairs with two less. Meadowbank were Wooden Spoonists on twenty-four, four of which had been gained off Albion Rovers. The usual exit of those players found wanting took place and during the close season others were signed on in the hope that they would gel with the more established players to come up with the right blend.

The close season heralded great changes in the board-room with David Forrester firstly being appointed a Director whilst continuing as Club Secretary and Bobby Flavell and a disillusioned Steven May resigning all within the Glasgow Fair holiday period. Local farmer Bobby Cameron was co-opted at the beginning of August with the specific remit of being in charge of the playing surface.

The Lanarkshire Football Association decided in their wisdom that rather than have meaningless mid-season matches, they would run a Mini-Lanarkshire Cup Tournament to be played on successive days just prior to the new season commencing. The venue for the first of these competitions was Fir Park, Motherwell and the Fans were offered the prospect of two semi-final games being played off on the Saturday with the Runners-Up match preceding the Lanarkshire Cup Final on the Sunday.

Season 1979/80
Accordingly, at Fir Park, on the 4th of August, Rovers were drawn against Hamilton Accies but found the going tough and the better prepared First Division team ran out emphatic winners by 2-0. Rovers' team was Balavage, Hay, McGregor, Hill, Leishman, Docherty, Coyle, Meikle, Franchetti, Campbell and Gillespie. The following day Rovers met Motherwell in the play-off for third and fourth place, and, in a poor match Motherwell won by 3-2. Airdrieonians deservedly won the tournament by defeating Hamilton in the Final.

The League programme started down at Dumfries against Queen of the South and Rovers were losing 2-0 until late in the game when a Campbell goal made it a grandstand finish but in the end Queens deserved their win. The first round League Cup two-leg opponents this year were East Stirlingshire with the first match at Falkirk. A late Franchetti penalty was enough to share the points with 'Shire at 1-1. Queen's Park came to Coatbridge in the first home match of the season and Rovers won by 3-0 with Rovers playing an unchanged team. With the Second Leg of the Cup tie ending up no scoring, Mr. McFaul decided that extra time was not necessary and ordered penalty kicks to decide the match, despite Rovers' protests that extra time was in the Rule Book. East Stirlingshire won by nine goals to eight with Gerry Laughlin missing from the spot for Rovers.

Next day Rovers appealed to the Scottish League on this irregularity and it was decided that a replay was necessary as extra time was not allowed by the Referee. Before that could happen, however, Rovers went up to Forfar, who were riding on a high, and, with Rovers losing 5-1 just after half-time, Balavage was stretchered off and Davy Main went into goal. The match finished up 6-2 for Forfar. On Monday, the 27th of August, the Second Leg of the Cup tie was replayed against East Stirlingshire and this time Rovers made no mistake by virtually winning the match by half-time scoring 3-1 at that stage and having a Franchetti goal in the second half to make the final score 4-1. On the Wednesday night Rovers travelled into Firhill for the First Leg Second Round Cup match and the Supports' spirits sagged when the 'Jags' went into a 2-0 lead mid-way through the second half. However, Ian Campbell scored two individualistic goals past Thistle's International goalkeeper Alan Rough to square the match at 2-2. All the credit in this match went to Rovers as Balavage once again was taken off after twenty minutes with a broken nose and Davy Main again displayed heroics in goal. On the Saturday the Second Leg match took place at Cliftonhill but despite Rovers being by far the more enterprising team, Thistle won by the only goal of the game scored in the second

ALBION ROVERS SEASON 1979/80

Standing: I. Gillespie, I. Campbell, P. Allan, J. Balavage, D. Hay, W. Leishman, H. Meikle.
Seated: J. Docherty, H. Hill, J. McGregor, W. McKee, J. Loughlin.

half.

Now out of the Cup, Rovers could concentrate on the League and the first match was scheduled the following Wednesday, though at Methill, and Rovers lost this one 1-0 and threw the match away by Ian Campbell missing a penalty. On the Saturday Cowdenbeath were beaten 2-1 when trialist Peter Houston had a fine display and was promptly signed after the match. Alloa Athletic lost at Coatbridge by 2-0 and Rovers won well at Meadowbank by 2-1 before East Stirlingshire got some revenge for their Cup exit at Falkirk by 2-0.

Two home defeats came next with Stranraer winning 3-1 and then Stenhousemuir by 2-1 to be followed by Brechin winning 2-0 on their home ground. With new public address equipment working for the home match against Falkirk, one thousand Fans saw Rovers fight back to share the points and four goals. A 2-0 victory at Montrose was followed by a fighting 2-2 draw at Hampden with George Dickson, formerly of Queen of the South, making his debut as central defender. A 5-0 victory over Forfar at Coatbridge was a fine beginning to November with Campbell boosting his goal tally for the season to eleven with a double.

Jim McGregor, who had joined the Club the previous season from East Stirlingshire and who trained with the players on the following Tuesday, died in his sleep during the night. His funeral service was on the Saturday morning with the Officials, Players and Supporters in attendance before going to Cowdenbeath to play a League match. The players' hearts were not in the game and it was to their credit that a 2-2 result was achieved.

In a Sunday match, Meadowbank were defeated 3-1 and Stenhousemuir were beaten by a similar score through at Larbert with Tony Coyle scoring the first goal in what turned out to be his last match. He was transferred to Stockport County for £25,000. Local boy, David Brand, was signed from Shettleston Juniors as a replacement and he took his place in the team the following week in the Scottish Cup First Round tie at Cowdenbeath. Despite scoring a goal, the young lad could not stimulate his mates enough and the Fifers won by 3-1.

The succeeding week at Brockville the pitch was in a dangerous condition with ice and frost. Despite Rovers' official complaint, Mr. McLeish of Stonehouse decided that the game should proceed. Rovers were two goals down before they knew what had hit them and eventually lost by 4-0. The referee also lost the place at one stage by taking the name of the wrong player for a field misdemeanour. Captain Main had a new full-back partner for the visit by Montrose when Liam Gallacher, formerly of Airdrieonians, lined up and Montrose, who were currently third top of the League were lucky to salvage a point in this one as Leishman uncharacteristically missed a penalty kick.

On New Year's Day Queen's Park came to Coatbridge and fought back to a 2-2 draw and against East Stirlingshire the following Saturday, Franchetti was ordered off. Irrespective of this, Rovers fought back with Campbell scoring in the last minute to square the match at 1-1. At Forfar a 2-2 draw was the result but Rovers lost Harry Meikle with a broken leg.

Cowdenbeath were beaten 1-0 with a first minute Houston goal as revenge for the Cup exit in December and the following Tuesday a Friendly was fixed up against a Celtic XI. With Rovers' team liberally sprinkled with trialists, a Leishman penalty saw the Coatbridge team run out winners by 1-0. The following week Rovers welcomed Jim Orr back to goal after a lay-off due to injury of more than a season and he put up the shutters in the 1-0 home victory over Alloa. For the next match against Brechin City, Ian Browning was signed from Clydebank and the former 'Steedman Babe' scored a hat-trick in the first half to demoralise City with Rovers going on to win by 4-0.

At Falkirk, Gallacher was ordered off and Browning and Main were booked as Rovers lost 1-0. Another away match, this time down at Palmerston, saw a fighting 3-3 draw and for the Tuesday home match against East Stirlingshire a poor defensive display cost Rovers dear and merited a 4-1 defeat. Motherwell were approached for Bruce Clelland on loan as he was currently not appearing in the first team but this was refused. Balavage was brought back to goal, in place of Orr, for the home match against East Fife in which Rovers, showing fine form, won by 5-1, followed by an away draw at Alloa, thanks to an equalising goal in the second half by Ian Browning.

At the 44th A.G.M. on the 20th March the accounts up to the 31st March 1979 showed a loss of £5,857. Tom Fagan was once again confirmed for yet another term as Chairman and his was the unpleasant task to divulge the Club debt had now risen to £35,910. Former Chairman Johnny Lees asked several questions at the meeting but did not receive any answers that were satisfactory to him.

Local lawyer, Jack McGoogan, was appointed to the Board and Rovers immediately turned on the style once more for the visit by Queen of the South. After an uninspiring first half, Rovers went into top gear in the second period and, with Peter Houston leading the way with a hat-trick, won the match by 5-1. Stranraer managed a draw at Coatbridge by 2-2 whilst the next week it took an Archie Rose own goal in the second half to break the deadlock of two stale teams to give Rovers the points. During the week Johnny Lees died quite suddenly.

Stranraer got due revenge at Stair Park on the Wednesday by 2-0 in a match which with only four remaining was Rovers' last reverse of the season. Willie Leishman showed his prowess from free kicks with his ninth goal of the season to set Rovers up for a convincing 4-1 victory at Montrose. The following Tuesday Mike Hill, the young provisionally signed goalkeeper, was given a run in goal and the lad acquitted himself well in a 1-1 draw. Another hat-trick by Houston, two of them coming within a minute, put Rovers well on the way to a 4-0 victory at home against East Fife with all the goals coming in the second half. In the last match of the season, Houston again saved Rovers' bacon with an equalising goal in the second half in a 1-1 draw with Rovers taking the opportunity to try out two new full-backs.

So finished the most successful season for years with the final placing being fourth with forty-four points from thirty-nine games. Falkirk won the Championship with fifty points, one more than fellow townies East Stirlingshire and Alloa were bottom on twenty-nine points.

The Social Club was opened in the downstairs function suite of the Casanova and this proved initially to be a money-spinner for the Club. Rovers' Support now looked confidently to the coming season in the knowledge that at last after many years there looked as though there were glimmers of a really worthwhile team capable of making a serious attempt for promotion and an end to the journeys to the far flung outposts of the Scottish League.

Season 1980/81
The Lanarkshire Cup Tournament was put into second place with Rovers competing this year in the Dryburgh Cup as a reward for being the highest goal scorers in the Second Division the previous season. Rovers drew Morton and the

First Round match took place on the 26th July when most folk were still on their Summer Holidays. The Premier League team, under the control of Benny Rooney immediately showed their class and moved into a 3-0 lead and despite a better show in the second half by Rovers the score ended 4-2 in favour of the home team. Thus ended Rovers' brief flurry in this Sponsored Cup represented by Balavage, Martin, Hamill, Meikle, Leishman, Main, Gillespie, Campbell, Franchetti, Houston and Brand. The following Tuesday, a Friendly against West Bromwich Albion was used as a warm-up for the Lanarkshire Cup matches and Rovers took the opportunity of giving their pool of players some needed match practice in the 3-2 defeat.

For the double-header tournament the venue this year was Douglas Park, Hamilton, for the County trophy in its 100th year of existence and Motherwell were Rovers' drawn opponents. The First Division side proved too strong for the Coatbridge team, who were never really in the hunt, and the 'Steelmen' won 4-1. The following day, Rovers were involved in the play-off situation once again this time against hosts Hamilton Accies who were out to prove that they were not the worst team in the County and Rovers were eaten up by a 5-2 score. This year Motherwell went on to defeat Airdrie in the Final.

The League campaign opened up with two away matches, the first being at Forfar where a Franchetti penalty in the second half shared the points at 1-1. This match was Billy Leishman's last game as he was transferred for £10,000 to fellow Second Division Dunfermline Athletic. At Stenhousemuir a fifth defeat out of six outings made Rovers' faithful wring their hands in despair at the inept display by the players who were showing none of their flair of the previous season. The first home League match, and only the second match played at Cliftonhill in seven games, was held on Sunday 24th August. This found Rovers in better form and, despite being one down at half time, Meadowbank were beaten by a strong second half performance with Rovers running out winners at 3-1.

Bells League Cup paired Rovers with St. Mirren and on the Tuesday, the Paisley team came to Coatbridge. In front of fifteen hundred fans, Rovers raised their game and took a deserved first-half lead. However, the superiority of technique and fitness in the second half saw the Saints coming back to win 2-1. The second leg of this match was at Love Street and, despite the inclusion of Alistair McPherson from Queen's Park in the defence, Saints were not to be denied on their own patch and they ran out winners by 5-0.

Back in the League Montrose were beaten 1-0 and in the end it didn't matter that Franchetti missed a penalty but Queen of the South were convincing winners at 4-0 at Coatbridge the following Thursday.

Two goals in the first half saw Rovers win at home against Cowdenbeath, with Balavage back in goal putting up the shutters on the Fife forwards. The next match was a 1-1 draw against East Fife at Methil. Rovers lost 3-2 against Brechin City at home and also by 1-0 at Alloa at September weekend. In mid-week Rovers had a fighting 1-1 draw at Shawfield in torrential rain but on the Saturday Arbroath hit Rovers for six with a fine attacking performance and all the Coatbridge side could muster was a solitary Mulvaney goal.

Only Balavage and Meikle kept their places for the long trip down to Stranraer but the mercurial Rovers came up trumps in this one winning by 4-1. Queen's Park fought out a share of four goals at Coatbridge and Cowdenbeath won comfortably enough by 2-1 through in Fife. A Franchetti penalty was enough to clinch a 2-1 victory at Montrose and two draws followed, starting with East Fife at home with no scoring and at Brechin with a score of 2-2.

Two home games were then played which just about summed up Rovers' season. League leaders Alloa came to Coatbridge looking for two points and were out-played and out-gunned by a fast moving Rovers' combine who won 3-1 whereas the following week Stranraer who were bottom of the League found Rovers on a day when they could do nothing right and the Stair Park team won by 3-1 leaving Rovers' fans champing at the bit.

A couple of aways saw Rovers draw 2-2 at Arbroath in a match where referee Tom Muirhead was injured in the first half and had to be replaced, whilst at Hampden Queen's Park won 2-0.

The New Year's Day match at Coatbridge found two new players being fielded and George Mackie from Partick Thistle had a fine game in the 2-1 win. Ex-Dundee forward Ian McDougall came on as a substitute and it was clear that these two experienced players could play a major part in Rovers' revival. A sharing of six goals against Clyde was a good preview for the Cup tie the following Monday against Arbroath making the third home game in a row. Ian Campbell scored a late goal to give Rovers another bite at the cherry through in Angus but on the Wednesday night, in atrocious conditions, a solitary goal was enough to put the Red Lichties through to the next round.

Clydebank, who were having goalkeeping difficulties, signed Mike Hill on loan whilst Forfar came to Coatbridge and won 4-2. Another defeat at Hampden by 3-1 was the last straw for Sam Goodwin and Martin Ferguson and both resigned from their coaching posts with Rovers committed to making a quick appointment to look after the on-field affairs. A Friendly match was arranged against a Rangers XI on the following Tuesday which ended up in an 8-2 romp for the Ibrox team.

Immediately following this match Harry Hood, the former Celtic and Clyde player, was appointed as Manager and former Celtic goalkeeper Evan Williams followed a week later as his assistant. Their first game in charge was on St. Valentine's Day and with referee Bob Valentine in the middle, all ended happily ever-after for Rovers with a 3-2 victory against East Fife. The other members of the 'Old Firm' provided an eleven on the next Tuesday but Rovers went down in this one 2-0. Manager Hood was using these games to see as many of the playing staff as possible and also to introduce players of his own choice.

A long trip to Brechin found City winning 2-1, despite Rovers being in the lead at half time and for their away match against Stenhousemuir, Jimmy Murray from Vale of Leven and Stuart Burgess were introduced to the defence which looked more solid than in recent times allowing Rovers to win by 3-0. Martin took Murray's place at Coatbridge against Arbroath but this seemed to disorganise the defence as Arbroath had only their third victory of the season by 4-2. Man of many clubs, Jim Dempsey, back from North America, gave the defence some stability and two 1-0 victories were chalked up, first of all at Alloa and then against the visiting Queen of the South. For the home match against Stranraer, Rovers had their best score of the season winning by 5-0. The only change in four games was Allan for Murray but Clyde finished Rovers' winning sequence by scoring four goals without reply at Shawfield.

The A.G.M. on the 5th of March saw the Board declare a profit of £37,917 and remain invested in the names of Messrs. Fagan, Forrester, Cameron and McGoogan. Thus the Club debt was reduced to £2,007.

Another home defeat by Cowdenbeath at 2-0 was followed by an easy defeat at Meadowbank by 2-1 which was annoying as Rovers were leading 1-0 at half time. Manager Hood was shedding players and Higgins, Docherty and Martin, were all freed. Two home matches had mixed fortunes with Rovers first of all winning 3-2 against Forfar but losing 2-0 against Stenhousemuir. McPherson and Franchetti then accepted frees to be followed sensationally by the resignations of Messrs. Hood and Williams themselves after a disagreement with the Board on policy.

With Rovers in turmoil both on and off the field, the last two matches were away from home and, although a fighting point was gained at Montrose at 1-1, Queen of the South proved to be too strong for the dispirited Rovers and won by a 3-0 margin. This game had an added bite to it that Queens' required to win to clinch promotion and hope that Cowdenbeath would lose or draw. As it turned out Cowdenbeath defeated themselves and Queens were promoted as runners up to the other Queen's from Hampden.

Rovers had suffered a serious slump of form and the fourth place in the previous season had become a twelfth position with only thirty-four points scored. It was no consolation that Stranraer only achieved twenty-two. There was a large clear-out of players but on looking back the Managerial difficulties obviously did nothing for the players cohesion or aspirations. Former Manager, Sam Goodwin, was appointed to the Board to look after the commercial interests on the 7th of May.

Season 1981/82
Prior to the season opening former English International centre forward of Hibs, Arsenal, Notts Forest, Juventus, etc., Joe Baker, was appointed as Coach and it was straight into the Lanarkshire Cup Tournament. Due to injuries and holidays, Rovers' pool was very limited and Ian Gillespie was fielded as substitute coming virtually straight off the plane from holiday. The competition this year took place at Broomfield and Rovers opened up the tournament by playing Hamilton Accies. It was an interesting first match of the season with Rovers giving their First Division opponents the run-around. Rovers eventually ran out winners by 3-1 qualifying to meet Motherwell in the Final.

After First Division Hamilton defeated Premier Division Airdrie in the play-off for third and fourth place, Rovers and Motherwell took the field for the Final. It was Rovers who took the play to the First Division team and were unlucky to be drawing 1-1 at half time. Try as they might, Rovers couldn't break the deadlock in the regulation ninety minutes and the tie went into extra time, much to the apprehension of leg-weary Rovers players. With full-time Motherwell mounting ever-increasing attacks on Rovers' goal, the Coatbridge boys found previously untapped reservoirs of energy and spirit as the play ended in the Motherwell penalty area and with no further scoring. As a decision had to be reached it was penalty play-off time and John Balavage now came into his own becoming Rovers' hero by saving three of the Motherwell club's attempts from the spot.

Captain Davy Main led his exhausted, but elated, players for the triumphant handing over of the Trophy, making a wee bit of history at the same time. Davy is only one of six Albion Rovers players to have been in two successful Lanarkshire Cup winning teams. Rovers' team was — Balavage, Murray, Main, Hamill, Burgess, Allan, Hill, McDonagh, Campbell, Houston and Hannigan, with substitutes Gormley and Gillespie.

Joe Baker had got off to a fine start and all Coatbridge now sat back to await the development of the team into promotion aspirants but little were we to know that the winning of the Cup virtually finished Rovers' season there and then with the

BALLBOYS 1981

Standing: Stephen Lindsay, James Dick, Desmond Crawford.
Kneeling: Alan McAlinden, Malcolm Marwick.

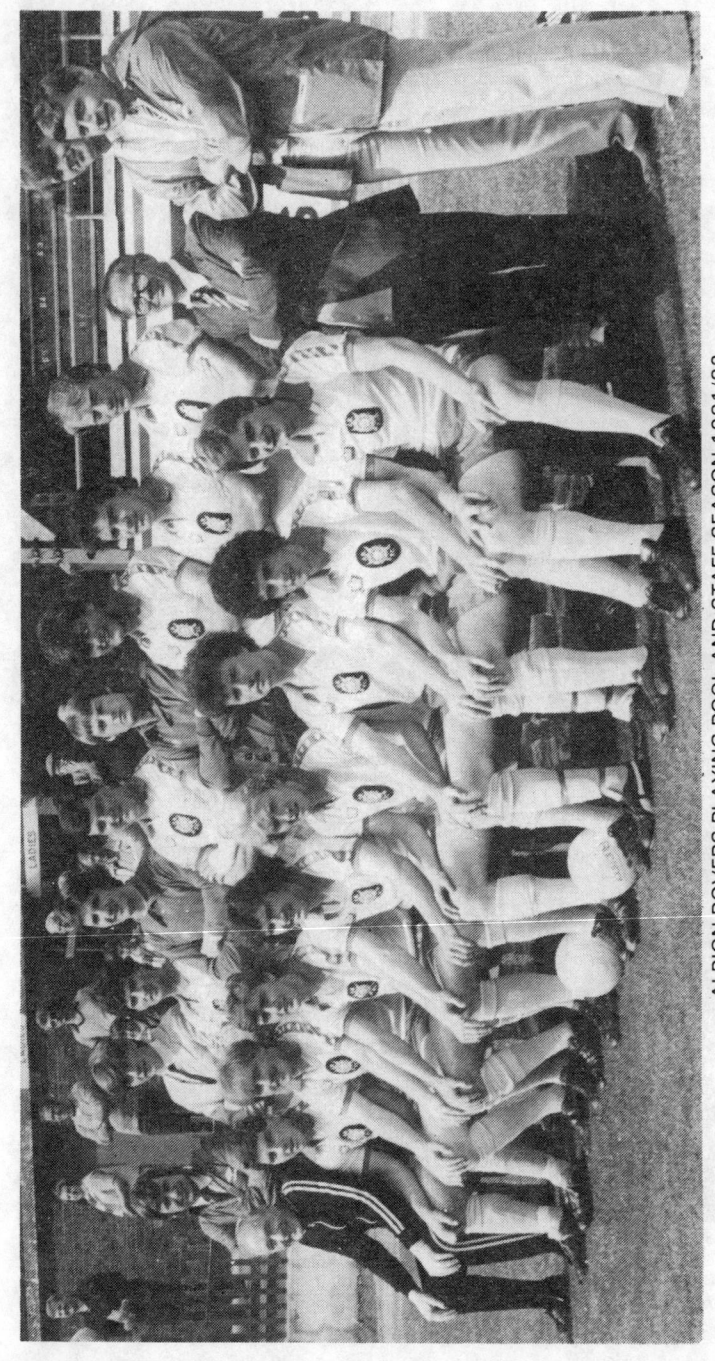

ALBION ROVERS PLAYING POOL AND STAFF SEASON 1981/82

Back Row: R. Ramsay (Asst. Coach), Sandy Ross, Jim Gormley, John Balavage, Peter Hamill, Alastair Purdie, Stewart Burgess.
Jim McDonagh, Ian Campbell, Jimmy Lawson (Groundsman), Colin McQueen, Joe Baker (Coach).
Front Row: Bob Muir (Physiotherapist), Tommy Murray, Peter Houston, Hugh Hill, Davie Main (Captain), Ian Gillespie, Scott Hannigan, Peter Allan and David Lapsley.

players subsequently sitting back expecting the results to come without due effort.

The League Cup campaign started on the 8th August at the Meadowbank Stadium when Thistle fought out a 2-2 draw. In this match Rovers played in their alternative strip of the Argentinian National colours of blue and white stripes with black pants. It is fair also to say that there the similarity ended and Rovers' play was less than pleasing. The first home game was a 1-1 draw against East Fife but against Stenhusemuir on the Saturday the Coatbridge fans found Rovers in County Cup form brushing aside the opposition by 5-2. Another bit of history was made in this match with Stuart Burgess scoring a hat-trick from his central defence position. The last time this was done was in 1894 when Davie Cross did a similar task from full back against Arthurlie.

However, the slump properly set in at Stranraer with the home team winning 2-0 and this was followed by a 4-0 drubbing at Arbroath with goalkeeper Purdie having an unhappy baptism and a weak defence giving him little cover. Ian Campbell was transferred to Montrose for £10,000 following this match and, with Balavage back in goal, Rovers overcame Cowdenbeath at Coatbridge by 2-0 on the start of the League programme but suffered the loss of Sandy Ross who required a cartilage operation. The trip to Monrose found Ian Campbell and his new mates too strong for Rovers by 4-2 and their bad luck continued with Peter Hamill then off with a broken bone in his foot. Back at Meadowbank, Rovers were 2-0 up and sitting in clover when the defence stopped contesting for the ball and Thistle banged in three goals to win by 3-2.

New signing Stevie Evans from Clyde made his debut at home against Stranraer and the new boy scored the first goal in a 4-0 victory which could have been greater if Hugh Hill had not missed a penalty in the first half. Rovers were in the wars the following Tuesday at Stenhousemuir when goalkeeper Purdie who had put up the shutters the previous Saturday had to be taken off requiring twelve stitches in a leg wound and expert emergency 'keeper Davie Main again took his place in goal. Rovers were further handicapped later on when Brian Gibson strained a ham string and even with both substitutes on Rovers were toiling. The 'Warriors', sensing a victory, were all over them but the game ended all square at 2-2.

Hugh Hill was then transferred to Arbroath for £7,000 and the sadly depleted Rovers' team lost not unexpectedly to East Fife by 3-0. Back home the following Wednesday Arbroath were defeated by two Evans' goals to nil and at Stirling, on September weekend Saturday, Rovers were confident of an away win as Stirling Albion had not won a match since January. Even with newly signed Gerry Collins from St. Roch's at inside right following his successful trial the previous week, Rovers could only lose by a penalty in the second half. During September Rovers had been advised by the S.F.A. that the signing of Jim McDonagh had been illegal and the lad reverted back to Livingstone United with Rovers also fined £100. This was disappointing as James had turned in ten consecutive performances before being left on the side-lines pending the decision of the Authorities. Rovers' fans were further disappointed when the next week the youngster signed for Airdrieonians.

Rovers now without Campbell, Hill and McDonagh, who were with other clubs and Ross and Hamill injured, fielded several trialists with a view to increasing the player pool but Berwick Rangers won virtually in the first half against a very disjointed Rovers' team by a 3-1 scoreline with a third defeat in a row coming at Brechin. Playing at the back was big Duncan Shields signed from Baillieston and the former skipper scored the first goal for Rovers but the home team ran out winners by 3-2. Forfar stole a point at Cliftonhill in a 3-3 match and Rovers visited Shawfield to take on top of the League Clyde who were unbeaten this season and got off to the best possible starts with two cracking goals in the first twenty minutes. Man of the match in this game was Gerry Collins who took up a central defending position when Shields had to go off early in the first half and Balavage kept his end up by saving a penalty. However, Clyde eventually did score with all their pressure and the last quarter of an hour was hectic with Rovers succeeding in winning at Shawfield for the first time since 1946. This match was an oasis in the desert of defeats and there were to be four other reverses immediately following, starting at home against Alloa by 5-1 and then Montrose by 2-0. Purdie was again given a chance in goal against Cowdenbeath through in Fife but the Fifers won 2-0 and it was back to Balavage for the next match against Stenhousemuir when Rovers fielded eleven positional changes. This drastic action had no possible benefit either for team work or result with the 'Muir winning very easily by 4-1. This ended a disastrous spell of nine matches with only three points scored out of the eighteen on offer.

With the news that Murray and Craig had been suspended for training misdemeanours, Gormley was freed and Burgess was stuck up the forward line. But it was left to top scorer Steve Evans to score his tenth goal of the season in the 1-0 victory. Burgess got on the scoreline the next week at Berwick but Rangers planted six behind Balavage in the match.

Derek Whiteford was engaged as Manager and the former Airdrieonians' player travelled with the team through to Arbroath to see a dispirited and disjointed team lose 4-0, in one of only four matches played in Scotland due to weather conditions. Joe Baker was kept on as Coach and it was left to the new duo to pick up the pieces as Rovers slumped to the lower reaches of the Second Division.

On the 2nd of January the long visit to Stranraer found this one of the very few games in British football to be played and Peter Houston scoring a fine goal in the first half giving new Manager Whiteford hope for the future. Rovers' task was made all the more difficult when Tom Murray was sent off after an hour and the players had to buckle down to ensure a win at full time by 1-0. Due to very bad weather conditions, there was no further matches until the 23rd January when Brechin City brushed Rovers' challenge aside to win 2-1 and then went on to travel to a Cup match against Inverness Caley the following day to win by 3-1.

The Second Preliminary round Cup tie hit Cliftonhill on the 20th January when Clachnacudden came to Coatbridge and fourteen hundred fans saw Rovers go into a first half lead through Peter Houston. This was equalised in the second half and, with the match looking like a replay in midweek at Inverness, Rovers got a winner with only three minutes to go. The prize for the Second Round contestants was a 'go' at Rangers at Ibrox in the Third Round. Eight thousand fans found Rovers outclassed but not outplayed. Although Rangers had a 3-0 lead at half time, Rovers were much better than that score would imply and despite the eventual 6-2 score Rovers gave evidence once again of being able to put on the style against a better class of opposition.

Come the Wednesday Clyde took revenge for their earlier defeat at Shawfield when Pat Nevin scored the only goal of the match in the second half in which Duncan Murray signed from Stonehouse Violet took his place in the centre of the defence. He was joined there in the following match at Alloa with the return of Billy Leishman from Dunfermline but this match also ended up a one goal defeat and youngster Murray started his senior career by being booked in both matches.

At Cowdenbeath on the Saturday Rovers won 3-2 with big men Burgess and Shields in the forward line and the former scored a couple and Houston the winner in this match where Rovers came back from being behind at half time. The other big man Shields scored Rovers' first goal in the home match against Montrose which saw the Angus team come back from Rovers leading at half time to a 2-2 result. Joe Baker left the Club during the week and Manager Whiteford was left to his own devices.

Captain Collins and his merry men won convincingly by 2-0 at Meadowbank but were never in the hunt at Berwick who ran out winners by 4-1. March was destined to be Rovers' best month as far as results were concerned, for following the Berwick disaster, the Wednesday match saw East Fife lose 1-0 at Coatbridge. On the Saturday Alloa drew 1-1 then another fine away victory at 4-1 over Stranraer found rampant Rovers beating Meadowbank clearly by 2-0 on the last day of the month.

The good form continued into April with Stirling losing 1-0 at Coatbridge but then five defeats in a row ensured Rovers would finish in the bottom area of the League. Rovers had no settled formation and started off their defeats by 4-1 up in Forfar in midweek with Brechin again winning 2-1 at Coatbridge on the Saturday. Another 2-0 defeat at Arbroath was followed on the next Wednesday by Forfar scoring three without reply, at Station Park. The run of defeats finished with Champions Clyde winning 3-2 at Coatbridge although former Clyde player Stevie Evans scored a couple against his old team.

Through at Methil, East Fife were held to a 1-1 draw thanks to a Hailey own goal, but the man of the match here was East Fife's Gordon Durie, with this youngster being a constant thorn in Rovers' flesh. The last match of the season

ALBION ROVERS CENTENARY GROUP 1982

Standing: Billy McNeil, Convener Burns Strathclyde Regional Council, Manager Derek Whiteford, Councillor John Dillon.
Seated: Tom Fagan and Provost Tom Clarke.

was at home against Stenhousemuir with trialist Sinnot of Armadale Thistle being the outstanding player afield and scoring Rovers' first goal in the 2-0 victory.

A disappointing season where the spectators' early expectations had never been realised meant Rovers climbed one place in the League but still finishing in a disappointing eleventh position with thirty-one points which was three less than the previous season. Stranraer were eleven points beneath them in bottom slot with Champions Clyde scoring fifty-nine points and Alloa going up on goal difference from Arbroath on fifty points.

Friday 21st May found Monklands District Council honouring the Club with a Civic Reception to commemorate the coming centenary in October of the year. This was held in the Municipal Buildings when members of the management, players and friends were entertained by Provost Tom Clarke, former player John Dillon now convener of Leisure and Recreational Services, District Councillors and Officials. A fine evening was held with main guests being Councillor Burns, Convener of Strathclyde Regional Council and Celtic Manager Billy McNeil.

Most of the players were retained and Manager Whiteford and his Assistant Bobby Ramsay set about putting them into the right frame of mind for the Centenary Season ahead. Rovers' fans hoped that a special effort would be produced by all concerned in this special year but had little to base their hopes on other than sheer speculation.

On the 27th of July the A.G.M. again confirmed Chairman Fagan for yet another year in the Chair with his co-Directors being David Forrester, Bobby Cameron, Jack McGoogan and Sam Goodwin. However, it had been a hard year and there was a loss of £5,506 to be explained away. Bobby Cameron the Farmer was to emigrate with his family to America within a few weeks and Rovers debt now stood at £3,499.

MONKLANDS DISTRICT COUNCIL

RECEPTION and DINNER
to mark THE CENTENARY OF
ALBION ROVERS FOOTBALL CLUB LTD.
(1882 — 1982)

MENU

Cream of Vegetable Soup
with Celery

or

Sea Food Cocktail

* * *

Salmon Mayonnaise

* * *

Entrecote Steak Chasseur
Brocolli Spears
Sauté Potatoes

* * *

Gateau and Fresh Cream

* * *

Cheese and Biscuits

* * *

Coffee

1982 Civic Reception Programme.

ALBION ROVERS CENTENERY PRESENTATION

Provost Clarke presents Tom Fagan with crystal bowl.

CHAPTER TWELVE

THE SECOND CENTURY

Season 1982/83 (Centenary Season)
The now customary mini-tournament for the Lanarkshire Cup took place, this time at Cliftonhill. Rovers were down to play Motherwell in the first match and being Cup holders and Hosts of the Competition, Rovers hoped to be the first host team to win the Trophy. A competent Motherwell team soon showed that this was not possible and Rovers were out virtually before the competition started by 2-0. Rovers' team was Balavage, Allan, Main, Leishman, Burgess, McGrath, Gibson, Collins, Houston, Evans and Conn. The following day Rovers met Airdrieonians in the play-off for the third and fourth positions and, in a match where the Diamonds were never in difficulty, Rovers ended up in last place losing 3-2. Motherwell ran out winners beating Hamilton in the Final.

With Collins unavailable for the opening League Cup match against Stranraer at Coatbridge, Billy Leishman donned the Captaincy and the Cup campaign started with a 2-2 draw. But at Meadowbank the following Wednesday the 'Jags' won 3-2. Collins returned for the home match against Stenhousemuir which ended up no scoring and the pathetic League Cup challenge was finished with two defeats both by 2-1, firstly at Cowdenbeath and then at home against Montrose. The latter was all the more depressing as Montrose played for virtually an hour with only ten men.

The Division Two campaign opened at Arbroath with the home team winning 3-1 and the experiment of Burgess in the forward line with Collins falling back turned out to be a flop. But the next Wednesday a re-arrangement of the forward ranks provided a 3-0 home victory against Stirling Albion. On the Saturday the match against East Fife looked like neither team would ever score with Rovers being the main culprits. Evans missed a penalty after half an hour and the only goal of the match was scored by Billy Leishman in the eighty-third minute when, after great frustration during the whole game, he decided to show the forwards how to do it with great success.

For the third consecutive match Rovers were unchanged for the visit to Stenhousemuir but the inconsistency of form showed itself once more and the 'Warriors' won by a first half goal to nothing, whilst at Montrose Rovers were unlucky to be held to a 3-3 draw. The only change made for the home match against Queen of the South was Balavage replacing Purdie in goal and this was a better performance, with Rovers winning 3-1. However, the same personnel lost at home by 2-0 to put the Manager back to the drawing board following this inept display.

At Firs Park, East Stirlingshire were held to a 1-1 draw, thanks to a Gibson penalty in the second half. Alec Livingstone signed from West Ham United took up the number eleven jersey for the home match against Brechin City which ended up no scoring. This match was the nearest to the Centenary date and prior to the match starting the Supporters' Club President, Helena Quinn, presented Chairman Fagan with a small gift to commemorate the fact. For the game at Meadowbank, Balavage returned in goal but, with Rovers winning 2-1 at half time, he remained in the Pavilion with Davie Main once more taking up the role of temporary goalkeeper. Despite a tremendous display by the rear guard, Thistle won in the end by 4-3.

Balavage didn't make the next match and Purdie was recalled at Berwick. He had no answer to the sharp-shooting Rangers' forwards who scored four goals without reply in a match where Captain Collins was ordered off. With news that Sandy Ross, Ferry and McGrath had all been freed, two home defeats were experienced, the first by Forfar at 1-0 and the second by 3-2 against Stranraer. In the last named match Conn missed a penalty which would have squared matters and this was all the more disappointing as he had been made Captain for this game.

The team was playing with little flair or enthusiasm but a fighting 2-2 draw at Stirling was followed by a 2-1 home victory over Montrose. December was destined to be memorable and as a prelude to the month, Queen of the South won handsomely by 5-0 at Palmerston at the end of November with Stevie Evans missing his first game of the season due to his marriage. Derek Whiteford and Bobby Ramsay were dismissed and Martin Ferguson appointed Manager. Martin, who had been Sam Goodwin's assistant, had recently been managing East Stirlingshire and it was against the Falkirk team that Rovers played their next match winning 3-1. Ferguson's first job was transferring Peter Houston to Falkirk and signing Bobby Gray from Stirling Albion. The new man took his place in midfield for the visit to Methil but East Fife were too strong, winning in the end by 4-3.

As a build-up to the Scottish Cup, on New Year's Day Stenhousemuir were defeated 2-1 at Coatbridge, whilst on the Monday at Stranraer a 5-1 victory was the satisfactory result. This was particularly important as Stranraer were the opponents the following Saturday at home in a Second Round Scottish Cup tie. In the Cup Rovers, who were always the better team, never looked like scoring and it was a great relief when Stevie Evans counted the only goal of the match in the second half. Ayr United were drawn away from home in the Third Round but before that time there were two League matches against the Angus clubs. The first was at home against Arbroath where, in a gale force wind Rovers, leading 1-0 at half time, succumbed to a superior Arbroath team to lose 3-1. Frank Grant made his debut at full back for the visit to Forfar but the team still went down 2-0.

The Support were not confident of success for the journey down to Ayrshire but were pleasantly surprised at the good form displayed by the team in the first half which ended no scoring. The home fans were by this time after the blood of Manager Willie McLean and their cries intensified when Rovers went two up with two fine opportunist goals by young Livingstone. Ayr knocked one back but the defence held firm and it was then on to a home game by Airdrieonians in two more weeks. Rovers' intervening matches were cancelled due to ground conditions but on the 19th February the Fourth Round match took place when three thousand fans found their day out spoiled by rival, bigoted chanting fans. With the match at no scoring and, after several scuffles on the terracing, a full blown riot took place with stones being hurled and fans spilling on to the pitch in their attempts to get away from the trouble spots. Referee Waddell stopped the match and announcements were made to regain order. However, it was fifteen minutes before the sorry scenes were finished, police moved in and the match restarted. Airdrie caught Rovers cold and scored two goals almost immediately on the restart and this was the half time score. A further goal was scored in the second half but Rovers had never fully recovered from the stoppage in the first half and it was Airdrie who proceeded to the Fifth Round in this their first victory in four outings in the Scottish Cup against Rovers.

For the League match at Brechin, Rovers were not at the races and City won 3-0 but a fighting display gained a 2-1 win at Montrose. Livingstone then emigrated to

Australia and Rovers missed his mobility in the home match against Berwick the following Wednesday. The match was already into injury time when Berwick scored the only goal of the match. Derek Woods was signed on loan from Clyde and the former Queen's Parker scored the first goal at home against Stranraer but again Rovers failed to last the pace and the South of Scotland team won 2-1. At Cowdenbeath, leading by a Bobby Gray goal, again the legs failed with the Fifers equalising in the last minute.

The following Saturday found Rovers having a rare success against Stirling Albion at Stirling winning 2-1, the winner being scored by substitute Dave Main with his first kick of the ball in the second half. Prior to the game the news was released that Annfield was being purchased by Stirling District Council and leased back to the Club, thus relieving them of a tremendous recurring financial problem. High flying Forfar visited Coatbridge the following week and, thanks to a first half Stevie Evans' goal, tasted defeat for the first time in twelve games.

At home against East Fife referee Thow had the fans going with some of his decisions in what turned out to be Davie Main's last match for the Club after six tremendous years of effort, whilst Sammy Conn was ordered off following two bookings. Again Rovers failed in the last minute at Stenhousemuir by the only goal of the match. With provisional signing Tony Gallagher from East Kilbride Thistle in the forward line the following Tuesday, second top Meadowbank were trounced 4-0 with the youngster scoring a fine double in one of the better all-round performances. At Brechin table-topping City learned from Meadowbank's mistakes and won comfortable by 3-0.

The first of three home matches the following Wednesday saw Cowdenbeath beaten 2-0 with Rovers' most recent signing, coloured teenager Victor Kasule coming on as substitute, score Rovers' second goal and show some early signs of undoubted class. Meadowbank pushing for promotion gained revenge and won 3-1 and Arbroath won 2-0 aided by Gray missing a penalty in the second half.

1983 crowds at Cliftonhill for cup tie.

With three games to go Rovers, who had been trying out several trialists in recent weeks, defeated East Stirlingshire 3-1 at Falkirk but lost 2-0 down at Palmerston against Queen of the South. The last game of the season was against Berwick Rangers at home and Rovers fielded new boys Boyle and McGorm and it was the last named who knocked in two goals in the first half against one by Berwick to win the match and promptly be offered signing-on terms.

Another disappointing season thus finished, although Rovers crept up one place in the League but were still tenth with thirty-four points which was exactly twenty behind Meadowbank who at fifty-five were one behind Champions Brechin. Montrose were bottom of the League with twenty-two. Martin Ferguson also submitted his resignation and joined St. Mirren during the close season in a coaching capacity. There was a higher than normal clear out when Billy Wilson was engaged as Manager coming from Kilsyth Rangers, he brought with him brother Jim, who was formerly on Rovers' books in the Sixties, a clutch of new signings from the junior ranks accompanied him together with one or two frees. There had been no agreement among the County teams regarding the Lanarkshire Cup tournament and this was not held as in previous seasons as a pre-season mini-tournament the intention being to play matches when possible during the season.

Season 1983/84
The League Cup campaign reverted to a two-leg arrangement with Queen of the South as opponents. The opening game of the season took place on the 13th August at Coatbridge and Manager Wilson's new signings were all displayed but Captain Collins got off on the wrong foot by being ordered off. This set the seal on capitulation of the points losing four goals without reply, all in the second half. Rovers were represented by Balavage, Rodgers, Deakin, Collins, Burgess, Gray, McCusker, McAteer, Gallagher, Reid and Gray. It was clear that success with Kilsyth Rangers was not any guarantee of success in Senior football and this was underlined when the return match the following Wednesday at Palmerston found the Queens winning by 2-1 on the day and 6-1 on aggregate.

League matches started off also at Cliftonhill with Gerry Collins back after his automatic one match suspension only to be promptly booked again together with three other Rovers' players. Kasule scored Rovers' goal in the second half but Stenhousemuir won easily enough by 2-1. This was Collins' last match being transferred to Ayr United. Two away defeats, firstly by 3-0 at Arbroath and then 3-1 at Stranraer came before the sixth defeat in a row found Montrose winning 2-0 at Coatbridge.

It seemed the only thing Rovers were good at at this stage was having players' names taken and they were leagues ahead of all other teams in Scotland but pointless in league success, being firmly at the foot of the Second Division. Dunfermline Athletic were the first team not to win against Rovers in a fighting 1-1 draw.

It was back to defeats however in the following two games with East Stirlingshire winning 3-2 at Coatbridge and Queen of the South 2-0 at Dumfries. There were grave questions as to the fitness of the Rovers' squad and a series of points were lost due to the team failing to last the pace.

The A.G.M. took place on the 22nd September when David Forrester was returned as retiring Director and Tom Fagan confirmed as Chairman. The Board was made up by Messrs. McGoogan and Goodwin. A loss was declared this time at £1,722 making an overall debit of £5,221.

The first of the lost points was in the home match against Stirling when a goal was conceded in the last ten minutes, the game finishing all square at 1-1. The same at Hampden with Queen's equalising with only eight minutes to go in another 1-1 draw. There was a real nail-biting finish with three goals in the last five minutes when Berwick ran out winners by 4-3 over the Border. A fight back from a half time deficit found Rovers at 1-1 when East Fife scored in the last minute to win 2-1 at Coatbridge and table-topping Forfar Athletic were losing 2-1 when they equalised in the second minute of injury time added on by Referee Hope. The final score here was 2-2. This made Rovers' points tally four out of a possible twenty-two and the Support was trying to stay loyal to the new Manager but finding things very difficult.

Stevie Evans, who had been in dispute with the Club re-signed on the basis that he was hardly likely to attract a signing offer if he was not match fit and he donned the number eleven shirt for the away visit to Cowdenbeath. Lo and behold! this was like a magic wand and Gallagher scored the only goal of the match with a fine header from a grand lob from the right by McQueen. With Rovers thinking of revivals Arbroath were defeated by 3-0 at Coatbridge but it was back to the old losing ways at Montrose the following week when referee Knowles ordered off Deakin for two bookings whilst yellow carding six other Rovers' players with some of his controversial decisions causing much of the trouble on the field. Not surprisingly Montrose won 3-1 whilst Queen's Park the following week came to Coatbridge and won 4-1.

Evans played his last game at Stirling in a very physical match where Rovers had Murray and Green ordered off and three other players booked. Rovers finishing up of course with nine men lost by 3-1. Stevie went to join George Caldwell and Gerry Collins at Ayr.

This was a dreadful prelude to the Scottish Cup match which was difficult enough being an away draw against Inverness Caledonian. The faithful few followed on and in the first half, with Rovers leading by a McGorm goal, it looked only a matter of time before Rovers added to their score but unfortunately with suspensions and injuries Rovers were pushed to field thirteen players and even Manager Wilson donned the track suit as second substitute. Early on McCusker was injured and Dow replaced his Captain whose influence in midfield was missed because Caley came back late in the game to win 2-1 thus making the journey back to Coatbridge very bitter and never-ending.

Back in the League, Queen of the South fought out a 1-1 draw and two Gallagher goals in the second half were enough to gain a point at 2-2 at East Stirlingshire. On the last day of the year, Stranraer were defeated 2-1 at Coatbridge with Tommy McAteer scoring a second half winner. On the Monday, amid torrential rain, the match against Stenhousemuir was started but there was no chance of the game finishing and referee Hope abandoned the match, with the score at 1-1, in the forty-first minute. Rovers played only one other match in January and this was on the 14th of the month through at Methil when they lost by the only goal of the game and young Robert Burns played his first match in goal. Again this was a late goal coming in the eighty-first minute. There was only one other game played in Scotland on the day due mainly to snow and blizzards.

February was a vast improvement with six points out of a possible ten. The improvement started at Stenhousemuir in the replayed match, which had earlier been abandoned, and ended up with the same score as at the abandonment 1-1 and, for the fourth consecutive away match, Dunfermline Athletic were beaten 2-1 with Rovers starting well scoring in the first minute and at one stage leading by

2-0. Murray was again ordered off in this game which saw Robert Burns signed and reserve goalkeeper Russell freed. The following Tuesday, a high scoring draw was fought out at Coatbridge with Berwick Rangers, the game ending 4-4 and Rovers were still in the scoring mood the following Tuesday winning 4-1 at Methil against East Fife.

However, Queen of the South won 4-1 with Rovers throwing away a grand opportunity to go into the lead in a goal-less first half when McGorm missed a penalty just before half time. Two away matches brought two defeats without scoring at Forfar by 1-0 and at Stranraer by 2-0. Rovers found themselves in a bit of a player crisis against Stirling Albion and had to field trialist Jeffries in goal for the match at Coatbridge which was a 4-1 defeat. The following Tuesday Cowdenbeath were beaten at Coatbridge by 2-0.

At Forfar the long trip seemed to be worthwhile, unfortunately pressure told in the end and Rovers' defence buckled to lose 1-0. There was little fight the following Saturday at Coatbridge when Montrose won 4-0, but a good all-round perfromance the following Saturday saw Rovers snatch a 3-2 win over Cowdenbeath.

The following Monday night Rovers went to Douglas Park on Lanarkshire Cup business with Hamilton Accies fielding virtually a second XI, although many of the players had first team experience. When Conn was ordered off for protesting at a penalty award in the first half, that finished any chance Rovers had of doing anything with the match. In fact, Hamilton won by 2-0 both their goals being scored from penalties.

Later in the week there was another bombshell for Rovers' fans, the managing duo of the Wilson brothers resigned leaving Rovers without a Manager for the visit by Queen's Park. It looked as if the fates were on Rovers' side and some of the luck they had had been getting all season found the match ending all square and Queen's missing two penalties.

The unemployed managerial duo of Benny Rooney and Mike Jackson, who had been out of work following their sacking from Greenock Morton the previous April, were fixed up on a temporary basis to assist Rovers and at the same time get themselves back into the swing of things with a Senior club. Jackson had, of course, already had a spell at Coatbridge as Ralph Brand's second-in-command in the Seventies. They looked about for some fresh blood to inject into the team and Bernie Slaven appeared in a number ten shirt for the trip to Berwick Rangers which ended up no scoring. For the home match against Stenhousemuir Gary Dickie was given an airing in the defence. This one also ended up a draw, this time 1-1. Roddy Hutchison, ex-Thistle, Morton, Hibs, Montrose, etc., had also been signed but the 'Warriors' refused to allow him to play.

For the visit to East End Park, Dunfermline Athletic were too strong for an inadequate Rovers' team, which also featured former Player of the Year, Andy Ritchie, as a substitute. When he came on latterly for Jim Deakin in the last few minutes, it was clear that he was not match fit. The following week saw a last home game and another defeat, this time at the hands of East Stirlingshire and Rovers job was made all the more difficult with Duncan Murray being ordered off for a record third time this season. The final match of the season was at Arbroath and this was one which Rovers won thanks to a Ritchie free kick special in the first half. Rovers ended up bottom of the Second Division for only the second time in their history with Forfar winning the title on sixty-three points accompanied upstairs by East Fife on forty-seven points.

In the short time they were at Cliftonhill, the new bosses looked the part and even had the players believing in themselves but it was too much to hope that they would be able to remain at Cliftonhill for long. The inevitable happened and when the Partick Thistle job became vacant, Benny Rooney was successful from the applicants received and he and Mike Jackson took over at Firhill looking to improve the fortunes of the 'Jags'. For their part, Rovers appointed Andy Ritchie as Player/Coach and the big, controversial Bellshill lad, who had in his career been the bane of every manager under whom he had served was, at a stroke now a manager himself. It was to be seen whether he could cope with the proposition but he had served under very experienced mentors in Jock Stein, Ally McLeod, Benny Rooney and Rovers were sure something must have rubbed off. There were few enough free transfers with the majority of players retained but fixed up for the new season were Bernie Slaven, Sandy Ross, back from Junior football and several untried youngsters. John Balavage was in dispute with the Club and Rovers had to look lively to sign a replacement.

Season 1984/85

The Lanarkshire Cup was reinstated as a Mini-Tournament, this year at Fir Park, and Motherwell were Rovers' opponents in the semi-final, The new player/coach kept McCusker as Captain and in a poor match Rovers had to admit defeat by 2-1. Scorer of the first Rovers' goal of the season was Tommy McAteer, a cool chip over the goalkeeper's head from halfway within the Motherwell half. Rovers were represented by Houston, Rodgers, Deakin, Clark, Gallagher, McCusker, Slaven, Ritchie, Conn, Ross and McAteer. Motherwell won the Cup from Airdrie in the final and there was no match for the third and fourth places.

In the first game of the League at home against Cowdenbeath a Sammy Conn goal in the first half was enough to separate the two teams. In the Skol League Cup the following Tuesday, Montrose came to Coatbridge and Rovers smashed their way to a 2-0 victory and the Ritchie led team was looking good.

The visit to Stenhousemuir on the Saturday found Rovers with a player revolt on their hands and it was only the intervention of David Letham, the League President and Jim Farry, the League Secretary, which persuaded the players to proceed with the match. It was hardly the right frame of mind to play the game and into the bargain Ritchie wanted to change the winning team and re-introduce himself into the forward line. However, a compromise was reached, he reverted to the substitutes' bench and Rovers had to end up content with a 1-1 draw. The following Wednesday, in the second round of the Cup, St. Johnstone were hosts to a Rovers' team who were brimming over with enthusiasm and it was totally against the run of play that the Saints were leading at half-time In a travesty of a result the home team ran out eventual winners by 2-1 with new boy Slaven scoring his fourth goal of the season and third in the Skol Cup.

For the League campaign proper Rovers were sitting relatively happily with three points out of a possible four when Queen of the South came to visit and Rovers got off to a famous start when Ritchie scored from a free kick in the first minute. However, Queens squared the match at 2-2 in the first half eventually running out winners by 4-3 in an exciting game. Young John Paisley made his debut in this match, coming on as a substitute for Gallagher, and made a little bit of history in so doing. His first touch of a ball in Senior football was to first time a volley past goalkeeper Davidson for Rovers' second goal just before half time. There was yet another Managerial bombshell at the end of this match with

ALBION ROVERS SEASON 1984/85

Back Row (left to right): Stephen Tennent, Sammy Conn, Alan Rodgers, Trialist, Tony Gallagher, Jim Woods.
Front Row (left to right): Joe Baker (Asst. Coach), John Greene, Jim Deakin, Bernie Staven, John Paisley, Kenny Clark, Jim McCusker (Captain), Victor Kasule, Andy Ritchie (Player-Coach).

player/coach Ritchie handing in his notice and advising the Board that he would not be back. From feeling aggrieved by losing both previous matches whilst being the better team, Rovers had no such excuses at Hampden the following week when, in a bad-tempered match, Conn was ordered off and two others were booked whilst Queen's were handing out a 5-1 drubbing. The Amateurs were winning 3-0 at half time, Rovers put on Paisley in the second half and he scored another goal within a minute but the 'Spiders' were not to be out-gunned in this one.

Former players Ray Franchetti and Duncan Shields were then appointed coaches in addition to Joe Baker and they were heartened by the attitude of the players at Arbroath the following Saturday. With Paisley on from the beginning in this one and scoring another goal, Rovers were shaping up into the team their earlier season promise had indicated. Robert Burns also returned to goal and, despite losing the first goal, Rovers looked much more like themselves winning 2-1. The first contest for the new Managerial trio was a visit from Alloa Athletic but, despite almost constant pressure, Rovers couldn't find a way past Donald Hunter who was making his last appearance in goal before leaving to join the Police Force and, as a consequence, Alloa won by the only goal of the fixture.

A second half hat-trick by Slaven won the away match against East Stirlingshire at 3-2 but Stranraer ran out winners by 2-1 at home with Rovers again scoring the first goal through Jim Deakin. Two away matches found varying fortunes with, first of all a nail-biting game at Annfield against Stirling Albion, Rovers winning 3-2 whilst at Montrose old pal Bruce Clelland was welcomed back to the fold but Montrose won by the only goal of the match. Dunfermline Athletic came and won 2-0 but with Rovers fighting every bit of the way the game hinged on centre half Gallagher being ordered off.

Worse was to follow the following week at Kirkcaldy with Raith Rovers ripping through the Coatbridge defence after a fairly even first half and Rovers were lucky to get away from this one with only a 3-0 defeat. Berwick Rangers lost to a late John Paisley goal and the boy was quickly donning the mantle of 'Super Sub'. Rovers said farewell to Stuart Burgess in this match being transferred to East Fife for an estimated £5,000. Another single goal home victory saw Arbroath beaten for the second time this season and the introduction of Derek Edgar, taking the place of the injured Kenny Clark.

The following Saturday a strong running Alloa team tore strips off Rovers' defence and, in a day of torrential rain, Rovers were well beaten by 4-0 at Recreation Park, New territory was broken for the next home match against Stirling Albion when the Commercial Manager fixed up the first match to be sponsored by local business and the confectionery firm of J.J. Lees, Plc., were forerunners in this type of venture. Unfortunately the Rovers' players couldn't match the Sponsors and the Stirling team ran out winners by 4-0. The following week the first round Scottish Cup tie took place down at Berwick with Bryan McKay from Shettleston making his debut at centre forward. Rovers didn't contest this one and lost by a 3-1 goal margin with Slaven scoring in the second last minute. This was the day when Stirling Albion defeated Selkirk 20-0 although they had shown no real signs of this kind of goal scoring prowess the week before.

This year's A.G.M. re-elected Jack McGoogan with Tom Fagan remaining as Chairman and the Board unchanged from the previous season. The loss this year had been £11,804 and the overall debit had alarmingly risen to £17,025 with no immediate prospect of improvement.

The only other game played in December was against Queen of the South at

Top money transfer Bruce Clelland in typical pose challenging McDart in the Lanarkshire Cup Match at Hamilton.

Dumfries when, with Rovers again scoring a first minute goal this time through Slaven, Queens eventually ran out winners by 3-2. Two of these goals were scored in the last few minutes and two of Queens' goals were from the penalty spot. The New Year's Day match at Coatbridge was a disappointing display and, although there was only another penalty goal between the two teams, Stenhousemuir deserved to win by a greater margin. Bad weather again clamped down and the only match played in January was at Cowdenbeath a fortnight later when with dreadful underfoot conditions, a no-scoring draw was played out.

Once football restarted again, Montrose came to Coatbridge and ran out winners by 4-1 whilst a late goal by Slaven gained a point in the 1-1 draw at Dunfermline. Arbroath lost for the third time this season, this time by 3-0, thanks to a Slaven hat-trick making his eighteenth of the season and putting him to the top of the Second Division scorer's lists. Eddie Farrell from Hamilton Accies also made his first appearance at full back. The next Tuesday, in a roughhouse affair, Rovers won by the only goal of the match but had Kasule ordered off against East Stirlingshire. Bruce Clelland scored his first goal since returning to the Club at Hampden in the first half but Queen's equalised in the second half to make the final score 1-1. Rovers freed both McCusker and Paisley and when Larbert was visited the following week both players lined up with the 'Warriors' against their former mates due to a severe player crisis at the Larbert Club. Slaven scored first but Paisley flipped one past his old mates before 'Muir who were showing more urgency scored a winner in the second half.

Kenny Clark was re-introduced to the forward line following a good recovery from his injury and Rovers started off as if they were going to annihilate Queen's Park but, despite being 3-1 up just before half time, a second half collapse saw the Glasgow team come back from the dead to square the game at 3-3. For the second time this season Stranraer came to Coatbridge and won by 2-1 in a match where Rovers looked strangely disinterested. Young Jim Creaney made his debut susbstituting for Greene. Berwick Rangers became the third home match in a row and Rovers gained ample revenge for the Scottish Cup defeat by turning on perhaps their best performance of the season so far and leading by 3-0 at half time. The fans were already counting the goals which would undoubtedly come in the second half but the English team had a different approach and came out fighting. By the end of the game Rovers were pleased to have hung on for a 3-2 victory. Stirling Albion without much difficulty despatched an inept Rovers' team at Stirling by 4-1 whilst Rovers, on the following Tuesday with an all-change line-up, gave Stranraer a goal of a start and then defeated them 3-2 at Stair Park. Raith Rovers opened April in gale swept conditions and won well in a fine attacking performance by 6-0 with the Coatbridge team having no answer to two fast wingers. Another away match found a single Slaven goal enough to defeat Berwick on the following Wednesday.

Slaven with twenty-seven goals to his credit and 'way out in front in the Second Division scorers scored two in the first half against table-topping Alloa, who were looking good for promotion. Just before half time the Wasps were awarded a penalty but this was missed and Rovers, after sustaining tremendous pressure, eventually ran out winners by 4-1 in a keen encounter. Alloa substitute Paterson broke a leg just after joining the fray and to make it thoroughly miserable for the visitors centre half Dall scored through his own goal in the very last minute. Dunfermline, who were third in line in the promotion stakes, visited Coatbridge the following Tuesday and a hard fought point at 1-1 was the result of a fast

Tony Gallagher

Jim Deakin

Victor Kasule

Alan Rodgers

entertaining game.

The match at Queen of the South was a real four pointer and it was Rovers who this time turned up trumps with Bernie Slaven scoring his thirtieth goal of the season from the penalty spot in the 2-1 victory. In so doing, he uplifted the Daily Record Trophy for the first Scottish player to score thirty goals in the season to which was added an additional prize of twelve bottles of champagne. Montrose clinched promotion in a 0-0 match at Links Park and their celebratory champagne had to be put on ice until they won the Championship the following week.

After a run of five games without defeat, Rovers again welcomed the Rovers, from Kirkcaldy, in an important fixture. If the Coatbridge team had any chance of climbing further up the League table, it had to be at the expense of Raith Rovers, who were currently experiencing their best spell of the season. Rovers were still smarting over the home defeat earlier in the month but the visitors slammed in another six goals without reply to ensure Rovers would have no chance of catching them in the League.

With two games left Rovers had a no-scoring away draw against East Stirlingshire with centre forward Mackay drafted into full back due to a shortage of players and he retained his position for the last match of the season, ironically enough against Cowdenbeath who, at the same venue, had started the League campaign back in August. The new full back scored with a fine header in the first half but the better organised Cowdenbeath team showed why they were sitting third in the League to score two second half goals and win deservedly by 2-1.

For the first time in several seasons, a respectable mid-table position was attained, eventually finishing in eighth place with thirty-nine points and Montrose running out Champions with fifty points followed upstairs by Alloa on forty-eight. Arbroath were bottom dogs with twenty-two points.

Only three players were freed in the close season and another award befell Bernie Slaven when he was voted the Second Division Players' Player of the Year at the Annual Sportsman's Dinner in Glasgow in May. Efforts were made during the close season to carry out improvements on the playing surface and the exterior of the grandstand was scheduled for re-surfacing. Following the tragic events at the European Cup Final in Brussels and the earlier tragedy at Bradford City's ground on the last day of the English season, Rovers along with all other Scottish clubs were looking closely into their safety aspects.

Commercial Manager, Robin Marwick, was immediately plunged into hectic work to bring the ground and facilities up to modern-day standards. Lack of finance over the years had resulted in only minimal maintenance being carried out and a visit by the League Management Committee found Cliftonhill the first casualty of the mid-summer football drama.

The ground was closed for football pending works being carried out to upgrade the grandstand, accesses, entrances and spectator comfort. Cliftonhill being one of the larger grounds had a greater number of problems than some of the smaller, more compact set-ups.

Season 1985/86

The Management made arrangements with near neighbours Airdrieonians to play the necessary home matches in the League campaign at Broomfield. This was a turning back of the clock to 1919 when Cliftonhill was being built. It was hoped that they would be as successful as in that earlier episode when Rovers won nine, lost two and drew one of the twelve games played before the triumphant opening

Bernie Slaven Scottish Top Scorer Season 1984/85.

at Cliftonhill when St. Mirren spoiled the celebrations by winning 2-0.

Before such requirements however, the mini-tournament for the Lanarkshire Cup at Hamilton found Rovers losing on a penalty kick out against Motherwell the match finishing 1-1 after extra time. McAteer and Mills being the culprits in a 5-4 defeat. Hamilton won 1-0 in the Final and again there was no match for the minor positions. Rovers were represented by Thompson, McKay (Paisley), Conn, Mills, Gallagher, Deakin, Kasule, Rodgers, Nolan (Greene), McAteer and Clelland.

The League campaign started at Berwick and again the match ended all square — this time by 0-0 and the future seemed promising. However, there were to be no further victories during August or September.

This season's Skol League Cup saw the long journey to Stranraer and the game was lost in the first five minutes with two sloppy goals the final score being 3-0. A first match at Broomfield found Stirling Albion too strong by 3-1 and the disappointment returned at Larbert with Stenhousemuir winning 4-2 and Alan Rodgers being ordered off.

Queen's Park in the second Broomfield match won with a goal in each half and Cowdenbeath by 3-0 in Fife ended with the luxury of a temporary 'keeper replacing their first choice who was injured saving Conn's weak penalty. Further ignominy in this match was Gallagher's early bath.

When with Scotland's World Cup squad at Ninian Park, Wales, on Tuesday 10th September, Rovers' most famous former player, Jock Stein, in front of the T.V. cameras was overcome with the pressures of office. Fans were appalled to watch the 'Big Man' stretchered away from the dug-out just as his Scottish players took a winning lead by means of a Davie Cooper penalty thus ensuring their appearance in the World Cup finals in Mexico in June, 1986. Later that evening all Scotland was shattered with the news that the National Team Supremo had died in the dressing room. Thus the former Rovers' player who had become a household name in every country in the world following his playing career at Celtic Park and managerial career at Easter Road, Dunfermline, Parkhead, Leeds and for Scotland but who had played more first team matches for Albion Rovers than for all his other clubs put together, was no more. All Scotland mourned his passing and none more so than the fans at Coatbridge who had seen the miner develop from the raw junior signed in December, 1942 into the mature player who left for pastures new in 1950 in non-league Welsh football and eventually a career as a top class coach and manager at the highest level.

At Broomfield the last "home" match found East Stirlingshire too good at snapping chances to win 2-1. The visit to Palmerston, never a happy hunting ground, found quite dreadful conditions with the League Programme decimated due to freak monsoon weather. Luckily the playing surface was in good condition at the start but quickly became a mud bath. Rovers, who had quickly gone into the lead were down 3-1 at half time and although getting one back just after half time lost the place in a goal-feast for the fans in a 5-2 defeat.

Top scorer of the previous season Bernie Slaven who had refused to re-sign had effectively put himself out of the game as there were no enquiries from other clubs. Rovers could have been doing with his goal-scoring prowess as the team had been playing reasonably well but with goals scarce a bottom table position was the obvious result.

Rovers bounced back from this bad result with their return to Cliftonhill for home matches. The ground was still closed but the grandstand and enclosure were available for matches with a crowd limit set by the Scottish League of 850.

Rovers' attendances over the past several seasons, apart from very individual one off games, was such that this crowd limit would be no inconvenience to them and they celebrated by two magnificent goals in the second half without reply in an explosive match. Jim Deakin and his immediate opponent were ordered off and there were wholesale bookings by the referee. For the first match at Perth in the League programme, two tough teams fought out a bruising match with Rovers losing 2-1 at half time but the roof caving in in the second half. Both Conn and Mills were ordered off and the Saints, against nine men, moved into a 4-1 score ably led by former Rover Stevie Evans. He latterly had a tackle on Alan Rodgers which meant the Rover had to be carried off and, with Rovers having used their substitutes, they were left with eight men to carry on. Needless to say the final score was 7-1.

Back at Cliftonhill, Arbroath, who had finished bottom of the table the previous season, were now under the able Managership of Jimmy Bone and they were unlucky to share the points in a no scoring draw as they had immeasurably the better of the play. Through at Meadowbank Stadium another draw, this time at 1-1 gave at least a glimmer of hope for the future.

However, the following Saturday at Dunfermline, it was back to square one with a heavy defeat by the homesters at 6-0 in what otherwise was an entertaining game.

The short lived unbeaten run at Cliftonhill came to an end when Stranraer won 3-2. Rovers threw this one away by losing two early goals but when Cowdenbeath visited seven days later, it was a different story and a late penalty by Alan Rodgers was sufficient to notch a win by 2-1.

November finished in complete disarray with two 5-1 defeats. The first was against East Stirlingshire when, with Rovers by far the better team and leading by a Bruce Clelland goal, right back McKay got into all sorts of bother, Rovers lost the equaliser and McKay was ordered off on half time. The ten men were blown apart in the second half when 'Shire went on to score four more goals without reply. At Coatbridge, Queen of the South were too good all through and in a competent display well deserved their 5-1 victory.

The Scottish Cup was next in line and Rovers had drawn a tough one in Gala Fairydean. The 'Dean' had the previous week won the South of Scotland Qualifying Cup for the fourth time in a row. They were convinced that they would be good enough for the bottom team in the Second Division but were blasted out of their complacency when Rovers went in at half time three goals up. Rovers increased their superiority in the second half by hammering in another five goals with the match ending up 8-1 when it could easily have gone into double figures. Last time Rovers had scored eight goals in any match was over twenty years earlier against Airdrieonians in the League Cup. The next Saturday, St. Johnstone were visitors for the third home game in a row and Rovers were confident in reversing the earlier scoreline at Perth but Saints, with former Rovers Balavage and Evans, were too physical and too good to win by a 4-2 margin.

On the 16th December the 49th A.G.M. was held at Cliftonhill covering the two years ending the 31st March 1985. Chairman Tom Fagan was unable to be present due to ill-health and Vice President David Forrester announced a loss of £5,003 in 1984 and a profit of £5,753 in 1985 giving an aggregate loss totalling £16,275. Mr. Fagan was again confirmed for another stint as Chairman and immediately following the meeting Robin Marwick was confirmed as a Director following his successful year and a half as Commercial Manager.

ALBION ROVERS SEASON 1985/86

Standing: A. Smith, D. Mills, R. W. Marwick, J. Greene, B. Clelland, J. Deakin, T. McAteer, J. Thompson, A. Rodgers, B. McKay, J. McKeown, T. Nolan, S. Goodwin, V. Kasule, G. Peacock, J. Grant.
Seated: T. Gemmell, D. Edgar, S. Conn, D. Forrester, A. Gallacher, J. Paisley, J. McGoogan.

1984 Grandstand before resurfacing.

1985 Grandstand after resurfacing.

With many games off in Scotland the trip through to Stirling found the pitch very soft and the rain and wind making conditions most unpleasant. With Rovers being clearly the better side, the game was won and lost in thirty seconds of farce. Centre-half Mills, watching four Stirling players standing in an offside position, was pushed in the back and he anticipated the referee's whistle by handling the ball when the cross came over. The whistle didn't come, other than the referee considering the offence had occurred in the penalty area and he gave a penalty which was promptly thumped away by Willie Irvine. Straight from the kick-off a cross from the right wing came off the goalkeeper on to Alan Rodgers for an own goal and the game was beyond Rovers once again.

With the last match of 1985 against Berwick Rangers being postponed, the New Year opened with two games scheduled against Queen's Park. The first was on New Year's Day at Hampden when again two goals, within a minute in the second half, were enough to defeat Rovers.

This was the final fling for the Franchetti/Shields association as they were dismissed as Coaches after some fifteen months and immediately the Directors went into conference to come up with a suitable replacement. After deliberations, the former Celt and Lisbon Lion, Tommy Gemmell, was fixed up as Manager.

The second game in four days against Queen's Park at Hampden, but this time in the Scottish Cup, then took place but unfortunately the introduction of the new boss was not enough to raise the adrenalin of the players to a satisfactory conclusion and the Amateurs won their third game of the season over the Coatbridge side by a 2-1 scoreline.

Following that disappointing Cup exit, the new Manager quickly settled down to knock his new charges into shape. The next weekend found a home match against Berwick Rangers and changes made in all departments. Despite much effort by the players, no goals were scored but a first point was chalked up. Weather continued to be pretty abysmal and on a quagmire of a pitch on the 18th January a third match in charge saw "Big Tam's" first victory in the home match against Meadowbank Thistle. The "Jags" went into an early lead but three tremendous goals in quick succession by Conn, Paisley and Kasule put Rovers in at half-time with their tails up. Despite a fine fight back in the second half, Thistle lost by 3-2. In this match Angus Smith signed on a month's trial from Hamilton Accies, added much pep to the forward line and contributed immensely to the overall improved performance.

On the last Saturday in January with Arbroath engaged on Cup business, the match at Gayfield was postponed and the manager contacted his former Celtic mate Davie Hay at Parkhead and fixed up a match with a Celtic XI. Football on the day was impossible and the referee abandoned the match at half-time with Rovers losing by 4-0 and the only winner really being the icy weather. The long journey down to Stranraer on the 1st February found Rovers in rampant form and a goal in each half was sufficient to keep the winning streak in motion but on the following Tuesday at Kirkcaldy in atrocious conditions Raith Rovers won by the only goal scored in the first half in a match which the Coatbridge side should really have won with something to spare.

There followed a month of inaction due to spartan weather conditions, with a prolonged snow and ice spell. Rovers' next match was on Tuesday 4th March at Arbroath which ended up at 1-1 each. With Angus Smith's trial period now ended Rovers introduced Paul Teeven from Bellshill Juniors on trial and he put on a good show. This was the start of a spell of seven games without a defeat and the fourth

1985/86 Directors.

away match in a row took place on the Saturday at Berwick. Two magnificent goals from Conn and Clelland overcame a first half deficit for a fine 2-1 victory and at home Stenhousemuir were held to a no-scoring draw. Cowdenbeath were then comprehensively defeated 2-0 through in Fife on the succeeding Tuesday, John Paisley scoring with his first touch as Substitute in the second half. Stranraer was again visited for a 3-2 victory in a match which Rovers made life difficult for themselves throwing away an early lead into a deficit just after half-time. But two-goal Alan Rodgers, ably assisted by Captain Sammy Conn, made the final result 3-2. The other South of Scotland team, Queen of the South, came to Coatbridge on the Tuesday and were quickly down to great two goals from Gallagher and Kasule but the strong running League leaders came back with two second half goals to share the points. Queen's went away with more than a point at the end of the game, signing Rovers' central defender Dougie Mills to assist their ultimately successful promotion challenge.

On the Saturday the other Queen's, from Hampden, fought back from a first half Alan Rodgers goal to share the points and two goals in a match which Rovers were unlucky not to win. Easter Monday saw Dunfermline Athletic as visitors and they easily brushed aside Rovers' challenge by 3-0. This match was played at Broomfield as Rovers' ground was still not able to take the tremendous travelling support carried by the Fifers. This turned out to be Rovers' largest crowd of the season of over 1,500. Thus ended a tremendous spell of points gathering and rekindling of interest in Coatbridge in the affairs of the 'Wee Rovers'. Ten points out of a possible fourteen was good business and Scottish Brewers recognised the amount of effort Tommy Gemmell was putting in as Manager by naming him their "Manager of the Month for March".

Unfortunately this success seemed to go to Rovers' head and a disastrous series of results were to follow with only two points gathered from the remaining sixteen on offer before the end of the season. At Arbroath the 'Red Lichties' won 2-0 and in mid-week Stirling Albion came to Coatbridge to win by the same score, despite the contribution by new signing Pat Morgan from Shettleston. After this match trialist Tom McDonald of St Roch's was signed. The second visit to Dunfermline on the Saturday saw Rovers unfortunate to lose by four clear goals but more importantly they lost central defender Tony Gallagher for the rest of the season with a ligament injury. In a disappointing match at Perth a second half penalty goal given for hands against the usually so-reliable Alan Rodgers, found Rovers in the unenviable position of having failed to score on five consecutive matches for only the second time in their 103 year history.

Meadowbank came to Coatbridge, still with an outside chance of promotion, and all eyes were on the Coatbridge side to consolidate their position off the bottom of the League as it was hoped that third or fourth bottom place might yet be possible. However, the match was a disaster with two goals lost in the first half and history of the wrong kind was made when, for the first time ever, a sixth game in a row without scoring a goal was recorded. There was gloom all round Cliftonhill. Rovers were missing their striker of last season Bernie Slaven and hadn't adequately replaced him throughout the season.

There was a flurry of trialists at this time. New players Morgan and McDonald were joined by Paul Teeven from Bellshill against East Stirlingshire on the last Tuesday in April and with the game in its final stages it looked as though Rovers were going to go seven games without scoring when two explosive goals by Captain Sammy Conn won the day and led to the young winger signing after the

Captain Sammy Conn welcoming new Manager Tommy Gemmell to Cliftonhill.

match following his good display.

At Kirkcaldy on the Saturday, Kasule got Rovers off to a fine start with a snappy goal in the first minute but the Fifers went quickly into a 2-1 lead before Rodgers restored parity from the penalty spot. But in the second half the 'Dark Blues' put on three goals without reply to run out easy winners by 5-2. The very last game in the Scottish Football League was played on Tuesday, 6th May when Stenhousemuir scored a late second half goal to win the final two points of the season.

Thus a disappointing end to the season left Tommy Gemmell thinking about what might have been and the knowledge that a lot of work would have to be put into the close season in preparation for a first full season for the enthusiastic manager.

Rovers had ended up in second bottom place with 24 points. There were free transfers for Tommy Nolan, Bruce Clelland and John Paisley, the latter for a second time in two seasons. Dunfermline won the Championship from Queen of the South by two points. Stranraer came bottom one point behind the Cliftonhillers.

The close season found much work being put out on improvements with the playing pitch receiving a much needed overhaul and entrances, terracing and accesses all being upgraded. A long-term ground redevelopment scheme was put into gear and the new beginning was begun. Rovers applied to the Scottish League to join a reserve team for the new term and Cliftonhill was throbbing once more.

"Home" match at Broomfield against Queen's Park 1985.

CONCLUSION

Thus our story ends for the time being—104 not out. That is a remarkable statistic considering the adversity which has often beset the Club. Lady Luck has never had a peg in the Coatbridge dressing-room but despite that there have been good times for players and fans alike.

Has not the Club played in the final of the foremost Cup in the land and also in the First Division from time to time? Have there not been players who have become household names in Scotland and beyond and who owe their beginnings to Coatbridge and Albion Rovers?

Modest success has come the way of the team over the years with a sprinkling of major trophy successes backed up with a more liberal spraying of lesser trophy successes. There have always been those dedicated to the best interests of the Club and it is no different today. The struggle is the same with only the names and times varying. Mediocrity has been the byword since the late 40's and it is now almost forty years since Rovers were last seen in the top division. The years ahead will be dedicated to bringing the good days back.

When the book is written detailing the second 100 years of this North Lanarkshire Club, who knows what glories the author will relate, what stars will have graced the hallowed turf. Success is long awaited in Coatbridge but meanwhile let this book serve as a memorial to all those who have given of their best, both on and off the pitch—those "Boys from the 'Brig"!

THE AUTHOR

Robin Marwick is married with three children and has lived all his live in the Monklands. From his earliest days he has been a staunch devotee of Albion Rovers, and from selling Programmes as a teenager in the 50s, he is now a Director of the Club. His children are continuing in this family tradition, which now spans four generations.

He is an Architect, practicing in Coatbridge, but his interests are many and varied. An involved member of various local and national organisations, he lives a very full life, gives freely of his time, especially to local groups and is a Justice of the Peace.

Although this is his first book, he has already experienced having his works published. A second book is already in draft form with the promise of more to come in the future.

APPENDIX 'A'

Player who represented Scotland whilst an Albion Rovers player

Jock White	I.R.		v Wales 1922

Players who represented Scotland after leaving Albion Rovers

Dave Haddow	G.	Rangers	v England 1894
Jock White	I.F.	Heart of Midlothian	v Ireland 1923
			v English League 1923 & 6
			v Irish League 1925 & 7
Duncan McKenzie	R.H.	Brentford	v Ireland 1938
Tom Kiernan	I.F.	Celtic	v English League 1947
Jock Stein	C.H.	Celtic	v English League 1954
Tony Green	I.F.	Blackpool	v Ireland 1971
			v England 1971
			v Wales 1972
Jim Brown	G.	Sheffield United	v Romania 1975

Players who represented other countries after leaving Albion Rovers

Ireland

Peter Boyle	L.B.	Sheffield United	v England 1901
			v England 1902
			v Scotland 1903
			v Wales 1903
			v England 1904

England

John Conlin	O.L.	Bradford P.A.	v Scotland 1906

Jamaica

Hugh Thom	C.H.	Eleven Caps in 1920's	

Northern Ireland

Danny Hegan	W.H.	Ipswich Town	v USSR 1969
		Wolverhampton Wanderers	v USSR 1971
			v Scotland 1972
			v England 1972
			v Wales 1972
			v Bulgaria 1972
			v Cyprus 1973

New Zealand

Sam Malcolmson	W.H.		v Fiji 1981
			v China 1981
			v Scotland 1982
			v Spain 1982

Canada

Eddie McLaine	C.F.	Car Steel Montreal	v U.S.A. 1926

APPENDIX 'B'

List of Managers

Name	Appointment	Termination	Reason
Archie Montgomery	June 1920 Also Club Secretary	Jan. 1922	Died 5/1/22
Willie Reid	Jan. 1922 Also Club Secretary	May 1929	Resigned to manage Dundee United
W. Webber Lees	May 1929 Also Club Secretary	June 1935	Reverted to Club Secretary
John Weir	June 1935	Mar. 1937	Resigned to be Chief Scout with Newcastle United
W. Webber Lees	Mar. 1937 Also Club Secretary	June 1949	Resigned to manage Dunfermline Athletic
Directors	June 1949	Aug. 1950	—
Bobby Beath	Aug. 1950	May 1952	Resigned
Tom Fagan	May 1952	1953	—
Jackie Hutton	1953	1961	Resigned
Dunky McGill	June 1961 Player/Manager	June 1962	Left to play at Stranraer
Willie Telfer	Aug. 1962	Mar. 1965	Resigned
Bobby Flavell	Mar. 1965	Sept. 1966	Resigned
Jackie Stewart	Sept. 1966	Nov. 1968	Resigned to manage Dumbarton
Jimmy Harrower	May 1969	Nov. 1969	Resigned
Bobby Flavell	Nov. 1969	May 1972	Resigned
Frank Beattie	June 1972	June 1973	Resigned
Ralph Brand	Aug. 1973	Mar. 1974	Resigned
George Caldwell	Aug. 1974	Aug. 1976	Resigned to coach Ayr United
Sam Goodwin	Aug. 1976	Feb. 1981	Resigned
Harry Hood	Feb. 1981	April 1981	Resigned
Joe Baker	July 1981	Feb. 1982	Resigned
Derek Whiteford	Dec. 1982	Dec. 1983	Resigned
Martin Ferguson	Dec. 1983	May 1983	Resigned to coach St. Mirren
Billy Wilson	July 1983	April 1984	Resigned
Benny Rooney	April 1984	May 1984	Resigned to manage Partick Thistle
Andy Ritchie*	June 1984	Sept. 1984	Resigned
Joe Baker*	Sept. 1984	Dec. 1985	Resigned
Ray Franchetti*	Sept. 1985	Jan. 1986	Resigned
Tommy Gemmell	Jan. 1986		

*Coach

APPENDIX 'C'

SCOTTISH CUP RECORD THROUGH THE YEARS

KEY
R = Rovers
O = Opposition
P = Preliminary Round
Q = Qualifying Cup

Season	Round	Opposition	Score R	Score O	Venue
1884/85	1st	Glengowan	1	2	a
1885/86	1st	Drumpellier	6	2	h
	2nd	Wishaw Swifts	2	2	h
	Replay	Wishaw Swifts	0	5	a
1886/87	1st	Clydebank	5	1	a
	2nd	Dykehead	7	0	h
	3rd	Thistle	4	7	h
	4th	Cambuslang	1	6	h
1887/88	1st	Airdriehill	12	0	h
	2nd	Rutherglen	6	3	a
	3rd	Northern	4	3	a
	4th	Bye	—	—	—
	5th	Our Boys (Dundee)	1	4	a
1888/89	1st	Bellshill	W	0	—
	2nd	Rutherglen	9	1	h
	3rd	Celtic	1	4	a
1889/90	1st	Carfin Shamrock	0	4	a
1890/91	1st	Carrington	2	1	a
	2nd	St. Mirren	1	5	a
1891/92	P1	Wishaw-Thistle	3	7	a
1892/93	P1	Shettleston Swifts	9	1	h
	P2	Carfin Hibs	10	0	h
	P3	Port Glasgow Athletic	4	2	h
	P4	Pollokshaws	2	1	a
	1st	Kilmarnock	1	2	h
1893/94	P1	Whitefield	W	0	—
	P2	Dykehead	5	1	h
	P3	Neilston	7	0	h
	P4	Falkirk	3	3	h
	Replay	Falkirk	5	2	h
	1st	Black Watch	6	0	h
	2nd	Celtic	0	7	a
1894/95	P1	Carfin	3	5	h
1895/96	Q1	Dykehead	1	0	h
	Q2	Wishaw Thistle	1	1	a
	Replay	Wishaw Thistle	5	1	h
	Q3	East Stirlingshire	0	2	h
1896/97	Q1	Royal Albert	1	4	a

Season	Round	Opposition	Score R	O	Venue
1897/98	Q1	Carfin Rovers	4	3	a
	Q2	Longriggend	3	0	h
	Q3	Port Glasgow Athletic	2	4	h
1898/99	Q1	Dykehead	4	2	h
	Q2	Vale of Leven	4	2	h
	Q3	Wishaw Thistle	1	5	a
1899/1900	Q1	Carfin Emmett	1	3	a
1900/01	Q1	Hamilton Academical	0	2	a Successful Protest
	Q1	Hamilton Academical	0	3	a
1901/02	Q1	Royal Albert	3	3	a
	Replay	Royal Albert	1	0	h
	Q2	Wishaw United	0	0	h
	Replay	Wishaw United	1	1	h
	2nd Replay	Wishaw United	2	2	a
	3rd Replay	Wishaw United	2	2	Broomfield
	4th Replay	Wishaw United	1	1	Fir Park
	5th Replay	Wishaw United	1	2	Douglas Park
1902/03	Q1	Royal Albert	1	0	a
	Q2	Motherwell	1	7	a
1903/04	Q1	Carfin Emmett	5	0	h
	Q2	Wishaw Amateurs	6	2	h
	Q3	Hamilton Academical	1	1	h
	Replay	Hamilton Academical	2	1	a
	Q4	Clyde	7	2	a
	Q5	Maxwelltown Volunteers	4	1	a
	Semi Final	Ayr	0	0	a
	Replay	Ayr	1	0	h
	Q Final	Arbroath	2	4	Dens Park
	1st	Kilwinning Eglinton	2	1	h
	2nd	Kilmarnock	2	2	a
	Replay	Kilmarnock	0	1	h
1904/05	Q1	Renton	2	3	a
1905/06	Q1	Vale of Leven	1	0	h
	Q2	Hamilton Academical	0	1	a
1906/07	Q1	Wishaw Thistle	2	1	a
	Q2	Hamilton Academical	2	1	a
	Q3	Renton	1	1	a
	Replay	Renton	3	3	h
	2nd Replay	Renton	1	3	Ibrox
1907/08	Q1	Royal Albert	3	1	a
	Q2	Dykehead	3	0	h
	Q3	Galston	1	5	h
1908/09	Q1	Clyde	0	1	h
1909/10	Q1	Dykehead	0	3	a
1910/11	Q1	Abercorn	4	0	h
	Q2	Morton	2	3	h
1911/12	Q1	Royal Albert	2	4	a

369

Season	Round	Opposition	Score R O	Venue
1912/13	Q1	Dykehead	2 0	h
	Q2	Wishaw Thistle	1 1	h
	Replay	Wishaw Thistle	0 0	a
	2nd Replay	Wishaw Thistle	0 1	Broomfield
1913/14	Q1	Paisley Academicals	6 1	h
	Q2	Dumbarton Harp	0 0	h
	Replay	Dumbarton Harp	4 1	a
	Q3	Dykehead	1 0	a
	Q4	Stevenston United	1 0	a
	Q5	Nithsdale Wanderers	3 0	a
	Semi Final	Arthurlie	3 0	h
	Final	Dundee Hibs	1 1	Tynecastle
	Replay	Dundee Hibs	1 1	Easter Road
	2nd Replay	Dundee Hibs	3 0	Tynecastle
	1st	Aberdeen	1 4	a
1914/15	Q1	Vale of Leven	1 3	a
1915/16 to 1918/19 NO COMPETITIONS				
1919/20	Q1	Paisley Grammar F.P.	3 1	h
	Q2	Renton	0 0	a
	Replay	Renton	2 0	h
	Q5	Royal Albert	— —	a Scratched
	1st	Dykehead	0 0	h
	Replay	Dykehead	2 1	a
	2nd	Huntingtower	W 0	
	3rd	St. Bernards	1 1	a
	Replay	St. Bernards	4 1	h
	4th	Aberdeen	2 1	h
	Semi Final	Rangers	1 1	Parkhead
	Replay	Rangers	0 0	Parkhead
	2nd Replay	Rangers	2 0	Parkhead
	Final	Kilmarnock	2 3	Hampden
1920/21	1st			
	2nd	Mid Annandale	3 1	h
	3rd	Armadale	2 2	a
	Replay	Armadale	0 0	h
	2nd Replay	Armadale	2 0	Hampden
	4th	Dundee	2 0	a
	Semi Final	Rangers	1 4	Parkhead
1921/22	1st	Johnstone	6 0	h
	2nd	Rangers	1 1	h
	Replay	Rangers	0 4	a
1922/23	1st	Hamilton Academical	0 1	a
1923/24	1st	Ayr United	1 3	a
1924/25	1st	Clyde	1 1	h
	Replay	Clyde	1 3	a
1925/26	1st	Nithsdale Wanderers	6 1	h
	2nd	Peebles Rovers	1 1	h
	Replay	Peebles Rovers	4 0	a
	3rd	Morton	0 1	a

Season	Round	Opposition	Score R	O	Venue
1926/27	1st	Elgin City	0	1	a
1927/28	1st	Glasgow University	5	1	h
	2nd	Brechin City	4	1	a
	3rd	Airdrieonians	3	1	h
	4th	Rangers	0	1	h
1928/29	1st	Galston	7	1	h
	2nd	Clackmannan	8	1	h
	3rd	Kilmarnock	0	1	h
1929/30	1st	Alloa	4	2	h
	2nd	Beith	2	1	h
	3rd	Montrose	2	2	h
	Replay	Montrose	1	3	a
1930/31	1st	Vale of Atholl	6	0	h
	2nd	Motherwell	1	4	a
1931/32	1st	Leith Athletic	1	1	a
	Replay	Leith Athletic	4	2	h
	2nd	Kilmarnock	0	2	a
1932/33	1st	Inverness Thistle	2	0	h
	2nd	Dumbarton	2	1	a
	3rd	Celtic	1	1	h
	Replay	Celtic	1	3	a
1933/34	1st	Vale Ocoba	4	1	h
	2nd	Kilmarnock	2	1	h
	3rd	Ross County	6	1	h
	4th	Motherwell	1	1	h
	Replay	Motherwell	0	6	a
1934/35	1st	Paisley Academicals	7	0	h
	2nd	Aberdeen	0	4	a
1935/36	1st	Rangers	1	3	h
1936/37	1st	Leith Athletic	4	4	a
	Replay	Leith Athletic	5	3	h
	2nd	Celtic	2	5	h
1937/38	1st	Dundee	4	2	h
	2nd	Ross County	5	2	a
	3rd	Falkirk	0	4	a
1938/39	1st	Aberdeen	0	1	a
1939/40	1st	Aberdeen	3	3	h
	Replay	Aberdeen	1	0	a
	2nd	Kilmarnock	1	2	a
1940/41 to 1945/46 NO COMPETITIONS					
1946/47	1st	Airdrieonians	3	0	h
	2nd	Dundee	0	3	a
1947/48	1st	Hibernians	0	2	h
1948/49	1st	Hamilton Academical	2	1	a
	2nd	Stenhousemuir	1	5	a
1949/50	1st	Alloa Athletic	1	0	h
	2nd	Dunfermline Athletic	1	2	a

Season	Round	Opposition	Score R	O	Venue
1950/51	1st	Stenhousemuir	1	1	h
	Replay	Stenhousemuir	2	1	a
	2nd	Clyde	0	2	h
1951/52	1st	Bye			
	2nd	Stranraer	1	1	h
	Replay	Stranraer	4	3	a
	3rd	Third Lanark	1	3	h
1952/53	1st	Bye			
	2nd	East Stirlingshire	2	0	h
	3rd	Queen of the South	0	2	a
1953/54	1st	Bye			
	2nd	Dundee	1	1	h
	Replay	Dundee	0	4	a
1954/55	5th	Clyde	0	3	a
1955/56	4th	Alloa	1	1	h
	Replay	Alloa	0	4	a
1956/57	1st	Vale of Atholl	8	2	h
	2nd	Peebles Rovers	2	2	a
	Replay	Peebles Rovers	6	0	h
	3rd	Vale of Leithan	2	0	h
	4th	Forres Mechanics	0	3	a
1957/58	1st	Berwick Rangers	3	1	h
	2nd	Heart of Midlothian	1	4	a
1958/59	1st	Celtic	0	4	a
1959/60	1st	Tarff Rovers	2	1	h
	2nd	Eyemouth United	0	1	a
1960/61	1st	Montrose	1	3	a
1961/62	1st	Bye			
	2nd	East Fife	0	1	a
1962/63	1st	Dundee United	0	3	a
1963/64	1st	Bye			
	2nd	Arbroath	4	3	h
	3rd	Kilmarnock	0	2	a
1964/65	P1	Brechin City	4	3	a
	P2	Queen's Park	0	0	a
	Replay	Queen's Park	1	1	h
	2nd Replay	Queen's Park	0	1	Firhill
1965/66	P1	Bye			
	P2	Berwick Rangers	0	0	a
	Replay	Berwick Rangers	3	0	h
	1st	Queen of the South	0	3	a
1966/67	P1	Bye			
	P2	Cowdenbeath	0	1	h
1967/68	P1	Bye			
	P2	Elgin City	1	3	a
1968/69	P1	Bye			
	P2	Stenhousemuir	0	1	a

Season	Round	Opposition	R	O	Venue
1969/70	P1	Bye			
	P2	Berwick Rangers	1	0	h
	1st	Dundee	1	2	h
1970/71	P1	Forfar Athletic	0	2	a
1971/72	1st	Bye			
	2nd	Queen's Park	3	2	h
	3rd	Celtic	0	5	a
1972/73	1st	Montrose	0	2	a
1973/74	1st	Berwick Rangers	0	0	a
	Replay	Berwick Rangers	2	0	h
	2nd	Queen of the South	0	1	a
1974/75	1st	St. Cuthbert's Wanderers	4	1	a
	2nd	Alloa Athletic	1	1	a
	Replay	Alloa Athletic	2	0	h
	3rd	Inverness Caledonian	1	0	a
	4th	Arbroath	0	2	a
1975/76	1st	Hawick Royal Albert	0	0	h
	Replay	Hawick Royal Albert	3	0	a
	2nd	Glasgow University	1	1	h
	Replay	Glasgow University	1	0	a
	3rd	Partick Thistle	1	2	h
1976/77	1st	Bye			
	2nd	Raith Rovers	2	1	h
	3rd	East Stirlingshire	3	0	a
	4th	East Fife	1	2	a
1977/78	1st	Bye			
	2nd	Buckie Thistle	1	0	h
	3rd	Morton	0	1	h
1978/79	1st	Dunfermline Athletic	2	2	a
	Replay	Dunfermline Athletic	2	3	h
1979/80	1st	Cowdenbeath	1	3	a
1980/81	1st	Bye			
	2nd	Arbroath	1	1	h
	Replay	Arbroath	0	1	a
1981/82	1st	Bye			
	2nd	Clachnacuddin	2	1	h
	3rd	Rangers	2	6	a
1982/83	1st	Bye			
	2nd	Stranraer	1	0	h
	3rd	Ayr United	2	1	a
	4th	Airdrieonians	0	3	h
1983/84	1st	Inverness Caledonian	1	2	a
1984/85	1st	Berwick Rangers	1	2	a
1985/86	1st	Gala Fairydean	8	1	h
	2nd	Queen's Park	1	2	a

APPENDIX 'D'

LEAGUE PLACINGS THROUGH THE YEARS

SEASON	P	W	D	L	F	A	Pts	Pos	Division
1882/91	Only Friendly or Cup Matches								
1891/92	22	15	1	6	88	51	31	2nd	Federation
1892/93	18	8	3	7	75	54	19	5th	Federation
1893/94	10	5	1	4	24	27	11	3rd	Alliance
1894/95	14	10	2	2	60	21	22	2nd	Alliance
1895/96	17	10	2	5	57	36	22	3rd	Alliance
1896/97	Friendlies Only								Friendlies
1897/98	14	5	3	6	26	34	13	4th	Combination
1898/99	18	4	2	12	32	51	10	10th	Combination
1898/99	8	3	0	5	13	18	6	4th	Lanarkshire
1899/1900	18	5	4	9	23	38	13	9th	Combination
1899/1900	7	5	1	1	14	5	11	1st	Lanarkshire Champions Unfinished
1900/01	18	7	3	8	36	42	17	6th	Combination
1900/01	5	3	2	0	9	4	8	2nd	Lanarkshire Unfinished
1901/02	14	11	2	1	40	10	24	1st	Combination Champions
1901/02	8	4	3	1	15	10	11	1st	Lanarkshire Champions
1902/03	18	13	3	2	59	20	29	1st	Combination Champions
1903/04	22	8	5	9	47	37	19	9th	Second

*2 Points Deducted for Fielding an unregistered player

SEASON	P	W	D	L	F	A	Pts	Pos	Division
1904/05	22	8	4	10	37	50	20	8th	Second
1905/06	22	12	3	7	48	29	27	3rd	Second
1906/07	22	10	3	9	43	36	23	6th	Second
1907/08	22	7	5	10	36	48	19	9th	Second
1908/09	22	9	2	11	37	48	20	10th	Second
1909/10	22	7	5	10	34	39	19	9th	Second
1910/11	22	10	5	7	27	21	25	3rd	Second
1911/12	22	6	1	15	19	37	13	11th	Second
1912/13	26	10	3	13	38	40	23	9th	Second
1913/14	22	10	7	5	38	33	27	2nd	Second
1914/15	26	9	7	10	37	42	25	9th	Second
1915/16	22	9	4	9	34	36	22	5th	Western
1916/17	19	4	6	9	28	28	14	7th	Western
1917/18	14	9	2	3	39	16	20	1st	Western Champions
1918/19	14	10	1	3	35	12	21	2nd	Western
1919/20	42	9	8	24	41	76	26	22nd	First
1920/21	42	11	12	19	57	68	34	17th	First
1921/22	42	17	10	15	55	51	44	11th	First
1922/23	38	8	10	20	38	64	26	19th	First
1923/24	38	15	12	11	67	53	42	5th	Second
1924/25	38	15	5	18	46	61	35	15th	Second
1925/26	38	16	6	16	78	71	38	9th	Second

SEASON	P	W	D	L	F	A	Pts	Pos	Division
1926/27	38	11	11	16	74	87	33	16th	Second
1927/28	38	17	4	17	79	69	38	8th	Second
1928/29	36	18	8	10	95	67	44	4th	Second
1929/30	38	24	6	8	101	60	54	3rd	Second
1930/31	38	14	11	13	80	83	39	9th	Second
1931/32	38	13	2	23	81	104	28	16th	Second
1932/33	34	19	2	13	82	57	40	5th	Second
1933/34	34	20	5	9	74	47	45	1st	Second Champions
1934/35	38	10	9	19	62	77	29	16th	First
1935/36	38	13	4	21	69	92	30	16th	First
1936/37	38	5	6	27	53	116	16	20th	First
1937/38	34	20	8	6	97	50	48	2nd	Second
1938/39	38	12	6	20	65	90	30	16th	First
1939/40	5	2	1	2	12	7	5	11th	First Unfinished
1939/40	30	15	2	13	61	60	32	7th	Western
1940/41	30	6	5	19	45	80	17	15th	Southern
1941/42	30	8	5	17	68	97	21	15th	Southern
1942/43	30	6	4	20	53	99	16	15th	Southern
1943/44	30	7	3	20	43	85	17	15th	Southern
1944/45	30	7	2	21	42	104	16	15th	Southern
1945/46	26	14	2	10	45	41	30	6th	B
1946/47	26	10	7	9	50	54	27	4th	B
1947/48	30	19	4	7	58	49	42	2nd	B
1948/49	30	3	2	25	30	105	8	16th	A
1949/50	30	10	7	13	49	61	27	11th	B
1950/51	30	14	4	12	56	51	32	8th	B
1951/52	30	6	10	14	39	57	22	14th	B
1952/53	30	5	4	21	44	77	14	16th	B
1953/54	30	12	7	11	55	63	31	7th	B
1954/55	30	8	10	12	50	69	26	11th	B
1955/56	36	8	11	17	58	82	27	17th	Second
1956/57	36	18	6	12	98	80	42	5th	Second
1957/58	36	12	5	19	53	79	29	17th	Second
1958/59	36	14	7	15	84	79	35	10th	Second
1959/60	36	14	8	14	71	78	36	10th	Second
1960/61	36	9	6	21	60	89	24	17th	Second
1961/62	36	10	5	21	42	74	25	18th	Second
1962/63	36	18	2	16	72	79	38	7th	Second
1963/64	36	12	12	12	67	71	36	9th	Second
1964/65	36	14	5	17	56	60	33	11th	Second
1965/66	36	18	7	11	58	54	43	7th	Second
1966/67	38	17	6	15	66	62	40	8th	Second
1967/68	36	14	9	13	62	55	37	8th	Second
1968/69	36	19	5	12	60	56	43	7th	Second
1969/70	36	14	5	17	53	64	33	11th	Second
1970/71	36	15	9	12	53	52	39	7th	Second
1971/72	36	7	6	23	36	61	20	18th	Second
1972/73	36	5	8	23	35	83	18	18th	Second

SEASON	P	W	D	L	F	A	Pts	Pos	Division
1973/74	36	7	6	23	38	72	20	17th	Second
1974/75	38	16	7	15	72	64	39	12th	Second
1975/76	26	7	10	9	35	38	24	9th	Second
1976/77	39	15	12	12	74	61	42	6th	Second
1977/78	39	16	8	15	68	68	40	8th	Second
1978/79	39	15	10	14	57	56	40	7th	Second
1979/80	39	16	12	11	73	56	44	4th	Second
1980/81	39	13	9	17	59	72	33	12th	Second
1981/82	39	13	5	21	52	74	31	11th	Second
1982/83	39	14	6	19	55	66	34	10th	Second
1983/84	39	8	11	20	46	76	27	14th	Second
1984/85	39	13	8	18	49	72	34	9th	Second
1985/86	39	8	8	23	38	86	24	13th	Second